CONSTRUCTION ADJUDICATION

CONSTRUCTION ADJUDICATION

HHJ Peter Coulson QC

OXFORD
UNIVERSITY PRESS

Great Clarendon Street, Oxford OX2 6DP

Oxford University Press is a department of the University of Oxford.
It furthers the University's objective of excellence in research, scholarship,
and education by publishing worldwide in

Oxford New York

Auckland Cape Town Dar es Salaam Hong Kong Karachi
Kuala Lumpur Madrid Melbourne Mexico City Nairobi
New Delhi Shanghai Taipei Toronto

With offices in

Argentina Austria Brazil Chile Czech Republic France Greece
Guatemala Hungary Italy Japan Poland Portugal Singapore
South Korea Switzerland Thailand Turkey Ukraine Vietnam

Oxford is a registered trade mark of Oxford University Press
in the UK and in certain other countries

Published in the United States
by Oxford University Press Inc., New York

© HHJ Peter Coulson 2007

The moral rights of the author have been asserted

Crown copyright material is reproduced under Class Licence
Number CPO1P000148 with the permission of OPSI and the
Queen's Printer for Scotland

Database right Oxford University Press (maker)

First published 2007

All rights reserved. No part of this publication may be reproduced,
stored in a retrieval system, or transmitted, in any form or by any means,
without the prior permission in writing of Oxford University Press,
or as expressly permitted by law, or under terms agreed with the appropriate
reprographics rights organization. Enquiries concerning reproduction
outside the scope of the above should be sent to the Rights Department,
Oxford University Press, at the address above

You must not circulate this book in any other binding or cover
and you must impose this same condition on any acquiror

British Library Cataloguing in Publication Data

Data available

Library of Congress Cataloging in Publication Data

Data available

Typeset by Cepha Imaging Private Ltd., Bangalore, India
Printed in Great Britain
on acid-free paper by the
MPG Books Group, Bodmin and King's Lynn

ISBN 978–0–19–923550–6

3 5 7 9 10 8 6 4

FOREWORD

It is difficult to believe that it is now nearly 10 years since the first adjudication under the 1996 Act. The process has represented a breath of fresh air for the construction industry and blown the cobwebs off the traditional methods by which the industry resolved its disputes. Latest court decisions on adjudication quickly became a major topic of interest. No construction law conference or publication was complete without a respectable update on the subject.

The introduction of a compulsory statutory dispute resolution process and the underlying requirement for a decision within 28 days led to early concerns but these have largely proved to be unfounded. That said, the Act and the default provisions of the Scheme failed to deal with major aspects of procedure, most importantly the basis for enforcement of decisions by adjudicators. This meant that it was left to the courts and in particular the Technology and Construction Court to deal with the gaps in the legislation and resolve fundamental questions of practice and procedure. The courts could, in principle, have treated the adjudication process as giving rise to only another contractual right so that decisions could be fully contested. Instead the courts have supported the process and made good the intention of the statute.

This makes it entirely appropriate that the first substantial legal text on construction adjudication should be written by Peter Coulson, now a distinguished judge in the Technology and Construction Court. Before his appointment to the bench Peter also had the advantage of dealing with adjudication as a practitioner at Keating Chambers. As a leading silk, he was involved in advising clients on the developing law. Now, in his current role he has, himself, made a major contribution to many aspects of that law.

From this wealth of experience, Peter has produced a clear and incisive text which covers every aspect of the subject in a methodical manner. It even covers the similar statutory procedures introduced in other countries and the proposed changes to the legislation here, which in this case includes Scotland. The text includes many helpful citations from the relevant judgments, amongst them those of an appropriately anonymous TCC Judge.

The publication of this text is timely. The law on many of the significant issues relating to adjudication has been made clear. Whilst there are still important aspects which arise, thanks to the many talented practitioners in this field, the immediate dust caused by the introduction of adjudication has settled. This book therefore reflects a more certain position than earlier texts.

I am delighted to have had some small role in encouraging Peter to write this text. It represents a major addition to legal texts on construction law. It will provide invaluable assistance not just for lawyers but for anyone involved in adjudication.

Sir Vivian Ramsey
Technology and Construction Court, London
October 2007

AUTHOR'S NOTE

I first mentioned the idea for this book to Vivian Ramsey in the autumn of 2001, as we crawled through the traffic on our way back from the Lord Chancellor's Breakfast. We agreed that there was a clear need for a book which contained a thorough review of all the cases concerned with adjudication, but that, since the sheer volume of cases at that time was so great, with no sign then of any slowing down, the moment for such a book had not yet come.

Time passed and, by the middle of 2006, it had become apparent that the number of cases concerning adjudication was at last decreasing and that a great many of the difficult questions raised by the Housing Grants, Construction and Regeneration Act 1996 had been answered by the TCC and the Court of Appeal. Finally, it seemed that the time was right for a comprehensive book about construction adjudication.

Because we have all got so used to it, it is difficult now to convey just how radical the 1996 Act seemed when it passed onto the statute book. It introduced a new mechanism by which the vast majority of construction disputes had to be resolved. Because construction disputes were seen as slow, and therefore expensive, the new procedure made speed the supreme virtue; no matter how complicated the dispute, no matter how voluminous the relevant paperwork, the adjudicator had to produce his decision within 28 days. In most cases, he could seek only an additional 14 days, and even then the referring party had to agree to it. Whilst this approach was justified on the basis that the adjudicator's decision would only be 'temporarily binding', it meant that the loser had to comply in full with the decision, no matter how outrageous it appeared, and could only challenge it later, in the sort of expensive court or arbitration proceedings which the Act was expressly designed to avoid.

In addition, the Act also re-wrote construction contracts to try and ensure that the smaller contractors were not kept out of their money by the larger organisations. They introduced the withholding notice procedure whereby, before the monies were due, the payer had to notify the payee as to what, if any, sums were being deducted from the payment and why. It also outlawed the 'pay-when-paid' system, whereby the larger contractors had passed onto their sub-contractors the financial difficulties of those higher up the contractual chain. Laudable although much of this undoubtedly was, it might be thought that the Act was rather contrary to the much-vaunted principles of the free market on which the outgoing government had staked so much.

Author's Note

Unsurprisingly, the 1996 Act, and the contractual adjudication schemes to which it gave rise, generated a large amount of litigation, as parties strove to discover the limits of the powers granted to adjudicators and the status and effect of their 'temporarily binding' decisions. The table of cases to this book contains close to 300 references, almost all of them dating from 1999 and onwards. On analysis, these authorities display a generally clear and consistent approach by judges at all levels to the underlying purpose of the 1996 Act and the need for the courts to support, without undue interference, the adjudication process.

Despite all of the potential anomalies and uncertainties created by the 1996 Act, there can be no doubt that the adjudication process has been a considerable success, and is a method of dispute resolution that is here to stay. I believe that its success has been down to a number of different factors, but I want here to spell out just two. One ingredient is the generally high standard of the written decisions produced by adjudicators. After an uncertain start, the inherent quality of these decisions has improved impressively over recent years; the various adjudication bodies have taken their obligations very seriously, particularly in respect of the training of would-be adjudicators, and have been rewarded with an increasingly high standard of finished product.

The other factor is the clarity with which the Court of Appeal have dealt with the adjudication issues which have been referred to them over recent years. A good many of the questions that were left unanswered, indeed confused, by the 1996 Act, have been given an unequivocal answer by the Court of Appeal in a series of clear and consistent judgments. As a result, the parties to a construction contract know very well in advance what the consequences are likely to be of any particular decision or dispute strategy which they might adopt in the particular adjudication with which they are concerned.

I should say a word about the structure of this book. Part I deals with the 1996 Act, and the particular type of adjudication which it introduced. Part II concerns other types of adjudication, and particularly the contractual adjudication procedures introduced by the standard forms of building and engineering contracts. Part III deals with the vexed question of the adjudicator's jurisdiction, and the extent to which he can make errors of fact and law. There is also a chapter on the closely related topic of fairness and natural justice. Part IV is concerned with the many points that commonly arise on applications to enforce the decision of the adjudicator.

It is right to say that Parts I–IV include many separate references to the same three dozen important cases. Whilst I have endeavoured to guard against repetition, the very nature of the disputes which commonly arise out of adjudicators' decisions means that the same cases are relevant under a number of different headings. This need to guard against too much repetition is made more difficult still by the

Author's Note

inescapable fact that one reported case might be relevant on two, three, or four different points of principle.

Part V is designed to provide a practical guide to adjudication: what to do, how to do it, when and why. An anonymous reviewer of my book proposal fairly suggested that, without it, there was a danger that the book might be a little grandiose, and of little help to those at what he called the 'muck and bullets' end of the adjudication process. I agreed wholeheartedly with that criticism and decided to devote a whole section of the book to what I hope is a comprehensive and helpful guide for those dealing with adjudications on a regular basis. Part VI is a short section, dealing with the current review of the 1996 Act, and the possible amendments to the statute which are being proposed.

There are, of course, a large number of people whom I would like to thank for their help in producing this book. Jackson and Ramsey JJ have been extremely encouraging and helpful, as have my colleagues at the TCC, both in and out of London. I have taken the advice of many construction lawyers and adjudicators whilst preparing the text: particular mention should be made of Paul Darling QC, the outgoing Chairman of TECBAR, and Matt Molloy, an experienced adjudicator who was a fount of good ideas for Part V. My publisher, Roxanne Selby, has been extremely enthusiastic from the outset, and I am very grateful to her, and everyone else at Oxford University Press, for all their help. Dominique Rawley, of Atkin Chambers, Merissa Martinez, of Trowers and Hamlins and Kate Williams, of Sirius Consulting (who together will produce a much-needed construction adjudication casebook next year) checked much of the text at very short notice, and suggested numerous improvements, almost all of which I gratefully accepted. David Grant, one of the clerks at Keating Chambers, carried out the huge task of compiling the original database. My wife, Ronnie, read uncomplainingly through the whole draft and even professed to find it interesting as she pointed out my many mistakes. And Liza Sanchez has, once again, carried out all the typing with the maximum of cheerfulness and the minimum of fuss.

I should like to dedicate this book to Tony Woolstone Esq, who first endeavoured to teach me some law whilst I was still at school, and to those amongst whom I learnt it: the Boys of '76 at Lord Wandsworth College, in Hampshire.

Peter Coulson
St Dunstan's House, EC4
17th July 2007

CONTENTS—SUMMARY

Table of Cases	xxiii
Table of Legislation, Treaties and Conventions	xxxv

PART I: STATUTORY ADJUDICATION

1. The Latham Report and its Aftermath	3
2. Part II of the Housing Grants Construction and Regeneration Act 1996	17
3. The Statutory Scheme	93

PART II: OTHER FORMS OF ADJUDICATION

4. Contractual Adjudication	147
5. Ad Hoc Adjudication	185
6. Adjudication in Other Jurisdictions	195

PART III: THE ADJUDICATOR'S JURISDICTION

7. General Principles	213
8. Errors of Law and Fact	263
9. Fairness	279
10. Abatement and Set-Off	311
11. Costs and Fees	335

PART IV: ENFORCEMENT

12. The Status and Effect of an Adjudicator's Decision	349
13. Principles of Enforcement	369
14. Adjudication Business in the TCC	381
15. Stay of Execution	395

PART V: A PRACTICAL GUIDE TO ADJUDICATION

16. Commencing an Adjudication	407
17. The Adjudication Itself	417
18. The Adjudicator's Decision	427

PART VI: THE FUTURE

19. The DTI Review and the Proposed Changes to the 1996 Act	435
Appendices	447
Index	471

CONTENTS

Table of Cases	xxiii
Table of Legislation, Treaties and Conventions	xxxv

I STATUTORY ADJUDICATION

1. The Latham Report and Its Aftermath

Introduction	1.01
The Main Recommendations of the Latham Report	1.07
Contract Terms	1.10
Adjudication	1.13
The Debates on the Bill	1.19
The Debates on the Scheme	1.31

2. Part II of the Housing Grants Construction and Regeneration Act 1996

General Purpose of Part II of the Act	2.01
Sections 104–105: Construction Contracts and Construction Operations	2.16
Section 104	2.18
Section 105	2.23
Exclusion Order 1998 (SI 1998 No 648)	2.37
Section 106: Residential Occupier	2.40
Section 107: Agreement in Writing	2.44
All, Not Part, of the Agreement Must be in Writing	2.46
Letters of Intent	2.60
Oral Variations	2.62
Implied Terms	2.67
Section 107(5)	2.69
Section 108: Adjudication	2.75
'A Dispute'	2.77
Notice at Any Time	2.85
28 Days	2.91
When Does the 28 Day Period Start to Run?	2.95

Is the Adjudicator Obliged to Complete the Decision Within 28 Days or Any Agreed Extended Period?	2.96
Is There Any Leeway Available to the Adjudicator When Communicating the Decision?	2.106
Impartiality/Fairness	2.109
Binding	2.116
Sections 109, 110 & 111: Payment Provisions	2.120
Payment Due Under the Contract	2.129
Set-Off	2.136
Nature and Timing of Withholding Notice	2.138
Relationship with Other Terms	2.142
Stay For Arbitration	2.148
Stay For Adjudication	2.152
Sections 112–115	2.153
Section 112: Suspension of Work	2.154
Section 113: 'Pay-When-Paid' Clauses	2.158
Section 114: The Scheme	2.162
Section 115: Service of Documents	2.164

3. The Statutory Scheme

Introduction	3.01
Part I of the Scheme—Adjudication	3.12
Notice of Adjudication	3.12
The Appointment of the Adjudicator	3.16
The Referral Notice	3.26
Referral Within 7 Days	3.29
More Than One Dispute	3.34
Resignation	3.39
Objection	3.48
Revocation	3.50
Powers of the Adjudicator	3.52
Acting Impartially	3.54
Taking the Initiative	3.57
Consideration of any Relevant Information	3.60
Time Limits	3.66
The Adjudicator's Decision	3.73
Opening Up, Revising and Reviewing	3.74

Interest	3.77
Costs	3.81
Reasons	3.83
Effect of the Decision	3.85
Binding Until the Dispute is Finally Determined	3.86
Enforcement of Peremptory Orders	3.94
Fees	3.95
Part II of the Scheme—Payment	3.97
Introduction	3.97
Entitlement to and Amount of Stage Payments	3.98
Dates for Payment	3.104
Final Date for Payment	3.108
Payment Notices and Withholding Notices	3.111
Prohibition of 'Pay-When-Paid'	3.114

II OTHER FORMS OF ADJUDICATION

4. Contractual Adjudication

The Importance of the Contractual Provisions	4.01
The JCT 1998 Form	4.06
Nomination	4.07
Referral Within 7 Days	4.11
More Than One Dispute	4.16
'Impartially'	4.17
Non-Compliance	4.18
28 Days	4.19
'Binding'	4.23
Final Certificates	4.25
Determination	4.26
Other Forms of JCT Contract	4.27
The JCT Adjudication Agreement	4.32
The Standard Forms of Sub-Contracts	
DOM/1	4.34
DOM/2	4.44
Other Standard Forms of Contract	
GC/Works	4.51
The ICE Form of Engineering Contract	4.54
NEC2	4.60
Contracts For Professional Services	4.61

Adjudication Rules	4.62
The TeCSA Rules	4.62
The CEDR Rules	4.71
The CIC Model Adjudication Procedure	4.72

5. Ad Hoc Adjudication

Introduction	5.01
The Relevant Authorities	5.03
Estoppel	5.12
Conclusion	5.14

6. Adjudication in Other Jurisdictions

Introduction	6.01
Australia	6.02
New South Wales	6.02
Overview	6.03
What Contracts does the NSW Act Apply to?	6.06
Can You Contract Out of the NSW Act?	6.09
Progress Payments and the Payment Claim	6.10
The Payment Schedule	6.12
Adjudication	6.13
Determination	6.18
Enforcement	6.20
Other Australian Jurisdictions	6.23
Singapore	6.29
New Zealand	6.35

III THE ADJUDICATOR'S JURISDICTION

7. General Principles

Introduction	7.01
What Happens if There Is a Jurisdictional Issue?	7.05
The Adjudicator's Power to Investigate His Own Jurisdiction	7.09
The Court's Investigation	7.16
Fundamental Principle	7.18
Was the Adjudicator Validly Appointed?	7.20
Was there a Construction Contract?	7.20
Was the Appointment in Accordance With the Contract?	7.25
Was the Contract in Writing?	7.28
Correct Parties	7.33

The Dispute	7.35
What was the Scope and Extent of the Dispute in the Notice of Adjudication?	7.35
Had that Dispute Crystallised Between the Parties Prior to the Notice to Refer?	7.46
Was the Dispute Referred to Adjudication a Single Dispute?	7.57
Insufficient Connection Between the Dispute Referred and the Adjudicator's Decision	7.64
The Relevance of Earlier Adjudication Decisions	7.71
Ousting the Jurisdiction of the Adjudicator in Other Ways	7.78
Making a Valid Objection on Jurisdiction	7.81
Summary of Principles Relating to Jurisdiction	7.83

8. Errors of Law and Fact

Introduction	8.01
Errors of Law/General	8.04
Errors of Law/Jurisdiction	8.14
Errors of Fact	8.18
'Slips'	8.24

9. Fairness

Introduction	9.01
Fairness/General	9.02
Size/Nature of Claim	9.04
Bias	9.11
Natural Justice/General	9.16
Natural Justice/Specific Instances	9.23
Separate Communications with the Parties	9.23
Failure to Consult	9.26
Taking Advice from Others	9.30
Indication of Preliminary View	9.33
Ambush	9.36
Effect of Earlier Adjudications	9.38
Miscellaneous	9.42
Human Rights	9.44
Unfair Terms in Consumer Contracts Regulations	9.49

10. Abatement and Set-Off

The Problem	10.01
Abatement/Set-Off Against a Sum Certified/Determined as Due	10.06
Abatement/Set-Off Against Sums Claimed	10.13
Set-Off Against the Adjudicator's Decision	10.20
The General Rule	10.21
The Exceptions	10.33
Liquidated Damages	10.35
Summary	10.38

11. Costs and Fees

Costs	11.01
The Usual Position	11.01
Ad Hoc Jurisdiction to Decide Costs	11.05
Particular Contract Provisions	11.07
The Adjudicator's Fees	11.12
Lien	11.19

IV ENFORCEMENT

12. The Status and Effect of an Adjudicator's Decision

Introduction	12.01
A Valid Decision	12.04
Compliance with Time Limits	12.06
Errors and Slips	12.09
The Decision Itself	12.15
Compliance with the Decision	12.16
Status of Decision	12.19
Temporary Finality/Generally	12.24
Temporary Finality/Subsequent Adjudications	12.27
Status in Later Court or Arbitration Proceedings	12.35
Winding Up/Bankruptcy	12.41
Protective Measures in Scotland	12.46

13. Principles of Enforcement

Introduction	13.01
General Approach	13.02
Was There a Construction Contract?	13.06
Was the Construction Contract in Writing?	13.08
Was More Than One Dispute Referred to the Adjudicator?	13.09
In What Circumstances is a Withholding Notice Necessary?	13.10
Can the Paying Party Set Off a Separate Claim Against the Sum Awarded by the Adjudicator?	13.12
In What Circumstances Might the Adjudicator be Found Guilty of Bias?	13.14
In What Circumstances Will the Court Consider Breaches of the Rules of Natural Justice?	13.16
Summary Judgment	13.18
Summary	13.20

14. Adjudication Business in the TCC

Introduction	14.01
Enforcement Generally	14.02
Summary Judgment in the TCC	14.05
Interest and Costs	14.12
The Consequences of Losing an Adjudication	14.15
Injunctions	14.20
Declaratory Relief	14.26
Staying Court Proceedings for Adjudication	14.30

15. Stay of Execution

Introduction	15.01
RSC Order 47	15.02
Cross-Claim of Judgment Debtor	15.04
Insolvency of Judgment Creditor	15.06
The Financial Difficulties of the Judgment Creditor	15.09

V A PRACTICAL GUIDE TO ADJUDICATION

16. Commencing an Adjudication

Introduction	16.01
Notice of Adjudication	16.02
Response to the Notice of Adjudication	16.07
Appointment of Adjudicator	16.10
A Challenge to the Nominated Adjudicator	16.16
Referral Notice	16.21

17. The Adjudication Itself

Directions	17.01
Response to Referral Notice	17.04
Referring Party's Reply	17.06
Meetings, Evidence and Hearings	
Meetings	17.08
Evidence	17.09
Hearings	17.11
Visits	17.13
Documentation	17.15
Timescale and Requested Extensions	17.19
Natural Justice	17.23
Conflict of Interest	17.24
Reciprocity	17.26
Inquisitorial or Adversarial?	17.28
Intimidatory Tactics	17.30

18. The Adjudicator's Decision

Reasons	18.01
Completion and Communication	18.03
Errors	18.06
Ancillary Matters	18.09
Fees and Costs	18.09
Effect of the Decision	18.12

VI THE FUTURE

19. The DTI Review and the Proposed Changes to the 1996 Act

Introduction	19.01
The Second Consultation Report	19.03
The Adjudication Framework	19.03
The Payment Framework	19.14
Improving the Right to Suspend Performance	19.28
Other Issues	19.31
Summary	19.36

APPENDICES

Appendix A: Part II of the Housing Grants, Construction and Regeneration Act 1996	449
Appendix B: Statutory Instrument 1998 No 648	457
Appendix C: Statutory Instrument 1998 No 649 (The Scheme)	461
Appendix D: Draft Directions in Adjudication Enforcement Proceedings	469
Index	471

TABLE OF CASES

A v B [2002] Scot CS 325 (CSOH). 4.67, 4.68
ABB Power Construction Ltd v Norwest Holst Engineering Ltd [2000] TCLR 831;
    77 Con LR 20; (2001) 17 Const LJ 246 . . . . 2.27, 2.32–2.34, 2.36, 7.20, 14.23n
ABB Zantingh Ltd v Zedal Building Services Ltd [2001] BLR 66; (2001) 3 TCLR 19;
    77 Con LR 32 . . . . 2.35, 7.16
Absolute Rentals Ltd v Gencor Enterprises Ltd (2001) 17 Const LJ 322;
    [2000] CILL 1637 . . . . 3.87, 15.16, 15.19
A C Yule & Son Ltd v Speedwell Roofing & Cladding Ltd [2007]
    EWHC 1360 (TCC) 2.101, 2.102, 2.104, 3.70, 3.71n, 4.21, 6.22n,
                                                                       11.21n, 12.06n, 17.22n
A&D Maintenance & Construction Ltd v Pagehurst Construction Services Ltd
    (2000) 16 Const LJ 199; [1999] CILL 1518 . . . . 2.89
AJ Brenton (t/a Manton Electrical Components) v Palmer (unreported,
    TCC 19 January 2001). 8.18, 8.20
Ale Heavy Lift v MSD (Darlington) Ltd [2006] EWHC 2080 (TCC). 2.74, 7.82,
                                                                              10.32n, 15.20
Allen Wilson Shopfitters v Buckingham [2005] EWHC 1165 (TCC);
    (2005) 102 Con LR 154 . . . . 3.93, 4.04n, 8.10, 9.57n
Allied London & Scottish Properties plc v Riverbrae Construction Ltd 2000 SLT 981;
    [1999] BLR 346; (2000) 2 TCLR 398 . . . . 8.08n, 10.21
Alstom Signalling Ltd v Jarvis Facilities Ltd [2004] EWHC 1285 (TCC) 2.127n, 2.133,
                                                                           3.101, 3.103, 12.04
AMEC Civil Engineering Ltd v Secretary of State for Transport [2004]
    EWHC 2339 (TCC); affirmed [2005] EWCA Civ 291; [2005] 1 WLR 2339;
    [2005] BLR 227; 101 Con LR 26 (CA). 7.54, 7.55
AMEC Capital Projects Ltd v Whitefriars City Estates Ltd [2004] EWHC 393 (TCC);
    (2004) 20 Const LJ 338; reversed [2004] EWCA Civ 1418; [2005] 1 All ER 723;
    [2005] BLR 1; 96 Con LR 142 (CA). 3.20, 3.57n, 3.84, 4.10, 7.03n, 7.04,
                                                              7.15, 7.24, 7.74n, 9.01, 9.15, 13.14, 13.15, 13.17
Andrew Wallace Ltd v Artisan Regeneration Ltd [2006] EWHC 15 (TCC). 7.34
Anisminic Ltd v Foreign Compensation Commission [1969] AC 147;
    [1969] 2 WLR 163; [1969] 1 All ER 208 (HL) 7.12n, 8.05, 8.06, 8.07, 8.08
Ardmore Construction Ltd v Taylor Woodrow Construction Ltd [2006]
    Scot CS 3 (CSOH); [2006] CILL 2309 . . . . 9.21, 9.34
A R T Consultancy Ltd v Navera Trading Ltd [2007] EWHC 1375 (TCC) 2.52n, 2.59, 7.30
A & S Enterprises Ltd v Kema Holding Ltd [2004] EWHC 3365 (TCC);
    [2005] BLR 76; [2004] CILL 2165 . . . . 9.43
Ashley House plc v Galliers Southern Ltd [2002] EWHC 274 (TCC);
    [2002] Adj LR 02/15 . . . . 15.12
Ashville Investments v Elmer Contractors [1989] QB 488; [1988] 3 WLR 867;
    [1988] 2 All ER 577; [1988] 2 Lloyd's Rep 73 (note) (CA) 7.23, 7.78n
Austin Hall Building Ltd v Buckland Securities Ltd [2001] BLR 274;
    (2001) 3 TCLR 18; 80 Con LR 115; (2001) 17 Const LJ 325 . . . . 2.114, 9.45, 9.48
Aveat Heating Ltd v Jerram Faulkus Construction Ltd [2007]
    EWHC 131 (TCC) 2.95, 2.100, 3.09, 3.30, 3.71n, 3.81n, 4.53, 4.73, 11.21n, 12.08

AWG Construction Services Ltd v Rockingham Motor Speedway Ltd [2004]
　　EWHC 888 (TCC); [2004] TCLR 6 .... 2.13–2.14, 2.92n, 3.57n,
　　　　　　　　　　　　　　　　　　　　　　　　　　　　7.53, 7.64, 9.05, 9.19n, 15.17, 15.19

BAL (1996) Ltd v Taylor Woodrow Construction Ltd [2004] All ER (D) 218 .... 9.32
Balfour Beatty Construction Ltd v London Borough of Lambeth [2002]
　　EWHC 597 (TCC); [2002] BLR 288; [2002] TCLR 25; 84 Con LR 1 .... 2.04, 3.41,
　　　　　　　　　　　　　　　　　　　　3.83, 4.17, 7.04, 9.19, 9.21, 9.27, 9.30, 9.31, 9.33n
Balfour Beatty Construction Ltd v Serco Ltd [2004] EWHC 3336 (TCC) 10.24, 10.31,
　　　　　　　　　　　　　　　　　　　　　　　　　　　　　　　　　　　　　10.33, 10.37
Ballast plc v The Burrell Company (Construction Management) Ltd 2001 SLT 1039;
　　2001 SCLR 837; [2001] BLR 529 .... 3.06, 7.12, 7.65, 8.08n, 8.12, 8.14
Barnes & Elliott Ltd v Taylor Woodrow Holdings Ltd [2003] EWHC 3100 (TCC);
　　[2004] BLR 111 .... 2.97, 2.106, 3.70, 3.71, 4.20, 4.22, 12.06
Barr Ltd v Law Mining Ltd [2001] Scot CS 152; (2001) 80 Con LR 134;
　　[2001] CILL 1764 .... 2.83, 4.55, 7.62, 13.09n
Beck Peppiatt Ltd v Norwest Holst Construction Ltd [2003] EWHC 822 (TCC);
　　[2003] BLR 316 ....7.50n, 7.52
Bennett v FMK Construction Ltd [2005] EWHC 1268 (TCC);
　　101 Con LR 92 .... 3.25, 4.14, 4.15, 7.43
Bennett (Electrical) Services Ltd v Inviron Ltd [2007] EWHC 49 (TCC) 2.52n, 2.54,
　　　　　　　　　　　　　　　　　　　　　　　　　　　　　　　　　　　　　2.61, 7.29n
Bickerton Construction Ltd v Temple Windows Ltd (unreported,
　　TCC 26 June 2001) 4.47, 7.67n
Bill Biakh v Hyundai Corp [1988] 1 Lloyd's Rep 187 .... 3.63
Bloor Construction (UK) Ltd v Bowmer & Kirkland London Ltd [2000] BLR 314;
　　[2000] BLR 764 .... 2.117, 2.118, 3.89, 6.19n, 8.26, 8.27, 8.29, 8.30,
　　　　　　　　　　　　　　　　　　　　　　　　　　　12.11, 12.12, 12.13, 18.07, 19.31n
Boddington v BT Police [1999] AC 143; [1998] 2 WLR 639; [1998]
　　2 All ER 203 (HL) 8.06n
Bothma (t/a DAB Builders) v Mayhaven Healthcare Ltd (TCC 16 November 2006);
　　[2007] EWCA Civ 527 .... 3.38, 7.61, 7.63, 7.82
Bouygues (UK) Ltd v Dahl-Jensen (UK) Ltd [2001] 1 All ER (Comm) 1041;
　　[2000] BLR 49; [2000] BLR 522; (2001) 3 TCLR 2 (CA). 2.04–2.09, 2.117,
　　　　　　　　　　　　　　　　　2.118, 4.64, 4.72, 7.04, 7.18n, 8.03, 8.04, 8.05, 8.08, 8.21,
　　　　　　　　　　　　　　　　　　8.25, 9.02, 12.09, 12.12, 12.25, 13.02, 13.03, 13.19,
　　　　　　　　　　　　　　　　　　　　　　　　　　　　　　13.20, 15.06, 15.07, 15.19
Bovis Lend Lease Ltd v Triangle Development Ltd [2002]
　　EWHC 3123 (TCC); [2003] BLR 31; 86 Con LR 26; [2003] CILL 1939 .. 2.140n, 10.02,
　　　　　　　　　　　　　　　　　　　　　　　　　　　　　　　　　　　　　10.31, 12.20
Bridgeway Construction Ltd v Tolent Construction Ltd [2000] CILL 1662 .... 11.07, 19.12
Broadwell (t/a Broadwell Construction) v k3D Property Partnership Ltd [2006]
　　AdjCS 04/21 .... 12.15
Brownlow Ltd v Dem-master Demolition Ltd (Sheriffdom of Lothian
　　and Borders 26 February 2004)... 2.64n
Bryen & Langley Ltd v Boston [2004] EWHC 2450 (TCC); [2005] BLR 28; 98
　　Con LR 82; reversed [2005] EWCA Civ 973; [2005] BLR 508 (CA)..... 9.55–9.56, 13.07
Buxton Building Contractors Ltd v Governors of Durand Primary School [2004]
　　EWHC 733 (TCC); [2004] BLR 474; 95 Con LR 120 ....3.60–3.61, 3.63,
　　　　　　　　　　　　　　　　　　　　　　　　　　　　　　　　　　3.65n, 4.04, 7.69

Cable & Wireless plc v IBM United Kingdom Ltd [2002] EWHC 2059; [2002]
　　2 All ER (Comm) 1041; [2002] CLC 1319; [2003] BLR 89 ....14.32, 14.34
Cape Durasteel Ltd v Rosser & Russell Building Services Ltd (1995) 46 Con LR 75 ...... 14.33

Table of Cases

Capital Structures plc v Time and Tide Construction Ltd [2006] EWHC 591 (TCC);
  [2006] BLR 226; [2006] CILL 2345 .... 7.32
Captiva Estates Ltd v Rybarn Ltd (In Administration) [2005] EWHC 2744 (TCC);
  [2006] BLR 66; [2006] CILL 2333 .... 2.38
Carillion Construction Ltd v Devonport Royal Dockyard Ltd [2003] BLR 79;
  [2003] TCLR 2 .... 2.64, 2.67n
Carillion Construction Ltd v Devonport Royal Dockyard Ltd [2005]
  EWHC 778 (TCC); [2005] BLR 310; 102 Con LR 167; affirmed [2005]
  EWCA (Civ) 1358; [2005] BLR 310; 104 Con LR 1 (CA) 2.15, 3.62–3.65,
            3.77–3.80, 3.81, 3.82, 4.04n, 7.03n, 7.04, 7.69, 7.84–7.85, 7.86,
            8.04, 9.01, 9.03n, 9.04n, 9.21, 9.33n, 12.25n, 369,13.17n, 13.21
Carl Construction (Scotland) Ltd v Sweeney Civil Engineering (Scotland)
  Ltd [2001] SCLR 95 .... 8.17
Cartwright v Fay (Bath County Court 9 February 2005) 4.33, 9.57n, 11.19n
Castle Inns (Stirling) Ltd v Clark Contracts Ltd [2007] Scot CS 21 (CSOH) 4.25, 7.74n
C & B Scene Concept Design Ltd v Isobars Ltd [2002] EWCA Civ 46; [2002]
  CLC 652; [2002] BLR 93 (CA) 2.09, 2.11–2.12, 3.05, 3.57n, 3.91, 3.92,
            3.93, 4.04, 4.46n, 7.04, 7.18, 8.03, 8.08, 8.09, 8.11, 9.17, 13.04
Chamberlain Carpentry and Joinery Ltd v Alfred McAlpine Construction
  Ltd [2002] EWHC 514 (TCC) 7.45
Channel Tunnel Group Ltd v Balfour Beatty Construction Ltd [1993] AC 334;
  [1993] 2 WLR 262; [1993] 1 All ER 664 (HL) 14.32, 14.34
Christiani & Nielsen Ltd v The Lowry Centre Development Co Ltd [2004] TCLR 2 ...... 5.05
CIB Properties Ltd v Birse Construction Ltd [2004] EWHC 2365 (TCC); [2005]
  1 WLR 2252; [2005] BLR 173 .... 2.93, 8.29, 9.06–9.07, 12.14
Citex Professional Services Ltd v Kenmore Developments Ltd [2004]
  Scot CS 20; A1195/02 .... 4.23n, 12.39
City Inn Ltd v Shepherd Construction Ltd 2002 SLT 781;
  2001 SCLR 961 .... 4.23, 12.38, 12.39
Clark Contracts Ltd v The Burrell Co (Construction Management)
  Ltd 2002 SLT 103 .... 2.132, 2.133, 10.09, 10.11, 10.18
Collins (Contractors) Ltd v Baltic Quay Management (1994) Ltd [2004]
  EWCA Civ 1757; [2005] BLR 63; [2005] TCLR 3; 99 Con LR 1 (CA) 2.150, 2.151,
                                                                          3.89, 7.55
Company (No 1299 of 2001), Re [2001] CILL 1745 .... 10.08, 12.43, 12.45
Comsite Projects Ltd v Andritz AG [2003] EWHC 958 (TCC);
  (2004) 20 Const LJ 24 .... 2.36
Connex South Eastern Ltd v MJ Building Services Group plc [2004] EWHC 1518;
  [2004] BLR 333; 95 Con LR 43; reversed [2005] EWCA Civ 193; [2005]
  1 WLR 3323; [2005] 2 All ER 871; [2005] BLR 201 (CA) 2.67–2.68, 2.90
Conor Engineering Ltd v Les Constructions Industrielles de la Mediterranée
  [2004] EWHC 899 (TCC); [2004] BLR 212 .... 2.36, 10.34
Construction Centre Group Ltd v Highland Council [2003] XA 123/02 Extra Division
  Inner House, Court of Session; 2002 SLT 1274; [2002] BLR 476 .... 2.140n, 4.57,
                                                                   4.58, 4.59, 10.37
Costain Ltd v Wescol Steel Ltd [2003] EWHC 312 (TCC) 4.36
Cott UK Ltd v FE Barber Ltd [1997] 3 All ER 540 .... 14.32, 14.34
Cowlin Construction Ltd v CFW Architects (A Firm) [2003] CILL 1961;
  [2003] BLR 252 .... 7.52
Cubitt Building & Interiors Ltd v Fleetglade Ltd [2006] EWHC 3413 (TCC);
  110 Con LR 36; [2007] CILL 2431 .... 2.14n, 2.24n, 2.96n, 2.100, 2.105,
            2.107, 2.166, 3.33n, 3.71n, 4.02, 4.13, 4.15, 4.18, 4.21, 4.33n, 4.36,
            7.43, 11.18, 11.21n, 11.22, 12.06n, 12.08, 12.13n, 16.13n, 18.04
Cygnet Healthcare Plc v Higgins City Ltd (2000) 16 Const LJ 394 .... 2.88

DGT Steel and Cladding Ltd v Cubitt Building & Interiors Ltd [2007]
    EWHC 1584 (TCC) 2.87n, 14.31, 14.34, 14.35, 14.36
DSND Sub–Sea v Petroleum Geoservices [2000] BLR 530 . . . . 7.32
David McLean Contractors Ltd v The Albany Building Ltd [2005]
    EWHC B5 (TCC) 7.74n, 10.30, 12.29
David McLean Housing Contractors Ltd v Swansea Housing Association
    Ltd [2002] BLR 125 . . . . 2.81, 2.149, 3.22, 4.03A, 7.58, 7.59, 7.80, 10.33, 12.19
Dawnays Ltd v FG Minter Ltd [1971] 1 WLR 1205; [1971] 2 All ER 1389 . . . . 1.01, 3.80,
    10.02, 10.03
Dean and Dyball Construction Ltd v Kenneth Grubb Associates Ltd [2003]
    EWHC 2465 (TCC); 100 Con LR 92 . . . . 2.53, 4.74, 8.08n, 9.25
Debek Ductwork Installation Ltd v TE Engineering Ltd (TCC Birmingham
    14 January 2002) 2.54, 2.64n
Deko Scotland Ltd v Edinburgh Royal Joint Adventure 2003 SLT 727 . . . . 4.69, 11.08
Director General of Fair Trading v First National Bank plc [2001] UKHL 52;
    [2002] 1 AC 481; [2001] 3 WLR 1297; [2002] 1 All ER 97 (HL) 9.50
Director General of Fair Trading v Proprietary Association of Great Britain [2000]
    All ER (D) 2425 . . . . 9.11n
Discain Project Services Ltd v Opecprime Developments Ltd [2001] BLR 287;
    (2001) 3 TCLR 17; 80 Con LR 95 . . . . 9.18, 9.19
Discain Project Services Ltd v Opecprime Developments Ltd (No 1) [2000]
    BLR 402; (2001) 3 TCLR 16 . . . . 2.110, 3.55n, 4.17n, 7.04, 9.26
Domsalla (t/a Domsalla Building Services) v Dyason [2007] EWHC 1174 (TCC);
    112 Con LR 95 . . . . 2.41, 4.05, 4.29, 7.01n, 9.57
Dumarc Building Services Ltd v Salvador Rico (Epsom County
    Court 31 March 2003) 4.30, 10.29n
Durabella Ltd v J Jarvis & Sons Ltd (2001) 83 Con LR 145 . . . . 2.161

Earls Terrace Properties Ltd v Waterloo Investments Ltd [2002] CILL 1889–1892 . . . . 2.22
Edmund Nuttall Ltd v RG Carter Ltd [2002] EWHC 400 (TCC); [2002] BLR 312;
    [2002] TCLR 27; 82 Con LR 24 . . . . 4.38, 4.40, 7.51, 7.53, 9.13n, 9.37
Edmund Nuttall Ltd v Sevenoaks DC (unreported, 14 April 2000) 8.27, 10.35,
    12.12, 18.07n
Elanay Contracts Ltd v The Vestry [2001] BLR 33; (2001) 3 TCLR 6 . . . . 9.44
Emcor Drake & Scull Ltd v Costain Construction Ltd [2004] EWHC 2439 (TCC);
    97 Con LR 142 . . . . 4.48, 4.49, 12.28
Epping Electrical Co Ltd v Briggs and Forrester (Plumbing Services) Ltd [2007]
    EWHC 4 (TCC); [2007] BLR 126; [2007] CILL 2438 . . . . 2.96n, 2.100, 2.107n,
    3.71n, 4.73, 11.23, 12.08

Faithful & Gould Ltd v Arcal Ltd (In Administrative Receivership)
    (TCC Newcastle No E190023). 11.19
Farebrother Building Services Ltd v Frogmore Investments Ltd [2001]
    CILL 1762–1764 . . . . 4.64, 4.65
Fastrack Contractors Ltd v Morrison Construction Ltd [2000] BLR 168;
    75 Con LR 33; (2000) 16 Const LJ 273 . . . . 2.80, 2.83, 7.05n, 7.09n,
    7.17, 7.48, 7.50, 7.58, 7.62, 7.66, 13.09n
Fencegate Ltd v James R Knowles Ltd [2001] CILL 1757 . . . . 2.19–2.20
Ferson Contractors Ltd v Levolex AT Ltd *see* Levolux AT Ltd v Ferson Contractors Ltd
Flannery Construction Ltd v M Holleran (2007) Ltd [2007] EWHC 825 (TCC) 2.54
Fredrick Mark Ltd v Schield [1972] 1 Lloyd's Rep 9; 1 BLR 32 (CA). 10.02n
Fulham Leisure Holdings Ltd v Nicholson Graham & Jones
    [2006] EWHC 2428 (Ch) 11.03n
FW Cook Ltd v Shimizu (UK) Ltd [2000] BLR 199 . . . . 7.37

Table of Cases

Galliford Try Construction Ltd v Michael Heal Associates Ltd [2003]
EWHC 2886 (TCC); 99 Con LR 19 .... 2.68, 5.09, 5.10, 5.15
Geris Handelsgesellschaft v les Constructions Industrielles de la
Mediterranée SA [2005] EWHC 499 (QB)............................. 10.33
Gibson Lea Retail Interiors Ltd v Makro Self Service Wholesalers Ltd
[2001] BLR 407 .... 2.21, 2.28
Gilbert Ash (Northern) Ltd v Modern Engineering (Bristol) Ltd [1974]
AC 689; [1973] 3 WLR 421; [1973] 3 All ER 195 (HL) 311, 10.01, 10.03
Gillies Ramsay Diamond v PJW Enterprises Ltd [2002] CILL 1901;
[2003] BLR 48 .... 2.18, 3.83, 8.08n
GKN Foundations Ltd v Wandsworth LBC [1972] 1 Lloyd's Rep 528;
1 BLR 38 (CA)... 10.02n
Glencot Development & Design Co Ltd v Ben Barrett & Son (Contractors)
Ltd [2001] BLR 207; (2001) 3 TCLR 11; 80 Con LR 14 .... 2.111, 3.54, 3.55,
4.17n, 9.12, 9.18, 9.24, 9.47
Gray & Sons Builders (Bedford) Ltd v Essential Box Co Ltd [2006]
EWHC 2520 (TCC); 108 Con LR 49; [2006] CILL 2395 .... 14.14
Griffin (t/a K&D Contractors) v Midas Homes Ltd (2000) 78 Con LR 152; (2002)
18 Const LJ 67 .... 2.163, 3.13n, 7.39, 11.15
Grovedeck Ltd v Capital Demolition Ltd [2000] BLR 181;
(2000) 2 TCLR 689 .... 2.70, 2.73, 7.13, 7.28, 7.59, 7.63, 13.09n, 19.04
Guardi Shoes Ltd v Datum Contracts [2002] CILL 1934 .... 12.44, 12.45

Halki Shipping Corp v Sopex Oils Ltd (The Halki) [1997] EWCA Civ 3062;
[1998] 1 WLR 726; [1998] 2 All ER 23; [1998]
1 Lloyd's Rep 465 (CA)................................... 2.150n, 4.40, 7.49, 7.52
Harlow & Milner v Teasdale (No 1) [2006] EWHC 54 (TCC) 12.41n, 14.04,
14.13n, 14.15–14.19
Harlow & Milner v Teasdale (No 2) [2006] EWHC 535 (TCC) 14.15–14.19
Harlow & Milner v Teasdale (No 3) [2006] EWHC 1708 (TCC);
[2006] BLR 359 .... 14.15–14.19
Hart Investments Ltd v Fidler [2006] EWHC 2857 (TCC); [2006] All ER (D) 232;
[2007] BLR 303; [2007] TLLR 1; (2007) 109 Con LR 14 .... 2.60, 2.100,
3.31–3.33, 3.71n, 11.21n, 12.08, 15.07, 16.13n
Harwood Construction Ltd v Lantrode Ltd (unreported,
TCC 24 November 2000)................................. 2.137, 10.22n, 15.08
Hayter v Nelson Home Insurance [1990] 2 Lloyd's Rep 265; 23 Con LR 88 .... 2.150n
Herschel Engineering Ltd v Breen Property Ltd [2000] BLR 272; (2000) 2 TCLR 473;
70 Con LR 1 .... 2.86, 2.88, 2.90, 14.33, 14.34, 15.11
Herschel Engineering Ltd v Breen Property Ltd (No 2) (unreported,
TCC 28 July 2000)... 15.13
HG Construction Ltd v Ashwell Homes (East Anglia) Ltd [2007]
EWHC 144 (TCC); [2007] BLR 175; 112 Con LR 128; [2007] CILL 2453 .. 7.74n, 9.41,
12.23, 16.19
Hillcourt v Teliasonera AB [2006] EWHC 508 (Ch)..................... 15.04, 15.05
Hills Electrical & Mechanical plc v Dawn Construction Ltd [2004] SLT 477 .... 3.07
Hillview Industrial Developments (UK) Ltd v Botes Building Ltd [2006] EWHC 1365
(TCC).. 10.32, 14.18n
Hitech Power Protection BV v MCI Worldcom Ltd [2002] EWHC 1953 .... 7.51
Holt Insulation Ltd v Colt International Ltd (unreported,
TCC Liverpool 23 July 2001)..3.44, 7.74
Homer Burgess Ltd v Chirex (Annan) Ltd 2000 SLT 277; [2000] BLR 124;
71 Con LR 245 .... 2.31, 2.36, 7.09n, 7.13

Table of Cases

Humes Building Contracts Ltd v Charlotte Homes (Surrey) Ltd (unreported,
    TCC Salford 4 January 2007) 9.21, 9.34
Hurst Stores and Interiors Ltd v ML Europe Property Ltd [2003]
    EWHC 1650 (TCC) 4.70

IDE Contracting Ltd v RG Carter Cambridge Ltd [2004] EWHC 36 (TCC);
    [2004] BLR 172; 102 Con LR 102 .... 3.23, 7.14, 7.24
Interserve Industrial Services Ltd v Cleveland Bridge (UK) Ltd [2006]
    EWHC 741 (TCC) 10.32, 14.18n

Jerome Engineering Ltd v Lloyd Morris Electrical Ltd [2002] CILL 1827 ..... 3.13n, 4.44, 7.40
John Mowlem Ltd v Hydra-Tight & Co plc (2002) 17 Const LJ 358 .... 3.08, 4.60, 14.23n
John Roberts Architects Ltd v Parkcare Homes (No 2) Ltd [2005]
    EWHC 1637 (TCC); [2005] BLR 484; reversed [2006] EWCA Civ 64; [2006]
    1 CLC 333; [2006] BLR 106; 105 Con LR 36 (CA) 335, 11.05n,
                                                    11.09–11.10, 11.11, 19.12n
Joinery Plus Ltd (In Administration) v Laing Ltd [2003] EWHC 3513
    (TCC); [2003] BLR 184; [2003] TCLR 4; 87 Con LR 87 .... 3.91, 3.92, 3.93,
                                                    4.46, 8.11, 12.14
JT Mackely & Co Ltd v Gosport Marina Ltd [2002] EWHC 1315 (TCC);
    [2002] BLR 367; [2002] TCLR 26 .... 4.56
JW Hughes Building Contractors Ltd v GB Metal Work Ltd [2003]
    EWHC 2421 (TCC) 7.11, 7.79, 9.42, 15.15

Keir Regional Ltd (t/a Wallis) v City & General (Holborn) Ltd [2006]
    EWHC 848 (TCC) 2.113, 3.65n, 9.21
King v Thomas McKenna Ltd [1991] 2 QB 480; [1991] 2 WLR 1234; [1991]
    1 All ER 653 (CA) 8.26n
KNS Industrial Services (Birmingham) Ltd v Sindall Ltd [2000] EWHC 75 (TCC);
    (2001) 3 TCLR 10; (2000) 75 Con LR 71; (2001) 17 Const LJ 170 .... 2.81, 3.28,
                                        4.35, 4.41, 4.43, 4.45, 4.52n, 7.44, 7.66, 10.14, 10.19

Latham Construction Ltd v Cross [2000] CILL 1568 .... 7.21, 7.78n
L Brown & Sons Ltd v Crosby Homes (North West) Ltd [2005]
    EWHC 3503 (TCC) 7.22, 7.23, 7.78
Lead Technical Services Ltd v CMS Medical Ltd [2007] EWCA Civ 316;
    [2007] BLR 251 (CA) 2.66, 7.27
Levolux AT Ltd v Ferson Contractors Ltd [2003] EWCA Civ 11; [2003]
    1 All ER (Comm) 385; [2003] BLR 118; [2003] TCLR 5 (CA) 2.119, 2.140n,
                                    4.51, 4.52, 7.04, 10.26–10.28, 10.29, 10.30,
                                    10.31, 10.37, 12.20, 13.13
Lindsay Parkinson (Sir) & Co v Triplan Ltd [1973] QB 609; [1973]
    2 WLR 632 (CA) 15.10, 15.13
Locabail v Bayfield [2000] QB 451; [2000] 2 WLR 870; [2000] 1 All ER 65 (CA) 9.11
London & Amsterdam Properties Ltd v Waterman Partnership Ltd [2003]
    EWHC 3059 (TCC); [2004] BLR 179; 94 Con LR 154;
    (2004) 20 Const LJ 215 .... 3.95, 8.08, 9.05, 9.36
Lovell Projects Ltd v Legg & Carver [2003] BLR 452 .... 4.28, 4.30, 7.53n, 9.52,
                                                    9.53, 9.55, 9.56
LPL Electrical Services Ltd v Kershaw Mechanical Services Ltd (unreported,
    2 February 2001) 7.40n

McAlpine PPS Pipeline Systems Joint Venture v Transco plc [2004]
    EWHC 2030 (TCC); [2004] BLR 352; 96 Con LR 69 ...... 3.57–3.58, 7.68, 7.69, 9.37

Macob Civil Engineering Ltd v Morrison Construction Ltd [1999]
    EWHC Technology 254; [1999] CLC 739; [1999] BLR 93; (1999)
    1 TCLR 113 .... 2.01, 2.03–2.04, 2.112, 7.18n, 8.04, 8.05, 8.18,
                                    9.17, 12.17, 12.25n, 13.02, 13.18, 13.20, 14.21, 14.22
Management Solutions and Professional Consultants Ltd v Bennett (Electrical)
    Services Ltd [2006] EWHC 1720 (TCC) 2.65, 2.66n
Martin Girt v Page Bentley [2002] EWHC 2434 (QB) 3.76
Mast Electrical Services v Kendall Cross Holdings Ltd [2007]
    EWHC 1296 (TCC); [2007] NPC 70 .... 2.58
Maxi Construction Management Ltd v Mortons Rolls Ltd [2001]
    Scot CS 199; [2001] CILL 1784 .... 2.126
Maymac Environmental Services Ltd v Faraday Building Services (2000)
    75 Con LR 101; [2001] CILL 1685 .... 4.34, 5.12
Mecright Ltd v TA Morris Developments Ltd (unreported,
    TCC 22 June 2001) 3.14– 3.15, 3.28, 7.38, 7.44
Medicaments, Re [2001] 1 WLR 700; [2001] UKCLR 550;
    [2001] ICR 564 (CA).. 9.11, 9.12
Melville Dundas Ltd (In Receivership) v George Wimpey UK Ltd [2005]
    SLT 24 (OH); reversed [2007] UKHL 18; [2007] 1 WLR 1136; 2007 SLT 413;
    2007 SCLR 429 (HL)..................... 2.134, 2.142, 2.146, 2.147, 4.26, 4.43,
                                                10.07, 10.12, 19.15n, 19.33, 19.35
Michael John Construction Ltd v Golledge [2006] EWHC 71
    (TCC); [2006] TCLR 3 .... 7.34, 7.58, 7.76, 9.14, 9.15, 9.32n, 15.14, 17.30n
Midland Expressway Ltd v Carillion Construction Ltd (No 3) [2006] EWHC 1505
    (TCC); [2006] BLR 325; 107 Con LR 205; [2006] CILL 2386 ....7.56, 11.11
Millers Specialist Joinery Co Ltd v Nobles Construction Ltd [2001]
    CILL 1770 .... 2.131n, 2.137, 10.15–10.16, 10.19
Mitsui Babcock Energy Services v Foster Wheeler Energia OY 2001 SLT 24 .... 2.34n
Mivan Ltd v Lighting Technology Projects Ltd [2001] ADJCS 04/09 (TCC) 3.44, 7.75
MJ Gleeson Group plc v Devonshire Green Holding Ltd (unreported,
    TCC Salford 19 March 2004)....................................... 10.29, 10.30
Modern Engineering Ltd v Gilbert-Ash [1974] AC 689; [1973] 3 WLR 421;
    [1973] 3 All ER 195 (HL).. 101, 1.03, 4.30
Mohammed v Dr Michael Bowles (Bankruptcy Registrar 2002) 4.28
Monmouthshire CC v Costelloe & Kemple Ltd [1965] 5 BLR 83 (CA) 7.49
Montan, The [1985] 1 WLR 625; [1985] 1 All ER 520; [1985]
    1 Lloyd's Rep 189 (CA)... 8.26n
Mott MacDonald Ltd v London & Regional Properties Ltd [2007]
    EWHC 1055 (TCC); [2007] CILL 2481 .... 2.61, 2.72, 2.108, 3.56, 3.71, 11.23
M Rhode Construction v Markham-David [2006]
    EWHC 814 (TCC) 2.106n, 2.165, 2.167
Multiconcept Developments Ltd v Abarus (CI) Ltd [2002] Adj LR 03/22 ...... 10.23n, 15.16n
Multiplex Constructions (UK) Ltd v Cleveland Bridge [2006] EWCA Civ 1834 .... 12.35n
Multiplex Constructions (UK) Ltd v Honeywell Control Systems [2007]
    EWHC 236 (TCC); [2007] BLR 167; [2007] Bus LR D13 .... 12.35n
Multiplex Constructions (UK) Ltd v Mott MacDonald Ltd [2007]
    EWHC 20 (TCC); 110 Con LR 63; [2007] CILL 2446 ....7.56, 12.35n
Multiplex Constructions (UK) Ltd v West India Quay Development Co (Eastern)
    Ltd [2006] EWHC 1569 (TCC); 111 Con LR 33 .... 7.64, 9.29, 15.16n

Nageh v Giddings [2006] EWHC 3240 (TCC); [2007] CILL 2420 .... 2.167
Naylor v Greenacres 2001 SLT 1092 ....3.46, 7.74n
Nikko Hotels (UK) Ltd v MEPC plc (1991) 2 EGLR 103;
    [1991] 28 EG 86 .... 2.05, 2.08, 8.02

Nolan Davis Ltd v Catton (TCC no 590 2000). 8.18, 8.19, 8.20, 11.06n, 15.16n
Nordot Engineering Services Ltd v Siemens plc [2001] CILL 1778 . . . . 185, 5.06,
  5.11, 5.15, 711
Northern Developments (Cumbria) Ltd v J & J Nichol [2000] BLR 158; (2000)
  2 TCLR 261 . . . . 2.09, 2.11, 2.130, 2.131, 3.81, 3.82, 4.45n, 7.36, 8.13, 11.05, 11.06
Nottingham Community Housing Association Ltd v Powerminster Ltd
  [2000] BLR 309; (2000) 2 TCLR 678; 75 Con LR 65 . . . . 2.29

Oakley v Airclear Environmental Ltd [2002] CILL 1824 . . . . 5.13
Orange EBS Ltd v ABB Ltd [2003] BLR 323; (2004) 20 Const LJ 30 . . . . 4.40, 7.52n
O'Reilly v Mackman [1983] 2 AC 287; [1982] 3 WLR 1096; [1982]
  3 All ER 1124 (HL) 8.05, 8.08
Outwing Construction Ltd v H Randell & Son Ltd [1999] BLR 156;
  64 Con LR 59; (1999) 15 Const LJ 308 . . . . 12.18

Palmac Contracting Ltd v Park Lane Estates Ltd [2005] EWHC 919 (TCC);
  [2005] BLR 301 . . . . 4.18, 4.36, 9.19n
Palmers Ltd v ABB Power Construction Ltd [1999] BLR 426; (2000)
  2 TCLR 322; 68 Con LR 52 . . . . 2.24–2.27, 2.34, 2.156
Parke v The Fenton Gretton Partnership [2001] CILL 1713 . . . . 12.42, 12.43, 12.45
Parsons Plastics (Research and Development) Ltd v Purac Ltd [2002]
  EWCA Civ 459; [2002] BLR 334; 93 Con LR 26; (2002)
  18 Const LJ 494 (CA). 5.08, 10.23–10.24, 10.27, 10.31, 10.33, 13.12, 13.13
Paul Jenson Ltd v Staveley Industries plc (unreported, Wigan County Court
  27 September 2001) 11.14
Pegram Shopfitters Ltd v Tally Weijl (UK) Ltd [2003] EWCA Civ 1750; [2004]
  1 WLR 2082; [2004] 1 All ER 818; [2004] 1 All ER (Comm) 593 (CA) 1.02n, 1.18,
  3.57n, 7.04, 7.09n, 7.27, 8.11, 8.14–8.15, 8.17, 13.06
Peterhead Harbour Trustees v Lilley Construction Ltd 2003 SLT 731;
  2003 SCLR 433 . . . . 4.59
Picardi (t/a Picardi) v Cuniberti [2002] EWHC 2923 (TCC); [2003] BLR 487;
  94 Con LR 81; (2003) 19 Const LJ 350 . . . . 2.41, 4.61, 9.51, 9.52, 9.53, 9.55, 9.57
Pierce Design International Ltd v Johnston [2007] EWHC 1691 (TCC) 2.147, 4.26,
  10.07, 19.35
Prentice Island Ltd v Castle Contracting Ltd (unreported, Sheriffdom Tayside,
  Central and Fife 15 December 2003) 3.47, 3.95, 7.75n, 11.15
Pring & St Hill Ltd v CJ Hafner (t/a Southern Erectors) [2002] EWHC 1775 (TCC);
  (2004) 20 Const LJ 402 . . . . 2.163, 3.36–3.37, 3.49, 7.26, 9.28
Project Consultancy Group v Grey Trust Trustees [1999] BLR 377; (2000) 2 TCLR 72;
  65 Con LR 146 . . . . 5.03, 5.05, 5.11, 5.15, 7.02, 7.03, 7.08, 7.12, 7.82, 8.18, 13.20
Pugh v Harris Calman Construction Ltd [2003] CLDC 30.6.03 . . . . 11.13

Quarmby v Larraby (unreported, TCC Leeds 2003) 7.23
Quietfield Ltd v Vascroft Construction Ltd [2006] EWHC 174 (TCC); 109 Con LR 29;
  [2006] CILL 2329; affirmed [2006] EWCA Civ 1737; [2007] BLR 67; [2007]
  CILL 2425; [2007] Bus LR D1 (CA) 7.77, 9.39, 9.40, 9.41, 12.30, 12.31–12.32

R v Cripps ex p Muldoon [1984] QB 686; [1984] 3 WLR 53; [1984]
  2 All ER 705 (CA) 8.26n
R v Gough [1993] AC 646; [1993] 2 WLR 883; [1993] 2 All ER 724 (HL). 3.54, 9.11, 9.12
R v Lord President of the Privy Seal ex p Page [1993] AC 682; [1993] 3 WLR 1112;
  [1993] 1 All ER 97 (HL). 8.06n
R v Soneji [2005] UKHL 49; [2006] 1 AC 340; [2005] 3 WLR 303; [2005]
  4 All ER 321 (HL) 2.102, 2.103, 2.104

Table of Cases

R v Wicks [1998] AC 92; [1997] 2 WLR 876; [1997] 2 All ER 801 (HL) 8.06n
Racal Communications Ltd, Re [1981] AC 374; [1980] 3 WLR 181;
    [1980] 2 All ER 634 (HL)... 8.06n
Rainford House Ltd v Cadogan Ltd [2001] EWHC Technology 18;
    [2001] BLR 416 .... 15.12, 15.19
Rankilor v Perco Engineering Services Ltd [2006] Adj LR 01/27 .... 9.35, 11.17
R Durtnell & Sons Ltd v Kaduna Ltd [2003] EWHC 517 (TCC); [2003] BLR 225;
    [2003] TCLR 7; 93 Con LR 36 .... 4.16, 7.13, 7.67, 12.23
Redworth Construction Ltd v Brookdale Healthcare Ltd [2006] EWHC 1994 (TCC);
    [2006] BLR 366; 110 Con LR 77; [2006] CILL 2373 .... 2.57, 5.09n, 8.23n, 12.21
Rentokil Allsa Environmental Ltd v Eastend Civil Engineering
    Ltd [1999] CILL 1506... 12.46
RG Carter v Edmund Nuttall Ltd (No 2) [2002] BLR 359 .... 4.35n, 9.13, 9.48
Ritchie Brothers (PWC) v David Philip (Commercials) Ltd 2005 1 SC 384;
    2005 SLT 341; [2005] BLR 384 (Appeal Court of Session); reversed 2004 SLT 471;
    [2004] BLR 379 (First Instance Court of Session)............ 2.95, 2.99, 2.100, 2.103,
        3.69, 3.70, 3.71, 4.15n, 4.21, 7.70, 11.21n, 12.06n, 12.07
RJ Knapman Ltd v Richards [2006] EWHC 2518 (TCC); 108 Con LR 64;
    [2006] CILL 2400 .... 8.23n, 10.32, 12.22
RJT Consulting Engineers Ltd v DM Engineering (Northern Ireland) Ltd [2002]
    EWCA Civ 270; [2002] 1 WLR 2344; [2002] CLC 905;
    [2002] BLR 217 (CA)...... 2.46–2.52, 2.55, 2.59, 2.64n, 2.68, 2.73, 7.29, 13.08, 19.04n
ROK Build Ltd v Harris Wharf Development Co Ltd [2006] EWHC 3573 (TCC)........ 7.33
RSL (South West) Ltd v Stansell Ltd [2003] EWHC 1390 (TCC)............ 4.45, 4.50, 9.20,
        9.28, 9.30, 9.31
Rupert Morgan Building Services (LLC) Ltd v Jervis [2003] EWCA Civ 1563;
    [2004] 1 WLR 1867; [2004] 1 All ER 529; [2004] BLR 18 (CA) 2.133, 10.10–10.12,
        10.19, 13.10, 13.11

Samuel Thomas Construction v Anon (unreported, 28 January 2000)................... 2.42
St Andrew's Bay Development Ltd v HBG Management Ltd 2003 SLT 740;
    2003 SCLR 526...................................... 3.70, 4.20, 11.21, 11.22
Save Britain's Heritage v No 1 Poultry Ltd [1991] 1 WLR 153; [1991] 2 All ER 10;
    89 LGR 809 (HL) 3.83
Shepherd Construction Ltd v Mecright Ltd [2000] BLR 489 .... 7.21, 7.23, 7.24, 7.78
Sherwood & Casson Ltd v MacKenzie [2000] 2 TCLR 418 ...... 2.09–2.10, 3.43, 7.72, 13.20
Shimizu Europe Ltd v Automajor Ltd [2002] EWHC 1571 (TCC); [2002] BLR 113;
    (2002) 18 Const LJ 259 .... 8.22, 8.23, 8.30, 12.23
Shimizu Europe Ltd v LBJ Fabrications Ltd [2003] EWHC 1229 (TCC);
    [2003] BLR 381 .... 2.140, 4.42, 4.51n, 4.65, 9.33
Simons Construction Ltd v Aardvark Developments Ltd [2003] EWHC 2472;
    [2004] BLR 117; [2004] TCLR 2; 93 Con LR 114 .... 2.98–2.99, 3.69, 12.06n
Sindall Ltd v Solland [2001] 3 TCLR 30; [2001] 3 TCLR 721 .... 2.81, 7.50, 7.52, 7.66
Skanska Construction UK Ltd v ERDC Group Ltd [2002] Scot CS 307;
    2003 SCLR 296..3.45, 7.75
SL Timber Systems Ltd v Carillion Construction Ltd 2002 SLT 997; 2001 SCLR 935;
    [2001] BLR 516 .... 2.131, 2.132, 10.10, 10.17, 10.18, 10.19
Solland International Ltd v Daraydan Holdings Ltd [2002] EWHC 220 (TCC);
    83 Con LR 109 .... 2.137, 3.90, 10.33
South Bucks BC v Porter (No 2) [2004] UKHL 33; [2004] 1 WLR 1953;
    [2004] 4 All ER 775; [2005] 1 P & CR 6 (HL)............................. 3.83
South West Contractors Ltd v Birakos Enterprises Ltd [2006] EWHC 2794 (TCC) 9.22n
Staveley Industries Plc v Odebrecht Oil and Gas Services Ltd (2001) 98(10) LSG 46 ...... 2.30

Stiell Ltd v Riema Control Systems Ltd 2000 SC 539; [2000] Scot CS 174;
    [2001] 3 TCLR 9 .... 4.71, 12.40, 12.46
Stirling v Westminster Properties Scotland Ltd [2007] Scot CS 117 (CSOH) 7.56
Stratfield Saye Estate Trustees v AHL Construction Ltd [2004] EWHC 3286 (TCC);
    [2004] All ER (D) 77 (Dec) 2.51–2.52, 2.56, 7.29
Strathmore Building Services Ltd v Grieg (t/a Hestia Fireside Design) [2000]
    ScotCS 133; (2001) 17 Const LJ 72 .... 2.138, 2.139
Stubbs Rich Architects v WH Tolley & Son Ltd (unreported, Gloucester County
    Court 8 August 2001).. 11.16
Summit Property Ltd v Pitmans [2001] EWCA Civ 2020; [2002] CPLR 97 (CA)....... 11.03n

Thomas-Frederic's (Construction) Ltd v Wilson [2003] EWCA Civ 1494; [2004]
    BLR 23; 91 Con LR 161; [2003] NPC 120 (CA) 2.55, 3.57n, 5.11, 5.15, 7.03,
                                                        7.33, 8.16n, 8.19, 8.20, 13.06
Thomas Vale Construction Plc v Brookside Syston Ltd [2006] EWHC 3637 .... 2.141
Tim Butler Contractors Ltd v Merewood Homes Ltd (2002) 18 Const LJ 74 ...... 2.124, 8.08n
Total M and E Services Ltd v ABB Building Technologies Ltd [2002]
    EWHC 248 (TCC); 87 Con LR 154; [2002] CILL 1857 .... 2.63, 2.66n, 11.04, 15.15
Try Construction Ltd v Eton Town House Group Ltd [2003] EWHC 60 (TCC);
    [2003] BLR 286; 87 Con LR 71; [2003] CILL 1982 .... 9.31

Vaultrise Ltd v Cook [2004] ADJCS 04/06 .... 3.75, 4.31, 7.80n, 9.43n
VHE Construction plc v RBSTB Trust Co Ltd [2000] EWHC Technology 181;
    [2000] BLR 187; (2000) 2 TCLR 278; 70 Con LR 51 .... 2.136, 2.140, 7.73,
                                                        10.21, 10.22, 10.31, 10.33, 12.19

Wagner v Laubscher Brothers & Co [1970] 2 QB 313; [1970] 2 WLR 1019 (CA)........ 15.04
Wates Construction Ltd v HGP Greentree Allchurch Evans Ltd [2005]
    EWHC 2174 (TCC); [2006] BLR 45; 105 Con LR 47 .... 14.14
Watkin Jones v LIDL [2002] EWHC 183 (TCC); 86 Con LR 155;
    [2002] CILL 1834, 1847 .... 7.53n
Watson Building Services Ltd v Harrison 2001 SLT 846 .... 3.22, 7.10, 7.12
Westdawn Refurbishments Ltd v Roselodge Ltd [2006] Adj LR 04/25 .... 2.54, 7.33
Westminster Building Co Ltd v Beckingham [2004] EWHC 138 (TCC);
    [2004] BLR 163; [2004] TCLR 8; 94 Con LR 107 .... 9.54, 9.55, 9.56
Westminster Chemicals and Produce Ltd v Eicholz & Loeser [1954]
    1 Lloyd's Rep 99 .... 5.01, 5.02
Whiteways Contractors (Sussex) Ltd v Impresa Castelli Construction United
    Kingdom Ltd [2000] EWHC Technology 67; (2000) 75 Con LR 92; (2000)
    16 Const LJ 453; [2000] CILL 1664 .... 4.42, 7.11n, 10.15, 10.16, 10.19
William Verry (Glazing Systems) Ltd v Furlong Homes Ltd [2005]
    EWHC 138 (TCC) 7.40, 7.54, 9.09, 9.39, 12.30
William Verry Ltd v London Borough of Camden [2006]
    EWHC 761 (TCC) 2.119, 3.33n, 10.37
William Verry Ltd v North West London Communal Mikva [2004]
    EWHC 1300 (TCC); [2004] BLR 308; 96 Con LR 96 .... 4.02n, 4.12, 4.13, 8.17
Wimbledon Construction Co 2000 Ltd v Vago [2005] EWHC 1086 (TCC);
    [2005] BLR 374; 101 Con LR 99........................... 15.10, 15.18, 15.20n
Woods Hardwick Ltd v Chiltern Air-Conditioning Ltd [2001] BLR 23 ..... 9.24, 10.14, 10.19
Workplace Technologies plc v E Squared Ltd [2000] CILL 1607 .... 14.23, 14.25

Yarm Road Ltd v Costain Ltd (unreported, 30 July 2001) 2.22n

AUSTRALIA

Brodyn Pty Ltd v Davenport (2004) 61 NSWLR 421;
    [2003] NSWSC 1019 .... 2.102, 2.103, 195, 6.21, 6.22
Emag Constructions Pty Ltd v High Rise Concrete [2003] NSWSC 903 .... 6.21
Leighton Contractors Pty v Campbelltown Catholic Club [2003] NSWSC 1103 .... 6.21n
McConnell Dowell Constructors (Aust) Pty Ltd v National Grid
    Gas plc [2007] BLR 92 .... 7.24, 7.78, 15.21
Musico v Davenport [2003] NSWSC 977 .... 6.21n
Okaroo Pty Ltd v Vos Construction & Joinery Pty Ltd [2005] NSWC 45 .... 6.07
Transgrid v Walter Construction Group [2004] NSWSC 21 .... 6.21n

TABLE OF LEGISLATION, TREATIES AND CONVENTIONS

A. UK Statutes	xxxv
B. UK Statutory Instruments	xxxvi
C. National Legislation from Other Jurisdictions	xxxvi

A. UK STATUTES

Arbitration Act 1996 . . . . 2.103
   s 9 . . . . 2.150, 3.87, 3.88
   s 42 . . . . 2.02, 3.94
   s 66 . . . . 12.19
Contracts (Rights of Third Parties)
   Act 1999 . . . . 4.33
Housing Grants, Construction
   and Regeneration Act 1996 . . . . v–vi, vii,
      1.30, 4.01, 4.28, 5.01, 6.02, 6.11,
      6.19, 6.31, 7.02, 7.18, 7.33, 7.48,
      7.50, 7.57, 8.04, 9.04, 9.44, 9.46,
      9.47, 9.51, 10.22, 10.24, 10.25,
      10.26, 10.39, 11.02, 11.24, 12.18,
      12.19, 12.35, 12.36, 12.46, 13.03,
      13.06, 13.08, 14.02, 14.19, 14.23,
      14.35, 15.01, 15.05, 15.15, 16.12,
      17.28, 19.09, 19.11, 19.26, 19.27,
      19.28, 19.30, 19.32
   Pt II 2.01, 2.04, 2.06, 2.10,
      2.22, 2.104, 2.106, 3.97, 449–455
   s 104 . . . . 2.16, 3.03, 7.20
   s 104(1) 2.17–2.18
   s 104(2) 2.17, 2.19
   s 104(5) 2.21
   s 104(6)(a) 2.22
   s 104(6)(b) 2.22
   s 105 . . . . 2.16, 7.20
   s 105(1) 1.22, 2.17, 2.23, 2.33,
      3.03, 5.06
   s 105(1)(a) 2.29–2.30
   s 105(1)(b) 2.26
   s 105(1)(c) 2.29–2.30
   s 105(1)(e) 2.23, 2.26
   s 105(2) 1.22, 2.17, 2.23, 2.25–2.26,
      2.31, 2.34, 3.03, 7.20
   s 105(2)(c) 2.26, 2.31, 2.33

   s 105(2(c)(i) 2.32, 2.35–2.36
   s 105(2)(c)(ii) 2.31
   s 105(3)(c) 2.29
   s 106 . . . . 2.40, 2.43, 9.51
   s 107 . . . . 2.44, 2.49, 2.55, 2.57,
      2.65–2.66, 2.68, 7.28
   s 107(2) 2.45–2.46, 2.48, 2.61
   s 107(3) 2.45, 2.62
   s 107(4) 2.45
   s 107(5) 2.45, 2.69–2.74, 7.59
   s 108 . . . . 2.75–2.76, 3.02, 4.02n,
      4.12, 7.54, 10.26, 11.01, 13.13
   s 108(1) 3.06, 4.60
   s 108(2) 2.114, 3.06, 4.60
   s 108(2)(a) 2.76, 2.89, 4.60
   s 108(2)(b) 3.29
   s 108(2)(c) 4.53, 7.69
   s 108(2)(d) 2.76
   s 108(3) 2.76, 2.116, 12.02n,
      12.16, 12.31, 12.32
   s 108(4) 3.06, 4.60, 10.16
   s 108(5) 4.01
   s 109 . . . . .2.120, 2.123, 2.142,
      2.143, 3.02, 3.03, 3.04, 4.04
   s 109(1) 2.124
   s 110 . . . . .2.120, 2.123, 2.126,
      2.130, 2.142, 2.143, 2.144, 3.03,
      3.04, 4.04, 10.04, 19.21
   s 110(1)(a) 2.126
   s 110(1)(b) 2.127
   s 110(2) 2.128–2.129, 2.131,
      2.132, 2.134, 2.135, 19.14,
      19.15, 19.17, 19.18, 19.20
   s 111 . . . . .2.120, 2.123, 2.131,
      2.142, 2.143, 2.147, 2.150,
      3.03, 3.04, 3.88, 4.26, 4.43,
      10.04, 10.12, 10.17, 10.21, 10.32,
      12.43, 12.44, 19.18, 19.21, 19.34

Housing Grants, Construction
and Regeneration Act 1996 (*cont.*)
  s 111(1) 2.128–2.129, 2.134, 2.135,
              2.136, 2.144, 2.145, 19.18
  s 112 . . . . 2.153, 2.154, 2.155, 2.157
  s 112(2) 2.156
  s 113 . . . . 2.153, 2.160
  s 113(1) 2.159, 2.161
  s 114 . . . . 2.153, 2.162
  s 114(4) 2.162, 2.163, 3.02, 3.07
  s 115 . . . . 2.153, 2.164, 2.166
  s 115(4) 2.165
Human Rights Act 1998 . . . . 2.114, 3.54,
                      9.45, 9.46, 9.48
Income and Corporation Taxes Act 1988
  s 562(2) 2.30
Late Payment of Commercial Debts
  (Interest) Act 1998 . . . . 3.80
Unfair Contract Terms
  Act 1977 . . . . 2.161, 3.97

B. UK STATUTORY INSTRUMENTS

Civil Procedure Rules 2.166
  Pt 1 . . . . 15.15
  Pt 7 . . . . 14.06
  Pt 8 . . . . 14.06
  Pt 24 . . . . 7.02, 7.14, 14.02,
              14.05, 14.08, 14.23, 15.15
  r 25 . . . . 14.24
Construction Contracts (England and
  Wales) Exclusion Order 1998,
  SI 1998 No 648 457–459
  para 3 . . . . 2.37
  para 4 . . . . 2.37
  para 5 . . . . 2.37
  para 6 . . . . 2.37–2.39
Insolvency Rules 1986, SI 1986 No 1925
  r 4.90 . . . . 15.06
Scheme for Construction Contracts
  (England and Wales) Regulations
  1998, SI 1998 No 649 . . . . . 1.33, 3.01,
                          461–468
Rules of the Supreme Court
  Ord 14 . . . . 1.03
  Ord 47 . . . . 15.01, 15.02
Unfair Terms in Consumer
  Contract Regulations 1999,
  SI 1999 No 2083 . . . . . 2.41, 4.29, 4.61
  reg 5(i) 9.49
  reg 5(ii) 9.49

C. NATIONAL LEGISLATION FROM OTHER JURISDICTIONS

Australia

NEW SOUTH WALES
Building and Construction Industry
  Security of Payment Act 1999 . . . . 6.01,
            6.02, 6.03–6.05, 6.07, 6.11
  s 4 . . . . 6.06n
  s 5(1) 6.06
  s 5(2) 6.06
  s 7(1) 6.06n
  s 8 . . . . 6.09
  s 12 . . . . 6.08
  s 13 . . . . 6.09
  s 14(3) 6.12n
  s 14(4) 6.12n
  s 16(4)(b) 6.13n
  s 17 . . . . 6.14n
  s 17(5) 6.15n
  s 20(2) 6.16n
  s 20(2B) 6.12n, 6.16
  s 21(3) 6.17
  s 21(4A) 6.17
  s 22(2) 6.18n
  s 22(3) 6.18n
  s 22(4) 6.19
  s 22(5) 6.19
  s 23 . . . . 6.20
  s 24(1) 6.20
  s 25(4) 6.20
  s 34 . . . . 6.09
Building and Construction
  Industry Security of Payment
  Act 2002 . . . . 6.05
  s 13(5) 6.10
  s 13(6) 6.10
Sub-contractors' Charges Act 1974 . . . . . 6.02

NORTHERN TERRITORY OF AUSTRALIA
Construction Contracts (Security of
  Payments) Act 2004 . . . . 6.23

QUEENSLAND
Building and Construction Industry
  Payments Act 2004 . . . . 6.23

VICTORIA
Building and Construction Industry
  Security of Payment Act 2002 . . . . . 6.23

WESTERN AUSTRALIA
Construction Contracts Act 2004 . . . . . . 6.23

EU

European Convention on Human
    Rights 1950
        Art 6 . . . . 2.114, 3.54, 9.44, 9.45,
                                9.46, 9.47

New Zealand

Construction Contracts Act 2002 . . . . . . 6.35
    s 25 . . . . 6.36n
    s 58 . . . . 6.36n
    s 58(1) 6.36n
    s 59 . . . . 6.36n
    s 61 . . . . 6.36n

Singapore

Building and Construction Industry
    Security of Payment
        Act 2004 . . . . 6.01, 6.29
    s 5 . . . . 6.30
    s 8 . . . . 6.30
    s 10 . . . . 6.30
    s 11 . . . . 6.30
    s 12 . . . . 6.30
    s 13 . . . . 6.30
    s 14 . . . . 6.30
    s 15 . . . . 6.30
    s 16 . . . . 6.31
    s 17 . . . . 6.31
    s 17(2) 6.31
    s 17(6) 6.31
    s 18 . . . . 6.32
    s 24 . . . . 6.34
    s 24(2) 6.34

Part I

STATUTORY ADJUDICATION

1. The Latham Report and its Aftermath	3
2. Part II of the Housing Grants Construction and Regeneration Act 1996	17
3. The Statutory Scheme	93

1

THE LATHAM REPORT AND ITS AFTERMATH

Introduction	1.01	The Debates on the Bill	1.19
The Main Recommendations of the Latham Report	1.07	The Debates on the Scheme	1.31
Contract Terms	1.10		
Adjudication	1.13		

'5.13 There are several ways to approach the concerns expressed by all sides of the construction process about contracts. They are:—

1. To do nothing.

2. To amend existing Standard Forms to meet some of the concerns.

3. To try to define what a modern construction contract ought to contain. If this can be achieved, there are then two further alternatives, which are to change existing contract forms to take account of such requirements and/or to introduce a new contract which will deliver them.

5.14 It is no longer possible to do nothing. That option can be discarded at once.'

From 'Constructing the Team' by Sir Michael Latham, Final Report, July 1994.

Introduction

A graph that indicated the health (and otherwise) of the construction industry in the UK in the twentieth century would make a startling sight: a bewildering series of peaks and troughs which often, but not always, mirrored the wider health of the UK economy. On occasions in the past, many have endeavoured to promote or otherwise help the construction industry, with a record of success that can only be described as mixed. Changing priorities amongst the senior judiciary have **1.01** not always helped to encourage stability and certainty. Thus, for example, in *Dawnays v Minter*,[1] Lord Denning MR decided, not for the first or the last time, that architects' certificates under standard forms of building contracts were, broadly speaking, to be regarded in the same way as a cheque or cash, and that, because 'cash flow was the very lifeblood of the enterprise', such certificates had to be honoured. He held that a certified sum had to be paid, regardless of the existence of cross-claims or other potential deductions. The principle, if that is what it was, in *Dawnays v Minter* was quickly overruled by the House of Lords in *Modern Engineering Ltd v Gilbert-Ash*.[2] In that case Lord Diplock famously observed that cash flow was the life blood of the village grocer, too.

1.02 The reason that these, and other reported cases concerned with interim payments, mattered so much was due to the volatility of the construction industry. A general building contractor who was not paid on time might find himself unable to complete the contract and, within weeks, out of business and bankrupt. These problems were exacerbated by the fact that, by their very nature, construction contracts have always generated disputes about payment. They last a good deal longer than most commercial contracts, thus increasing the chances of things going wrong somewhere along the line. Most disputes arising in connection with commercial contracts concern defects of one sort or another; in construction contracts, it is common for there to be complaints about defects and delays, as well as the inevitable disputes about variations and extra expense.[3]

1.03 Following the decision in *Modern Engineering*, an employer who wanted to avoid making an interim payment to his contractor was often able to do so by putting together some kind of cross-claim which, even if it was rather thin, would be good enough to avoid summary judgement being given on the contractor's claim under RSC Order 14. For many years it was felt that this was an unsatisfactory state of affairs and that, in the right circumstances, something should be done to tip the balance at least a little way back in favour of the claiming party, even at the temporary expense of those who had to pay. This was the genesis of compulsory adjudication. However, it took a major recession before the idea became more widely advocated.

1.04 By the early 1990's, it was generally considered that the construction industry in the UK was in the grip of a major and deep-seated crisis. The general recession of

---

[1] [1971] 1 WLR 1205.
[2] [1974] AC 689.
[3] In his judgment in *Pegram Shopfitters Ltd v Tally Wiejl (UK) Ltd* [2003] EWCA Civ 1750, May LJ said: 'Construction contracts do by their nature generate disputes about payment. If there are delays, variations or other causes of additional expense, those who do the work often consider themselves entitled to additional payment. Those who have the work done often have reasons, good or bad, for saying that the additional payment is not due.'

the late 1980's/early 1990's had hit the construction industry hard. The decline in property prices led to a reduction in work, and the wider financial constraints meant that contractors and sub-contractors were continually starved of the necessary cash flow. It was calculated that, by 1993, construction output was some 39 percent below its 1990 peak, compared to a reduction of just three percent in the manufacturing industry.[4]

However, the difficulties in the industry went much wider than the general effects of the recession. Another major concern was the high cost of the UK construction industry, particularly when compared with costs in Europe and in the USA. Allied to the concerns about high cost were worries about the high proportion of disputes within the construction industry, the length of time that it took for such disputes to be resolved, and their cost. It was, for instance, noteworthy that during this period of recession for the industry, there was a significant increase in the volume of work for those directly concerned with construction disputes, including barristers, solicitors, claims consultants and other construction professionals. **1.05**

The problems within the construction industry mattered because the industry itself comprised such a major part of the UK economy overall. For example, in 1993, the value of output in the whole construction industry was £46.3 billion, which represented about eight percent of Gross Domestic Product.[5] With as many as 200,000 contractors in the UK, the health of the industry plainly mattered to the health of the UK economy as a whole. **1.06**

The Main Recommendations of the Latham Report

On 5 July 1993, it was announced in the House of Commons that there was to be a Joint Review of Procurement and Contractual Arrangements in the United Kingdom Construction Industry. The Review was funded by the Department of the Environment, together with four industry organisations and two groups representing clients. The Review was conducted by Sir Michael Latham. An Interim Report, entitled 'Trust and Money', was published in December 2003. The Final Report, entitled 'Constructing the Team', was published in July 1994. This latter document is referred to below as 'the Latham Report'. **1.07**

The Latham Report was extremely wide-ranging. Although this book, of necessity, concentrates on those aspects of the Latham Report that relate to **1.08**

---

[4] See paragraph 2.6 of the Latham Report.
[5] This statistic can be found at paragraph 2.1 of the Latham Report. The source is given as the Department of the Environment.

construction contracts and the efficient resolution of construction disputes, it should be noted that the Report dealt with a wide variety of topics, including the 'Role of Clients', 'The Design Process', 'Selection and Tendering Procedures', 'Team Work on Site' and even 'Liability Post-Completion'. A number of the recommendations in these areas have yet to be implemented.

1.09 The two most radical aspects of the Latham Report concerned its recommendation of particular payment provisions to be implied into building contracts, and its unequivocal recommendation of a new type of mandatory dispute resolution mechanism known as adjudication.

Contract Terms

1.10 Despite the wide range of available Standard Forms of Construction and Engineering Contracts, it appears that Sir Michael Latham was unimpressed with their applicability to what he called the 'reality on modern construction sites'.[6] He considered that certain common features of all construction and engineering contracts were desirable and should include:—

(a) a general duty to trade fairly, with specific requirements relating to payment and related issues;
(b) clearly defined work stages, including milestones or other forms of activity schedules;
(c) the pre-pricing of any variations;
(d) an adjudication system which was independent of contract administration.[7]

The recommendations for 'the most effective form of contract in modern conditions'[8] identified 13 specific elements which, in Sir Michael Latham's view, should be included in any contract.

1.11 The Report was particularly critical of what were described as 'unfair conditions' that were regularly included within construction contracts. Paragraph 8.9 of the Report (Recommendation 25) recommended that there should be a 'Construction Contract Bill' which should state that particular actions were unfair or invalid. These included any attempt:

(a) to amend or delete those sections of the contract relating to times and conditions of payment, and the right of interest on late payments;
(b) to seek to deny or frustrate the right of immediate adjudication to any party to the contract or sub-contract, where it has been requested by that party;

---

[6] See paragraph 5.17(2) of the Latham Report.
[7] See paragraph 5.17(4) of the Latham Report.
[8] See paragraph 5.18 of the Latham Report.

(c) to refuse to implement the decision of the adjudicator;
(d) to seek to exercise any right of set-off or contra-charge without:
 (i) giving notification in advance;
 (ii) specifying the exact reason for deducting the set-off; and
 (iii) being prepared to submit immediately to adjudication and accepting the result;
(e) to seek to set off in respect of any contract other than the one in progress.

1.12 In addition, the Report concluded unequivocally that 'pay-when-paid' clauses should be expressly declared unfair and invalid.[9] In making this recommendation, the Report was essentially accepting the submissions made to the review by the Constructors Liaison Group and the Confederation of Construction Specialists, representing sub-contractors, who were particularly upset at the widespread use of such provisions. Of course, it was the sub-contractors who often bore the financial burden of the insolvency or failure of a company much higher up the contractual chain. Thus, in the many pieces of satellite litigation arising out of the building of the first tower at Canary Wharf, and major developments such as the Hatfield Galleria development over the A1 in Hertfordshire, the financial difficulties of the employers were passed on, via 'pay-when-paid' clauses, to those sub-contractors who had actually carried out the work and were therefore most at risk if the relevant payments were not made.

Adjudication

1.13 The entirety of Chapter 9 of the Latham Report was given over to a discussion about Dispute Resolution. This highlighted the adversarial attitudes in the UK construction industry. Whilst it maintained that 'the best solution is to avoid disputes,'[10] the Report realistically accepted that a certain number of disputes were inevitable. The unequivocal recommendation in the Report was that the best way of resolving such disputes was by way of adjudication: indeed, at paragraph 9.4, the conclusion was that a system of adjudication 'must become the key to settling disputes in the construction industry'.

1.14 The Latham Report identified a number of key elements of the adjudication process that it was recommending. Amongst other things, the Report stated that there was no inherent reason why adjudication should not be used for any size of contract. It recommended that there should be no restriction on the issues to be placed before the adjudicator for decision and no specified 'cooling off period' before the adjudicator could be called in. It recommended that the adjudicator be

---

[9] See paragraph 8.10 of the Latham Report.
[10] See paragraph 9.3 of the Latham Report.

named in the contract before the work started and could then be called in when necessary. The Report also stated that:

> As well as dealing with disputes between clients and main contractors, the contract documents must specify that the adjudicator must have equal scope to determine disputes between contractors and sub-contractors, and between sub-contractors and sub-sub-contractors. Jurisdiction on sub-contract issues should not be limited to disputes over set-off. It should encompass any matter which can also be within the scope of resolution under the main contract.[11]

1.15 It is interesting to note that, even at this stage, the Report grappled with the extent to which the decisions of adjudicators should be final and binding. It is clear that at least one well-known construction claims consultant recommended that, once an adjudicator had reached his decision, no appeal or reference to the High Court should be permitted under any circumstances. However, the Report concluded that this was going too far. At paragraph 9.7, it was recorded that:

> It is correct that the authority of the adjudicator/expert must be upheld, and that the decision should be implemented at once. Such published experience as exists of adjudication—and it does not seem very extensive at main contract level, because the possibility of the system being used appears to induce the parties to reach their own settlement without recourse to it—suggests that it is successful in reducing disputes without further appeal or litigation. But it would be difficult to deny a party which feels totally aggrieved by an adjudicator's decision any opportunity to appeal either to the courts or arbitration. I doubt whether such a restriction would be enforceable.

1.16 Accordingly, the Latham Report recommended that, whilst an adjudication result had to be implemented at once, it could subsequently be overturned by the courts or an arbitrator after practical completion. Thus, as the Report made plain, 'if the award of the adjudicator involves payment, it must be made at once'.[12] The Report also stated that, unless there was some exceptional or important issue of law which had to be brought to court immediately, the courts should only be approached as a last resort, and after practical completion of the contract.

1.17 Accordingly, at paragraph 9.14, the Report set out its recommendations as to adjudication:

> I have already recommended that a system of adjudication should be introduced within all the Standard Forms of Contract (except where comparable arrangements already exist for mediation or conciliation) and that this should be underpinned by legislation. I also recommend that:—
>
> 1. There should be no restrictions on the issues capable of being referred to the adjudicator, conciliator or mediator, either in the main contract or sub-contract documentation.

---

[11] See paragraph 9.5 of the Latham Report.
[12] See paragraph 9.7(2) of the Latham Report.

2. The award of the adjudicator should be implemented immediately. The use of stakeholders should only be permitted if both parties agree or if the adjudicator so directs.
3. Any appeals to arbitration or the courts should be after practical completion, and should not be permitted to delay the implementation of the award, unless an immediate and exceptional issue arises for the courts or as in the circumstances described in (4) . . .
4. Resort to the courts should be immediately available if a party refuses to implement the award of an adjudicator. In such circumstances, the courts may wish to support the system of adjudication by agreeing to expedited procedures for interim payment.
5. Training procedures should be devised for adjudicators. A Code of Practice should also be drawn up under the auspices of the proposed Implementation Forum.

1.18 In these recommendations, the concept of mandatory adjudication was born. It should not, however, be thought that this was the first time that such a dispute resolution mechanism had been invented. Indeed, as May LJ pointed out in *Pegram Shopfitters Ltd v Tally Weijl (UK) Ltd*,[13] 'those who consider and make policy for the building industry, including the government, have taken a general view over the years that a temporary balance should in appropriate circumstances fall in favour of those who claim payment, at the temporary expense of those who pay' with the result that, prior to the Latham Report, a number of standard forms of building and engineering contracts already made provision for a type of adjudication process. What was radical about the recommendations in the Latham Report was that adjudication would now be the compulsory first step in any dispute arising under most construction and engineering contracts.

The Debates on the Bill

1.19 The Housing Grants Construction and Regeneration Bill was introduced early in 1996. One of its main features were the complex provisions concerning what were 'construction operations' (which were covered by the Bill and therefore subject to the detailed adjudication provisions) and what was outside the definition of 'construction operations', which would have the effect of excluding the underlying contracts from the scope of the Bill. The debates in Parliament, particularly those in the House of Lords, foreshadowed the disputes which arose in the TCC (Technology and Construction Court) in the early days of adjudication, as to whether or not a particular operation or activity was within or outside the Act. It is difficult, even now, to see quite why, if adjudication was the effective solution to dispute resolution that its advocates proclaimed it to be, it was thought necessary to exclude from its reach so many operations which would ordinarily be within

---

[13] [2003] EWCA Civ 1750.

the rubric of 'construction activities', and thus deprive so many parties within the construction industry of its alleged benefits.

1.20 It is instructive to take just one example from the debates to illustrate the nice distinctions that were being, and continue to be, made. In the House of Lords on 28 March 1996, Lord Howie of Troon used by way of example the component parts of the then-new Waterloo International Terminal. He made the point that the steel train shed was made in a factory and then brought on site and assembled. As a result, that element of this major project would be excluded from the Bill because of the distinction between manufacture and construction. However the undercroft was formed of massed concrete which was carried out on site, and would therefore be included within the Bill. However, he then went on to say that, to the extent that parts of the undercroft were pre-cast concrete elements, manufactured elsewhere, those might be outside the Bill after all. Earl Ferrers seemed rather reluctant to discuss the precise consequences of the Bill for particular industries, saying that 'those muddy what we seek to do in the Bill'.[14] Having conceded that 'this is not a simple area', he confirmed that 'the fitting in of a part manufactured elsewhere' was part of the manufacturing process and was not therefore a construction activity. It seems a pity that no-one pointed out that the simple task of bricklaying, the quintessential 'construction activity', could be described as 'the fitting in of a part manufactured elsewhere', and was thus, at least on one analysis, excluded from the Bill.

1.21 Some members of the House of Lords could not understand why certain industries had asked to be excluded from the Bill given that the principal aim of the Bill appeared to be:

> ... to ensure that where we have a contractual morass within the construction industry there is a fall-back position to protect everyone in the industry from the previous regime of litigation concerning contracts that have not been fulfilled adequately and endless arbitration and disputes procedures. It is a fall-back position to protect the people operating within the industry rather than an imposition of some new series of regulations, red tape and other paraphernalia. If one looks at it in that light, the arguments from the processing industry, the mining industry and the small contractor effectively fall away.[15]

This point was later reflected in the debate in the House of Commons, when one MP, not unreasonably, made this comparison:

> There is no more reason to exclude the process industries than to exempt drivers who have never had an accident from obeying the Highway Code. This is a good Bill, and we should include all the industries that are relevant to construction, not leave out the process industries because they have largely been able to manage their affairs

---

[14] See Hansard, 28.3.96, column 1858.
[15] See the speech of Lord Monkswell, Hansard 28.3.96, column 1865.

reasonably well in the past. There can be problems, and the industries would benefit from the legislation.[16]

1.22 Whatever the intrinsic merits of these points, they were not successful. When the Bill passed into law, it included a lengthy definition of the works included within 'construction operations' (section 105(1)), and it also allowed the exclusion of a number of different industries and activities which might ordinarily be thought of as encompassing 'construction operations' (section 105(2)).

1.23 Another point that arose during the debates in the House of Lords was the extent to which it was necessary to exclude smaller contracts from the provisions of the Bill including, of course, the requirement for adjudication. At one stage, a minimum limit of £25,000 was suggested.[17] Although this suggestion was received sympathetically, in the end the Bill passed into law with no such lower limit. However, the fact that the Bill excluded contracts with residential occupiers, and contracts which would take less than 45 days to complete, made it less important to exclude small value works, since small scale work would be likely to be carried out as part of domestic refurbishment, or take a short period to complete, and would therefore be excluded in any event.

1.24 Unsurprisingly, there was a considerable debate about the extent to which the decision of the adjudicator would be binding. Lord Lucas made it clear, on behalf of the Government, that many parties wanted adjudication to resolve disputes only until practical completion of the contract, and that this was perfectly acceptable.[18] However, difficulties arose from the proposed fall-back position that, if the contract did not provide to the contrary, the adjudicator's decision would be final. As Lord Berkeley put it:

> I do not believe that there is any situation in which the adjudication could be made binding on all contracts. If there is a serious problem, one cannot expect disputes worth tens or hundreds of millions of pounds to be resolved in four weeks.[19]

However, the debate on this topic revealed a lack of clarity as to the extent to which an adjudicator's decision would be binding. Despite Lord Lucas registering his 'surprise' that arrangements could be contemplated that allowed a dispute involving £1 million or £100 million to be settled in 28 days by a single individual, choosing his own evidence and with no form of appeal, it was pointed out that there was a risk that the Bill, and the provisional version of the scheme included within it, provided for just that. The uncertain nature of the status of the

---

[16] Taken from the speech of Mr Peter Thurnham, MP for Bolton North-East in the debate on 8 July 1996 (Hansard, column 94).
[17] See the speech of Viscount Ullswater, Hansard 28.3.96, column 1865.
[18] Hansard 28.3.96, column 1909.
[19] Hansard 28.3.96, column 1911.

adjudicator's decision was exacerbated when it was said that 'binding' meant that the decision was 'the end of it unless you have a dispute which can be taken to the court. That is a strictly limited category connected with areas of law and misbehaviour.'[20]

1.25 Unsurprisingly, there was grave concern that, on this point at least, the Government's proposals were moving away from the type of adjudication envisaged in the Latham Report. That allowed for a decision which was binding until practical completion and had to be complied with, but with no fetters or restrictions on the type or nature of the challenge that could be made after practical completion. This point was made in the debate in the House of Lords by Lord Howie of Troon who referred, not for the first time, to a confusion in the Bill between adjudication and arbitration. He made plain that it was inherently impractical to have a situation in which, after just 28 days, the adjudicator's decision was binding and could only be reviewed on a point of law. He said that the adjudicator's decision must be subject to revisitation 'not only on points of law but on whether he was correct in his decision in terms of the contract and the context in which the contract was carried out'. In the end, it was this view that prevailed.

1.26 The Bill also included a proposed scheme for adjudication, withholding notices and the like, to be incorporated into all contracts which made no express provision for such matters. In the debates in both the House of Lords and the House of Commons, it can be seen from Hansard that, whilst there was a general level of agreement as to the provisions in the Bill, there was widespread dismay at the provisions of the proposed scheme for adjudication itself. Again, many of the difficulties appear to arise from a confusion between adjudication and arbitration.[21] There was also concern as to the over-complex nature of the scheme originally proposed, leading to the conclusion that, although the scheme had been 'conceived with the best intentions . . . it is really a monster'.[22] These criticisms reflected comments made by industry professionals: the Institute of Civil Engineers described the scheme as originally proposed as 'dismal', whilst the Building Employers Confederation said that they had given the scheme 'the thumbs down'. The Constructors' Liaison Group described the proposed scheme as 'quite appalling' and the Official Referee's Solicitors Association (now TeCSA) described it as 'misconceived'.[23]

1.27 On 7 May, the Bill was debated in the House of Commons. The majority of the debate was given over to other elements of the Bill. There was, however, a useful

---

[20] Hansard 28.3.96, column 1911, taken from the speech of Lord Lucas.
[21] See the speech of Lord Howie of Troon, Hansard 28.3.96, columns 1933 and 1934.
[22] Lord Howie of Troon, Hansard 28.3.96, column 1934.
[23] All the references are taken from the speech of Lord Berkley, Hansard 1.4.96, column 13.

introduction to the system of adjudication proposed in the Bill. The Minister for Construction Planning and Energy Efficiency, Mr Robert B Jones, said:

> The Bill promotes a clear system of dispute resolution called adjudication. The industry is clear about what it means by that: it wants a mechanism that produces a fast and impartial resolution of a dispute and allows the contract to continue. The industry does not want the decision necessarily to be the final one. It wants to ensure that disputes are tested at the time, on the spot and are resolved quickly to the parties satisfaction.
>
> Our provisions provide a right to refer construction disputes for adjudication. We expect that entitlement to be met normally by the construction industry deciding, as a matter of course, to include adjudication arrangements in its contracts. The Government are challenging the industry to take action to improve its contractual practice and to introduce the sort of adjudication arrangements that best suit it. The best outcome must be that there is no need for a fall-back.
>
> However, we have a view about the minimum standards that contractual adjudication must satisfy. They relate to speed of decision, impartiality and the freedom for an adjudicator to investigate disputes and reach his own conclusion.[24]

1.28 The reports in Hansard reveal that, when the Bill went into Committee, many of the potential anomalies in the definition of 'construction operations' were trotted out all over again. There was much debate about the nice differences between construction maintenance and construction repair. One MP made the justifiable point about these debates that:

> We are returning to definitional problems . . . which have bedevilled the industry. There will be a field day for lawyers and a wonderful opportunity for people to find ways of frustrating the good intentions of the Bill and Sir Michael Latham's Report.[25]

However, this intervention failed to persuade those responsible for the Bill to omit the various complex definitions of what was within, and what was beyond, the reach of the new compulsory adjudication process.

1.29 There was also a significant debate about the effect of an adjudicator's decision. However, there seemed to be widespread agreement that, at least until practical completion, the adjudicator's decision was not simply to be regarded as a recommendation or advisory, but a decision which had to be complied with. There was reference to the representation provided to the Committee by Professor John Uff CBE QC, who said that the objective should be to ensure 'decisions of temporary finality only'.[26] However, no amendment to the Bill, to make clear the precise status of the adjudicator's decision, was accepted.

---

[24] Hansard, 7.5.96, column 52.
[25] From the speech of Mr Nick Raynsford, MP for Greenwich, Hansard, 13.6.96, column 292.
[26] Hansard, 18.6.96, columns 331 and 332: Standing Committee F.

1.30 The last debate in the Commons occurred on 8 July 1996. Some of the points identified above were revisited in argument but with little effect on the Bill. However, although it then received the Royal Assent, the Housing Grants Construction and Regeneration Act did not come into effect until 1 May 1998. This was principally because of the delays in the formulation of an acceptable scheme for adjudication. The relevant sections of the 1996 Act are attached at Appendix A.

The Debates on the Scheme

1.31 As noted above, the original scheme for adjudication proposed in 1996 as part of the Bill attracted far more opprobrium than the Bill itself. This was largely the result of attempts to limit the ways in which an adjudicator's decision might be capable of later challenge. In the debate in the House of Lords on 22 April 1996, Lord Ackner referred to the extensive criticism of the proposed scheme and said:

> What I have always understood to be required by the adjudication process was a quick, enforceable interim decision which lasted until practical completion when, if not acceptable, it would be the subject matter of arbitration or litigation. That was a highly satisfactory process. It came under the rubric of 'pay now, argue later', which was a sensible way of dealing expeditiously and relatively inexpensively with disputes which might hold up the completion of important contracts.
>
> What is being proposed here is a speedy, fast-track arbitration which produces a binding conclusion, not open to any challenge after practical completion, but fixed and firm for all time in a wholly unrealistic time scale . . . What on earth is the point of rushing through an arbitration which is to be final and binding in a situation probably of great complexity and, what is worse, one where the speed can be frustrated by applications to the court of the kind envisaged by the new Arbitration Bill which will become an Act in 1996? Because of the finality which it is suggested is to be ingrained in the adjudication, the courts will obviously be listened to. So there will be delay and frustration in the sense that payment will be put off and the adjudication process which is designed will be self-defeating for a reason which I find difficult to follow.[27]

1.32 As a result of this decisive intervention, and other points made during the debates about the scheme, it was decided that further consultation would be necessary before the scheme was finalised. In November 1996, once the Bill had received Royal Assent in July 1996, the Department of the Environment sent out a consultation paper, seeking responses as to the nature and extent of the scheme.

---

[27] Hansard, 22.4.96, columns 989–990.

The eventual result of this consultation paper was the Scheme for Construction **1.33** Contracts (England and Wales) Regulations 1998. In the discussions on these Regulations in the relevant Committees of the House of Commons and the House of Lords, it quickly became apparent that many of the concerns, raised by Lord Ackner and others two years previously, had been dealt with in the new version of the scheme, particularly in the removal of the provisions making an adjudicator's decision binding for all time. There was broad agreement as to the contents of the proposed scheme; it was felt that, finally, the concepts of arbitration and adjudication had been distinguished, and that the scheme allowed for a decision which was binding and had to be complied with, although it could be challenged either in arbitration or in the courts. The Regulations, and the Scheme for which they provided, came into effect on 1 May 1998. They are attached as Appendix C.

2

PART II OF THE HOUSING GRANTS CONSTRUCTION AND REGENERATION ACT 1996

General Purpose of Part II of the Act	2.01
Sections 104–105: Construction Contracts and Construction Operations	2.16
Section 104	2.18
Section 105	2.23
Exclusion Order 1998 (SI 1998 No 648)	2.37
Section 106: Residential Occupier	2.40
Section 107: Agreement in Writing	2.44
All, Not Part, of the Agreement Must be in Writing	2.46
Letters of Intent	2.60
Oral Variations	2.62
Implied Terms	2.67
Section 107(5)	2.69
Section 108: Adjudication	2.75
'A Dispute'	2.77
Notice at Any Time	2.85
28 Days	2.91
When Does the 28 Day Period Start to Run?	2.95
Is the Adjudicator Obliged to Complete the Decision Within 28 Days or Any Agreed Extended Period?	2.96
Is There Any Leeway Available to the Adjudicator When Communicating the Decision?	2.106
Impartiality/Fairness	2.109
Binding	2.116
Sections 109, 110 & 111: Payment Provisions	2.120
Payment Due Under the Contract	2.129
Set-Off	2.136
Nature and Timing of Withholding Notice	2.138
Relationship with Other Terms	2.142
Stay For Arbitration	2.148
Stay For Adjudication	2.152
Sections 112–115	2.153
Section 112: Suspension of Work	2.154
Section 113: 'Pay-When-Paid' Clauses	2.158
Section 114: The Scheme	2.162
Section 115: Service of Documents	2.164

'We do not intend that adjudication should be used simply to postpone resolving disputes. We have had enough of disputes within the construction industry. Government, the industry and its clients want to see an end to them: they are expensive and damaging to the industry's productivity and reputation.'

Robert Jones, Minister for Construction, Planning and
Energy Efficiency, Hansard, 7.5.96, column 54.

General Purpose of Part II of the Act

2.01 The provisions relating to adjudication are set out in Part II of the 1996 Act. They are included at Appendix A. The Scheme for Construction Contracts is at Appendix C. The first case in which the principles behind Part II were considered by the courts was *Macob Civil Engineering Ltd v Morrison Construction Ltd*.[1] The adjudicator had directed that Morrison should pay Macob £302,366.34 plus VAT, interest and fees. The principal dispute in the adjudication concerned the agreement between the parties as to the relevant dates for payment. The adjudicator decided that he could not determine what agreement, if any, had been reached on this point and, in the absence of an adequate contractual mechanism for determining the dates when payments became due, he applied the payment provisions of Part II of the Scheme for Construction Contracts (SI 1998 No 649). As a result of those provisions, he held that Morrison's notice of intention to withhold payment was out of time.

2.02 Morrison contended, amongst other things, that the decision was invalid. Their main argument was that the adjudicator had failed to give the parties the opportunity to make representations on the question of whether the mechanism for payment was ambiguous and therefore inadequate within the meaning of the Act. It was also said that he had acted in breach of natural justice because he had invoked Section 42 of the Arbitration Act 1996 (peremptory orders) without giving the parties the opportunity to make representations on that point.

2.03 Morrison argued that, to be enforceable under the Act, an adjudicator's decision had to be a lawful and valid decision. Thus, they said, where the validity of a decision was challenged, that decision could not be binding or enforceable until the validity of the decision had been determined or agreed. Dyson J (as he then was) rejected that argument. He said:

> It will be seen at once that, if this argument is correct, it substantially undermines the effectiveness of the scheme for adjudication. The intention of Parliament in enacting the Act was plain. It was to introduce a speedy mechanism for settling disputes in

---

[1] [1999] BLR 93.

construction contracts on a provisional interim basis, and requiring the decisions of adjudicators to be enforced, pending the final determination of disputes by arbitration, litigation or agreement: see s108(3) of the Act and paragraph 23(2) of Part I of the Scheme. The timetable for adjudication is very tight (see s108 of the Act). Many would say unreasonably tight, and likely to result in injustice. Parliament must be taken to have been aware of this. So far as procedure is concerned, the adjudicator is given a fairly free hand. It is true (but hardly surprising) that he is required to act impartially (s108(2)(e) of the Act and paragraph 12(a) of the Part I of the Scheme). He is, however, permitted to take the initiative in ascertaining the facts and the law (s108(2)(f) of the Act and paragraph 13 of Part I of the Scheme). He may, therefore, conduct an entirely inquisitorial process, or he may, as in the present case, invite representations from the parties. It is clear that Parliament intended that the adjudication should be conducted in a manner which those familiar with the grinding detail of the traditional approach to the resolution of construction disputes apparently find difficult to accept. But Parliament has not abolished arbitration or litigation of construction disputes. It has merely introduced an intervening provisional stage in the dispute resolution process. Crucially, it has made it clear that decisions of adjudicators are binding and are to be complied with until the dispute is finally resolved.

2.04 *Macob* is the starting point for a series of reported cases which have explained in some detail the purpose of Part II of the Act in general and the adjudication process in particular. The vast majority of those cases confirm 'that the purpose of adjudication is not to be thwarted by an overly sensitive concern for procedural niceties'.[2] In many ways the stark reality of the Act, and the courts' approach to its general purpose, was made plain early on in the case of *Bouygues (UK) Ltd v Dahl-Jensen (UK) Ltd*.[3] In that case Bouygues had purported to determine the sub-contract in question and Dahl-Jensen left site. Subsequently, Dahl-Jensen issued a notice to adjudicate claiming a variety of sums by way of additional payment, damages for breach of contract, and delay and disruption costs. The adjudicator's decision was based on his calculations of the sums due to the respective parties under each head of claim. This gave rise, on his calculations, to a balance due to Dahl-Jensen of approximately £200,000. However, in undertaking these calculations, the adjudicator had taken a gross sum, including retention, and deducted from it the amount actually paid during the sub-contract works. Those amounts did not include any retention because none had by then fallen due. As a result of this failure to compare like with like, the adjudicator incorrectly awarded Dahl-Jensen the release of all the retention by way of his decision. Had he undertaken the calculation properly, the net result of his award would have been completely different, with a sum of £140,000 being due from Dahl-Jensen to Bouygues.

---

[2] HHJ Lloyd QC in *Balfour Beatty Construction Ltd v The Mayor & Burgesses of the London Borough of Lambeth* [2002] EWHC 597; [2002] BLR 288 at paragraph 27.

[3] [2000] BLR 49. The judgments in the Court of Appeal are at [2000] BLR 522.

2.05 Unsurprisingly perhaps, Bouygues refused to comply with the adjudicator's decision. The matter came originally before Dyson J. He decided that, in considering whether the adjudicator's decision was enforceable, the court should adopt an approach similar to that applied by Knox J in *Nikko Hotels (UK) Ltd v MEPC Plc*.[4] That was a rent review case in which the tenants contended that the expert's decision was a nullity because it was based on a misinterpretation of the rent review clause. Knox J held that the expert's decision was conclusive and not open to review on the grounds that it was erroneous in law, unless it could be shown that the expert had not performed the task assigned to him. He said:

> If he has answered the right question in the wrong way, his decision will be binding. If he has answered the wrong question, his decision will be a nullity.

2.06 Dyson J concluded that, by effectively ordering the release of the retention, the adjudicator had plainly made a mistake. However, he accepted the argument put forward by Bouygues that the mistake was made in the adjudicator's calculation of the value of the disputes that were referred to him, and that the adjudicator had not made a mistaken decision to deal with (or purport to deal with) a dispute that was outside his jurisdiction. Although the Judge found that it was common ground that Dahl-Jensen was not yet entitled to the release of the retention, he said that the adjudicator did not purport to determine that Dahl-Jensen was entitled to the release of such retention. He went on to say that it was not difficult to make mistakes in doing calculations of this type, particularly when an adjudicator was working under the severe time constraints imposed by the 1996 Act. He concluded that the error derived from the adjudicator's miscalculation of the amount of the overpayment in the counterclaim and that there could be no doubt that what the adjudicator was doing in his counterclaim analysis was calculating the amount of the overpayment. He was, therefore, doing precisely what he had been asked to do; he was answering the right question, but in the wrong way.

2.07 Dyson J then went on to address the consequences of that conclusion:

> 35. Mr Furst submits that, if Dahl-Jensen is permitted to enforce a decision which is plainly erroneous, Bouygues will suffer an injustice, and this will bring the adjudication scheme into disrepute. But as I said in *Macob*, the purpose of the scheme is to provide a speedy mechanism for settling disputes in construction contracts on a provisional interim basis, and requiring the decisions of adjudicators to be enforced pending final determination of disputes by arbitration, litigation or agreement, whether those decisions are wrong in points of law or fact. It is inherent in the scheme that injustices will occur, because from time to time adjudicators will make mistakes. Sometimes those mistakes will be glaringly obvious and disastrous in their consequences for the losing party. The victims of mistakes will usually be able to recoup their losses by subsequent arbitration or litigation, and possibly even by subsequent adjudication.

---

[4] [1991] 2 EGLR 103.

Sometimes they will not be able to do so, where, for example, there is intervening insolvency, either of the victim or of the fortunate beneficiary of the mistake.

Dyson J reiterated the difference between an erroneous decision that the adjudicator was entitled to reach, and a decision that was outside his jurisdiction:

> 36. Where the adjudicator has gone outside his terms of reference, the court will not enforce his purported decision. This is not because it is unjust to enforce such a decision. It is because such a decision is of no effect in law. In deciding whether a decision has been made outside an adjudicator's terms of reference, the court should give a fair, natural and sensible interpretation to the decision in the light of the disputes that are the subject of the reference. There will be some cases where it is clear that the adjudicator has decided an issue that was not referred to him or her. But in deciding whether the adjudicator has decided the wrong question, rather than given the wrong answer to the right question, the court should bear in mind that the speedy nature of the adjudication process means that mistakes will inevitably occur, and, in my view, it should guard against characterising a mistaken answer to an issue that lies within the scope of the reference as an excess of jurisdiction.

2.08 Bouygues appealed, but their appeal was refused. Buxton LJ dismissed the argument based on the plain injustice of the mistake, considering that Dyson J had been quite right when he pointed out that the possibility of such an outcome was inherent in the exceptional and summary procedure provided by the 1996 Act. He made the point that unfairness in a specific case could not be determinative of the true construction or effect of the Scheme for Construction Contracts in general.[5] Chadwick LJ also agreed with and upheld the approach based on *Nikko Hotels*. He said:

> 28 I am satisfied, for the reasons given by Buxton LJ, that in the present case, the adjudicator did confine himself to the determination of the issues put to him. This is not a case in which he can be said to have answered the wrong question. He answered the right question. But, as is accepted by both parties, he answered that question in the wrong way. That being so, notwithstanding that he appears to have made an error that is manifest on the face of his calculations, it is accepted that, subject to the limitations to which I have already referred, his determination is binding upon the parties.

2.09 The decision in *Bouygues* set out clearly the courts' approach to the general purpose and policy behind the adjudication provisions of the 1996 Act. A more detailed analysis of the general purpose and effect of the provisions of Part II of the 1996 Act can be traced through three other early cases: *Sherwood & Casson Ltd v MacKenzie*,[6] *Northern Developments v J & J Nichol*[7] and the decision of the Court of Appeal in *C&B Scene v Isobars*.[8]

---

[5] [2000] BLR 522 at 525, paragraph 15.
[6] A decision of HHJ Thornton QC, dated 30 November 1999, reported at [2000] 2 TCLR 418.
[7] [2000] BLR 158.
[8] [2002] BLR 93.

2.10 In *Sherwood & Casson Ltd v MacKenzie*, HHJ Thornton QC summarised the approach of the courts to the 1996 Act in five propositions, as follows:

> 1. A decision of an adjudicator whose validity is challenged as to its factual or legal conclusions or as to procedural error remains a decision that is both enforceable and should be enforced.
> 2. A decision that is erroneous, even if the error is disclosed by the reasons, will still not ordinarily be capable of being challenged and should, ordinarily, still be enforced.
> 3. A decision may be challenged on the ground that the adjudicator was not empowered by the HGCRA to make the decision because there was no underlying construction contract between the parties or because he had gone outside his terms of reference.
> 4. The adjudication is intended to be a speedy process in which mistakes will inevitably occur. Thus, the court should guard against characterising a mistaken answer to an issue, which is within an adjudicator's jurisdiction, as being an excess of jurisdiction. Furthermore, the court should give a fair, natural and sensible interpretation to the decision in the light of the disputes that are the subject of the reference.
> 5. An issue as to whether a construction contract ever came into existence, which is one challenging the jurisdiction of the adjudicator, so long as it is reasonably and clearly raised, must be determined by the court on the balance of probabilities with, if necessary, oral and documentary evidence.

2.11 This approach was adopted by HHJ Bowsher QC in *Northern Developments v JJ Nichol* who expressly followed the five propositions set out by Judge Thornton in *Sherwood & Casson*.[9] These five principles were also cited with approval by Sir Murray Stuart Smith in his judgment in *C&B Scene*.

2.12 In *C&B Scene*, the Recorder at first instance refused C&B Scene's application for summary judgment and gave Isobars permission to defend on the basis that the points that they raised as to the errors made by the adjudicator were at the very least arguable. The Court of Appeal allowed C&B Scene's appeal, notwithstanding the fact that the Court accepted, for the purposes of the argument, that the adjudicator had made an error in law. Sir Murray Stuart-Smith said:

> 22. The real question is whether this error on the part of the adjudicator went to his jurisdiction, or was merely an erroneous decision of law on a matter within his jurisdiction. If it was the former the Recorder was right to hold that summary judgment should not be entered. If it was the latter, then in my judgment the proper course, subject to any question of stay of execution, is that the claimant is entitled to summary judgment.
>
> 23. The whole purpose of Section 108 of the Act, which imports into construction contracts the right to refer disputes to adjudication, is that it provides a swift and effective means of resolution of disputes which is binding during the currency of the contract and until final determination by litigation or arbitration, Section 108(3). The provisions of Sections 109–111 are designed to enable the contractor to obtain

---

[9] In addition, Judge Bowsher cited with approval the statement by HHJ Hicks QC in *VHE v RBSTB* [2000] BLR 157 that the courts had no general appellate jurisdiction over adjudicators.

payment of interim payments. Any dispute can be quickly resolved by the adjudicator and enforced through the courts. If he is wrong, the matter can be corrected in subsequent litigation or arbitration. . . .

30. It is important that the enforcement of an adjudicator's decision by summary judgment should not be prevented by arguments that the adjudicator has made errors of law in reaching his decision, unless the adjudicator has purported to decide matters which are not referred to him. He must decide as a matter of construction of the referral, and therefore as a matter of law, what the dispute is that he has to decide. If he erroneously decides that the dispute referred to him is wider than it is, then, in so far as he has exceeded his jurisdiction, his decision cannot be enforced. But in the present case there was entire agreement to the scope of the dispute, and the adjudicator's decision, albeit he may have made errors of law as to the relevant contractual provisions, is still binding and enforceable until the matter is corrected in the final determination.

2.13 It is a theme regularly taken up in the later decisions of the TCC and the Court of Appeal, when setting out how and why the adjudicator's decision should be enforced provided that he had the jurisdiction to reach it, no matter how mistaken that decision might seem, to emphasise that the decision is of a temporary nature only. Just as Sir Murray Stuart-Smith pointed out in the above passage that any mistakes could be corrected in subsequent litigation and arbitration, the courts have generally observed that the justification for enforcing a decision which may be wrong in fact or in law is because that is consistent with the 'pay now, argue later' philosophy built into the Act itself.[10] It is worth noting, as some dissenting voices have pointed out, that in larger construction disputes, the sums of money at stake in an adjudication are very significant, and, since the parties have to bear their own costs of the adjudication process, a party can lose a very considerable sum in adjudication and face no realistic prospect of recovering that sum for months, if not years. It is plain that this is the other side of the adjudication coin and one that has not received very much publicity. However, the point was made expressly by HHJ Toulmin CMG QC in *AWG Construction Services Ltd v Rockingham Motor Speedway Ltd*.[11] There, Judge Toulmin picked up the point from the judgment of Dyson J in *Macob* where it had been noted that the decision of the adjudicator was 'merely introduced [as] an intervening stage in the dispute resolution process'. Judge Toulmin went on to observe:

122. The word 'mere' was entirely appropriate to characterise the summary and inexpensive procedure that was envisaged by Parliament. It is a less appropriate description of a process which has already cost over £1 million. The court has to grapple with a procedure which Parliament introduced to provide a quick, easy and cheap provisional answer so that, in particular, sub-contractors were not unjustly kept out of their money. It has developed into an elaborate and expensive procedure

---

[10] See paragraph 1.31 above.
[11] [2004] EWHC 888 (TCC).

which is wholly confrontational, a full-scale trial normally, on the documents, of the issues referred to the adjudicator (not necessarily the whole dispute) within a timetable of 42 days from notice of adjudication to decision by the adjudicator. . .

123. The claimant has the considerable advantage in a complex adjudication that it can choose when to start the adjudication, having taken the time it has needed to prepare. It will then impose a very tight timetable on the defendant and frequently on the adjudicator. It is with this in mind that I raise the possibility that there may be disputes which are so complex and the advantages so weighted against a defendant that there is a conflict between the right to refer to adjudication and to obtain a decision under s108(2)(c) and (d) of the Act, and the adjudicator's duty to act impartially under s108(e) of Act and that this may be a conflict which it is impossible to resolve.

2.14 The remarks made by Judge Toulmin in *AWG* will strike a chord with anybody who has acted for the responding party in adjudication, who can often be given very little time to respond to a case of inordinate detail, on which millions of pounds may turn, of which it has had very little prior notice. On one view, it is a matter for the adjudicator to decide whether or not he can fairly and properly arrive at a conclusion within the 28 days, or any extended period that may be agreed, and if he cannot, he should refuse the appointment.[12] However, the cases are not littered with examples of adjudicators taking that course. Often, the material relied on by both sides in an adjudication will grow significantly during the 28 day period, making it impossible for the adjudicator to produce a realistic assessment of how long he might need to produce a fair decision, and preventing efficient case management by either the adjudicator or the parties.[13] There is little doubt, therefore, that the potential abuse of the 1996 Act, as outlined by Judge Toulmin, remains a real risk in the UK construction industry. However, in general, the courts, and in particular the Court of Appeal, have not been persuaded that such considerations ought to colour their approach to the general purpose of the 1996 Act, and the enforcement of the decisions of adjudicators.

2.15 The most recent re-statement of the general purpose of the adjudication provisions within the 1996 Act can be found at paragraphs 85 to 87 of the judgment of Chadwick LJ in *Carillion Construction Ltd v Devonport Royal Dockyard Ltd*,[14] which are set out verbatim at paragraph 7.85 below. Chadwick LJ emphasised that the courts would enforce the decision of an adjudicator unless it was one of those rare instances when the question that the adjudicator decided was not the question referred to him or the way in which he has gone about the adjudication was obviously unfair. He noted that the adjudicator's task was simply to find an

---

[12] In some Australian states, the adjudicator has the express power to rule that a particular dispute is not suited to the adjudication process.

[13] In *Cubitt Building & Interiors Ltd v Fairglade Ltd* [2006] EWHC 3413 (TCC), at paragraph 15 of his judgment, the TCC Judge described this process as 'creep'.

[14] [2005] EWCA (Civ) 1358.

interim solution which met the needs of the case, and that the need to have the 'right' answer had been subordinated to the need to have an answer quickly. He also said that adjudication under the 1996 Act was not intended to provide definitive answers to complex questions. It might be thought that this was an unequivocal statement as to the general purpose and effect of the 1996 Act: if the adjudicator had the jurisdiction to reach the decision he did, and if he arrived at that conclusion in a way that was not obviously unfair, it will be enforced, no matter how wrong it may ultimately prove to be.

Sections 104-105: Construction Contracts and Construction Operations

Sections 104 and 105 of the 1996 Act provide as follows: 2.16

104-(1) In this Part a "construction contract" means an agreement with a person for any of the following—

(a) the carrying out of construction operations;

(b) arranging for the carrying out of construction operations by others, whether under sub-contract to him or otherwise;

(c) providing his own labour, or the labour of others, for the carrying out of construction operations.

(2) References in this Part to a construction contract include an agreement—

(a) to do architectural design or surveying work, or

(b) to provide advice on building, engineering interior or exterior decoration or on the laying-out of landscape,

in relation to construction operations.

(3) References in this Part to a construction contract do not include a contract of employment (within the meaning of the Employment Rights Act 1996).

(4) The Secretary of State may by order, add to, amend or repeal any of the provisions of sub-section (1)(2) or (3) as to the agreements which are construction contracts for the purposes of this Part or are to be taken or not to be taken as included in references to such contract.

No such order shall be made unless a draft of it has been laid before and approved by resolution of each House of Parliament.

(5) Where an agreement relates to construction operations and other matters, this Part applies to it only so far as it relates to construction operations.

An agreement relates to construction operations so far as it makes provision of any kind within sub-section (1) or (2).

(6) This Part applies only to construction contracts which—

(a) are entered into after the commencement of this Part, and

(b) relate to the carrying out of construction operations in England, Wales or Scotland.

(7) This Part applies whether or not the law of England and Wales or Scotland is otherwise the applicable law in relation to the contract.

105(1) In this Part "construction operations" means, subject as follows, operations of any of the following descriptions—
- (a) construction, alteration, repair, maintenance, extension, demolition or dismantling of buildings, or structures forming, or to form, part of the land (whether permanent or not);
- (b) construction, alteration, repair, maintenance, extension, demolition or dismantling of any works forming, or to form, part of the land, including (without prejudice to the foregoing) walls, roadworks, power-lines, telecommunication apparatus, aircraft runways, docks and harbours, railways, inland waterways, pipe-lines, reservoirs, water-mains, wells, sewers, industrial plant and installations for purposes of land drainage, coast protection or defence;
- (c) installation in any building or structure of fittings forming a part of the land including (without prejudice to the foregoing) systems of heating, lighting, air-conditioning, ventilation, power supply, drainage, sanitation, water supply or fire protection or security or communications systems;
- (d) external or internal cleaning of buildings and structures, so far as carried out in the course of their construction, alteration, repair, extension or restoration;
- (e) alterations which form an integral part of, or are preparatory to, or are for rendering complete, such operations as are previously described in this sub-section, including site clearance, earth-moving, excavation, tunnelling and boring, laying of foundations, erection, maintenance or dismantling of scaffolding, site restoration, landscaping and the provision of roadways and other access works;
- (f) painting or decorating the internal or external surfaces of any building or structure.

(2) The following operations are not construction operations within the meaning of this Part—
- (a) drilling for, or extraction of, oil or natural gas;
- (b) extraction (whether by underground or surface working) of minerals; tunnelling or boring, or construction of underground works, for this purpose;
- (c) assembly, installation or demolition of plant or machinery or erection or demolition of steelwork for the purposes of supporting or providing access to plant or machinery, on a site where the primary activity is—
    - (i) nuclear processing, power generation, or water or effluent treatment, or
    - (ii) the production, transmission, processing or bulk storage (other than warehousing) of chemicals, pharmaceuticals, oil, gas, steel or food and drink;
- (d) manufacture or delivery to site of—
    - (i) building or engineering components or equipment,
    - (ii) materials, plant or machinery, or
    - (iii) components for systems of heating, lighting, air-conditioning, ventilation, power supply, drainage, sanitation, water supply or fire protection, or for security or communications systems,

    except under a contract which also provides for their installation;
- (e) the making, installation and repair of artistic works, being sculptures, murals and other works which are wholly artistic in nature.

(3) The Secretary of State may by order add to, amend or repeal any of the provisions of sub-section (1) or (2) as to the operations and work to be treated as construction operations for the purpose of this Part.

(4) No such order shall be made unless a draft of it has been laid before and approved by resolution of each House of Parliament.

2.17 We have already seen[15] that much of the debate in both Houses of Parliament at the Bill stage centred upon the apparent contradictions encompassed in these sections. Despite the many effective points made during those debates, the Act was passed in the somewhat unusual form set out above. Thus there is a wide definition of construction contracts in s104(1) and s104(2); this wide definition is then the subject of detailed exposition at s105(1), before being the subject of a number of potentially wide exceptions (s105(2)). It is difficult not to feel instinctive sympathy with those who pointed out during the Parliamentary debates that these definitions were likely to lead to just the sort of disputes that the Act itself was designed to avoid. Be that as it may, the effect of these sections is to state that the 1996 Act applies to all contracts related to the carrying out of construction operations: there are then lengthy lists of what are included within construction operations, and what operations, for the purposes of the Act, are very firmly excluded. As was envisaged by Parliament, there have now been a number of reported cases on these provisions.

Section 104

2.18 The provisions at s104(1) have not caused significant difficulty. In *Gillies Ramsay Diamond v PJW Enterprises Ltd*[16] a decision of the Outer House of the Court of Session, a contractor was successful in adjudication on his claim against the employer, PJW, largely as a result of the failure by the employer's architect, GRD, to issue written instructions. PJW then issued its own adjudication against GRD alleging professional negligence. One of GRD's arguments was that, since he was the contract administrator, such work did not fall within the definition of a construction contract in s104(1). The court disagreed, finding that contract administration services amounted to 'arranging for the carrying out of construction operations by others, whether under sub-contract . . . or otherwise'. The court held that it was of the essence of a contract administrator's function to arrange for the carrying out of the construction operation by means of advising on consultations required, orchestrating tenders, programming, certifying and controlling finances. The court held that, without such measures, the construction operations would not be carried out, and certainly would not be performed in a satisfactory way.

2.19 S104(2) is designed to ensure that contracts for the provision of professional services in connection with construction operations were firmly caught by the

---

[15] See Chapter 1, paragraphs 1.19–1.22 above.
[16] [2002] CILL 1901–1903.

provisions of the 1996 Act. However, s104(2) has been treated as referring only to professional services associated with actual construction operations. Thus, in *Fencegate Ltd v James R Knowles Ltd*[17] James R Knowles, the well-known construction claims consultants, provided a range of services to Fencegate in connection with a construction arbitration. Thereafter disputes arose as to Knowles' entitlement to fees, and these were referred to adjudication. Although the adjudicator awarded Knowles £31,000 odd, Fencegate applied to the court for a declaration that the adjudicator had no jurisdiction because the contract between themselves and Knowles was not within s104(2). HHJ Gilliland QC, sitting at the TCC in Salford, rejected the submission that the giving of factual evidence by an architect, designer or surveyor at an arbitration fell within the words of s104(2)(a) of the 1996 Act. He held that it was not the 'doing' of architectural designing or surveying work itself. He decided that, although the reporting back to the client of what had been discovered upon a survey will form an essential part of the services which the surveyor has agreed to provide and should be regarded as part of the actual survey (and therefore included in the 'doing' of the work), the giving of factual evidence at an arbitration or in court of what had been found in the course of that survey was a significantly different activity from actually surveying the property and reporting to the client. The Judge also held that assisting in an arbitration was not the same thing as providing advice on building or engineering. As a result, he held that the contract fell outside s104(2) of the 1996 Act and the adjudicator had no jurisdiction to decide the fee dispute referred to him.

2.20 S104(5) has given rise to a certain amount of difficulty. As Judge Gilliland pointed out in *Fencegate*[18] it is difficult to see what s104(5) adds to s104(2), particularly given that s104(2) itself imposes a requirement that matters which are not themselves construction operations are only brought within the definition of a construction contract (and thus within Part II of the Act) if they relate to construction operations. Judge Gilliland concluded that s104(5) was intended to make clear that, where a contract related both to construction operations and to other activities, the contract was to be treated as severable between those parts which related to construction operations, and those parts which related to other activities, and that Part II, and the other provisions for adjudication, were to apply to the contract only in so far as the contract related to construction operations. This seems a sensible and practical interpretation of the Act and would appear to be the only way in which real effect can be given to s104(5).

2.21 In *Gibson Lea Retail Interiors Ltd v Makro Self Service Wholesalers Ltd*[19] Gibson Lea were employed by Makro to supply and install shop fittings at four cash and

---

[17] [2001] CILL 1757–1759.
[18] [2001] CILL 1757–1759 at paragraph 7.
[19] [2001] BLR 407.

carry stores. Gibson Lea wished to issue adjudication proceedings and, when Makro took the point that the shop fittings works were not construction operations within s.104 of the Act, Gibson Lea sought a declaration that the works which were the subject matter of the four contracts were indeed construction operations. Makro's principal argument was that the works were not construction operations but, in the alternative, they argued that, even if some of the works undertaken by Gibson Lea could be regarded as construction operations within the meaning of the Act, it was plain that other items of work which they carried out were not within that description. Thus it was argued that, at best, the Act only applied to some of the items supplied under the contracts. In support of this submission, Makro relied on s104(5). HHJ Seymour QC found that Makro were right and that the shopfitting work being carried out by Gibson Lea was not within the definition of construction operations. However, he expressly found that, had it been necessary to do so, he would have found that, on any view, the works which Gibson Lea had agreed to undertake included specific operations which were undoubtedly not construction operations, and that Makro's submissions as to the meaning and effect of s104(5) were therefore correct.

2.22 S104(6) provides two limits to the applicability of the Act. Sub-section (a) makes it clear that the Act applies only to construction contracts which were entered into after the commencement of that Part of the Act and sub-section (b) makes plain that the Part only applies to the carrying out of construction operations in England, Wales or Scotland. There have been a number of disputes as to the commencement provisions. In *Earls Terrace Properties Ltd v Waterloo Investments Ltd*[20] HHJ Seymour QC had to deal with a situation where the construction contract was dated 4 December 1996, which was before the commencement of Part II of the Act. The contract was later varied by agreement on 20 July 1998. That variation did not affect the content of the services to be provided, although it did alter the fee arrangements. The Judge held that the provisions of the 1996 Act did not apply to the first agreement because of s104(6)(a). The question was whether the 1998 agreement made any difference. The Judge concluded that the 1998 agreement was not itself a construction contract and that it would be a bizarre consequence if the effect of the making of such an agreement brought the original contract within Part II of the Act. As to s104(6), the Judge said this:

> By making the provision which it did in s104(6) of the 1996 Act, Parliament plainly intended that the far reaching, and to some extent possibly draconian, provisions of Part II of the 1996 Act should only apply to construction contracts which were made at a date after which the parties making the contract were aware that the provisions of Part II were going to apply to that contract. Parliament therefore seems deliberately to have wished not to bring within the scope of Part II of the 1996 Act contracts

---

[20] [2002] CILL 1889–1892.

which were made at a time at which the parties could not have envisaged that provisions such as those which the 1996 Act made in relation to adjudication would be thrust upon them.

He concluded that the variations made in the 1998 agreement were simply variations to sums of money which were payable in respect of services which had themselves not altered and therefore it was not contemplated that that variation could or would bring the original contract within the scope of Part II of the Act.[21]

Section 105

2.23 The drafting of s105 has given rise to a raft of problems. Many of these are inherent in the structure of this section itself. S105(1) purports to define what is meant by 'construction operations' for the purposes of the 1996 Act. S105(1)(e) widens the definition further because it includes 'operations which form an integral part of, or are preparatory to, or are for rendering complete, such operations as are previously described in this sub-section . . .' However, s105(2) then seeks to identify a number of operations which, for the purposes of the Act, are not to be construed as 'construction operations' even if an ordinary, common sense view would be that such activities plainly were construction operations.

2.24 The operation of these sections was one of the matters considered by HHJ Thornton QC in *Palmers Ltd v ABB Power Construction Ltd*.[22] He concluded that the right approach was as follows:

> 24. In considering the somewhat convoluted section 105 of the HGCRA, it is helpful first to notice one of its most important features. This is that there are some operations which fall within the definition, provided by section 105(1), and would therefore appear to be construction operations and yet are not such operations as a result of section 105(2) of the Act. This is because sub-section 105(1) states, somewhat inelegantly, that sub-section (1) applies 'subject as follows' which, in its context, means that sub-section (1) is to apply unless sub-section (2) also applies. If sub-section (2) applies, sub-section (1) is not to apply. The inapplicability of sub-section 105(1) arises in any particular case even though most, if not all, of the relevant operations described in sub-section (2) also fall within one of the descriptions of relevant operations set out in sub-section (1).

---

[21] The decision in *Earls Terrace* is, perhaps, to be contrasted with the decision of HHJ Havery QC in *Yarm Road Ltd v Costain Ltd* (unreported) 30.7.01. There the original sub-contract was dated 7 August 1995, which was before Part II of the 1996 Act came into force. There was a novation agreement dated 14 August 1998. Judge Havery held that the novation agreement discharged the original sub-contract and created a fresh sub-contract the subject matter of which was the carrying out of construction operations. The Judge therefore concluded that the novation agreement fell within s104(6)(a).

[22] [1999] BLR 426.

In *Palmers v ABB*, the claimant sub-contractor sought a declaration that the work **2.25** that was the subject matter of its sub-contracts was within the 1996 Act because it comprised 'construction operations'. ABB argued that the work was excluded by s105(2) because the sites where the work was being carried out had, as their primary activity, the generation of power. The scaffolding provided by Palmers was used to provide temporary access and support to the structural frame within which ABB were installing boilers and associated pipe work. The scaffolding therefore required almost constant modification to provide the necessary access whilst the works being carried out by ABB were progressed.

Judge Thornton held that ABB's work was a construction operation within **2.26** s105(1). He held that the assembly and fixing to the land of industrial plant and similar features were included within s105(1)(b). He then went on to consider the scaffolding being provided by Palmers and said that, by reference to s105(1)(e), 'it might be thought that there was no question but that the scaffolding work was preparatory to one of the operations "previously described"'. But, as he went on to note, the assembling and erecting of the boiler by ABB also fell within the ambit of s105(2)(c), which was one of the exclusions to the Act. ABB argued that Palmers' scaffolding work was similarly excluded. They maintained that 'previously described in this sub-section' was a reference to those operations previously described which were not, additionally, included in sub-section (2), so that it was said that such operations were not 'previously described in this sub-section' but were operations which were subsequently described in sub-section (2), and therefore excluded. The Judge held, by reference to the Act itself (and, if there was any doubt about it by reference to the Parliamentary debates), that the relevant words suggested that s105(1)(e) was not incorporating the exclusions provided by sub-section 105(2). The Judge said:

> 34 ... If the words had been intended to exclude from sub-section 105(1)(e) preparatory operations for those operations which, although apparently within the ambit of sub-section 105(1), are not to be treated as being so because they are also within the definition of excluded construction operations that are set out in sub-section 105(2), it would have been a more natural use of language to use these words: 'such construction operations as are previously defined by this sub-section' rather than the words actually used: 'such operations as are previously described in this sub-section'. By widening the relevant reference from 'construction operations' to 'operations' and by referring to operations that are 'described in this sub-section' rather than to operations that are 'defined by this sub-section' the draftsman of the HGCRA appears to be pointing to operations which fit the words of sub-section (1) even if they fall outside its ambit by virtue of sub-section (2). In other words, scaffolding which is preparatory to an excluded construction operation may, nonetheless, itself be a construction operation.

This was an important decision because it meant that a sub-contractor who was **2.27** carrying out an activity further down the contractual chain, which activity was plainly a 'construction operation' within the meaning of s105(1) would not be deprived of his right to adjudication merely because the site on which he was working, or the work of the main contractor for whom he was providing certain services, may fall within s105(2) and therefore be excluded by the Act. However, Judge Thornton's decision must be contrasted with the decision in *ABB Power Construction Ltd v Norwest Holst Engineering Ltd*,[23] discussed further below.

2.28 An argument as to the relationship between the two principal parts of s105 also arose in *Gibson Lea v Makro*.[24] In that case the principal argument was whether shopfitting amounted to 'construction operations'. Makro's argument, which was accepted by the Judge, was that the items supplied by Gibson Lea to Makro were, insofar as they were installed, not fixtures and therefore did not form part of the land. Thus they were not a construction operation within s105(1)(a). However, as part of the argument before the court, Gibson Lea contended that a purposive approach should be adopted to s105 and that, effectively, the right way to define 'construction operations' under s105(1) was to include everything which arguably fell within those words, unless the operation was specifically excluded by s105(2). The submission was also that it was appropriate to have regard to the terms of s105(2) to indicate that which would fall within the definition of 'construction operations', but for its express exclusion by sub-section 105(2). The Judge concluded that, since s105(1)(a) was clear and not ambiguous, and that since the shopfitting works in that case plainly did not fall within s105(1)(a), the Act did not apply. However, although the judgment does not address expressly the wide argument put forward by Gibson Lea, noted above, it is submitted that their proposition cannot be right. If a wide interpretation of the expression 'construction operations' was to be adopted, with only the express exclusions at s105(2) to define those operations by way of limited exception, the Act would have said that. Instead, the Act at s105(1) sets out a whole list of matters which are 'construction operations'. It is suggested, therefore, that if, on the evidence, the work being done does not fall within s105(1) it is not a construction operation, regardless of the position under s105(2).

2.29 The inter-relationship between the various sub-sections of s105(1) have themselves caused difficulty. In *Nottingham Community Housing Association Ltd v Powerminster Ltd*[25] the relevant contract provided for an annual service by Powerminster of each gas appliance in the properties owned by the housing association. Powerminster made a claim in adjudication for unpaid sums under the contract, and the housing association countered by contending that it was not a construction contract within the meaning of the Act. The housing association's

---

[23] [2000] TCLR 831, discussed at paragraphs 2.32–2.34 below.
[24] [2001] BLR 407.
[25] [2000] BLR 309.

principal argument was that, although sub-section (a) of s105(1) included within the definition of 'construction operations', the 'construction alteration, repair, maintenance, extension, demolition or dismantling of buildings', paragraph (c) of s105(3), which expressly referred to 'systems of heating', related only to the installation of such a system. Thus the argument was that repair and maintenance of systems of heating were not within 105(1)(c) and was therefore not a construction operation within the meaning of the Act. Dyson J concluded that the maintenance and repair of heating systems which had been installed in a building were operations within sub-section (a) and that it would be surprising if it were otherwise. However, that left the difficulty of paragraph (c), which, on its face, was limited to installation, and did not include maintenance and repair. Counsel for Powerminster accepted that, on his construction of sub-section (a), sub-section (c) was redundant. However, Dyson J said that he was not persuaded by the redundancy argument and that, whatever the reason for including sub-section (c) he was not persuaded that its inclusion should lead him not to give sub-section (a) what he considered to be its clear and true meaning. He therefore held that the contract was a construction contract within the meaning of the Act.

2.30 Another example of the court's approach to s105(1) can be found in *Staveley Industries Plc v Odebrecht Oil and Gas Services Ltd*.[26] There Odebrecht sub-contracted to Staveley the design, engineering, supply, delivery, installation, testing and commissioning of various electrical and telecommunications equipment for installation in the modules that were intended to be the living quarters for operatives at an oil and gas rig. Staveley sought a declaration that this was a construction contract and contended that the work fell within s105(1)(c), as well as s105(1)(a). The defendant said that the work did not come within 105(1)(a) or (c) because the modules did not form part of the land. HHJ Havery QC ruled that the contract was not a construction contract. He held that the reference to 'the land' in s105(1) referred to the land where the building or structure was situated when built. Furthermore, since the provisions of section 105(1) were derived from section 562(2) of the Income and Corporation Taxes Act 1988, which Act included a provision for offshore installations (which was not included within s105(1) of the 1996 Act), it seemed clear that there was no intention to include offshore installations within the 1996 Act.

2.31 Inevitably, the principal source of dispute in this part of the 1996 Act has been the exclusions contained within s105(2). The vast bulk of these disputes have centred on cases where the party anxious to avoid the adjudication process has argued that the work in question (often being carried out by a sub-contractor or a

---

[26] [2001] 98(10) LSG 46.

sub-sub-contractor) is being performed at a site where the primary activity is, say, power generation or bulk storage pursuant to 105(2)(c).[27] The first of these disputes to come to court was the decision of the Outer House of the Court of Session (Lord MacFadyen) in *Homer Burgess Ltd v Chirex (Annan) Ltd*.[28] There the pursuers were engaged to construct pipework at the defender's site, which pipework ran between various pieces of machinery and equipment and by which ingredients and pharmaceuticals in the process of manufacture were conveyed from one stage of the manufacturing process to another. The adjudicator decided that this was a construction contract because, as an engineer, he regarded 'plant' as being a device or a piece of apparatus in which part of the process was effected, and he therefore concluded that the installation of the pipework was not the installation of 'plant' within s105(2)(c). The court held that the adjudicator was wrong in law in defining 'plant' in the way in which he did and that, given that this was a decision which went to his jurisdiction, it was one which the court was entitled to review. Lord MacFadyen found that the pipework was part of the plant being assembled and installed at the defender's site and that, without that pipework, the individual pieces of machinery or equipment would be unable to operate. Given that the pipework was in a real sense part of the apparatus which the defenders were going to use in order to carry out their business of manufacturing pharmaceuticals, the installation of that pipework was an operation that fell within the scope of the exception in s105(2)(c)(ii).

2.32 The decision in *Homer Burgess* was considered by HHJ Lloyd QC in *ABB Power Construction Ltd v Norwest Holst Engineering Ltd*.[29] In that case ABB were building three boiler houses as part of a project to extend the existing power station in Aberdeen. The area of the extension was separated from the existing power station by a fence. ABB engaged Norwest Holst as sub-contractors to carry out insulation/cladding works to boilers, ducts, pipework, drums and tanks. Norwest Holst also prefabricated the materials off site. ABB contended the sub-contract was for the assembly or installation of plant on a site where the primary activity was power generation and that, in consequence, the exception at 105(2)(c)(i) applied. Norwest Holst argued, amongst other things, that the work was not a site where the primary activity 'is' power generation but was work on a site where the primary activity would be power generation in the future. In addition they argued that there were two sites: the existing site and the site of the new extension.

2.33 Judge Lloyd held that the words in s105(2)(c) 'assembly, installation . . . of plant' included insulation or cladding of pipework, because without insulation or

---

[27] See for example, *Palmers v ABB* analysed at paragraphs 2.25–2.27 above.
[28] [2000] BLR 124.
[29] [2000] TCLR 831.

cladding the boilers and the associated plant would simply not function. Thus work which would otherwise be a construction operation under s105(1) would not be a construction operation by reason of s105(2)(c), assuming always that installation was undertaken on a site, such as a site for nuclear processing or power generation, that was within that sub-section. He also decided that s105(2)(c) applied to work on a site where the activity will be one of those described in the section when the works are completed, and not only to a site where the activity 'is' such an activity. He treated the site as a single site where power generation was the primary activity, notwithstanding the existence of the fence.

In reaching his decision, Judge Lloyd appeared to take a different approach to that of Judge Thornton in *Palmers v ABB*.[30] At paragraph 14 of his judgment in *ABB v Norwest Holst*, Judge Lloyd said: **2.34**

> 14 ... It is in my judgment clear from the language used in Section 105(2) that it was intended that, if the regimes were not to apply, it would be invidious if they applied to some but not all construction contracts on a site or for a project. Defining the exempt construction operations by reference to the nature of the project or by reference to a site should minimise the possibility that, for example, one contractor or sub-contractor would think that it was better or worse off than another working alongside it, or preceding or following it. That would not be conducive to the purpose of the legislation and would be inimical to the establishment or maintenance of harmonious working relationships and the concept of team work. Section 105(2) plainly reflects the fact that the majority of construction work done for the purposes set out in paragraphs (a) to (d) is carried out by contractors responsible for design or performance and for owners or employers most of whom take an active interest in seeing that every aspect of their project should be properly planned and coordinated. Such involvement minimises the incidence of disputes at every level or tier. The object of this sub-section is therefore that all the construction operations necessary to achieve the aims or purposes of the owners or of the principal contractors (as described in it) would be exempt. If these approaches are correct then an interpretation should be given to Section 105(2) which would further and not thwart them.

The exception at 105(2)(c)(i), concerned with power generation, led to a common argument that wherever power generation plant could be found at a site, the relevant contract or sub-contract was excluded from the workings of the Act. This fallacious argument was dealt with by HHJ Bowsher QC in *ABB Zantingh v Zedal Building Services Ltd*.[31] The dispute concerned two large printing sites owned by the Miller Colour Print Group in Watford and Oldham. At each site they decided to build a diesel-powered generation station to supply power to their printing operations. ABB Zantingh agreed to design, build and maintain the power generation stations, and they sub-contracted to Zedal, the defendant, the supply, **2.35**

---

[30] See also the decision of the Outer House in *Mitsui Babcock Energy Services v Foster Wheeler Energia OY* [2001] SLT 24.
[31] [2001] BLR 66.

installation, labelling, termination and testing of all field wiring. Disputes arose and Zedal appointed an adjudicator. ABB Zantingh challenged the adjudicator's jurisdiction on the basis that this was not a construction contract, because the work was exempted by s105(2)(c)(i). Judge Bowsher rejected this argument. He said that, if the sites were defined as the whole areas occupied by Miller at Oldham and Watford, then it could not conceivably be said that the primary activity of those sites was power generation. He said that, taking those sites as a whole, power generation could only be regarded as ancillary to the primary activity of printing colour magazines, whether or not any excess power which might be generated at the sites could be sold to others. He went on to find that the exception at s105(2)(c) only related to sites where the primary activity was power generation and that there was no statutory exception in relation to sites where the secondary or tertiary activity was power generation. He therefore concluded that the exception did not apply and that the relevant sub-contract was a construction contract within the meaning of the Act.

2.36 Similarly pragmatic conclusions were reached in two later cases, *Comsite Projects Ltd v Andritz AG*[32] and *Conor Engineering Ltd v Les Constructions Industrielles de la Mediterranée*.[33] In *Comsite* the claimant argued that the work sub-contracted to them by AAG, which included the installation of wiring and building services to a dryer building that formed part of a new waste water treatment works, was within the definition of construction operations under s105(1). AAG argued that the work fell within s105(2)(c)(i) and was therefore excluded. HHJ Kirkham concluded that the building services which Comsite were to install were physically integral to the building, but not integral to the dryer plant. There was no reason to suppose that the dryer plant was not capable of operating without any of the services to be installed pursuant to the sub-contract. Accordingly, adopting the approach in *Homer Burgess v Chirex* and *ABB Power v Norwest Holst*, the Judge concluded that none of the services supplied under the sub-contract were connected to the plant or used to enable the plant physically to be operated. Their purpose and function were simply related to the building, which involved not only the plant but also other areas of activity. The sub-contract was therefore a construction contract within s105(1). Similarly, in *Conor*, the dispute concerned a waste incineration plant which, when in operation, turned the water in the pipes surrounding the furnace into steam, which was then used to produce electricity. Mr Recorder Blunt QC found that the prime purpose of the plant was the incineration of waste and that the principal physical activity at the site was also the incineration of waste. He accepted the argument that the generation of electricity was simply 'a spin-off' from the incineration process. He decided that he could

---

[32] [2003] EWHC 958 (TCC).
[33] [2004] EWHC 899 (TCC).

not conclude that the principal purpose of the site was power generation, and he therefore rejected the submission that the work fell within the exception at s105(2)(c)(i).

Exclusion Order 1998 (SI 1998 No 648)

2.37 It is convenient here to consider the terms of the Exclusion Order (SI 1998 No 648), which excludes certain contracts from the ambit of the 1996 Act which would otherwise fall within it. A copy of the Statutory Instrument appears at Appendix B. Paragraph 3 excludes certain agreements under statute; paragraph 4 excludes private finance initiatives; paragraph 5 excludes Finance Agreements, as defined by the Order; and paragraph 6 excludes Development Agreements, again as defined by the Order.

2.38 There are no reported cases under paragraphs 3-5 inclusive of the SI. In *Captiva Estates Ltd v Rybarn Ltd (In Administration)*[34] HHJ Wilcox had to consider paragraph 6, concerned with development agreements. A development agreement was excluded from the ambit of the 1996 Act 'if it includes provision for the grant or disposal of a relevant interest in the land on which take place the principal construction operations to which the contract relates'. The order goes on to define a relevant interest in land as either freehold or 'a leasehold for a period which is to expire no earlier than 12 months after the completion of the construction operations under the contract'. In *Captiva*, the contract granted Rybarn options for the grant of leases for seven of the flats that were the subject of the development. The terms of the contract which created that option meant that, on the due exercise by Rybarn of the option, Captiva had an estate or interest taken away without its consent and vested in another. Thus the Judge found that this was a relevant interest in land for the purposes of the Exclusion Order and was caught by paragraph 6 of the Exclusion Order. Thus he concluded that the contract was excluded from the Act and the adjudication was invalid.

2.39 It is not clear precisely what Parliament had in mind when they excluded development agreements from the ambit of the 1996 Act. Furthermore, paragraph 6 of the Order is broadly drafted, such that, as in *Captiva*, it covered a contract where only seven out of 28 flats were the subject of the relevant option. As the learned editors of the Building Law Reports point out, the wide words of paragraph 6 appear to provide parties with a route by which they might effectively contract out of the 1996 Act, provided of course that they were willing to incorporate an option in relation to a relevant interest in respect of part of the ongoing development.

---

[34] [2005] EWHC 2744 (TCC); [2006] BLR 66.

Section 106: Residential Occupier

2.40 Section 106 of the 1996 Act provides as follows:

106–(1) This Part does not apply—
  (a) to a construction contract with a residential occupier (see below), or
  (b) to any other description of construction contract excluded from the operation of this Part of order of the Secretary of State.

(2) A construction contract with a residential occupier means a construction contract which principally relates to operations on a dwelling which one of the parties to the contract occupies, or intends to occupy, as his residence.

In this sub-section "dwelling" means a dwelling-house or a flat; and for this purpose—

"dwelling-house" does not include a building containing a flat; and

"flat" means separate and self-contained premises constructed or adapted for use for residential purposes and forming part of a building from some other part of which the premises are divided horizontally.

(3) The Secretary of State made by order amend sub-section (2).

(4) No order under this section shall be made unless a draft of it has been laid before and approved by resolution of each House of Parliament.

2.41 The importance of this section has been diminished over the years, as the standard forms of building contract have incorporated their own forms of adjudication agreement. Thus, if a residential occupier signs a building contract which incorporates, for instance, one of the JCT standard forms, then he is prima facie agreeing to adjudication in the event of disputes, despite the fact that he is a residential occupier within the meaning of the Act. Accordingly, this exception now only applies in situations where there is no express agreement to adjudicate. However, it remains of some significance, not least because it has been relied on to argue that, even where an express agreement to adjudicate was incorporated into the contract with the residential occupier, the agreement was invalid pursuant to the terms of the Unfair Terms in Consumer Contract Regulations. Thus, in *Picardi v Cuniberti & Cuniberti*[35] HHJ Toulmin CMG QC found that the adjudication provisions should have been (and were not) drawn to the residential occupier's attention. He referred to adjudication as 'an unusual procedure', and that Parliament had specifically excluded private dwelling houses from its application. Therefore, he said, a contract provision that, despite this exclusion, adjudication is to be adopted is clearly an unusual provision which must be brought to the specific attention of the lay party if it is later to be validly invoked.[36] This is perhaps to be contrasted with the decision of HHJ Thornton QC in *Steve Domsalla (t/a Domsalla*

---

[35] [2003] BLR 487.
[36] For a fuller discussion of this topic, see paragraphs 9.49–9.58 below.

Building Services) v Kenneth Dyason,[37] in which the residential occupier had signed a standard form with an adjudication provision. The Judge rejected the suggestion that the adjudication provisions were somehow not binding on the employer, and he also rejected the submission that such provisions were unfair pursuant to the Unfair Terms in Consumer Contracts Regulations. However, he did find that, on the facts, the withholding notice provisions were unfair.

2.42 In *Samuel Thomas Construction v Anon*[38] the adjudicator had decided that the builder's contract was not with a residential occupier, and was therefore caught by the 1996 Act. The contract in question concerned the refurbishment of a number of farm buildings. One barn was being refurbished so that the employers could live in it. However, the contract also encompassed barn A, which was being refurbished for onward sale, as well as other barns and a garage block. The adjudicator decided that, where the construction contract was for two dwellings, one of which was to be occupied by one of the parties and one of which was not, the contract in question could not be said principally to relate to operations on a dwelling which one of the parties to the contract intended to occupy. He therefore decided that he had the necessary jurisdiction to adjudicate. This decision was upheld by His Honour Judge Overend, sitting as the TCC Judge in Exeter.

2.43 One complication arising from these provisions concerns the work done to the common parts of a building which might be divided into flats, one of which is owned by the residential occupier employing the contractor. It would appear that, if the contract was solely for work in respect of those common parts, the exception at s106 would not apply because it could not be said that the construction contract principally related to operations in the flat occupied by the employer. It may be more difficult to say whether or not the exception applied if the contract was for both work to the common parts and work to the employer's own flat.

Section 107: Agreement in Writing

2.44 Section 107 of the Act provides as follows:

> 107–(1) The provisions of this Part apply only where the construction contract is in writing, and any other agreement between the parties as to any matter is effective for the purposes of this Part only if in writing.
>
> The expressions "agreement", "agree" and "agreed" shall be construed accordingly.
>
> (2) There is an agreement in writing—
> (a) if the agreement is made in writing (whether or not it is signed by the parties),

---

[37] [2007] EWHC 1174 (TCC).
[38] (Unreported) 28.1.00.

(b) if the agreement is made by exchange of communications in writing, or
(c) if the agreement is evidenced in writing.

(3) Where parties agree otherwise than in writing by reference to terms which are in writing they make an agreement in writing.

(4) An agreement is evidenced in writing if an agreement made otherwise than in writing is recorded by one of the parties, or by a third party, with the authority of the parties to the agreement.

(5) An exchange of written submissions in adjudication proceedings, or in arbitral or legal proceedings in which the existence of an agreement otherwise than in writing is alleged by one party against another party and not denied by the other party in his response constitutes as between those parties an agreement in writing to the effect alleged.

(6) References in the Part to anything being written or in writing included being recorded by any means.

2.45 At first sight, this is a rather curious set of provisions. They appear to be designed to achieve two different results. On the one hand, sub-sections (2), (3), (4) and (5) are all intended to ensure that there will be an agreement in writing for the purposes of the 1996 Act, even if there is not a completed contract form. On the other hand, the underlying principle of the section is a recognition that, if the terms of the contract are in doubt, particularly if the argument concerns what was said and/or agreed during particular conversations, then it would be an impossible task for an adjudicator to decide the underlying dispute in circumstances where the relevant terms of the contract itself are in issue.[39]

All, Not Part, of the Agreement Must be in Writing

2.46 The most important sub-section is sub-section (2). This appears to recognise that it is common in the UK construction industry for the parties to work quite happily on the basis of an agreed contract, without a formalised set of contract documents in place. Thus the sub-section provides that there is an agreement in writing, whether or not that agreement is actually signed, or if the agreement is made by an exchange of letters, or if there is some other way in which the agreement can be said to be evidenced in writing. The leading case on this sub-section is the Court of Appeal decision in *RJT Consulting Engineers Ltd v DM Engineering (NI) Ltd*.[40]

---

[39] To the concern of some commentators the DTI 2nd Consultation Report now proposes that these provisions are scrapped in their entirety, leaving the adjudicator with the difficulty of trying to work out what the contract terms were, when they were not recorded in writing, and when there may be a major debate about what was agreed. This is explored further in Chapter 19 below.

[40] The first instance decision was that of HHJ Mackay QC, the TCC Judge in Liverpool, reported at [2001] CILL 1766–1768. The Court of Appeal decision, which allowed the appeal from Judge Mackay's decision, is reported at [2002] BLR 217.

2.47 RJT agreed to complete the design of some mechanical engineering works for DM. The agreement was oral. DM complained about the quality of the design and commenced adjudication proceedings. RJT maintained that, because the contract was oral, the adjudicator had no jurisdiction. HHJ Mackay QC rejected that argument. He referred to the correspondence, which made reference to an oral agreement, and concluded that there was sufficient material to bring the agreement within s107(2). He said:

> It seems to me that if I were to find that it is necessary to have a recitation of the terms of an agreement when the existence of the agreement, the parties to the agreement and the nature of the work and the price of the agreement are plainly to be found in documentary form, but nonetheless in a contract worth more than three-quarters of a million pounds because the initial agreement was oral, it is not caught by the Act, and it seems to me such an attempt would run contrary not only to the terms of the Act but contrary to my duty to carry out what I believe to be the law at any particular time. And therefore, adopting that methodology, I hold that it is not necessary to have the terms identified and the extensive documentary evidence in this case is well sufficient to bring it within the adjudication proceedings . . .

2.48 RJT appealed. The Court of Appeal allowed the appeal. One strand in the judgments of both Ward LJ and Auld LJ was the absence, in the written material before them, of a clear record of the terms that had been agreed orally. As Auld LJ put it at paragraph 21 of the judgment, 'the material terms of the agreement were insufficiently recorded in writing in any of those forms'. However, it is clear from the judgment of Ward LJ that the majority of the Court of Appeal were persuaded that, as a matter of principle, it was important for the purposes of s107(2) that *all* of the material terms were recorded in writing in order for the contract to come within the relevant sub-section. At paragraph 12 of his judgment Ward LJ said:

> [s107] must be seen against the background which led to the introduction of this change. In its origin it was an attempt to force the industry to submit to a standard form of contract. That did not succeed but writing is still important and writing is important because it provides certainty. Certainty is all the more important when adjudication is envisaged to take place under a demanding timetable. The adjudicator has to start with some certainty as to what the terms of the contract are.

2.49 As to the requirements of s107 itself, Ward LJ, at paragraph 19 of his judgment, was unequivocal:

> On the point of construction of section 107, what has to be evidenced in writing is, literally, the agreement, which means all of it, not part of it. A record of the agreement also suggests a complete agreement, not a partial one. The only exception to the generality of that construction is the instance falling within sub-section 5 where the material relevant parts alleged and not denied in the written submissions in the adjudication proceedings are sufficient. Unfortunately I do not think sub-section 5 can so dominate the interpretation of the section as a whole so as to limit what needs to be evidenced in writing simply to the material terms raised in the arbitration.

Ward LJ was, however, anxious to ensure that this point did not lead to what he described as 'jurisdictional wrangling' and he expressed the hope that adjudicators would be robust in excluding the trivial from the ambit of the agreement. Robert Walker LJ agreed with the judgment of Ward LJ.

2.50 Although the third member of the Court of Appeal, Auld LJ, agreed that the appeal should be allowed, he appeared to express himself in rather different language, emphasising (as already noted) that it was only the 'material' terms which had to be in writing. For this reason, the decision of the Court of Appeal in *RJT Consulting* has been summarised in three propositions:[41]

(a) a contract is not evidenced in writing merely because there are documents which indicate the existence of a contract;

(b) all the terms of the oral agreement must be evidenced in writing;

(c) alternatively, as per Auld LJ, the material terms of the agreement must be evidenced in writing.

2.51 This summary highlights the potentially important difference between the majority and Auld LJ. Is it all the terms that have to be in writing, or just the material terms, and, if the latter, how can it be determined what is 'material' and what is not? The answer to this potential difficulty was provided by Jackson J in *Trustees of the Stratfield Saye Estate v AHL Construction*.[42] The Judge pointed out that the remarks of Auld LJ were not the views of the majority, and that it was not possible to regard them 'as some kind of gloss upon or amplification of the majority. The reasoning of Auld LJ, attractive though it is, does not form part of the ratio of *RJT*.' Therefore, as he stressed, what mattered was the recording of all the contract terms in writing.

2.52 The principles in *RJT*, as explained by Jackson J in *Stratfield Saye*, have been applied in a number of subsequent cases.[43] It is instructive to take a number of examples to see the courts' general approach to ensuring that, wherever possible, an objection raising a deficiency in the written record of the contract terms will not usually be permitted to frustrate the enforcement of the adjudicator's decision.

2.53 In *Dean & Dyball Construction Ltd v Kenneth Grubb Associates Ltd*[44] Dean & Dyball were contractors building a marina at Watchet in Somerset. They engaged Grubb to carry out related design work. Grubb sent Dean & Dyball a letter, called

---

[41] See the decision of HHJ Bowsher QC in *Carillion Construction Ltd v Devonport Royal Dockyard* [2003] 79, at 83, paragraph 25.

[42] [2004] EWHC 3286 (TCC); [2004] All ER (D) 77 (DEC).

[43] See, by way of example, *Bennett Electrical Sevices Ltd v Inviron Ltd* (paragraph 2.61 below) and *A.R.T. Consultancy Ltd v Navera Trading Ltd* (paragraph 2.59 below).

[44] [2003] EWHC 2465.

the proposal letter, in May 2000, which said that his offer was open for a period of 30 days. The proposal was not accepted in that time but, on 23 August 2000, Dean & Dyball accepted the proposal and said that: 'Our official appointment letter will follow in due course'. In fact, no such letter was sent. HHJ Seymour QC held that the absence of such a letter did not prevent the finding that the parties had entered into a binding contract. The Judge went on to reject the submission that, in some way, the contract was partly oral and partly in writing, and concluded that the contract was evidenced in writing and was therefore within the provisions of s107(2).

2.54 Two more recent cases from the TCC in Birmingham, and two from London, show the courts' general approach to disputes concerning terms allegedly agreed orally.

(a) In *Debeck Ductwork Installation Ltd v TE Engineering Ltd*,[45] HHJ Kirkham was dealing with an application to enforce an adjudicator's decision. The claimant, Debeck, claimed that there was a fax, sent by them to the defendant, which evidenced the agreement in writing. On the facts, the Judge rejected that submission. She found that the fax in question did not set out or record all of the matters on which Debeck itself sought to rely in pursuing its claim. For example, the fax did not explain, even in summary terms, the scope of the work to be undertaken. In addition, the fax made no mention of a number of further terms of the contract on which the defendant relied, including issues concerning specification, quality and timing. The Judge concluded that it was quite wrong for Debeck to argue that it was entitled to rely on a document which did not contain all the relevant terms, and then to ignore, and invite the Court to disregard, the additional terms which the defendant said had been agreed orally. The Judge therefore concluded that Debeck could not show that there was an agreement that had been evidenced in writing and that the adjudicator did not have the necessary jurisdiction to decide the dispute.

(b) In *Westdawn Refurbishments Ltd v Roselodge Ltd*[46] HHJ McCahill QC refused the summary enforcement of an adjudicator's decision because he concluded that many of the contract terms, including the important agreements as to when an invoice would be rendered, and when the interim payments would be made, were agreed orally. The case is interesting because the referring party was obviously aware of the potential difficulties with its case on the contract, and argued before the adjudicator that, because no terms were agreed orally, the contract must therefore have been made up of written terms and/or terms to be implied from various statutes. This was not only wrong on the facts of

---

[45] Unreported, 14.1.02, HHJ Kirkham (sitting at the TCC in Birmingham).
[46] [2006] Adj LR 04/25.

the case, but it is also thought that, even if it could have been shown that nothing was agreed orally, it is potentially dangerous for a claimant to put its case on a contract in writing in such a nebulous way.

(c) In *Bennett Electrical Services v Inviron Ltd*,[47] HHJ Wilcox held that a letter of intent, which was plainly marked 'subject to contract' could not evidence or give rise to a binding contract. Further, even if it did, it could not be said that all the terms of the contract were in writing, in accordance with *RJT*. He therefore held that the adjudicator had no jurisdiction.

(d) In *Flannery Construction Ltd v M Holleran (2007) Ltd*,[48] the same Judge concluded that the various documents relied on as forming the contract did not identify with any certainty the scope of the works or how that scope might be varied in the future. He also found that the documents evidenced a major (and unresolved) difference between the parties, because one side wanted one overall 'framework' agreement to cover all the various sites where work was to be performed, and the other wanted a series of discrete contracts. The failure to reach agreement on this fundamental issue was another reason why the Judge concluded that the defendant had a strong arguable case that there was no concluded contract at all, and certainly no contract in accordance with s107.

2.55 In addition to *RJT*, the other main Court of Appeal authority on this specific topic is *Thomas-Fredric's (Construction) Ltd v Keith Wilson*[49] in which the principal point contained the identity of one of the parties. Although the underlying agreement was oral, it was evidenced by a letter dated 6 August 2002, which had been signed by Mr Wilson, the Appellant, 'on behalf of Gowersand Ltd'. The contractors made arrangements to transfer the NHBC Certificate to Gowersand. However, thereafter, they contended that, after all, they had contracted directly with Mr Wilson. The Judge held that that was indeed the case. However, Simon Brown LJ had 'the greatest difficulty with this conclusion';[50] as he pointed out, the adjudicator's jurisdiction under the 1996 Act only arose in respect of a construction contract in writing and, in this case, the only agreement that was relied on was the letter of 6 August 2002 which was expressly signed, not on behalf of Mr Wilson himself, but on behalf of the company, Gowersand. Simon Brown LJ referred back to the decision of the Court of Appeal in *RJT Consulting* and said that, in the absence of any evidence that Mr Wilson, rather than Gowersand, was the contracting party, there could be no claim against him personally; there was simply

---

[47] [2007] EWHC 49.
[48] [2007] EWHC 825 (TCC).
[49] [2003] EWCA Civ 1494.
[50] See paragraph 13 of the judgment.

no written contract to which he was a party. Accordingly, the appellant had not submitted to the adjudicator's jurisdiction and the appeal was allowed.

2.56 There have been a number of other decisions under s107 in the TCC, in addition to those cited at paragraph 2.54 above. The first was that of Jackson J in *Trustees of the Stratfield Saye Estate v AHL Construction Ltd*,[51] noted above. In that case, Jackson J concluded that there was a contract between the parties for a defined scope of work. He then had to decide whether or not that contract was in writing for the purposes of s107(2). Having said that an agreement was only evidenced in writing for the purposes of section 107 if all the express terms of that agreement are recorded in writing, and that it was not sufficient merely to show that all terms material to the issues under adjudication have been recorded in writing, he concluded that, on the facts before him, all the express terms of the agreement between the parties had been recorded in writing.

2.57 In *Redworth Construction Ltd v Brookdale Healthcare Ltd*[52] the contract between the parties was evidenced in a variety of documents and oral agreements. The claimant contractor commenced adjudication by referring to one such document, but omitting any reference to others. The adjudicator decided on that limited basis that there was a written contract and that he did have the necessary jurisdiction. In the subsequent enforcement proceedings, HHJ Havery QC found that Redworth could not go beyond the matters on which they had relied in the adjudication in support of their argument that the adjudicator had the necessary jurisdiction. He said that they had elected to rely on those matters, and they could not both approbate and reprobate their earlier arguments. They had put their argument in such a way as to obtain a benefit and thus it would not be just to allow them to resile from that election. The Judge went on to point out that, on the evidence, certain terms of the contract were not in writing. In particular, the date of possession, the contract period and the date for completion of the works were not agreed in writing. The completion date was only ever agreed orally. Thus, given that the claim before the adjudicator was for the recovery of sums withheld because the contract overran that date, the Judge had no hesitation in concluding that the contract was not a contract in writing within the meaning of section 107 of the Act. The adjudicator did not therefore have the necessary jurisdiction.

2.58 The most recent case on the topic is *Mast Electrical Services v Kendall Cross Holdings Ltd*.[53] In that case, there were three different sites and a plethora of tenders, revised tenders and other correspondence on each. In respect of each alleged contract,

---

[51] [2004] EWHC 3286 (TCC); [2004] All ER (D) 77 (DEC).
[52] [2006] EWHC 1994 (TCC).
[53] [2007] EWHC 1296 (TCC).

Jackson J doubted there was a contract at all and noted that, even if there was, the documents relied on did not record basic matters like agreed rates of payment. Indeed, on the facts, he concluded that debates about what the rates should be were never resolved. The adjudicator had originally resigned because there was no contract in writing in accordance with the 1996 Act; Jackson J concluded that he had been right to do so.

2.59 Of course, there is a significant difference between the situation where there is one contract, and some of its terms are not in writing, and the situation where the parties reach separate agreements in relation to different aspects of the work. Thus, in *A.R.T. Consultancy Limited v Navera Trading Limited*[54] the parties had reached an oral agreement in respect of certain design works and subsequently agreed a written contract in connection with the work on site. The adjudicator's decision related solely to the claims under the written contract. The TCC Judge concluded that the contract complied with the principles set out in *RJT*, and that the existence of an earlier agreement, in respect of anterior design works, did not deprive the adjudicator of jurisdiction.

Letters of Intent

2.60 There have been three recent decisions on whether 'contracts' which were in the form of simple letters of intent complied with s107. In all three cases, the answer was, perhaps unsurprisingly, in the negative. In *Hart Investments Ltd v Fidler & Ors*[55] the employer's agent sent the contractor a letter of intent in conventional terms. No formal contract was ever agreed and the work was therefore carried out in accordance with the 'fall-back' provisions of the letter, to the effect that the employer would reimburse the contractor's reasonable costs. The TCC Judge was aware that similar arrangements to such a letter of intent were common in the UK construction industry and that, up until that point, there had been no reported case on whether such an arrangement complied with s107(2)(c) of the 1996 Act. He concluded that it did not. First, he said it was not easy to say that such a loose arrangement constituted a binding/enforceable contract at all. Even if it did, the sort of clarity of terms envisaged by s107(2)(c) and the Court of Appeal in *RJT* was wholly absent. He pointed out that, on the facts in that case, it was unclear whether there was any agreement on matters which might be regarded as the minimum necessary for a building contract, namely agreement as to parties, work scope, price and time. He said that the biggest difficulty came with the consideration of the contract work scope. The work scope was work which would, or might be, the subject of orders in the future, whether written or oral. It was not discernible

---

[54] [2007] EWHC 1375 (TCC).
[55] [2006] EWHC 2857 (TCC); [2007] BLR 30.

from the letter of intent. Such a definition was a recipe for confusion and dispute, and the very situation which s107(2)(c) was designed to avoid. Furthermore the Judge concluded that the fact that all of these arrangements were designed to be a full-back position, only relevant at all if no formal/full contract was ever concluded, also militated against the conclusion that this was a contract in writing containing all the terms that had been agreed by the parties. On the contrary, it was designed to provide a very basic framework that would only be operated if a formal/full contract was not agreed.

The same conclusion in respect of a similar letter of intent was reached by HHJ Wilcox in *Bennett (Electrical) Services Ltd v Inviron Ltd*.[56] There the Judge observed that the fixed price in the letter of intent was £169,157 but, in the usual way, a great deal of extra work had been instructed because the claimant contractor's valuation of all the works carried out was £542,287, of which £203,763 had already been paid. The Judge concluded that a number of issues had been discussed at one particular meeting, including working hours, mechanisms of payment, variations, insurance and health and safety. However none of those matters were the subject of recorded written agreement. He also pointed out that one of the claims before the adjudicator for additional monies was not defined by any written contract terms, because the default provisions in the letter of intent made no provision for price and rates, the method of assessing and timing and the payment of such additional monies. Accordingly he concluded that there was no written contract in accordance with s107. Likewise, at paragraphs 49–52 of his judgment in *Mott MacDonald Limited v London & Regional Properties Limited*,[57] HHJ Thornton QC set out his conclusions as to why the letter of intent in that case was not in accordance with s107(2) of the 1996 Act. He noted that many of the core terms of the parties' agreement were inferred by conduct or were evidenced in other documents which were not relied on by the referring party in the adjudication. **2.61**

Oral Variations

It is common in the UK construction industry for parties to agree, part way through the contract, to make changes either to the work scope, or to the terms of the contract itself, or to both work scope and contract terms. There can then be arguments to the effect that the contract no longer complies with section 107, and it is in such instances that section 107(3) can often be relevant. **2.62**

---

[56] [2007] EWHC 49 (TCC).
[57] [2007] EWHC 1055 (TCC).

2.63 In *Total M E Services Ltd v ABB Building Technologies Ltd*,[58] HHJ Wilcox was dealing with the common situation where, although the original contract in writing was for a lump sum, additional works were ordered. It was argued that the mechanism by which additional works were ordered and paid for was an oral variation to the written contract and, since that variation was not recorded in writing, the contract was not within s107(2). Judge Wilcox rejected that submission, basing his decision on s107(3) ('an agreement otherwise than in writing by reference to terms which are in writing'). He held that the adjudicator made his decision on the basis of a dispute that arose out of a single written construction contract as varied orally by the parties. He concluded that the varied contract was clearly within the provisions of s107, notwithstanding the fact that it was evidenced partly in writing and partly orally. He therefore decided that the adjudicator had the necessary jurisdiction.

2.64 A different result, on rather different facts, arose in the first dispute in *Carillion Construction Ltd v Devonport Road Dockyard*.[59] In that case, there was a written construction contract between the parties. Part way through the contract there was a meeting on the 30 October 1999 which, on Carillion's case, led to a binding agreement which revised the basis of payment to the sort of 'costs reimbursable' arrangement so popular with contractors. Although this was disputed by Devonport, the adjudicator decided that a binding agreement had been reached varying the terms such that Carillion were entitled to be reimbursed their costs. Devonport defended the summary judgment application on the basis that the adjudicator had no jurisdiction to reach that decision. HHJ Bowsher QC referred to *RJT Consulting*. He then identified certain documents in the evidence and said that, although they demonstrated that there was a discussion about whether the contract should become costs reimbursable, they did not evidence any agreed contract, because the documents conflicted. He went on at paragraph 4 to say:

> It is a simple proposition, and easy to accept, that once a construction agreement in writing is before an adjudicator he has the jurisdiction to construe its express terms and to decide what, if any, terms are to be implied or incorporated by reference. But it is quite a different thing to suggest that once a construction agreement is before an adjudicator, he has jurisdiction to decide on the existence of an oral agreement not evidenced in writing just because it follows and amends the written agreement. I am not considering what in the construction industry would come under the normal heading of "variations made pursuant to a term of the contract". What is in issue is an alleged oral agreement that radically changed the written agreement (if it was made)...

---

[58] [2002] EWHC 248 (TCC).
[59] [2003] BLR 79.

He therefore concluded that the adjudicator did not have the jurisdiction to enter into the adjudication at all.⁶⁰

2.65 An example of what Judge Bowsher called 'variations made pursuant to a term of the contract' arose in *Management Solutions and Professional Consultants Ltd v Bennett (Electrical) Services Ltd*.⁶¹ In that case, the defendant, Bennett, contended that the effect of oral instructions which varied the scope of the work or added extra work was to remove the contract from s107 of the 1996 Act because the whole of the agreement was not in writing or evidenced in writing. HHJ Thornton QC noted that the relevant contractual term provided that no variation to the work was to be carried out without Bennett issuing a written instruction to carry out that variation. The requirement that such variations had to be in writing could be waived by agreement, so that the requirement for a written variation was not a pre-condition to a variation instruction being issued or taking effect where the parties agreed, expressly or by implication, that the varied work could be carried out as instructed orally. The Judge concluded that the entirety of the contract was in writing; that the contract allowed the work scope to be changed within the limits provided for by the written contractual provisions so that, although the works could be varied, such variations did not vary the contract but were merely instructions issued under the contract and with the authority of the contractual provisions. He also found that the disputed variations were undertaken under the terms of the contract and within its scope, even if such variations were oral and not evidenced in writing. If the instructions were issued orally by Bennett then the resulting work was carried out by agreement and the only consequence was that the contractual requirement that a variation should be evidenced in writing was waived by both parties.

2.66 Accordingly, the mere fact that there were oral instructions or oral variations will not, of itself, take the contract outside the scope of s107.⁶² What matters is the nature and effect of any such oral agreement. It is respectfully suggested that it is no more than common sense that a written contract which permits variation instructions should be caught by s107, regardless of whether those subsequent variations were oral or in writing. But other types of subsequent oral instruction

---

60 In *Brownlow Ltd v Dem-master Demolition Ltd* (unreported 26.2.04, a decision of the Sheriffdom of Lothian Borders) there was a dispute about the letters exchanged between the parties and whether or not they comprised an agreement in writing. It appears that the letters did not contain a detailed description of the work that was to be carried out. Despite the citing of a number of the relevant authorities, including *Debeck*, and *RJT Consulting*, the Sheriff found that the documents came within s107 and that therefore there was an agreement in writing. On the face of it this looks a surprising decision but it is difficult, without sight of the letters themselves, which are not set out in the judgment, to form a concluded view.
61 [2006] EWHC 1720 (TCC).
62 As demonstrated by the decisions in *Total M&E* and *Management Solutions*.

or agreement will be treated differently. An example can be found in the Court of Appeal decision in *Lead Technical Services Ltd v CMS Medical Ltd*.[63] In that case the principal issue concerned the precise form of contract that had been agreed by the parties, because that dictated whether or not the adjudicator had been rightly appointed. However, from paragraph 16 onwards of his judgment, Moses LJ dealt with a separate contention as to why the adjudicator had no jurisdiction. This was by reference to an alleged oral agreement that the claimant's fees were to be capped at £20,000. It was CMS's case that there was such an oral agreement in place and that, in consequence, there was no contract in writing as defined by s107. Moses LJ identified the various elements of the evidence that supported CMS's contention and noted that the Judge at first instance did not deal with these points at all. He concluded that the Judge was 'miles away' from justifying a summary judgment dismissing those assertions and that there was a real prospect, based on cogent grounds, of establishing that the adjudicator had acted without jurisdiction (because the contract was partly written and partly oral). The Court of Appeal therefore concluded that the Judge had erred in enforcing the adjudicator's decision.

Implied Terms

2.67 In *Connex v MJ Building Sevices Group PLC*[64] HHJ Havery QC found that there were no express terms of the agreement that were not in writing. In any event, he decided that, because there was a reference in a set of minutes to Connex giving an instruction to MJ that the project be carried out immediately, the conclusion was irresistible that this instruction constituted an acceptance of MJ's tender. He further concluded that, since the minutes were written with the authority of the parties, they constituted evidence falling within s107(4) of the Act of the acceptance. Although this decision went to the Court of Appeal[65] this part of the Judge's decision was not appealed, and was therefore not considered by the Court of Appeal.[66]

2.68 One of the arguments that arose in *Connex* was the question of implied terms. It had been submitted there that it was manifestly not the intention of Parliament to exclude from the jurisdiction of an adjudicator contracts that contained implied terms. Judge Havery accepted what he called 'that very reasonable proposition'. The same point arose in *Galliford Try Construction v Michael Heal Associates Ltd*.[67] There HHJ Seymour QC concluded that no contract had been made at all. However, at paragraph 29 of his judgment, he went on to consider the issue as to

---

[63] [2007] EWCA Civ 316.
[64] [2004] EWHC 1518.
[65] [2005] EWCA Civ 193.
[66] See also HHJ Bowsher QC in *Carillion Construction Ltd v Devonport Royal Dockyard Ltd* [2003] BLR 79, in which he said at paragraph 34 that an adjudicator could consider implied terms.
[67] [2003] EWHC 2886 (TCC).

whether, if there had been a contract, it could be said to be in writing within the meaning of s107. He referred to the decision in *RJT Consulting* and observed that the Court of Appeal did not consider what the position would be if a contract included terms which were to be implied. He said:

> It may be that the mischief which Parliament was anxious to avoid does not arise in a case in which terms fall to be implied into a contract as a matter of law, regardless of the actual intention of the parties. However, it could arise in an acute form if it were suggested that a contract, not otherwise complete, could be completed after it had been executed by the implication of terms which were said to represent the actual, but unexpressed, intention of the parties.

It is respectfully suggested that Judge Seymour was quite right to differentiate between implied terms in this way. The usual terms which are implied into construction contracts as a matter of law, such as terms as to reasonable quality, fitness for purpose and the like, could not possibly be said to render a contract outside the terms of s107. However, implied terms which are relied on because of, say, particular conversations between the parties, or a particular course of dealing in the past, and which are not set out in the documents put forward under s107, would probably take the contract outside the terms of s107, and therefore deny the adjudicator any jurisdiction.

Section 107(5)

2.69 The provisions of s107(5) are, on their face, surprising. They appear to be designed to prevent a party from appearing to accept the existence of an agreement in writing during the adjudication itself, and then, at a later date, arguing before the court that there was, in truth, no such agreement. It is, in one sense, a form of statutory estoppel.

2.70 The leading case on this provision is the decision of HHJ Bowsher QC in *Grovedeck Ltd v Demolition Ltd*.[68] In that case, the relevant demolition sub-contracts were oral, so, on its face, the Act did not apply. However, the claimants contended that the events in the adjudication conferred a jurisdiction upon the adjudicator pursuant to s107(5). This was an ambitious submission, given that the defendants challenged and denied the jurisdiction of the adjudicator in every communication after his appointment. As Judge Bowsher observed, 'freedom of contract has fallen but I cannot believe that it has fallen that far'.[69] He also had to deal with the problem of s107(5). He said:

> On one reading of section 107(5), if one party to an adjudication alleges the existence of an oral agreement and the other does not deny the existence of an oral

---

[68] [2000] BLR 181.
[69] See 185, paragraph 27.

agreement, then there is an agreement in writing "to the effect alleged", that is, in the terms alleged by the claimant, even though the other party hotly denies, as he did here, that the agreement was in the terms alleged. Parliament cannot have intended such an unjust result.

2.71 Judge Bowsher was persuaded to look at the reports in Hansard. As a result he concluded:

> 29. If one reads section 107(5) without the words "in adjudication proceedings or" it is clear that the intention of Parliament was that a contract should be treated as a contract in writing if in arbitral or litigation proceedings *before* the adjudication proceedings in question an oral contract had been alleged and admitted. I also would read the words "and not denied" as meaning that the alleged terms of the contract were not denied. By adding the words "in adjudication proceedings or", Parliament intended to add a reference to *other preceding* adjudication proceedings. There was no intention by Parliament to provide that submissions made by a party to an unauthorised adjudication should give to the supposed adjudicator a jurisdiction which he did not have when he was appointed.
>
> 30. Read in that way, the sub-section has an entirely sensible and practical intention and purpose and I so read it. Disputes as to the terms, express and implied, of oral construction agreements are surprisingly common and are not readily susceptible of resolution by a summary procedure such as adjudication. It is not surprising that Parliament should have intended that such disputes should not be determined by Adjudicators under the Act, but if in any case such room for dispute has been removed by previous formal and binding legal submissions, then the adjudicator has jurisdiction.

2.72 In a similar way, in *Mott MacDonald Limited v London & Regional Properties Limited*,[70] it was argued on behalf of the claimant that, even if the contract itself was not in writing, the pleadings exchanged in the adjudication were sufficient to bring it within s107(5). There, the claimant had referred to a contractually binding letter of intent and, in response, the defendant had simply said that the adjudicator should give effect to the express, clear and unambiguous wording agreed in that letter. Judge Thornton analysed the pleadings and the adjudication correspondence in detail, and concluded that the response was not one that could be described as 'not denying the existence of an agreement that was not in writing'. Section 107(5) was not, therefore, engaged.

2.73 These decisions therefore limit the potential effect of s107(5). It is submitted that they do so in an entirely sensible and practical way, and in a manner which is entirely consistent with the principle that Ward LJ emphasised in *RJT Consulting Engineers*: the critical importance of contracts being in writing was because the summary adjudication procedure could only work if there were not disputes about

---

[70] [2007] EWHC 1055 (TCC).

the terms of the very contract under which the adjudicator had been appointed.[71] It should, however, be noted that in *RJT Consulting*, the Court of Appeal expressly chose not to rule upon or decide the issue before Judge Bowsher in *Grovedeck*. Thus the particular point in that case, and the specific limitation placed on s107(5) by Judge Bowsher QC, remains to be considered by an appellate court.

2.74 It should not, however, be thought that the result of these cases is that s107(5) has been rendered inoperable. For example, in *Ale Heavy Lift v MSD (Darlington) Ltd*,[72] it was argued that the adjudicator had no jurisdiction to hear the dispute because there were effectively two contracts, and the second was not in writing. HHJ Toulmin CMG QC held that, as a result of the exchange of written submissions in the adjudication, there was, pursuant to s107(5), an agreement in writing to the effect alleged. The Judge, in reaching this conclusion, was clearly influenced by the fact that no jurisdictional challenge had been made to the adjudicator at the time.

Section 108: Adjudication

2.75 S108 of the 1996 Act reads as follows:

> 108(1) A party to a construction contract has the right to refer a dispute arising under the contract for adjudication under a procedure complying with this section.
> For this purpose "dispute" includes any difference.
> (2) The contract shall—
> (a) enable a party to give notice at any time of his intention to refer a dispute to adjudication;
> (b) provide a timetable with the object of securing the appointment of the adjudicator and referral of the dispute to him within 7 days of such notice;
> (c) require the adjudicator to reach a decision within 28 days of referral or such longer period as is agreed by the parties after the dispute has been referred;
> (d) allow the adjudicator to extend the period of 28 days by up to 14 days, with the consent of the party by whom the dispute was referred;
> (e) impose a duty on the adjudicator to act impartially; and
> (f) enable the adjudicator to take the initiative in ascertaining the facts and the law.
> (3) The contract shall provide that the decision of the adjudicator is binding until the dispute is finally determined by legal proceedings, by arbitration (if the contract provides for arbitration or the parties otherwise agree to arbitration) or by agreement. The parties may agree to accept the decision of the adjudicator as finally determining the dispute.

---

[71] This is why some commentators consider it to be slightly curious that the DTI now seem to be so keen to do away with this safeguard altogether.
[72] [2006] EWHC 2080 (TCC).

(4) The contract shall also provide that the adjudicator is not liable for anything done or omitted in the discharge or purported discharge of his functions as adjudicator unless the act or omission is in bad faith, and that any employee or agent of the adjudicator is similarly protected from liability.

(5) If the contract does not comply with the requirements of sub-section (1) to (4), the adjudication provisions of the Scheme for Construction Contracts apply.

(6) For England and Wales, the scheme may apply the provisions of the Arbitration Act 1996 with such adaptions and modifications as appear to the Minister making the scheme to be appropriate. For Scotland the scheme may include provision conferring powers on courts in relation to adjudication and provision relating to the enforcement of the adjudicator's decision.

2.76 The general aims and intention of these provisions relating to adjudication have been addressed in paragraphs 2.01–2.15 above. The detailed issues that arise out of these specific provisions form a major part of the remainder of this book. Accordingly, this part of Chapter 2 will deal in outline only with five particular elements of s108 that have been the source of controversy. They are: the reference to 'a dispute' throughout the section (paragraphs 2.77–2.84 below); the meaning to be given to the phrase 'at any time' in s108(2)(a) (see paragraphs 2.85–2.90 below); the effect of the 28 days provision at s108(2)(d) (see paragraphs 2.91–2.107 below); the extent of the duty to act impartially (see paragraphs 2.109–2.115 below); and the binding nature of the decision referred to at s108(3) (see paragraphs 2.116–2.119 below).

'A Dispute'

2.77 There have been two distinct types of debate concerning the references to 'a dispute' throughout s108. The first type, of which there are a large number of reported cases, concerns the appropriate approach to deciding whether or not 'a dispute' had crystallised at the time of the notice of the intention to refer that dispute to adjudication. It was frequently argued by responding parties in the adjudication that the alleged dispute which the referring party had raised was not a matter which had previously arisen. The argument was that such a claim, since it has not been considered, let alone rejected, by the responding party, could not be said to be in dispute. Often, the referring party was successful on the reference and the responding party refused to pay the sum awarded by the adjudicator, leading to contested enforcement proceedings. The responding party, being the defendants in the enforcement proceedings, would argue that a dispute had not crystallised at the time of the notice to refer, and therefore the adjudicator did not have the necessary jurisdiction. This is an important point and is considered in some detail in Chapter 7 below, particularly at paragraphs 7.35–7.56. In short, the courts have endeavoured to avoid a legalistic approach to the meaning of the word 'dispute', and have been quick to conclude that a claim which has gone unanswered, even for a comparatively short time, is disputed for the purposes of the 1996 Act.

2.78 The other type of debate arising out of the words 'a dispute' concerns the clear use in s108 of the singular word 'dispute'. The 1996 Act was designed to provide a swift summary procedure in relation to a specific, clear-cut dispute. Only one dispute can be referred to the adjudicator at any given time. Of course, during the currency of a construction contract, a variety of disputes may arise between the employer and the main contractor or between the main contractor and his sub-contractors. How is the expression 'a dispute', in the singular, to be interpreted in such circumstances?

2.79 This is one of the perennial areas of debate under the 1996 Act which has yet to be considered by the Court of Appeal. It is dealt with in detail in paragraphs 7.57–7.63 below. However, by way of an introduction to the point, it is right to say that, at first instance, the courts have taken a relatively broad interpretation of the expression 'a dispute' and have made plain that a number of different claims (both money claims and, say, claims for extensions of time) can be encompassed within a single dispute.

2.80 The starting point is the decision of HHJ Thornton QC in *Fastrack Contractors Ltd v Morrison Construction Ltd & Anor*.[73] In that case, the claim was for measured work, variations, prolongation costs, loss and expense and loss of profit as a result of repudiation. It was effectively Fastrack's claim for outstanding sums following the termination of the contract. Judge Thornton concluded that such a claim, which was disputed by Morrison, comprised 'a dispute' (in the singular) for the purposes of the Act and was not an attempt to refer more than one dispute to the same adjudicator. He said at paragraph 20 of his judgment:

> It is to be noted that the HGCRA refers to a "dispute" and not to "disputes". Thus, at any one time, a referring party must refer a single dispute, albeit that the Scheme allows for disputing parties to agree, thereafter, to extend the reference to cover "more than one dispute under the same contract" and "related disputes under different contracts". During the course of a construction contract, many claims, heads of claim, issues, contentions and causes of action will arise. Many of these will be, collectively or individually, disputed. When a dispute arises, it may cover one, several or many of one, some or all of these matters. At any particular moment in time, it will be a question of fact what is in dispute. Thus the "dispute" which may be referred to adjudication is all or part of whatever is in dispute at the moment that the referring party first intimates an adjudication reference. In other words, the "dispute" is whatever claims, heads of claim, issues, contentions or causes of action that are then in dispute which the referring party has chosen to crystallise into an adjudication reference. A vital and necessary question to be answered, when a jurisdictional challenge is mounted, is what was actually referred? That involves a careful characterisation of the dispute referred to be made. This exercise will not necessarily be determined solely by the wording of the notice of adjudication since this document, like any

---

[73] [2000] BLR 168.

commercial document having contractual force, must be construed against the underlying factual background from which it springs and which will be known to both parties.

2.81 This inclusive approach was followed by HHJ Lloyd QC in a trio of cases which he decided subsequently: *KNS Industrial Services (Birmingham) Ltd v Sindall Ltd*,[74] *Sindall Ltd v Solland*[75] and *David McLean Housing Contractors Ltd v Swansea Housing Association Ltd.*[76] In that last case, the notice to refer identified what were called six separate disputes, including claims for loss and expense, extensions of time, valuation of variations and the valuation of measured work. The Judge concluded that, despite the words used in the notice, the matters referred to adjudication constituted one single dispute because, on the facts, the dispute between the parties was what sum should have been paid by the employer as a result of the claimant's single payment application number 19.

2.82 As a result of this approach, it has not been common for a claim by a contractor to have been incapable of being presented as one single dispute.[77] This is particularly so in respect of a claim made at the end of the contract. Thus, although those responsible for the 1996 Act probably did not envisage it being used for this purpose, a contractor with a complex final account claim is entitled to argue that his claim is, in essence, one single claim for an unpaid sum and that therefore he is entitled to adjudicate his final account claim, no matter how large the claim might be and no matter how voluminous the supporting documentation. One of the more extreme examples of this was the adjudication claim in *CIB Properties Ltd v Birse Construction Ltd*.[78] In that case, there was a disputed termination of the contract and, in the first adjudication, the adjudicator had ruled that the termination was the responsibility of the contractor. Some time later the employer, CIB, then made a claim for the financial consequences of the termination which was said to amount to £15 million. The claim encompassed numerous different heads of loss and was supported by documents that filled in excess of 50 lever arch files. It was, however, impossible to argue that this was anything other than a single dispute: it was a single, disputed claim that the £15 million was due to CIB as a result of Birse's responsibility for the termination of the contract. Whether such a result is

---

[74] [2001] 17 Const LJ.
[75] [2001] 3 TCLR 30.
[76] [2002] BLR 125.
[77] There have been two reported cases where the court has concluded that two disputes were referred simultaneously, and the adjudicator lacked jurisdiction as a result. They are *Grovedeck Ltd v Capital Demolition Ltd* [2000] BLR 181, where there were disputes on two different contracts, and *David and Teresa Bothma (In Partnership) T/A DAB Builders v Mayhaven Healthcare Limited* (16.11.06, TCC in Bristol), where the notice of adjudication talked of *disputes*, and there was no link between the contractor's financial claim and his claim for an extension of time. These cases are dealt with in greater detail in paragraphs 7.60 and 7.61 below.
[78] [2005] 1 WLR 2252.

what the framers of the 1996 Act had in mind when they created the adjudication process is, perhaps, another question.[79]

2.83 The inclusive approach adopted by the courts at first instance, beginning with *Fastrack*, was questioned by Lord MacFadyen in *Barr Ltd v Law Mining Ltd*.[80] Lord MacFadyen pointed out that there was some force in the criticism of Judge Thornton's inclusive analysis in *Fastrack* because, if everything currently in dispute between the parties formed a single dispute, s108 was restricted in scope and might even be deprived of content. However, having made that point, he was not persuaded that, on the facts in *Barr*, the adjudicator had fallen into error in holding that the matters referred to him constituted a single dispute. The adjudicator had decided that it was open to him to regard the matters before him as one dispute and the Judge could not say that he was wrong to have taken that view.

2.84 As noted above, the argument that more than one dispute was referred to the adjudicator often arises during enforcement proceedings to support an argument that the adjudicator had acted beyond his jurisdiction. Accordingly, the various authorities that have arisen out of this argument are analysed in greater detail in Chapter 7 below.[81]

Notice at Any Time

2.85 S108(2)(a) allows a party to give notice of his intention to refer a dispute to adjudication 'at any time'. Arguments as to how this provision should be interpreted have arisen in three factual situations: first, where there were already ongoing court/arbitration proceedings between the parties; secondly, where the underlying contract has come to an end; and thirdly, where there was a delay between the relevant events and the commencement of the adjudication proceedings. Each situation is dealt with below.

2.86 In *Herschel Engineering Ltd v Breen Property Ltd*,[82] Herschel obtained judgment in default of defence in respect of their claim for unpaid invoices. Judgment was subsequently set aside and Breen were given unconditional leave to defend. Herschel served a notice of appeal on 14 January 2000 and the appeal was set down for 24 May 2000. However, immediately prior to serving its notice of appeal, on 13 January, Herschel referred the dispute arising from the non-payment of the invoices to adjudication. Breen sought an injunction restraining Herschel from

---

[79] Despite the fact that courts have, from time to time, expressed doubts about such a consequence, no enforcement proceedings have yet failed because of the size and extent of the dispute referred to adjudication.
[80] (2001) 80 Con LR 134.
[81] See in particular paragraphs 7.57–7.63.
[82] [2000] BLR 272.

proceeding with the adjudication on the grounds that the court should not countenance two concurrent proceedings.

2.87 Dyson J refused the injunction. He accepted that there was a well-established line of authority to the effect that party A should not normally make the same claim against party B in different proceedings, because such conduct would be oppressive and unjust to B, and gave rise to the risk of inconsistent findings. This applied both to concurrent court proceedings and to concurrent court and arbitration proceedings. However, he rejected the submission that there was a close analogy between the position of an arbitrator and that of an adjudicator. An adjudicator's decision was only of temporary effect. It gave rise to no estoppel. Thus he concluded that the principles deriving from the authorities as to concurrent proceedings had no application to adjudication. The Judge went on at paragraph 19 of his judgment:

> If Parliament had intended that a party should not be able to refer a dispute to adjudication once litigation or arbitration proceedings had been commenced, I would have expected this to be expressly stated. The relationship between adjudication on the one hand and litigation and arbitration on the other, was what informed the content of section 108(3) of the Act. The aggrieved claimant should not have to wait many months, if not years, before his dispute passed through the various hoops of a full blown action or arbitration.

He concluded that the words 'at any time' meant what they said, and that was so even if, in the meantime, separate court proceedings had been commenced.[83]

2.88 However, it should not be thought that concurrent proceedings will always be allowed: it will always depend on the facts. Thus, in *Cygnet Healthcare Plc v Higgins City Ltd*[84] there was a dispute between the parties as to whether or not there was a contract. The parties agreed that that dispute should be referred to an ad hoc arbitration and an arbitrator was appointed. However, at the same time, Cygnet commenced an adjudication to reclaim monies due to alleged delays and consequential losses. That claim necessarily involved the adjudicator in considering the 'contract/no contract' issue. The adjudicator awarded Cygnet certain sums pursuant to that claim and they commenced enforcement proceedings. The enforcement application failed. HHJ Thornton QC held that the dispute as to whether or not a contract existed had been validly referred to the ad hoc arbitration and thus, if the court were to entertain the claimant's application to enforce, it would necessarily have to determine the very question that the parties had

---

[83] It should also be noted that Dyson J was not asked to stay the TCC proceedings whilst the adjudication took place. That was the application successfully made in *DGT Steel & Cladding Ltd v Cubitt Building & Interiors Ltd* [2007] EWHC 1584 (TCC), discussed below at paragraphs 14.31–14.36.

[84] (2000) 16 Const LJ 394.

agreed to refer to arbitration. The Judge distinguished the decision in *Herschel*, on the grounds that, in *Cygnet*, the parties had entered into an ad hoc arbitration agreement which covered one of the very disputes that was immediately thereafter referred to the adjudicator. The Judge considered that, in all the circumstances, the party's ad hoc arbitration agreement should be enforced and he declined to entertain Cygnet's applications.

As noted above, it has been unsuccessfully argued that, in circumstances where the underlying contract has come to an end, the adjudication provisions must also be regarded as inoperable. In *A&D Maintenance & Construction Ltd v Pagehurst Construction Services Ltd*[85] the contract came to an end in November 1998 and the adjudication, comprising a claim for the balance due for work done, took place in February/March 1999. HHJ Wilcox rejected the submission that, because the contract had come to an end, the sub-contractor was unable to make a claim in accordance with its provisions. The Judge noted that s108(2)(a) expressly provided that the party could give a notice 'at any time'. He pointed out that, even if the contract had been terminated, the matters referred to the adjudicator remained in dispute under the contract. As a result the adjudication provisions clearly remained operative, in precisely the same way as the arbitration clause would also remain operative. **2.89**

In *Connex South Eastern Ltd v MJ Building Services Group Plc*[86] the Court of Appeal had to consider a submission that it was an abuse of process for MJ to start adjudication proceedings on 13 February 2004 when, 15 months beforehand, on 29 November 2002, they had written to Connex stating that the latter's conduct amounted to a repudiatory breach of contract which MJ accepted, thereby terminating the contract. It was argued by Connex that this delay amounted to 'an abuse of process' and that the phrase 'at any time' could not be read literally. The argument was that the whole point of adjudication was to arrive at a quick, cheap, temporary decision and that if, as a result of the passage of time, it was no longer possible to have a quick, cheap and temporary adjudication, then it was an abuse of process to permit an adjudication to take place. Dyson LJ adopted precisely the same approach as he had adopted in *Herschel*.[87] He said: **2.90**

> I cannot accept these submissions. The phrase "at any time" means exactly what it says. It would have been possible to restrict the time within which an adjudication could be commenced, say, to a period by reference to the date when work was completed or the contract terminated. But this was not done. It is clear from Hansard

---

[85] [1999] CILL 1518.
[86] [2005] EWCA Civ 193.
[87] It does not appear from the judgment in the Court of Appeal that *Herschel v Breen* was cited to the Court of Appeal in *Connex*. However, that seemed to have made no difference since Dyson LJ followed precisely the same approach as he had adopted in *Herschel v Breen* five years before.

that the question of the time for referring a dispute to adjudication was carefully considered, and that it was decided not to provide any time limit for the reasons given by Lord Lucas. Those reasons were entirely rational. There is, therefore, no time limit.

28 Days

2.91 The 28 day period was deliberately designed to ensure a swift response to the dispute being referred to the adjudicator. Depending on the size of the claim being referred, and the extent and effect of any decision on the claim, those involved in dealing with adjudications on a regular basis know that the amount of work necessary to prepare a party's case can be significant. It is a very demanding process, not least for the adjudicator, who not only has to understand the arguments being put forward by both sides, but has to reach a clear and cogent decision, and publish it, all within 28 days of the referral. This has given rise to a number of practical difficulties.

2.92 There will be disputes which, when they are referred to the adjudicator, are so extensive that they are simply not capable of being fairly determined within the 28 days.[88] It is for the adjudicator to decide whether or not he is capable of arriving at a fair conclusion within the limited period available to him. If he is not, then he should decline the reference.

2.93 Problems can occur when the issues involved in the resolution of the single dispute turn out to be much more extensive than had originally been envisaged. In *CIB Properties Ltd v Birse Construction Ltd*[89] the adjudicator, a well-known construction QC, sought a number of extensions during the adjudication itself, as a result of the size and scope of the submissions being exchanged between the parties. Eventually, the adjudication took about three months. In an ordinary case, the position is that the referring party can agree unilaterally to extend the adjudication for an additional 14 days (making a total of 42 days in total). Although s108(2)(d) would not appear to allow the parties the opportunity to agree that the adjudicator can have additional time, s108(2)(c) is not so restricted, so further extensions beyond the 42 days can be granted, provided that both sides agree.

2.94 There have been a number of recent decisions concerned with the 28 day (or agreed extended) period and an adjudicator's obligation to comply therewith. These are analysed below. The first question is: when does the 28 days start to run? The second is whether or not the adjudicator is obliged to complete the decision

---

[88] This, of course, was what Judge Toulmin had in mind in his remarks in *AWG Building Services*, quoted at paragraph 2.13 above.
[89] [2005] 1 WLR 2252.

within the 28 day (or agreed extended) period. The third is whether, if he has completed his decision on time, the adjudicator is entitled to a further period, following the expiry of the 28 days, in which to communicate that decision to the parties.

When Does the 28 Day Period Start to Run?

In *Ritchie Brothers (PWC) Ltd v David Philip (Commercials) Ltd*[90] at first instance, Lord Eassie expressed the view that, in paragraph 19 of the Scheme, the "date of the referral notice" meant the date of despatch of that notice. However, in *Aveat Heating Ltd v Jerram Falkus Construction Ltd*[91] HHJ Havery QC considered that that was inconsistent with s108(2)(c) of the Act. He concluded that something could not be referred to another person unless that person received it; it might be sent with the intention of referring it but, if the document was never received, the notice was never referred. He therefore concluded that 'referral takes place upon receipt of the notice by the adjudicator'. Thus, the 28 days, or any agreed extended period, starts to run from the date that the referral notice was received by the adjudicator. On the facts of *Aveat*, Judge Havery concluded that the decision was reached within the agreed extended period. It is thought that, to the extent that there is a conflict between these two approaches, Judge Havery's reasoning is to be preferred. **2.95**

Is the Adjudicator Obliged to Complete the Decision Within 28 Days or Any Agreed Extended Period?

It would appear that, on the basis of the case law as it presently stands, the answer to this question is an unequivocal Yes. At the outset of any consideration of this point, it must be noted that the courts have repeatedly held that the completion of the decision, and its subsequent communication to the parties, are separate events. Although it has been regularly argued that the decision is not complete until it has been communicated to the parties, it has just as regularly been held that that is a fallacious submission.[92] Further, it will be noted from the authorities analysed below that, whilst there is some leeway in relation to the time for communication of the decision, the decision itself must be completed within the 28 days or the agreed extended period. **2.96**

In *Barnes & Elliott Ltd v Taylor Woodrow Holdings Ltd & Anor*[93] HHJ Lloyd QC was principally concerned with a decision which was completed within the **2.97**

---

[90] [2004] BLR 379.
[91] [2007] EWHC 131 (TCC).
[92] This argument has been repeatedly rejected by the TCC Judges, most recently in *Epping Electrical Co Ltd v Briggs & Forrester (Plumbing Services) Ltd* [2007] EWHC 4 (TCC) and *Cubitt Building and Interiors Ltd v Fleetglade Ltd* [2006] EWHC 3413 (TCC).
[93] [2003] EWHC 3100 (TCC); [2004] BLR 111.

relevant period but not delivered until after the expiry of that period. This was one of the many cases in which the Judge made plain that there were two stages, namely the completion of the decision and then the subsequent notification of that decision. Judge Lloyd emphasised that an adjudicator was not entitled to complete the decision outside the time allowed and that the Act only conferred authority to the adjudicator to make a decision within the 28 day period or such extended period as was agreed by the parties.

2.98 A decision which it is thought is incapable of being reconciled with the Act, and the other authorities, is *Simons Construction Ltd v Aardvark Developments Ltd*.[94] This dispute did not arise under the Act and the Scheme, but was instead a case under a particular contractual form of adjudication. However, the contractual stipulation was that the adjudicator had to give his decision in that case by 17 June. He in fact gave it on 25 June. HHJ Seymour QC held that the decision was binding, provided only that the adjudication agreement had not already been terminated as a result of the adjudicator's failure to produce a decision in the relevant time scale, and that a fresh notice of referral had not already been given by one of the parties. He appeared to base this decision on various provisions within the Scheme. On the face of it, it is difficult to see how a decision that was not reached within 28 days could be valid, given the emphasis in the 1996 Act on the necessity of the adjudicator's decision being completed within that time scale.

2.99 The decision in *Simons Construction* was the subject of sustained criticism by the Lord Justice Clerk (Gill) in *Ritchie Brothers (PWC) Ltd v David Philip (Commercial) Ltd*[95] and it was not followed in that case by the Court of Session. On the facts of *Ritchie*, the decision was due on 16 October but the adjudicator had requested the contractors to consent to an extension until 23 October. The decision was not delivered to the parties until 27 October. The Lord Justice Clerk concluded that the decision was not within the adjudicator's jurisdiction because it was a decision reached out of time. He emphasised that the 28 day period meant what it said. He rejected the suggestion that the adjudicator was entitled to reach his decision at any time during an indefinite period after the expiry of the 28 days, so long as neither of the parties had served a fresh notice of adjudication. In a short concurring judgment, Lord Nimmo Smith said that: 'If a speedy outcome is an objective, it is best achieved by adherence to strict time limits.' He added that: 'If certainty is an objective, it is not achieved by leaving the parties in doubt as to where they stand after the expiry of the 28 day period.' The adjudicator's decision was therefore held to be a nullity.

---

[94] [2003] EWHC 2474; [2004] BLR 117.
[95] [2005] SLDT 341.

2.100 Although the decision in *Ritchie* was a majority decision, it was the first by an appellate court on the point. It has been followed by the TCC in London in a number of subsequent cases. In *Hart Investments Ltd v Fidler & Anor*[96] the TCC Judge concluded that the decision in *Ritchie* was a correct statement of the law and that a decision reached outside the 28 day period would be a nullity unless there was an agreed extension of that period. In *Cubitt Building & Interiors Ltd v Fleetglade Ltd*[97] the same Judge repeated that view, concluding that adjudicators do not have the jurisdiction to grant themselves extensions of time without the express consent of both parties. Although it is unclear whether either of these cases was cited to HHJ Havery QC in *Epping Electrical Co Ltd v Briggs & Forrester (Plumbing Services) Ltd*,[98] he reached the same conclusion in that case. Having noted that *Ritchie* was the only decision on the point by an appellate court, Judge Havery said that it would be anomalous and undesirable if the 28 day provision was interpreted in different ways in the two jurisdictions. Whilst strictly he was not bound by the decision in *Ritchie*, he considered that he ought to follow it. The same Judge repeated that conclusion in the later case of *Aveat Heating Ltd v Jerram Falkus Construction Ltd*.[99]

2.101 The most recent decision in which the TCC emphasised the importance of compliance with the 28 day (or the agreed extended) period is *A C Yule & Son Ltd v Speedwell Roofing & Cladding Ltd*.[100] There, as a result of Speedwell's request for further time to make representations on one particular aspect of the case, the adjudicator had sought a consequential extension of two days to complete his decision. Yule had agreed to his request. Although Speedwell did not respond to the request itself, they conducted themselves in a way that was only consistent with an extension of time having been agreed. Following the adjudicator's decision, which was provided during the two day extension period, Speedwell took the point that the decision was invalid because they had not consented to the requested extension. The TCC Judge rejected that contention, saying that there was a clear obligation on the part of both parties to the adjudication to respond plainly and promptly to an adjudicator's request for further time. If, in breach of that obligation, one party failed to respond at all, there was a very strong case for saying that that party had accepted, by their silence, the need for the required extension. As the Judge put it, 'The adjudicator can do no more than work out that he needs a short extension, and seek agreement from the parties to such an extension. Common sense, as well as common courtesy, requires a prompt response.' He went on to find that Speedwell's conduct was only consistent with

---

96 [2006] EWHC 2857 (TCC); [2007] BLR 30; [2007] TLLR 1; (2007) 109 Con LR 14.
97 [2006] EWHC 3413 (TCC).
98 [2007] EWHC 4 (TCC).
99 [2007] EWHC 131 (TCC).
100 [2007] EWHC 1360 (TCC).

their having agreed to an extension of time and, even if he was wrong about that, he concluded that Speedwell were estopped from belatedly taking the point that the decision was invalid because it had not been completed in time.

2.102 Although the Judge's conclusion meant that the adjudicator's decision was valid, and was therefore enforced by way of summary judgment, *Yule* is also of some additional significance because, in shortly addressing the claimant's alternative arguments, the TCC Judge considered afresh the consequences of non-compliance with the statutory or agreed period. Although his remarks were necessarily brief, they constitute the first time in which the courts have expressly considered the contention, by reference to the House of Lords decision in *R v Soneji*,[101] and the Australian case of *Brodyn Pty Ltd v Davenport and Anor*,[102] that what matters is not the language in which the statutory requirement of completion within 28 days is expressed, but the consequences of non-compliance with that period. It has been suggested in some quarters that *Ritchie*, and the other cases referred to in the preceding paragraphs, were wrongly decided, because they placed too much emphasis on the mandatory requirements of the 1996 Act, and gave insufficient weight to the consequences of a finding that a decision, provided out of time, was a nullity.

2.103 The Judge made five points in rejecting the argument that *Ritchie*, and the cases that followed it, were wrongly decided. First, he did not consider that such an approach, which was clearly applicable to the sort of 'one-chance only' applications sometimes required by the criminal law (and which lay at the heart of the debate in *R v Soneji*), was necessarily applicable to the field of private dispute resolution. He made the point that the Arbitration Act 1996 stipulated tight time limits for applications to appeal against or set aside an arbitrator's award, and that there were numerous decisions of the Commercial Court and the Court of Appeal which made plain that a failure to comply with those time limits was almost always fatal to an application made out of time, regardless of the consequences. Secondly, he concluded that, because adjudication was a process in which accuracy had been sacrificed for speed, it would be contrary to the whole basis of adjudication for speed suddenly to become less important, with the pace of any given adjudication to be dictated, not by the statutory requirements, but 'by a complex (and potentially ever-changing) kaleidoscope of factors comprised of the consequences of the adjudicator's failure to comply with those requirements'. Thirdly, he pointed out that the mere fact that the decision was a nullity was not an end to the process (unlike the confiscation order application at issue in

---

[101] [2006] 1 AC 340.
[102] 61 NSWLR 421. This case is considered in Chapter 6 below, in the context of adjudication in Australia.

R v Soneji), because a fresh adjudication could always be commenced if the first decision was a nullity. In addition, the extent of the delay and the amount of any wasted costs in the event of a further adjudication might be small. Fourthly, he distinguished the decision of the Court of Appeal of New South Wales in *Brodyn Pty Ltd v Davenport and Anor*,[103] on the basis that the adjudication provisions under consideration in that case were very different to those provided by the Scheme for Construction Contracts. There was, for example, no obligation that the adjudicator 'shall' complete his decision within a particular time.[104]

2.104 The fifth and final point that the Judge made in *Yule*, in concluding that the 28 day (or any agreed extended) period was to be regarded as mandatory, was his view that, in a speedy process like adjudication, the need for certainty was paramount. He considered that that certainty would be lost if the 28 days was no longer regarded as a clear and mandatory requirement, but merely a guideline. Equally, he said, certainty would be lost if an adjudicator was given as long as he wanted to provide an enforceable decision, provided only that the parties could not show clear prejudice as a result of any delays beyond the 28 day (or agreed extended) period. Thus he concluded that, even if he was persuaded to adopt the approach in *R v Soneji*, in construing the 1996 Act as a whole (and paragraph 19 of the Scheme in particular) he would come to the same conclusion, namely that the benefits of speed and certainty underpinned the statutory requirement that the decision of the adjudicator shall be provided within 28 days (or any agreed extended period), and not thereafter. He concluded that the 1996 Act and the Scheme were to be construed purposively to ensure that those objectives were maintained.

2.105 Accordingly, unless and until this issue is reviewed by the Court of Appeal, it seems clear that the adjudicator must endeavour to complete his decision within 28 days, or the extended period, and his failure to do so will mean that his decision is a nullity. Furthermore, for the reasons explained by the TCC Judge in *Cubitt Building & Interiors Ltd v Fleetglade Ltd*[105] this could, in certain circumstances, deprive one of the parties to the contract of a substantive and permanent remedy (such as where the challenge to the Final Certificate has to be made within a certain period, otherwise the Certificate becomes binding). It is therefore important for everybody, including the adjudicator, to ensure that his decision is completed within the relevant period.

---

[103] (2004) 61 NSWLR 421.
[104] Furthermore, a closer examination of the decision in *Brodyn* makes clear that the NSW Court of Appeal were not dismissing the notion that a failure to comply with statutory requirements and time limits rendered an adjudicator's decision unenforceable: see paragraphs 6.21–6.22 below.
[105] [2006] EWHC 3413 (TCC).

Is There Any Leeway Available to the Adjudicator When Communicating the Decision?

2.106 Just as the authorities are clear that an adjudicator does not have the right or ability to extend time unilaterally to complete his decision, they also demonstrate that he does have some leeway in the communication of that decision. Thus, in *Barnes v Elliott* (paragraph 2.97 above), the adjudicator completed his decision within time but, due to a mix-up as to the method of delivery, it was not provided to the parties until one day after the expiry of the relevant period. Judge Lloyd decided that an error which resulted in a delay of a day, or possibly of two days, in the communication of the decision, was in all the circumstances excusable. He held that it was within the tolerance and commercial practice which one had to afford to the 1996 Act and to the contract. A valid decision reached within 28 days did not become unauthorised and invalid merely because, as a result of an error by the adjudicator in despatching the decision, it did not reach the parties within the time limit.[106]

2.107 In *Cubitt Building & Interiors Ltd v Fleetglade Ltd*[107] the adjudicator's decision was dated the last day of the agreed extended period. However, the decision was not provided to the parties until just after noon the following day. There was extensive argument to the effect that the decision had not been completed within time and/ or that the decision should have been communicated immediately, and not over 12 hours late. The TCC Judge expressed his concern that it had been necessary for him to consider in detail the evidence of the adjudicator's thinking on an almost hour-by-hour basis. He concluded that the communication just after noon the following day complied with the adjudicator's obligation to communicate the decision forthwith but warned that, in the days of email and fax, the time for the communication of the decision following its completion should be very short—a matter of a few hours at most. He struggled to see how any decision not communicated at the latest by the middle of the day after the final deadline, as in *Cubitt*, could be said to have been communicated 'forthwith'. He said that the safest thing for an adjudicator to do, if the decision had reached the last date of the 28 day period, was to email that decision during that final day.[108]

2.108 On the facts in *Mott MacDonald Limited v London & Regional Properties Limited*,[109] the decision was completed before the end of the period, but was not communicated until after the expiry of the period. This delay arose because of the adjudicator's

---

[106] It is respectfully suggested that it was this point which Jackson J had in mind when, in *M Rhode Construction v Nicholas Markham-David* [2006] EWHC 814 (TCC) he said that 'a slight delay is not fatal to the decision'.

[107] [2006] EWHC 3413 (TCC).

[108] In both *Cubitt* and *Epping Electrical*, there was a delay because the adjudicator wrongly considered that he was entitled to a lien in respect of his fees. This question is dealt with in greater detail in paragraphs 11.18–11.23 below.

[109] [2007] EWHC 1055 (TCC).

insistence on recovering his fees before he released his decision.[110] The delay was held to be outside the requirements of the 1996 Act, and the decision was not enforced.

Impartiality/Fairness

2.109 Again, the question as to whether or not an adjudicator has to comply with the rules of natural justice, and the extent to which it is necessary for him so to comply, has been a major feature of arguments as to the enforceability or otherwise of adjudicators' decisions. Accordingly, this important jurisdictional point is dealt with in some detail in Chapter 9 below. However, it is instructive to note at this point the courts' general approach to the adjudicator's obligation, pursuant to s108(2)(e), to act impartially.

2.110 The nature and extent of the adjudicator's obligation to act impartially was first considered by the courts in *Discain Project Services Ltd v Opecprime Developments Ltd*.[111] In that case the adjudicator had two private conversations with employees of the contractor which, although he did not initiate them, were not recorded and communicated to the defendant. On the application for summary judgment, HHJ Bowsher QC said that he found the fact of these discussions 'distasteful, and I cannot bring myself to enforce an adjudication which has been arrived at in that way'. The matter then went to a full hearing, with evidence.[112] In his final judgment, Judge Bowsher made plain that he did not criticise the adjudicator for misuse of his inquisitorial powers, but did criticise him because he failed to use his powers to control the conduct of the proceedings in order to prevent one party approaching him in a way that the adjudicator felt improper.

2.111 The Judge found that, as a matter of general principle, the adjudicator had to conduct the proceedings in accordance with the rules of natural justice or as fairly as the limitations imposed by Parliament permit. In so deciding, he followed the same approach as HHJ Lloyd QC in *Glencot Development & Design Co Ltd v Ben Barrett & Son (Contractors) Ltd*.[113]

2.112 Judge Bowsher was obviously concerned that, in arriving at the conclusion that the adjudicator was obliged to act in accordance with the rules of natural justice (and in this case, had failed so to do) he was expressing a view that was contrary to that expressed by Dyson J in *Macob*. It will be remembered that there, Dyson J had indicated that, even if the adjudicator had reached his decision by making a

---

[110] An adjudicator is not entitled to exercise a lien in this way: see paragraphs 11.19–11.24 below.
[111] [2000] BLR 402.
[112] [2001] BLR 287.
[113] [2001] BLR 207.

procedural error which invalidated that decision, 'it is still a decision on the issue' and was therefore to be enforced. Judge Bowsher concluded that that cannot have been what Dyson J meant in *Macob*, saying:

> On the other hand, with all respect, it is a startling proposition that an adjudicator's decision, if arrived at in serious breach of a principle of natural justice, must as a matter of law nevertheless be enforced in circumstances where payment under an invalid decision could easily turn out to be irretrievable and precipitate the insolvency of the party affected (particularly where, as here, there had not even been a decision by the adjudicator on the merits, but only a procedural one shutting out consideration of any defence or cross-claim). Even given the inherent and obvious pro-producer and anti-customer and anti-paymaster bias of the HGCRA's statutory adjudication proposals, it is submitted that, in the absence of express wording, Parliament can only have intended adjudicator's decisions validly arrived at on the merits or law of a properly referred dispute to be binding on the parties for the comparatively lengthy period which could be involved before final judgment or award and almost inconceivable that Parliament intended to accord to adjudicators' decisions or conduct an immunity and enforceability not accorded by the law to arbitrators in their awards or even to the judiciary and their judgments.

2.113 For the reasons explored in the detailed analysis of the cases under this topic at Chapter 9 below, an adjudicator is generally obliged to act impartially; this means that, within the confines of the particular adjudication and the time limits imposed, he must obey the rules of natural justice. On the other hand, as we shall see, the courts will not allow a simple assertion of a breach of these rules to be used to avoid the enforcing of an adjudicator's decision. Before deciding not to enforce the adjudicator's decision on this ground, the courts will want to be sure, not only that any alleged breach of natural justice has been clearly and obviously demonstrated from the papers, but that also the breach had such a decisive effect upon the adjudicator's decision-making process that the decision itself has been invalidated. Thus, in *Kier Regional Ltd v City & General (Holborn) Ltd*[114] Jackson J held that, although the adjudicator ought to have taken two experts' reports into account in reaching his decision, the error did not invalidate that decision because it was clear that the adjudicator had considered each of the arguments that had been advanced by the relevant party. At worst, it was an error of law, not a breach of natural justice, and therefore one which did not invalidate the decision.

2.114 A related question is the extent to which the provisions of s108(2) amount to a breach of the Human Rights Act 1998, and the European Convention on Human Rights Article 6, which provides that everyone is entitled to a fair and public hearing within a reasonable time. In *Austin Hall Building Ltd v Buckland Securities Ltd*[115] it was argued that the adjudication process was in breach of the Human

---

[114] [2006] EWHC 848 (TCC).
[115] [2001] BLR 274.

Rights legislation. HHJ Bowsher QC rejected that submission. He doubted whether the adjudicator was a public authority and that, even if there was a right to a public hearing, that right could be waived and such waiver could be inferred by a failure to ask for a public hearing. However, the Judge's principal reason for rejecting the submission was that section 6(2) of the Human Rights Act made plain that sub-section (1) did not apply to any particular act if 'as a result of one or more provisions of primary legislation, the authority could not have acted differently'. The Judge held that, in order to comply with the 28 day time limit provided by the 1996 Act, the adjudicator could not have acted differently in imposing the time limits that he imposed on the parties, about which the defendant subsequently complained. Thus the adjudicator was acting in accordance with primary legislation and could not be criticised for imposing the time limits that he did. This important strand of the Judge's conclusion on the Human Rights issue is set out verbatim in paragraph 9.46 below.

2.115 In addition, in *Austin Hall*, the Judge made the point at paragraph 68 of his judgment, that adjudications were governed by the rules of natural justice and that those rules were not very far different from Article 6 of the Convention. He reiterated the point that the adjudicator was constrained to impose the time limits that he did, and as a result could not be criticised for breaching the rules of natural justice.

Binding

2.116 Clearly, the extent to which the adjudicator's decision was binding was one of the most important elements of the Bill and was the subject of extensive debate.[116] However, s108(3) has not, of itself, engendered very much controversy. The parties to a construction contract are aware that the decision of an adjudicator is binding until the matter is taken either to court or to a final determination by an arbitrator. As previously noted, the arguments as to whether or not the decision is binding have tended to revolve around questions of the enforceability of the decision, and those issues have themselves turned, in the main, on arguments as to the adjudicator's jurisdiction.

2.117 However, there has been dispute about the binding nature of decisions which contain a palpable error. As we saw from the decision of the Court of Appeal in *Bouygues*, the general position is that, if the adjudicator was answering the question that he had been asked by the parties, then it mattered not whether there were errors of fact or law in that decision: it was still enforceable. However, this question arose even more starkly in *Bloor Construction (UK) Ltd v Bowmer & Kirkland*

---

[116] Please see Chapter 1 above.

(London) Ltd.[117] In that case the adjudicator faxed to the parties a decision at 3.32 pm on 11 February 2000. The decision stated that Bowmer should pay Bloor a total of £122,098.76. Bowmer realised that the adjudicator had failed to deduct the payments on account that they had already made. The error was pointed out to him and on the same day, at 5.53 pm, he sent out a corrected decision which confirmed that, once due allowance was taken for the payments on account, no further sum was due to Bloor. The adjudicator said that his first decision was 'an obvious slip'. Bloor sought to enforce the adjudicator's first and uncorrected decision. HHJ Toulmin CMG QC categorised the error as 'a slip'. He said that, in the absence of any specific agreement to the contrary, a term could and should be implied into the contract allowing the adjudicator to correct an error arising from an accidental error or omission. He said that the purpose of adjudication was to enable broad justice to be done between the parties and that that would be achieved if the parties were taken to agreeing that the adjudicator could correct an obvious mistake of the sort which he had made in that case.

2.118 It is respectfully submitted that the decision in *Bloor* was based on contractual common sense. Some commentators have suggested that the problem with the result is that it is difficult to say that it was not contrary to the reasoning of both Dyson J and the Court of Appeal in *Bouygues*. However, it is thought that the two can be reconciled. *Bloor* was a strong case on the facts, because the adjudicator accepted that there had been an error and rectified it immediately. If the parties are in dispute as to the obviousness (or otherwise) of the alleged 'slip', or the adjudicator does not accept that an error had been made, or does accept it but only some time after the publication of the decision, then it is thought that the approach in *Bouygues* will remain appropriate. This is discussed in greater detail in paragraphs 8.24–8.30 below.

2.119 The leading case on the proper construction of the word 'binding' in s108(3) is the Court of Appeal case of *Ferson Contractors v Levolux AT Limited*,[118] referred to in detail in paragraphs 10.26 – 10.28 below. In *William Verry Ltd v London Borough of Camden*,[119] Ramsey J referred to that decision and said that the Court of Appeal 'set out in clear terms the principle which applies to the implementation of the intention of Parliament. . . . In my judgment, the effect of those statutory provisions [particularly s108] and of the passages in *Levolux* is generally to exclude a right of set-off from an adjudicator's decision.'

---

[117] [2000] BLR 314.
[118] [2003] BLR 118.
[119] [2006] EWHC 761.

Part II of the Housing Grants Construction and Regeneration Act 1996

Sections 109, 110 & 111: Payment Provisions

The relevant sections of the 1996 Act read as follows: 2.120

109–(1) A party to a construction contract is entitled to payment by instalments, stage payments or other periodic payments for any work under the contract unless—
- (a) it is specified in the contract that the duration of the work is to be less than 45 days, or
- (b) it is agreed between the parties that the duration of the work is estimated to be less than 45 days.

(2) The parties are free to agree the amounts of the payments and the intervals at which, or circumstances in which, they become due.

(3) Any absence of such agreement, the relevant provisions of the Scheme for Construction Contracts apply.

(4) References in the following sections to a payment under the contract include a payment by virtue of this section.

110–(1) Every construction contract shall—
- (a) provide an adequate mechanism for determining what payments become due under the contract, and when, and
- (b) provide for a final date for payment in relation to any sum which becomes due.

The parties are free to agree how long the period is to be between the date on which the sum becomes due and the final date for payment.

(2) Every construction contract shall provide for the giving of notice by a party not later than five days after the date on which a payment becomes due from him under the contract, or would have become due if—
- (a) the other party had carried out his obligations under the contract; and
- (b) no set-off or abatement was permitted by reference to any sum claimed to be due under one or more other contracts,

specifying the amount, if any, of the payment made or proposed to be made, and the basis on which that amount was calculated.

(3) If or to the extent that a contract does not contain such provision as is mentioned in sub-section (1) or (2), the relevant provisions of the Scheme for Construction Contracts apply.

111–(1) A party to a construction contract may not withhold payment after the final date for payment of a sum due under the contract unless he has given an effective notice of intention to withhold payment.

The notice mentioned in section 110(2) may suffice as a notice of intention to withhold payment if it complies with the requirements of this section.

(2) To be effective such a notice must specify—
- (a) the amount proposed to be withheld and the ground for withholding payment, or
- (b) if there is more than one ground, each ground and the amount attributable to it,

and must be given not later than the prescribed period before the final date for payment.

(3) The parties are free to agree what that prescribed period is to be.

In the absence of such agreement, the period shall be that provided by the Scheme for Construction Contracts.

(4) Where an effective notice of intention to withhold payment is given, but on the matter being referred to adjudication it is decided that the whole or part of the amount should be paid, the decision shall be construed as requiring payment not later than—
  (a) seven days from the date of the decision, or
  (b) the date which apart from the notice would have been the final date for payment,
whichever is the later.

2.121 At the heart of these provisions is the attempt to ensure that every construction contract contains a transparent and straightforward mechanism for the payment to the contractor of interim payments on account (sometimes called instalments or progress payments). In addition it recognises that, although there will inevitably be a period between the date on which a payment becomes due, and the final date on which that sum must be paid, it imposes an obligation on the payer to notify the payee well in advance of the final date for payment how much is going to be paid and how that sum has been calculated. If the payer wishes to withhold part or all of a sum otherwise due under the contract, then a withholding notice must be served, again well in advance of the final date for payment, which makes it crystal clear what is being withheld and why.

2.122 The mischief at which s110 is aimed is clear: too often in the past, construction contracts, particularly sub-contracts, were either absurdly complex or vague as to what sums would become due and when. Section 110 is designed to do away with such uncertainty. The mischief that s111 is aimed at is more subtle but was, prior to the 1996 Act, a major source of dispute and difficulty within the construction industry. It was common for contractors and, particularly sub-contractors, to carry out a large amount of work and comply with the contractual mechanism in respect of payment. The contractor or sub-contractor would then confidently expect to be paid only to receive at, or sometimes after the final date for payment, an indication that the monies would not be forthcoming as a result of an alleged defect or other deficiencies in the contractor's work. Sometimes, the out-of-pocket contractor or sub-contractor would have no idea why the sums were not being paid until, once he had issued his writ and issued his application for summary judgment, he would be informed, sometimes for the first time, that the payer had a set-off and counterclaim which extinguished his claim. It was notoriously easy for unscrupulous payers, be they employers or main contractors, to put together a sufficiently intimidating counterclaim to ensure that the payee did not receive the sums due at the summary judgment hearing. In order to destroy such abuses once and for all, s111 created the system of withholding notices, whereby if the payer had a genuine reason not to pay sums otherwise due, they had to spell that reason out in advance of the payment becoming due.

2.123 Accordingly, these three sections of the 1996 Act are designed to introduce into most construction contracts three distinct arrangements: a system of stage payments (s109); a clear mechanism by which those stage payments become due and finally payable (s110); and the mechanism by which the payer must notify the payee of its intention to withhold payment (s111). Each section is considered briefly below. It is unsurprising that it is in relation to s111 that the majority of the authorities occur.

2.124 Most construction contracts, and certainly all the standard forms in common use, provide for a system of stage payments. The purpose of s109(1) is to ensure that, save in smaller contracts where the work will take less than 45 days, all contracts provide for a stage payment mechanism. In *Tim Butler Contractors Ltd v Merewood Homes Ltd*[120] the defendant contended that s109 did not apply because the duration of the work was less than 45 days. The adjudicator held that the duration of the works under the contract was not specified or agreed as less than 45 days, concluding that the parties had agreed price, terms and conditions and the date of commencement, but had reached no agreement as to the duration of the works. Although there was a programme which showed a four week duration, the adjudicator found that that did not form part of the contract between the parties. The adjudicator therefore decided in favour of the claimant.

2.125 The enforcement application was heard by HHJ Gilliland QC in the TCC in Salford, when he too rejected the defendant's submission. He concluded that the question as to whether a construction contract came into existence which entitled the claimant to stage payments was a dispute as to the terms of the contract. It was not a dispute which went to the jurisdiction of the adjudicator. The adjudicator had to decide what the agreed terms were and, in particular, whether or not the programme was a term of the contract. The adjudicator did so and concluded that the programme was not a term of the contract. The Judge found that the adjudicator was entitled to reach that view and, whether it was right or wrong, it was a decision within his jurisdiction. The decision was therefore enforced.

2.126 S110(1) requires that every construction contract must provide an adequate mechanism for determining what payments were due under the contract and when, and, in respect of each payment, providing a final date for such payment. The problem that arose in *Maxi Construction Management Ltd v Morton Rolls Ltd*[121] is

---

[120] [2002] 18 Const LJ 74.
[121] [2001] CILL 1784–1787.

not uncommon. There, the payment provisions of the contract had been amended to include two distinct stages. The first was the agreement of the contractor's valuation by the employer's agent, whilst the second stage envisaged an application by the contractor for payment of the sum that had been agreed. Lord MacFadyen concluded that such a regime was not in accordance with s110(1)(a). A requirement that a valuation be agreed by the employer's agent before a claim for payment could be made was not necessarily incompatible with s110(1)(a), provided always that there was a timetable for the process of agreement, and, just as importantly, a means of resolving a failure to reach any such agreement. The amendments in the contract under consideration included no such timetable and no such mechanism. Thus, failure on the part of the employer's agent to agree a valuation could hold up the making of claim for payment indefinitely. Thus the Judge concluded that the contract did not provide an adequate mechanism for determining when payments became due under the contract. Accordingly, the Scheme for Construction Contracts was implied instead.

2.127 S110(1)(b) is plainly important because it requires each construction contract to provide a final date by which each stage payment must be paid. This provision was considered by HHJ Lloyd QC in *Alstom Signalling Ltd v Jarvis Facilities Ltd*.[122] In that case the adjudicator found that the contract did not satisfy s110(1)(b) because, he said, the final date for payment was capable of being unilaterally altered. The Judge rejected that analysis. He said that the payment terms in the sub-contract that he was considering related up the contractual chain to the main contract with Railtrack. The contract provided that payment would be made within seven days of a Railtrack certificate. The Judge held that there was therefore certainty as to the final date for payment, namely seven days after the Railtrack certificate, and the fact that Railtrack, possibly in breach of its own contract with Alstom, might fail to issue that certificate did not mean that, for the purposes of s110(1)(b), there was no final date for payment. The Judge pointed out that the final date for payment remained seven days after the issue of the certificate. He also made the important point that the fact that a date was set by reference to a future event did not render it any the less a final date. The event on which the payment might turn could be a stage, or milestone date, or completion, practical or substantial. It could be the result of an action by a third party, such as a certificate under a superior contract or transaction. However, provided that the event was readily recognisable and would produce a date by reference to which the final date could be set, there was no reason why the event could not provide for a final date for payment in accordance with s110(1)(b).

---

[122] [2004] EWHC 1285 (TCC).

S110(2) imposes upon the payer the obligation to notify the payee, not later than five days after the date on which a payment become due, the amount of the payment that was being or would be made, and the basis on which that amount was calculated[123]. As pointed out above, this was of important practical significance to the payee, because it meant that he would be promptly notified if the employer intended not to pay the full amount that the payee was expecting. As s111(1) makes expressly clear, such a notice could also constitute a withholding notice under s111. It is therefore instructive to turn to the authorities under that section, and the inter-relationship between s110 and s111. This is analysed under five sub-headings: what is meant by 'a payment due' (paragraphs 2.129–2.133 below); the extent, if at all, to which the payer is entitled to set off against sums otherwise due (paragraphs 2.136–2.137 below); the nature and timing of the withholding notice under s111 (paragraphs 2.138–2.141 below); the inter-relationship with these provisions and other terms of the contract (paragraph 2.142 below); and the inter-relationship between these provisions and a party's right to seek a stay for arbitration (paragraphs 2.148–2.151 below).   **2.128**

Payment Due Under The Contract

There was for many years after the 1996 Act came into force a debate about the right approach to the payee's entitlement to a payment due under the contract. These debates principally arose under those contracts which did not contain a regime by which interim payments were certified or authorised by the employer's agent. The most extreme position adopted by the payee was that, if it claimed £X under the contract, and there was no notice under s110(2) or no withholding notice from the payer in accordance with s111, it was said that the payee was entitled to £X. At the other extreme, it was said by the payer that a payment that was 'due' could only be identified as such following a detailed investigation by the adjudicator, and the court, as to whether the sums claimed were actually due. This, of course, would have allowed the payer a broad licence to investigate every element of the sum claimed, both in the adjudication and in court on the enforcement application, on the basis that, if it was not due, s110(2) could not apply. Eventually, it has been demonstrated that, as a generality, neither of these extreme positions is right, and that everything turns on the terms of the contact and, in particular, whether or not the contract provides for a payment mechanism by reference to the certificates or valuations of a third party.   **2.129**

The high watermark of the payee's approach, to the effect that, in the absence of a withholding notice, a sum claimed was a sum due under the contract in   **2.130**

---

[123] Under a contract with a certificate regime, this provision is superfluous, and the DTI 2nd Consultation Report (June 2007) proposes amendments to the 1996 Act accordingly: see paragraph 2.134 below.

Statutory Adjudication

accordance with s110 can be found in the decision of HHJ Bowsher QC in *Northern Developments (Cumbria) Ltd v J&J Nichol*.[124] In that case the contractor made an application for payment and 14 days later the employer sent a withholding notice. Thereafter, the contract was terminated and the employer made a claim for repudiation. The adjudicator refused to consider the alleged repudiation because it was not a matter within the withholding notice. Judge Bowsher agreed with that. However, in his judgment he appeared to suggest that a contractor was entitled to the sum claimed, save for any points expressly raised by the employer in a withholding notice. At paragraph 29 he said:

> The intention of the statute is clearly that if there is to be a dispute about the amount of the payment required by section 111, that dispute is to be mentioned in a notice of intention to withhold payment not later than five days after the due date for payment... There is to be no dispute about any matter not raised in a notice of intention to withhold payment. Accordingly, in my view, the Adjudicator had no jurisdiction to consider any matter not raised in the notice of intention to withhold payment in this case.

2.131 That passage in the judgment of Judge Bowsher was interpreted by some as meaning that any disputes as to payment, including whether or not a particular part of the claim was due under the contract, had to be identified in a withholding notice and, if it was not in a withholding notice, it could not be raised by the employer. However, that interpretation of Judge Bowsher's judgment missed the simple point that, if the claim was based simply on a contractor's application for payment, it was open to the employer to challenge the application on the basis that at least some of the sums claimed were not due under the contract. This was not a question of withholding anything from sums otherwise due; it was making the point that some of the sums claimed were simply not due in the first place. This distinction was explained by Lord MacFadyen in *SL Timber Systems v Carillion Construction Ltd*.[125] In that case, the adjudicator decided that the main contractors had failed to serve notices in accordance with s110(2) and that therefore the sub-contractors were entitled to the sums that they claimed without any scrutiny of the substance of their applications. Lord MacFadyen concluded that that approach was wrong in principle. As to s111 he said:

> The section is not, in my opinion, concerned with every refusal on the part of one party to pay a sum claimed by the other. It is concerned, rather, with the situation where a sum is due under the contract, and the party by whom that sum is due seeks to withhold payment on some separate ground. Much of the discussion of the section in the cases has been concerned with what circumstances involve "withholding" payment and therefore require a notice. Without the benefit of authority, I would have been inclined to say that a dispute about whether the work in respect of which

---

[124] [2000] BLR 158.
[125] [2001] BLR 516.

the claim was made had been done, or about whether it was properly measured or valued, or about whether some other event on which a contractual liability to make payment depended had occurred, went to the question of whether the sum claimed was due under the contract, therefore did not involve an attempt to "withhold . . . a sum due under the contract", and therefore did not require the giving of a notice of intention to withhold payment. On the other hand, where there was no dispute that the work had been done and was correctly measured and valued, or that the other relevant event had occurred, but the party from whom payment was claimed wished to advance some separate ground for withholding the payment, such as a right of retention in respect of a counterclaim, that would constitute an attempt to "withhold . . . a sum due under the contract", and would require a notice of intention to withhold payment.

The Judge considered what Judge Bowsher had said in *Northern Developments*. He concluded that if Judge Bowsher meant that, without a section 111 notice, there could be no dispute of any sort as to whether the sum claimed was properly due, the Judge had taken too broad a view of the effect of s111.[126]

2.132 The distinction between the case where the payee's claim was based simply on an application for payment, the detail of which might be legitimately disputed by the payer, and the case where the payee's claim was based on a certificate or valuation authorised by the employer's agent, in which case there could be no legitimate complaint that, under the contract, the sums certified were due, was made in clear terms by Sheriff J A Taylor in *Clark Contracts Ltd v The Burrell Co (Construction Management) Ltd*.[127] In that case, the main contractor's claim was based on an interim certificate. Accordingly, Sheriff Taylor distinguished the situation under consideration in *SL Timber* because, in *Clark*, there was no dispute that the architect had issued an interim certificate. The certificate functioned as a notice under s110(2). The Sheriff found that the contractors became entitled to payment of the sum certified within 14 days of the certificate being issued and that amounted to an entitlement to payment of a sum due under the contract. Thus, if the employers wanted to avoid a liability to make that payment, they had to issue a notice in

---

[126] It should be noted that precisely the same conclusion was arrived at by HHJ Gilliland QC in *Millers Specialist Joinery Co Ltd v Nobles Construction Ltd* [2001] CILL 1770–1773. In his judgment in that case, Judge Gilliland said at paragraph 22: 'If it were correct that the effect of a failure to serve a valid note of intention to withhold payment under s111 was that the amount of the valuation or invoice was to be regarded as a sum "due under the contract", the consequence would appear to be that neither an adjudicator nor the court could properly refuse to order payment in full even though it might be perfectly clear, for example, that the work or the materials claimed for had not been carried out or supplied, or that the wrong rate or price had been claimed or that there had been some other error in the invoice or valuation. If the effect of a failure to serve a notice under the section is to deprive the payer of the right to refuse payment on the basis that the sum from which the deduction is sought to be made is not properly due and payable, it is difficult to see on what basis the court could refuse to give judgment for the full amount or what cause of action the payer would subsequently have to recover the payment.'
[127] [2002] SLT 103.

accordance with s111(1) of the 1996 Act. There was no such notice and therefore the sum was due.[128]

2.133 This distinction, between sums claimed on the one hand and sums certified on the other, was emphasised by the Court of Appeal in *Rupert Morgan Building Services (LLC) Ltd v Jervis & Anor*.[129] In that case, there was a certificate. Jacob LJ referred to Sheriff Taylor's analysis in *Clark* and concluded that, if a sum had been certified under the contract, it was therefore 'due' and could not be opened up by the adjudicator, and if an employer wanted to withhold money from a certified sum, he had to serve notice in accordance with s111. Jacob LJ also pointed out that, not only was Sheriff Taylor's analysis obviously right, it had a series of advantages. It avoided difficult distinctions between sums due, counterclaims and abatement. It provided a fair solution, because the money was held, at least temporarily, by the party in whose favour the certificate had been issued, but did not prevent later repayment if it was subsequently shown that the sum certified was not due. It meant that a valid withholding notice provided following the issue of a certificate had to be clear and specific. And it provided relief to the sub-contractor against the potentially overbearing actions of the main contractor, which was one of the principal purposes of the 1996 Act in the first place. The relevant passage from the judgment of Jacob LJ can be found at paragraph 10.12 below. This approach was subsequently adopted by HHJ Lloyd QC in *Alstom Signalling Ltd v Jervis Facilities Ltd*:[130] see in particular paragraphs 23 and 27 and 31–36 of his judgment. The distinction between sums certified and sums simply claimed under the contract is of particular importance in the context of abatement and set-off, and is dealt with in greater detail in Chapter 10 below.

2.134 Accordingly, under a contract that provides for interim certificates, the certificate is itself likely to operate as a notice under s110(2) of the Act, because the certificate specifies 'the amount of the payment made or proposed to be made, and the basis on which that amount was calculated'. Indeed, as a result of this perceived duplication, the DTI Report of June 2007 for the 2nd Consultation on the proposed changes to the 1996 Act suggests the amendment of clause 110(2) 'by allowing a notice or certificate from a third party to act as section 110(2) payment notice.[131] It may be that, in taking up this point, they were prompted by the remarks of Lord Hoffmann in *Melville Dundas Ltd (in receivership) and others v George Wimpey UK Ltd and another*,[132] when he said that 'Serving a notice under

---

[128] See also *Re A Company (No 1299 of 2001)* (2001) CILL 1745.
[129] [2004] 1 WLR 1867.
[130] [2004] EWHC 1285 (TCC).
[131] See paragraphs 19.14 onwards below.
[132] [2007] UKHL 18; [2007] 1 WLR 1136. This important case is addressed in greater detail in paragraphs 2.142–2.146 below.

section 110(2) seems to have no consequences (except that it may stand as a notice under section 111(1)) and there is no penalty for not doing so. The purpose of section 110(2) is therefore something of a puzzle. It seems to have dropped from heaven into the legislative process on its last day in the House of Commons... the amendment by which it was inserted was neither explained nor debated.'

2.135 Whilst a notice under s110(2) is superfluous under a contract with a certificate regime, it is suggested that it is an important document for a construction contract under which the contractor makes a monthly claim for an interim payment, the employer considers the detail of that claim, and then decides what is due. Once the employer has reached his conclusion as to what is due, the contractor is entitled to know what he is being paid, and how that figure has been arrived at. That is the information which the s110(2) notice must contain and that is why it is so important: it fixes the amount of the sum due. It should also be noted that one of the DTI proposals is for the s110(2) and s111(1) notice provisions to be streamlined, so that the latter is simply a revision of the former.[133]

Set-Off

2.136 One of the most common situations arising in and after adjudication proceedings is the attempt by the payer to raise a set-off in respect of sums otherwise due. This has generated a large amount of case law, which is analysed in greater detail in Chapter 10 below. The principal difficulty arises when a paying party seeks to raise a set-off, in circumstances where there has been no effective withholding notice in accordance with s111(1). This issue first came before the courts in *VHE Construction Plc v RBSTB Trust Co Ltd*.[134] The second adjudicator found a net sum due to the contractors. Thereafter, the employer's project manager notified the contractors that they intended to deduct the vast majority of the sum otherwise awarded by the adjudicator by reference to their cross-claim for liquidated damages for delay. The employer paid the difference and the contractor issued proceedings for the sum that had been deducted. His Honour Judge Hicks QC said that he was quite clear that s111(1) excluded the right to deduct money in exercise of a claim to set-off in the absence of an effective notice of intention to withhold payment. He concluded that the words 'may not withhold payment' are ample in which to have the effect of excluding set-offs and there was no reason why they should not mean what they say.

2.137 This point has been reiterated on a number of occasions. HHJ Gilliland QC came to the same conclusion in *Millers Specialist Joinery*.[135] HHJ Seymour QC also

---

[133] See paragraphs 19.20–19.21 below.
[134] [2000] BLR 187.
[135] [2001] CILL 1770–1773.

Statutory Adjudication

decided the point in the same way in both *Solland International Ltd v Daraydan Holdings Ltd*[136] and in *Harwood Construction Ltd v Lantrode Ltd*.[137] In the latter case, the Judge said that: 'if a set-off was not excluded by section 111 it is difficult to see how the scheme has any practical value'.

Nature and Timing of Withholding Notice

2.138 In order to comply with s111, a withholding notice must be in writing. In *Strathmore Building Services Ltd v Colin Scott Greig (Trading as Hestia Far Side Design)*[138] Lord Hamilton in the Court of Session said that, although the words 'in writing' are not expressly used in s111, it was unmistakable that writing in some form was required. A telephone message, even one referring to a particular letter of earlier date, will not, therefore, suffice.

2.139 An effective withholding notice cannot be provided prior to the making of the relevant application for payment. In *Strathmore Building Services Ltd*, it was submitted that, whilst s111(2) provided that a notice must be given not later than a particular time, it did not prohibit a valid notice from being served at any earlier time, even before the relevant application for payment. Lord Hamilton rejected that submission. He said that the purpose of s111 was to provide a statutory mechanism on compliance with which (but only on compliance with which) a party otherwise due to make a payment may withhold such payment. He said it clearly envisaged a notice being a considered response to the application for payment, in which response it was specified how much of the sum applied for it was proposed to withhold, and the ground or grounds for withholding such an amount. He concluded that such a response could not effectually be made prior to receipt of the application for payment itself.

2.140 Clearly, if a withholding notice was not issued the requisite time before the final date for payment, it was ineffective: see *VHE v RBSTB*;[139] and a number of other cases that reached the same conclusion.[140] But, on the unusual facts of *Shimizu Europe Ltd v LBJ Fabrications Ltd*[141] HHJ Kirkham was able to distinguish these cases and find that a much later withholding notice was valid. The reason was that, in his decision, the adjudicator decided that Shimizu must pay LBJ a particular sum not later than 28 days after LBJ had delivered a VAT invoice. On 21 February 2003, LBJ, who accepted that payment did not become due until after delivery by

---

[136] [2002] EWHC 220 (TCC).
[137] Unreported, 24.11.00.
[138] [2001] 17 Const LJ 72.
[139] [2000] BLR 187.
[140] See, for example, *Ferson Contractors Ltd v Levolux* [2002] EWCA Civ 11; *The Construction Centre Group Ltd v Highland Council* [2002] BLR 476; and *Bovis Lend Lease Ltd v Triangle Development Ltd* [2003] BLR 31.
[141] [2003] BLR 381.

them of a VAT invoice, submitted an invoice for the awarded sum. Four days later, on 25 February 2003, Shimizu gave notice of their intention to withhold payment on the grounds of set-off. The Judge concluded that, unlike the circumstances in *VHE*, Shimizu had served a valid withholding notice after the decision but before the final date for payment. She concluded that Shimizu had a statutory right to withhold (provided that the correct steps were taken) including the giving of an effective withholding notice no later than the prescribed period before the final date for payment. Thus *Shimizu* was not a case of a contractual provision overriding the effect of an adjudicator's decision. In that case Shimizu were exercising a right given to them by the Act to withhold against a sum which an adjudicator had decided would, in the future, become due. On the basis of the adjudicator's decision, there remained 28 days after the provision of the invoice in which a withholding notice could be served. Since it was served in that time, Shimizu were entitled to rely on it.

The courts will take a commonsense, practical view of the contents of a withholding notice and will not adopt an unnecessarily restrictive interpretation of such a notice. A good example of this is the decision of HHJ Kirkham in *Thomas Vale Construction Plc v Brookside Syston Ltd*[142] in which the claimant, TVC, sought a declaration that the withholding notice was invalid. The Judge went through the various criticisms, and rejected them one by one, describing them as 'artificial and contrived'. It is thought that, provided that the notice makes tolerably clear what is being withheld and why, the court will not strive to intervene or endeavour to find reasons that would render such a notice invalid or ineffective. **2.141**

Relationship with Other Terms

Because the provisions of the Act at sections 109–111 must apply to all construction contracts, there can sometimes be difficulties in correlating the provisions of those sections with the particular contract terms themselves. Of course, if a contract clause falls outside the terms of sections 110 and 111, then it is the Act that must prevail. An example of these difficulties arose starkly in *Melville Dundas Ltd (in receivership) v George Wimpey UK Ltd*,[143] the only adjudication case thus far to go to the House of Lords. There the contractors sought almost £400,000 against the employers, despite the fact that, by the time they commenced their proceedings, they were in receivership. The final date for payment of the sum due was 16 May 2003. No withholding notice was served: the final date for such a notice would have been 11 May. Administrative receivers of the contractors were appointed on 22 May, and the employer determined the contractors' employment **2.142**

---

[142] [2006] EWHC 3637 (TCC).
[143] Outer House of the Court of Session: [2005] SLT 24. House of Lords: [2007] UKHL 18; [2007] 1 WLR 1136.

under the contract on 30 May. The employer relied on clause 27.6.5.1 of the JCT Standard Form of building contract which provided, subject to certain provisos, that the provisions of the contract which required any further payment to the contractors 'shall not apply'. The contractors argued that this clause was, in effect, providing for a scheme for withholding payment but that, since no withholding notice in accordance with s111 had been given, the clause was not in accordance with the 1996 Act, and the employers could not withhold the payment in question. The contractors argued that the clause of the contract dealing with the position on termination had to be read to avoid conflict with s111. In the Outer House of the Court of Session, Lord Clarke concluded that s111 did not subvert the contractual arrangement. The clause dealing with termination was an entirely separate mechanism and that sections 109-111, being concerned with cash flow, were not intended to apply in such circumstances. The Judge also held that, by reference to s110(1), the parties had agreed that the original date for payment of sums due under the contract could be altered in the event of the contract being determined so that 'the final date for payment' of the sum in question had not yet arrived.

2.143 His decision was reversed by the Inner House, but reinstated by the House of Lords, by a majority of 3:2, on slightly different grounds. Lord Hoffmann concluded that, on the facts of that case, there were two particular factors which led him to conclude that the clause in question fell within the scope of sections 110 and 111 of the 1996 Act: the insolvency of the contractors, which meant that any payment by the employer might not be recovered subsequently, and the fact that it was impossible for the employers to have issued a withholding notice prior to 16th May, because the receivership had not occurred at that date. As to the importance of the insolvency, he said at paragraph 13:

> A provision such as clause 27.6.5.1, which gives the employer a limited right to retain funds by way of security for his cross-claims, seems to me a reasonable compromise between discouraging employers from retaining interim payments against the possibility that a contractor who is performing the contract might become insolvent at some future date (which may well be self-fulfilling) and allowing the interim payments system to be used for a purpose for which it was never intended, namely to improve the position of an insolvent contractor's secured or unsecured creditors against the employer.

2.144 As to the impossibility point, Lord Hoffmann said at paragraph 20:

> In the case of clause 27.6.5.1 the contractor will have been given notice of why the payment is being withheld because he will have received the notice of determination. But the retrospective operation of the clause means that he will not have received it within the time stipulated in the statute. It seems to me, however, that it would be absurd to impute to Parliament an intention to nullify clauses like 27.6.5.1, not by express provision in the statute, but by the device of providing a notice of

requirement with which the employer can never comply. Section 111(1) must be construed in a way which is compatible with the operation of clause 27.6.5.1.

And at paragraph 22 he reiterated that:

> The problem arises because I very much doubt whether Parliament, in enacting section 111(1), took into account that parties would enter into contracts under which the ground for withholding a payment might arise *after* the final date for payment. One cannot therefore find an answer in a close examination of the language of the section. I would prefer simply to lex non cogit ad impossibilia and that on this ground section 111(1) should be construed as not applying to a lawful ground for withholding payment of which it was in the nature of things not possible for notice to have been given within the statutory time frame. That may not be particularly elegant, but the alternative is to hold that the parties' substantive freedom of contract has been indirectly curtailed by a mere piece of machinery, the operation of which would serve no practical purpose. This I find even less attractive.

2.145 The two dissenting speeches were given by Lord Mance and Lord Neuberger of Abbotsbury. At paragraph 77 Lord Neuberger said this:

> In addition, it seems to me that it would cut across the purpose of section 111(1) if what appeared to be a final date for payment with its concomitant prohibition on refusal to pay, could somehow be retrospectively vitiated simply because the contract has been brought to an end. If, as I see it, the purpose of sections 110 and 111 is to assist the cash flow for contractors and subcontractors, then it seems to me that it would be inconsistent with the way in which section 111 is expressed and also with its purpose, if it ceased effectively to be effective on the determination of the contract, at least in a case such as this, where the determination occurs after the final date for payment has passed.

There are a number of commentators who consider that this approach is more consistent with the underlying purpose of the 1996 Act. It was not, however, the view of the majority.

2.146 Thus, under the JCT Standard Form (and the other forms with similar terms), it seems clear that the insolvency of the contractor will operate to prevent further payments, even if those payments were due under the contract at the time of the insolvency or the appointment of administrators. The absence of a withholding notice will be no bar to the employer withholding further payments if it was impossible for a notice specifying the insolvency/administration, and the consequential determination, to be served in time. However, the difficulty with the majority view in *Melville Dundas* is the possible extent of its effect in cases of determination; on one view, taken to its logical conclusion, a clause like 27.6.5.1 could operate to allow an employer who had not paid sums due under the contract, and who had not served any withholding notices, subsequently to determine that contract, and rely on the clause to justify a position that no further money was payable. The DTI were sufficiently troubled about the potential uncertainties introduced by the decision to identify their concerns in the Report for the 2nd Consultation on the 1996 Act, and to suggest that the rule in *Melville Dundas* was—or certainly should be—limited to circumstances of bankruptcy and liquidation.[144]

2.147 At present, the only case in which the effect of the decision in *Melville Dundas* has been considered is *Pierce Design International Limited v Mark Johnston and Another*.[145] In that case, sums were due to the contractors and not paid. There had been no withholding notices. Subsequently, there were disputes about defects and delay, and the employers determined the contract. They relied on clause 27.6.5.1 as a defence to the claim for the sums due, and relied on the approach in *Melville Dundas*. The contractor argued that, in the absence of the contractor's insolvency or any impossibility in serving withholding notices, the clause could not operate to prevent the contractor from enforcing his entitlement to the interim payments that were due: if it did, it fell foul of s111. This argument was rejected by the TCC Judge, who pointed out that the House of Lords had decided that the clause complied with the Act, and it could not therefore be argued to the contrary. However, he went on to hold that the proviso to the clause, that it could not be used to prevent the enforcement of amounts which the employer 'has unreasonably not paid . . . and which have accrued 28 days or more before the date of determination of the employment of the contractor . . .' (which proviso had not been relevant on the facts in *Melville Dundas*), took effect in circumstances where there had been no withholding notices in respect of the sums which had fallen due months before the determination. He concluded that, in such circumstances, the contractors were entitled to recover those sums by way of summary judgment.

Stay For Arbitration

2.148 It is sometimes argued by the payer seeking to avoid the consequences of an unfavourable adjudicator's decision that the action to enforce that decision should be stayed for arbitration because there is a dispute as to whether the sum claimed is due. In the ordinary case, such an argument could not succeed. The whole purpose of the Act is to ensure that the decision is binding until it is challenged in arbitration or in court. Accordingly, in the ordinary case, the sum awarded by an adjudicator must be paid by the paying party and he cannot seek to avoid that result by staying the enforcement proceedings for arbitration.

2.149 In *David McLean Housing Contractors Ltd v Swansea Housing Association Ltd*[146] the claimant contractors made a claim for a variety of matters including loss and expense and an extension of time. Once the adjudicator had reached his decision,

---

[144] See paragraphs 19.33–19.35 below.
[145] [2007] EWHC 1691 (TCC).
[146] [2002] BLR 125.

the employer issued a certificate in accordance with that decision but, on the same day, notified the contractors that their claim for liquidated and ascertained damages would be deducted from the payment due. The contractors sought summary judgment on the sums found due to them by the adjudicator and the defendant counterclaimed for liquidated damages. One of the arguments was in relation to the contractors' application that the employer's counterclaim for liquidated damages should be stayed for arbitration. HHJ LLoyd QC dismissed that application on the grounds that the actions taken by the contractors to invoke the assistance of the court to enforce the adjudicator's decision, which were intimately connected with the subject matter of the counterclaim, and to have the counterclaim struck out, constituted steps in the action. He concluded that they were inconsistent with the right to have a dispute arbitrated and had to be regarded as steps in the proceedings. Thus he dismissed the application for a stay.

2.150 There was a different result in *Collins (Contractors) Ltd v Baltic Quay Management (1994) Ltd*.[147] In that case the contract was in the JCT minor works form. The employer failed to pay on interim certificate 5, by which time practical completion had been achieved. The contractors purported to determine the contract and at the same time wrote a letter enclosing their final account. The employer did not pay either the sum due under certificate 5 or the sums claimed in the final account, but their solicitors maintained that the dispute had to be resolved by adjudication or arbitration. However, when the contractors started proceedings, it was in the courts. The claim included the assertion that s111 applied to the contract and that no withholding notice had been served. The employer sought a stay of the proceedings under section 9 of the Arbitration Act and the Judge at first instance granted the stay. The contractors appealed. In the Court of Appeal, the contractors argued that the effect of s111 was that where, as here, a notice of intention to withhold payment had not been given by an employer, the employer was not entitled to withhold payment and the contractors were accordingly entitled to judgment in the amount wrongfully withheld. The Court of Appeal rejected that submission, finding that the arbitration clause was in very wide terms and that, if there was a dispute or difference, the court was obliged to grant a stay. Clarke LJ (as he then was) said that, assuming that the employer had no defence to the claim under certificate 5, there was nothing in s111 to deprive the employer of his right to a stay. He said that s111 was concerned only with the substantive rights of the parties and was not concerned with the question whether the claim for the monies wrongfully withheld should be determined by the court or by an arbitrator.[148]

---

[147] [2004] EWCA Civ 1757.
[148] The Court of Appeal followed the approach in *Hayter v Nelson* [1990] 2 Lloyd's Rep 265 and *The Halki* [1998] 1 WLR 726 to the effect that, even if one party to arbitration agreement claims that there is no dispute because he is entitled to the sum sought, the matter still has to go to arbitration because there is still 'a dispute'.

2.151 Of course, what went wrong in *Collins* was that the contractors failed to pursue their claims in adjudication. On the facts of the case, it would appear that the employer had no defence to the claim based on certificate 5 and that therefore the adjudicator would have been bound to award the contractors the sum due on that certificate in any event. If the employers still failed to pay, the contractors could then have commenced enforcement proceedings in the TCC, which could not have been defeated by an application for a stay.

Stay For Adjudication

2.152 On a slightly different, but related point, the court can sometimes be asked to stay existing court or arbitration proceedings, in order to allow an adjudication to take place. The general position appears to be that, if there is a binding adjudication agreement between the parties, it will be for the party resisting the stay to show why a stay should not be granted. This point is dealt with in detail in paragraphs 14.30–14.36 below.

Sections 112–115

2.153 These miscellaneous provisions of the 1996 Act provide as follows:

> 112–(1) Where a sum due under a construction contract is not paid in full by the final date for payment and no effective notice to withhold payment has been given, the person to whom the sum is due has the right (without prejudice to any other right or remedy) to suspend performance of his obligations under the contract to the party by whom payment ought to have been made ("the party in default").
>
> (2) The right may not be exercised without first giving to the party in default at least seven day's notice of intention to suspend performance stating the ground or grounds on which it is intended to suspend performance.
>
> (3) The right to suspend performance ceases when the party in default makes payment in full of the amount due.
>
> (4) Any period during which performance is suspended in pursuance of the right conferred by this section shall be disregarded in computing for the purposes of any contractual time limit the time taken, by the party exercising the right or by a third party, to complete any work directly or indirectly affected by the exercise of the right.
>
> Where the contractual time limit is set by reference to a date rather than a period, the date shall be adjusted accordingly.
>
> 113–(1) A provision making payment under a construction contract conditional on the payer receiving payment from a third person is ineffective, unless that third person, or any other person payment by whom is under the contract (directly or indirectly) a condition of payment by that third person, is insolvent.
>
> [Sub-sections (2), (3) and (4) are concerned with the test for insolvency for a company, a partnership and an individual.]

114–(1) The Minister shall by Regulations make a scheme ("the Scheme for Construction Contracts") containing provision about the matters referred to in the preceding provisions of this Part.

(2) Before making any Regulations under this section the Minister shall consult such persons as he thinks fit.

(3) In this section "the Minister" means—

(a) for England and Wales, the Secretary of State, and

(b) for Scotland, the Lord Advocate.

(4) Where any provisions of the Scheme for Construction Contracts apply by virtue of this Part in default of contractual provision agreed by the parties, they have effect as implied terms of the contract concerned.

(5) Regulations under this section shall not be made unless a draft of them has been approved by resolution of each House of Parliament.

115–(1) The parties are free to agree on the manner of service of any notice or other document required or authorised to be served in pursuance of the construction contract or for any of the purposes of this Part.

(2) If or to the extent that there is no such agreement the following provisions apply.

(3) A notice or other document may be served on a person by any effective means.

(4) If a notice or other document is addressed, pre-paid and delivered by post—

(a) to the addressee's last known principal residence or, if he is or has been carrying on a trade, professional business, his last known principal business address, or

(b) where the addressee is a body corporate, to the body's registered or principal office,

it shall be treated as effectively served.

(5) This section does not apply to the service of documents for the purposes of legal proceedings, for which provision is made by rules of the court.

(6) References in this part to a notice or other document include any form of communication in writing and references to service shall be construed accordingly.

Section 112: Suspension of Work

At common law, the position is that, if an employer fails to pay one instalment or stage payment in accordance with the contract, it is a question in each case whether such failure amounts to a repudiation of the contract. Generally, the courts have held that failure to pay one instalment out of many due under the terms of a contract is not ordinarily sufficient to amount to a repudiation of the contract.[149] In addition, the courts have said that a failure to pay a stage payment is less likely to amount to repudiation if the failure occurs towards the end of the contract.[150]

2.154

---

[149] See *Mersey Steel & Iron Co Ltd v Naylor* [1884] 9 App Cas 434, HL; *Decro-Wall International S.A. v Practitioners in Marketing* [1971] 1 WLR 361, CA; *Lakshmijit v Faiz Sherani* [1974] AC 605, PC; and *Afovos Shipping v Pagnan* [1983] 1 WLR 195, HL.

[150] *Cornwall v Henson* [1900] 2 Ch 298, CA.

2.155 Thus, the principal purpose of s112 was to allow the contractor who had not been paid in accordance with the contract the right to suspend work until payment was made, but avoiding any question of repudiation of the contract itself. This provides a neat solution to the 'all-or-nothing' arguments that arise if a contractor, who has not been paid a stage or instalment, walks off site.

2.156 It is important, however, to note that s112(2) makes any such suspension of work conditional upon the provision by the contractor to the employer of a notice of intention to suspend performance. In *Palmers Ltd v ABB Power Construction Ltd*[151] HHJ Lloyd QC stressed the importance of the notification provisions and said that the statutory right to suspend must be proceeded by such a notice. In that case, there was a dispute about the validity of the suspension notice. The Judge said that he would not determine such issues, leaving them instead to the adjudicator, on the basis that 'the dispute as to whether Palmers had complied with the statutory precondition to a lawful suspension of work will fall within the jurisdiction of the adjudicator when appointed and it is more appropriate for Palmers, in the first instance, to have recourse to that dispute resolution procedure'.

2.157 There are few reported instances of contractors suspending work in the way envisaged by s112. There are two reasons for this. One is the inherent caution that all contractors have about taking such a potentially radical step. Even though the Act encourages the contractor to suspend work due to non-payment, the contractor is acutely aware that some sort of procedural error—the failure to serve a notice for example—might lead to allegations that he wrongfully repudiated the contract. The other is the sheer inconvenience, disruption and cost of suspending work, only for the employer belatedly to pay up, so that re-mobilisation then has to take place. The DTI 2nd Consultation Report suggests ways in which this second concern might be addressed,[152] but it is thought that such changes are unlikely to lead to a major increase in temporary suspensions of work.

Section 113: 'Pay-When-Paid' Clauses

2.158 During the late 1980's and the early 1990's, 'pay-when-paid' clauses became common in construction and engineering contracts and sub-contracts. They were a way in which, in particular, the main contractor passed down the contractual chain the risk that, during the currency of the project, the employer might no longer be in a position to meet its obligations when they fell due. This was, on one view, grotesquely unfair because, although the main contractor was often in a position to carry out a financial check on the employer and, if concerned, able to obtain bonds and other financial security, the sub-contractors down the

---

[151] [1999] BLR 426.
[152] See paragraphs 19.28–19.30 below.

contractual chain could do neither. They faced a stark choice: carry out the work and risk not getting paid for reasons which had nothing to do with either them or their direct employers, or lose the contract. The courts endeavoured to provide such assistance as they could in circumstances where the employer had gone into liquidation with the sub-contractors having not been paid and the main contractor arguing that the 'pay-when-paid' provision provided it with a complete defence. One common argument was the suggestion that the 'pay-when-paid' provisions only applied during the currency of the contract and, once the contract had come to an end, the payment of the sub-contractor was no longer dependent on whether or not the main contractor had itself been paid.

2.159 The difficulty with this approach was that it was very often a contrived attempt to provide the sub-contractor with a remedy in a situation where the sub-contractor had all the merits, but where the clause of the contract that the sub-contractor had signed did, on its face, provide a complete defence. As a result of these difficulties and concerns, the Latham Report came to the unequivocal conclusion that 'pay-when-paid' clauses should be prohibited. However, the 1996 Act was not quite so clear cut. It is true that s113(1) made ineffective any provision in a construction contract that made payment conditional on the payer receiving payment from a third party. However, that wide provision was then subject to a potentially wide exception, namely that the provision was not ineffective if the third person who was making the original payment was insolvent. This might be regarded as a rather significant exception, given that the principal problem with 'pay-when-paid' clauses was that they were triggered, not by a simple refusal to pay by the employer up the contractual chain, but because that employer had gone into receivership or liquidation. In other words, the principal problem identified in the Latham Report, of sub-contractors going unpaid because of financial events about which they could do nothing, remained a risk enshrined in the exception to s113(1).

2.160 It is interesting to record, however, that (with one exception, addressed below) s113 has not generated any reported cases. It would appear that most parties within the construction industry are operating on the basis that the 1996 Act outlaws 'pay-when-paid' provisions and that, as a result, no such provisions are being drafted or included in the contracts that are actually being let. Thus it appears that the Latham Report has had the desired effect, and has, in practice, outlawed 'pay-when-paid' provisions, even though, for the reasons set out above, it might be thought that this has happened in a rather roundabout way.

2.161 The exception referred to above is the case of *Durabella Ltd v J Jarvis & Sons Ltd*.[153] The judgment of HHJ Lloyd QC needs to be treated carefully because, following the late settlement of the case, he only delivered part of the full judgment which he

---

[153] [2001] 83 Con LR 145.

would otherwise have handed down. The Judge concluded that the contract contained a pay-when-paid clause. Durabella purported to attack the clause on the basis of the Unfair Contract Terms Act 1977. In developing this submission, it was suggested that s113 of the 1996 Act was relevant to the consideration of reasonableness. This submission was rejected by the Judge. This was mainly because, as he pointed out, the 1996 Act had been carefully drawn up to exempt particular construction operations, because certain sectors of the construction industry had been found to be already so well organised that no regulation of any of their contracts or sub-contracts (including the use of 'pay-when-paid' clauses) was needed. Thus the Judge said that it was difficult to conclude that, but for s113(1), the 'pay-when-paid' clause was perceived throughout the construction industry as unreasonable in itself. If it were then Parliament would have prohibited it throughout the industry; the absence of such an industry-wide prohibition strongly suggested that in some areas 'pay-when-paid' provisions were not only regarded as not unreasonable, but as a fair apportionment of some of the common risks of contracting. In addition, the Judge noted that s113(1) only made such a clause ineffective as regards financing the work, and did not affect its application in the event of insolvency. For all these reasons, the Judge declined to say that the 'pay-when-paid' provision under consideration, in so far as it was conditional on payment being received by Jarvis from another, was unreasonable in itself although, as he pointed out, particular circumstances might lead it to be unreasonable.

Section 114: The Scheme

2.162 S114 introduced The Scheme for Construction Contracts ('the Scheme'), a detailed series of provisions containing, in relatively simple terms, all the provisions in sections 109–113. S114(4) makes plain that, if the construction contract between the parties does not contain these or similar provisions, then, by default, the Scheme applies and has the effect of implied terms of the construction contract. The provisions of the Scheme, and the many authorities dealing with its provisions, are analysed in detail in Chapter 3 below. The Scheme itself is at Appendix C.

2.163 In *Griffin & Anor (t/a K&D Contractors) v Midas Homes Ltd*[154] HHJ Lloyd QC held that the adjudicator had the jurisdiction to make part of the decision that he did, but not the remaining part. There then arose a problem in relation to the apportionment of his fees. The Judge referred to the fact that the Scheme took effect as implied terms of the contract pursuant to s114(4). In those circumstances, the Judge concluded that, whilst the claimant was entitled to that proportion of the adjudicator's fees that related to the matter on which the adjudicator

---

[154] [2000] 78 Con LR 152.

had the jurisdiction to decide in the claimant's favour, the claimant had not been entitled to exercise its right to call for adjudication in respect of the other part of the decision and that, in such circumstances, the claimant had to pay the costs of that element of the adjudication. In *Pring & St Hill Ltd v CJ Hafner (t/a Southern Erectors)*[155] the TCC Judge was concerned with paragraph 8(2) of the Scheme which provided that an adjudicator could, with the consent of all parties, adjudicate at the same time on related disputes under different contracts. The Judge found that, pursuant to the mechanism at s114(4) of the 1996 Act, that paragraph took effect as a contractual term and therefore entitled the defendant to give (or withhold) its consent prior to the adjudication of its dispute by a particular adjudicator.

Section 115: Service of Documents

Section 115 is concerned with the service of documents in and for the purposes of adjudication. The section makes clear that, for the purposes of adjudication, the more formal provisions of the CPR relating to service of court documents do not apply. Thus, for example, effective service can be achieved by posting the document in question to the addressee's last known principal residence or principal business address. **2.164**

In practice, this can mean that an adjudication can take place with the responding party not even aware of it. However, in *M Rohde Construction v Nicholas Markham-David*[156] Jackson J allowed the defendant to set aside judgment in default, which judgment was itself based on the decision of an adjudicator. The claimant contended that the adjudication documents had been sent to the defendant's last known principal residence and that this constituted effective service under s115(4) of the 1996 Act. However, Jackson J was concerned that, on the evidence before him, the defendant could easily have been contacted at another address altogether and that there was a serious issue between the parties, namely whether the claimant had available during the adjudication a ready means of contacting the defendant, which the claimant chose neither to use nor to communicate to the adjudicator. Accordingly, Jackson J set aside the judgment obtained in default on the basis that there was a triable issue between the parties. He said that if it turned out that the claimant had taken a deliberate decision, which deprived the defendant of the opportunity to make representations in the adjudication, then he considered that this might be one of those rare and exceptional cases in which the court would decline to enforce an adjudicator's decision by reason of a breach of natural justice. **2.165**

---

[155] [2002] EWHC 1775 (TCC).
[156] [2006] EWHC 814 (TCC).

2.166 In *Cubitt Building & Interiors Ltd v Fleetglade Ltd*[157] the referring party took a number of points about its alleged failure to comply with the seven day period for the service of the referral notice. One of the arguments adopted was the suggestion that the Civil Procedure Rules were incorporated into the adjudication process. This would have meant that the service of a document by fax after 4 pm would lead to a deemed date for service on the following business day, which, on the facts of that case, would have meant that the seven day period had not been breached. The TCC Judge pointed out that s115 made no reference to the CPR, except at sub-section 115.5, which was concerned with the service of enforcement proceedings in the courts. He therefore said that s115 was inconsistent with the suggestion that the CPR should be incorporated wholesale into the adjudication process: if that was the intention, s115 would have said so. Although the Judge recognised that the CPR was a set of common sense, practical rules governing the service of court documents, and that there might be exceptional adjudications in which it might be appropriate to have regard to its terms, they were not generally incorporated into the adjudication process. Furthermore, as the Judge pointed out, it was the referring party, Cubitt, who had chosen to serve the particular document in question at 4.42 pm. If he acceded to their request that the CPR should apply, so that the deemed time for service of this document was the following day, then he would effectively be giving Cubitt relief from their own decision to serve the document at the time that they did. The Judge said he would be very reluctant to re-write history by arriving at a different date for the service of the original notice of adjudication.

2.167 The courts will endeavour to avoid a situation where a purely technical point about service is relied on to prevent the enforcement of the adjudicator's decision. In *Nageh v Richard Giddings*,[158] there had been an adjudicator's decision against the defendant, and a summary judgment enforcing that decision. The defendant tried unsuccessfully to set aside judgment on the grounds that he was unaware of either the adjudication or the court proceedings. However, the court found that his challenge had been raised many months after he became aware of them, and therefore much too late. In addition, in the absence of any evidence that the claimant had deliberately used the wrong address, or knew of some other effective address for the defendant which could have been utilised, the potential challenge based on *M Rohde* did not arise. The application to set aside the summary judgment was dismissed.

---

[157] [2006] EWHC 3413 (TCC).
[158] [2006] EWHC 3240 (TCC).

3

THE STATUTORY SCHEME

Introduction	3.01	Costs	3.81
Part I of the Scheme—Adjudication	3.12	Reasons	3.83
Notice of Adjudication	3.12	Effect of the Decision	3.85
The Appointment of the Adjudicator	3.16	Binding Until the Dispute is Finally Determined	3.86
The Referral Notice	3.26	Enforcement of Peremptory Orders	3.94
Referral Within 7 Days	3.29	Fees	3.95
More Than One Dispute	3.34	Part II of the Scheme—Payment	3.97
Resignation	3.39	Introduction	3.97
Objection	3.48	Entitlement to and Amount of Stage Payments	3.98
Revocation	3.50		
Powers of the Adjudicator	3.52	Dates for Payment	3.104
Acting Impartially	3.54	Final Date for Payment	3.108
Taking the Initiative	3.57	Payment Notices and Withholding Notices	3.111
Consideration of any Relevant Information	3.60		
Time Limits	3.66	Prohibition of 'Pay-When-Paid'	3.114
The Adjudicator's Decision	3.73		
Opening Up, Revising and Reviewing	3.74		
Interest	3.77		

'The essence of an adjudication is that it should be quick . . . as the Minister knows and as Clause 106 allows, that adjudication produces rough justice, but it is a rough justice which can be put right at a later stage.'

Lord Howie, Hansard, 22.4.06, column 985, proposing an alternative to the scheme then being proposed.

'Is this cheap and cheerful, or just quick and dirty?'

Lord Lucas, Hansard, 22.4.06, column 996, responding to an alternative proposal to the scheme as then formulated.

Introduction

3.01 As noted in Chapter 1, the Scheme as originally proposed attracted a large amount of criticism. Following consultation, the revised Scheme, which came into force on 1 May 1998, was regarded much more favourably. The Scheme, introduced by SI 1998 No 649, is set out in full at Appendix C.

3.02 The Scheme is designed as a fall-back position; if the construction contract in question does not contain the adjudication provisions set out in s108, or if it does not include the payment provisions set out in s109 of the 1996 Act, then the provisions of the Scheme apply as implied terms of the contract (s114(4)). Although many of the standard forms of construction and engineering contracts now contain specific adjudication and payment provisions which comply with the Act, so the parties do not need to have regard to the Scheme, there are many construction contracts, particularly for smaller works, which do not contain such provisions. In addition, there are instances of contract clauses which, although they have been drafted with the intention of meeting the provisions of the 1996 Act, fail to do so. Thus the provisions within the Scheme remain of significance.

3.03 In order to work out whether or not the adjudication and/or payment provisions of the Scheme apply, it is necessary to ask a number of related questions. The first question is to determine whether or not the contract under consideration is a construction contract within the meaning of s104. That in turn will depend on whether or not the work that is being carried out pursuant to the contract is a 'construction operation' within the meaning of s105(1). It will also be necessary to consider whether the operation in question is excluded by s105(2). Assuming that the contract in question is a construction contract, the second issue is whether that contract contains adjudication provisions of the kind set out in s108 and payment provisions as set out in ss109–111. If the contract contains such provisions then the Scheme is irrelevant. If, however, the contract does not contain the adjudication and payment provisions provided for by the 1996 Act, then the Scheme will come into effect as implied terms of contract.

3.04 An obvious issue arising out of the interrelationship between any given contract and the provisions of the Scheme was the extent to which the latter overrode the former. If, for example, the contract contained some of the payment provisions required by ss109–111 of the Act, but omitted others, does the Scheme apply in full, regardless of the express terms of the contract, or does the Scheme apply only to fill in the gaps within the contract itself?

This question was first raised in *C&B Scene Concept Design Ltd v Isobars Ltd*.[1] **3.05**
In that case, although Clause 30 of the JCT Standard Form of Building Contract with Contractor's Design required the parties to elect between two alternatives for interim payments, the parties had failed to select one of the two options. At first instance, the Recorder found that the whole of Clause 30, not just the provisions as to how and when the interim payments were to be made, fell away and were replaced wholesale by the Scheme. On appeal, the defendant who had made that submission was no longer represented. The claimant contended that the Recorder had been wrong to replace the entirety of Clause 30 with the Scheme, relying on the words in s110(3) which implied the Scheme 'if or to the extent that a contract' did not contain the relevant provision. However, because ultimately it did not affect the outcome of the appeal, Sir Murray Stuart Smith was content to assume, without deciding, that the Recorder had been right on that point.

The point also arose tangentially in *Ballast Plc v The Burrell Company (Construction* **3.06**
Management) Ltd.[2] In that case the adjudicator decided that he was unable to reach a decision. The Court of Session decided that this decision was itself a nullity and that it was unacceptable for the adjudicator to wash his hands of the dispute which had been referred to him and refuse to decide it. In arriving at his decision, Lord Reid concluded that the adjudicator was not exercising a jurisdiction created by statute, and that the adjudicator's approach would not be warranted if the adjudication procedure had been one expressly incorporated into the contract, since the adjudicator's powers and duties would then be created and defined by the contract. He went on to say that it was possible that an adjudication might be governed partly by express contract terms and partly by the Scheme, since the contract might comply only in part with the requirements of s108(1)(2)(4). This suggested that, in Lord Reid's opinion, the provisions of the Scheme would be implied into the contract only and to the extent that it was necessary so to do, in order to make good the gaps in the original contract framework.

The issue, as to whether the Scheme applied wholesale to a non-compliant con- **3.07**
tract, or only to the extent that it was necessary to fill the gaps, arose starkly in the Scottish case of *Hills Electrical & Mechanical Plc v Dawn Construction Ltd*.[3] In that case, the sub-contractors maintained that the contract between the parties failed to provide dates on which they should make applications for payment, so that they could be incorporated into the main contractor's application for payment under the main contract with the employer. Therefore, they said, the Scheme should apply instead. This was important to the sub-contractors because, although

---

[1] The decision of Mr Recorder Moxon Browne QC is reported at [2001] CILL 1781–1783. The decision of the Court of Appeal is reported at [2002] 1 BLR 93.
[2] [2001] BLR 529.
[3] [2004] SLT 477.

the terms of the contract did expressly provide for a final date of payment of any sums due under the contract, being 28 days after the day on which the sum fell due, the sub-contractor's argument, that the Scheme applied wholesale, meant that the 17 day provision in Part II, paragraph 8(2), of the Scheme would apply instead. This was crucial because the employer had gone into administration after the 17 day period had expired but before the expiry of the 28 days. Thus the main contractor would be liable to the sub-contractors if the 17 days, derived from the Scheme, applied as the final date for payment, but there would be no such liability if the 28 days in the contract was the applicable term. Lord Clarke had no difficulty in deciding against the sub-contractors, on the basis that the Scheme only applied to the extent that the express terms of the contract omitted particular requirements of the 1996 Act. He said:

> 18. I approach the question which was raised at the debate from the starting point that it is to be assumed, as a matter of statutory interpretation, that the legislature intended to innovate on parties' freedom of contract only to the extent that this was clearly provided for, either expressly or by clear implication by the terms of the legislation itself. It appears to me that that approach is expressly recognised in various parts of the legislation dealing with the payment provisions in construction contracts ... s114(4) provides that where any provision of the scheme does apply to a construction contract, in default of a contractual provision agreed by the parties, the effect is that the scheme's provision becomes an implied term of the contract in question. That sub-section begins with the words "where *any provisions* of the Scheme". The emphasised words, in my judgment, clearly envisage that it was not intended by the legislature that expressly agreed terms relating to the matters covered by the scheme were to be supplanted by the provisions of the scheme simply because of the fact that the parties had omitted to provide for one or other of the matters desiderated by the legislation or had failed to deal with it adequately, having regard to the statutory provisions.

3.08 However, this should not necessarily be regarded as the last word on the subject, as a result of two decisions of the TCC in London. In the first, *John Mowlem Ltd v Hydra-Tight Ltd*,[4] HHJ Toulmin CMG QC suggested that the extent to which a contractual mechanism failed to comply with the 1996 Act might ultimately be irrelevant because, if it failed to comply, then the entire machinery was tainted and fell by the wayside. In those circumstances it would be replaced by the provisions of the Scheme. The case is discussed in greater detail in paragraph 4.60 below.

3.09 As HHJ Havery QC pointed out in *Aveat Heating Ltd v Jerram Falkus Construction Ltd*,[5] although Judge Toulmin had merely indicated that this may be the answer to this issue, *Mowlem* had been taken as authority for this proposition in *Keating*

---

[4] [2002] 17 Const LJ 358.
[5] [2007] EWHC 131 (TCC).

on Construction Contracts (8th edn, Sweet and Maxwell, 2006), at paragraph 17.014. Judge Havery also observed that the text of the relevant paragraph was actually at odds with its footnote. He therefore considered the point afresh and concluded that the words of the 1996 Act were clear: either the parties agreed their own terms and conditions which complied with the requirements of the Act, or the provisions of the Scheme applied. He went on:

> It is true that the Act does not say that if the Scheme applies, the contractual adjudication provisions are void. But if they are not void, then the contract contains competing and to some extent mutually contradictory provisions. One could then make sense of the contract only if, in the case of every pair of mutually contradictory provisions, only one member of the pair were to be treated in any given case as prevailing over the other. I unhesitatingly follow Judge Toulmin in reaching the conclusion that that is not the intention of the legislation. The solution stated in the text of *Keating* is simpler. It is that the two sets of adjudication provisions, contractual and the Scheme, exist as alternative packages, only one of which (at the option of the party initiating the adjudication) applies in any given case.

For these reasons he concluded that the footnote in *Keating* was correct and that, if any part of the contractual mechanism did not comply with the 1996 Act, the Scheme applied wholesale.

3.10 Thus, for the present, the position remains unclear. There are two Scottish authorities which suggest that it is only those parts of the contractual mechanism which do not comply with the Scheme which require to be replaced, and that the other parts of the mechanism remain as before. On the other hand, there are two TCC decisions which suggest to the contrary, and that a 'piecemeal' result is a recipe for potential confusion and uncertainty. Those latter cases incline to the view that, if one part of the mechanism is non-compliant, then the mechanism must be replaced in its entirety. The learned editors of *Keating* also appear, for the reasons explained by Judge Havery, to support this view. It would seem that this is an important matter which will have to be resolved by an appellate court.[6]

3.11 The detailed provisions of the Scheme are divided into two parts. Part I is concerned with the detailed provisions as to adjudication. Part II is concerned with the provisions relating to payment, withholding notices and the like. The specific requirements under each Part of the Scheme are discussed below.

---

[6] This point is further considered at paragraph 3.97 below.

Part I of the Scheme—Adjudication

Notice of Adjudication

3.12 Paragraph 1 of Part 1 of the Scheme provides as follows:

1–(1) Any party to a construction contract (the "referring party") may give written notice (the "notice of adjudication") of his intention to refer any dispute arising under the contract to adjudication.

(2) The notice of adjudication should be given to every other party to the contract.

(3) The notice of adjudication shall set out briefly—
   (a) the nature and a brief description of the dispute and of the parties involved,
   (b) details of where and when the dispute has arisen,
   (c) the nature of the redress which is sought, and
   (d) the names and addresses of the parties to the contract (including, where appropriate, the addresses which the parties have specified for the giving of notices).

3.13 It is impossible to over-emphasise the importance of the notice of adjudication. It is the cornerstone of both the adjudicator's jurisdiction and the scope and limit of the referring party's claim in the adjudication.[7] Although the significance of the notice of adjudication is dealt with in greater detail at paragraphs 7.35–7.45 below, it is important to note at this stage that the notice must identify carefully the dispute and the nature of the redress sought. Numerous problems in adjudication and adjudication enforcement have arisen out of the referring party's failure to provide an adequate notice of adjudication, and his subsequent attempts to make good that omission in the referral notice (Part 1, paragraph 7) and other documents served in the adjudication. The courts have made it plain that this is not a legitimate approach.

3.14 In *Mecright Ltd v TA Morris Developments Ltd*[8] Morris had commenced adjudication proceedings against Mecright. In Morris' notice of adjudication, they sought first a declaration that the sub-contract had been cancelled by them in accordance with the sub-contract and, secondly, recovery of damages arising out of the cancelled sub-contract. In their response document, Mecright sought, amongst other things, the value of work at the time that they were instructed to cease work, and the cost to them of what they said was the wrongful repudiation by Morris. The adjudicator concluded that Morris had indeed repudiated the sub-contract and awarded the responding party monies both for works carried out under the sub-contract and in consequence of the repudiation. Morris contended that the

---

[7] See, for example, *Ken Griffin v Midas Homes Ltd* [2001] 78 Con LR 152 *and Jerome Engineering v Lloyd Morris* [2002] CILL1827.

[8] Unreported, 22.6.01, a decision of HHJ Seymour QC in the TCC in London.

adjudicator did not have the jurisdiction to arrive at such a decision and relied on the proposition that the jurisdiction of the adjudicator derived from the terms of the notice of adjudication set out in paragraph 1 of Part 1 of the Scheme. Mecright argued that, because paragraph 20 of Part 1 of the Scheme allowed the adjudicator to take into account 'any other matters which the parties to the dispute agree should be within the scope of the adjudication or which are matters under the contract which he considers are necessarily connected with the dispute', the adjudicator was entitled to reach the decision he did.

3.15 HHJ Seymour QC said:

> Grammatically, the language used suggests that what the adjudicator may do is to take these other matters into account in determining the dispute or disputes otherwise referred to him for decision. However, it seems to me that, upon proper construction, what the words which I have quoted mean is that, first, the adjudicator can decide any matters which the parties to the adjudication agree after all the initial notice of adjudication should be within the scope of the adjudication but were not originally; and second, that he can decide any matter arising under the relevant contract which he considers is necessarily connected with the dispute. As what is contemplated in relation to the first of these alternatives is that something which was not originally within the scope of the adjudication is brought within it by the agreement of the parties and that the adjudicator is entitled, but not bound, to decide such matters, it must follow that the matters are 'other disputes'. If that is correct, again, in my judgment, it follows that the matters under the contract which he considers are necessarily connected with the dispute mentioned next in paragraph 20 are other disputes which are aspects of or the resolution of which is necessary to resolve the dispute or disputes the subject of the notice of adjudication.

Judge Seymour said that the essence of the dispute described in the notice was whether, in the circumstances, Morris had been entitled to determine its contract with Mecright and, if so, what sum Morris was entitled to as a consequence. He therefore accepted Morris' submission that a dispute as to how much Mecright was entitled to be paid in respect of the execution of the sub-contract works, or as a result of the wrongful determination of its contract by Morris, was not, on a proper construction of the notice of adjudication, included within the dispute that was referred by that notice. He therefore agreed with the submission that the adjudicator did not have the jurisdiction to reach his decision.

The Appointment of the Adjudicator

3.16 Paragraphs 2–6 inclusive of Part I of the Scheme provide as follows:

> 2–(1) Following the giving of a notice of adjudication and subject to any agreement between the parties to the dispute as to who shall act as adjudicator—
>
> (a) the referring party shall request the person (if any) specified in the contract to act as adjudicator, or

(b) if no person is named in the contract or the person named has already indicated that he is unwilling or unable to act, and the contract provides for a specified nominating body to select a person, the referring party shall request the nominating body named in the contract to select a person to act as adjudicator, or

(c) where neither paragraph (a) nor (b) above applies, or where the person referred to in (a) had already indicated that he is unwilling or unable to act and (b) does not apply, the referring party shall request an adjudicator nominating body to select a person to act as adjudicator.

(2) A person requested to act as adjudicator in accordance with the provisions of paragraph (1) shall indicate whether or not he is willing to act within two days of receiving the request.

(3) In this paragraph, and in paragraphs (5) and (6) below, an "adjudicator nominating body" shall mean a body (not being a natural person and not being a party to the dispute) which holds itself out publicly as a body which will select an adjudicator when requested to do so by a referring party.

3. The request referred to in paragraphs 2, 5 and 6 shall be accompanied by a copy of the notice of adjudication.

4. Any person requested or selected to act as adjudicator in accordance with paragraphs 2, 5 or 6 shall be a natural person acting in his personal capacity. A person requested or selected to act as an adjudicator shall not be an employee of any of the parties to the dispute and shall declare any interest, financial or otherwise, in any matter relating to the dispute.

5–(1) The nominating body referred to in paragraphs 2(1)(b) and 6(1)(b) or the adjudicator nominating body referred to in paragraphs 2(1)(c), 5(2)(b) and 6(1)(c) must communicate the selection of an adjudicator to the referring party within five days of receiving a request to do so.

(2) Where the nominating body or the adjudicator nominating body fails to comply with paragraph (1), the referring party may—

(a) agree with the other party to the dispute to request a specified person to act as adjudicator, or

(b) request any other adjudicator nominating body to select a person to act as adjudicator.

(3) The person requested to act as adjudicator in accordance with the provisions of paragraphs (1) or (2) shall indicate whether or not he is willing to act within two days of receiving the request.

6–(1) Where an adjudicator who is named in the contract indicates to the parties that he is unable or unwilling to act, or where he fails to respond in accordance with paragraph 2(2), the referring party may—

(a) request another person (if any) specified in the contract to act as adjudicator, or

(b) request the nominating body (if any) referred to in the contract to select a person to act as adjudicator, or

(c) request any other adjudicator nominating body to select a person to act as adjudicator.

(2) The person requested to act in accordance with the provisions of paragraph (1) shall indicate whether or not he is willing to act within two days of receiving the request.

The Statutory Scheme

3.17 At first sight, these provisions relating to the appointment of an adjudicator appear overly complex. However, given the range of points that have been taken in some of the reported cases as to the appointment of the adjudicator, it is perhaps sensible that they strive to cover every eventuality. There is no doubt that the best course for the parties to a construction contract to adopt is to name the adjudicator in the contract (paragraph 2(1)(a)), with a specified nominating body also identified in the contract in case the named adjudicator is unable or unwilling to act. At the very least, it is sensible for the parties to identify a specified nominating body in the contract. This avoids the sort of unseemly scramble, which has been known, whereby each party is keen to be the referring party in the adjudication, and they head off to two different nominating bodies to try and get an adjudicator appointed first.

3.18 Pursuant to paragraph 2(2) a person requested to act as adjudicator (either because he is named in the contract or because he has been selected by an adjudicator nominating body) must indicate within two days of receiving the request whether or not he is willing to act. Paragraph 4 makes clear that any such adjudicator cannot be an employee of any of the parties and must declare any financial or other interest that he may have in any matter relating to the dispute.

3.19 Under paragraph 5 of Part 1 of the Scheme, the nominating body must communicate the selection of an adjudicator to the referring party within five days of receiving the request. It is extremely important that the nominating body complies with (or even endeavours to improve upon) this period, because the referring party only has seven days from the date of the notice of adjudication to provide the referral notice (as required by paragraph 7(1) of the Scheme). If they fail to comply with that timescale, the referring party may go elsewhere, or agree the appointment of a particular person with the other side. Paragraph 6 is designed to deal with the position where the adjudicator named in a contract is unable or unwilling to act, or does not respond within two days. In those circumstances the referring party can go either to another person or the nominating body set out in the contract or request any other nominating body to select an adjudicator.

3.20 There have been a number of cases where an adjudicator has been named in the contract and, for whatever reason, he has been unable to act as adjudicator. In *AMEC Projects Ltd v Whitefriars City Estates Ltd*[9] HHJ Toulmin CMG QC was dealing with a contract where the person named in the contract was a Mr George Ashworth. This should have been a reference to a Mr Geoffrey Ashworth. The contract allowed the managing partner of Mr Ashworth's firm to select a replacement if he was unavailable to deal with a dispute that was referred to him. Mr Ashworth had died by the time that the dispute was referred. The referring party argued that there was no machinery under the contract for appointing an adjudicator as a result of the death

---

[9] [2004] EWHC 393 (TCC).

of Mr Ashworth, and that in consequence, pursuant to paragraph 2(1)(c), it could request an adjudicator nominating body to select a person to act as adjudicator. The referring party obtained an adjudicator nominated by the RIBA. The responding party argued that, because the terms of the contract specified that, if the individual named as the adjudicator was unavailable, either party could apply to the managing partner for a replacement, that is what should have happened and that the adjudicator appointed by the RIBA had no jurisdiction.

3.21 Judge Toulmin held that, because Mr Ashworth had died before the matter was referred, the contractual provisions did not apply; the reference to the managing partner was intended only to occur if, during an ongoing adjudication, the adjudicator 'dies or becomes ill or is unavailable for some other cause'. In consequence, the Judge concluded that the death of Mr Ashworth meant that the contract provisions were no longer workable and the Scheme applied instead. Thus the adjudicator had been rightly appointed in accordance with paragraph 2(1)(c) of Part 1 of the Scheme. This part of the judgment was upheld in the Court of Appeal.[10] Dyson LJ agreed that the provisions in the contract relating to the possibility of a reference to the managing partner or director could not apply before the person originally named had been appointed as the adjudicator.

3.22 Precisely the same approach to the nomination provisions had been adopted in two earlier cases. In *Watson Building Services Ltd v Harrison*[11] the Outer House (Lady Paton) was dealing with a dispute as to the incorporation of certain adjudication and other provisions into the contract between the parties which, so it was said by the responding party, meant that the adjudicator, appointed under the Scheme, had no jurisdiction. She concluded that, whatever clauses might or might not have been incorporated into the sub-contract, a set of adjudication provisions had not been incorporated. She therefore concluded that the provisions of the Scheme applied. This, in turn, meant that the adjudicator had been properly appointed and had the jurisdiction to deal with the dispute referred to him. Similarly, in *David McLean Housing Ltd v Swansea Housing Association Ltd*[12] there was a dispute over the appointment of an adjudicator, who was selected by the RICS in accordance with the Scheme. The defendant argued that, pursuant to the contract, the correct appointing body was the Chartered Institute of Arbitrators. HHJ Lloyd QC held that, on a proper construction of the contract documents, there was no provision to which the reference to the Chartered Institute of Arbitrators could attach. Accordingly, the contract did not contain a valid appointment mechanism and the Scheme applied. Thus the appointment of the adjudicator was in accordance with the implied terms of the contract.

---

[10] [2004] EWCA Civ 1418.
[11] [2001] SLT 846.
[12] [2002] BLR 125.

3.23 It is important that, if the person named in the contract is unwilling or unable to act as adjudicator, he must make that clear to all parties. In *IDE Contracting Ltd v RG Carter Cambridge Ltd*[13] the person named in the contract made it clear to the referring party that his other work commitments meant that he was unable to act. Thus the referring party's Notice of Adjudication informed the responding party that the Chartered Institute of Arbitrators would be requested to nominate an adjudicator and that the named person had declined to act. The responding party did not want an adjudicator selected at random and proposed various alternative adjudicators but that offer was not taken up. The Chartered Institute of Arbitrators named a Mr Smalley. The responding party therefore made clear that it was their case that Mr Smalley had no jurisdiction.

3.24 HHJ Havery QC had to consider the detailed provisions of paragraph 2(1)(b) of Part 1 of the Scheme. He said:

> 9. . . . What is intended, in my judgment, is that the notice of adjudication comes first. Then the referring party is to request the person specified in the contract to act as adjudicator, unless he has already indicated to the parties that he is unwilling or unable to act. The request must doubtless be in writing since it must be accompanied by a copy of the notice of adjudication. The person specified must indicate within two days whether or not he is willing to act. If he indicates that he is not, then provided that that indication is made to all parties the referring party may proceed under paragraph 6(1)(b) to request the nominating body to select a person to act as adjudicator. What happened here is that no request at all was made under paragraph 2(a). The procedure was bypassed. And it is in my judgment implicit in paragraph 2(b), as it is explicit in paragraph 6, that the unwillingness or inability of the specified person to act should be indicated to all parties.

In consequence, the Judge concluded that the referring party's failure to comply with these provisions deprived the adjudicator of jurisdiction.

3.25 Where an adjudicator resigns in the erroneous belief that the proceedings are fatally flawed, the adjudicator's inability to adjudicate on the dispute will be cured by a further referral, provided that the second referral occurs within the necessary time limits: see *Tracy Bennett v FMK Construction Ltd*.[14]

The Referral Notice

3.26 Paragraph 7 of Part 1 provides as follows:

> 7–(1) Where an adjudicator has been selected in accordance with paragraphs 2, 5 or 6, the referring party shall, not later than seven days from the date of the

---

[13] [2004] BLR 172.
[14] [2005] EWHC 1268 (TCC).

notice of adjudication, refer the dispute in writing (the "referral notice") to the adjudicator.

(2) The referral notice shall be accompanied by copies of, or relevant extracts from, the construction contract and such other documents as the referring party intends to rely upon.

(3) The referring party shall, at the same time as he sends to the adjudicator the documents referred to in paragraphs (1) and (2), send copies of those documents to every other party to the dispute.

3.27 The referral notice is the referring party's principal opportunity to set out in detail its claim or case. In larger adjudications, such a document is not unlike a detailed statement of claim, with appendices containing copies of the relevant extracts from the contract, and other documents which the referring party considers are important or helpful to its case. It is important that the referring party makes every effort to ensure that the referral notice is as full as possible. Not unreasonably, adjudicators, and responding parties, are unhappy when, following the production of the responding party's response to the referral notice, the referring party seeks permission from the adjudicator to put in a reply, which very often contains material which could and should have formed part of the referral notice.

3.28 Although it is important for the referring party to ensure that the referral notice is as clear and detailed as possible, it is important to ensure that, unless there is express agreement otherwise, the referral notice does not seek to enlarge the dispute that was the subject of the notice of adjudication. The following cases are relevant on this point:

(a) In *KNS Industrial Services (Birmingham) Ltd v Sindall Ltd*[15] HHJ Lloyd QC expressly warned that the further documents which came into existence following the notice of adjudication, such as the referral notice, 'do not cut down or, indeed, enlarge the dispute (unless they contain an agreement to do so)'.

(b) Precisely the same conclusion was reached by HHJ Seymour QC in *Mecright Ltd v TA Morris Developments Ltd*,[16] the case already referred to at paragraphs 3.14–3.15 above, where Mecright's cross-claims, which had not been identified in the notice of adjudication, were subsequently upheld by the adjudicator. The Judge declined to enforce the award because, he said, the adjudicator did not have the jurisdiction to decide claims that were not identified as part of the dispute set out in the notice of adjudication. Mecright had argued that the scope of the dispute referred to the adjudicator could be ascertained not

---

[15] [2001] 17 Const LJ 170.
[16] Unreported, 22.6.01, HHJ Seymour QC sitting at the TCC in London.

simply from the notice of adjudication but also from the referral notice and the response. Judge Seymour rejected that argument. He said:

> The basic scheme of adjudication, in accordance with the Scheme, is that what is referred is a single dispute. Paragraph 8 of Part 1 of the Scheme provides for an adjudicator, with the consent of all parties, to deal with more than one dispute at a time, although he is not bound to do so. That provision seems to me directed principally at an agreement made at the stage before adjudication procedure really gets underway for, as I have already pointed out, paragraph 20 seems to deal with the position if an agreement is made to expand the scope of an adjudication once it is in progress. Nevertheless, at whatever stage the consent or agreement of all parties is relevant, it seems to me that such consent or agreement must be express, and is not to be implied from conduct or in some other way. . . . While, as I have pointed out, my view and that of other Judges is that those who describe a dispute which they wish to refer to adjudication in vague terms have only themselves to blame if the scope of what has been referred appears to be wider than what they may have thought, it seems to me to be wrong in principle to expose those involved in an expeditious process such as adjudication to the requirement to take care to express themselves during the process in such a way that it cannot be said that, by words or conduct, they have unintentionally consented or agreed to some process other than that upon which they were initially engaged.

Referral Within 7 Days

3.29 Section 108(2)(b) of the 1996 Act provides that the contract 'shall provide a timetable with the object of securing the appointment of the adjudicator and referral of the dispute to him within 7 days of such notice'. Paragraph 7(1) of the Scheme is couched in stronger language: '. . . the referring party *shall*, not later than seven days from the date of the notice of adjudication, refer the dispute . . . to the adjudicator' (emphasis added).

3.30 The first point to note is that there is a debate as to whether the referral means the dispatch of the notice to the adjudicator, or his or her receipt of that notice.[17] In *Aveat Heating Ltd v Jerram Falkus Construction Ltd*,[18] HHJ Havery QC said that 'a thing is not referred to another unless that other receives it . . . the word is unambiguous. Referral takes place upon receipt of the notice by the adjudicator.' It is therefore prudent to assume that what matters is not the sending of the document but its receipt by the adjudicator.

3.31 The more important question concerns the language of paragraph 7(1) of the Scheme and, in particular, whether those words are directory or mandatory. The learned editor of *Emden's Construction Law* (Butterworths Law) at Section V

---

[17] See the discussion at paragraph 2.95 above.
[18] [2007] EWHC 131 (TCC).

at 87–92 suggests that the words are directory. However, in *Hart Investments Ltd v Fidler & Anor*[19] the TCC Judge reached a different conclusion. He said that, although his initial reaction was that it might be harsh to say that a delay of, say, one day in the provision of the referral notice rendered the adjudication a nullity, even if the objection was taken at the time, on a more detailed analysis, all kinds of difficult questions arose if the failure to comply with the time period was ignored. What if the delay was not one day, but one month? What if important events occurred during the period of any delay in the provision of a referral notice which put the responding party in a much worse position as against the referring party than it would have been if there had been no delay? If the words 'not later than 7 days' are to be qualified in some way, then how is such a qualification to be formulated, let alone assessed?

3.32 The Judge repeated the point made numerous times before, that the whole purpose of adjudication was that speed was given precedence over accuracy and that what mattered was a quick decision, not necessarily a correct one. If the timetable could be extended without consent, even at the beginning, let alone at the end of the relevant period, there was a great danger of uncertainty and of a watering-down of the critical importance of the timetable on which the entire adjudication process was based. He therefore found that the word 'shall' in the Scheme was mandatory and that the referring party had therefore to serve the referral notice on the adjudicator within seven days.

3.33 It should be noted that, as the Judge pointed out in *Hart*, if there was a delay in the provision of the referral notice, the responding party might well consent, expressly or by implication, to waive the irregularity. The important point in *Hart* was that there was no such waiver and the responding party immediately took the point as to delay. The referring party therefore had the opportunity to start again but he failed to take it, thereby taking the risk that, as turned out to be the case, the adjudicator's decision was a nullity.[20]

---

[19] [2006] EWHC 2857 (TCC); [2007] BLR 30.
[20] Clause 41A of the JCT Standard Form of Building Contract is in similar form to the Scheme and again requires that the party giving notice 'shall refer the dispute or difference to the Adjudicator within 7 days of the notice'. In *Cubitt Building & Interiors Ltd v Fleetglade Ltd* [2006] EWHC 3413 (TCC) the TCC Judge concluded that the word 'shall' was mandatory and was not merely a provision allowing the referring party to use his best endeavours to take those steps within the specified period. He said that the requirement was that those events shall happen within a certain timeframe and that therefore the provisions were mandatory. In reaching this conclusion he distinguished the decision of HHJ Thornton QC in *William Verry v North West London Communal Mikva* [2004] BLR 3008, which he said was a particular decision on its own facts.

More Than One Dispute

Paragraph 8 of Part I of the Scheme provides as follows: **3.34**

> 8–(1) The adjudicator may, with the consent of all the parties to those disputes, adjudicate at the same time on more than one dispute under the same contract.
>
> (2) The adjudicator may, with the consent of all the parties to those disputes, adjudicate at the same time on related disputes under different contracts, whether or not one or more of those parties is a party to those disputes.
>
> (3) All the parties in paragraphs (1) and (2) respectively may agree to extend the period within which the adjudicator may reach a decision in relation to all or any of these disputes.
>
> (4) Where an adjudicator ceases to act because a dispute is to be adjudicated on by another person in terms of this paragraph, that adjudicator's fees and expenses shall be determined in accordance with paragraph 25.

The intention of these provisions is to allow an adjudicator the ability to deal with more than one dispute at the same time, and to deal with the same or related disputes under different contracts, if the underlying subject matter is the same or similar. However, the key ingredient in these provisions is the consent of all parties. Although the two ways in which the scope of the decision-making process could be enlarged arise out of common sense and practicality, the Scheme recognises that such arrangements can only be appropriate when all parties consent. So, for example, the same dispute, as to who was responsible for a crane collapse which caused a man's death and a month's delay on site, might arise under the main contract, and under one or more of the sub-contracts. In many ways it makes a lot of sense to have one adjudicator appointed to decide the question of liability and then to apply that answer across all of the various contracts to which it might be relevant. But he can only do that if all the parties consent. The sub-sub-contractor may be unwilling to allow the dispute to be fought out in a multi-party adjudication and might prefer to deal with the dispute only with the party with which it had a contract. Without consent, only a single dispute can be referred to adjudication: see paragraphs 7.57–7.63 below. **3.35**

This question of consent was at the heart of the decision of HHJ Lloyd QC in *Pring & St Hill Ltd v CJ Hafner t/a Southern Erectors*.[21] In that case, the adjudicator had originally been appointed to decide an adjudication which arose between the main contractor McAlpine, and their sub-contractor, PSH, in connection with damaged glazing. In that first adjudication, the adjudicator found that PSH were obliged to pay a sum to McAlpine. Later, PSH started adjudication proceedings against Southern Erectors (SE) who were, as the Judge found, one of four **3.36**

---

[21] [2002] EWHC 1775 (TCC).

potential sub-sub-contractors who might have caused or contributed to the damage to the glazing. The same adjudicator who had decided the dispute between McAlpine and PSH was appointed to adjudicate the dispute between PSH and SE. He was also appointed to adjudicate the dispute between PSH and another sub-sub-contractor, JCH. SE objected to his appointment, both in terms of his previous involvement in the adjudication between McAlpine and PSH, and also to the proposal that their adjudication with PSH ran in parallel with PSH's adjudication with JCH. The adjudicator rejected these challenges and made a decision against SE. At the enforcement proceedings, SE's objections were argued out before HHJ Lloyd QC.

3.37 The first point that arose was the meaning and effect of paragraph 8(2) of Part 1 of the Scheme. PSH accepted that the dispute between PSH and SE and the dispute between PSH and JCH were related for the purposes of paragraph 8(2). PSH contended that paragraph 8(2) did not apply, however, because it was directed solely to an adjudicator conducting two or more adjudications at the same time, in a consolidated manner. On the other hand, SE argued that the words of paragraph 8(2) were not as narrow as that and were concerned precisely with the mischief which arose in that case. SE submitted that the purpose of paragraph 8(2) was to prevent an adjudicator deciding one adjudication, whether consciously or not, in the light of what he might learn or be told (or find out, carrying out his investigative powers) in the other, related adjudication. Judge Lloyd said:

> 16. ... In my judgment paragraph 8(2) is intended to cover, and does cover, a variety of circumstances. It is intended to cover all the situations in which there may be related disputes under different contracts, whether or not the parties are the same and whether or not there may permissibly be consolidation of the two proceedings. It applies whenever one party needs to know or may need to know, *before* allowing the adjudication to proceed in that way, whether the adjudicator is going to have to pass on information or may acquire information which would not be available in the other adjudication to which it is not a party. In other words, they are all circumstances where, as a matter of principle, a party's rights to the resolution of a dispute, privately and confidentially, would or might be infringed by the introduction of a third party, either in the same proceedings or by having the dispute determined by a person who would or could acquire knowledge from the other proceedings but which could not be used in the resolution of the dispute, yet might either consciously or unconsciously influence its outcome.

Accordingly, Judge Lloyd held that, although the appointment of the adjudicator in that case might have been validly made, it was necessarily a condition of appointment which was dependent upon the consent of all the parties. Paragraph 8(2) took effect as a contractual term and SE were entirely within their rights and acting reasonably by withholding their consent to the appointment of the adjudicator. The adjudicator had erred in going ahead without the consent of the parties.

In *David and Teresa Bothma (In Partnership) T/A DAB Builders v Mayhaven Healthcare Limited*[22] the Judge described the result in *Pring* as a logical, if harsh result, because if an award were produced under the Scheme resolving more than one dispute, it would be impossible to determine by any process of severance which part of the award should be enforced and which part of the award should be discarded. On the facts of *Bothma*, where the notice of adjudication referred to as many as four different 'disputes', ranging from sums due by way of interim payment to the validity of all architect's instructions to date and the date for completion of the contract, the Judge concluded that the adjudicator did not have the necessary jurisdiction, in particular because more than one dispute had been referred to him at the same time, and the defendant had made a proper and timeous objection on that ground at the outset. Permission to appeal was refused, and the Court of Appeal expressly agreed with the Judge's approach.[23]

3.38

Resignation

Paragraph 9 of Part 1 of the Scheme provides as follows:

3.39

9–(1) An adjudicator may resign at any time on giving notice in writing to the parties to the dispute.

(2) An adjudicator must resign where the dispute is the same or substantially the same as one which has previously been referred to adjudication, and a decision has been taken in that adjudication.

(3) Where an adjudicator ceases to act under paragraph 9(1)—

   (a) the referring party may serve a fresh notice under paragraph 1 and shall request an adjudicator to act in accordance with paragraphs 2 to 7; and
   (b) if requested by the new adjudicator and insofar as it is reasonably practicable, the parties shall supply him with copies of all documents which they had made available to the previous adjudicator.

(4) Where an adjudicator resigns in the circumstances referred to in paragraph (2), or where a dispute varies significantly from the dispute referred to him in the referral notice and for that reason he is not competent to decide it, the adjudicator shall be entitled to the payment of such reasonable amount as he may determine by way of fees and expenses reasonably incurred by him. The parties shall be jointly and severally liable for any sum which remains outstanding following the making of any determination on how the payment shall be apportioned.

Paragraph 9 envisages the resignation of an adjudicator in two distinct circumstances. Under paragraph 9(1), the adjudicator may resign at any time, merely by giving notice in writing to the parties. This, obviously, is at the adjudicator's

3.40

---

[22] (Unreported) 16.11.06, a decision of HHJ Havelock-Allan QC, sitting in the TCC in Bristol.
[23] [2007] EWCA Civ 527.

discretion. He may resign because of ill health or because of some other unexpected event occurring after his acceptance of the appointment but before the expiry of the 28 days. The other principal circumstance which may lead an adjudicator to decide to resign under paragraph 9(1) is if, once the adjudication is up and running, it becomes apparent to the adjudicator that the issues involved are not capable of fair resolution within the strict statutory time limit, even if extended by 14 days.

3.41 The courts have pointed out on a number of occasions that, if an adjudicator considers that he is not able to deliver a fair or just result within the time scale of the adjudication, he should resign. As HHJ Lloyd QC put it in *Balfour Beatty v Lambeth Borough Council*,[24] if an adjudicator cannot fairly and reasonably arrive at a decision within the allotted time, and the parties refuse to extend that time, 'an adjudicator ought not to make a decision at all and should resign'. This is because what matters is not the size or complexity of the adjudication itself, but whether or not the adjudicator considers that he is capable of reaching a fair decision in the statutory (or any agreed extended) period. This point is explored further in the chapter concerned with fairness, at paragraphs 9.04–9.10 below.

3.42 The other circumstance in which paragraph 9 contemplates the resignation of the adjudicator is much more specific. If the dispute is the same or substantially the same as one which has previously been referred to adjudication, and a decision has been taken in that earlier adjudication, then paragraph 9(2) is unequivocal: in such circumstances, the adjudicator must resign. Doubtless as a result of this finality, there have been a large number of reported cases in which the responding party has sought a declaration or a finding that the adjudicator should have resigned and that, in consequence, he had no jurisdiction to give the decision he did. This topic is addressed below at paragraphs 7.71–7.77 (jurisdiction) and 12.27–12.34 (enforcement).

3.43 Perhaps unsurprisingly, the majority of the reported cases demonstrate a practical willingness on the part of the courts to find that the disputes in question were not the same or substantially the same, and that, in consequence, the arbitrator was not obliged to resign. The first of these decisions was that of HHJ Thornton QC in *Sherwood & Casson Ltd v MacKenzie*.[25] In that case, Sherwood were MacKenzie's sub-contractor. The first adjudication concerned Sherwood's claim by reference to interim application 3, with MacKenzie submitting two lists of contra charges. The adjudicator decided that dispute. Thereafter, Sherwood prepared a final account which included a variation account which listed the same variations that had been included within application 3, and one or two other items. Many of the

---

[24] [2002] BLR 288.
[25] [2000] 2 TCLR 418.

sums were different to those claimed in the first adjudication and additional supporting documentation was provided. The final account was disputed and there was a second adjudication. The adjudicator decided that a further sum was due to Sherwood; MacKenzie failed to pay and Sherwood brought a claim for summary judgment. Judge Thornton made clear that the court could conduct an inquiry 'for the limited purpose of ascertaining whether or not two separate disputes are substantially the same'. He said that the court was not concerned to investigate the merits of the disputes, let alone resolve them. He emphasised that the court would give considerable weight to the decision of the adjudicator and would only embark on a jurisdictional inquiry in the first place where there were substantial grounds for concluding that the adjudicator had erred in concluding that there was no substantial overlap. In that case, having investigated the question of overlap, the Judge concluded that the disputes were not the same or substantially the same. The final account claim involved a loss and expense claim which had not been made in the first adjudication and, although the variation claims were similar in factual content, they raised separate disputes because of the timing and context in which they were raised. He therefore decided that the disputes were clearly different and the adjudicator had the jurisdiction to arrive at his second decision.

3.44 The problem of overlap between different adjudications can go to the subsequent adjudicator's jurisdiction (where the relevant cases are addressed in paragraphs 7.71–7.77 below) and to broader questions of fairness (where the relevant cases are addressed in paragraphs 9.38–9.41 below). It is, however, instructive to note at this stage the courts' general approach to paragraph 9(2) of the Scheme. In *Mivan Ltd v Lighting Technology Projects Ltd*[26] LTP issued a notice of adjudication to recover the balance on their interim payment applications. Mivan said there had been an over-payment but LTP pointed out that, in the absence of withholding notices, the sums applied for became due. The adjudicator agreed with that and ordered Mivan to pay the balance. They did so and then, having issued a valid withholding notice, issued their own notice of adjudication to recover the alleged overpayment. LTP raised the point at paragraph 9(2) of Part 1 of the Scheme and invited the adjudicator to resign. He did not do so and found in Mivan's favour. LTP refused to repay the money, asserting that the decision was a nullity and unenforceable. On the enforcement application, LTP contended that the subject matter of the second adjudication was the same or substantially the same as the first adjudication and that therefore the adjudicator should have resigned. HHJ Seymour QC disagreed. He said that the dispute in the first adjudication was whether or not the invoices were payable in the absence of a withholding notice, whereas the second adjudication was concerned with (different) questions

---

[26] [2001] ADJCS 04/09, a decision of HHJ Seymour QC in the TCC in London on 9 April 2001.

of repayment. The second adjudication was therefore a separate and distinct dispute and thus the second adjudicator's decision was enforced by way of summary judgment. The same reasoning led to the same result in *Holt Insulation Ltd v Colt International Ltd*.[27] Importantly, one of the reasons for HHJ MacKay QC's decision in *Holt* was that the notices of adjudication in the two adjudications were 'crucially different'.

3.45 In *Skanska Construction UK Ltd v The ERDC Group Ltd & Anor*[28] the Outer House (Lady Paton) considered a situation where, in the first adjudication, the adjudicator ruled that the respondents were not due anything because of the lack of sufficient information. The respondents commenced a second adjudication some time later with some similar claims and some new claims, and with more supporting information. The adjudicator decided that he had the jurisdiction to deal with the second adjudication and gave a decision in favour of the respondents. The petitioners sought judicial review of that decision. The court concluded that the dispute referred to the second adjudicator was not substantially the same as the dispute referred to the first adjudicator. The court held that the situation was similar to that in *Sherwood & Casson Ltd*, because a different stage in the contract had been reached and different contractual provisions applied. The Judge also pointed out that considerably more information was available by the time of the second adjudication and, as she put it, 'different considerations and perspectives may apply'.

3.46 However, it should not be thought that it is inevitable that a court will conclude that the disputes were not the same or substantially the same. In *Naylor v Greenacres*[29] the first adjudication had been instigated by the petitioner seeking entitlement to payment in the sum of £19,484.17. The respondents defended the claim on the basis of defective work to the concrete ice rink slab, but the adjudicator decided that the petitioner was entitled to the full amount sought. Shortly thereafter, the respondents initiated a second set of adjudication proceedings which identified the dispute as the failure to supply and install the slab in accordance with the contract. The court held that this was the same dispute as had already been referred to adjudication because it was concerned with the correct execution of the contract work. Thus the arbitrator did not possess any jurisdiction to decide the second adjudication.

3.47 Difficulties concerning the adjudicator's entitlement to fees can arise in circumstances where the adjudicator has to resign if the circumstances set out in paragraph 9(2) of Part 1 of the Scheme arose. In *Prentice Island Ltd v Castle*

---

[27] Unreported, 23.7.01, a decision of HHJ MacKay QC sitting at the TCC in Liverpool.
[28] [2003] SCLR 296.
[29] [2001] SLT 1092.

Contracting Ltd[30] there was a dispute as to whether or not the adjudicator should have resigned because the dispute was the same or substantially the same as an earlier dispute which had been resolved in adjudication. Unusually, the issue as to whether or not the dispute was the same or substantially the same as a previous reference had still to be argued out, and thus the correctness or otherwise of the assertion to that effect was not in issue in the reported case, which was concerned solely with the adjudicator's entitlement to fees. The court concluded that, whatever the position as to resignation, an adjudicator who is appointed to deal with a second adjudication is a validly appointed adjudicator, albeit subject to a duty to resign from that office if the circumstances set out in paragraph 9(2) of Part 1 of the Scheme applied. As the court pointed out, the provisions of paragraph 9(2) assume a validly appointed adjudicator. Thus the structure of the Scheme envisages that the adjudicator might have to decide whether or not the dispute is the same or substantially the same as an earlier dispute which had already been adjudicated. Even if an adjudicator in good faith fell into error on that question and continued to act in circumstances in which he ought to resign, the court concluded that he remained in post as a validly appointed adjudicator, unless and until he resigned or was stopped from acting by the court. He was therefore entitled to be remunerated according to the work undertaken by him in the capacity as adjudicator.

Objection

Paragraph 10 of Part 1 of the Scheme provides as follows: **3.48**

> 10. Where any party to the dispute objects to the appointment of a particular person as adjudicator, that objection shall not invalidate the adjudicator's appointment nor any decision he may reach in accordance with paragraph 20.

The purpose of this paragraph of the Scheme is clear: the mere fact that one party objects to the appointment of a particular person as an adjudicator will not invalidate the appointment or, therefore, any decision that the adjudicator might make. Anything less, and the wily responding party could always ensure that the adjudication was ineffective by raising spurious objections to the appointment of any individual as the adjudicator. In *Pring & St Hill Ltd v CJ Hafner t/a Southern Erectors*,[31] as already noted, the adjudicator dealt with the sub-contract adjudication, despite the fact that the responding party objected on the basis that he had previously dealt with the same underlying issue in an adjudication involving other parties. **3.49**

---

[30] Unreported, 15.12.03, a decision of R A Dunlop QC, Sheriff Principal, Sheriffdom of Tayside Central and Fife.
[31] [2002] EWHC 1775 (TCC).

The Judge concluded that, given the absence of consent, the adjudicator had no jurisdiction pursuant to paragraph 8(2) of the Scheme. In that case it had also been argued that, by reference to paragraph 10 of the Scheme, one party could not invalidate the appointment, even by raising a fundamental objection to the adjudicator's jurisdiction. This argument was unsuccessful. The Judge concluded that paragraph 10 of Part 1 of the Scheme was concerned with the consequences of an objection to the appointment of a particular person to be the adjudicator and had nothing to do with whether that person, if otherwise validly chosen and appointed, had the necessary jurisdiction. Thus the objections to the adjudicator in that case, which had been raised at the outset, were not thwarted by paragraph 10.

Revocation

3.50 Paragraph 11 of Part 1 of the Scheme provides as follows:

> 11–(1) The parties to a dispute may at any time agree to revoke the appointment of the adjudicator. The adjudicator shall be entitled to the payment of such reasonable amount as he may determine by way of fees and expenses incurred by him. The parties shall be jointly and severally liable for any sum which remains outstanding following the making of any determination on how the payment shall be apportioned.
>
> (2) Where the revocation of the appointment of the adjudicator is due to the default or misconduct of the adjudicator, the parties shall not be liable to pay the adjudicator's fees and expenses.

3.51 These provisions speak for themselves. In the same way as paragraph 9(1) gives the adjudicator the ability to resign on notice at any time, so paragraph 11(1) allows the parties to agree to revoke his appointment at any time. Unless the revocation is due to the default or misconduct of the adjudicator, the parties are jointly and severally liable for his fees. If the revocation is due to his default or misconduct, then the adjudicator is not entitled to such fees. It is perhaps noteworthy that there has been no reported case in which the proviso to paragraph 11(2) has been found to operate.

Powers of the Adjudicator

3.52 The powers of the adjudicator are set out in detail in paragraphs 12–19 inclusive of Part 1 of the Scheme. They provide as follows:

> 12. The adjudicator shall—
>   (a) act impartially in carrying out his duties and shall do so in accordance with any relevant terms of the contract and shall reach his decision in accordance with the applicable law in relation to the contract; and
>   (b) avoid incurring unnecessary expense.

13. The adjudicator may take the initiative in ascertaining the facts and the law necessary to determine the dispute and shall decide on the procedure to be followed in the adjudication. In particular he may—

 (a) request any party to the contract to supply him with such documents as he may reasonably require including, if he so directs, any written statement from any party to the contract supporting, or supplementing the referral notice and any other documents given under paragraph 7(2),
 (b) decide the language or languages to be used in the adjudication and whether a translation of any document is to be provided and if so by whom,
 (c) meet and question any of the parties to the contract and their representatives,
 (d) subject to obtaining any necessary consent from a third party or parties, make such site visits and inspections as he considers appropriate, whether accompanied by the parties or not,
 (e) subject to obtaining any necessary consent from a third party or parties, carry out any test or experiments,
 (f) obtain and consider such representations and submissions as he requires, and, provided he has notified the parties of his intention, appoint experts, assessors or legal advisers,
 (g) give directions as to the timetable for the adjudication, any deadlines, or limits as to the length of written documents or oral representations to be complied with, and
 (h) issue other directions relating to the conduct of the adjudication.

14. The parties shall comply with any request or direction of the adjudicator in relation to the adjudication.

15. If, without showing sufficient cause, a party fails to comply with any request, direction or timetable the adjudicator made in accordance with his powers, fails to produce any document or written statement requested by the adjudicator, or in any other way fails to comply with a requirement under these provisions relating to the adjudication, the adjudicator may—

 (a) continue the adjudication in the absence of that party or of the document or written statement requested,
 (b) draw such inferences from that failure to comply as circumstances may, in the adjudicator's opinion, be justified, and
 (c) make a decision on the basis of the information before him attaching such weight as he thinks fit to any evidence submitted to him outside any period he may have requested or directed.

16–(1) Subject to any agreement between the parties to the contrary, and to the terms of paragraph (2) below, any party to the dispute may be assisted by, or represented by, such advisers or representatives (whether legally qualified or not) as he considers appropriate.

(2) Where the adjudicator is considering oral evidence or representations, a party to the dispute may not be represented by more than one person, unless the adjudicator gives directions to the contrary.

17. The adjudicator shall consider any relevant information submitted to him by any of the parties to the dispute and shall make available to them any information to be taken into account in reaching his decision.

18. The adjudicator and any party to the dispute shall not disclose to any other person any information or document provided to him in connection with the adjudication which the party supplying it has indicated is to be treated as confidential, except to the extent that it is necessary for the purposes of, or in connection with, the adjudication.

19–(1) The adjudicator shall reach his decision not later than—
  (a) twenty eight days after the date of the referral notice mentioned in paragraph 7(1), or
  (b) forty two days after the date of the referral notice if the referring party so consents, or
  (c) such period exceeding twenty eight days after the referral notice as the parties to the dispute may, after the giving of that notice, agree.

(2) Where the adjudicator fails, for any reason, to reach his decision in accordance with paragraph (1)—
  (a) any of the parties to the dispute may serve a fresh notice under paragraph (1) and shall request the adjudicator to act in accordance with paragraphs 2 to 7; and
  (b) if requested by the new adjudicator and insofar as it is reasonably practicable, the parties shall supply him with copies of all documents which they had made available to the previous adjudicator.

(3) As soon as possible after he has reached a decision, the adjudicator shall deliver a copy of that decision to each of the parties to the contract.

3.53 A number of particular points need to be made about these paragraphs concerning impartiality (paragraphs 3.54–3.55 below); the taking of the initiative by the adjudicator (paragraphs 3.57–3.58 below); the adjudicator's consideration of any relevant information submitted to him (paragraphs 3.60–3.65 below); and the time limits referred to in paragraph 19 (paragraphs 3.66–3.71 below). Again, it should be noted that more detailed consideration of the interface between the rules of natural justice and the constraints of the adjudication process can be found in Chapter 9 below.

Acting Impartially

3.54 This topic is dealt with in detail at Chapter 9 below. What follows is a brief introduction to the concepts of impartiality and fairness within the constraints of the statutory adjudication process. In *Glencot Development & Design Co Ltd v Ben Barrett & Son (Contractors) Ltd*,[32] HHJ Lloyd QC considered the meaning of the word 'impartially'. He concluded that it had to be given the same meaning as at common law or in Article 6 of the Human Rights Convention, as applied by the Human Rights Act 1998. Even though an adjudicator was not a classic judicial tribunal, in practice an adjudication was probably closer to an arbitration than an expert determination. It may not take place in public but it had been instituted by Parliament in order to provide a determination of rights which, albeit the effect of

---

[32] [2001] BLR 207.

any decision is ultimately reversible, will nonetheless have immediate practical and potentially far-reaching impact. He said that the appropriate test was that identified by the House of Lords in *R v Gough*[33] where, at the end of his speech, Lord Goff said:

> Finally, for the avoidance of doubt, I prefer to state the test in terms of real danger rather than real likelihood, to ensure that the court is thinking in terms of possibility rather than probability of bias. Accordingly, having ascertained the relevant circumstances, the court should ask itself whether, having regard to those circumstances, there was a real danger of bias on the part of the relevant member of the tribunal in question, in the sense that he might unfairly regard (or have unfairly regarded) with favour, or disfavour, the case of a party to the issue under consideration by him . . .

3.55 Judge Lloyd went on, at paragraph 20 of his judgment in *Glencot*, to rule that the adjudicator had to conduct the proceedings in accordance with the rules of natural justice or as fairly as the limitations imposed by Parliament permitted.[34] He concluded that the test for apparent bias was an objective test. The views of the adjudicator were either irrelevant or not determinative. The test was whether the 'circumstances would lead a fair-minded and informed observer to conclude that there was a real possibility or a real danger, the two being the same, that the tribunal was biased'. On the facts of *Glencot*, the adjudicator conducted a mediation process which failed to resolve the dispute but which involved him talking privately to representatives of both sides. The Judge concluded that any fair-minded and informed observer would have concluded that his participation in these lengthy discussions meant that there was a real possibility that he was biased.

3.56 In *Mott MacDonald Ltd v London & Regional Properties Ltd*,[35] the adjudicator wrongly sought to impose a lien on his fees, and made it a pre-condition that the referring party must pay all his fees before the decision was released. HHJ Thornton QC held that this was a breach of rule 12(a) and that the adjudicator appeared to lack impartiality by giving at least the impression, through the operation of this pre-condition that he was financially beholden to the referring party.

Taking the Initiative

3.57 Paragraph 13 allows the adjudicator to take the initiative in ascertaining the facts and the law necessary to determine the dispute and then goes on to identify, at sub-paragraphs (a)–(h) inclusive, various ways in which this initiative may be taken. However, although this suggests a relatively wide power on the part of the adjudicator to get to what he considers to be the heart of the dispute and to decide it,

---

[33] [1993] AC 646.
[34] For a similar approach, see, amongst others, *Discain Project Services Ltd v Opecprime Development Ltd* [2000] BLR 402.
[35] [2007] EWHC 1055 (TCC).

there are in practice a number of important restraining factors.[36] One is the limitation on his jurisdiction created by the notice of adjudication. A good example of the clash between the power to take the initiative, and the limitations imposed on the adjudicator by the terms of the notice, is the case of *McAlpine PPS Pipeline Systems Joint Venture v Transco Plc*.[37] In that case McAlpine commenced an adjudication claiming interest as a result of Transco's alleged failure promptly to certify the amounts due to McAlpine on the occurrence of particular 'compensation events'. Transco denied the claim, and argued that no proper details of these events had ever been provided. In its reply to Transco's response, McAlpine served in excess of 500 pages of appendices which sought to argue the underlying compensation events, rather than simply the claim for interest. It was said that this was necessary in order to deal with Transco's assertion that McAlpine had failed to provide the appropriate detail of the factual background for the compensation events in relation to which interest was claimed. The adjudicator said that, in order to reach a conclusion as to the entitlement to interest, he had to decide, in respect of each compensation event, which party was responsible for the delay in certification. The adjudicator found that McAlpine had to provide considerable further material if he was to find in their favour. Transco complained that the reply, and the adjudicator's response, raised an entirely different case to that in the notice of adjudication, and the adjudicator did not have the jurisdiction to consider these new issues.

3.58 HHJ Toulmin CMG QC held that the dispute that was referred to the adjudicator was McAlpine's claim for interest payments and that the basis of that claim was that set out in the notice of adjudication, namely that payments in respect of various compensation events had not been certified when they ought to have been. He decided that Transco's response was legitimate, because it confined its contention to the simple proposition that McAlpine could not succeed on the basis on which the claim had been put forward. The Judge found that the Transco response deliberately stopped short of setting out an affirmative contention on each individual claim. The Judge found that the adjudicator had been right to conclude that this was not an ambush by Transco but a reiteration of the stance which they had adopted since the dispute started. It was not Transco's fault that McAlpine had not provided sufficient substantiation originally. The Judge went on to conclude that the adjudicator had no jurisdiction to go beyond the dispute as set out in the notice of adjudication. In the face of Transco's submissions on jurisdiction, the adjudicator had no basis for embarking on a consideration of what he regarded as the real dispute. Despite the provisions of paragraph 13 of the Scheme, with its

---

[36] The relevant cases are cited in Chapter 9, and include *Pegram, AMEC v Whitefriars, Thomas-Frederic's, C&B Scene*, and *AWG*.
[37] Unreported, 12.5.04, a decision of HHJ Toulmin CMG QC sitting at the TCC in London.

express reference to the adjudicator taking the initiative, the adjudicator had no jurisdiction to embark on a course which was outside the terms of the referral notice without the agreement of both parties. At paragraph 146 of his judgment, the Judge said:

> Unfortunately, it is not enough for the adjudicator to say that he was sure that both parties would want to conclude the matter without recourse to further proceedings. If the existing referral does not enable him to deal with the dispute in the way in which he wishes, he is powerless to alter the terms of the referral in the absence of the agreement of both parties. So long as the dispute remains before him, he must decide only the issues referred to him.

In consequence, the Judge found that the adjudicator had gone beyond the terms of the dispute referred to him and that he had no jurisdiction to do so. He therefore declined to enforce the decision.

3.59 Although, on the face of the Scheme, it would appear that an adjudicator has wide powers to adopt an inquisitorial approach to the dispute, a number of factors mean that, in reality, those powers have to be exercised with considerable care. The restraint imposed by the terms of the notice of adjudication has already been considered. In addition, the adjudicator has a short period in which to complete his decision, and this tends to mean that, from a practical point of view, it is much easier for the adjudicator to decide between the opposing cases put forward by the parties than embark on a lengthy investigation of his own into points not apparently raised by either side. Further, both paragraph 17 of the Scheme and the rules of natural justice mean that any new information unearthed or different approach adopted by the adjudicator has to be shared with the parties, and, if it is a matter of importance, their views have to be sought on it prior to the production of the decision itself.[38] Again, this tends to result in a process that is more like an arbitration or a case in court than an inquisitorial, fact-finding exercise.

Consideration of any Relevant Information

3.60 The provision at paragraph 17 of Part 1 of the Scheme is in mandatory terms: the adjudicator 'shall consider' any relevant information submitted to him. This has given rise to a number of attacks on the decisions of adjudicators on the basis that the adjudicator failed to consider a particular element of relevant information and therefore was in breach of his obligations identified at paragraph 17. Perhaps the high watermark of this approach can be found in the decision of HHJ Thornton QC in *Buxton Building Contractors Ltd v The Governors of Durand Primary School*.[39] In that case, the contract administrator had issued a certificate of making good

---

[38] See in particular paragraphs 9.26–9.35 below.
[39] [2004] EWHC 733 (TCC); [2004] 1 BLR 474.

defects and a further certificate, described as an interim certificate, which certified that the second tranche of the retention fund should be released to the contractors, Buxton. He did not, however, issue a final certificate. Accordingly, Buxton were in difficulties because, although they obviously wanted to be paid the second tranche of the retention, there was no contract machinery which allowed the payment of that sum, because there was no final certificate. There was a sum which was due but which could not be shown to be payable. In those circumstances, Buxton operated paragraph 8 of Part II of the Scheme which provided that a contractor in Buxton's position could serve a claim on the employer, which then made the final date for payment 17 days from the service of that claim. Buxton sent an invoice to trigger the 17 day period. The school had always maintained that no sums were due because of defects in the work. Prior to the release of the retention certificate the school had served a general notice of an intention to withhold payment and, before the issue of Buxton's invoice and before the date for payment of the invoice sum, they had also served details of the sum to be withheld and of the reasons for withholding. In the adjudication, Buxton said that the only issue was whether the certified sum was due and payable and said that the documents from the school did not amount to a withholding notice under the Scheme. The adjudicator decided the point in favour of Buxton, concluding that no withholding notice had been served by the school and that the supervising officer had to be presumed to have taken the school's claim into account in computing the sum being certified as due.

3.61 Judge Thornton concluded that the adjudicator's decision showed that he had not considered at all the nature, content, validity or quantification of the school's cross-claim; he did not investigate the material provided to him by the school; he did not decide whether the school's cross-claim had in fact been taken into account by the supervising officer when certifying but instead made an erroneous assumption that it had been; he did not consider whether the certificate that was issued had any contractual validity, and instead wrongly assumed that the certificate was one that was duly authorised by the contract conditions and that its payment was provided for by those conditions; and he did not take into account or consider the validity of the correspondence from the school which amounted, or arguably amounted, to a valid withholding notice that had been served timeously. Judge Thornton concluded that there was a fundamental flaw that attached to the adjudicator's decision. That flaw was that the decision had been reached, or must be taken to have been reached, without the adjudicator having considered or decided upon the contents of the submissions, documents and issues referred to him by the school. Having been invited by Buxton to ignore those documents, it appears that that is what the adjudicator did. The adjudicator's failure, said the Judge, amounted to a serious irregularity and a serious failure to conform to paragraph 17 of Part I of the Scheme. The adjudicator's decision was therefore not enforced.

3.62 The decision in *Buxton* was considered by Jackson J in the case of *Carillion Construction Ltd v Royal Devonport Dockyard*.[40] Devonport were the main contractors and Carillion were sub-contractors. During the course of the works, Devonport agreed variations to the main contract with the employer, which gave rise to a number of interim uplifts to the 'target cost' payable under the sub-contract. Carillion referred the question of the amount it was entitled to be paid to an adjudicator. The adjudicator disregarded the negotiations between Devonport and the employer, saying they were irrelevant to the question of target cost as between the parties and disregarded an alternative calculation of the target cost put forward by Devonport. He instead concluded that Carillion were entitled to be paid a sum which reflected the defects in Carillion's work, but that Devonport's cross-claim in respect of defects should be reduced by 20%. The adjudicator made an award in Carillion's favour. Devonport refused to pay and Carillion brought enforcement proceedings. Devonport submitted that the adjudicator had acted without jurisdiction and in breach of natural justice in declining to consider the matters put forward by Devonport in the adjudication and that he had failed to give the parties an opportunity to comment on the reduction to Devonport's defects claims. In short it was submitted that the adjudicator had not considered the relevant information submitted to him.

3.63 At paragraph 81 of his judgment, Jackson J identified a total of five propositions which he considered were relevant to the debate about the adjudicator's obligations to consider the evidence and give reasons for his decision. The first two are relevant to the adjudicator's powers in respect of evidence:[41]

> 1. If an adjudicator declines to consider evidence which, on his analysis of the facts or the law, is irrelevant, that is neither (a) a breach of the rules of natural justice nor (b) a failure to consider relevant material which undermines his decision on *Wednesbury* grounds or for breach of paragraph 17 of the Scheme. If the adjudicator's analysis of the facts or the law was erroneous, it may follow that he ought to have considered the evidence in question. The possibility of such error is inherent in the adjudication system. It is not a ground for refusing to enforce the adjudicator's decision. I reach this conclusion on the basis of the Court of Appeal decisions mentioned earlier. This conclusion is also supported by the reasoning of Steyn J in the context of arbitration in *Bill Biakh v Hyundai Corporation*.[42]
>
> 2. On a careful reading of His Honour Judge Thornton's judgment in *Buxton Building Contractors Ltd v Governors of Durand Primary School*[43] I do not think that this judgment is inconsistent with proposition 1. If, however, Mr Furst is right and

---

[40] [2005] EWHC 778 (TCC).
[41] The other three propositions are set out in paragraph 3.83 below.
[42] [1988] 1 Lloyds Rep 187.
[43] [2004] 1 BLR 474.

if *Buxton* is inconsistent with proposition 1, then I consider that *Buxton* was wrongly decided and I decline to follow it . . .

3.64 Jackson J then applied these propositions to the facts. He dismissed Devonport's case that the adjudicator failed to have regard to all the relevant material. He said that it was clearly an issue for the adjudicator to decide whether the negotiations between Devonport and the employer were relevant to the assessment of target cost and, if so, how. The adjudicator concluded that those negotiations were not relevant and whether he was right or wrong in that conclusion could not affect the validity of his decision. More generally, Jackson J pointed to the fact that the adjudicator had received literally hundreds of pages of legal argument and that he had done 'a remarkable job in keeping abreast of the battle and in keeping under control the torrent of incoming material'. The adjudicator had made it plain in his written decision which arguments he accepted and how his figures were calculated. There was no need for him to recite and address particular arguments in his decision. The challenge to the adjudicator's jurisdiction failed.

3.65 Jackson J's decision was upheld in the Court of Appeal.[44] Chadwick LJ concluded that it was 'beyond argument' that the Judge was correct to take the view he did of the adjudicator's approach to the question of 'target cost'. Chadwick LJ also held that the Judge was right to reject the attack on the adjudicator for a breach of natural justice. As to the propositions set out in paragraph 81 of the judgment of Jackson J, Chadwick LJ said that the Court of Appeal was in broad agreement with those propositions, which were themselves indicative of the approach which courts should adopt when required to address a challenge to the decision of an adjudicator appointed under the 1996 Act. However, he made it plain that the Court of Appeal was less confident than Jackson J had been that the decision in *Buxton* could be reconciled with the first of those propositions. The Court of Appeal endorsed that first proposition and, to the extent that *Buxton* was inconsistent with it, they said that the Judge was right not to follow it.[45]

Time Limits

3.66 Paragraph 19 of the Scheme provides for three options. Option 1 is the statutory period for the adjudication, namely 28 days. Option 2 provides for an extension of 14 days to that period, at the sole discretion or request of the referring party, making a total of 42 days. However, that option is only available to the adjudicator if the referring party requests or consents to it. Option 3 allows for an

---

[44] [2005] EWCA Civ 1358.
[45] *Buxton* was also doubted in *Kier Regional Limited v City & General (Holborn)* [2006] EWHC 848 (TCC).

unlimited extension(s) to the 28 day period, provided that both parties to the adjudication consent to such extension(s).

3.67 The difficulties created by these time limits will usually arise in the larger adjudications. There may be some adjudications which, once they are up and running, cannot fairly be disposed of within the 28 days or, indeed, within the 42 days. In those circumstances, it is submitted, the adjudicator has a choice. He should seek an appropriate extension of time from both parties. If he does not get such an extension of time then, if he considers that he cannot dispose of the adjudication fairly within the time limit that he has been given, he should resign in accordance with his power under paragraph 9 of Part I of the Scheme.

3.68 The practical difficulty that can arise is where the material that each party is seeking to rely on in the adjudication grows over the course of the 28 days. The adjudicator may seek an extension of time on the basis of one set of material and then be provided with a further two dozen lever arch files which make it necessary for him to seek a further extension. In those circumstances, the parties are placed in a very difficult position. On the one hand, they will be instinctively unhappy about the extension of the adjudication process, particularly in circumstances where the adjudicator has no power to award costs.[46] On the other hand, if the parties are, say, three weeks into a lengthy adjudication and they have already spent a good deal of money on the process, they will naturally be reluctant to deprive the adjudicator of the extension that he requires, thereby rendering all that expenditure futile. In *CIB Properies Ltd v Birse Construction Ltd*[47] the adjudicator was faced with a voluminous claim with an equally voluminous response. The adjudicator sought a number of extensions of time as the process went on and, mindful of the practical realities of the position, the parties granted the adjudicator those extensions. Eventually the adjudication process took about three months.

3.69 Difficulties can arise if the adjudicator fails to deliver his decision within the 28 day period and no extension has been agreed. There is a full discussion of this topic at paragraphs 2.91–2.108 above. Under the Scheme, the position can be shortly stated. Although, in *Simons Construction Ltd v Aardvark Developments Ltd*[48] the adjudicator provided his decision eight days beyond the 28 day time limit, and HHJ Seymour QC held that the decision was binding, his reasoning (that a decision was always valid provided only that the adjudication agreement, if any, had not already been terminated for failure to produce a decision within the relevant time scale and that a fresh notice of adjudication had not already been given by one of the parties) was criticised and not followed in *Ritchie Brothers (PWC)*

---

[46] See the discussion at paragraphs 11.01–11.06 below.
[47] [2005] 1 WLR 2252; [2005] BLR 173.
[48] [2003] EWHC 2474; [2004] BLR 117.

Ltd v David Philp (Commercials) Ltd.[49] Instead it was held that the adjudicator's decision was reached out of time (and that after a purported extension that was also consented to by the pursuers out of time), and that the adjudicator did not retain his jurisdiction. The court decided that the true interpretation of paragraph 19 of Part I of the Scheme was that the jurisdiction ceased on the expiry of the time limit if it had not already been extended in accordance with paragraph 19(1). The Lord Justice Clerk (Gill) concluded that Judge Seymour's interpretation of paragraph 19 could not be justified. Lord Abernethy, who gave a dissenting judgment, supported the approach of Judge Seymour.

3.70 In *Ritchie*, there was an alternative argument, to the effect that the failure to provide a decision within the time limit stipulated by the Scheme was a technical failure rather than a fundamental error or impropriety. The pursuers relied on the reasoning of Lord Wheatley in *St Andrew's Bay Development Ltd v HB Management Ltd*.[50] However, the Lord Justice Clerk rejected this argument as well, pointing out that it provided no hard and fast criteria by which a court could determine for how long after the time limit a failure to reach a decision could be considered to be merely technical, or in what circumstances the jurisdiction could be said to come to an end. In reaching this view, the Judge relied in part on HHJ Lloyd QC's judgment in *Barnes & Elliott Ltd v Taylor Woodrow Holdings Ltd*.[51] In that case there was a decision within the time limit, but a failure to communicate it until the following day. Judge Lloyd held that the decision had been arrived at timeously. The Lord Justice Clerk pointed out that this meant that, on the facts, *Barnes & Elliott* was distinguishable from *Ritchie*, but that in any event he considered that Judge Lloyd was correct to say that s108 of the 1996 Act only conferred authority to make a decision within the 28 day period or such other period as it provides.

3.71 The approach in *Ritchie* has been expressly adopted by the TCC Judges in London, including most recently in *AC Yule & Son v Speedwell Roofing and Cladding Ltd*[52] which was also a dispute under the Scheme. There, the TCC Judge rejected the contention that the most important factor in deciding whether a decision produced out of time was a nullity was the consequence of non-compliance, as opposed to the mandatory language of the Scheme itself. The other more recent cases in which the TCC have adopted the approach in *Ritchie* are listed below.[53]

---

[49] [2005] SLT 341.
[50] [2003] SLT, particularly at page 744 F–G.
[51] [2003] EWHC 3100; [2004] BLR 111.
[52] [2007] EWHC 1360 (TCC).
[53] See, for example, *Hart v Fidler and Anor* [2006] 2857 (TCC); *Cubitt Building & Interiors Ltd v Fleetglade Ltd* [2006] EWHC 3413 (TCC); *Epping Electrical Co Ltd v Briggs and Forrester (Plumbing Services) Ltd* [2007] EWHC 4 (TCC); *Aveat Heating Ltd v Jerram Falkus Construction Ltd* [2007] EWHC 131 (TCC); and *AC Yule & Son Limited v Speedwell Roofing & Cladding Limited* [2007] EWHC 1360 (TCC). These cases are discussed in detail in paragraphs 2.91–2.108 above.

The Statutory Scheme

Accordingly, it would seem clear that, as things presently stand, the adjudicator must reach his decision within the 28 day period set out in paragraph 19(1) of the 1996 Act or, alternatively, within any extended period agreed by the parties. If the decision is not reached within that period, the decision is a nullity (see *Ritchie* and the cases cited in paragraphs 2.91–2.108 above). If the decision is completed within the correct period, and is communicated the following day, then the decision is probably not a nullity (see *Barnes & Elliott* and *Cubitt Building & Interiors Ltd v Fleetglade Ltd*).

Paragraph 19(3) of the Scheme requires the adjudicator to deliver his decision to the parties 'as soon as possible after he has reached a decision'. In *Mott MacDonald*,[54] the decision was completed on about 8th December, but was not sent to the parties until 13th December. The delay arose out of the adjudicator's insistence on being paid his fees before he communicated the decision. It was held that this delay was contrary to rule 19(3) and, in part for this reason, the decision was not enforced.

3.72

The Adjudicator's Decision

Paragraphs 20–22 of Part I of the Scheme provide as follows:

3.73

> 20. The adjudicator shall decide the matters in dispute. He may take into account any other matters which the parties to the dispute agree should be within the scope of the adjudication or which are matters under the contract which he considers are necessarily connected with the dispute. In particular he may—
> (a) open up, revise and review any decision taken or any certificate given by any person referred to in the contract unless the contract states that the decision or certificate is final and conclusive,
> (b) ecide that any of the parties to the dispute is liable to make a payment under the contract whether in sterling or some other currency and, subject to Section 111(4) of the Act, when that payment is due and the final date for payment,
> (c) having regard to any term of the contract relating to the payment of interest decide the circumstances in which, and the rates at which, and the periods for which simple or compound rates of interest shall be paid.
>
> 21. In the absence of any directions by the adjudicator relating to the time for performance of his decision, the parties shall be required to comply with any decision of the adjudicator immediately on delivery of the decision to the parties in accordance with this paragraph.
>
> 22. If requested by one of the parties to the dispute, the adjudicator shall provide reasons for his decision.

---

[54] [2007] EWHC 1055 (TCC).

Opening Up, Revising and Reviewing

3.74 Paragraph 20(a) of Part 1 of the Scheme gives the adjudicator the same express powers as an arbitrator under the standard forms of building contract to open up, revise and review previous decisions of the contract administrator or architect. This is obviously an extremely important power, because it allows the adjudicator to correct errors which he may perceive in previous interim payment certificates or previous awards of extensions of time and/or loss and expense. Indeed, taken to its logical conclusion, this power could allow an adjudicator to declare that, say, a practical completion certificate must be issued, in circumstances where the contract administrator or architect has refused to issue such a certificate. It must be questionable whether, save in exceptional circumstances, it can ever be appropriate for an adjudicator, appointed to consider a dispute within 28 days, to substitute his own view on a matter such as practical completion, particularly in circumstances where the contract administrator has been involved in the day-to-day detail throughout the currency of the contract.

3.75 In *Vaultrise Ltd v Paul Cook*[55] the claimant contractor made a final account claim, pointing out that there should have been a final certificate but none had been issued. The adjudicator found for the claimant. In the enforcement proceedings, the defendant asserted that his obligation to pay was triggered only by certificates issued under the contract and that, since there was no final certificate, the adjudicator had no power to issue such a certificate. The Judge rejected that submission, finding that an adjudicator could consider whether or not a certificate should have been issued and, if a certificate was outstanding, he could determine the appropriate sum due. The Judge said that the adjudicator had the jurisdiction to find, as he had done, that a final certificate should have been issued on or before a particular date and to determine the amount due from the defendant to the claimant. There was no reason why a dispute as to whether or not a certificate should have been issued (and, if so, what the certificate should say) should not be referred to adjudication.

3.76 It is also important for the parties to make clear to the adjudicator precisely what previous decisions they want opened up and reviewed and how any sums which are sought are made up. In *Martin Girt v Page Bentley*[56] the contractor claimed some £60,000 odd from the employer, who said that in fact there had been an overpayment. The adjudicator set out what should have happened and referred to the relevant tax considerations. The adjudicator was concerned that, since it was unclear that the claimant had the necessary registration cards and tax certificates, he should only award the claimant a sum due net of tax. Accordingly the sum of just £18,000 odd was awarded to the claimant. The defendant argued that the

---
[55] [2004] Adj CS 04/06.
[56] [2002] EWHC 2434.

whole investigation into the tax position was a frolic of the adjudicator's own making and that this foray outside his jurisdiction fatally tainted the award. Judge Wilcox pointed out that, if anybody had suffered as a result of the tax point, it was the claimant, because the appropriate certificate would have enabled a gross payment to have been made, and there was such a certificate produced and filed with the Inland Revenue. The Judge found that the adjudicator had the jurisdiction to reach the decision that he did and that, in any event, any prejudice resulting from the arguable breach of natural justice was visited on the claimant, not the defendant. Since the claimant did not seek to impugn the award, the decision would be enforced.

Interest

3.77 One of the many issues in *Carillion Construction Ltd v Devonport Royal Dockyard*[57] was the nature and scope of paragraph 20(c) of Part 1 of the Scheme. Devonport argued that this provision only allowed the adjudicator to award interest if the underlying contract between the parties provided that such interest was payable. Carillion argued that paragraph 20(c) created a free-standing right on the part of the adjudicator to award interest. Jackson J concluded that paragraph 20(c) did indeed create a free-standing right to award interest. There were, he said at paragraph 123 of his judgment, five reasons for this decision:

1. As a matter of impression this seems to me to be the more natural meaning of sub-paragraph (c), when read in the context of the whole of paragraph 20 of the Scheme.
2. In my view it is reading too much into the second and third sentences of paragraph 20 to hold that everything in sub-paragraphs (a),(b) and (c) must arise from some other express term of the contract.
3. It makes obvious commercial sense for an adjudicator to have the power to award interest. The Scheme takes effect as a set of implied terms in many construction contracts pursuant to Section 114(4) of the 1996 Act. I would certainly expect the Scheme to include a power to award interest.
4. In my view, the phrase in paragraph 20(c) "having regard to any term of the contract relating to the payment of interest . . ." means that if there is any such term, the adjudicator must have regard to it. In other words, the free-standing right conferred by paragraph 20(c) does not override any express term of the contract dealing with interest.
5. If paragraph 20(c) had the meaning for which Mr Furst contends, it would be unnecessary. The clause would be saying that which was self-evident.

3.78 In the Court of Appeal,[58] Chadwick LJ, giving the judgment of the court, said that the court had reached the same conclusion as Jackson J on the question of interest. However, their reasons were very different. Chadwick LJ did not accept that,

---

[57] [2005] EWHC 778 (TCC).
[58] [2005] EWCA Civ 1358.

if paragraph 20(c) had the meaning for which Devonport contended, it would be unnecessary. It would, for example, enable the adjudicator to decide whether the circumstances in which the contract provided for the payment of interest had arisen, the date from which interest was payable under the contractual provisions and, if not specified in the contract, the rate at which and the basis on which interest should be paid. Chadwick LJ said that the real question was the effect to be given to the words 'in particular' which precede the three sub-paragraphs (a)-(c) in paragraph 20 Part 1 of the Scheme. He thought that the words 'in particular' should bear their usual and natural meaning so that what came after them was intended to be a particularisation of what had gone before. It elaborated and explained what had gone before but it did not add to it. Thus he concluded that the adjudicator could decide questions as to interest but only if those questions were matters in dispute which had been properly referred to him or were questions which the parties had agreed were within the scope of the adjudication or were questions which the adjudicator considered to be 'necessarily connected with the dispute'. Thus, contrary to the judgment of Jackson J, he concluded that there was no free-standing power to award interest. However, he went on to find that, in that case, the parties to the dispute agreed that the question of whether interest should be paid on monies outstanding was within the scope of the adjudication and the parties had conferred on the adjudicator the jurisdiction to award interest.[59]

3.79 Accordingly, in one sense, the position in relation to interest under paragraph 20(c) has been clarified by the decision of the Court of Appeal in *Carillion*: there is no free-standing power on the part of the adjudicator to award interest and paragraph 20(c) does not provide it. Thus the adjudicator only has the power to award interest if that issue had been referred to him or had been agreed by the parties to be within the scope of the adjudication or was a matter which the adjudicator considered to be necessarily connected with the dispute. The parties can, as they did in *Carillion*, give the adjudicator the jurisdiction to consider questions of interest and, in so doing, confer on an adjudicator a jurisdiction to award interest which he would not otherwise have had.

3.80 However, the decision in *Carillion* does not address the different question of whether an adjudicator has the inherent power to award interest in any event, regardless of paragraph 20. It may be that a referring party could seek interest in reliance upon the Late Payment of Commercial Debts (Interest) Act 1998, or as damages for late payment in accordance with the principle in *FG Minter v Dawnays*.[60] There is, however, no authority as yet for either proposition.

---

[59] It is worth noting that this agreement was inferred by the Court of Appeal from relatively scant material.
[60] 13 BLR 1.

Costs

This topic is dealt with in detail in Chapter 11 below. It seems clear that an adjudicator does not have the power to order one side to pay the other side's costs. In *Northern Developments (Cumbria) Ltd v J&J Nichol*[61] HHJ Bowsher QC considered an award of costs made by an adjudicator. The Judge concluded that, pursuant to the Scheme, an adjudicator had no jurisdiction to decide that one party's costs of the adjudication be paid by another party. It is respectfully submitted that this is a correct interpretation of the Scheme: certainly neither paragraph 20 nor, for that matter, paragraph 25 which deals with fees and expenses, makes any reference to the question of costs. By analogy with the reasoning of Chadwick LJ in *Carillion*, there is therefore nothing in the scheme which gives the adjudicator a free-standing right to award costs.[62]

3.81

But, just as the Court of Appeal in *Carillion* found that the parties had agreed, in that case, and on those facts, that the adjudicator did have the jurisdiction to decide interest, so, in *Northern Developments*, the parties were found by Judge Bowsher to have agreed that the adjudicator should deal with the question of costs. The Judge said at paragraph 44:

3.82

> Provided they do not detract from the requirements of the Act and the Scheme, the parties are free to add their own terms and there is no reason why they should not expressly agree that the Adjudicator should have power to order one party to an adjudication to pay the costs of the other party. There would be no difficulty if such an agreement were made expressly and in writing. From a policy point of view, there is much to be said for a requirement that such an agreement can only be made expressly and in writing.

The Judge then went on to conclude that, in the circumstances of that case, there was an implied agreement between the parties that the adjudicator should have jurisdiction to award costs.

Reasons

At paragraph 81 of his judgment in *Carillion*, Jackson J identified three principles relevant to paragraph 22 of Part 1 of the Scheme, namely the provision by the adjudicator of reasons. These three propositions follow on from propositions 1 and 2 identified at paragraph 3.63 above. They were:

3.83

> 3. It is often not practicable for an adjudicator to put to the parties his provisional conclusions for comment. Very often those provisional conclusions will represent some intermediate position, for which neither party was contending. It will only be

---

[61] [2000] BLR 158.
[62] *Aveat* is also authority for the general proposition that the adjudicator has no general power to award costs.

in an exceptional case such as *Balfour Beatty v The London Borough of Lambeth*[63] that an adjudicator's failure to put his provisional conclusions to the parties will constitute such a serious breach of the rules of natural justice that the Court will decline to enforce his decision.

4. During argument, my attention has been drawn to certain decisions on the duty to give reasons in a planning context. See in particular *Save Britain's Heritage v No 1 Poultry Ltd*[64] and *South Bucks BC & Anor v Porter (No 2)*.[65] In my view, the principles stated in these cases are only of limited relevance to adjudicators' decisions. I reach this conclusion for three reasons:

   (a) Adjudicators' decisions do not finally determine the rights of the parties (unless all parties so wish).
   (b) If reasons are given and they prove to be erroneous, that does not generally enable the adjudicator's decision to be challenged.
   (c) Adjudicators often are not required to give reasons at all.

5. If an adjudicator is requested to give reasons pursuant to paragraph 22 of this Scheme, in my view a brief statement of those reasons will suffice. The reasons should be sufficient to show that the adjudicator has dealt with the issues remitted to him and what his conclusions are on those issues. It will only be in extreme circumstances, such as those described by the Lord Justice Clerk in *Gillies Ramsay*,[66] that the court will decline to enforce an otherwise invalid adjudicator's decision because of the inadequacy of the reasons given. The complainant would need to show that the reasons were absent or unintelligible and that, as a result, he had suffered substantial prejudice.

3.84 It is respectfully submitted that these three propositions represent clear guidance, both to adjudicators and to those involved in adjudication, as to what needs to be included within the adjudicator's reasons and what course the adjudicator should follow to make sure that his decision is clear and intelligible. These propositions were endorsed by Chadwick LJ in the Court of Appeal.[67] In addition, the following points should also be noted:

   (a) In *AMEC v Whitefriars*,[68] Dyson LJ said that an adjudicator did not have to invite the parties to make representations or to give reasons in respect of a challenge to jurisdiction: see paragraph 7.15 below.
   (b) In *Multiplex Constructions (UK) Ltd v West India Quay Development Co (Eastern) Ltd*,[69] Ramsey J confirmed that there was no duty to give reasons unless asked, and that, even if there were, such reasons could be cursory.

---

[63] [2002] EWHC 597 (TCC)
[64] [1991] 1 WLR 153.
[65] [2004] 1 WLR 1953.
[66] [2003] BLR 48.
[67] [2005] EWCA Civ 1358, at paragraph 84.
[68] [2004] EWCA Civ 1418.
[69] [2006] EWHC 1569 (TCC).

Effect of the Decision

Paragraphs 23–26 of Part 1 of the Scheme provide as follows: **3.85**

23–(1) In his decision, the adjudicator may, if he thinks fit, order any of the parties to comply peremptorily with his decision or any part of it.

(2) The decision of the adjudicator shall be binding on the parties, and they should comply with it until the dispute is finally determined by legal proceedings, by arbitration (if the contract provides for arbitration or the parties otherwise agree to arbitration) or by agreement between the parties.

24. Section 42 of the Arbitration Act 1996 shall apply to this Scheme subject to the following modifications—

(a) in sub-section (2) for the word "tribunal" wherever it appears there shall be substituted the word "adjudicator",
(b) in sub-paragraph (b) of sub-section (2) for the words "arbitral proceedings" there shall be substituted the word "adjudication",
(c) sub-paragraph (c) of sub-section (2) shall be deleted, and
(d) sub-section (3) shall be deleted.

25. The adjudicator shall be entitled to the payment of such reasonable amount as he may determine by way of fees and expenses reasonably incurred by him. The parties shall be jointly and severally liable for any sum which remains outstanding following the making of any determination on how the payment shall be apportioned.

26. The adjudicator shall not be liable for anything done or omitted in the discharge or purported discharge of his functions as adjudicator unless the act or omission is in bad faith, and any employee or agent of the adjudicator shall be similarly protected from liability.

Binding Until the Dispute is Finally Determined

The concept of 'temporary finality' has been discussed at 2.116–2.119 above. It is **3.86** the essence of the adjudication process, as set out in Part 1 of the Scheme, that the adjudicator's decision is binding on the parties until it is reviewed either in court or in arbitration. This is one of the principal reasons why the courts have endeavoured to ensure that, if the adjudicator has fairly answered the right question, then his decision will be enforced, no matter whether the court might have come to a different decision on the facts or on the law.

In the early days of the adjudication process, the point was sometimes taken that, **3.87** if the loser disputed the adjudicator's decision, that was a dispute within the meaning of s9 of the Arbitration Act and therefore there should be a stay for arbitration. In the earliest decision on this point, *Absolute Rentals Ltd v Glencor Enterprises Ltd*[70] HHJ Wilcox concluded that by virtue of the 1996 Act and the Statutory

---

[70] CILL July–August 2000, pages 1637–1638.

Scheme, the determination of the adjudicator and its enforcement was entirely without prejudice to the final merits and determination by the arbitrator. As a result, he concluded that no stay for arbitration was appropriate. He said that the suggestion that the enforcement judgment should be stayed pending the outcome of the claim because of the claimant's potentially perilous financial position was not appropriate because it would frustrate the Scheme. In refusing to grant the stay for arbitration or to stay the judgment, Judge Wilcox memorably described adjudication as 'a robust and summary procedure and there may be casualties...'

3.88 Judge Wilcox's clear reasons for the enforcement of the adjudicator's decision, and his refusal to grant a stay for arbitration, were, it is submitted, entirely in accordance with the principal purpose of the 1996 Act in general and the Scheme in particular. It would plainly make a nonsense of the adjudication process if the losing party could avoid the consequences of an adjudicator's decision by claiming that he disputed that decision and that that dispute should be referred to arbitration. Although some views which have been expressed to the contrary, it is thought that this principle is entirely unaffected by the more recent decision of the Court of Appeal in *Collins (Contractors) Ltd v Baltic Quay Management (1994) Ltd*,[71] previously referred to at paragraph 2.150 above. In that case, the claim that was stayed for arbitration was an ordinary civil action for sums due under the final account. For reasons which were unexplained, the contractors had not pursued their claims in an adjudication. Thus the Court of Appeal had a relatively simple task in concluding that, because of the clear provisions of the arbitration agreement which the parties had agreed, the court proceedings should be stayed pursuant to s9 of the Arbitration Act. Although there was some discussion in the judgment about s111 of the 1996 Act, this was on a separate point[72] and was wholly unconcerned with the enforcement of an adjudicator's decision.

3.89 In the vast majority of cases, the decision that is binding in accordance with paragraph 23(2) is the decision communicated by the adjudicator to the parties. It is submitted that it is a very rare case that would allow an adjudicator to legitimately revise his original decision as a result of 'an obvious slip'. However, as discussed in paragraphs 2.117–2.118 above, the particular circumstances of *Bloor Construction (UK) Ltd v Bowmer & Kirkland (London) Ltd*[73] persuaded HHJ Toulmin CMG QC that there was an implied term allowing an adjudicator to correct an error arising from an accidental slip or omission and that the correction being made within 3 hours of the incorrect decision was acceptable in all the circumstances.

---

[71] [2004] EWCA Civ 1757.
[72] The issue discussed at paragraphs 2.119–2.120 above.
[73] [2000] BLR 314.

The Statutory Scheme

Furthermore, there can be no doubt that the parties are obliged to comply with **3.90**
that binding decision.[74] That is what paragraph 23(2) says in express terms.
Although some standard forms of building contract incorporate provisions that
appear to make the adjudicator's decision binding, they do not always expressly
provide that the parties must comply with it. However, as HHJ Seymour QC
pointed out in *Solland International Ltd v Daraydan Holdings Ltd*[75] such provi‑
sions can only be sensibly construed as meaning that the decision is binding and
the parties are obliged to comply with it. He relied, as part of his reasoning, on the
clear words of paragraph 23(2).

One area in which it has often been argued that the decision is not binding is **3.91**
where it is suggested that the adjudicator had regard to the wrong terms of the
contract. In *Joinery Plus Ltd v Laing Ltd*[76] HHJ Thornton QC drew a distinction
between a situation where the correct contractual provisions were misconstrued
by the adjudicator and where the adjudicator construed and applied the wrong
conditions. In the former case, he said, the parties were clearly bound by the adju‑
dicator's decision and he explained the Court of Appeal decision in *C&B Scene*[77]
as being such a case. In *Joinery Plus*, Judge Thornton concluded that he was
dealing with a case where the adjudicator had construed and applied the wrong
conditions and that, as a consequence, the decision was a nullity.

It is difficult not to be sympathetic to Judge Thornton's proposition in *Joinery Plus* **3.92**
that, given that the adjudicator had decided the case by reference to the wrong set
of conditions and without recourse to the correct contractual documentation, his
errors went to the heart of his jurisdiction and were so fundamental that they
meant that he had not merely answered the right question in the wrong way, but
had answered the wrong question altogether. On the other hand, the problem
with this approach is that there may be a fine line between an error of law which
the adjudicator had the jurisdiction to make, and an error of law which meant that
his ultimate decision was outside his jurisdiction. After all, it may be said that a
mistaken decision, say, as to the extent of the work scope under a contract was not
an error of law but one which went to the fundamental question that an adjudica‑
tor should be asking himself. In addition, it is not easy to reconcile Judge Thornton's
reasoning with the decision of the Court of Appeal in *C&B Scene Concept v
Isobars*.[78] Although Judge Thornton said that that was a decision where the
adjudicator incorrectly applied the agreed terms, that may not necessarily be an
accurate summation of the point in issue in *C&B Scene*. Moreover, *C&B Scene* is

---

[74] See, in particular, Chapters 7 and 13 below.
[75] [2002] EWHC 220 (TCC).
[76] [2003] BLR 184.
[77] [2002] BLR 93.
[78] [2002] BLR 93.

itself in some ways an unsatisfactory decision, because some of the important points that it raised were not fully argued out due to the fact that only one party was represented.

3.93 It is submitted that, save in perhaps exceptional cases, it is inappropriate for a court being asked to enforce the decision of an adjudicator to embark on a lengthy investigation into the adjudicator's consideration of the relevant terms of the contract. It is thought that the approach of the Court of Appeal in *C&B Scene* is the one that is applicable in the vast majority of cases. In that case, the adjudicator had to resolve as a matter of law whether particular clauses applied or not and, if they did, what their effect was. Even if the adjudicator was wrong as to the application of those clauses, that was not a matter that prevented the enforcement of the decision. In *Allen Wilson Shop Fitters v Anthony Buckingham*[79] there was a dispute about how the claimant's financial entitlement arose because of the employer's decision to sack the contract administrator. The claim in the adjudication was put by reference to the payment provisions in the Scheme, rather than the payment mechanism in the contract. The TCC Judge concluded that the precise nature of the contractual payment machinery was an issue which did not and could not affect the enforcement proceedings; it was a matter for the adjudicator and, whether he was right or wrong, the court could not review the correctness of that decision in enforcement proceedings. The TCC Judge followed the Court of Appeal in *C&B Scene*. It is submitted that *Joinery Plus* is perhaps best treated as a case on exceptional facts, and not a decision of general application.

Enforcement of Peremptory Orders

3.94 Paragraph 24 of Part 1 of the Scheme incorporates the provisions of Section 42 of the Arbitration Act 1996. Section 42 is concerned with the court's power to make an order requiring a party to comply with the peremptory order of an arbitrator. Those powers are therefore expressly provided to the court to ensure that parties comply with decisions of the adjudicator. The TCC has now developed its own summary procedure by which the decisions of adjudicators can be enforced, and the reasons for non-compliance can be examined. This is discussed in detail in paragraphs 14.02–14.11 below.

Fees

3.95 Chapter 11 deals in detail with the principles concerned with the adjudicator's entitlement to fees, and their calculation. In respect of adjudications under the Scheme, Paragraph 25 of Part 1 sets out the adjudicator's entitlement to the payment of his fees. In *London & Amsterdam Properties Ltd v Waterman*

---

[79] [2005] 102 Con LR 154.

Partnership Ltd[80] there was a complaint about the adjudicator's fee proposals, it being argued that the adjudicator's appointment was at variance with the Scheme and that therefore the adjudicator had no jurisdiction. HHJ Wilcox accepted that the adjudicator's fee proposal included the words 'for each hour during which I engage myself upon this adjudication' which did not appear in the Scheme. However, he found that, as a yardstick to ascertaining the final entitlement of the adjudicator, an hourly rate for time actually spent was both sensible and reasonable. Whilst the Judge accepted that the arrangement was notionally open-ended and could therefore be abused by an inexperienced adjudicator, he concluded that the adjudicator in the instant case was an experienced professional nominated by the RICS whose fee proposals were clearly 'modest and reasonable by any token'. The Judge therefore rejected the submission that the adjudicator's fee proposals made after his appointment were at variance with the Scheme.

The provisions of paragraph 25 also arose for consideration in *Prentice Island Ltd v Castle Contracting Ltd*.[81] In that case the Sheriff had concluded that the adjudicator was properly appointed and that, even if he was wrong about that, so that the adjudicator should have resigned pursuant to paragraph 9(2) of the Scheme, that did not affect his entitlement to fees. The Sheriff said that it was to be expected that paragraph 25 should be found in that part of the Scheme dealing with the effects of the decision, since it was the issue of the decision that exhausted the referral process, and it was at that stage that the adjudicator became entitled to determine his fee. He considered that it was because of that association that special provision was made in paragraph 9(4) for the circumstances in which the referral does not run its full course, thus making it clear that the adjudicator was nevertheless entitled to be remunerated for the process on which he had been engaged up until that point. Essentially, the Sheriff rejected the suggestion that the adjudicator's entitlement to fees under paragraph 25 was in any way conditional on the validity of the adjudicator's decision. Where a decision was issued, thus bringing to an end the process in respect of which the adjudicator was appointed, and marking the first occasion on which he could determine the reasonable amount of his fees and expenses incurred by him in that process, the communication of the decision triggered the adjudicator's entitlement to be paid his fees.

3.96

---

[80] [2004] BLR 179.
[81] Unreported, 15.12.03, a decision of R A Dunlop QC, Sheriff Principal in the Sheriffdom of Tayside Central and Fife.

Part II of the Scheme—Payment

Introduction

3.97 The point has already been made that there is a debate as to whether the specific provisions within Parts I and II of the Scheme apply to construction contracts as a means of filling in any gaps in those contacts, or by way of wholesale replacement. This is particularly important in relation to the provisions in Part II of the Scheme, relating to payment. It is quite common for construction contracts to include a number of provisions in relation to payment but to omit one or perhaps two of the specific detailed provisions set out in Part II. It is no coincidence that most of the authorities concerning whether or not the Scheme applied in whole or just in part to make good the omissions were cases concerned with these payment provisions. As discussed in paragraphs 3.04–3.10 above, the courts in Scotland have apparently concluded that the detailed provisions within the scheme apply only to the extent that the contract does not contain that particular provision, whilst a number of the TCC Judges have reached the opposite conclusion. Whilst the point must await final resolution by the Court of Appeal, it is perhaps worth noting that, by analogy with the operation of the Unfair Contract Terms Act 1977, it may well be that a non-compliant term brings down the whole contractual mechanism, and requires the implication of the Scheme. Under UCTA, if a term is unfair, it is struck out altogether. The court does not attempt to redraft the contract term in question, seeing what can be salvaged and what must be deleted because it is unfair. If the same approach is adopted here, a contract with, say, payment terms which did not comply with the 1996 Act in a particular respect would be made subject to the implication of the Scheme in its totality, rather than leaving the parties with their rights and liabilities to be the subject of a contract which was created, essentially, by the court, as a mixture of the terms that had been agreed (where they complied with the Act), and the terms to be implied from the Scheme (where the express terms did not comply with the 1996 Act).

Entitlement to and Amount of Stage Payments

3.98 Paragraphs 1 and 2 of Part II of the Scheme provide as follows:

1. Where the parties to a relevant construction contract fail to agree—
    (a) the amount of any instalment or stage or periodic payment for any work under the contract, or
    (b) the intervals at which, or circumstances in which, such payments become due under that contract, or

(c) both of the matters mentioned in sub-paragraphs (a) and (b) above,
the relevant provisions of paragraphs 2 to 4 below shall apply.

2–(1) The amount of any payment by way of instalments or stage or periodic payments in respect of a relevant period shall be the difference between the amount determined in accordance with sub-paragraph (2) and the amount determined in accordance with sub-paragraph (3).

(2) The aggregate of the following amounts—
   (a) an amount equal to the value of any work performed in accordance with the relevant construction contract during the period from the commencement of the contract to the end of the relevant period (excluding any amount calculated in accordance with sub-paragraph (b)),
   (b) where the contract provides for payment for materials, an amount equal to the value of any materials manufactured on site or brought onto site for the purposes of the works during the period from the commencement of the contract to the end of the relevant period, and
   (c) any other amount or sum which the contract specifies shall be payable during or in respect of the period from the commencement of the contract to the end of the relevant period.

(3) The aggregate of any sums which have been paid or are due for payment by way of instalments, stage or periodic payments during the period from the commencement of the contract to the end of the relevant period.

(4) An amount calculated in accordance with this paragraph shall not exceed the difference between—
   (a) the contract price, and
   (b) the aggregate of the instalments or stage or periodic payments which have become due.

3.99 Paragraph 1 of Part II of the Scheme emphasises the importance of stage payments. All construction contracts must include provisions relating to the amount of such stage payments, and the intervals at which and the circumstances in which such payments become due. If the construction contractor does not include some or all of these provisions, then the detailed provisions in paragraphs 2, 3 and 4 of the Scheme will be implied into the contract.

3.100 Paragraph 2 is concerned with the amount of such stage payments. Put shortly, the amount is to be the difference between the amount calculated in accordance with sub-paragraph (2) and the amount which has been paid, or is due for payment (sub-paragraph (3)). Sub-paragraph (2) calculates the value of the work done to date, including, where relevant, payments for materials and other matters specified in the contract. What is the 'value of work?' That is defined in paragraph 12 of Part II of the Scheme as meaning:

> An amount determined in accordance with the construction contract under which the work is performed or where the contract contains no such provision, the cost of any work performed in accordance with that contract together with an amount equal to any overhead or profit included in the contract price.

3.101 Paragraph 2(2)(a) and paragraph 12 of Part II of the Scheme were considered by HHJ Lloyd QC, in *Alstom Signalling Ltd v Jarvis Facilities Ltd*.[82] Judge Lloyd QC commented that, for the purposes of the Scheme, the value of the work carried out is the value placed upon it by the proper operation of the construction contract. Under the particular contract in that case, which involved a certification process, the amount was the amount that Alstom considered should be included in a certificate, having taken into account any answers to any questions or queries that they may have had as to the build up of each interim account.

3.102 Most construction and engineering contracts provide for a process by which a third party, usually the architect or the contract administrator, will issue a certificate identifying the sum to be paid on an interim basis by the employer. There will usually be a mechanism which allows the contractor to identify the sums which the contractor says should be included within that certificate and a period in which the architect or contract administrator considers the claim by the contractor and arrives at his own certification. The sum certified is then due and must be paid no later than the date specified in the contract. Such an arrangement would obviate the implication of paragraphs 1 and 2 of the Scheme because it provides for a system of stage payments. Other common forms of contract which would again obviate paragraphs 1 and 2 of Part II of the Scheme are those which provide for a lump sum payment, specified in the contract, on a monthly or periodic basis. Other, more simple contracts, may not make it clear how the stage payments are to be calculated, and it is those contracts in respect of which paragraphs 1 and 2 of the Scheme are now principally relevant. It is worth noting that, as a result of the definition of 'value of work' in paragraph 12, if the construction contract contains no provision which would allow the parties to arrive at the 'value of work', then the default position is that the contractor is entitled to the cost of the work that he has performed, together with overheads and profit. Thus, it is plainly in the employer's interest to ensure that there is a workable mechanism by which the value of work can be objectively ascertained. If it cannot, then the employer runs the risk that the default position will apply, and the contractor will be entitled to his costs, plus an allowance for overheads and profit.

3.103 Paragraph 2(4) seeks to provide a cap on the amount of any stage payments. The cap is said to be the difference between the contract price and the aggregate of the instalments for stage payments. It is slightly unclear what the purpose of paragraph 2(4) really is. If it is intended to state that the total amount of interim payments cannot be greater than the contract price, it might not be thought to have added very much, particularly as paragraph 12 defines the 'contract price' as 'the entire sum payable under the construction contract in respect of the work'.

---

[82] [2004] EWHC 1285 (TCC).

As Judge Lloyd QC pointed out in *Alstom*, the use of the word 'entire' is unfortunate because it has connotations of 'entire contracts'. Judge Lloyd went on:

> It means the final sum due. The Scheme has to cover a wide variety of contracts. It is not to be assumed that in promulgating Part II of the Scheme the Government was unaware of re-measurement contracts or other contracts in which the contract price is no more than the tender sum and the 'price' is arrived at by the application of rates and prices to the quantities of work executed. In order to find out what is meant by the 'entire sum' it is necessary to examine the construction contract, to ascertain the work done under it and then to determine what is payable for that work. The buffer [the total amount of interim payments could not be greater than the contract price] may still apply e.g. where interim payments prove to be over-estimates or other mistaken assessments. It is probably directed to mundane situations where a contractor or sub-contractor is paid generally on account what is asked for (e.g. by way of 'drawings') which then get close to the total sum payable. It is aimed at over-payments which are always difficult to recover.

Accordingly, adopting this common sense analysis, Judge Lloyd concluded that, in that case, the 'entire sum' was what turned out to be payable to Jarvis, the contractors, in accordance with the detailed provisions of the contract.

Dates for Payment

Paragraphs 3–7 inclusive of Part II of the Scheme provide as follows: **3.104**

> 3. Where the parties to a construction contract fail to provide an adequate mechanism for determining either what payments become due under the contract, or when they become due for payment, or both, the relevant provisions of paragraphs 4 to 7 shall apply.
>
> 4. Any payments of a kind mentioned in paragraph 2 above shall become due on whichever of the following dates occurs later—
>   (a) the expiry of seven days following the relevant period mentioned in paragraph 2(1) above, or
>   (b) the making of a claim by the payee.
>
> 5. The final payment payable under a relevant construction contract, namely the payment of an amount equal to the difference (if any) between—
>   (a) the contract price, and
>   (b) the aggregate of any instalment or stage or periodic payments which have become due under the contract,
>
> shall become due on the expiry of—
>   (a) 30 days following completion of the work, or
>   (b) the making of a claim by the payee, whichever is the later.
>
> 6. Payment of the contract price under a construction contract (not being a relevant construction contract) shall become due on
>   (a) the expiry of 30 days following the completion of the work, or
>   (b) the making of a claim by the payee, whichever is the later.

7. Any other payment under a construction contract shall become due
   (a) on the expiry of seven days following the completion of the work to which the payment relates or
   (b) the making of a claim by the payee,
   whichever is the later.

3.105 These paragraphs are implied into a construction contract where that contract does not have an adequate mechanism for determining what payments become due under the contract and/or when they become due. Paragraph 4 provides that stage payments become due on the later of two dates: the expiry of seven days following the relevant period, or the making of a claim by the payee. The relevant period is defined in paragraph 12 of the Scheme as being either the period specified in the contract or, if there is no such period, a period of 28 days. Thus, pursuant to paragraph 4 an interim payment will become due on the latest of two dates, either the expiry of seven days after the 28 day period, or when the payee makes a claim for the stage payment.

3.106 Paragraph 5 deals with final payments, and provides that the final payment will be due on the later of two dates: the making of the claim or 30 days following completion of the work. Paragraph 5 applies to what is called a 'relevant construction contract' which is defined in paragraph 12 as a construction contract 'other than one which specifies that the duration of the work is to be less than 45 days or in respect of which the parties agree that the duration of the work is estimated to be less than 45 days'. Curiously, paragraph 6 applies to construction contracts which are not relevant construction contracts, which must mean contracts which specify the duration at less than 45 days or where the parties agree that the work will take less than 45 days. However, paragraph 6 appears not to differ from paragraph 5 in any relevant particular, providing again that the final date for payment is 30 days after the completion of the work, or on the date of the making of the claim by the payee, whichever is the later.

3.107 Paragraph 7 of Part II of the Scheme appears to be a catch-all provision which states generally that any other payment under a construction contract becomes due on the expiry of seven days following the completion of the work to which the payment relates. To that extent, therefore, it is consistent with paragraph 4(a), which also refers to the expiry of seven days following the relevant period.

Final Date for Payment

3.108 Paragraph 8 of Part II of the Scheme provides as follows:

> 8–(1) Where the parties to a construction contract fail to provide a final date for payment in relation to any sum which becomes due under a construction contract, the provisions of this paragraph shall apply.

The Statutory Scheme

(2) The final date for the making of any payment of the kind mentioned in paragraphs 2, 5, 6 or 7 shall be 17 days from the date that payment becomes due.

3.109 Paragraph 8 of Part II provides that a stage payment that is due must be paid no later than 17 days from the date that it became due. Thus, supposing a contractor started work on 1 January, then, pursuant to paragraph 2(1) he would be entitled to a stage payment in relation to the work carried out up until 28 January. Pursuant to Clause 4(a) that sum would become due on 4 February (being seven days after the expiry of the 28 day period) and that payment would have to be made no later than 21 February (17 days later).

3.110 There are a number of reported cases in which the contract under consideration failed to provide a final date for payment, and the provisions of paragraph 8 of Part II of the Scheme had to be applied. Thus, in *Buxton Building Contractors Ltd v The Governors of Durand Primary School*[83] there was no final certificate so there was no mechanism under the contract by which the second tranche of the retention monies would become payable. In those circumstances, Buxton could and did operate paragraph 8 of Part II of the Scheme. In the absence of a prescribed date for payment, Buxton issued an invoice for the sum due (paragraph 5(b)) and the making of that claim triggered the 17 day period in paragraph 8(2). Similarly, in *Hills Electrical and Mechanical Plc v Dawn Construction Ltd*[84] the sub-contractors were desperate to ensure that the 17 day period in paragraph 8(2) applied, rather than the 28 day period allowed for in the contract, since the parties were agreed that there was only a valid claim if the final date for payment was 17 days after the payment became due, rather than 28. The court rejected that case on the grounds that the Scheme was only implied to the extent that the contract did not expressly provide for a particular element of the relevant payment provisions. Since this contract did include a provision for the final date for payment (28 days) there was no room or need to imply the 17 days from the Scheme. The claim therefore failed.

Payment Notices and Withholding Notices

3.111 Paragraphs 9 and 10 of Part II of the Scheme provide as follows:

Notice specifying amount of payment

9. A party to a construction contract shall, not later than five days after the date on which any payment—
   (a) becomes due from him, or

---

[83] [2004] EWHC 733 (TCC).
[84] [2004] SLT 477.

> (b) would have become due, if—
>> (i) the other party had carried out its obligations under the contract, and
>> (ii) no set-off or abatement was permitted by reference to any sum claimed to be due under one or more other contract,
>
> give notice to the other party to the contract specifying the amount (if any) of the payment he has made or proposes to make, specifying to what the payment relates and the basis on which that amount is calculated.
>
> Notice of intention to withhold payment
>
> 10. Any notice of intention to withhold payment mentioned in Section 111 of the Act shall be given not later than the prescribed period, which is to say not later than seven days before the final date for payment determined either in accordance with the construction contract or where no such provision is made in the contract, in accordance with paragraph 8 above.

3.112 The principles relating to the notices specifying the amount of payment and withholding notices have been discussed at paragraphs 2.121–2.147 above. It is instructive to work out precisely how these provisions operate. Let us return to the example of the contractor who started work on the 1 January pursuant to a contract to which the Scheme applied in full. In those circumstances, the sum was due to the contractor on 4 February. Accordingly, no later that the 9 February, the payer must make plain to him what sum he is going to pay, specifying to what the payment relates and the basis on which that amount is calculated. If a sum is to be deducted then it is often appropriate for any such amount to be identified in that notice. Paragraph 10 of Part II of the Scheme makes plain that, in any event, any amount that it is to be withheld must be identified not later than seven days before the final date for payment. In this example, the final date for payment was 21 February (17 days after 4 February). Thus the withholding notice would have to be issued no later than 14 February.

3.113 The principal area of contention to which these provisions have given rise is the extent to which an employer can seek to avoid making payments of the sum due by reference to cross-claims and other matters. In addition, there were numerous disputes about how the sum due was calculated, particularly under contracts which did not provide for a certification regime. The cases dealing with these disputes are set out in detail at Chapter 10 below.

Prohibition of 'Pay-When-Paid'

3.114 Paragraph 11 of Part II of the Scheme provides as follows:

> 11. Where a provision making payment under a construction contract conditional on the payer receiving payment from a third party is ineffective as mentioned in Section 113 of the Act, and the parties have not agreed other terms for payment, the relevant provisions of—
>> (a) paragraphs 2, 4, 5, 7, 8, 9 and 10 shall apply in the case of a relevant construction contract; and

(b) paragraphs 6, 7, 8, 9 and 10 shall apply in the case of any other construction contract.

3.115 This paragraph is perhaps rather less complicated than it looks. Essentially it is providing that, where a contract contains a prohibited 'pay-when-paid' mechanism, the Scheme provisions, discussed above, will apply in full. The only exception to that is that, for construction contracts for less than 45 days, the relevant paragraph is 6 rather than paragraphs 4 and 5, the difference of course being that, for a shorter contract, it is unnecessary to make provisions for stage and final payments. The provisions of the 1996 Act dealing with pay-when-paid clauses are dealt with at paragraphs 2.158–2.161 above.

Part II

OTHER FORMS OF ADJUDICATION

4. Contractual Adjudication	147
5. Ad Hoc Adjudication	185
6. Adjudication in Other Jurisdictions	195

4

CONTRACTUAL ADJUDICATION

The Importance of the Contractual Provisions	4.01	DOM/1	4.34
		DOM/2	4.44
The JCT 1998 Form	4.06	Other Standard Forms of Contract	4.51
Nomination	4.07	GC/Works	4.51
Referral Within 7 Days	4.11	The ICE Form of Engineering Contract	4.54
More Than One Dispute	4.16		
'Impartially'	4.17	NEC/2	4.60
Non-Compliance	4.18	Contracts For Professional Services	4.61
28 Days	4.19	Adjudication Rules	4.62
'Binding'	4.23	The TeCSA Rules	4.62
Final Certificates	4.25	The CEDR Rules	4.71
Determination	4.26	The CIC Model Adjudication Procedure	4.72
Other Forms of JCT Contract	4.27		
The JCT Adjudication Agreement	4.32		
The Standard Forms of Sub-Contracts	4.34		

'It seems to me that if the contractual adjudication provisions comply with the Act, then they must be at the forefront of the court's consideration of the parties' respective rights and liabilities. I would respectfully venture the opinion that, in some of the reported cases, the focus has been too much on the 1996 Act (and s.108 in particular) and not enough on the relevant terms of the parties' contract.'

His Honour Judge Coulson QC in *Cubitt Building and Interiors Ltd v Fleetglade Ltd* [2006] EWHC 3413 (TCC).

The Importance of the Contractual Provisions

The 1996 Act requires all construction contracts to have an adjudication procedure which complies with s108: see s108(5). The same section makes plain that if the construction contract in question does not contain adjudication provisions   **4.01** that comply with s108 (1)–(4), then the Scheme for Construction Contracts will then apply. It is therefore envisaged that the construction contract will include its own adjudication provisions. All of the standard forms of building and engineering contracts have been amended to include provisions, which can often be quite lengthy, to provide for adjudication. Some of those provisions, and the adjudication rules which have also been produced for incorporation into such contracts, are dealt with below. However, before dealing with some of the points that have arisen on those express terms and particular rules, it is important first to consider the interplay between the contractual provisions, the 1996 Act and the Scheme.

4.02 If a construction contract contains a set of adjudication provisions, then the first question to be asked is whether those provisions comply with s108 (1)–(4) of the 1996 Act. If they do not, the Scheme applies. If, on the other hand, the adjudication provisions in the construction contract do comply with s108 then those contractual provisions become determinative of the parties' rights and obligations in respect of adjudication. In *Cubitt Building and Interiors Ltd v Fleetglade Ltd* [2006] EWHC 3413 (TCC), the parties were agreed that the contract contained provisions which complied with the 1996 Act and that, in those circumstances, all that mattered were those contractual provisions. The TCC Judge expressly accepted the proposition that, whilst the parties could not contract out of the 1996 Act, if the contractual provisions complied with the Act, then they had to be at the forefront of the Court's consideration of the parties' respective rights and liabilities. The Judge went on to suggest that, in some at least of the reported cases, too great an emphasis had been placed upon the operation of s108, and not enough on the relevant contractual provisions.[1]

4.03 Accordingly, provided that the relevant contractual provisions comply with the 1996 Act, it does not matter if they contain additional or supplementary provisions. The mere fact that the contractual provisions contain terms which are different to those envisaged by the 1996 Act does not matter, provided always that the requirements of the 1996 Act are included within those provisions. Provisions which add to the basic requirements of the Act are perfectly acceptable; provisions which alter or omit those basic requirements are not.

4.03A It will sometimes be the case that, although the parties have contracted on a standard form which has been amended in an attempt to comply with the 1996 Act, that contract may, on analysis, fail to comply with the basic requirements of the Act, in which case the Scheme will apply. So, in *David McLean Housing Contractors*

---

[1] For example, in *William Verry v North West London Communal Mikva* [2004] BLR 3008, the TCC Judge's approach was based on a careful analysis of s108, not the operative words of the contract which, potentially at any rate, had a different emphasis.

Ltd v Swansea Housing Association Ltd,[2] the parties contracted on the JCT 1981 form (with Contractor's Design) which had been amended to allow for adjudication. However, the unfortunate manner in which the contract documents were compiled, which included deletions, additions and various omissions, led the Judge to conclude that the contract did not meet the requirements of s108 of the 1996 Act and the Scheme took effect instead.

4.04 The failure of the contract to comply with the 1996 Act will not be limited to the precise adjudication provisions that it contains. It is, of course, necessary for all construction contracts to contain the relevant provisions for interim and final payment set out in ss109 and 110. Thus, in the same way, a standard form contract may, on the face of it, comply with those provisions, but may have been amended or otherwise altered such that the contract actually made does not comply with the 1996 Act. In that event the Scheme for Construction Contracts would be incorporated into the contract instead. Thus, in *C & B Scene Concept Design Ltd v Isobars Ltd*,[3] the payment provisions in the JCT form required the parties to elect which of two alternatives for interim payments they had chosen. The parties failed to make that choice and, therefore, there were no contractual provisions as to how much should be paid by interim payments and when those payments should be made. Thus the Scheme was implied.[4] A different sort of difficulty arose in *Buxton Building Contractors Ltd v The Governors of Durand Primary School*.[5] There, although the contract envisaged that the second tranche of the retention fund would be released by way of a final certificate, the contract administrator chose not to issue a final certificate, but instead issued an interim certificate requiring the employer to pay the second tranche of the retention monies. That was not a certificate authorised by the JCT form. In those circumstances, as the Judge noted, the contractor operated paragraph 8 of Part II of the Scheme for Construction Contracts which applied to claims for payment where there were no adequate contractual payment provisions.[6]

4.05 There is one last, but potentially very important, general point to be made about contractual adjudication. There is a view that, whilst an adjudicator can make errors of law and fact in statutory adjudications, which will not affect the validity and enforceability of the decision, the same is not true of a decision in

---

[2] [2002] BLR 125.
[3] [2002] BLR 93.
[4] A similar result eventuated in *Allen Wilson v Buckingham* [2005] EWHC 1165 (TCC). In both cases, this potential confusion formed the basis of a plea by the losing party that the adjudicator lacked jurisdiction to reach the decision that he did. In both cases, this argument failed.
[5] [2004] EWHC 733 (TCC).
[6] The correctness of the decision in *Buxton* was doubted by the Court of Appeal in *Carillion*. However, the TCC Judge's analysis of the interplay between the contractual provisions and the Scheme was not doubted.

a purely contractual adjudication. The culmination of this view can be seen in *Steve Domsalla (t/a Domsalla Building services) Ltd v Kenneth Dyason*,[7] where HHJ Thornton QC decided that what he called the 'unreviewable error doctrine' arose out of the statutory underpinning of adjudication, so as to give effect to the statutory policy of a contractor's cash flow. He said that a consumer contract was not subject to that same policy. The obvious difficulty with this approach is that it would give rise to major differences on enforcement, depending solely on the original basis of the appointment of the adjudicator. In addition, it might be said to ignore the point that statutory adjudication operates by way of the implication of the Scheme into the construction contract. On that basis, it could be said that all adjudication is contractual in one way or another. It is to be hoped that this potentially important point is clarified when the case is heard by the Court of Appeal.

The JCT 1998 Form

4.06 The JCT Standard Form of contract in most common use is the 1998 Edition, which also forms the basis of the With Contractor's Design version of the same terms. Although there are a number of minor variations to the JCT provisions, depending on which version is being used, it is perhaps helpful to set out in full Clause 41A of those provisions:

> 41A Adjudication
>
> 41A-1 Clause 41A applies where, pursuant to article 5, either Party refers any dispute or difference arising under this Contract to adjudication.
>
> 41A-2 The Adjudicator to decide the dispute or difference shall be either an individual agreed by the Parties or, on the application of either Party, an individual to be nominated as the Adjudicator by the person named in the Appendix ('the nominator'). Provided that
>
> 41A-2.1 no Adjudicator shall be agreed or nominated under clause 41A-2 or clause 41A-3 who will not execute the Standard Agreement for the appointment of an Adjudicator issued by the JCT (the 'JCT Adjudication Agreement') with the Parties; and
>
> 41A-2.2 where either Party has given notice of his intention to refer a dispute or difference to adjudication then
>
> – any agreement by the Parties on the appointment of an adjudicator must be reached with the object of securing the appointment of, and the referral of the dispute or difference to, the Adjudicator within 7 days of the date of the notice of intention to refer (see clause 41A-4.1);

---

[7] [2007] EWHC 1174 (TCC).

- any application to the nominator must be made with the object of securing the appointment of, and the referral of the dispute or difference to, the Adjudicator within 7 days of the date of the notice of intention to refer.

Upon agreement by the Parties on the appointment of the Adjudicator or upon receipt by the Parties from the nominator of the name of the nominated Adjudicator the Parties shall thereupon execute with the Adjudicator the JCT Adjudication Agreement.

41A-3 If the Adjudicator dies or becomes ill or is unavailable for some other cause and is thus unable to adjudicate on a dispute or difference referred to him, the Parties may either agree upon an individual to replace the Adjudicator or either Party may apply to the nominator for the nomination of an adjudicator to adjudicate that dispute or difference; and the Parties shall execute the JCT Adjudication Agreement with the agreed or nominated Adjudicator.

41A-4.1 When pursuant to article 5 a Party requires a dispute or difference to be referred to adjudication then that Party shall give notice to the other Party of his intention to refer the dispute or difference, briefly identified in the notice, to adjudication. If an Adjudicator is agreed or appointed within 7 days of the notice then the Party giving the notice shall refer the dispute or difference to the Adjudicator ("the referral") within 7 days of the notice. If an Adjudicator is not agreed or appointed within 7 days of the notice the referral shall be made immediately on such agreement or appointment. The said Party shall include with that referral particulars of the dispute or difference together with a summary of the contentions on which he relies, a statement of the relief or remedy which is sought and any material he wishes the Adjudicator to consider. The referral and its accompanying documentation shall be copied simultaneously to the other Party.

41A-4.2 The referral by a Party with its accompanying documentation to the Adjudicator and the copies thereof to be provided to the other Party shall be given by actual delivery or by FAX or by special delivery or recorded delivery. If given by FAX then, for record purposes, the referral and its accompanying documentation must forthwith be sent by first class post or given by actual delivery. If sent by special delivery or recorded delivery the referral and its accompanying documentation shall, subject to proof to the contrary, be deemed to have been received 48 hours after the date of posting subject to the exclusion of Sundays and any Public Holiday.

41A-5.1 The Adjudicator shall immediately upon receipt of the referral and its accompanying documentation confirm the date of that receipt to the Parties.

41A-5.2 The Party not making the referral may, by the same means stated in clause 41A-4.2, send to the Adjudicator within 7 days of the date of the referral, with a copy to the other Party, a written statement of the contentions on which he relies and any material he wishes the Adjudicator to consider.

41A-5.3 The Adjudicator shall within 28 days of the referral under clause 41A-4.1 and acting as an Adjudicator for the purposes of S.108 of the Housing Grants, Construction and Regeneration Act 1996 and not as an expert or an arbitrator reach his decision and forthwith send that decision in writing to the Parties. Provided that the Party who has made the referral may consent to allowing the Adjudicator to extend the period of 28 days by up to 14 days; and that by agreement between the Parties after the referral has been made a longer period than 28 days may be notified jointly by the Parties to the Adjudicator within which to reach his decision.

41A-5.4 The Adjudicator shall not be obliged to give reasons for his decision.

Other Forms of Adjudication

41A-5.5 In reaching his decision the Adjudicator shall act impartially and set his own procedure; and at his absolute discretion may take the initiative in ascertaining the facts and the law as he considers necessary in respect of the referral which may include the following:

-5.1 using his own knowledge and/or experience;

-5.2 subject to clause 30.9, opening up, reviewing and revising any certificate, opinion, decision, requirement or notice issued, given or made under the Contract as if no such certificate, opinion, decision, requirement or notice had been issued, given or made;

-5.3 requiring from the Parties further information than that contained in the notice of referral and its accompanying documentation or in any written statement provided by the Parties including the results of any tests that have been made or of any opening up;

-5.4 requiring the Parties to carry out tests or additional tests or to open up work or further open up work;

-5.5 visiting the site of the Works or any workshop where work is being or has been prepared for the Contract;

-5.6 obtaining such information as he considers necessary from any employee or representative of the Parties provided that before obtaining information from an employee of a Party he has given prior notice to that Party;

-5.7 obtaining from others such information and advice as he considers necessary on technical and on legal matters subject to giving prior notice to the Parties together with a statement or estimate of the cost involved;

-5.8 having regard to any term of the Contract relating to the payment of interest, deciding the circumstances in which or the period for which a simple rate of interest shall be paid.

41A-5.6 Any failure by either Party to enter into the JCT Adjudication Agreement or to comply with any requirement of the Adjudicator under clause 41A-5.5 or with any provision in or requirement under clause 41A shall not invalidate the decision of the Adjudicator.

41A-5.7 The Parties shall meet their own costs of the adjudication except that the Adjudicator may direct as to who should pay the cost of any test or opening up if required pursuant to clause 41A-5.5.4.

41A-5.8 Where any dispute or difference arises under clause 8-4.4 as to whether an instruction issued thereunder is reasonable in all the circumstances the following provisions shall apply:

-8.1 The Adjudicator to decide such dispute or difference shall (where practicable) be an individual with appropriate expertise and experience in the specialist area or discipline relevant to the instruction or issue in dispute.

-8.2 Where the Adjudicator does not have the appropriate expertise and experience referred to in clause 41A-5.8.1 above the Adjudicator shall appoint an independent expert with such relevant expertise and experience to advise and report in writing on whether or not any instruction issued under clause 8-4.4 is reasonable in all the circumstances.

-8.3 here an expert has been appointed by the Adjudicator pursuant to clause 41A-5.8.2 above the Parties shall be jointly and severally responsible for the expert's fees and expenses but, in his decision, the Adjudicator shall direct as to who should pay the fees and expenses of such expert or the proportion in which such fees and expenses are to be shared between the Parties.

-8.4 Notwithstanding the provisions of clause 41A-5.4 above, where an independent expert has been appointed by the Adjudicator pursuant to clause 41A-5.8.2 above, copies of the Adjudicator's instructions to the expert and any written advice or reports received from such expert shall be supplied to the Parties as soon as practicable.

41A-6.1 The Adjudicator in his decision shall state how payment of his fee and reasonable expenses is to be apportioned as between the Parties. In default of such statement the Parties shall bear the cost of the Adjudicator's fee and reasonable expenses in equal proportions.

41A-6.2 The Parties shall be jointly and severally liable to the Adjudicator for his fee and for all expenses reasonably incurred by the Adjudicator pursuant to the adjudication.

41A-7.1 The decision of the Adjudicator shall be binding on the Parties until the dispute or difference is finally determined by arbitration or by legal proceedings or by an agreement in writing between the Parties made after the decision of the Adjudicator has been given.

41A-7.2 The Parties shall, without prejudice to their other rights under this Contract, comply with the decision of the Adjudicator; and the Employer and the Contractor shall ensure that the decision of the Adjudicator is given effect.

41A-7.3 If either Party does not comply with the decision of the Adjudicator the other Party shall be entitled to take legal proceedings to secure such compliance pending any final determination of the referred dispute or difference pursuant to clause 41A-7.1

41A-8 The Adjudicator shall not be liable for anything done or omitted in the discharge or purported discharge of his functions as Adjudicator unless the act or omission is in bad faith and this protection from liability shall similarly extend to any employee or agent of the Adjudicator.

Nomination

4.07 The nomination of the adjudicator under these provisions can happen in one of two ways. The more usual path to nomination is that envisaged in Clause 41A.2 above, whereby the parties either agree a particular person to act as the adjudicator or the adjudicator is nominated by a person or body named in the contract and referred to as 'the nominator'. In most cases, the nominator will be a professional body, such as the RICS and the ACIA, or TeCSA and TECBAR. Given the tight timetable applicable to adjudications, the nominator needs to nominate an adjudicator promptly and difficulties might arise if there are any delays.[8]

---

[8] See for example the judgment in *Cubitt Building and Interiors Ltd v Fleetglade Ltd* [2006] EWHC 3413 (TCC), in particular paragraph 46.

4.08 There will sometimes be disputes about the person nominated by the nominator to act as the adjudicator. This is a particular problem on major contracts where there has been a long-running series of individual disputes which have been referred to adjudication. Often a party who was successful in an earlier adjudication wants the same adjudicator to be nominated again, whilst the party who was unsuccessful will seek to have somebody else appointed in their stead. Both parties will make their cases to the nominator, who then has to decide whom to nominate. There are no authorities expressly dealing with this problem and with the way in which the nominator should deal with it. It is suggested that, where points are raised about the nomination of a particular person to act as adjudicator, the nominator has an obligation to consider all such points fully. Ultimately, however, it will be up to the nominator to weigh in the balance the advantages inherent in the nomination of an adjudicator who is already familiar with the basic contractual landscape, and the problems of nominating an individual against whom one party has raised an express objection. It is thought that, unless the objection is obviously spurious, it may well be the best course for the nominator to nominate a new adjudicator.

4.09 The other way in which adjudicators are appointed is when they are expressly named in the contract. Many of the large infrastructure projects of recent years, such as the Wembley Stadium contracts, provided for named adjudicators. The advantage of that process is that the nomination exercise is unnecessary, which saves time and potential dispute. The disadvantage can be if one or other of the parties to the contract forms the view that the adjudicator named in the contract is either not up to the task, or has apparently reached an unreasonably adverse opinion of that party's overall position.

4.10 If the named adjudicator is unable to accept the appointment, the JCT Form contains an express provision to deal with such an eventuality:

> If the Adjudicator dies or becomes ill or is unavailable for some other cause, and is thus unable to adjudicate on a dispute or difference referred to him then
> 1. Either party may apply to the individual named as the Adjudicator in Appendix 1 to replace the Adjudicator to adjudicate that dispute or difference, save that
> 2. If the individual named as the Adjudicator in Appendix 1 is unavailable then either Party may apply to the partner or director who is managing (for the time being) the practice of such named individual . . .

In *Amec Projects Ltd v Whitefriars City Estates Ltd* [2004] EWHC 393 (TCC) the adjudicator named in the JCT contract had died before the adjudication. The TCC Judge found that there was no one else who was qualified to act as the adjudicator under the terms of the contract and that in any event, since the dispute had not been referred to the adjudicator prior to his death, the contractual provisions noted above, as to the making of an application to the manager of the practice, did not apply. Accordingly, the nomination provisions in the Scheme for Construction

Contracts were applicable. That part of the decision was upheld by the Court of Appeal.[9]

Referral Within 7 Days

4.11 In order to ensure that the adjudication follows an appropriately tight timetable, Clause 41A is designed to ensure that the dispute is referred to the adjudicator within seven days of the original notice of intention to refer. This can be seen in Clause 41A.2.2 ('with the object of securing the appointment of, and the referral of the dispute or difference to, the Adjudicator within 7 days of the date of the notice of intention to refer...') and Clause 41A.4.1 ('If an Adjudicator is agreed or appointed within 7 days of the notice then the Party giving the notice shall refer the dispute or difference to the Adjudicator ('the referral') within 7 days of the notice'). These latter provisions have created a certain amount of difficulty.

4.12 In *William Verry v North West London Communal Mikva*[10] HHJ Thornton QC was dealing with a dispute that had arisen under these provisions. The adjudicator had been appointed promptly and given directions which required the referring party to serve the referral notice eight days after the adjudication notice. The referring party complied with that order. After the adjudication, the responding party subsequently objected, saying that the referral notice was invalid because it was provided more than seven days after the notice of intention to refer. The Judge rejected that argument. It is clear from paragraph 30 of his judgment that, perhaps unsurprisingly, one of the principal reasons for his decision was that the referral notice had been served in accordance with the adjudicator's directions and, since no point had been taken on the validity of the directions themselves, it was difficult to say that a referral notice served in accordance with the adjudicator's directions was somehow invalid. It appears that the Judge's analysis of the position concentrated on s108 of the 1996 Act, and not the words of the contract itself.

4.13 The decision in *William Verry* was considered in *Cubitt Building & Interiors Ltd v Fleetglade Ltd*,[11] another case about these JCT Conditions. There, the TCC Judge concluded that, on the particular facts of *William Verry*, the decision was entirely reasonable and sensible, but was, for various reasons, to be regarded as a case on its own particular facts. Further, to the extent that Judge Thornton suggested that the seven day period referred to in clause 41A was directory, the Judge in *Cubitt* came to a different view. He said that the requirement in Clause 42A 4.1 that the referring party 'shall refer the dispute or difference... within 7 days of the notice' was a mandatory requirement. He said that the language admitted of no other

---

[9] [2004] EWCA Civ 1418.
[10] [2004] BLR 308.
[11] [2006] EWHC 3413 (TCC).

conclusion, because the word used was 'shall', not 'may'. It was not a provision allowing the referring party to use his best endeavours to take these steps within the specified period. The requirement was that these events shall happen within a certain time frame. For these reasons, he concluded that the provisions in Clause 41A 4.1 were mandatory. He summarised his conclusion as follows:

> 28. In my judgment, a necessary ingredient of the swift adjudication process is certainty. Parties need to know where they stand, who must do what, and by when. Once the process is up and running, it should run like clockwork. Clause 41A is plainly designed to achieve that. Take for example its provisions in respect of the referral notice. The Clause envisages two very common situations. The first is when the adjudicator has been appointed within seven days of the adjudication notice. If that has happened, the referral notice, which triggers the adjudicator's power to issue directions and so on, must be served within that period. But unlike the Scheme for Construction Contracts, Clause 41A expressly recognises that sometimes, because of the involvement of a nominating body and the delays that that can bring, the adjudicator may not be appointed until after the seven day period has expired. Under Clause 41A that does not invalidate the adjudication; it simply means that the referral notice must be served immediately on the appointment of the adjudicator . . .
>
> 29. The specific point of principle raised by Issue 1 is, of course, whether the words in Clause 41A.4.1 are mandatory or discretionary; and, if mandatory, how they are to be interpreted. I am in no doubt that the words are mandatory. The language admits of no other conclusion. The word that is used repeatedly is the word "shall". It is not "may"; it is not a provision allowing the referring party to use his best endeavours to take these steps within the specified period. The requirement is that these events shall happen within a certain time frame. I consider therefore that the provisions are mandatory.

4.14 It is of course much easier to see how and why the words in Clause 41A.2.2 ('with the object of securing') have been regarded as directory, not mandatory. In *Mr Tracy Bennett v FMA Construction Ltd*[12] the concerns about the validity of the notice of adjudication were heightened by the fact that the dispute concerned a final certificate, so that there was the risk that, if the adjudication was invalid, the final certificate would be binding. In that case, the contractor's solicitors served a notice of intention to refer on 6 April 2005 but did not apply to the nominator until 13 April. An adjudicator was nominated on 14 April 2005 but the referral notice was not sent to him until 18 April. The supporting documents were then sent the following day. The employer took the point that Clause 41A.2.2 had not been complied with, because the application to the nominator was not made until the afternoon of the seventh day after the service of the notice of intention to refer the dispute to adjudication. The adjudicator concluded that the adjudication was probably fatally flawed and resigned on 21 April 2005. The following day,

---

[12] [2005] EWHC 1268 (TCC).

the notice of intention to refer was re-served and the same adjudicator was re-appointed on 26 April. The original referral notice was deemed to have been re-served on 28 April. The delay allowed the employer to contend that the second notice of intention to refer was served more than 28 days after the date of the final certificate and thus the final certificate was binding. Judge Havery rejected that submission, finding that the words in Clause 41A.2.2 were 'merely directory' and that the first notice of intention to refer was sufficient to comply with the contractual provisions so as to prevent the final certificate from being conclusive evidence in respect of those matters which the contractors wished to challenge. It does not appear that the arguments in *Bennett* dealt with Clause 41A.4.1, although it would appear that it was that provision that was of particular relevance to the seven day period.

4.15 Accordingly, the operation of the seven day period envisaged in Clause 41A is not entirely free from doubt. Whilst the words in Clause 41A.2.2 were plainly directory (as Judge Havery found in *Bennett*) the words in Clause 41A.4.1, which were not considered in *Bennett*, were treated as mandatory in *Cubitt*. However, given the recent trend of authorities which have highlighted the importance of complying with the strict timetables in adjudication,[13] it is thought that the courts will be likely in future to treat the word 'shall' in such contract provisions as mandatory, providing a requirement which must be complied with. Parties whose contracts incorporate Clause 41A or similar should endeavour to ensure that the referral notice is ready to be served at the same time or shortly after the notice of intention to refer.

More Than One Dispute

4.16 One of the fundamental principles of adjudication is that only one dispute can be referred to the adjudicator at any one time.[14] That is made plain in the 1996 Act and is one of the features of the Scheme for Construction Contracts. There is, however, some suggestion that Clause 41A allows 'any number of disparate disputes can simultaneously be the subject of one notice of adjudication': see paragraph 41 of the judgment of HHJ Seymour QC in *R Durtnell and Sons Ltd v Kaduna Ltd*.[15] It is not immediately apparent from the judgment what part of Clause 41A the Judge considered permitted such an interpretation. Moreover, if it were right, it would appear to render the JCT adjudication provisions at odds

---

[13] See, for example, *Richie Brothers v David Philip* [2005] BLR 384 and the various subsequent decisions of the TCC referred to in paragraphs 2.91–2.107 above.
[14] See the full discussion of this point at paragraphs 7.57–7.63 below.
[15] [2003] BLR 225.

with the 1996 Act. It is thought, therefore, that the decision in *Durtnell* should be treated with considerable caution.[16]

'Impartially'

4.17 Clause 41A.5.5 requires the adjudicator to act 'impartially'. As a consequence of this express provision, HHJ Lloyd QC in *Balfour Beatty Construction Ltd v The Mayor and Burgesses of the London Borough of Lambeth*[17] found that the adjudicator had to conduct the proceedings in accordance with the rules of natural justice or as fairly as the limitations imposed by Parliament permit.[18] In *Balfour Beatty*, Judge Lloyd concluded that, although 'the purpose of adjudication is not to be thwarted by an overly sensitive concern for procedural niceties', the provisions of Clause 41A 'envisage that some basic procedural principles have to be applied in order that each party is treated fairly'. He held that although the adjudicator had the power to set his own procedure, he could not do so without first informing the parties of the procedure which he was going to adopt. And although the adjudicator had to take the initiative in ascertaining the facts and the law, he was obliged in principle to inform the parties of the information that he obtained from his own knowledge and experience or from other sources, and of the conclusions that he might reach having taken those sources into account. Fairness and impartially are dealt with in greater detail in Chapter 9 below.

Non-Compliance

4.18 Clause 41A.5.6 expressly provides that a failure to comply with any of the adjudicator's requirements, or with any provision or requirement under Clause 41A, 'shall not invalidate the decision of the adjudicator'. At first sight, this looks to be a wide saving provision, which, if taken to its logical conclusion, could excuse extensive delay on the part of either the referring or the responding party. Indeed, it has been argued that the provision could operate to provide an adjudicator with the necessary jurisdiction even if, for example, he was not appointed until long after the seven day period had expired. However, the authorities make clear that Clause 41A.5.6 cannot be interpreted in this way. In *Palmac Contracting Ltd v Park Lane Estates Ltd*,[19] HHJ Kirkham QC held that the effect of the clause was

---

[16] It should also be noted that the main thrust of the decision in *Durtnell*, to the effect that there could be no dispute relating to extensions of time until the architect had considered further applications for an extension of time under the contract, is the subject of considerable criticism in the commentary in the BLR.

[17] [2002] EWHC 597 (TCC).

[18] In expressing that conclusion, Judge Lloyd was referring to a previous decision of his, namely *Glencot Developments v Ben Barrett* [2001] BLR 207 and a number of other cases including *Discain Projects Services Ltd v Opec Prime Ltd* [2000] BLR 402.

[19] [2005] EWHC 919 (TCC).

not such as to validate the appointment of an adjudicator invalidly appointed. She said that its scope was limited to procedural steps within a validly constituted adjudication. That view was echoed in *Cubitt*.[20] At paragraph 50 of his judgment in that case, having referred to *Palmac*, the TCC Judge said:

> In my view, Clause 41A.5.6 is concerned with procedural relief. It cannot confer jurisdiction to an adjudicator who does not have any jurisdiction in the first place. An adjudicator, in order to have the power to make directions, must be in receipt of a valid referral notice. If that has not happened, then Clause 41A.5.6 cannot rescue the situation. Take as an example an adjudicator who was appointed in a situation where there is then no referral notice for three months. In such circumstances the responding party is entitled to say, if and when the belated referral notice turns up, that the adjudicator had no power to make any directions at all. Under Clause 41A the referral notice would be a nullity. It would make a nonsense of the whole adjudication process if the referring party could then rely on Clause 41A.5.6 to argue that the much-delayed referral notice had not invalidated the decision of the adjudicator.

28 Days

4.19 As previously noted, under the 1998 Act, an adjudicator has 28 days to produce his decision, or longer if an extended period is agreed by the parties. Clause 41A.5.3 of the JCT provisions reflects this requirement. This provision has been the subject of a number of reported cases, each stemming from the adjudicator's failure to produce his decision within the 28 days or the agreed extended period. The cases are analysed at paragraphs 2.91–2.107 above. In summary, it is possible to trace a clear development in the courts' attitude to adjudicators who unilaterally grant themselves more time to complete their decision than is permitted by the JCT Conditions.

4.20 In *St Andrews Bay Development Ltd v HBG Management Ltd*,[21] where the contract incorporated the JCT Conditions, With Contractor's Design (including Clause 41A), the adjudicator should have reached her decision on 5 March but did not provide the decision until 7 March, with the reasons being communicated three days later on 10 March. It was contended that, since the decision was out of time, it was ultra vires. Lord Wheatley agreed that the adjudicator was not entitled to delay communication of the decision until her fees were paid.[22] However, he went on to find that the delay, although a serious matter, was not of sufficient significance to render the decision a nullity. He said that the production of a decision two days outwith the time limit provided was not such a fundamental

---

[20] [2006] EWHC 3413 (TCC), paragraphs 49 and 50.
[21] [2003] SLT 740.
[22] For a fuller discussion of an adjudicator's ability (or lack of it) to exercise a lien on the decision in respect of his fees, see paragraphs 11.19–11.24 below.

error or impropriety that it should eviscerate the entire decision. By contrast, in *Barnes & Elliott Ltd v Taylor Woodrow Holdings Ltd*,[23] HHJ Lloyd QC had to deal with a situation where the decision had been reached within the agreed time scale, but was not communicated to the parties until the following day. Again it was argued that that decision was a nullity. Again the Judge refused to accept that proposition and found that there should be some flexibility in the communication of the decision. However, Judge Lloyd made it clear that this was because the decision had been arrived at in time and was therefore, in principle, authorised and valid. He stressed that this form of contract only conferred authority on the adjudicator to make a decision within the 28 day period, or such other period as was agreed. This, therefore, appeared to differentiate between a decision not reached within the 28 days, which was, prima facie, outside the contractual provisions, and a decision reached within the 28 days but communicated thereafter which, on the facts of that case, Judge Lloyd held was within the contract.

4.21 A number of more recent decisions have emphasised the importance of the 28 day period in these and similar contractual provisions.[24] *Richie Brothers (PWC) Ltd v David Philip (Commercials) Ltd*[25] has already been referred to at paragraph 2.99. Likewise *Cubitt Building & Interiors Ltd v Fleetglade Limited*,[26] a case where the contract incorporated the JCT Conditions (and where the TCC Judge concluded that adjudicators did not have the jurisdiction to grant themselves extensions of time without the express consent of both parties), is referred to in detail in paragraph 2.100 above. On the facts of that case, he concluded that the decision was reached within the agreed extended period and its communication the following day complied with the requirement 'forthwith' to send the decision to the parties. The adjudicator's decision was therefore not a nullity. Finally, *AC Yule & Sons Ltd v Speedwell Roofing & Cladding Ltd*,[27] which is dealt with in detail in paragraphs 2.101–2.104 above, reiterates the same approach and explains why it is the mandatory nature of the statutory period, rather than the consequences of non-compliance with that period, which matters most.

4.22 Although *Yule* was a decision under the Scheme, both *Barnes & Elliott* and *Cubitt* were concerned expressly with clause 41A of the JCT Contract. It is thought that there is no substantive difference between the JCT Conditions and the Scheme on this point. As to the need for communication 'forthwith', given the immediacy of electronic communication, any decision reached under clause 41A ought to be completed and communicated to the parties by the end

---

[23] [2004] 1 BLR 111.
[24] They are cited at paragraph 3.71 above (footnote 46).
[25] [2005] 1 BLR 384.
[26] [2006] EWHC 3413 (TCC).
[27] [2007] EWHC 1360 (TCC).

of the last day of the extended period, and certainly not later than part-way through the following day.

'Binding'

Clause 41A.7.1 makes plain that the decision of the adjudicator 'shall be binding on the parties until the dispute or difference is finally determined by arbitration or by legal proceedings'. This concept of temporary finality is discussed in detail below at paragraphs 12.24–12.34. A point that has risen under these provisions is the status of the adjudicator's decision in any subsequent proceedings. In *City Inn Ltd v Sheppard Construction Ltd*[28] it was argued that the effect of the adjudicator's decision was to throw onto the responding party the burden of showing that the extension of time which the adjudicator awarded was not justified. It was argued that the binding quality of the adjudicator's decision continued, not merely until the dispute was made the subject of litigation, but until the court proceedings were finally determined so that during the proceedings, the adjudicator's decision remained binding and had to be rebutted by the party arguing for a different result.[29]

4.23

This argument was rejected by the court. It was held to be no part of the function of an adjudicator's decision to reverse the onus of proof in any subsequent arbitration or litigation to which the parties resort to obtain a final determination of the dispute between them. It was held that such an approach read too much into the words 'binding until the dispute or difference is finally determined'. The court concluded that the burden of proof in any such subsequent arbitration or litigation lay where the law placed it, and was unaffected by the terms of the adjudicator's decision.

4.24

Final Certificates

In common with many standard forms of building and engineering contracts, the JCT Forms include provisions for final certificates, which if not challenged within a specified period, becoming conclusive evidence on a range of matters. One way in which they can be challenged is by a reference to adjudication. The point has already been made[30] that this might have fatal consequences for the challenge if, due to no fault on the part of the contractor, the decision is a nullity. In *Castle Inns (Stirling) Limited v Clark Contracts Limited*,[31] the issue was slightly different, although the underlying problem was the same. The particular clause of the

4.25

---

[28] [2002] SLT 781.
[29] See also *Citex Professional Services Ltd v Kenmore Developments Ltd* [2004] ScotCS 20; A1195/02.
[30] See paragraph 2.105 above.
[31] [2007] CSOH 21.

Scottish version of the JCT Standard Form in issue allowed disputes, on which an adjudicator had given a decision after the final certificate, to be finally determined in arbitration or court proceedings, provided that they were commenced within 28 days of the decision. This time bar only operated on disputes which had been decided by an adjudicator; there was no equivalent bar on disputes which had not been decided by the adjudicator. The pursuers needed to demonstrate that their claim in court raised an issue which the adjudicator had not decided (so the time bar was irrelevant). Lord Drummond Young decided that, although the adjudication had been concerned with a delay claim, which was also the subject matter of the litigation, the former related to payments of loss and expense to a shopfitting contractor, whilst the latter comprised the pursuers' claim for loss of profit in consequence of the late opening of the store. There was therefore no time bar. Of course, if the detailed analysis had been resolved the other way, it would have left the pursuers without a claim.

Determination

4.26 The House of Lords case of *Melville Dundas v George Wimpey UK Ltd*[32] has already been considered in detail in paragraphs 2.142–2.147 above. Their Lordships, by a majority, decided on the facts of that case that clause 27.6.5.1 of the JCT Standard Form was not inconsistent with s111 of the 1996 Act in permitting an employer to rely on the provision that no further payment was required following determination, in circumstances where the claimant contractor was insolvent and it had been impossible for withholding notices to be served in time. In *Pierce Design International Limited v Mark Johnston and Another*,[33] the TCC Judge held that this ruling in respect of clause 27.6.5.1 could not be distinguished merely because there was no insolvency, and (arguably at any rate) no impossibility in serving proper withholding notices. However, he concluded that the proviso to the clause, which prohibited the employer from relying on it to prevent enforcement of sums due which were 'unreasonably not paid' by the employer, meant that, on the facts of that case (unlike the situation in *Melville Dundas*), the clause did not provide a defence to the claim, since the failure to pay sums which were due under the contract, and in respect of which there had been no withholding notices, was an unreasonable non-payment on the part of the employer. In that case, the proviso operated to ensure that the contractor was not prevented from recovering the outstanding interim payments.

---

[32] [2007] UKHL 18; [2007] 1 WLR 1136.
[33] [2007] EWHC 1691 (TCC).

Other Forms of JCT Contract

4.27 All of the other JCT forms of main contract contain the same or very similar adjudication provisions. However, a number of important decisions relating to particular clauses of particular JCT forms have played a role in the development of the practice and principle of adjudication and enforcement of adjudicator's decisions. Some of the more important are noted below.

4.28 The JCT Minor Works Form is commonly used for lower value works, and is thus often used for contracts concerned with the refurbishment and extension of domestic dwellings. In *Lovell Projects Ltd v Legg & Carver*[34] the Judge held that the supplemental adjudication procedures added to the form by way of condition D complied with the 1996 Act. Thus, although the work related to the refurbishment of a dwelling house by a residential occupier, (which was of course exempted by the 1996 Act) the fact that the contract expressly provided for adjudication meant that the employer could not argue that the adjudication provisions were somehow inapplicable.[35] Similarly, in *Mohammed v Dr Michael Bowles*,[36] although the applicant argued that the contract was exempt because it was with a residential occupier, the argument was rejected by the registrar who concluded that the contract, in the JCT Minor Works Form, adopted the framework of the dispute resolution procedure contained in the 1996 Act. He concluded that the adjudicator had determined the issue as to the appropriate contract terms, and it was not for the court to look behind the adjudicator's decision.

4.29 A similar argument, that a residential occupier who had agreed the JCT Minor Works Form should not be bound by the adjudication provisions therein, was rejected by HHJ Thornton QC in *Steve Domsalla (t/a Domsalla Building Services) v Kenneth Dyason*.[37] The Judge also rejected the contention that the adjudication provisions were rendered unfair by the Unfair Terms in Consumer Contracts Regulations, saying at paragraph 93 of his judgment that they did not substantially alter the balance of the parties' rights and obligations. However, on the particular facts of that case, where the contract had been negotiated by Mr Dyason's insurers (who had also appointed the contract administrator) and he was simply the titular employer, the Judge found that the withholding notice

---

[34] [2003] BLR 452.
[35] In *Lovell*, there was also an argument that, pursuant to the Unfair Terms in Consumer Contracts Regulations 1999, the adjudication provisions were unfair because they had not been individually negotiated. The argument failed. The issues raised by the 1999 Regulations are dealt with below at paragraphs 9.49–9.57.
[36] [2002], a decision of the Bankruptcy Registrar.
[37] [2007] EWHC 1174 (TCC).

Other Forms of Adjudication

provisions of the Minor Works Form were unfair and thus not binding on him as the employer.

4.30 Clause 2.3 of the Minor Works Form deals with liquidated damages and permits the employer to deduct liquidated damages from any monies due to the contractor. In *Dumarc Building Services Ltd v Salvador Rico*[38] the Judge refused to allow the employer to set off against an adjudicator's award an amount of liquidated damages. He said that the effect of the employer's submissions was to add into Clause 2.3 the words 'including sums owed under an adjudication'. He concluded that there was no right to set off for liquidated damages provided by Clause 2.3 and to hold otherwise 'would drive a coach and horses' through the 1996 Act and the detailed provisions the parties had agreed upon to resolve disputes by way of adjudication. The Judge in *Lovell* reached the same conclusion, deciding that, although the starting presumption was that each party was entitled to a set off as per *Modern Engineering v Gilbert Ash*,[39] the amended terms of the Minor Works Form plainly rebutted that presumption. He concluded that they amounted to clear and unequivocal words whereby the parties agreed that a set off would only be permitted when a withholding notice had been served. One of the many provisions of the Minor Works Form to which the Judge had regard in reaching this conclusion was Supplemental Condition D7.2 which provided that the parties agreed to comply with the decision of the adjudicator.

4.31 The Intermediate Form, known as the IFC, also contains similar provisions to those discussed above. Also, like all other JCT contracts, it provides a contractual regime whereby the contract administrators/architect issues certificates and reaches decisions as a result of the quasi-arbitral role created by the contract. In *Vaultrise Ltd v Paul Cook*[40] the point was taken that the issuing of certificates, such as the certificate of practical completion, was a matter for the contract administrator and only he, or an arbitrator, had the power to open up and revise such certificates. It was said that an adjudicator did not have that power. The TCC Judge concluded otherwise, finding that an adjudicator had the power to consider whether or not a certificate should have been issued and, if a missing certificate was due, he could determine the appropriate sum outstanding. In the instant case the adjudicator had found that a final certificate should have been issued and he went on to determine the amount that that certificate should have identified. He said that the sum was due from the employer to the contractor. The Judge concluded that that was a dispute which the adjudicator had every reason to determine, describing it as 'a perfectly valid dispute fit for adjudication'.

---

[38] In the Epsom County Court, decision of His Honour Judge Hull QC.
[39] [1974] AC 689.
[40] [2004] ADJCS 04/06.

The JCT Adjudication Agreement

The JCT adjudication provisions set out above envisage that, in the event of an adjudication, the parties to the contract and the adjudicator will agree a tri-partite agreement, in standard form, referred to as the JCT Adjudication Agreement. This records the appointment of the adjudicator and the acceptance of that appointment by the parties. It requires the adjudicator to observe the adjudication provisions which already bind the parties and makes the parties jointly and severally liable for the adjudicator's fees. It also contains termination provisions which allow the parties jointly to terminate the adjudication agreement. There is an express provision that, if that joint termination was as a result of the failure by the adjudicator to give his dispute within the time-scales in the adjudication provisions or at all, the adjudicator was not entitled to recover his fees. **4.32**

The Agreement is important for two reasons. First, it allows the adjudicator a direct route against the parties if his fees are not paid, and avoids the rather convoluted reliance on the Contracts (Rights of Third Parties) Act 1999 which, in *Cartwright v Fay*[41] provided the adjudicator's only route to recovering his fees against the defendant. More importantly, it binds the adjudicator to the adjudication provisions in the JCT Form. It therefore makes the adjudicator contractually liable to produce his decision within 28 days or any agreed extended period. If he does not, he is in breach of contract. Moreover, although Clause 41A.8 appears to give the adjudicator immunity from anything done in the discharge of his functions, it must be arguable that his failure to produce a decision within the 28 days or the agreed extended period would have represented a complete failure on his part to discharge his functions at all, and the immunity may well be inoperative.[42] **4.33**

The Standard Forms of Sub-Contracts

DOM/1

There are often disputes, further down the contractual chain, as to whether the standard sub-contract conditions were incorporated. In *Maymac Environmental Services v Faraday Building Services*,[43] HHJ Toulmin CMG QC found that a sub-contract which incorporated the DOM/1 terms had come into existence and that, although the terms were modified and expanded as the work progressed, **4.34**

---

[41] 9 February 2005, Bath County Court.
[42] See *Cubitt Building and Interiors Ltd v Fleetglade Ltd* [2006] EWHC 3413, paragraph 91.
[43] (2000) 75 Con LR 101.

the adjudicator had the necessary jurisdiction. In any event, Faraday had agreed to the adjudication of the dispute and could not now argue that they were not bound by the result.

4.35 One of the most important features of the 1996 Act, and the Scheme for Construction Contracts, was the maintenance of cash-flow to domestic sub-contractors, who were perceived to have suffered significantly as a result of the financial constraints and the tough commercial line adopted by many main contractors in the early 1990's. Once the Act was in force, the DOM/1 Sub-Contract Conditions were amended to provide for adjudication.[44] In *KNS Industrial Services (Birmingham) Ltd v Sindall Ltd*[45] HHJ Humphrey Lloyd QC held that, not only were the adjudication provisions in accordance with the 1996 Act, but so too were the contractual provisions concerned with interim payments and withholding notices. The Judge held that the DOM/1 terms met the requirements of the 1996 Act and that therefore the provisions of s110 were no longer relevant, because the terms of the sub-contract were the material provisions. As for s111, the DOM/1 terms provided that the prescribed period (ie, the final date for a withholding notice before the final date for payment) was five days before the final date for payment, and incorporated wholesale into clause 21.3.2 the provisions of s111.

4.36 The adjudication provisions in the DOM/1 Conditions are set out in Clause 38A. Amongst other things, this provides that all relevant notices and other documents served as part of the adjudication had to be sent by fax and first class post forthwith to the address of the other party. In *Costain Ltd v Wescol Steel Ltd*[46] the point was taken that the documents were not served in accordance with this provision and that therefore the reference to adjudication was invalid. The Judge rejected this contention, relying on the words of Clause 38A.5.6 of DOM/1, which provided that any failure to comply with any requirement under Clause 38A 'shall not invalidate the decision of the adjudicator'. The Judge held that this rendered the provisions and requirements of Clause 38A non-mandatory so far as the validity of any decision of the adjudicator was concerned. It is respectfully suggested that this was a correct application of the proviso to Clause 38A.5.6, because it was concerned with a potential procedural problem (in that case, the precise form of service). It is to be contrasted with the decisions in *Palmac*[47] and *Cubitt*[48] where

---

[44] Originally, there was a provision in the DOM/1 conditions which stipulated that the parties had to mediate before they could refer their dispute to adjudicate. HHJ Thornton QC held in *RG Carter v Edmund Nuttall Ltd* [2002] BLR 359 that this pre-condition sought to fetter the unqualified entitlement to adjudication provided by the 1996 Act, and was therefore unenforceable.
[45] [2001] 17 Const LJ 170.
[46] [2003] EWHC 312 (TCC).
[47] [2005] EWHC 919 (TCC).
[48] [2006] EWHC 3413 (TCC).

the TCC Judges made plain that this potentially wide catch-all proviso could not give an adjudicator jurisdiction in circumstances where, for whatever reason, he did not have the necessary jurisdiction in the first place.

4.37 Clause 38A of DOM/1 provided that 'any dispute or difference arising under the sub-contract may be referred to adjudication'. This, of course, is very similar wording to all other standard forms of sub-contract. However, it is under the DOM/1 provision that there have been a number of cases in which the proper meaning of the word 'dispute' has been canvassed. The debate concerned an interpretation of the word 'dispute' which required the dispute set out in the notice of intention to refer to one that had plainly arisen between the parties prior to the service of the notice ('the restricted view'). The alternative argument was that the word 'dispute' had a wider meaning and that a dispute arose once money was claimed and not admitted or paid ('the wider approach'). There is a full discussion as to these competing views, and the clear settlement of this debate in favour of the 'wider approach' in paragraphs 7.46–7.56 below. For present purposes, it is sufficient to identify the two competing cases arising out of the DOM/1 form.

4.38 In *Edmund Nuttall Ltd v RG Carter Ltd*[49] the referring party sought an entitlement to an extension of time from the responding party. Having failed to obtain that extension, the referring party issued a notice of intention to refer. The referral notice set out a detailed claim for an extension of time, together with loss and expense. The basis of that claim was considered by the Judge to be materially different to the claim that had been made under the contract. HHJ Seymour QC concluded that the real question was not whether there was a dispute at the time of the notice of referral, but whether the dispute which the adjudicator decided was that which formed the subject matter of the notice. He said that if the adjudicator had adjudicated on a 'dispute' which was not the subject of that notice, he had no jurisdiction to decide the dispute. The Judge said that, for there to be a dispute, there must have been an opportunity for the protagonists each to consider the position adopted by the other and to formulate arguments of a reasoned kind. He said that where a party has an opportunity to consider the position of the opposite party and to formulate arguments in relation to that position, what constitutes a 'dispute' between the parties was not only a 'claim' which had been rejected, but the whole package of arguments advanced and facts relied on by each side. He concluded that adjudication was only appropriate after there had been attempts to resolve the dispute by an open exchange of views and that, therefore, a party in adjudication could not abandon wholesale facts and arguments that had

---

[49] [2002] BLR 312.

Other Forms of Adjudication

previously been relied on, even if the claim remained the same. The relevant part of his judgment is set out verbatim at paragraph 7.51 below.

4.39 In consequence of these views, Judge Seymour concluded that the 'dispute' advanced in the adjudication was different to that which had arisen between the parties and was referred to in the notice of intention to refer. He therefore concluded that the adjudicator did not have the necessary jurisdiction and dismissed the claim to enforce the decision. This decision has been the subject of a certain amount of criticism, and it has not been followed in a number of subsequent cases.[50] It is, in many ways, the high water mark of the restricted view of the word 'dispute'.

4.40 The approach in *Nuttall* is to be contrasted with the approach of HHJ Kirkham in *Orange EBS Ltd v ABB Ltd*.[51] In her judgment the Judge concluded that she was bound by the decision of the Court of Appeal in *Halki Shipping Corporation v Sopex Oils Ltd*,[52] namely that 'there is a dispute once money is claimed unless and until the defendants admit that the sum is due and payable'. She therefore found that a dispute had arisen because the claim had been neither admitted nor paid and that sufficient time had elapsed between the making of the claim and the issue of the notice of intention to refer. The Judge did not embark on a detailed comparison of the basis of the claim as submitted under the contract and the claim that was referred to adjudication. This wider approach to the question of whether or not a 'dispute' had crystallised at the time of the notice of adjudication, must be regarded as the correct analysis in law, for the reasons explained at paragraphs 7.52–7.54 below.

4.41 There have been a number of cases concerned with the operation of the payment and withholding provisions at Clause 21 of DOM/1. In *KNS Industrial Services (Birmingham) Ltd v Sindall Ltd*,[53] already referred to in paragraph 4.35 above, KNS contended that the adjudicator had had no authority to make deductions from sums otherwise due to them because Sindall had not given notice of intention to withhold in respect of amounts for non-compliant work. Despite this, the adjudicator had set off against KNS's gross valuation sums to reflect these allegations. The Judge pointed out that the term 'withhold' was used to cover both the situation where, in arriving at a valuation, the contractor had not taken account of a counter-vailing factor, as well as the situation where there was to be a reduction in or deduction from an amount that had been declared or thought to be due. In the former case the word 'withhold' may not always be

---

[50] For a fuller discussion of this point please see paragraphs 7.46–7.56 below.
[51] [2003] BLR 323.
[52] [1998] 1 WLR 726.
[53] [2001] 17 Const LJ 170.

correct, for one cannot withhold what is not due. He concluded that the adjudicator was right to make a deduction for non-compliant work because there was plainly a dispute about the valuation of the work and KNS were not entitled to be paid for work that was not in accordance with the contract.

4.42 The DOM/1 Conditions, and clause 21 in particular, were also at the heart of the decision in *Shimizu Europe Ltd v LBJ Fabrications Ltd*,[54] previously referred to at paragraph 2.140 above, where the relevant facts are set out. The Judge allowed Shimizu to set off a separate claim against the amount awarded by the adjudicator because the adjudicator had found that the sum due to LBJ was not to be paid by Shimizu until 28 days after LBJ had delivered a VAT invoice, as required by Clause 21.2.4. Although the adjudicator had decided that Shimizu had no right to set off (against the sum which would become due to LBJ) the sums which Shimizu had identified and claimed in the adjudication, he did not decide that Shimizu had no future right of set-off. Because he had identified a sum to be paid to LBJ 28 days after the provision of an invoice, pursuant to Clause 21, Shimizu were able to serve a fresh withholding notice in respect of the sum claimed on that invoice. LBJ's claim was therefore dismissed. It is clear that this judgment was based entirely on the wording of the adjudicator's original decision: had he, for example, found that the sum was due forthwith, there would have been no opportunity for Shimizu to serve a withholding notice. Generally, adjudicators tend to require the sum to be paid immediately and thus preclude the possibility of fresh withholding notices. In addition, it should be noted that most of the arguments in which the losing party has sought to set up some sort of set-off or cross-claim against the sum decided by the adjudicator have failed: see the discussion at paragraphs 10.20–10.37 below. In *Whiteways Contractors (Sussex) Ltd v Impresa Castelli Construction United Kingdom Ltd*[55] the Judge rejected the argument that the loser had set up an effective abatement from sums due. It is interesting to note that the analysis in the judgment is undertaken almost exclusively by reference to sections 110 and 111 of the 1996 Act, even though the DOM/1 terms of sub-contract were incorporated. However, on the abatement point, nothing turned on it, because the provisions were so very similar.

4.43 Another feature of the judgment of HHJ Lloyd QC in *KNS* was its consideration of Clause 29 of DOM/1, dealing with determination. Clause 29.6.3 provided that in the event of determination, the contractor was not bound to make any further payment to the sub-contractor until after completion of the works and the making good of defects, at which point the sub-contractor had to apply for payment and, if a net sum was due, the contractor had to pay it. The Judge

---

[54] [2003] BLR 381.
[55] [2000] 16 Const LJ 453.

concluded that s111 of the 1996 Act did not apply instead of clause 29.6, because the clause was part of a typical, self-contained code applicable when the sub-contractor was in serious and irreparable default. The adjudicator had, in fact, required the contractor to make a modest payment to the sub-contractor, notwithstanding the provisions of Clause 29.6.3, which the Judge described as inexplicable but concluded that it was a mistake that he had the jurisdiction to make. In any event, the point did not matter because the payment had been made in any event. In addition, it should be noted that the particular (sub-contract) determination clause in *KNS* was not very different to the (main contract) determination clause under consideration in *Melville Dundas*, and the conclusion in each case was essentially the same.[56]

DOM/2

4.44 The adjudication provisions at Clause 38A of the DOM/2 Standard Form are very similar to those incorporated into the DOM/1 Form. In *Jerome Engineering Ltd v Lloyd Morris Electrical Ltd*[57] the TCC Judge found that, unusually, the contract provisions required the relief sought to be stated in the referral notice, not within the notice of adjudication. The point had been taken that the notice of adjudication had referred to a valuation dispute but had not sought any express relief or any payment award. The referral notice did include an express claim for £122,604. The TCC Judge concluded that, despite this anomaly, the notice of adjudication could not have left the responding party in any doubt that the referring party was referring the dispute to adjudication because they wanted payment of that which, at least on an interim basis, was due to them. However, even if he was wrong about that, the Judge concluded that both the notice of adjudication and the referral notice were in full compliance with Clause 38A because, pursuant to the contract, it was only the latter document which had to specify the relief. This decision was based four square upon the precise terms of DOM/2. It should be noted that, if the adjudication had occurred under the Scheme for Construction Contracts, the result might have been different because the Scheme expressly requires the notice of intention to refer to identify the relief claimed.

4.45 There are a number of cases under these forms of sub-contract in which the loser has sought to argue that, where a valid objection is taken to part of an adjudicator's decision, that part can be regarded as 'severable', thus allowing those parts upon which the objection might bite to be separated out from those parts which are unaffected by the complaint. In relation to the DOM/2 conditions,

---

[56] See paragraph 4.26 above.
[57] [2002] CILL 1827–1828.

this argument was expressly labelled as 'misconceived' by HHJ Seymour QC in *RSL (South West) Ltd v Stansell Ltd.*[58] Judge Lloyd reached a similar view on the facts of *KNS*, although he accepted that there might be instances where the decision can be severed, so that the authorised part can be saved and the unauthorised elements set aside. The practical difficulties involved in even attempting such an exercise will depend on the facts of the particular case, and the nature and form of the decision itself.

4.46 The DOM/2 Conditions have also featured in a number of cases concerned with jurisdiction.[59] For example, in *Joinery Plus Ltd (In Administration) v Laing Ltd*[60] HHJ Thornton QC was faced with an adjudicator's decision which was expressly based on the JCT Works Sub-Contract. In fact, the parties were agreed that the sub-contract incorporated the DOM/2 Conditions. The Judge concluded that the decision had been reached by reference to the wrong conditions of contract and without recourse to the correct contractual documentation and that, as a consequence, the adjudicator had not decided the dispute which had arisen under the relevant contract and he had not decided it in accordance with the provisions of that contract. The Judge concluded that these errors went to the heart of the adjudicator's jurisdiction and that the decision was therefore a nullity.[61]

4.47 The decision in *Bickerton Construction Ltd v Temple Windows Ltd*[62] is another case where the DOM/2 Conditions applied but where the adjudicator was found to have exceeded his jurisdiction. The Judge found that both parties had understood and proceeded on the basis that the adjudicator would not be dealing with the final account between them but his decision was based on a figure which reflected the total value of the work carried out by the sub-contractor. The adjudicator had the jurisdiction to determine what sums could be validly withheld from sums otherwise due to the sub-contractor but he had no jurisdiction to decide the final account figure, the determination of which had been expressly excluded from the scope of the adjudication. Thus the court concluded that the adjudicator had exceeded his jurisdiction and he was not entitled to direct that a sum of money be paid by the sub-contractor to the contractor.

---

[58] [2003] EWHC 1390 (TCC). This case is referred to in greater detail at paragraph 4.50 below.
[59] See for example *Northern Developments (Cumbria) Ltd v J&J Nichol* [2000] BLR 158.
[60] [2003] BLR 184.
[61] As the learned editors of the BLR point out, the decision in *Joinery Plus* might be difficult to reconcile with the decision of the Court of Appeal in *C&B Scene Concept v Isobars* [2002] BLR 93. In that case, the adjudicator may have made an error in relation to the relevant contract terms but the Court of Appeal held that that did not constitute a decision in excess of the adjudicator's jurisdiction. Although Judge Thornton described *C&B Scene* as a case where the correct contractual provision was misconstrued by the adjudicator, that may not be an entirely accurate representation of what he did.
[62] Unreported, 26 June 2001, TCC.

4.48 The DOM/2 conditions include detailed provisions, at clause 11, dealing with delay. On any major contract or sub-contract, the parties' rights and liabilities in relation to delay will change as delaying events occur. This will often lead to procedural difficulties because a party may seek an extension of time on one basis, and that claim for an extension may be referred to an adjudicator. If that party seeks a further extension of time the second adjudicator cannot reach any decision that is inconsistent with or cut across the decision of the first adjudicator.[63] In *Emcor Drake & Skull Ltd v Costain Construction Ltd*,[64] HHJ Havery QC decided that Clause 11.7 of DOM/2 permitted the main contractor to grant more than one extension of time and that, accordingly, there could be more than one adjudication on the issue as to the sub-contractor's entitlement. As to the main issue of fact, namely whether the second adjudicator had reconsidered facts and matters that had previously been adjudicated upon, the Judge concluded that he had not.

4.49 The decision in *Emcor Drake & Skull* is important for another reason, although the matter is only referred to in passing at the end of the judgment. One of the arguments advanced by the contractor in seeking to resist the enforcement of the adjudicator's decision concerned the scope of the documentation raised in the adjudication itself. The complaint was that there was something like 5,000 pages said to be relevant to the referral notice and that, in consequence, it was unfair and an abuse of the adjudication process to require the contractor to respond to those facts and matters in the second adjudication. Judge Havery rejected this submission in robust terms:

> The necessity to respond quickly to vast quantities of paperwork is one of the well-known hazards of the adjudication process. That cannot of itself be a ground for contending that there has been an abuse of process. In my judgment, the fact that the same documentation appears in two successive adjudications is a wholly insufficient ground for describing what happened as an abuse of process.

This was just one of a number of occasions when the point as to the size and scale of the 'dispute' has led the losing party to claim that the adjudicator's decision was not enforceable. There is a wider discussion about this topic in paragraphs 9.04–9.10 below. However, by reference to the authorities cited there, the present position appears to be that, if the adjudicator is content that he can reach a fair decision within the 28 days or the agreed extended period, then the losing party will not be able to avoid enforcement of that decision on this ground.

---

[63] For a more detailed discussion on the problems created by serial adjudications, please see paragraphs 7.71–7.77 and 9.38–9.41 above.
[64] [2004] EWHC 2439.

Finally, adjudications carried out pursuant to the DOM/2 provisions have **4.50** been the subject of some criticism as a result of an alleged failure to comply with the rules of natural justice. One decision in this category is the decision of HHJ Seymour QC in *RSL (South West) Ltd v Stansell Ltd*[65] referred to above. The Judge had to consider whether the adjudicator had acted impartially in accordance with Clause 38A.5.5 in circumstances where, in breach of an agreement reached with the parties, he had relied on the report of a programming expert which had not been disclosed to them. The Judge held that it was elementary that the rules of natural justice required that a party to a dispute resolution procedure should know what the case against him might be and should have an opportunity to meet it. He concluded that the mere fact that the adjudicator had taken into account, in reaching his decision in relation to extensions of time, a report which was not disclosed to the parties was sufficient to conclude that the decision was reached in breach of the rules of natural justice and should not be enforced. It is important to note that the Judge reached this conclusion notwithstanding the fact that the time constraints were such that it was difficult to see how the adjudicator could have invited further submissions on the report and still reached his conclusion within the allotted period.[66]

Other Standard Forms of Contract

GC/Works

Many large-scale infrastructure projects carried out on behalf of Government **4.51** Departments and Agencies are let on versions of the GC/Works Contract and Sub-Contracts. The decision of HHJ Wilcox in *Levolux A.T. Ltd v Ferson Contractors Ltd*[67] was concerned with two different aspects of the GC/Works Sub-Contract. The defendant failed to pay the sum awarded by the adjudicator and argued that they were entitled to set-off against that sum their own claim for the costs of completion. The Judge found that, although Clause 38A.11 of the contract form allowed either party to raise 'any right of set-off, counterclaim or abatement in connection with the enforcement of an adjudicator's decision', the set-off had to be the subject of a proper withholding notice. Under this form of contract there was no fresh right to set-off following the adjudicator's decision.[68]

---

[65] [2003] EWHC 1390 (TCC).
[66] For a detailed discussion of the adjudication cases concerned with natural justice, please see Chapter 9 below.
[67] [2002] BLR 341.
[68] This, of course, was different to the result in *Shimizu v LBJ Fabrications* [2003] BLR 381, but as explained at paragraph 4.42 above, *Shimizu* turned on the particular terms of the adjudicator's decision and, in particular, his ruling that the sum would not be due and payable to the

4.52 *Levolux* is also important because of the court's consideration of the determination provisions in Clause 29 of the GC/Works sub-contract. The defendant sought to rely on these provisions to argue that, following the service of the determination notice, it was not bound to make any further payment to the claimant until after the works and the making good had been completed. Judge Wilcox rejected this argument, saying that, on the facts, the claimant was owed monies at the time that work was suspended; that the adjudicator found that the claimant was entitled to suspend the works; and that the purported determination was wrongful. In those circumstances, there was no bar on the payment of the sums found due by the adjudicator. In addition, the Judge also concluded that the words in Clause 29.8.1 to monies 'that may be due or accruing due from the contractor or to the sub-contractor shall cease to be due or accrue due . . .' did not include monies due under an adjudicator's award within his jurisdiction.[69] This conclusion was also upheld by the Court of Appeal.

4.53 Clause 38A of the GC/Works Sub-Contract is concerned with adjudication. Clause 38A.5 provides that 'the adjudicator shall notify its decision to the Contractor and the Sub-Contractor not earlier than 10 and not later than 28 days from receipt of the notice of referral, . . . the adjudicator's decision shall nevertheless be valid if issued after the time allowed . . .' In *Aveat Heating Ltd v Jerram Falkus Construction Ltd*[70] HHJ Havery QC concluded that this open-ended ability on the part of the adjudicator to provide a valid decision after the 28 days or any extended period was contrary to s108(2)(c) of the 1996 Act. As a result, he decided that the contractual adjudication mechanism fell by the wayside and that it had to be replaced by the Scheme.

The ICE Form of Engineering Contract

4.54 The best-known standard form in respect of civil engineering works is the ICE Conditions. Following the 1996 Act, supplementary provisions were drafted to include expressly for adjudication. The terms of the ICE conditions which have arisen most often in adjudication cases are Clause 60 (concerned with interim payments, withholding notices and the like) and Clause 66 (the procedure

---

sub-contractor until 28 days after the service of a VAT invoice. This allowed time for the service of a fresh withholding notice.

[69] This decision can be contrasted with *KNS* although, in reality, each turned on its own particular facts, the terms of the contracts in question, and the precise terms of the adjudicators' respective decisions.

[70] [2007] EWHC 131 (TCC).

whereby the parties seek the engineer's decision on a particular dispute between them).

4.55 In *Barr Ltd v Law Mining Ltd*,[71] the ICE Conditions 5th Edition were incorporated into the contract but they had been modified by a letter which provided that payment for work would be 30 days after certification. The parties disagreed how this would work in practice. In his decision the adjudicator identified the competing arguments and then went on to find that both payment mechanisms put before him failed to comply with s110 of the 1996 Act, because they failed to provide a mechanism for determining when a payment became due under the contract. He therefore concluded that the Scheme had to be implied. The court concluded that, in arriving at this conclusion the adjudicator did not exceed his jurisdiction, even if his decision might be wrong in law. His decision did not result from his failure to address the correct question, and his decision was therefore upheld.

4.56 As to the operation of clause 66, that vital component of the dispute resolution mechanism offered by the ICE Conditions, there are a trio of cases dealing with the interaction between adjudication, the engineer's decision, and arbitration. In *JT Mackley & Co Ltd v Gosport Marina Ltd*[72] there had been two adjudications which had resulted in decisions in principle favourable to the contractor. Subsequently, the contractor sought and obtained an engineer's decision as to the value of their works. Three months later, the employer's solicitors purported to serve a joint notice of dispute and notice to refer to arbitration on both the contractor and the engineer. The employer's complaint was that the works had not been properly designed and/or carried out by the engineer and the contractor. The contractor contended that the joint notice to refer was invalid because a decision of the engineer was a condition precedent to the entitlement of any party to refer a dispute to arbitration, and the employer could not somehow attempt to do both simultaneously. The employer contended that an engineer's decision was not required where what the party issuing the arbitration notice wanted to do was to challenge the decision of an adjudicator. The Judge rejected the employer's argument, deciding that the fact of a previous adjudication and the existence of an adjudicator's decision had nothing to do with any subsequent arbitration in which the correctness of that decision might be disputed. The Judge pointed out that the adjudicator's decision was temporarily binding until there was a later arbitration and any such arbitration had to be carried out in accordance with the arbitration clause in the contract. That required that there had first to be a decision of the

---

[71] [2001] Scot CS 152; 80 Con LR 134.
[72] [2002] BLR 367.

engineer under clause 66. The Judge therefore granted a declaration that the joint notice to refer was invalid.

4.57 In *The Construction Centre v Highland Council*[73] the defenders failed to pay the sum found due by the adjudicator of more than £5.5 million, and instead, within seven days of his decision, served a notice of intention to withhold. They argued that the arbitration provisions of the contract did not permit the arbitrator to take account of a final decree of the court pronounced in accordance with the adjudicator's decision, and that therefore they would be irredeemably prejudiced if there was judgment against them for the £5.5 million. This argument was rejected by Lord MacFadyen who ruled that the pursuers were contractually entitled to require the defenders to implement the adjudicator's provisional determination of the dispute, whether it be right or wrong. In consequence, any decree pronounced in that action was not a finding by the court that the adjudicator was right and it would therefore have no effect on the final determination of the dispute by the arbitrator. In line with other decisions[74] the court held that the service of a withholding notice after the publication of the adjudicator's decision did not entitle the defenders to withhold payment and that s111 was intended to apply only to the withholding of payments in respect of which the contract provided a final date for payment; it did not apply to payments due in consequence of an adjudicator's decision.

4.58 The decision *The Construction Group Centre Ltd* is also important for another reason. The claim which was the subject of the (invalid) withholding notice was a set-off in respect of liquidated damages. The court held that, whilst the scope of an adjudication was defined by the notice of adjudication, any ground that justified non-payment of the sum sought fell within the scope of the adjudication. Thus the court ruled that the adjudicator could not have declined to allow the defenders to plead the cross-claim for liquidated damages had they chosen to do so. Their failure to raise the matter in the adjudication was another reason why they were not entitled, after the event, to rely on their alleged cross-claim.

4.59 The third case concerned with clause 66 of the ICE Conditions of Contract is another Scottish case, *Peterhead Harbour Trustees v Lilley Construction Ltd*.[75] There, the employer argued that, because the payment dispute had been referred to adjudication, and that adjudication had taken place, the terms of clause 66 did not admit the possibility of subsequent arbitration in respect of the same subject matter and that by triggering the adjudication, the contractor had stepped outside the provisions of clause 66. This argument was rejected by the court in similar

---

[73] [2002] BLR 476.
[74] See paragraphs 10.20–10.32.
[75] Scots Law Times, 2003, 731.

terms to the decision in *The Construction Centre Group*. The adjudicator's decision in favour of the contractor had been paid. There remained a dispute as to the extent of the defendant's contractual entitlement to payment which was described by the court as a dispute 'that can competently be resolved in accordance with the provisions of clause 66'. Moreover the court held that there was nothing in the provisions of clause 66 that would preclude the contractor from serving a notice of dispute in the terms of clause 66(2) as a necessary preliminary step to having the dispute between the parties resolved by arbitration. The earlier decision of the engineer was not a final determination of the dispute between the parties.

NEC/2

One of the many NEC family of standard form building and engineering contracts is the clumsily titled Option Y (UK) 2. These provisions were the subject of a close analysis by HHJ Toulmin CMG QC in *John Mowlem & Co Plc v Hydra-Tight & Co Plc*.[76] The Judge concluded that Clauses 90.1 to 90.4 of Y (UK) 2 did not comply with s108(1) and (2)(a) of the 1996 Act because they did not give the parties an immediate right to refer at any time (or to give notice of an intention to refer) a dispute to adjudication. The contractual mechanism there set out was described as a notification of dissatisfaction which delayed a referral to adjudication for four weeks, during which time the parties had an opportunity to meet and resolve their differences. During that time the parties were to endeavour to agree that a dispute 'shall not have arisen' and that therefore there was no matter which could be referred to adjudication. That was plainly different to the 1996 Act, which provided that a party to a construction contract must have an immediate right to give notice of an intention to refer a dispute to adjudication. In addition, the Judge concluded that Clause 90.1 and following did not provide a timetable for the securing of the appointment of an adjudicator, and referral of a dispute to him, within seven days. For these reasons, the Judge concluded that the Scheme for Construction Contracts must apply. The Judge considered whether, if some parts of the sub-contract complied with the 1996 Act, they could be retained and the Act only used to substitute for or fill in those parts of the sub-contract which were contrary to the Act. He concluded that the words of the 1996 Act were clear and that, if any part of the sub-contract does not comply with the Act, s108(1)(2)(4) and/or the provisions of the Scheme must apply instead.[77]

4.60

---

[76] [2001] 17 Const LJ 358.
[77] See paragraphs 3.04–3.10 above.

Contracts For Professional Services

4.61 The standard forms of contract governing the engagement of construction professionals also contain adjudication provisions. Thus the ACE Conditions of Engagement incorporate adjudication provisions and stipulate that any adjudication will take place in accordance with the Construction Industry Council Model Adjudication Procedure. A number of particular aspects of that procedure are discussed in paragraphs 4.73–4.75 below. Similarly, the RIBA Conditions of Engagement in respect of the engagement of architects, contain an adjudication clause. In *Picardi v Cuniberti & Cuniberti*[78] the Judge concluded that, contrary to the claimant's submissions, the RIBA conditions of engagement were never agreed by the defendants. However, even if he had concluded that the contract incorporated the RIBA Conditions, the Judge indicated that he would have decided that the adjudication provisions would have been excluded pursuant to the *Unfair Terms in Consumer Contracts Regulations* 1999 on the basis that adjudication was an unusual procedure which, in the 1996 Act, specifically excluded private dwelling houses. Thus, if the claimant had wanted to obtain the defendant's agreement to adjudicate disputes related to works carried out at private dwelling houses, the particular adjudication provisions of the RIBA Conditions of Engagement would have had to have been drawn to the defendant's attention.

Adjudication Rules

The TeCSA Rules

4.62 Following the change of name of the Official Referee's Court to the Technology and Construction Court, the specialist solicitors practising in that field changed their name from ORSA to TeCSA. In both guises, they have created specific rules for the prompt and efficient resolution of disputes by way of adjudication. Large parts of those rules reflect the 1996 Act and the Scheme. However, some of the specific rules have been the subject of particular comment by the courts.

4.63 Rules 11 and 12 of Version 1.3 of these rules seek to add an important gloss on the provisions of the 1996 Act. They provide as follows:

> 11. The scope of the adjudication shall be the matters identified in the notice requiring adjudication, together with:
>
> > (1) any further matters which all Parties agree should be within the scope of the adjudication;

---

[78] [2003] BLR 487. For a fuller discussion of the Unfair Terms in Consumer Contracts Regulations 1999, please see paragraphs 9.49–9.58 below.

(2) any further matters which the Adjudicator determines must be included in order that the adjudication may be effective and/or meaningful.

12. ... The Adjudicator may rule upon his own substantive jurisdiction and as to the scope of the Adjudication.

As explained in more detail in paragraphs 7.35–7.45 below, the notice of intention to refer a dispute to adjudication is commonly regarded as the sole source of the adjudicator's jurisdiction, so that a dispute not identified there cannot be later raised by the claimants during the adjudication. It will be seen that rule 11 of the TeCSA Rules gives the adjudicator the power to widen the scope of the adjudication if he considers that to be 'effective and/or meaningful'. This is potentially a significant power which an adjudicator under these Rules may be able to use to address other related matters, and which, by way of contrast, an adjudicator under the Scheme for Construction Contracts would not have.

4.64 Furthermore, it is generally accepted that an adjudicator cannot issue a binding decision on his own jurisdiction unless the parties have expressly agreed to be bound by that decision.[79] However, it has been argued that rule 12 allows the adjudicator to make a binding decision on his own jurisdiction. In *Farebrother Building Services Ltd v Frogmore Investments Ltd*[80] HHJ Gilliland QC concluded that rule 12 meant that an adjudicator's decision that a particular issue was within his jurisdiction was binding on the parties. He distinguished the decision in *Bouygues*[81] on the grounds that that did not apply to adjudications carried out pursuant to the TeCSA Rules. He concluded that if, by mistake, the adjudicator decided that something was within his jurisdiction when, on the proper construction of the notice, it was not, then the rules provided that he could rule on his substantive jurisdiction and it was not a matter with which the court could interfere. Thus he ruled that such a decision was binding until it was set aside, and the court could not intervene at the enforcement stage.

4.65 The decision in *Farebrother* is difficult to reconcile with the conclusion of HHJ Kirkham in *Shimizu Europe Ltd v LBJ Fabrications Ltd*,[82] a case already referred to at paragraphs 2.140 and 4.42 above Judge Kirkham considered rules 11 and 12, and also rule 33, which provides that, save in the case of bad faith on the part of the adjudicator, no party shall make any application to the court whatsoever in relation to the conduct of the adjudication or the decision of the adjudicator until such time as the adjudicator has made his decision and until the party making the application has complied with any such decision. She concluded that the rules did

---

[79] See, for example, *Nordot v Siemens* [2001] CILL 1778–1779. This topic is addressed in paragraphs 7.09–7.15 below.
[80] [2001] CILL 1762–1764.
[81] [2000] BLR 49.
[82] [2003] BLR 381.

not have the effect of preventing a party from asking the court to construe a decision and the rules could not oust the jurisdiction of the court. She said, at paragraph 48 of her judgment:

> The [TeCSA] Rules presuppose that the decision would be one validly made within an adjudicator's jurisdiction. So, for example, if LBJ were to make a claim for summary judgment to enforce the decision, the rules would not prevent Shimizu raising a jurisdictional argument as a defence; if the decision is without jurisdiction, it will not be summarily enforced. In circumstances where a party is able to persuade the court that the adjudicator did not have jurisdiction, it would at the least be harsh, and in my judgment contradictory and inappropriate, to require that party first to comply with the decision.

4.66 As a matter of principle it is respectfully suggested that Judge Kirkham's approach is to be preferred. Whilst rule 12 allows the adjudicator to rule on his own substantive jurisdiction, there is nothing in the TeCSA Rules to indicate that such a decision is to be treated as binding and/or not open to review by the court. The wording of rule 12 allows the adjudicator to rule on his own jurisdiction and in most cases it is appropriate for the adjudicator to do just that. But if one party takes a jurisdictional objection, both to the adjudicator and, in any enforcement proceedings, to the court, then the court is obliged to review that jurisdictional challenge, and if the court concludes that the jurisdictional challenge is valid, then that would be enough to render the decision unenforceable. It would be inappropriate to conclude that rule 12 somehow provides the necessary jurisdiction to an adjudicator who, without rule 12, would not have the jurisdiction to entertain the dispute. Such a view is also consistent with general principle, as noted at paragraphs 7.09–7.15 below.

4.67 In *A v B*[83] the court was concerned with the TeCSA Rules relating to enforcement. Rule 14 provides that the adjudicator's decision 'shall be binding until the dispute is finally determined by legal proceedings, by arbitration . . . or by agreement', and rule 28A expressly states that:

> Every decision of the Adjudicator shall be implemented without delay. The parties shall be entitled to such reliefs and remedies as are set out in the decision, and shall be entitled to summary enforcement thereof, regardless of whether such decision is or is to be the subject of any challenge or review. No party shall be entitled to raise any right of set-off, counterclaim or abatement in connection with any enforcement proceedings.

In addition, paragraph 2.1 of Appendix 8 to the Rules provided that:

> (f) Notwithstanding rules 14 and 33, no party shall, save in the case of bad faith on the part of the Adjudicator make any application whatsoever to a competent court in relation to the conduct of the Adjudication or the decision of the Adjudicator until

---

[83] 17 December 2002, Outer House, Court of Session; (2002) CA 110/02.

the earlier of the Actual Completion date of the last Phase or termination of this sub-contract...

This was similar to the provision considered by HHJ Kirkham in *Shimizu*.

4.68 The defenders in *A v B*[84] argued that paragraph 2.1(f) prevented the pursuers from enforcing the adjudicator's decision because actual completion had not taken place. The court rejected this argument on two alternative grounds. If paragraph 2.1(f) of Appendix 8 had the effect contended for by the defenders, it was incompatible with s108(3) of the 1996 Act, and was accordingly of no legal effect. But, in the alternative, as a matter of construction, paragraph 2.1(f) of Appendix 8 was to be construed as relating only to judicial review of an adjudicator's decision, and not to proceedings to enforce such a decision.

4.69 Rule 21A of the TeCSA Rules allows the adjudicator to make awards of costs (or, in Scotland, judicial expenses). In *Deko Scotland Ltd v Edinburgh Royal Joint Venture*[85] the adjudicator had taken advantage of this power to include, along with the decision awarding sums to the contractors, a ruling that the employer was to pay half of the contractor's costs. The reason the costs were reduced to half was that the adjudicator concluded that much of the time spent in connection with the adjudication was taken up with matters for which the contractor was wholly unsuccessful, and he said that he had apportioned the costs accordingly. The contractor pursued a claim for its expenses in court. The employer successfully attacked the claim on two grounds. First, it was argued that the claim had to be limited to legal costs and should not include the fees of a claims consultant and a surveyor. Secondly, they also argued that any award of expenses by an adjudicator was subject to taxation and that any proceedings for enforcement had to be based on an account of expenses that had either been taxed or had been agreed. The court upheld both of these submissions. The case is of relevance because of the clear equation between (English) costs and (Scottish) expenses in the judgment of Lord Drummond Young. The Judge also concluded that the provisional nature of an adjudicator's decision had no bearing on the need for taxation which was required in order to prevent successful parties to legal proceedings from making excessive claims for expenses. He said that that requirement existed whether or not the result of the legal proceedings was fully determinative of the party's rights and was liable to be undone by other proceedings.

4.70 It remains an open question as to whether an adjudicator appointed under the TeCSA Rules is obliged to give reasons if the parties do not agree that he should. In *Hurst Stores and Interiors Ltd v ML Europe Property Ltd*,[86] a substantive judgment

---

[84] (2002) CA 110/02.
[85] Scots Law Times 2003, 727.
[86] [2003] EWHC 1650 (TCC).

dealing with a challenge to the earlier findings of an adjudicator, the adjudicator had said that, pursuant to rule 27 of the TeCSA Rules, he was not obliged to give reasons because, although one party had requested such reasons, the other party had not agreed to the provision of such reasons.

The CEDR Rules

4.71 There are fewer reported cases on the CEDR Rules. One of them is *Stiell Ltd v Riema Control Systems Ltd*.[87] That was directly concerned with paragraphs 12 and 13 of the CEDR Rules which provided that the decision of the adjudicator was final and binding upon the parties unless one or other of the parties issued, within the specified time, a written notice of its dissatisfaction. If such a notice of dissatisfaction was provided, the dispute would be finally determined by court proceedings or by reference to arbitration and, in such proceedings, neither the court nor the arbitrator would be bound by the decision of the adjudicator, and indeed would have the power to review and revise such a decision. This led to an unsatisfactory situation in *Stiell* because, although the pursuers had been partially successful, they were obliged to issue a notice of dissatisfaction in respect of that part of the decision which was adverse to them. The defendant paid the sum identified by the adjudicator. Thereafter the defendant sought to discharge the interim protective measures, namely the warrant for arrestment on the defendant, whose underlying basis was the proposition that the defendant did, or even might, owe the pursuer more than it had then paid. Surprisingly, the court decided that the decision of the adjudicator did not change matters and that the pursuer's claim for the sums (which the adjudicator had determined were not due) was a pure debt and not dependent upon a contingency. The interim measures therefore remained in place. It is difficult not to agree with the learned commentators of the Technology and Construction Law Report that in England and Wales, a different approach would have been adopted.

The CIC Model Adjudication Procedure

4.72 Reference has already been made to the CIC Model Adjudication Procedure.[88] A number of the more important paragraphs of this procedure are set out in the judgment of Dyson J in *Bouygues*.[89] They included paragraph 1, which stipulates that the object of adjudication is to reach a fair, rapid and inexpensive decision upon a dispute arising under the contract; paragraph 4, which provides that the decision shall be binding until the dispute is finally determined by legal

---

[87] [2001] 3 TCLR 9. See also paragraph 12.40 below.
[88] See paragraphs 2.04–2.08 above.
[89] [2000] BLR 49.

proceedings, arbitration or agreement; paragraph 5 which provides that the adjudicator's decision shall be implemented by the parties without delay whether or not the dispute was to be referred to legal proceedings or arbitration; and paragraphs 8 and 14 which contain familiar provisions in relation to the notice of intention to refer and the referral notice. Paragraph 20 allows the adjudicator to deal with matters other than those set out in the notice, but only if those matters are agreed by the parties and the adjudicator, and not otherwise. In accordance with those rules, Dyson J concluded that the adjudicator's jurisdiction to decide the disputes derived from the Model Procedure and, to the extent that he purported to decide matters which did not fall within the scope of paragraph 20 (and which therefore had not been referred to him), his decision did not come within paragraphs 4 and 5 and was void.

4.73 The CIC Procedure has been called into serious doubt as a result of two decisions of HHJ Havery QC in the London TCC. In the first, *Epping Electrical Co Ltd v Briggs & Forrester (Plumbing Services) Ltd*[90] the Judge had to consider rule 25 of the CIC Procedure which provided that 'if the adjudicator fails to reach his decision within the time permitted by this procedure, his decision shall nonetheless be effective if reached before the referral of the dispute to any replacement adjudicator . . . ' Judge Havery said that the apparent effect of this rule, which would allow the adjudicator to reach an effective decision beyond the 28 day period, was inconsistent with s108(2) of the Act. As a result, he concluded that the CIC Procedure was not compliant and that the Scheme must apply instead. He revisited that decision in *Aveat Heating Ltd v Jerram Falkus Construction Ltd*[91] (which was not concerned with the CIC Procedure but a particular provision of GC/Works Sub-Contract Conditions which also purported to suggest that the adjudicator's decision would be valid if issued after the time allowed). Again Judge Havery concluded that such a provision was not in accordance with the Act and that, in consequence, the Scheme must apply.

4.74 Another of the unusual features of at least one version of the CIC Model Procedure was that it expressly permitted the adjudicator to conduct separate interviews with the parties and their respective experts. In *Dean & Dyball Construction Ltd v Kenneth Grubb Associates Ltd*[92] the defendant objected to the adjudicator's decision on the grounds that he had followed an unfair procedure, notwithstanding that it was a procedure expressly permitted by the CIC Model Adjudication Procedure. HHJ Seymour QC said that if there was no express provision in the relevant adjudication procedure which allowed this course, he had 'some doubts' that such a course could ever be proper without the tribunal indicating to the

---

[90] [2007] EWHC 4 (TCC).
[91] [2007] EWHC 131 (TCC).
[92] [2003] EWHC 2465 (TCC).

absent party what had been said. However, the Judge decided that on the material before him, the defendants' argument really amounted to no more than 'the somewhat unpromising proposition that the procedure, if operated in accordance with its express terms, could be operated unfairly'. The Judge went on to conclude that on the material before him, there had been no unfairness and that there was no suggestion that the adjudicator had regard to any evidence given on behalf of the claimant of which the defendant was unaware or which it did not have an opportunity to answer.

4.75 The CIC Procedure, at paragraphs 28 and 29, makes plain that the parties must bear their own costs and expenses incurred in the adjudication and that the parties would be jointly and severally liable for the adjudicator's fees and expenses. However, in *Bridgeway Construction Ltd v Tolent Construction Ltd*[93] the parties had deleted those paragraphs and instead agreed that the party serving the notice of adjudication would bear all the costs and expenses incurred by both parties and all of the adjudicator's fees and expenses. Bridgeway served a notice of adjudication and were successful but, in accordance with the contract, the adjudicator required them to pay the costs. Tolent paid the sum ordered under the adjudication decision, less its own legal costs and other expenses. Bridgeway were then obliged to contend that the amendments to the contract to which they had agreed were ineffective because they inhibited parties from pursuing the remedies provided by the adjudication procedure. This argument was rejected by HHJ MacKay QC who had no difficulty in deciding that the contracting parties could agree what they liked and that it was not for a disappointed party to seek to argue that the contract which he had freely agreed was in some way wrong or invalid. The decision of the adjudicator was therefore upheld.

---

[93] [2000] CILL 1662–1664.

5

AD HOC ADJUDICATION

Introduction	5.01
The Relevant Authorities	5.03
Estoppel	5.12
Conclusion	5.14

'I can see no reason, as a matter of law, why parties cannot agree to abide by the decision of a third party if they so wish. Clearly that is appropriate in the case of arbitration. Why should it not be appropriate in the case of adjudication, I ask?'

His Honour Judge Gilliland QC,
in *Nordot Engineering Services Ltd v Siemens Plc*
(SF00901 TCC 16/00; CILL, September 2001).

Introduction

5.01 In addition to statutory adjudication under the 1996 Act, and contractual adjudication pursuant to the terms of the contract in question, there is a third way in which parties to a contract can agree, or be deemed to have agreed, to submit their dispute to adjudication. That is by reference to what is called in the authorities ad hoc adjudication, whereby the parties agree, or are deemed to have agreed, to confer jurisdiction onto an adjudicator to decide the particular dispute that has arisen between them. Because this is a matter entirely for the agreement of the parties, such an adjudication may arise in respect of contracts other than construction contracts, or in respect of contracts for the provision of work and services which would otherwise be excluded by the provisions of the 1996 Act.[1]

---

[1] See the detailed discussion as to construction operations excluded by the 1996 Act at paragraphs 2.23–2.43 above.

5.02 It has long been the position that an arbitrator can derive a full jurisdiction from the ad hoc agreement of the parties. In *Westminster Chemicals and Produce Ltd v Eicholz & Loeser* [1954] 1 LLR 99 at 105–106, Devlin J (as he then was) was concerned with a situation where it was said that the arbitrator had ad hoc jurisdiction to deal with the dispute. The Judge said that if two people agreed to submit a dispute to a third person, then the parties agreed to accept the award of that person, or, putting it another way, they had conferred jurisdiction on that third person to determine their dispute. If, however, one of the parties thinks that the dispute that has arisen is outside the agreement to refer disputes to a third person, then that party can protest the jurisdiction of the arbitrator, and to contend that he had not agreed to abide by the award. It was held that a party who had made that position clear at the outset can then take part in the arbitration without losing his rights to reactivate the jurisdiction argument at an appropriate stage. For obvious reasons, the approach and reasoning in *Westminster Chemicals* has been considered and applied in a number of the adjudication cases concerned with ad hoc jurisdiction, dealt with in chronological order below.

The Relevant Authorities

5.03 The first adjudication dispute in which the question of ad hoc jurisdiction arose was *The Project Consultancy Group v The Trustees of The Gray Trust*.[2] In that case there was a dispute as to whether the contract in question was a construction contract or had been entered into before 1 May 1998 (the starting date for the 1996 Act). Dyson J, as he then was, rejected the claimant's first argument, to the effect that the defendant could not challenge the adjudicator's decision on his own jurisdiction. Much of the judgment is concerned with the subsidiary contention by the claimant, to the effect that there was an ad hoc submission of the jurisdiction issue to the adjudicator, with the result that his decision was binding. It was argued that the defendant had submitted that question to the adjudicator for his decision and had agreed to be bound by it. Dyson J expressly confirmed that the principles enunciated by Devlin J in *Westminster Chemicals* were 'equally applicable to an adjudication'. In other words, it was open to the parties to a contract to confer an ad hoc jurisdiction on an adjudicator and that, if that is what they had done, they would be bound by the result. The Judge then turned to consider the facts in order to ascertain whether or not the parties had given the adjudicator the necessary ad hoc jurisdiction. He concluded that they had not. He pointed to the defendant's solicitors' letter of 9 March 1999 which said in terms that the 1996 Act did not apply and that the notice of reference to adjudication was invalid. The letter

---

[2] [1999] BLR 377.

went on to make plain that, if the claiming party proceeded with the adjudication, the defendant would dispute the adjudicator's jurisdiction and that, if a decision was made despite such objections, the defendant would not comply with any such decision on the basis that it had been made without jurisdiction. It might be thought that the effect of such a letter was entirely obvious. However, as can often be the case, the position was muddled by the formal documents exchanged in the adjudication in which, amongst other things, the defendant had set out in detail its case on the jurisdictional issue. The claimant (referring party) relied on that document as demonstrating that the responding party was conferring ad hoc jurisdiction on the adjudicator to decide the issue.

5.04 Dyson J rejected that contention in a passage of his judgment which is equally applicable to the majority of cases in which a submission of ad hoc jurisdiction is maintained by the referring party, despite the evidence of clear antecedent objections from the responding party:

> 15. In my view, the defendant's solicitors' letter of 9 March 1999 stated in the clearest terms that the defendants protested the adjudicator's jurisdiction, and that they would not recognise and comply with any decision to award money to the claimant. The letter also made it clear that, if the adjudication proceeded, they reserved their right to participate, but without prejudice to their contention that there was no jurisdiction. I do not consider that there can be any reasonable doubt as to the meaning of the letter. The only real question is whether, by participating in the adjudication process, the defendants waived the jurisdiction point, and agreed to submit to abide by the decision of the adjudicator on that issue. The only material relied on by Ms Rawley is the content of the defendant's response to which I have already referred. But, in their response, the defendants continued to assert that the adjudicator had no jurisdiction. This stance was entirely consistent with what was said in the letter of 9 March. It is a question of fact whether a person submits to the jurisdiction of a third person … In my view, the defendants never departed from the position which they expressed very clearly in their solicitor's letter of 9 March 1999. They did not submit to the jurisdiction of the adjudicator.

5.05 The next case in time was *Christiani & Nielsen Ltd v The Lowry Centre Development Co Ltd*.³ This was a case in which HHJ Thornton QC found that the adjudicator had the necessary jurisdiction because the contract was caught by the provisions of the 1996 Act. However, he considered at the outset of his judgment whether the parties had agreed to vest in the adjudicator an ad hoc jurisdiction, to determine his own jurisdiction, which decision would then be binding. Judge Thornton agreed, at paragraph 14 of his judgment, that the parties could have agreed to vest the adjudicator with the power to decide whether or not the relevant contract under which the dispute arose was entered into before 1 May 1998 (and was thus not caught by the 1996 Act), although he warned that the status of such

---

3 HHJ Thornton QC, June 29, 2000 (TCC). The case was not reported until [2004] TCLR 2.

a decision, and the extent to which it could be challenged, could only be decided following a consideration of the express and implied terms of the agreement to confer such ad hoc jurisdiction. He considered the facts and the correspondence and, in a similar way to Dyson J in *Project Consultancy*, concluded that the documents exchanged between the parties and provided to the adjudicator setting out their respective submissions on the jurisdiction issue did not amount to an agreement between the parties to confer an ad hoc jurisdiction on the adjudicator. He concluded that the provision of such submissions had to be seen against the background of the responding party's continuing protest as to jurisdiction and he decided that the responding party had not agreed to confer on the adjudicator the necessary jurisdiction to enable him to decide his own jurisdiction. This was despite the fact that the adjudicator apparently thought that that is what had happened.

5.06 These two decisions are to be contrasted with the decision of HHJ Gilliland QC in *Nordot Engineering Services Ltd v Siemens Plc*.[4] In that case, it was suggested that the work that was the subject matter of the contract was not a construction operation as defined by s105(1) of the 1996 Act. It was argued by Siemens that, because the 1996 Act had expressly excluded contracts such as the one between themselves and Nordot (because, so they said, the work that was the subject matter of that contract was not a construction operation within the meaning of the Act) it was not open to the parties to confer an ad hoc jurisdiction on the adjudicator. Judge Gilliland rejected that contention. He said:

> ... It seems to me that the submission that it is not open to the parties to confer jurisdiction on an adjudicator is not sound in principle. I can see no reason, as a matter of law, why parties cannot agree to abide by the decision of a third party if they so wish. Clearly that is appropriate in a case of arbitration. Why should it not be appropriate in the case of adjudication I ask? If the parties with their eyes open enter into an agreement to the effect that 'the adjudicator will decide this question and we will be bound by his decision', why should the court not give effect to that agreement? There can be no public policy against that and the mere fact that the system of adjudication is established by statute does not, it seems to me, make any difference. One could say exactly the same thing, as a matter of principle, in relation to the question of arbitration. There is no obligation to agree to arbitration before the parties agree to it. Similarly if parties wish to resolve a dispute and submit it to an adjudicator who derives his jurisdiction from the statute nevertheless, it seems to me, it is open to the parties to confer that jurisdiction on him by agreement should they wish.

5.07 Judge Gilliland also emphasised the need for a clear jurisdictional objection to be lodged by the party who did not wish to enter into such an agreement. He then went on to consider, on the facts of the case, whether it could properly be said that there had been a submission to the ad hoc jurisdiction of the adjudicator. He said

---

[4] (SF00901 TCC 16/00) dated 14 April 2000. Also reported at CILL, September 2001.

that such a finding depended on the fair reading and interpretation of the correspondence which passed between the parties. He concluded that, in all the circumstances, the parties had agreed to confer an ad hoc jurisdiction on the adjudicator. This was principally because the responding party had written to the adjudicator and, having made the point that they did not consider that the work was a construction operation under the 1996 Act, went on to say in clear terms:

> 'We will, however, abide by your decision in this matter and will comply with whatever direction you deem appropriate.'

In the circumstances, the Judge concluded that the statement that the defendant would abide by the adjudicator's decision in the matter was clear and unequivocal, and that it amounted to an agreement that the adjudicator had the ad hoc jurisdiction to decide the point.

5.08 There are a number of other reported cases in which it was concluded that the adjudicator had been given an ad hoc jurisdiction, and the parties were bound by the result. In *Parsons Plastics (Research and Development) Ltd v Purac Ltd*[5] there was a dispute as to whether the subject matter of the contract was a construction operation. However, the parties agreed to submit to an ad hoc adjudication under the terms of the contract between them. The referring party was successful but, instead of paying the sum awarded by the adjudicator, the responding party issued a withholding notice. The referring party argued that, although the adjudication was an ad hoc referral, the decision was final and binding and should be enforced as if it had been made under the Act. Their enforcement application failed, both at first instance and in the Court of Appeal. However, it is clear from the judgment of Pill LJ that the referring party's failure was not due to the nature of the adjudication itself (the ad hoc nature of the adjudication did not appear to be in issue), but to the fact that, pursuant to the particular terms of the contract in question, the responding party had a right to set-off its counterclaim against the sums awarded by the adjudicator.[6]

5.09 In *Galliford Try Construction Ltd v Michael Heal Associates Ltd*[7] there were a whole series of issues for the Judge to decide. In the end he refused to give summary judgment to enforce the adjudicator's claim, principally because the formation and terms of the contract which the referring party had urged on the adjudicator was very different to the terms of the contract which they maintained at the enforcement hearing.[8] However, along the way, HHJ Seymour QC decided that the

---

[5] [2002] BLR 334, CA.
[6] For the importance of this decision in connection with a losing party's ability to set off against the sum awarded by the adjudicator, see paragraphs 10.23 and 10.24 below.
[7] [2003] EWHC 2886 (TCC).
[8] Judge Seymour was particularly damming of this process and said: 'Galliford thus seems to be playing fast and loose with the process of adjudication, shifting its ground opportunistically to meet

referring party was correct in its submission that, by reference to the correspondence, there was a clear agreement between the party's respective solicitors that, if the mediation failed, the disputes would be submitted to the adjudication of a named adjudicator. In particular, he decided that the expression 'without prejudice to our contentions on jurisdiction' was, in all the circumstances, insufficient to amount to an objection to the adjudicator reaching a binding decision on the point in question. He also found that, in any event, that reservation had been overtaken by the subsequent course of the correspondence.

5.10 The decision in *Galliford Try* is also important because Judge Seymour made the point that it was not just a question of working out whether or not the adjudicator had the necessary ad hoc jurisdiction, but, if so, what the terms were of that agreement. What is it that the parties were getting?[9] Judge Seymour said:

> 42. There is no reason in law why parties to a dispute may not agree, if they wish, to submit disputes which have already arisen to adjudication, even if otherwise the agreement between the parties made no provision for adjudication and the provisions of the 1996 Act were inapplicable. Adjudication may be a useful means of seeking to resolve disputes in areas quite outside the construction industry. However, it remains to consider what is the effect in law of agreeing to submit to adjudication disputes which have already arisen. In other words, what exactly is it the parties agree to if they agree to submit disputes to adjudication?

5.11 In addition to *Project Consultancy*, perhaps the most important decision on ad hoc jurisdiction is the Court of Appeal case of *Thomas-Fredric's (Construction) Ltd v Keith Wilson*.[10] In that case, the claimant contractor asserted that there had been an ad hoc adjudication, and that the defendant/appellant had agreed to be bound by the result. The Court of Appeal found that the adjudicator had reached the wrong conclusion on the underlying issues as to the true identity of the contracting parties. However, as noted in paragraph 16 of his judgment, Simon Brown LJ went on to say that, nevertheless, such a decision would be binding and enforceable if it could be shown that the appellant had agreed to accept that ruling. Having referred to *Project Consultancy* and *Nordot*, Simon Brown LJ then turned to the facts and documents in the case and, having reviewed them, concluded that it was impossible to say that the appellant had submitted to the jurisdiction of the

---

the challenge of the moment. No court can be expected to treat phlegmatically a case in which a successful party to an adjudication comes before it saying: "*I know that I have succeeded in the adjudication on a basis which I now recognise was wrong in law, but the adjudicator decided what he was asked to decide and it is just tough luck for the defendant*". That attitude seems to come very close to an abuse of the process of adjudication.' A similar result, albeit expressed in less extravagant language, can be found in *Redworth Construction Limited v Brookdale Healthcare Limited* [2006] EWHC 1994 (TCC), a decision of HHJ Havery QC.

[9] This echoed the similar question raised by Judge Thornton in *Christiani & Neilson* at paragraph 20 of his judgment.
[10] [2003] EWCA Civ 1494.

adjudicator in the full sense described by Judge Gilliland in *Nordot*. Instead, he decided that the appellant's position was very similar to the objection taken by the responding party in *Project Consultancy*. He concluded that the adjudicator had not been asked to make a decision on the jurisdictional issue, and had certainly not been asked in such a way as to indicate that the appellant would then accept the adjudicator's ruling upon it. He was therefore entitled to challenge the decision as one which had been made without the necessary jurisdiction, and the Court of Appeal concluded that, because he had a more than respectable case that he was not a party to the underlying contract, the decision would not be enforced.

Estoppel

5.12 Unsurprisingly perhaps, as an alternative to the suggestion that the parties conferred an ad hoc jurisdiction on the adjudicator to decide the dispute between them, referring parties have, in the alternative, contended that the loser is now estopped from denying that the adjudicator had the necessary jurisdiction. In *Maymac Environmental Services Ltd v Faraday Building Services Ltd*[11] the principal dispute was whether or not there was a construction contract between the parties. HHJ Toulmin CMG QC held that there was. However, even assuming that he was wrong about that, the Judge had no hesitation in going on to conclude that Faraday were estopped by representation and convention from now arguing that the 1996 Act and the Scheme did not apply. The Judge found that Faraday had consented to submit to the adjudication and, in so doing, had admitted that there was a contract to which the Act and the Scheme applied. The adjudication was conducted on that basis. Thus Faraday could not now argue that the Act and the Scheme did not apply. Assuming that no contract existed and that the referral was not under the Act, the referral had still been made on the basis that the adjudication would take place, by agreement between the parties, on the same terms as the Act and the Scheme. Such an agreement was enforceable on the same basis as if the Act had applied.

5.13 Similarly, in *William Oakley & David Oakley v Airclear Environmental Ltd and Airclear TS Ltd*[12] Etherton J upheld the County Court Judge's view that there was an estoppel by convention and that the two parties had proceeded under a mutual assumption (which had been communicated between them) that a code of dispute resolution was available to resolve a dispute that had arisen between them. On the particular facts of that case there was a common assumption by the first

---

[11] [2001] CILL 1685.
[12] [2002] CILL 1824.

respondent and the appellants that their contractual relations were governed by the NAAM/T and NAM/SC forms of contract, including the express adjudication provisions contained therein.

Conclusion

5.14 The message from the authorities discussed above is clear. If the responding party objects to the jurisdiction of the adjudicator, then such objection should be identified in clear terms in the immediate response to the notice of intention to refer. Thereafter, even if the adjudicator calls for detailed arguments as to the jurisdiction position, the responding party can participate in such a process, provided that he makes clear reference to the fact that his participation and submissions are without prejudice to his primary position that the adjudicator does not have the requisite jurisdiction. Any suggestion that the responding party will accept or abide by the result (as happened in *Nordot*) may well be fatal to the objection and may well be taken to confer ad hoc jurisdiction on the adjudicator.

5.15 Concern was expressed that the general making of jurisdictional challenges by the responding party might give rise to extensive difficulties with the enforcement of adjudicator's decisions. This concern was articulated by the editors of the Building Law Reports in their editorial on *Project Consultancy*:[13]

> The possibilities of challenging the jurisdiction of an adjudicator are broad if not infinite. This decision confirms that any arguable challenge to the jurisdiction of the adjudicator will secure that the decision of the adjudicator is summarily unenforceable. If the decision is not enforceable immediately, the underlying dispute going to the jurisdiction of the adjudicator has to be resolved either by the court or in a ppropriate cases by the arbitrator. Accordingly one of the principal objects of the 1996 Act, namely the prompt resolution of disputes, is necessarily but effectively undermined.

This concern is addressed in greater detail in paragraphs 7.02–7.03 below. It has largely proved unfounded. Of course, one of the ways in which a jurisdictional challenge has been met is for the referring party to argue that, even if there was an original difficulty with the adjudicator's jurisdiction, the responding party waived such difficulties by agreeing to confer upon the adjudicator an ad hoc jurisdiction. In *Thomas-Fredric's*, Simon Brown LJ summarised the proper approach to allegations of ad hoc jurisdiction in two propositions:

> (1) If a defendant to a Part 24(2) application has submitted to the adjudicator's jurisdiction in the full sense of having agreed not only that the adjudicator should rule

---

[13] [1999] BLR 377 at 379.

on the issue of jurisdiction but also that he would then be bound by that ruling, then he is liable to enforcement in the short term, even if the adjudicator was plainly wrong on the issue.

(2) Even if the defendant has not submitted to the adjudicator's jurisdiction in that sense, then he is still liable to a Part 24(2) summary judgment upon the award if the adjudicator's ruling on the jurisdictional issue was plainly right.

It is thought that, in the light of this clear statement of principle, following as it did the remarks of Dyson J, to similar effect, in *Project Consultancy*, it will only be in clear cases, such as *Nordot* and *Galliford Try*, where the court will be persuaded that, despite earlier protests, the responding party eventually submitted to the adjudicator's jurisdiction (in the full sense of being bound by his decision on jurisdiction), by way of an ad hoc agreement.

6

ADJUDICATION IN OTHER JURISDICTIONS

Introduction	6.01	The Payment Schedule	6.12
Australia	6.02	Adjudication	6.13
New South Wales	6.02	Determination	6.18
Overview	6.03	Enforcement	6.20
What Contracts does the NSW Act Apply to?	6.06	Other Australian Jurisdictions	6.23
Can You Contract Out of the NSW Act?	6.09	**Singapore**	6.29
Progress Payments and the Payment Claim	6.10	**New Zealand**	6.35

'What the legislature has effectively achieved is a fast track interim progress payment adjudication vehicle. That vehicle must necessarily give rise to many adjudication determinations which will simply be incorrect. That is because the adjudicator in some instances cannot possibly, in the time available and in which the determination is to be brought down, give the type of care and attention to the dispute capable of being provided upon a full curial hearing... The nature and range of issues legitimate to be raised, particularly in the case of large construction contracts, are such that it often could simply never be expected that the adjudicator would produce the correct decision. What the legislature has provided for is no more or no less than an interim quick solution to progress payment disputes which solution *critically* does not determine the parties' rights inter se. Those rights may be determined by curial proceedings, the court then having available to it the usual range of relief, most importantly including the right to a proprietor to claw back progress payments which it had been forced to make through the adjudication determination procedures.'

Einstein J in *Brodin Pty v Davenport* [2003] NSWC 1019, at paragraph 22

Introduction

6.01 The perceived advantages of adjudication have led to its introduction, in various guises, in a number of other countries. The Building and Construction Industry Security of Payment Act 1999 (NSW) ('NSW Act') introduced adjudication in respect of progress payments to New South Wales, and has become a model for a number of other similar pieces of legislation in other jurisdictions. It is dealt with in some detail below. Other Australian states which now provide for adjudication include Victoria and Queensland. The Building and Construction Industry Security of Payment Act 2004 introduced adjudication to Singapore and there is also similar legislation in place in New Zealand.

Australia

New South Wales

6.02 In some Australian states, there was already legislation which offered sub-contractors down the contractual chain some protection against the insolvency of employers and main contractors.[1] However, it was recognised that these provisions did not assist with improving the cash flow to the sub-contractors carrying out the bulk of the work on any construction site. In New South Wales, it was recognised that what was required was legislation which provided a quick enforcement process in relation to progress payments. The principle behind the NSW Act was that the dispute being decided in adjudication was the sub-contractors' right to progress payments, not final liabilities, so that any potential injustice done during the adjudication could, at least in principle, be corrected in the determination of those final liabilities in arbitration or litigation. Essentially, the NSW Act transfers the payment risk to the party up the contractual chain until there is a final determination. The NSW Act, which has been copied in other states, has been described in these terms:

> Its genius is its ability to get money into the hands of contractors and sub-contractors without the need for full scale litigation. To put it in terms of the adage, it has created a situation where possession is nine parts of the law, [and] that possession passes to the lower tier contractor.[2]

---

[1] See, for example, the Sub-contractors' Charges Act 1974 (NSW).
[2] 'Statutory Adjudication in Australia' by Professor Doug Jones, Adjudication Society, London Branch, 21 November 2006.

It is therefore instructive to consider the detail of the NSW Act and to see where it is similar to, and where it differs from, the Housing Grants Construction and Regeneration Act 1996.

Overview

6.03 The NSW Act provides that, in circumstances where a construction contract makes provision for progress payments, the contractor's contractual entitlement is underwritten by the statute. It works in a relatively simple way. The contractor makes a 'payment claim' setting out the amount it claims to be due. The owner must respond with a 'payment schedule' setting out the amount the owner believes to be due and giving reasons for any differences from the payment claim. If the amount shown in the schedule is less than the amount claimed, or if there is simply no response from the owner to the payment claim, then the contractor can apply for adjudication. The owner is entitled to make a written response to the contractor's adjudication application. Thereafter the procedure is at the discretion of the adjudicator. A determination must be made within ten business days of the adjudicator notifying the parties of his/her acceptance of the appointment. Thereafter, if the owner does not pay the amount due pursuant to the adjudicator's determination, the contractor is entitled to give notice of an intention to suspend work and may also obtain an 'adjudication certificate' which can be filed in court as a judgment for a debt.

6.04 If the contractor does not make provisions for progress payments then, rather like the Scheme for Construction Contracts in England, Wales and Scotland, the NSW Act provides for certain default provisions to take effect. These provide the contractor with an entitlement to monthly progress payments. He can then utilise the process noted above.

6.05 It is worth noting that, in its early days, the NSW Act was remarkably ineffective, despite the fact that it had such a precise goal (namely improving the cash flow of sub-contractors by tightening up interim payment provisions). There were two reasons for this. First, when the contractor issued proceedings to enforce the adjudication determination as a debt, the owner was able to bring a cross-claim as a defence in order to defeat those proceedings. Because the original NSW Act did not contain effective provisions in respect of withholding notices/set-off, employers/owners were able to defeat the interim claims by continued use of the set-off mechanism. Secondly, an owner was entitled to choose to provide security for the amount of the interim payment determined in adjudication, pending the outcome of final dispute resolution proceedings. This of course meant that there had to be full scale arbitration or litigation before the progress payment was actually recovered by the contractor, thus defeating the whole purpose of the NSW Act. In consequence, in 2002, the Building and Construction Industry Security of

Other Forms of Adjudication

Payment Amendment Act (NSW) ('2002 Amendments') was passed, and the NSW Act, as amended, has proved to be very popular.[3]

What Contracts does the NSW Act Apply to?

6.06 The NSW Act applies to any construction contract, whether written or oral, or partly written and partly oral.[4] A 'construction contract' is defined as a 'contract or other arrangement under which one party undertakes to carry out construction work or to supply related goods and services, for another party'.[5] One broad similarity with the 1996 Act is that, in s5(1), the NSW Act defines 'construction work' in some detail. It also contains, at s5(2), a series of exclusions. However, the principal difference is that what is excluded is limited to 'the drilling for, or extraction of, oil or natural gas' and 'the extraction . . . of minerals, including tunnelling or boring, or constructing underground works, for that purpose'. Thus the whole raft of processes and industries which are excluded by operation of the 1996 Act are included within the NSW Act.

6.07 Another difference is that the construction contract in question does not have to be in writing, let alone have all its terms set out in writing. Indeed, the NSW Act goes even further: it does not require the existence of a formal contract and covers work done pursuant to 'an arrangement'. It was held in *Okaroo Pty Ltd v Vos Construction & Joinery Pty Ltd*[6] that 'arrangement' meant a transaction or relationship which is not enforceable at law as a contract would be'. Nicholas J considered that this wide definition would not only include all contracts, but all non-enforceable relationships as well. Accordingly, all that matters when investigating whether the contract or arrangement was a construction contract for the purposes of the Act was to see 'whether it is one under which one party undertakes to carry out construction work, or to supply related goods and services, for another party. There is no other requirement or qualification which is expressly or by implication included in the definition which must be satisfied.'[7]

6.08 Other contracts to which the NSW Act specifically does not apply include loan agreements; contracts with a home owner who resides in, or intends to reside in, the dwelling where the work is carried out; contracts where the consideration is related not to the value of the work performed but to some other method of remuneration, such as a concession or right to demand a toll; where the party is an employee of the party for whom the work is carried out; and when the construction work or related goods and services are carried out and supplied

---

[3] During the first four years of the operation of the Act, only 116 adjudication applications were made. In the two years following the 2002 Amendments, there were over 1000 adjudications.
[4] s7.1.
[5] s4.
[6] [2005] NSWSC 45.
[7] *supra*, paragraph 42 of the judgment of Nicholas J.

Adjudication in Other Jurisdictions

outside New South Wales. Also, precisely in line with the 1996 Act, the NSW Act renders void 'pay when paid' provisions affecting construction contracts.[8]

Can You Contract Out of the NSW Act?

Section 34 of the NSW Act renders it impossible to exclude the operation of the Act by contracting out. Thus construction work carried out in New South Wales under a contract that purports to be governed by the law of another jurisdiction will still fall under the scope of the NSW Act. That said, it is also important to note that the adjudication mechanism provided by the NSW Act does not limit or exclude any other entitlement that a claimant may have under a construction contract or any other remedy that the claimant may have for recovering such other entitlement. In other words, the benefits conferred by the NSW Act are wholly additional to the parties' contractual rights and remedies.

6.09

Progress Payments and the Payment Claim

Section 8 of the NSW Act entitles a person, who has undertaken to carry out construction work, or to supply related goods and services, to regular progress payments. In order to recover a progress payment, section 13 entitles such a person to serve a payment claim. The payment claim must identify the construction work or related goods and services to which the progress payment relates; indicate the amount claimed; and state that the claim is made under the NSW Act. The inclusion in such a payment claim of disputed claims for delay and disruption costs will not render a payment claim invalid.[9] The payment claim is made at the date determined by the contract or, where there is no express provision for interim applications in the contract, it must be made on the last day of the month in which the work was first carried out, and then the last day of each subsequent month. The 2002 Amendments stipulate that the payment claim must be served within a period determined by the construction contract, or twelve months after the construction work was carried out, whichever is the later.[10] In addition, the 2002 Amendments, at s13(5) and s13(6), make plain that, whilst the claimant cannot serve more than one claim in respect of each reference date, a claimant can claim previous unpaid amounts in a subsequent claim. This would appear to allow, and even encourage, serial adjudication.

6.10

Of course, the biggest difference between the NSW Act and the 1996 Act is that the latter is concerned with all disputes which might arise under the construction contract, whilst the former is limited to progress payments (although, as noted, these can include sums by way of loss and expense). In this way, many of the

6.11

---

[8] s12.
[9] See *Walter Construction Group Ltd v CPL (Surrey Hills) Pty Ltd* [2003] NSWSC 266, paragraph 107.
[10] s13(4).

disputes which have arisen in England, Wales and Scotland, and in particular the difficulties of accommodating an adjudicator's decision on a claim for, say, an extension of time within the on-going contractual machinery, simply do not arise. The NSW Act is therefore even more focussed upon the importance of maintaining cash-flow.

The Payment Schedule

6.12 The respondent, being the person on whom the payment claim has been served, may reply to the claim by providing a payment schedule to the claimant. The time for response is within the time required by the relevant construction contract or ten business days (whichever expires earlier).[11] The payment schedule must identify the payment claim to which it relates and the portion of the payment (if any) that the respondent proposes to make. If it is less than the amount claimed, the schedule must indicate why the scheduled amount is less and, if the respondent is withholding payment for any reason, the schedule must also indicate the respondent's reasons for withholding that payment.[12] The payment schedule is important because, in any subsequent adjudication, the respondent is not permitted to rely on any reasons or grounds for non-payment that have not already been specified in the payment schedule.[13] If the respondent does not provide a payment schedule within the time required, the respondent becomes liable to pay the claimed amount on the due date for the progress payment. If a payment schedule has been provided, the respondent is liable to pay the amount (if any) proposed in the schedule.

Adjudication

6.13 If the respondent fails to serve a payment schedule, or serves a payment schedule but then fails to pay in accordance with it, a statutory debt arises and the claimant may either commence litigation to recover the sum or make an adjudication application. If litigation is commenced then the claimant can apply for summary judgment, because the respondent is not entitled to bring any cross-claim or raise any defence in relation to matters arising under the construction contract.[14] If the respondent fails to pay the scheduled amount, an adjudication application must be made within twenty business days after the due date for payment. Where no schedule was provided at all, the claimant must give a notice of intention to make an adjudication application within twenty business days following the due date for payment. The respondent may provide a payment schedule within five

---

[11] s14(4).
[12] s14(3).
[13] s20(2B).
[14] s16(4)(b).

business days of the notice. The adjudication application must then be made within ten business days after the expiry of the five day period.

6.14 Of course, the most common situation in which a dispute will arise will be where the respondent provides a payment schedule but where that schedule indicates an amount significantly less than the sum claimed by the claimant. In those circumstances, the claimant's only option will be to commence adjudication. That adjudication must be commenced within ten business days of receipt of the payment schedule.[15]

6.15 The adjudication process is subject to the strict timetable imposed by the NSW Act. The adjudication application must be made in writing; it must be made to the authorised nominating authority; it must identify the payment claim and schedule to which it relates; and it may contain submissions relevant to the application itself. The authorised nominating authority must refer the application to an adjudicator as soon as practicable.[16] The Act does not specify the precise form of the claimant's submissions, but it is commonplace for such submissions to include not only legal argument but also evidence and documentation on which the adjudicator can rely. The adjudication application is then served on the respondent.

6.16 In circumstances where the respondent has provided a payment schedule, the respondent may lodge a response to the adjudication application within five days of receipt of the application, or two days of the receipt of notice of the adjudicator's acceptance of the application. The response must be in writing and identify the adjudication application to which it relates. The response may also contain relevant submissions.[17] As noted above, the response cannot include any reasons for withholding payment which were not already stated in the payment schedule. Although there is no corresponding statutory limitation on the claimant, it was held in *John Holland Pty Ltd v Cardno MBK (NSW) Pty Ltd*[18] that a claimant could not, by way of his submissions, assert a basis for the claim not included in the payment claim. The reason given was one of procedural fairness; if new matters were raised the respondent would then be unable to respond to such matters by operation of s20(2B) of the NSW Act.

6.17 The adjudicator has ten days to determine the adjudication unless the parties agree to give him further time pursuant to s21(3). The ten days start from the end of the period within which a response may be lodged. The adjudicator may request further written submissions and may carry out an inspection or site visit.

---

[15] s17.
[16] s17(5).
[17] s20(2).
[18] [2004] NSWSC 258.

He may also require an informal conference at which, as s21(4A) makes plain, the parties are 'not entitled' to legal representation.

Determination

6.18 The adjudicator must determine the amount of payment, the date on which the amount becomes payable, and the rate of interest payable on the amount. In reaching his determination, the adjudicator may only consider the Act, the construction contract, the payment claim, the payment schedule and the results of any inspection carried out by the adjudicator.[19] The determination must be in writing and must include reasons.[20] The amount of the progress payment must be calculated in accordance with the terms of the contract and, if there is no express provision to allow such a calculation, then the amount has to be calculated on the basis of the value of the construction work carried out. Section 10 sets out the relevant valuation process. If the work cannot be valued in accordance with a detailed methodology provided by the contract, it must be valued with regard to the contract price; any other rates or prices in the contract; any variation agreed to by the parties by which the price is to be adjusted by a specific amount; the estimated cost of remedying any defect; and the value of materials and components if they have become the property of the party for whom the construction work is being carried out.

6.19 Section 22(4) provides that, once an adjudicator has determined the value of the work or related goods and services, that value would then be applicable in any subsequent adjudication, unless either party satisfies the later adjudicator that the value of work has changed since the previous determination. Also in a departure from the 1996 Act, s22(5) of the NSW Act contains an express provision dealing with slips or clerical errors. In such circumstances the adjudicator may on his/her own initiative, or on the application of either party, amend the determination by correcting the slip.[21]

Enforcement

6.20 The NSW Act also contains detailed provisions in respect of enforcement. Following the determination of the amount due by the adjudicator, the respondent is required to pay the amount five days after the determination is served on the respondent, or at a later date decided by the adjudicator.[22] If the respondent fails to pay then the claimant can request an adjudication certificate from an

---

[19] s22(2).
[20] s22(3).
[21] Of course, this is in line with the decision in *Bloor Construction v Bowmer & Kirkland* [2000] BLR 764. In addition, the DTI 2nd Consultation Report on the proposed amendments to the 1996 Act seeks to introduce a similar 'slip' rule.
[22] s23.

authorised nominating authority.[23] The certificate identifies the names of the claimant and respondent, the sum required to be paid, and the date on which payment was due. It may also include any interest that is due and payable. The certificate is then filed with a court and becomes enforceable as a judgment of that court for a debt. If the respondent seeks to have the judgment set aside, he has very limited room for manoeuvre. He is not entitled to bring any cross-claim, to raise any defence in relation to matters arising under the construction contract, or to challenge the adjudicator's determination.[24] As a result, the adjudicator's determination will only be set aside in very limited circumstances, explored in paragraph 6.21 below. In addition, if the sum determined by the adjudicator is not paid, the claimant may also serve on the respondent a notice of the claimant's intention to suspend construction work. The claimant is entitled to suspend work two business days after notice has been given. The respondent is liable to pay any loss or expense incurred as a result of the respondent removing from the contract any part of the work or supply. The claimant is not liable for any loss or damage suffered by the respondent as a consequence of work not being carried out during the suspension.

6.21 The severe statutory limitations on the respondent's ability to challenge the adjudicator's determination led to a number of cases in which it was held that a jurisdictional error on the part of the adjudicator rendered an adjudication determination voidable.[25] In *Brodyn Pty Ltd v Davenport*[26] the NSW Court of Appeal overturned this line of cases, indicating that jurisdictional error was not a helpful category to apply to the NSW Act. Instead, the NSW Court of Appeal concluded that a determination could only be set aside where:

(a) One of the essential pre-conditions for the existence of an adjudicator's determination had not been met. Such pre-conditions are matters such as the existence of a construction contract, the service of a payment claim and so on. Such essential pre-conditions were to be distinguished from mere 'detailed requirements', such as the time constraints set out in the Act.
(b) The determination was not a bona fide attempt by the adjudicator to exercise the power afforded to it under the Act. At first sight, this appears to be a very limited ground of challenge, applicable where there is fraud on the part of the claimant in which the adjudicator is also involved.

---

[23] s24(1).
[24] s25(4).
[25] See, for example, *Musico & Others v Davenport & Others* [2003] NSWSC 977; *Leighton Contractors Pty Ltd v Campbelltown Catholic Club* [2003] NSWSC 1103 and *Transgrid v Walter Construction Group* [2004] NSWSC 21.
[26] [2004] 61 NSWLR 421.

(c) The determination had arisen as a result of a substantial denial of natural justice. The NSW Court of Appeal in *Brodyn* held that a failure by the adjudicator to consider the submissions provided by the parties would amount to a substantial denial of natural justice, although simply misinterpreting these submissions or misapplying the law would not. In addition, the NSW Court of Appeal approved the decision in *Emag Constructions Pty Ltd v High Rise Concrete*,[27] which was a case where the determination was set aside because the court held that failure to comply with the timing and service requirements of the Act amounted to a breach of natural justice.

6.22 Accordingly, in New South Wales, there is an effective and popular adjudication mechanism relating to claims for interim payments. There are some similarities, and some specific differences, between the NSW Act and the Housing Grants Construction and Regeneration Act. Broadly, they are designed to have the same effect. In addition, whilst it has been argued that the English courts should adopt the same line as the NSW Court of Appeal in *Brodyn*, the slightly different approach in that case can be traced back to the different provisions of the NSW Act.[28] Moreover, it is thought that, in the light of what the NSW Court of Appeal said about natural justice in *Brodyn*, it may well be thought that the differences between the courts' overall approach to adjudication in Australia, on the one hand, and in England, Wales and Scotland, on the other, are in practice of narrow compass.

Other Australian Jurisdictions

6.23 Statutory adjudication has been introduced in a number of other Australian states and territories including Victoria (the Building and Construction Industry Security of Payment Act 2002, recently amended); Queensland (The Building and Construction Industry Payments Act 2004); Western Australia (Construction Contracts Act 2004); and the Northern Territory of Australia (Construction Contracts (Security of Payments)) Act 2004).

6.24 These various Acts all apply to construction contracts. They create a statutory right on the part of the contractor to progress payments. They entitle the contractor to serve payment claims on the principal and require the principal to issue a response to such claims. Although the precise definition of a 'pay-when-paid' clause varies from Act to Act, such provisions are rendered of no effect. They also create a protected right for the contractor to suspend work for non-payment of

---

[27] [2003] NSWSC 903.
[28] In *A C Yule & Sons Ltd v Speedwell Roofing & Cladding Ltd* [2007] EWHC 1360 (TCC) the TCC Judge distinguished *Brodyn* on the basis that, for example, the time limits in the 1996 Act were mandatory and those in the NSW Act were not.

amounts due, although there are variations as to when the right to suspend work is triggered.

All these Acts provide a right for a party to a construction contract to refer disputes to adjudication. The Queensland and Victoria Acts define adjudication in a broadly similar way to the NSW Act. Under each of these Acts, a person is entitled to make an adjudication application only in relation to a payment claim which has been disputed or ignored.[29] The Western Australia Act widens the range of adjudication by providing that a party to a contract may apply to have any 'payment dispute' adjudicated, except if an adjudication application has already been made, or the dispute is the subject of an order of judgment or other finding by an arbitrator or court.[30] A 'payment dispute' is defined as including non-payment of a payment claim, or non-return of retention monies or security at the appropriate time. The Western Australia Act specifically provides that adjudicators' decisions for payments other than for final payments will be taken to be payments on account but, unlike the NSW Act, it appears that a final determination of rights and liabilities (subject always to subsequent arbitration or litigation) is possible in the adjudication. **6.25**

All of these statutes adopt a process of swift adjudication so as to provide a prompt interim resolution of payment disputes. They are also similar in that they provide for adjudication as an additional dispute resolution process, leaving the existing contractual processes intact. Thus, if a party is dissatisfied with an adjudication determination, it can take that dispute to court or arbitration in accordance with the terms of the contract. **6.26**

In Queensland and Victoria, as in New South Wales, the referral of a payment dispute to adjudication is in the hands of the claimant alone. In Western Australia and the Northern Territories, either party may initiate the referral. The application for adjudication, and any response, must contain certain prescribed information and must set out or have attached to it all the information and documentation on which the party making it relies. Also under the Acts in Western Australia and the Northern Territories, an adjudicator is obliged to dismiss any adjudication application if he is satisfied that it is not possible to make a fair determination because of the complexity of the matter or because the time frame for the determination is insufficient. This is to be contrasted with the Acts in NSW, Queensland and Victoria, which all require a decision within ten days, no matter how complicated the dispute might be. **6.27**

All of the Acts noted above provide that the decision of the adjudicator is binding on the parties, unless and until the dispute is resolved by a court, arbitrator or **6.28**

---

[29] Queensland Act, s21; Victoria Act, s18.
[30] WA Act, s25.

some other form of alternative dispute resolution. In addition, in all jurisdictions, where an adjudication determination is made to the effect that one party is liable to make a payment to another, the liable party must pay the sum determined in the adjudication within a prescribed period. In default, the adjudication determination may be enforced as a judgment debt, on which statutory interest accrues.

Singapore

6.29 In Singapore, the Building and Construction Industry Security of Payment Act 2004 ('the Singapore Act') came into being in response to growing concerns about cash flow problems besieging the construction industry there.[31] At the turn of the new Millennium, the construction industry in Singapore had been in steady decline due to the effects of lower tender prices, compounded by wide-ranging payment problems. The Singapore Act was closely modelled upon and derived much of its inspiration from the NSW Act. However, it also introduces a number of powers which are entirely new.

6.30 Section 5 of the Act entitles any person who has carried out any construction work, or supplied any goods or services, under a contract, to a progress payment. Section 8 deals with the due date for payment in respect of progress payments. Sections 10 and 11 mirror the NSW Act in setting out a detailed regime in respect of payment claims and payment responses. Section 12 permits a claimant who has failed to receive payment by the due date of the response to make an adjudication application. Adjudication applications are dealt with in section 13. Section 14 deals with the appointment of the adjudicator and section 15 the adjudication response of the other party.

6.31 Section 16 of the Act is concerned with adjudication procedures. This requires the adjudicator, in a way similar to the Housing Grant, Construction and Regeneration Act 1996, to act independently, impartially and in a timely manner. It expressly requires him to 'comply with the principles of natural justice'. Section 17 sets out the relevant time limits. They are extremely tight, and the adjudicator is required to determine an adjudication application within seven days after the commencement of the adjudication, if the adjudication relates to a construction contract and the respondent has failed to make a payment response and to lodge an adjudication response by the commencement of the adjudication, or has failed to pay the response amount which has been accepted by the claimant by the due date. In any other case, the adjudicator has 14 days after the commencement of adjudication

---

[31] See page ix of the *Annotated Guide to the Singapore Act* by Wong Partnership, Sweet & Maxwell Asia, 2004.

to determine the adjudication application, unless a further extension is agreed by the parties. Section 17(2) requires the adjudicator to determine the adjudicated amount (if any) to be paid by the respondent to the claimant, the date on which the amount is payable, the interest payable on the adjudicated amount, and the proportion of the costs of the adjudication payable by each party to the adjudication. The determination must include reasons. Sub-section (6) also permits an adjudicator to rectify a clerical mistake or error.

6.32 Section 18 of the Singapore Act introduces an entirely new concept, namely an adjudication review application. It permits an aggrieved respondent to apply for a review of the adjudication application by the authorised nominating body. Where in any adjudication application the adjudicated amount exceeds the relevant response amount by the prescribed amount or more, the respondent who is aggrieved may lodge an application for review with the same authorised nominating body with which the application for the adjudication was lodged originally. The application for review must be lodged by the respondent within seven days of service of the adjudication determination. No application for review can be lodged by the respondent unless he has paid the adjudicated amount to the claimant. The authorised nominating body appoints a review adjudicator, or a panel of review adjudicators, who follow the procedure set out in section 19 of the Singapore Act. They can substitute the adjudication determination for any determination that they consider appropriate or refuse the adjudication review application.

6.33 At first sight, it would appear that this review process is contrary to the whole purpose of the Singapore Act and the adjudication process for which it provides. However, given that the respondent must pay the adjudicated sum to the claimant, no matter how excessive he considers it to be, it is thought that the review process will be of limited application, and likely to prove relevant only where large sums are at stake. It should also be noted that only the aggrieved respondent can trigger the review process.

6.34 Another feature of the Singapore Act which does not find expression either in the Housing Grants Construction and Regeneration Act or the NSW Act, is section 24, which is concerned with direct payment from the principal. Where a respondent has failed to pay the whole or any part of the adjudicated amount to the claimant, the principal of the respondent may make payment of the amount outstanding, or any part thereof, in accordance with the procedure set out in section 24(2). This direct payment clause allows the employer to by-pass the main contractor in making payments direct to the sub-contractors and, at the same time, setting off an equivalent amount from sums otherwise due to the main contractor. This is designed to benefit the employer, by providing them with a discretionary right to assume payment obligations on behalf of the main contractor and alleviate the sub-contractor's cash-flow problems in the interests of minimising disruption or delay to the project, which will occur if the sub-contractor continues to be unpaid. The direct payment provision also encourages sub-contractors to bid for work because they will regard it as an added assurance that, if the main contractor gets into financial difficulties, they will be paid direct by the employer.

New Zealand

6.35 In New Zealand, statutory adjudication was introduced by the Construction Contracts Act 2002. This is also similar to the NSW Act. It creates a statutory right to progress payments; it provides for payment claims and responses; it renders pay when pay provision is of no effect; it may create a right for the contractor to suspend work for non-payment. Under the New Zealand Act, the right to suspend arises in three sets of circumstances: firstly, where the principal has failed to provide a payment schedule in response to a payment claim; secondly, where the principal has failed to pay an amount set out in a payment schedule; and thirdly, where the principal has failed to pay an amount set out in an adjudicator's determination.

6.36 The New Zealand Act also provides a right for a party to a construction contract to refer disputes to adjudication. In this regard, the New Zealand Act is similar to the Housing Grants Construction and Regeneration Act, because what can be referred is any sort of dispute, not just an unpaid progress payment. Thus, in New Zealand, a party to a construction contract has the right to refer a dispute (which includes a disagreement) to adjudication, except where it is the subject of an international arbitration agreement.[32] However, a different regime applies to enforcement. In New Zealand, a determination on the matter of a payment is enforceable and may be recovered as a debt due in any court.[33] On the other hand, a determination about the 'rights and obligations' of the parties is not enforceable, which means that if a party fails to comply with it, the other party may bring proceedings to enforce it, but the court need only have regard to, and not be bound by, the adjudicator's determination.[34] It is thought that this may create potential difficulties: although it will often be simple to differentiate between a determination requiring payment and a determination of the parties' rights and obligations, there will be other occasions when they may well amount to precisely the same thing. A claim for a specific sum may turn on whether or not the contractor is responsible under the contract for a particular

---

[32] s25.
[33] ss58 and 59.
[34] ss58(2) and 61.

element of the work or whether it is work that he was required to do by way of a variation. In those circumstances it may be difficult to say that the determination of the amount is enforceable (because it might be said that it was a determination of rights and liabilities), even though it appears reasonably clear that that was the intention of the legislature.

PART III

THE ADJUDICATOR'S JURISDICTION

7. General Principles	213
8. Errors of Fact and Law	263
9. Fairness	279
10. Abatement and Set-Off	311
11. Costs and Fees	335

7

GENERAL PRINCIPLES

Introduction	7.01	Was the Dispute Referred to Adjudication a Single Dispute?	7.57
What Happens If There is a Jurisdictional Issue?	7.05	Insufficient Connection Between the Dispute Referred and the Adjudicator's Decision	7.64
The Adjudicator's Power to Investigate His Own Jurisdiction	7.09	The Relevance of Earlier Adjudication Decisions	7.71
The Court's Investigation	7.16	Ousting the Jurisdiction of the Adjudicator in Other Ways	7.78
Fundamental Principle	7.18	Making a Valid Objection on Jurisdiction	7.81
Was the Adjudicator Validly Appointed?	7.20	Summary of Principles Relating to Jurisdiction	7.83
Was there a Construction Contract?	7.20		
Was the Appointment in Accordance With the Contract?	7.25		
Was the Contract in Writing?	7.28		
Correct Parties	7.33		
The Dispute	7.35		
What was the Scope and Extent of the Dispute in the Notice of Adjudication?	7.35		
Had that Dispute Crystallised Between the Parties Prior to the Notice to Refer?	7.46		

'. . . an adjudicator has jurisdiction to make a mistake, as long as he asks himself a question or questions which have actually been referred to him for decision and seeks to answer such question or questions.'

His Honour Judge Seymour QC in *Shimizu Europe Ltd v Automajor Ltd* [2002] BLR 113.

Introduction

7.01 The TCC and the Court of Appeal have repeatedly made it plain that errors of fact, errors of law and procedural errors will not, without more, justify a failure to comply with the adjudicator's decision.[1] As a result, the grounds for impeaching such a decision are extremely limited. By far the most common attack on the decision of an adjudicator is the submission that the adjudicator had no jurisdiction to reach that decision. Because courts have been clear that a decision will be summarily enforced unless it is one which the adjudicator did not have the jurisdiction to reach, commercial necessity has led defendants to take all manner of points to support the proposition that the adjudicator had no relevant jurisdiction.

7.02 Once the 1996 Act came into force, there was concern that imaginative defendants would be able to invent spurious arguments that would call into question the adjudicator's jurisdiction, thereby defeating the claimant's enforcement application under CPR Part 24. In one of the earliest cases, *The Project Consultancy Group v The Trustees of the Gray Trust*,[2] previously noted at paragraphs 5.03–5.04 above in the context of ad hoc jurisdiction, Dyson J concluded that such fears were exaggerated. He said that he thought that it would only be in comparatively few cases that jurisdiction arguments would even be possible and, whenever they were advanced, both the adjudicator and the court would be 'vigilant to examine the arguments critically'. However, despite this, he concluded that it must be open to a defendant in enforcement proceedings to challenge the decision of an adjudicator on the grounds that he was not empowered by the 1996 Act (or the contract) to make the decision. The editors of the Building Law Reports, in their commentary on the case, expressed their concern about this conclusion, stating that 'the possibilities of challenging the jurisdiction of an adjudicator are broad, if not infinite'.[3] They went on to say that, in their view, the decision in *Project Consultancy* confirmed that any arguable challenge to the jurisdiction of the adjudicator would ensure that the decision was summarily unenforceable and that, as a result, one of the principal objects of the 1996 Act was effectively undermined.

---

[1] Neither this Chapter, nor Chapters 8 (Errors of Law and Fact) and 12 (Enforcement) endeavours to draw any distinction between errors of law and fact made in statutory adjudication and errors of law and fact in contractual adjudication. All three Chapters assume that what HHJ Thornton QC in *Steve Domsalla (t/a Domsalla Building Services) v Kenneth Dyason* [2007] EWHC 1174 (TCC) called 'the doctrine of unreviewable error of an adjudicator within jurisdiction' applies equally to both types of adjudication. Permission to appeal has been given on the Judge's finding in that case that there is a significant difference between the two.

[2] [1999] BLR 377.

[3] The full text of this passage can be found at paragraph 5.15 above.

In practice, the fears of the editors of the Building Law Reports have not generally **7.03**
materialised. Although there are a number of reported cases in which the court has
concluded that the adjudicator did not have the necessary jurisdiction to reach his
decision, such results are significantly outweighed by the cases in which such
jurisdictional challenges have failed.[4] It is thought that this situation has arisen
because the courts have indeed been vigilant to examine critically all jurisdiction
arguments. Although in *Thomas Frederic's (Construction) Ltd v Keith Wilson*[5]
Simon Brown LJ (as he then was) readily recognised the concern that the adjudication process might be emasculated by jurisdictional challenges, he repeated the
views of Dyson J in *Project Consultancy*, and concluded that it was only if the
defendant had advanced a properly arguable jurisdictional objection, with a realistic prospect of success, that he could hope to resist the summary enforcement of
an adjudicator's decision. He said that a defendant who had agreed to be bound
by the adjudicator's ruling on the issue of jurisdiction would be liable to enforcement in the short term, even if the adjudicator was plainly wrong on the jurisdiction point. Furthermore, even if the defendant had not submitted to the
adjudicator's jurisdiction in that sense, he was still liable for summary judgment if
the adjudicator's ruling on the jurisdictional issue was plainly right. But, as both
these cases acknowledged, that approach would still leave a handful of cases where,
even in the short term, an adjudicator's decision did not bind the parties, namely
those situations in which, as Simon Brown LJ put it, 'a respectable case has been
made out for disputing the adjudicator's jurisdiction'.

The importance of a jurisdictional challenge to the adjudicator's decision (as **7.04**
opposed to complaints about errors of law or fact) can be seen in the four general
principles identified by Jackson J at paragraph 80 of his judgment in *Carillion
Construction v Devonport Royal Dockyard Ltd*.[6] These four general principles were
based on five decisions of the Court of Appeal and two decisions of the TCC.[7]
They were formulated as follows:

---

[4] Indeed, it is worth noting that, certainly prior to the Court of Appeal decisions in *AMEC v
Whitefriars* [2004] EWCA Civ 1418 and *Carillion Construction Ltd v Devonport Royal Dockyard Ltd*
[2005] EWCA Civ 1358, there were more first instance decisions in which the adjudicator's decision
was not enforced because of a breach of the rules of natural justice of one sort or another than there
were decisions in which it was concluded that the adjudicator had exceeded his jurisdiction.
[5] [2003] EWCA Civ 1494. This case has already been referred to, again in the context of ad hoc
jurisdiction, in paragraphs 5.11 and 5.15 above.
[6] [2005] BLR 310.
[7] The cases were: *Bouygues (UK) Ltd v Dahl-Jenson (UK) Ltd* [2001] All ER (Comm) 1041;
[2000] BLR 522; *C&B Scene Concept Design Ltd v Isobars Ltd* [2002] BLR 93; *Levolux AT Ltd v
Ferson Contractors Ltd* [2003] EWCA Civ 11; 86 Con LR 98; *Pegram Shopfitters Ltd v Tally Weijl
(UK) Ltd* [2003] EWCA Civ 1750; [2004] 1 All ER 818; *Amec Projects Ltd v Whitefriars City Estates
Ltd* [2004] EWCA Civ 1418 [2005] BLR 1, *Discain Project Services Ltd v Opec Prime Development
Ltd* [2000] BLR 402 and *Balfour Beatty Construction Ltd v Lambeth London Borough Council* [2002]
BLR 288.

The Adjudicator's Jurisdiction

(1) The adjudication procedure does not involve the final determination of anybody's rights (unless all the parties so wish).
(2) The Court of Appeal has repeatedly emphasised that adjudicator's decisions must be enforced, even if they result from errors of procedure, fact or law: see *Bouygues*, *C&B Scene* and *Levolux*.
(3) Where an adjudicator has acted in excess of his jurisdiction or in serious breach of the rules of natural justice, the court will not enforce his decision: see *Discain*, *Balfour Beatty* and *Pegram Shopfitters*.
(4) Judges must be astute to examine technical defences with a degree of scepticism consonant with the policy of the 1996 Act. Errors of law, fact or procedure by an adjudicator must be examined critically before the court accepts that such errors constitute excessive jurisdiction or serious breaches of the rules of natural justice: see *Pegram Shopfitters* and *Amec*.

In the Court of Appeal[8] Chadwick LJ said at paragraph 52 that he did not understand there to be any challenge to those principles and they were fully supported by the authorities, as demonstrated by Jackson J in his judgment. They make a convenient starting point for any consideration of the significance, range and limits of the adjudicator's jurisdiction.

What Happens if There Is a Jurisdictional Issue?

7.05 If the responding party challenges the jurisdiction of the adjudicator, it has four options.[9] Firstly, the responding party can agree to refer the dispute as to the adjudicator's jurisdiction to the same adjudicator, and to be bound by the result. If the responding party agrees to that course, and the appointed adjudicator accepts the reference to him of this secondary dispute, the jurisdiction of the adjudicator can then be resolved as part of the reference. The important thing about this option is that the responding party is bound by the adjudicator's decision and cannot subsequently challenge it, or seek to resist enforcement on the grounds that the adjudicator lacked the necessary jurisdiction. In consequence, there have been a large number of cases in which the claimant has argued that the defendant agreed to be bound by the adjudicator's decision on jurisdiction, and the defendant has denied such an agreement. Those cases are analysed in paragraphs 7.09–7.15 below.

---

[8] [2005] EWCA Civ 1358.
[9] The four options are discussed in paragraph 31 of the judgment of HHJ Thornton QC in *Fastrack Contractors Ltd v Morrison Construction Ltd* [2000] BLR 168.

Secondly, the referring party can seek to refer the dispute as to jurisdiction to a second adjudicator but, since that would not halt the first adjudication, and since that first adjudication has to be completed within the 28 day timescale, this is not an option that is commonly pursued. Thirdly, the referring party can seek a declaration from the TCC that the proposed adjudicator lacked jurisdiction. This is the procedure that was followed in a number of the reported cases and the TCC is often able to deal with such disputes at short notice: see paragraphs 14.26–14.28 below. However, it is an option which requires a certain amount of co-operation between the parties to the adjudication and the adjudicator himself. **7.06**

The final option is perhaps the one most commonly adopted. The responding party, who does not accept the jurisdiction of the adjudicator, can set out in clear terms the grounds of its objection. Thereafter, having fully reserved its position, the responding party can participate in the adjudication, and will, if the adjudicator requires it, make submissions as to how and why it is said that the adjudicator does not have the necessary jurisdiction. Thereafter, if the referring party is successful in both its jurisdictional and its substantive case, and seeks to enforce the decision, the responding party, having properly reserved its position, can seek to challenge the validity of the adjudicator's decision on the grounds of his lack of jurisdiction. **7.07**

It is the potential blurring of the divide between the first and the final option of those noted above which has given rise to so many of the reported cases. *Project Consultancy*[10] is a good example of this trend. The defendant made plain at the outset that it did not accept that the adjudicator had any jurisdiction, because the contract was concluded before 1 May 1998 and the 1996 Act therefore did not apply to it. The defendant's solicitors wrote in clear terms to say that the adjudicator had no jurisdiction, inviting the claimant to withdraw the reference and warning the claimant that if it proceeded with the adjudication, the defendant would not comply with any award and would raise the jurisdiction point on enforcement. That is exactly what happened. The referring party/claimant argued that, because the adjudicator had asked for, and the parties had provided, submissions on the jurisdiction question, there had been an ad hoc agreement between the parties that they would be bound by the adjudicator's decision. In other words, the argument was that the parties had taken the first option noted in paragraph 7.05 above. Dyson J rejected that argument and said that, on the facts, the position was as set out in the fourth and final option, set out in paragraph 7.07 above. He found that the defendant's solicitors had written in the clearest terms to explain why, on their analysis, the adjudicator did not have the necessary jurisdiction and to warn that the claimant that they **7.08**

---

[10] [1999] BLR 377.

would not recognise and comply with any decision that the adjudicator reached. The Judge then went on to consider the facts and stated that the question of whether, and if so when, a contract was ever concluded between the parties was by no means straightforward. He found it impossible to resolve the issues with any degree of confidence because he had not seen all the relevant documents and did not know the full story. Therefore, because it was impossible to resolve those issues at a summary hearing, he dismissed the application to enforce the adjudicator's decision.

The Adjudicator's Power to Investigate His Own Jurisdiction

7.09 There is no doubt that an adjudicator can investigate any partial or full challenge to his jurisdiction.[11] If, following such an investigation, the adjudicator considers that the challenge was well-founded, he must then decline to adjudicate on the dispute. If he concludes that the challenge should fail, and that he has the necessary jurisdiction to decide the dispute, he must then proceed with the substance of the adjudication. But, unless the parties had agreed to be bound by the result of the adjudicator's investigation into his own jurisdiction, the adjudicator's ruling on the jurisdiction issue will not be determinative and the challenger can defeat the enforcement proceedings by showing a respectable case that the adjudicator did not have the necessary jurisdiction, and was wrong to conclude to the contrary.[12] The parties can agree to be bound by express agreement; implied agreement (often where the jurisdiction dispute has been referred to the adjudicator for determination and no objection or reservation has been made;[13]) or unilateral waiver of any jurisdictional objections.

7.10 This fine line, between an agreement to allow the adjudicator to reach a conclusion on the jurisdiction point, and an agreement to be bound by that conclusion, explains why there are so many cases in which the successful party has sought to argue that the loser agreed to be bound by the adjudicator's decision on jurisdiction. To some extent at least, such arguments have been assisted by a lack of clarity in one or two of the reported cases as to the precise reasons for the court's conclusion that, notwithstanding the jurisdiction argument, the adjudicator's decision should be enforced. In particular, there was, in the early days, a failure properly to differentiate between, on the one hand, the adjudicator's power to investigate and rule on his own jurisdiction and, on the other, his (much more

---

[11] See *Fastrack Contractors Ltd v Morrison Construction Ltd* [2000] BLR 168, paragraph 32.
[12] Authority for this proposition can be found in *Grovedeck v Capital Demolitions* [2000] BLR 181; *Homer Burgess v Chirex* [2000] BLR 124; and at paragraph 10 of the judgment of May LJ in *Pegram Shopfitters Ltd v Tally Weijl (UK) Ltd* [2003] EWCA Civ 1750.
[13] See Chapter 5 above.

limited) ability to produce a binding determination on such an issue. A number of these decisions were based on a finding, sometimes not expressly made clear, that the parties had reached an ad hoc agreement to be bound by the adjudicator's conclusion as to jurisdiction. Thus, in *Watson Building Services Ltd v Harrison*,[14] a decision of the Outer House, Lady Paton construed the formal documents exchanged in the adjudication as confirming that, although at the outset the employer had challenged the adjudicator's jurisdiction, he had also agreed that, if the adjudicator concluded that he did have the necessary jurisdiction, he could and should proceed to determine the merits of the parties' disputes. She concluded that, considering the employer's actions and the terms of his formal response in the adjudication, it was not open to the employer later to seek to challenge the adjudicator's decision on his jurisdiction. In other words, any earlier reservation of the employer's position on the jurisdiction point had been lost, and a subsequent agreement to be bound by the decision had been reached.

In two English cases, the court concluded, again on the construction of the relevant documents, that the parties had reached an ad hoc agreement to be bound by the adjudicator's decision on his own jurisdiction.[15] In *JW Hughes Building Contractors Ltd v GB Metal Work Ltd*[16] Forbes J decided that both parties agreed, by their conduct, to the adjudicator having the necessary jurisdiction to deal with all issues relating to his jurisdiction in accordance with the terms and conditions that he had proposed. The Judge accepted the submission that, by reason of the way in which the matter was dealt with before the adjudicator, there was an ad hoc agreement by the parties to the effect that the adjudicator had jurisdiction to make a binding decision on the issue.[17] Similarly, in *Nordot Engineering Services Ltd Siemens Plc*,[18] HHJ Gilliland QC concluded that the responding party's express agreement to 'abide by your decision in this matter [the decision on jurisdiction]' amounted to an ad hoc agreement on their part to accept the result of the adjudicator's determination of their jurisdictional challenge.[19]

7.11

---

14 [2002] Scots Law Times 846.
15 For a full discussion of the adjudicator's ad hoc jurisdiction, please see Chapter 5 above.
16 [2003] EWHC 2421 (TCC).
17 This is perhaps one of the rulings on this topic which is less than clear. There was no dispute that both parties had asked the adjudicator to rule on his jurisdiction. The question was whether the parties had agreed to be bound by the result. The difference between the adjudicator's investigation into his jurisdiction and the binding nature of his determination of that issue is not explored in the judgment in *JW Hughes*.
18 [2001] CILL 1778.
19 A further example of the situation where one party transmuted an agreement to ask the adjudicator to investigate the jurisdictional issue into an agreement to be bound by his decision on the point is *Whiteways Contractors (Sussex) Ltd v Impresa Castelli Construction United Kingdom Ltd* [2000] 16 Const LJ 453. HHJ Bowsher QC concluded that the adjudicator's decision on jurisdiction was simply part of his overall decision and was therefore binding on the parties until the dispute or difference was finally determined by arbitration or legal proceedings. He made no separate

7.12 It rapidly became apparent that there was a significant difference between those cases in which the parties had agreed to be bound by the adjudicator's decision on jurisdiction and those (much more common) cases, such as *Project Consultancy*, where the challenger was happy for the adjudicator to investigate and rule on the issue but made it plain that, since he challenged the adjudicator's jurisdiction in any event, he would not (indeed, logically could not) be bound by the result of that investigation. Thus, in *Ballast Plc v The Burrell Company (Construction Management) Ltd*[20] the Outer House was again concerned with the validity of an adjudicator's ruling on his own jurisdiction. Lord Reid distinguished *Watson* on the basis that that was a case where the parties had requested the adjudicator to determine the validity of his own appointment and, in effect, his own jurisdiction. He said that situation raised specific issues as to the effect of the parties' agreement, rather than illustrating any general point as to the extent to which an adjudicator's decision on a jurisdictional challenge will have binding effect. As a general principle, Lord Reid concluded that the adjudicator could not determine with binding effect the extent of his own jurisdiction, because the limits of that jurisdiction were determined by the notice of adjudication and the provisions of the Scheme, and could not be narrowed or extended by the adjudicator's misconstruction of those limits. It is respectfully suggested that this must be right as a matter of law. Lord Reid concluded on the facts of *Ballast* that the adjudicator had misconstrued his powers and failed to exercise his jurisdiction to determine the referred dispute. As a result, he found that the adjudicator's decision was a nullity.[21]

7.13 There are a number of decisions in which the courts have restated the principle that, in the ordinary case and without specific agreement, the adjudicator does not have jurisdiction to decide his own jurisdiction. In *Grovedeck Ltd v Capital Demolition Ltd*[22] HHJ Bowsher QC said that a party who protested the jurisdiction of the adjudicator may invite him to enquire into his jurisdiction, but not to decide it. Similarly, in *Homer Burgess Ltd v Chirex (Annan) Ltd*[23] Lord MacFadyen ruled that the temporarily binding quality accorded to decisions of an adjudicator was accorded only to decisions on matters of dispute arising under a construction contract. Thus, if there was an issue as to whether a particular dispute arose under a construction contract or not, that was a preliminary issue which the adjudicator

---

finding of any ad hoc agreement. The subsequent cases have demonstrated that this is perhaps too simplistic an approach.

[20] [2001] BLR 529.

[21] Lord Reid's reasoning relied on the decision of the House of Lords in *Anisminic Ltd v Foreign Compensation Commission* [1969] 2 AC 147 and their Lordship's conclusion that it could not be for the Commission to determine the limits of its own powers. The decision in *Ballast* is analysed further at paragraph 8.12 below.

[22] [2000] BLR 181.

[23] [2000] BLR 124 at 134.

had to address, but was not itself a dispute arising under a construction contract. Therefore, he concluded that a decision by an adjudicator, as to whether a particular dispute or a particular aspect of a dispute fell within his jurisdiction, was not one which was exempted from review by the courts.[24] Furthermore, the courts have been quick to emphasise, when conducting such a review, that the alleged agreement to the adjudicator reaching a binding decision on the jurisdiction point must be looked at realistically. Thus, in *R Durtnell & Sons Ltd v Kaduna Ltd*[25] the dispute was whether, in his decision, the adjudicator had exceeded his jurisdiction because, so it was said, he had dealt with extensions of time in circumstances where no such dispute had arisen between the parties. The claimant argued that the defendant had agreed to the adjudicator determining the issues relating to extensions of time. The TCC Judge concluded that the adjudicator had had no jurisdiction to make the assessments that he purported to make regarding the grant of an extension of time for completion of the works. He also found that the defendant had not waived his right to raise the jurisdictional objection. He concluded that the matters which the adjudicator purported to decide without the necessary jurisdiction were not such that the defendant either did appreciate, or should have appreciated, prior to the publication of the adjudicator's decision, that they would be included in that decision. Thus the question of waiver of such rights did not arise and the defendant had not lost the right to challenge the adjudicator's jurisdiction.

7.14 It is important to note that, if the defendant identifies a clear challenge to the adjudicator's jurisdiction, and can demonstrate an arguable case to this effect in any subsequent CPR Part 24 proceedings, then the decision of the adjudicator will not be summarily enforced, even if the defendant had not suffered prejudice as a result of the process. In *IDE Contracting Ltd v RG Carter Cambridge Ltd*[26] HHJ Havery QC concluded that the contractual provisions relating to the appointment of the adjudicator had not been complied with and that such non-compliance deprived the adjudicator of the requisite jurisdiction. He also found that the defendant had not submitted to the adjudicator's jurisdiction in the full sense of having agreed, not only that the adjudicator should rule on the issue of jurisdiction, but also that it would be bound by that ruling. The Judge went on to say that, although the defendant alleged that it had been prejudiced as a consequence of the adjudicator's decision, the state of the evidence was not such as to show convincingly that such prejudice had occurred. However, although the Judge was not satisfied that the defendant had therefore suffered prejudice, he concluded that it was unnecessary for the defendant to show actual prejudice,

---

[24] Lord MacFadyen's approach was, of course, echoed by Lord Reid in *Ballast*.
[25] [2003] BLR 225.
[26] [2004] BLR 172.

because the defendant had not submitted to the adjudicator's jurisdiction. In the circumstances of that case, that was all that was required to ensure that the decision could not be enforced.

7.15 Finally on this topic, it is instructive to note that the Court of Appeal ruled in *AMEC Projects Ltd v Whitefriars City Estates Ltd*[27] that the adjudicator was not obliged by the 1996 Act, or the general common law, to give the parties the opportunity to make representations to him on questions of jurisdiction. At paragraph 41 of his judgment in that case, Dyson LJ said:

> A more fundamental question was raised as to whether adjudicators are in any event obliged to give parties the opportunity to make representations in relation to questions of jurisdiction. I respectfully disagree with the judge's view that the requirements of natural justice apply without distinction, whether the issue being considered by the adjudicator is his own jurisdiction or the merits of the dispute that has been referred to him for decision. The reason for the common law right to prior notice and an effective opportunity to make representations is to protect the parties from the risk of decisions being reached unfairly. But it is only directed at decisions which can affect parties' rights. Procedural fairness does not require that parties should have the right to make representations in relation to decisions which do not affect their rights, still less in relation to 'decisions' which are nullities and which cannot affect their rights. Since the 'decision' of an adjudicator as to his jurisdiction is of no legal effect and cannot affect the rights of the parties, it is difficult to see the logical justification for a rule of law that an adjudicator can only make such a 'decision' after giving the parties an opportunity to make representations. The matter can be tested in this way. Let us suppose that the court were to hold that an adjudicator was right to 'decide' that he had jurisdiction, but that he had reached this 'decision' without giving the parties an opportunity to make representations on the point. The court would not declare the 'decision' to be void. It would not do so because the adjudicator's 'decision' was of no legal effect. No useful purpose would be served by such a declaration, not least because the court had held that the adjudicator did in fact have jurisdiction. The court would not grant any relief for the supposed breach of natural justice in such a case. It seems to me that this demonstrates that the rules of natural justice have no part to play in relation to issues that the decision-maker has no power to decide.

Notwithstanding this conclusion, Dyson LJ went on to suggest that, where time permitted, adjudicators would be well advised to give the parties the opportunity to make representations on jurisdictional issues: his point was simply that an adjudicator who did not allow parties such an opportunity would not ordinarily be acting in breach of natural justice. Of course, the position might well be different in the situation where the parties had agreed to be bound by the adjudicator's ruling on the jurisdiction issue: in those circumstances, it is thought that the adjudicator must invite and consider appropriate submissions from the parties in order to allow the proper and fair disposition of the jurisdiction dispute.

---

[27] [2004] EWCA Civ 1418.

The Court's Investigation

What happens when a jurisdictional challenge arises? In *ABB Zantingh Ltd v Zedal Building Services Ltd*[28] there was a jurisdictional challenge to the adjudicator. He adjourned the proceedings, with the agreement of both parties, pending resolution by the court of the dispute relating to his jurisdiction. HHJ Bowsher QC agreed that this was an entirely proper course in the circumstances of that case, partly because, if the adjudicator had decided the matter himself, the dispute would almost inevitably have come to the court and possibly to the Court of Appeal. However, in more recent years, the trend has been for the adjudicator to rule on his own jurisdiction and for the challenger, if unsuccessful, to repeat the jurisdictional challenge on the enforcement application. **7.16**

The question then arises: how should the court approach its investigation into the jurisdictional challenge? Almost invariably, the adjudicator's ruling on his own jurisdiction will be bound up within his reasoned decision. The general rule, of course, is that the court should not unpick that decision to gauge whether or not it contains errors of law or fact. On the other hand, it is necessary for the court, when investigating the validity or otherwise of any jurisdictional challenge, to examine the detail of the decision. The proper approach of the courts to such a dispute was addressed by HHJ Thornton QC in *Fastrack Contractors Ltd v Morrison Construction Ltd*.[29] He concluded that the court would give appropriate weight to any findings of fact made by the adjudicator and relevant to the jurisdictional challenge, but would not be bound by them and would either have to hear out the challenge with evidence or, if that could not be provided, determine the challenge on such material as was available, and either enforce or decline to enforce summarily the whole or part of the adjudicator's decision, depending on the court's decision on the jurisdictional issue. **7.17**

Fundamental Principle

The fundamental principle that governs all enquiries into the adjudicator's jurisdiction can be simply stated. If a dispute has arisen between two parties to a construction contract and the adjudicator is validly appointed to decide that dispute, then, provided his decision attempts to answer that dispute, his decision will be binding in accordance with the 1996 Act, regardless of errors of fact or law or procedure. If, on the other hand, he was not validly appointed, or he decided something other than the dispute that was referred to him, his decision will be **7.18**

---

[28] [2001] BLR 66.
[29] [2000] BLR 168, at paragraph 32.

unenforceable because it would have been made without jurisdiction.[30] Thus it follows that it is not enough for the defendant to show an error on the part of the adjudicator. What matters, in the words of Sir Murray Stuart-Smith in *C&B Scene* is whether the error on the part of the adjudicator went to his jurisdiction, or was merely an erroneous decision of law (or fact) on a matter within his jurisdiction. If it was the former, the decision would be unenforceable; if it was the latter, the decision would be enforceable by way of summary judgment.

7.19 Therefore the potential issues that might arise on any investigation of the jurisdiction of the adjudicator can be sub-divided under a number of separate headings. First, the court may have to consider whether or not the adjudicator was validly appointed, and this might in turn involve a consideration of such issues as to whether or not the contract between the parties was a construction contract; whether or not the appointment was in accordance with the contractual provisions; and whether or not the contract was in writing. Next, the court may have to consider the nature, scope and extent of the dispute as stated in the notice of adjudication, to ensure that it was that dispute, and no other, which the adjudicator decided in his written decision. This again breaks down into a number of separate issues. What was the dispute in the notice of adjudication? Had that dispute crystallised between the parties prior to the service of the notice of adjudication? Was the dispute that was referred to the adjudicator a single dispute? Furthermore, there are other issues which can be relevant to jurisdiction, such as whether the decision improperly trespassed on previous adjudication decisions under the same contract, or whether the adjudicator's jurisdiction was ousted in some other way. All of these topics are dealt with below.

Was the Adjudicator Validly Appointed?

Was There a Construction Contract?

7.20 If there was no contractual mechanism which expressly allowed for the appointment of an adjudicator, then the Scheme for Construction Contracts would be implied, provided of course that the contract between the parties was a construction contract, in accordance with s104 and s105 of the 1996 Act.[31] Accordingly, in a dispute about the adjudicator's jurisdiction to decide a dispute under the Scheme, it may be necessary to consider whether there was a construction contract in existence. In practice, this might well involve an analysis of the subject matter of the contract in question, to see whether the operations being

---

[30] See, by way of example only, *Macob v Morrison* [1999] BLR 93; *Bouygues v Dahl-Jenson* [2000] BLR 522; and *C&B Scene v Isobars* [2002] BLR 93.
[31] Please see Chapter 2 above and in particular paragraphs 2.16–2.36.

General Principles

carried out on site meant that the contract was expressly excluded from the 1996 Act by operation of s105(2). In *ABB Power Construction Ltd v Norwest Holst Engineering Ltd*[32] ABB were carrying out extensive works at a power station which comprised the construction of three new boiler houses. They subcontracted the insulation and cladding of the boilers and pipework to Norwest Holst. Norwest Holst gave a notice of adjudication under the sub-contract. ABB contended that the adjudicator had no jurisdiction, because the work in question was expressly exempted from the operation of the 1996 Act by s105(2). Before any further steps were taken to progress the adjudication, the TCC was asked to rule, by way of a declaration, as to the adjudicator's jurisdiction. The Judge concluded that great care had been taken in selecting the construction operations that were to be exempt from the 1996 Act, and that the operation in question was one of those operations which were exempted by s105(2). He therefore held that the adjudicator had no jurisdiction. Thus, although there was no adjudicator's decision for the court to consider in that case, the Judge still had to embark on a detailed investigation into precisely what ABB were doing under the main contract, and what Norwest Holst were doing under the sub-contract, in order to decide the nature of the operations on site and to see whether they were excluded by s105(2). It does not appear that, in *ABB*, there was a significant dispute on the facts, but it can readily be seen that there might well be circumstances in which, if there were such disputes, the court might have to consider detailed (and even contested) evidence about the works on site, before reaching a conclusion as to whether or not the operation in question was included within or exempted from the operation of the 1996 Act.

7.21 It is often the case that the parties to a construction contract can find themselves embroiled in disputes from an early stage, and they may seek to resolve such disputes by entering into a second, settlement agreement which compromises all claims and cross-claims under the original contract. In such cases, it may be a difficult question of construction as to whether the second agreement is a construction contract or a contract pursuant to which the adjudicator has been validly appointed. In *Shepherd Construction Ltd v Mecright Ltd*[33] there was a dispute about such a settlement agreement, with the referring party contending that it had entered into that agreement under duress.[34] HHJ Lloyd QC held that any dispute under the settlement agreement could not be a dispute 'under' the original contract, because the original contract had been replaced by the settlement agreement. The Judge therefore granted the declaration that the adjudicator had no jurisdiction. A similar view to the effect that a settlement agreement was

---

[32] [2000] TCLR 831. See the discussion of this case at paragraphs 2.32–2.33 above.
[33] [2000] BLR 489.
[34] The detailed facts of the case are set out in paragraph 7.78 below.

not a construction contract within the meaning of s108 was expressed by HHJ MacKay QC in *Lathom Construction Ltd v Brian Cross and Ann Cross*.[35]

7.22 However, it is suggested that, in the light of more recent decisions, these cases should be treated with a certain amount of caution. As Ramsey J pointed out in *L Brown & Sons Ltd v Crosby Homes (North West) Ltd*,[36] the dispute as to the status of any settlement agreement breaks down into two separate stages. First, the court must determine whether the second or settlement agreement was or was not a variation of the original contract. If the second agreement was simply a variation of the first, then the dispute resolution provisions in the first agreement continue to be relevant to any dispute under the second agreement. On that analysis, the second agreement would have no effect upon the adjudicator's jurisdiction. The second stage in the court's consideration of this issue only arises if it has concluded that the settlement agreement is not a variation of the original agreement, but is instead a separate and stand-alone contract. It then becomes a question of whether, as a matter of construction of that separate agreement, the adjudicator was validly appointed. Even if the settlement agreement was a separate, stand-alone agreement, the dispute resolution procedures in the first agreement may still apply to a dispute which arises under the settlement agreement, provided that the drafting of one or both of them makes that position clear.

7.23 On this analysis, whether or not the second settlement agreement allows for adjudication will almost always depend on the drafting of the particular agreements in question. Thus, in *Shepherd*, HHJ Lloyd QC decided that a provision in the original agreement which permitted a party to refer to adjudication 'any dispute or difference arising under it' was not wide enough to cover disputes arising in respect of the second agreement,[37] whilst in *Quarmby v Larraby*[38] HHJ Grenfell decided, again as a matter of construction, that disputes that arose under the contract which had not been caught by the settlement agreement could still be adjudicated. Similarly, in *L Brown*, Ramsey J concluded that a clause which allowed disputes to be referred to adjudication that arose under, out of, or in connection with the original contract did allow a party to refer a dispute which arose in respect of the second agreement. It is respectfully suggested that this distinction is not only right, but it is also entirely in line with the Court of Appeal decision in *Ashville Investments v Elmer Contractors*[39] in which it was held that the

---

[35] [2000] CILL 1568.
[36] [2005] EWHC 3503 (TCC).
[37] See also *Capital Structures v Time & Tide* [2006] EWHC 591, in which HHJ Wilcox decided that a dispute about economic duress did not arise under the contract.
[38] [2003] Leeds TCC.
[39] [1989] QB 488; [1988] 3 WLR 867.

words 'in connection with' in an arbitration clause were wide enough to allow an arbitrator to deal with claims for rectification and misrepresentation.

These, and a number of other cases on the same topic, were discussed by Jackson J in *McConnell Dowell Constructors (Aust) Pty Ltd v National Grid Gas Plc*.[40] In that case, he concluded that the supplemental agreement was simply a variation of the original agreement, and that therefore the original dispute resolution provisions still applied. The principal reason for his decision was the continuing existence of obligations under the original contract. That therefore made it a very different situation to that in *Shepherd*, where the second agreement was expressed to be in full and final settlement of all the referring party's claims under the original contract.

7.24

Was the Appointment in Accordance With the Contract?

The vast majority of construction and engineering contracts now contain detailed adjudication provisions. However, this does not mean that there will be no jurisdictional challenge to the appointment of a particular adjudicator to decide a dispute arising under the contract. There are a number of cases in which the appointment provisions in the contract have broken down, or proved impossible to operate: in those cases, the courts have endeavoured to take a pragmatic view of the appointment provisions, but with the clear understanding that an appointment which cannot be justified under the contract is invalid, and results in a complete absence of jurisdiction. Thus, in *AMEC Projects Ltd v Whitefriars City Estates Ltd*[41] both the TCC Judge at first instance and the Court of Appeal construed the contract in a practical fashion so as to ensure that, because the mechanism of nominating the parties' first choice adjudicator had broken down, there was a workable fallback position. Accordingly, in that case it was held that the adjudicator, who had been appointed following the death of the adjudicator named in the contract, had the appropriate jurisdiction. That is to be contrasted with the decision in *IDE Contracting Ltd v RG Carter*[42] where the appointment of the adjudicator was patently not in accordance with the express terms of the contract, and HHJ Havery QC had no realistic alternative but to find that the adjudicator's decision was unenforceable.

7.25

In *Pring and St Hill Ltd v C J Hafner (trading as Southern Erecters)*[43] the Scheme was implied into the contract. Paragraph 8(2) of the Scheme stipulates that the adjudicator can adjudicate at the same time on related disputes under different

7.26

---

[40] [2007] BLR 92.
[41] [2004] EWCA Civ 1418.
[42] [2004] BLR 172.
[43] [2002] EWHC 1775 (TCC). This case has been discussed, in the context of paragraph 8(2) of the Scheme, at paragraphs 3.36–3.37 above.

contracts, but the provision made plain that this could only happen with the consent of all the parties to those disputes. The TCC Judge concluded on the evidence that the defendant had made it clear that it did not want the adjudicator to deal with two related disputes simultaneously, one of which did not involve the defendant at all. In the light of that clear statement, the Judge found it extremely difficult to understand how or why the adjudicator could possibly have thought that he could go ahead and deal with the two disputes together. He therefore concluded that the adjudicator had not acted in accordance with his appointment (because he had considered other matters involving other parties) and that, in the light of the clear objection to the approach he adopted, he lacked the necessary jurisdiction.

7.27 Of course, if there is a real dispute between the parties as to the terms of the contract that they have agreed then, depending on the precise nature of the dispute, it can often be difficult for an adjudicator to assume a valid appointment. The dispute between the parties as to the terms of the contract between them in *Pegram Shopfitters Ltd v Tally Weijl (UK) Ltd*[44] meant that it could not safely be assumed that the adjudicator had been validly appointed, so his decision was not enforced.[45] The Court of Appeal reached a similar conclusion in *Lead Technical Services Ltd v CMS Medical Ltd*.[46] In that case, there was a dispute between the parties as to the precise terms of the contract which had been agreed, with CMS, the responding party, arguing that an earlier agreement had been supplanted by a deed of appointment which contained different terms, and a different adjudicator nominating body. The adjudicator concluded that he had been appointed in accordance with the earlier contract, and not the subsequent deed of appointment and that was a view supported by the TCC Judge at first instance in Leeds. However, in the Court of Appeal, Moses LJ demonstrated that CMS had a real prospect of proving that the agreement between the parties was that which was contained in the subsequent deed. If that was so, the adjudicator had no jurisdiction because he had been appointed by the wrong body. In those circumstances, the Court of Appeal overturned the decision of the Judge and refused to enforce the adjudicator's decision.

Was the Contract in Writing?

7.28 One of the most important features of the 1996 Act was the stipulation that, in order for the contract to be a construction contract, it had to be in writing. The cases in which this aspect of the provisions of s107 has been considered by the courts are set out in detail in Chapter 2 (paragraphs 2.44–2.74) above. The courts

---

[44] [2003] EWCA 1750.
[45] See the full discussion of this case at paragraphs 8.14–8.16 below.
[46] [2007] EWCA Civ 316.

have construed the provisions in s107 relatively strictly, and rejected various attempts to widen the application of the section, in large measure because the requirement that the terms be in writing was designed to promote certainty. Thus in *Grovedeck Ltd v Capital Demolition Ltd*[47] the claimants accepted that the underlying contracts were oral. However, they maintained that the simple existence of the referral notice, and the response to the referral notice, brought the oral contracts within the ambit of the 1996 Act. HHJ Bowsher QC acknowledged that, on one reading of s107(5), if one party to an adjudication alleged the existence of an oral agreement, and the other did not deny the existence of an oral agreement, then there was an agreement in writing 'to the effect alleged', even though the responding party hotly denied, as was the case in *Grovedeck*, that the agreement was in the terms alleged. The Judge concluded that Parliament cannot have intended such an unjust result. He went on to find that disputes as to the terms, whether express or implied, of oral construction agreements were surprisingly common and were not readily susceptible of resolution by a summary procedure such as adjudication. In consequence, he said that it was not therefore surprising that Parliament should have intended that such disputes should not be determined by adjudicators under the 1996 Act.

7.29 As noted in paragraphs 2.46–2.51 above, the leading case on this area of the law is the Court of Appeal decision in *RJT Consulting v DM Engineering*.[48] In that case, overturning the decision of the Judge at first instance, Ward LJ said that the agreement had to be evidenced in writing and that meant 'all of it, not part of it. A record of the agreement also suggests a complete agreement, not a partial one.' Although Auld LJ appeared to suggest in his judgment that it was only the material terms of the agreement that had to be recorded in writing, this was not the view of the majority. Subsequently, in *Trustees of the Stratfield Saye Estate v AHL Construction Ltd*[49] Jackson J dealt expressly with the differing approaches of the majority and Auld LJ in *RJT*, and concluded that an agreement is only evidenced in writing for the purposes of s107(2)–(4) if all the express terms of that agreement are recorded in writing. He found that it was not sufficient to show that all terms material to the issues within the adjudication in question had been recorded in writing.[50]

7.30 It is of course incumbent on the party protesting the adjudicator's jurisdiction on this ground to demonstrate at least an arguable case that there were other terms

---

[47] [2000] BLR 181.
[48] [2002] BLR 217.
[49] [2004] EWHC 3286 (TCC).
[50] The same approach was adopted by HHJ Wilcox in *Bennett (Electrical) Services Limited v Inviron Limited* [2007] EWHC 49 (TCC).

not recorded in writing. In *A.R.T. Consultancy Limited v Navera Trading Limited*,[51] the defendant alleged that there were other terms that were agreed orally, thus depriving the adjudicator of jurisdiction. On analysis, the TCC Judge found that this contention related to the design element of the works, which had been carried out some time earlier. The argument presupposed that this design element was intended to be part and parcel of the agreed contract for the works on site. The Judge concluded that there was no basis for this assumption and that, on the evidence, the parties had intended that the construction work itself would be let as a separate contract. All the terms of that contract were in writing; the existence of a separate, earlier agreement in relation to the design works, which the adjudicator had ignored for the purposes of his decision, was irrelevant and did not deprive the adjudicator of jurisdiction. The decision was therefore enforced.

7.31 If all the terms of a construction contract are not in writing, then the contract does not comply with the 1996 Act and the adjudicator will not have been validly appointed. Of course, different considerations will apply in circumstances where there is an agreed contractual mechanism for adjudication in writing, but where some of the other contract terms are not in writing. Take, for example, an agreement whereby the parties agree the incorporation of a standard form which contains an adjudication provision. Prima facie therefore, they have agreed to adjudicate any disputes that might arise between them. However, it may also be that some of the other terms of the contract were agreed orally. What then is the position? It is thought that, whilst such an issue will almost always turn on the facts, an adjudicator appointed under the agreed adjudication provisions in such a case will have been validly appointed. This is because, if there was a written agreement between the parties to adjudicate their disputes, and if the contract complies with the Act (so that, for example, there was a written agreement to refer disputes to adjudication), then it will be unnecessary to demonstrate that, in addition, all of the other express terms of the contract were also in writing.

7.32 It should also be noted that a defendant may be able to avoid the consequences of an adjudicator's decision, at least in the short term, if he can demonstrate an arguable case that the relevant construction contract, even if in writing, was entered into as a result of economic duress. In this area of the law, the leading case on economic duress is the decision of Dyson J in *DSND Sub-Sea v Petroleum Geoservices*[52] which makes clear the practical difficulties faced by a party who wishes to allege that a contract is voidable as a result of economic duress. Despite these difficulties, in *Capital Structures Plc v Time and Tide Construction Ltd*[53] HHJ Wilcox concluded that the defendant had demonstrated 'an arguable, albeit shadowy, case as

---

[51] [2007] EWHC 1375 (TCC).
[52] [2000] BLR 530.
[53] [2006] EWHC 591 (TCC).

General Principles

to economic duress' and an arguable case that they had elected to have the relevant contract (which was in fact a settlement agreement) set aside. He therefore gave leave to defend, but only on terms that the defendant company paid into court the amount awarded by the adjudicator's decision.

Correct Parties

Although it may seem trite, the reported cases demonstrate that, in order for an adjudicator to reach a decision which the courts will subsequently enforce, the parties to the adjudication must also be the parties to the relevant construction contract. There are a number of authorities which demonstrate this principle. **7.33**

(a) The Court of Appeal decision referred to above, *Thomas-Frederic's (Construction) Ltd v Keith Wilson*,[54] demonstrates that, if there is a respectable case that a defendant can mount to demonstrate that he was not a party to the relevant contract, and that therefore the adjudicator had no jurisdiction to make any decision binding on him, then such a decision will not be enforced.

(b) A subsequent example of the same principle can be found in *Rok Build Ltd v Harris Woolf Development Company Limited*.[55] There, HHJ Wilcox concluded that all but one of the points taken by the defendants amounted to a 'mere scramble to find reasons to defeat the claim for summary judgment'. However, the exception was the argument in respect of the correct identity of the claimant. The claimant, Rok Build Ltd, had commenced an adjudication against the defendants, who immediately pointed out that the claimant had no standing, because the contractor named in the contract was not Rok Build, but Walter Llewellyn & Sons Ltd. At some stage, there had apparently been a de facto substitution of Rok Build Ltd for the titular contractor, Walter Llewellyn & Sons Ltd, but there was no evidence as to when it happened, what the circumstances were that gave rise to it, and what agreement or acquiescence was shown by the defendant to the changed state of affairs. Judge Wilcox concluded that, on the evidence before him, it was reasonably arguable that the claimant as described in the enforcement proceedings had no right whatsoever to refer a dispute to adjudication under the contract, and it therefore followed that it was at least arguable that the claimant was not entitled to summary judgment. The adjudicator's decision was therefore not enforced.

(c) In *Westdawn Refurbishments Ltd v Roselodge Ltd*,[56] HHJ McCahill QC had already found that, because the contract terms were not all in writing, he

---

[54] [2003] EWCA 1494.
[55] [2006] EWHC 3573 (TCC).
[56] [2006] Adj LR 04/25.

could not summarily enforce the adjudicator's decision. Accordingly he considered, but did not decide, the second point in the case, which was to the effect that, because the claimant had not been a party to the original construction contract, but was instead an assignee, he could not invoke the adjudication process. Having weighed up the competing contentions, and observed that the fact of an assignment (and the existence of potentially competing rights of assignor and assignee) made the situation potentially much more complicated than had been envisaged by the 1996 Act, the Judge concluded that 'the arguments that would deny an assignee a remedy are not insubstantial'.

7.34 However, the authorities also demonstrate that the court will need to be persuaded that there is good evidence that the referring party is not the party named in the contract before it will even consider granting leave to defend in any summary judgment application for the enforcement of the decision. Thus, in *Andrew Wallace Ltd v Artisan Regeneration Ltd*[57] the defendants argued that, since they had contracted with Mr Andrew Wallace as an individual, and not with his company, the claimant company was not entitled to enforce the adjudicator's decision. The position was muddled by the fact that Mr Wallace had, on occasion, issued invoices in his own name rather than in the name of the company. However the TCC Judge found that the position was fully explained in the contemporaneous correspondence and that there was no doubt that the defendants were well aware that the contract was with the company, not the individual. She found that, on analysis, the invoices were not inconsistent with that conclusion. Therefore, she held that, on the evidence, the defendants' prospects of success on this point were fanciful, not real, and she entered summary judgment against them. A similar result occurred in *Michael John Construction Ltd v Golledge & Ors*.[58] This was an unusual case involving arguments about the capacity of the various parties pursued by the claimant contractor in two separate adjudications concerning the same outstanding sums. The facts of the case are set out in paragraph 7.76 below. In the enforcement hearing, counsel for the various defendants took the point that, having decided the liability of specific individuals in one capacity, the adjudicator could not decide the second dispute on a different basis as to capacity. This was described as 'the jurisdictional bind' that the claimant contractor had got itself into. The TCC Judge rejected this submission, pointing out that, in reality, the disputes in the two adjudications had been different, and there was no question of 'double jeopardy'. Furthermore, he said that it would be 'monstrous' if the claimant, who had not been told by the defendant the true position as to the identity of the relevant individuals before the start of the first adjudication, was to

---

[57] [2006] EWHC 15 (TCC).
[58] [2006] EWHC 71 (TCC).

General Principles

be deprived of its contractual remedy because of that failure, over which it had had no control.

The Dispute

What was the Scope and Extent of the Dispute in the Notice of Adjudication?

7.35 Without any doubt, the most important document in the adjudication process is the notice of intention to refer a dispute to adjudication, commonly known as the notice of adjudication. The authorities make it clear that any jurisdictional issues will be considered by reference to the nature, scope and extent of the dispute identified in the notice of adjudication.[59] Unless there is an express agreement by the parties, and the adjudicator, either to widen or to narrow the extent of the dispute in the notice of adjudication, it is that dispute alone which the adjudicator has the jurisdiction to decide.

7.36 In *Northern Developments (Cumbria) Ltd v J&J Nichol*[60] J&JN had made an application for payment on 13 July. On 29 July NDCL wrote a letter purporting to be a notice of intention to withhold payment. On 6 August J&JN withdrew from site and NDCL treated this action as a repudiatory breach of contract. The dispute which was referred to adjudication by J&JN in their notice of adjudication was in respect of the outstanding monies. Accordingly, when NDCL responded by seeking to set-off the damages which they claimed arose out of J&JN's repudiation of the contract, J&JN said that the adjudicator did not have the jurisdiction to deal with that claim. HHJ Bowsher QC accepted that submission, concluding that the adjudicator had no jurisdiction to consider any matter not raised in the notice of adjudication, which was itself concerned with the validity or otherwise of the notice of intention to withhold payment of 29 July. That was the document that triggered the dispute that was subsequently referred to adjudication. The adjudicator had expressly excluded the repudiation issue from his decision, so it could not be impeached, even though he had in fact decided not to consider the repudiation claim for another reason, which was wrong in law. This error was irrelevant and the decision was enforced.

7.37 Similarly, in *FW Cook Ltd v Shimizu (UK) Ltd*[61] the TCC Judge found that the notice of adjudication was drafted rather loosely. It appeared to indicate simply that the referring party wanted to obtain decisions on certain items in dispute, in the hope that other matters might well be resolved, once the adjudicator's decision

---

[59] See also paragraphs 3.12–3.15 above.
[60] [2000] BLR 158.
[61] [2000] BLR 199.

on the specific items had been given. Accordingly, the Judge ruled that the notice to refer did not seek to obtain a definitive decision from the adjudicator as to how much the next interim payment should be, but simply sought a decision on a number of elements in the overall final account. Thus, he said, the adjudicator's decision did not mean that the sums that he had identified were immediately payable, because that would involve a consideration of overall liability, and that was not the question the adjudicator had been asked to decide. For these reasons, the Judge concluded that, if the adjudicator had intended to direct that certain sums should be paid, then he had done something which he was not authorised to do. He would not have had the jurisdiction to reach such a decision. However, the Judge found on the facts that the adjudicator had not fallen into error because he had merely provided the parties with the third party assistance which had been sought in the notice of adjudication.

7.38 Also in similar vein was the decision of HHJ Seymour QC in *Mecright Ltd v T&A Morris Developments Ltd*[62] where he analysed the notice of adjudication carefully and concluded that it did not include a dispute as to how much Mecright was entitled to be paid in respect of the execution of the sub-contract works, or what was due as a result of the allegedly wrongful determination of its contract by Morris. The Judge therefore found that the adjudicator had no jurisdiction to decide that a sum was due to Mecright in respect of the execution of the sub-contract works. The decision was not summarily enforced.

7.39 There are a number of reported cases in which the court's analysis of the dispute contained in the notice of adjudication led to the conclusion that the adjudicator had exceeded his jurisdiction when, in his decision, he considered and purported to decide other issues which had not been referred to him. In *Griffin & Anor (t/a K&D Contractors) v Midas Homes Ltd*,[63] HHJ Lloyd QC explained in some detail the purpose and function of a notice of adjudication. He said:

> The purposes of such a notice are first, to inform the other party of what the dispute is; secondly, to inform those who may be responsible for making the appointment of an adjudicator, so that the correct adjudicator can be selected; and finally, of course, to define the dispute of which the party is informed, to specify precisely the redress sought, and the party exercising the statutory right and the party against whom a decision may be made so that the adjudicator knows the ambit of his jurisdiction.

In that case the notice of adjudication of 3 May 2000 identified the dispute by reference to two earlier letters, which had therefore themselves to be analysed to see the precise nature of the dispute referred to the adjudicator. The Judge concluded that, in consequence of the notice, the adjudicator had the jurisdiction to deal

---

[62] TCC, 26.6.01, unreported. This case is the subject of a more detailed analysis at paragraphs 3.14–3.15 above.
[63] [2000] 78 Con LR.

with two outstanding invoices, and he held that the decision was enforceable in respect of those sums. However, he concluded that, because other invoices and general claims were not identified in the notice of 3 May 2000, the adjudicator did not have the jurisdiction to make a decision about those other invoices or claims.[64]

There are a number of reported cases in which the court has concluded that, on a proper analysis of the notice of adjudication, the adjudicator had the necessary jurisdiction to reach all aspects of his decision. So in *Jerome Engineering Ltd v Lloyd Morris Electrical Ltd*[65] it was held that an adjudication notice which omitted an express request for relief, and simply made reference to a failure to make payment in accordance with the DOM/2 standard form of sub-contract, was sufficient to permit the adjudicator to require the contractor to make an interim payment to the sub-contractor.[66] Likewise, in *William Verry (Glazing Systems) Ltd v Furlong Homes Ltd*,[67] the TCC Judge's construction of the notice of adjudication provided a complete answer to the jurisdiction point. In that case, Furlong, the main contractor, sent Verry, the sub-contractor, a notice of adjudication which, amongst other things, asked the adjudicator 'to decide that the extension of time granted by Furlong to 2 February 2004 is correct'. The Judge concluded that this meant that the adjudicator had to decide whether the existing extension granted by Furlong was correct, which therefore meant that he also had to consider all Verry's claims for extension of time, whenever made. The request was not limited to an investigation as to whether or not the extension that had been granted was correct *at the time that it was granted*, and on the information that was available when it was granted; the dispute which, on a proper construction of the notice of adjudication, had been referred to the adjudicator was a much wider dispute than that. In addition, it was found that, because Furlong had referred to adjudication their existing entitlement to liquidated damages, it was impossible for the adjudicator to decide such entitlement to liquidated damages without first deciding Verry's existing entitlement to an extension of time, again regardless of their previous claims. Accordingly, for these two separate reasons, as a matter of construction of the notice to intention to refer to adjudication, the court

7.40

---

[64] The same Judge was obliged to consider in some detail the notice in the case of *David McLean Housing Ltd v Swansea Housing Association Ltd* [2002] BLR 125. The notice identified six 'matters in dispute' although the Judge concluded that, in effect, they were all aspects of one dispute and that the notice was valid. The decision is discussed in greater detail in paragraph 7.59 below.

[65] [2002] CILL 1827.

[66] HHJ Havery QC reached a similar conclusion in *LPL Electrical Services Ltd v Kershaw Mechanical Services Ltd* (2.2.01, unreported) where he concluded that, on a proper construction of the notice to refer, the claimant was seeking payment of all outstanding sums, although the notice only specifically referred to the most recent interim application for payment.

[67] [2005] EWHC 138 (TCC).

concluded that the adjudicator had the jurisdiction to consider *de novo* Verry's entitlement to an extension of time.

7.41 One of the most common debates relating to the scope and extent of the dispute that was referred to adjudication by the notice concerns whether or not the dispute thus being referred to adjudication properly included any cross-claim. In *VHE Construction Plc v RBSTB Trust Co Ltd*[68] the second adjudicator identified a sum of £254,000 odd payable by RBSTB in a written decision dated 9 November 1999. Two days after the decision, RBSTB notified VHE that they intended to deduct most of that sum by way of liquidated damages, and they merely paid the small balance between the two figures. VHE sought and obtained summary judgment for the remainder of the sum due in accordance with the second adjudicator's decision. HHJ Hicks QC decided that s111(4) of the 1996 Act required that an effective notice of withholding payment must precede the referral to adjudication; if it did, the notice of adjudication must include a reference to the effect of that withholding notice and the validity of the grounds for withholding payment which it asserts.

7.42 The importance of ensuring that the notice of adjudication properly describes the relevant dispute is even more pronounced if the dispute relates to the contents of a final certificate. Many of the JCT Standard Forms of Building Contract contain detailed provisions relating to the issue of a final certificate which, unless challenged within a set period, becomes conclusive evidence on a variety of potentially significant matters. If a final certificate is challenged, then the challenger is required to issue a notice of adjudication within a specified period (not usually longer than 28 days), and it therefore becomes critically important for the challenger to ensure that every element of his challenge to the final certificate is enshrined in the notice of adjudication; otherwise, if a point of challenge is omitted from the notice, the final certificate will become conclusive evidence in respect of that omitted matter. In such circumstances, there is a potential benefit to be gained by the party who is content with the final certificate in taking technical points about the notice of adjudication and/or the conduct of the adjudication to which it gives rise because, if such arguments are successful and, say, the decision is a nullity, the final certificate will not have been challenged in time.

7.43 The courts are astute to the consequences of such arguments. Thus, in *Mr Tracy Bennett v FMK Construction Ltd*[69] the court rejected a number of technical points which would have ruled the notice, and therefore the adjudicator's decision, invalid. In particular, the TCC Judge concluded that a first notice of adjudication

---

[68] [2000] BLR 187. This decision is discussed in greater detail, in connection with the principles relating to set-off and withholding notices, in paragraphs 10.21–10.22 below.
[69] [2005] EWHC 1268 (TCC).

General Principles

was sufficient to comply with the final certificate provisions in the contract, and prevented the final certificate from becoming conclusive evidence, even though that notice was replaced by a later notice of adjudication which was served outside the period prescribed by the contract for a challenge to the final certificate. In similar vein, there was a potential problem with the adjudicator's jurisdiction in *Cubitt Building & Interiors Ltd v Fleetglade Ltd*[70] where the referral notice was allegedly served more than seven days after the notice of adjudication. If that criticism had been sustained, and it deprived the adjudicator of jurisdiction, then the period under the contract for challenging the final certificate would have elapsed, and no subsequent notice would have been served in order to rectify any default. The court concluded that, because the adjudicator was only appointed very late on day seven, it was in accordance with the contract and the 1996 Act if the referral notice was served promptly on the following day, which is what happened. This meant that the adjudicator did have the necessary jurisdiction and that the challenge to the final certificate had not been lost. Both cases serve as an eloquent warning to those who wish to challenge a final certificate that they need to do so promptly and in clear terms. It can also be worthwhile for a challenger in such circumstances to issue both a notice of adjudication and a claim form (or arbitration notice) at the same time, so as to ensure that an error by the adjudicator later during the reference does not create an insurmountable procedural difficulty.

7.44 It is the notice of adjudication which defines the limits of the adjudicator's jurisdiction. It is extremely important that the parties in adjudication understand that the later documents, and in particular the more detailed referral notice, do not extend the adjudicator's jurisdiction beyond that which is set out in the notice of adjudication. In *KNS Industrial Services Ltd v Sindall Ltd*[71] HHJ Lloyd QC noted in trenchant terms that the further documents which come into existence following the notice of adjudication, such as the referral, 'do not cut down, or, indeed, enlarge the dispute (unless they contain an agreement to do so)'. This conclusion was endorsed by HHJ Seymour QC in *Mecright Ltd v T&A Morris Developments Ltd*[72] where the Judge went on to say that the basic scheme of adjudication was that what was referred was a single dispute, and that an adjudicator could only deal with more than one dispute at a time if there was clear and express consent to this from the parties. Such consent is not to be implied from conduct or by the construction of documents other than the notice of adjudication. Indeed, Judge Seymour emphasised the importance of the notice of adjudication in the summary process. He said:

---

[70] [2006] EWHC 3413 (TCC).
[71] [2001] 17 Const LJ 170.
[72] 22.6.01, unreported.

There is implicit within it [adjudication] a risk of injustice; but Parliament has considered that risk to be acceptable because an adjudication is of limited temporal effect and only of an interim nature. While, as I have pointed out, my view and that of other judges is that those who describe a dispute which they wish to refer to adjudication in vague terms have only themselves to blame if the scope of what has been referred appears to be wider than what they may have thought, it seems to me to be wrong in principle to expose those involved in an expeditious process such as adjudication to the requirement to take care to express themselves during the process in such a way that it cannot be said that by words or conduct, they have unintentionally consented or agreed to some process other than that upon which they were initially engaged. This risk is eliminated if, as it seems to me to be right, any consent or agreement for the purposes of the Scheme has to be express.

7.45 In many ways, the sorts of issues which commonly arise in respect of the dispute that was the subject of the notice of adjudication can be exemplified in another case of Judge Seymour's, namely *Chamberlain Carpentry and Joinery Ltd v Alfred McAlpine Construction Ltd*.[73] There was a notice of adjudication which contained a series of elements of Chamberlain's account which, on their case, McAlpine had failed to pay. The adjudicator found in their favour and McAlpine resisted enforcement. The first complaint was that the notice contained more than one dispute. The second was that the adjudicator's decision requiring McAlpine to pay sums arising out of a particular application for payment did not arise from the notice of adjudication, and there was no correlation between the notice and the valuation exercise that had been undertaken by the adjudicator. The complaint was, therefore, that the adjudicator had exceeded his jurisdiction by having regard to points made elsewhere than in the notice of adjudication. As to the first point, the Judge concluded that what Chamberlain referred to adjudication by their notice of adjudication was a dispute as to how much it should be paid by McAlpine; that was a single dispute and the fact that, in order to reach a conclusion as to the sum due, it would be necessary to consider a number of elements which Chamberlain contended were relevant to the overall calculation of the payment did not mean that there was in reality a series of disputes as to what was payable under a number of different heads. As to the second point, however, the Judge rejected Chamberlain's argument that it was appropriate to consider the adjudicator's jurisdiction by reference to the referral notice, which had in fact been sent under cover of the notice of adjudication. Instead, the Judge concluded that, although a valid notice of adjudication may incorporate by reference other documents and, if it did, it must be construed together with those incorporated documents, the referral notice was not incorporated into the notice of adjudication because it had been merely sent with the notice of adjudication and was nowhere referred to within in. Although, at first sight, that looks to be a rather

---

[73] [2002] EWHC 514 (TCC).

legalistic approach, it should be noted that, on the facts, the Judge concluded that the notice of adjudication had properly described the dispute that was subsequently determined by the adjudicator in his decision, and he therefore had the appropriate jurisdiction to arrive at the sum due to Chamberlain. The decision was therefore enforced.

Had that Dispute Crystallised Between the Parties Prior to the Notice to Refer?

Responding parties often complain that the adjudicator's decision can concentrate on matters which, at the time of the issue of the notice of adjudication, the defendant did not even realise were in dispute. The complaints are either of 'ambush', with the notice of adjudication purporting to identify a dispute of which the responding party was either unaware or had had only a few days to consider, or 'creep', where the responding party thought that the dispute involved a short, self-contained matter but which, because of the way in which the referring party put it in the adjudication, involved a much more extensive trawl through hitherto unchartered territory. In these instances, responding parties complain that the purported dispute in the notice of adjudication was either no such thing, because the dispute had not crystallised between the parties—indeed, had not even been discussed—at the time of the issue of the notice of adjudication or, alternatively, that whilst the notice of adjudication appeared to identify a dispute which the responding party was aware of and was capable of addressing, the dispute which the adjudicator ended up deciding was very different, and had never arisen until the process of adjudication itself. **7.46**

In principle, the answer to these difficulties is straightforward. The dispute in the notice of adjudication must have crystallised between the parties prior to the service of that notice, even though such crystallisation may require no more than the service of a claim by the claiming party and subsequent inactivity, for a fairly short period, by the responding party. The adjudicator is obliged to decide that dispute and cannot seek to widen his jurisdiction, without the parties' consent, to deal with other matters which are not referred to, either expressly or by implication, in the notice of adjudication. In practice, in the early days of adjudication, it was a little unclear as to how the courts might approach the question of whether a dispute (and, if so, what dispute) had arisen between the parties. In more recent years, it is submitted that the necessary clarity has been provided by a number of decisions in the TCC. **7.47**

The starting point for a consideration of what is meant by the word 'dispute' is *Fastrack Contractors Ltd v Morrison Construction Ltd*.[74] HHJ Thornton QC **7.48**

---

[74] [2000] BLR 168.

pointed out that the 1996 Act, and the whole process begun by the notice of adjudication, required there to be a dispute that had already arisen between the parties to a construction contract. Any selection or acceptance of appointment by an adjudicator, and/or any subsequent adjudication and decision, which were not confined to that pre-existing dispute, would be undertaken without jurisdiction. He went on at paragraph 27 to say:

> A 'dispute' can only arise once the subject-matter of the claim, issue or other matter has been brought to the attention of the opposing party and that party has had an opportunity of considering and admitting, modifying or rejecting the claim or assertion.

7.49 In arriving at this conclusion, HHJ Thornton relied on two non-adjudication cases: *Halki Shipping Corporation v Sopex Oils Ltd*[75] and *Monmouthshire County Council v Costelloe & Kemple Ltd*.[76] In *Halki* the Court of Appeal confirmed that a 'dispute', the existence of which was the statutory pre-condition of a party being entitled to enforce an arbitration clause and to have legal proceedings stayed for arbitration under the Arbitration Act 1996, had a wide meaning and included any claim which the opposing party had been notified of, and which that party had refused to admit or had not paid, whether or not there was any answer to that claim in fact or in law. Judge Thornton concluded that the cases showed that a claim and its submission do not necessarily constitute a dispute and that a dispute only arose when a claim had been notified and then rejected. However, a rejection can occur when an opposing party refuses to answer the claim, and a dispute can arise when there has been a bare rejection of the claim to which there is no discernable answer in fact or in law.

7.50 In accordance with the reasoning in *Fastrack*, HHJ Lloyd QC in *Sindall Ltd v Abner Solland & Ors*[77] said that the absence of a reply to a claim or an assertion may give rise to the inference that there was a dispute, and that this would therefore cover the situation where the responding party was guilty of prevarication. The Judge said, 'for there to be a dispute for the purposes of exercising the statutory right to adjudication it must be clear that a point has emerged from the process of discussion or negotiation has ended and that there is something which needs to be decided'. His judgment itself is analysed at paragraph 7.66 below. These two decisions, early on in the life of the 1996 Act, with their emphasis on the need for an opportunity for the responding party to consider the claim, and a requirement for the process of discussion or negotiation to have ended before a dispute could be said to have arisen, led to the suggestion in some quarters that the London

---

[75] [1998] 1 WLR 726.
[76] [1965] 5 BLR 83.
[77] [2001] 3 TCLR 712.

General Principles

TCC Judges were taking a more restricted approach to the meaning of 'dispute' in adjudication than was being utilised elsewhere.[78]

Furthermore, this view was apparently confirmed by two decisions of HHJ Seymour QC dealing with the need for the 'crystallisation' of the dispute prior to the service of the notice of adjudication. In *Edmund Nuttall Ltd v R G Carter Ltd*[79] Judge Seymour concluded that, for a dispute to have arisen, there must have been an opportunity for each of the protagonists to consider the position adopted by the other and to formulate arguments of a reasoned kind. At paragraph 36 of his Judgment, he said:

7.51

> 'It may be that it can be said that there is a 'dispute' in a case in which a party which has been afforded an opportunity to evaluate rationally the position of an opposite party has either chosen not to avail himself of that opportunity or has refused to communicate the results of his evaluation. However, where a party has had an opportunity to consider the position of the opposite party and to formulate arguments in relation to that position, what constitutes a 'dispute' between the parties is not only a 'claim' which has been rejected, if that is what the dispute is about, but the whole package of arguments advanced and facts relied upon by each side. No doubt, for the purposes of a reference to adjudication under the 1996 Act or equivalent contractual provision, a party can refine its arguments and abandon points not thought to be meritorious without altering fundamentally the nature of the 'dispute' between them. However, what a party cannot do, in my judgment, is abandon wholesale facts previously relied upon or arguments previously advanced and contend that because the 'claim' remains the same as that made previously, the 'dispute' is the same . . . The whole concept underlying adjudication is that the parties to an adjudication should first themselves have attempted to resolve their differences by open exchange of views and, if they are unable to, they should submit to an independent third party for decision the facts and argument which they have previously rehearsed among themselves. If adjudication does not work in that way there is the risk of premature and unnecessary adjudications in cases in which, if any one party had had an opportunity to consider the arguments of the other, accommodation might have been possible.

On the facts, the Judge concluded that the dispute that was referred to adjudication was the existing claim for an extension of time, not the new claim for an extension that was advanced by reference to an expert's report that was only provided for the purposes of the adjudication itself. Similarly, in *Hitec Power Protection BV v MCI Worldcom Ltd*[80] the same Judge concluded that there was no dispute between the claimant and the defendant in relation to the matters set out in the notice of adjudication served on behalf of the claimant, because the issues there identified did not arise between the parties to the adjudication, but between

---

[78] See paragraph 3 of the judgment of Forbes J in *Beck Peppiatt Ltd v Norwest Holst Construction Ltd* [2003] EWHC 822 (TCC) in which the Judge identified defendant's counsel's express submission to this effect.
[79] [2002] BLR 312.
[80] [2002] EWHC 1953.

the claimant and those third parties who had placed a series of separate purchase orders. The Judge said that, by the time the matter was determined by the adjudicator, the claim against the defendant was put on a completely different contractual basis to that which had been stated at the time that the notice of adjudication was served and that, in those circumstances, the adjudicator did not have the necessary jurisdiction to decide the dispute on the basis of the new, and different, case.

7.52 To the extent that some of the judgments noted above might be said to have stemmed from an overly-restrictive interpretation of the word 'dispute' (as opposed to being a series of cases merely decided on their own specific facts), a series of more recent decisions have made it plain that the word 'dispute' is not to be given a restrictive or particular meaning for the purposes of adjudication. Thus, in *Beck Peppiatt Ltd v Norwest Holst Construction Ltd*[81] Forbes J rejected the contention that *Fastrack* suggested a more restricted approach to the meaning of 'dispute' (or that it had been so interpreted by the TCC Judges) for the purposes of adjudication in a way that was inconsistent with *Halki*. He went on expressly to approve what Judge Lloyd said in *Sindall v Solland*, commenting that, in his view, Judge Lloyd's comments were not in conflict with the approach of the Court of Appeal in *Halki*. He reiterated that the word 'dispute' was an ordinary English word which should be given its ordinary English meaning and that each case had to be determined on its own facts. He expressly rejected the suggestion that the word 'dispute' should be given some form of specialised meaning for the purposes of adjudication. This approach was followed by HHJ Kirkham in *Cowlin Construction Ltd v CFW Architects (A Firm)*.[82] In that case, Cowlin submitted a claim on 27 February 2002. CFW did not admit that the sum claimed by Cowlin was due and payable and, on 18 May 2002, Cowlin issued a notice of adjudication. The Judge said that, applying the test in *Halki*, because CFW had not accepted the claim by 18 May, even though they had not expressly rejected it, there was a dispute between the parties by that date. She went on to say that, in the same way as the Court of Appeal in *Halki* declined to construe the word 'dispute' more narrowly in the context of arbitration, there was similarly no reason to construe the word 'dispute' more narrowly in the context of adjudication.[83]

7.53 There were then a number of TCC decisions in which the point was reiterated that the word 'dispute' should not be given a restricted meaning merely because

---

[81] [2003] BLR 316.
[82] [2003] CILL 1961; [2003] BLR 252–254.
[83] The same Judge reached the same conclusion in *Orange EBS Ltd v ABB Ltd* [2003] BLR 323. A final account claim had been provided on 2 December 2002 and no response had been received by 6 January when the notice of intention to refer was issued. The Judge concluded in accordance with *Halki* that a dispute had arisen by 6 January. This case is also referred to at paragraph 4.40 above.

the adjudication process was a summary one, some of which dealt expressly with Judge Seymour's reference to a 'package of arguments' in *Nuttall*.[84] Many of the cases noted in the preceding paragraphs were summarised in the judgment of HHJ Toulmin CMG QC in *AWG Construction Services Ltd v Rockingham Motor Speedway Ltd*.[85] The Judge expressly said that, to the extent that *Nuttall* suggested that a dispute could consist only of the issues referred to adjudication and only those facts and matters set out in the notice of adjudication and/or the referral notice, he regarded that as too rigid a principle, and contrary to the approach in *Halki* and the other cases noted above. He said that, following *Halki*, a wide interpretation should be given to the word 'dispute' so that the adjudicator's jurisdiction was preserved wherever possible. He concluded that, although each case depended on its own facts and the context in which the referral to adjudication occurred, it was important that a court should approach the question of what comprised the dispute 'with robust commonsense, which takes into account the nature of the dispute and the manner in which it has been presented to the adjudicator'. He reiterated therefore that, within the limits that he described, the adjudicator was not confined to considering rigidly only the package of issues, facts and arguments which had been referred to him.

7.54 The pragmatic approach described by Judge Toulmin, and the wide interpretation given to the word 'dispute' to which he also refers, can be seen in the five most recent decisions on this issue. First, in *Amec Civil Engineering Ltd v The Secretary of State for Transport*[86] Jackson J considered all of the authorities identified above and summarised them into seven propositions, at paragraph 68 of his judgment, as follows:

1. The word 'dispute' which occurs in many arbitration clauses and also in section 108 of the Housing Grants Act should be given its normal meaning. It does not have some special or unusual meaning conferred upon it by lawyers.
2. Despite the simple meaning of the word 'dispute', there has been much litigation over the years as to whether or not disputes existed in particular situations. This litigation has not generated any hard-edged legal rules as to what is or is not a dispute. However, the accumulating judicial decisions have produced helpful guidance.
3. The mere fact that one party (whom I shall call 'the claimant') notifies the other party (whom I shall call 'the respondent') of a claim does not automatically and immediately give rise to a dispute. It is clear, both as a matter of

---

[84] See, by way of example, the two decisions of HHJ Moseley QC in *Watkin Jones v LIDL* [2002] CILL 1834–1836 and 1847–1849, and *Lovell Projects Ltd v Legg & Carver* [2003] BLR 452.
[85] [2004] EWHC 888 (TCC).
[86] [2004] EWHC 2339 (TCC).

language and from judicial decisions, that a dispute does not arise unless and until it emerges that the claim is not admitted.

4. The circumstances from which it may emerge that a claim is not admitted are Protean. For example, there may be an express rejection of the claim. There may be discussions between the parties from which objectively it is to be inferred that the claim is not admitted. The respondent may prevaricate, thus giving rise to the inference that he does not admit the claim. The respondent may simply remain silent for a period of time, thus giving rise to the same inference.

5. The period of time for which a respondent may remain silent before a dispute is to be inferred depends heavily upon the facts of the case and the contractual structure. Where the gist of the claim is well known and it is obviously controversial, a very short period of silence may suffice to give rise to this inference. Where the claim is notified to some agent of the respondent who has a legal duty to consider the claim independently and then give a considered response, a longer period of time may be required before it can be inferred that mere silence gives rise to a dispute.

6. If the claimant imposes upon the respondent a deadline for responding to the claim, that deadline does not have the automatic effect of curtailing what would otherwise be a reasonable time for responding. On the other hand, a stated deadline and the reasons for its imposition may be relevant factors when the court comes to consider what is a reasonable time for responding.

7. If the claim as presented by the claimant is so nebulous and ill-defined that the respondent cannot sensibly respond to it, neither silence by the respondent nor even an express non-admission is likely to give rise to a dispute for the purposes of arbitration or adjudication.

Adopting these principles, the Judge concluded that a dispute had arisen on the facts of *Amec* by the time of the notice of adjudication. This result was upheld in the Court of Appeal,[87] who expressly endorsed his seven principles. A similar result occurred in *William Verry (Glazing Systems) Ltd v Furlong Homes Ltd*[88] in which the TCC Judge observed that the restrictive approach in *Nuttall* (if that is what it was) had not been followed in subsequent cases, and that instead the courts had taken a robust view as to whether a dispute had arisen in any given case, having regard to its particular facts.

7.55 The only other Court of Appeal decision in this area of adjudication law[89] is *Collins (Contractors) Ltd v Baltic Quay Management (1994) Ltd*.[90] In his judgment

---

[87] [2005] EWCA Civ 291.
[88] [2005] EWHC 138 (TCC).
[89] In addition to the appeal in *Amec*, cited at footnote 87.
[90] [2004] EWCA Civ 1757.

in that case, Clarke LJ (as he then was) referred expressly to the seven propositions outlined by Jackson J in *Amec* (and quoted in full in paragraph 7.54 above). He accepted those propositions as broadly correct and endorsed the general approach that, while the mere making of a claim did not amount to a dispute, a dispute would be held to exist once it can reasonably be inferred that the claim was not admitted. He noted that Jackson J did not endorse the suggestions in some of the earlier cases, either that a dispute may not arise until negotiation or discussion had been concluded or that a dispute should not be lightly inferred, and he expressed the opinion that Jackson J was right not to do so. Indeed, he went on to say that negotiation and discussion were likely to be more consistent with the existence of a dispute, albeit an as yet unresolved dispute, than with an absence of a dispute. He concluded that, in such circumstances, the court was likely to be willing readily to infer that a claim was not admitted and that a dispute existed so that it could be referred to arbitration or adjudication.

7.56 Two of the most recent decisions in this area of the law are both decisions of Jackson J. In *Midland Expressway Ltd & Anor v Carillion Construction Ltd & Ors*[91] he adopted the principles endorsed by the Court of Appeal in *Amec* and noted that the contractual definition in that case of 'construction dispute' was very similar to the definition of the word 'dispute' given by the Court of Appeal in *Amec*. In *Multiplex Constructions (UK) Ltd v Mott MacDonald Ltd*[92] the same Judge rejected what he described as the 'unreal and artificial' interpretation of the dispute between the parties urged upon him by the defendant, Mott MacDonald, favouring a broad interpretation of the relevant correspondence so as to not unduly circumscribe the scope of the dispute before the adjudicator. In *John Stirling v Westminster Properties Scotland Limited*[93] Lord Drummond Young followed the approach in *Amec* and concluded on the facts that a dispute as to an interim certificate existed prior to the notice of adjudication. He said that a claim had been asserted, no sum had been paid, and the defenders had failed to advance any reason to explain such non-payment. That, he said, was 'sufficient for the inference that the defenders disputed the pursuers' claim. If that were not so, a party could adopt the tactic of simply failing to respond to repeated invoices, claim letters and the like, and thus substantially delay any reference to adjudication.'

Was the Dispute Referred to Adjudication a Single Dispute?

7.57 The 1996 Act makes it clear that only a single dispute can be referred to an adjudicator at any one time. The obvious explanation for this is that adjudication is a fast and summary process and it would become unworkable if an adjudicator had to

---

[91] [2006] EWHC 1505 (TCC).
[92] [2007] EWHC 20 (TCC).
[93] [2007] Scot CS CSOH 117.

deal with more than one dispute at the same time. It also appears that the contractual adjudication provisions drafted by the various professional bodies are also generally designed to anticipate the reference of a single dispute at any one time, although some particular standard terms expressly allow for multiple references at the same time. Single dispute requirements can be problematic when, under most construction contracts, the potential range of dispute is considerable, from arguments over proper payment for original work and variations, to debates about responsibility for delays and defects. In addition, many of these issues might crystallise out of a single claim for an interim payment, or on a final account. The obvious question then arises: when does a contractor's claim involve the reference to adjudication of more than one dispute, thus depriving the adjudicator of jurisdiction? The answer, in the cases thus far, perhaps surprisingly, is almost never.

7.58 Again, the starting point for consideration of this topic is the decision of HHJ Thornton QC in *Fastrack Contractors Ltd v Morrison Construction Ltd*.[94] In a much cited passage, Judge Thornton defined a single dispute as follows:

> During the course of a construction contract, many claims, heads of claim, issues, contentions and causes of action will arise. Many of these will be, collectively and individually, disputed. When a dispute arises, it may cover one, several or many of one, some or all of these matters. At any particular moment in time, it will be a question of fact what is in dispute. Thus the 'dispute' which may be referred to adjudication is all or part of whatever is in dispute at the moment that the referring party first intimates an adjudication reference. In other words, the 'dispute' is whatever claims, heads of claim, issues, contentions or causes of action that are then in dispute which the referring party has chosen to crystallise into an adjudication reference.

This passage has been cited with approval in a number of cases including, in particular, *David McLean Housing Ltd v Swansea Housing Association Ltd*[95] and *Michael John Construction v Golledge*.[96] There can be no doubt, therefore, that the courts have again taken a broad interpretation of the words 'dispute', with the result that if, for example, a contractor's application for an interim payment involves claims for variations, extensions of time and loss and expense, the rejection of that application, or its part-payment, will result in a single dispute, even if the investigation into the claims for payment will be entirely separate from

---

[94] [2000] BLR 168.
[95] [2002] BLR 125.
[96] [2006] EWCA Civ 71 (TCC). In that case, it was suggested that a contractor's claim for money due brought against a number of individuals (because it was unclear who the employer was) involved two separate disputes: who was the paying party and how much did he owe? The TCC Judge rejected this argument, saying that 'it would be contrary to the whole purpose of adjudication if such a simple dispute could then be broken down into its component parts, to enable the Defendants to be able to say that, because the dispute incorporates more than one issue, there must be more than one dispute'.

the investigation into the claims for an extension of time and consequential loss and expense, which latter issue also carries with it the inherent assertion that the employer is not entitled to liquidated damages for the same period of delay.

7.59 In *David McLean Housing Contractors Ltd v Swansea Housing Association Ltd*[97] the contractor sought to be paid by reference to interim payment application number 19, provided some months after practical completion. The claim included claims for payment for measured work and variations and for direct loss and expense. It was not paid, and there was a notice of adjudication which identified six separate 'matters in dispute'. HHJ Lloyd QC concluded that what was referred to adjudication was a single dispute, namely what payment ought to have been made as a result of interim payment application number 19. The fact that this application contained various elements, including measured work, variations and loss and expense, which were subsequently reflected in the notice of adjudication, did not mean that there was more than one dispute between the parties. The Judge also rejected the contention that the fact that one element in the notice of arbitration was a claim for an entitlement to extension of time (rather than a money claim) meant that this, at least, was a separate dispute; because application number 19 included a claim for loss and expense, the Judge said that that could not properly be ascertained or determined until any right to extension of time had also been determined. The Judge stressed that the interpretation of the notice of adjudication had to be approached by the court 'in a sensible manner and to try to give effect to its intentions, whilst bearing in mind the purposes of adjudication and the presumed intentions of the parties to be inferred from the contract'.

7.60 Because of the wide interpretation given to the word 'dispute' in this context, it is perhaps unsurprising that there are few reported cases in which it was found that the notice of adjudication referred more than one dispute to adjudication, and was therefore invalid. In *Grovedeck Ltd v Capital Demolition Ltd*,[98] HHJ Bowsher QC had already ruled that the contract was not in writing and therefore did not comply with s107(5) of the 1996 Act, so the adjudicator did not have the appropriate jurisdiction in any event. His remarks as to the reference of more than one dispute are therefore strictly *obiter*. However, Judge Bowsher concluded that the claimant's reference to adjudication of claims arising for work carried out on behalf of the defendant on two separate sites amounted to an attempt to refer more than one dispute to adjudication, and thus amounted to another ground for refusing to enforce the adjudicator's decision.

---

[97] [2002] BLR 125.
[98] [2000] BLR 181.

7.61 In *David and Teresa Bothma (In Partnership) T/A DAB Builders v Mayhaven Healthcare Limited*[99] the notice of adjudication stated that 'disputes have now crystallised between the parties as follows . . .' and went on to identify four separate disputes, including the date for completion, the non-withdrawal of the notice of non-completion, the sum of valuation number 9, and the 'scope and validity of architect's instructions issued to date'. The Judge found that, on the facts, the extension/completion issue was unconnected to the financial claim, and that, in consequence, two independent disputes were referred to the adjudicator. He therefore concluded that the adjudicator did not have the jurisdiction to decide those multiple disputes, and the decision was not enforced. Permission to appeal was refused,[100] Waller LJ noting that, although the employer had not taken the specific point about multiple disputes when the adjudication was first referred to the adjudicator, 'the employer made it clear that he reserved his position in relation to jurisdiction in very wide terms', and that was sufficient to defeat any question of waiver.

7.62 It is right to note that doubts have been expressed as to the potentially wide application of Judge Thornton's words in *Fastrack*. In *Barr Ltd v Law Mining Ltd*[101] Lord MacFadyen agreed that it was not a correct approach to sub-divide and analyse what was in substance one dispute into its component parts, and to label each part a separate dispute. However, he went on to say that a realistic view must be taken, and that there was some force in the criticism of the width of Judge Thornton's interpretation of the word 'dispute' in *Fastrack*. Indeed he went as far as to say that, if everything currently in dispute between the parties formed a single dispute, paragraph 8(1) of the Scheme was fairly restricted in scope or perhaps even deprived of content altogether. However, the Judge went on to note that the adjudicator had dealt with (and rejected) the 'several disputes' argument, having concluded that it was open to him to regard the matters referred to him as comprising one dispute. The Judge said that, despite what he had said about Judge Thornton's analysis, he was not persuaded that the adjudicator was wrong to take that view. The adjudicator's decision was therefore enforced.

7.63 It would appear, therefore, that a party refers a single dispute to adjudication if it can be demonstrated that his claim, which may be made up of several different elements, can be fairly described as a single, disputed claim for a sum due (or some other relief, like an extension of time) under the contract. In those circumstances, it is always important to ensure that the notice of adjudication is carefully drafted

---

[99] 16.11.06, a decision of HHJ Havelock-Allan QC, sitting at the TCC in Bristol.
[100] [2007] EWCA Civ 527.
[101] [2001] Scot CS 152; 80 Con LR 134.

General Principles

and does not refer to disputes in the plural.[102] If a contractor or a sub-contractor is making a claim pursuant to the payment provisions of the contract then, provided that such a claim can legitimately include a wide range of different elements, such a claim is likely to give rise to a single dispute. It is thought that it will be rare for the court to decide that a claim in relation to one contract and one site gives rise to more than one dispute, unless the referring party is making two different and unrelated claims (such as occurred in *Bothma*), or seeking two different declarations as to its contractual entitlement which involve entirely different aspects of the contract. Therefore, for example, a contested claim for a declaration that a sub-contractor is entitled to an extension of time of 15 weeks may well be a separate dispute from the same sub-contractor's claim, also hotly denied, that condition X of the sub-contract should be interpreted in such a way as to give rise to a particular method of valuing variations, or that condition Y meant that he had no design co-ordination obligation. In practical terms, it is thought likely that a notice to refer will usually fall foul of the stipulation that it must contain a reference to only one dispute only where, as in *Grovedeck*, there is an attempt to refer disputes arising under more than one contract in a single notice of adjudication, or where, as in *Bothma*, the notice of adjudication refers to a number of disputes which, on analysis, are independent of one another.

Insufficient Connection Between the Dispute Referred and the Adjudicator's Decision

There are a number of reported cases in which the courts have concluded that the adjudicator did not have the necessary jurisdiction to arrive at his decision. A number of them can be categorised as examples of a situation in which there was ultimately insufficient connection between the dispute that was referred to the adjudicator, and his written decision. Thus, in *AWG Construction Services Ltd v Rockingham Motor Speedway Ltd*[103] HHJ Toulmin CMG QC held that, as a matter of construction, the notice of adjudication served by Rockingham encompassed a claim that AWG were negligent in designing the race track for reasons which had been set out in the referral notice and the expert's report. As the adjudication developed, Rockingham's case altered and the issue of inadequate drainage became the central plank of their criticism of AWG. The Judge concluded that it was significant that Rockingham's own advisers had failed to include for additional drainage in their own remedial scheme. He found that the case in respect of drainage was essentially new, and emerged only during the adjudication. It was therefore different to that referred by way of the

7.64

---

[102] Guidance as to the drafting of the notice of adjudication is dealt with in greater detail in Chapter 16 below.
[103] [2004] EWHC 888 (TCC).

notice of adjudication. Therefore the adjudicator's decision, which relied so heavily on the drainage criticisms, went beyond the dispute which was referred to him; he answered a question which had not been referred to him and his decision was not enforced. In *Multiplex Constructions Ltd v West India Quay Developments*,[104] the same point was argued, but on the facts Ramsey J concluded that the adjudicator's decision determined the dispute which had been referred to him.

7.65 Furthermore, it should be noted that this lack of correlation between the dispute referred and the decision does not only arise where the decision goes beyond that which was originally referred. In *Ballast Plc v The Burrell Company (Construction Management) Ltd*[105] Ballast made a claim for sums due. The adjudicator refused to grant the relief sought and stated that the central request to assess the value of work done was 'not valid' because of what he described as a failure on the part of the parties to abide strictly by the terms of the JCT contract. Lord Reid said that the adjudicator's approach was wrong in law and in consequence the adjudicator had failed to exercise his jurisdiction to determine the dispute. His decision was therefore a nullity.

7.66 The courts' broad interpretation of the word 'dispute' will mean, however, that many jurisdictional challenges will be doomed to fail. The best example of this is perhaps *Sindall Ltd v Abner Solland & Ors*.[106] In that case, HHJ Lloyd QC concluded that the notice of adjudication did not include the reference of a disputed claim for an extension of time because, at the time of the notice, Sindall were waiting to hear from the contract administrator and had not treated the administrator's failure to express any opinion as giving rise to a dispute. Thus the adjudicator did not have authority to reach a decision on the amount of the extension of time as such. However, the Judge went on to find that the principal dispute referred to adjudication was whether or not Sindall's employment had been wrongfully terminated. That issue turned on whether the contract administrator had been right to say that, at the time of termination, the state of progress on site was sufficient to justify the conclusion that Sindall were not proceeding regularly and diligently with the work. Therefore, in order to decide the wrongful determination issue, the adjudicator had to have regard to Sindall's entitlement to an extension of time at the relevant date. In those circumstances, the Judge concluded that the adjudicator had not arrived at any decision which was beyond his authority or jurisdiction. In arriving at that conclusion, Judge Lloyd referred to an earlier decision of his also involving Sindall, namely *KNS Industrial Services (Birmingham) Ltd v Sindall Ltd*.[107] In that case, he referred

---

[104] [2006] EWHC 1569 (TCC); 111 Con LR 33.
[105] [2001] BLR 529.
[106] [2001] 3 TCLR 712.
[107] [2000] 75 Con LR 71.

not only to Judge Thornton's definition of a dispute in *Fastrack*, but he went on to say that:

> A party to a dispute who identifies the dispute in simple or general terms has to accept that any ground that exists which might justify the action complained of is comprehended within the dispute for which adjudication is sought.

7.67 Notwithstanding the wide interpretation of the word 'dispute' in the authorities, there are still many authorities where the courts have concluded that the adjudicator's decision bears insufficient relationship to the dispute that was originally referred to him. Thus in *R Durtnell & Sons Ltd v Kaduna Ltd*[108] HHJ Seymour QC found that the notice of adjudication served by Durtnell contained only one limited claim in respect of an extension of time. The adjudicator, however, did not limit his decision on extensions of time to that one specific matter, and instead dealt generally with Durtnell's entitlement. The Judge concluded that he did not have the jurisdiction to do so. He reasoned that there could be no dispute as to an entitlement to an extension of time in a situation where the claim for that extension had been referred to the architect, and the time for him to make a determination of that claim, as set out in the contract, had not yet expired. Although the Judge accepted that it was not expressly made a condition precedent in the contract that any dispute referred to adjudication should first have been referred to the architect, he went on to say that it was not easy to see how a dispute as to the contractor's entitlement to an extension of time under the express terms of the contract could arise until that had happened, and the architect had either made his determination, or the time permitted for his doing so had expired.[109]

7.68 Often, an adjudicator is at least tempted to exceed his jurisdiction because the dispute that has been referred to him is of narrow compass, and he can see an opportunity for resolving a wider dispute to be of assistance to the parties. Of course, unless the parties expressly consent to such an exercise, the adjudicator simply has no jurisdiction to proceed in this way. Thus, in *McAlpine PPS Pipelines Systems Joint Venture v Transco Plc*[110] the Judge concluded, on the facts set out at paragraphs 3.57–3.58 above, that the notice of adjudication identified the dispute as being limited to McAlpine's claim for interest payments. Although that claim had arisen because, according to McAlpine, payments in respect of various compensation events had not been certified when they ought to have been, there

---

[108] [2003] BLR 225.
[109] A similar result occurred in *Bickerton Construction Ltd v Temple Windows Ltd* (TCC unreported 26.6.01) where HHJ Kirkham held that the adjudicator did not have the jurisdiction to decide the final account figure, because the ongoing consideration of that claim under the contract meant that it had been expressly excluded from the dispute referred to him.
[110] TCC, unreported, 12 May 2004.

was no reference to adjudication of the compensation events themselves, or the information that McAlpine had originally provided in support of those claims. Transco's response was simply to dispute the claim on the basis that it could not succeed. What, therefore, was missing was any reference to adjudication of the underlying disputes concerning the compensation events themselves, and the adequacy (or otherwise) of the information originally supplied in support of those claims. Unhappily, the adjudicator had concluded that he was sure that both parties wanted him to deal with those other matters, because he believed that the parties wanted him to conclude the underlying dispute 'without recourse to further proceedings'. This was a fatal error: it was certainly not what Transco wanted from the adjudication. As Judge Toulmin said, if the existing notice of adjudication did not enable the adjudicator to deal with the dispute in the way in which he wanted, then in the absence of the express agreement of both sides, he was powerless to alter the terms of the notice or widen the scope of the dispute. So long as it was just the original dispute which remained before him, he had to decide only those limited issues which had been referred to him, and he therefore had no basis for embarking on a consideration of what he regarded as the real dispute. As a result of the adjudicator's erroneous view of his own jurisdiction, new issues were introduced in the course of the adjudication without the agreement of Transco, both by McAlpine and by the adjudicator himself. The adjudicator therefore exceeded his jurisdiction because the decision he eventually produced bore no correlation to the narrow dispute that had been originally referred to him, and his decision was not enforced.

7.69 In contrast to the particular criticism of the decision in *McAlpine*, the adjudicator in *Buxton Building Contractors Ltd v The Governors of Durand Primary School*[111] was also held to have exceeded his jurisdiction, but this time because he did not deal with the entirety of the dispute that had been properly referred to him. The contractor made a claim based on a certificate that had been issued after practical completion, in circumstances where no final certificate could be issued because the administrator was aware that the school had a cross-claim in respect of defects. The adjudicator decided that the sum certified was due and that because no withholding notice had been served by the school, he could not consider the cross-claim for defects. The Judge concluded that the decision demonstrated that the adjudicator had not considered the nature, content, validity or quantification of the cross-claim and did not investigate the material provided to him by the school, having made an erroneous assumption that the cross-claim had been taken into account by the supervising officer when issuing his certificate. HHJ Thornton QC held that there was a fundamental flaw in the decision, which was that it had

---

[111] [2004] EWHC 733 (TCC).

been reached without the adjudicator having considered or decided upon the contents of the submissions, documents and issues referred to him by the school. He had thus failed to decide the entirety of the dispute referred to him in accordance with s108(2)(c). It is, however, important to note that in *Carillion Construction Ltd v Devonport Royal Dockyard Ltd*[112] Chadwick LJ expressly doubted that the decision in *Buxton* was consistent with the proposition that an adjudicator who declined to consider evidence which he thought was irrelevant did not act outside his jurisdiction. It is therefore a case which must be treated with some caution.

7.70 Finally, in order to produce a decision in accordance with his jurisdiction, an adjudicator must comply with the time limits in the 1996 Act, or, if those time limits are set out in the contract, the relevant contractual provisions. If he fails to comply with those time limits, the adjudicator acts outside his jurisdiction and his belated decision is a nullity. That was the clear effect of the decision in *Richie Brothers (PWC) Ltd v David Philip (Commercials) Ltd*.[113] There, the Court of Session decided by a majority that a decision that was not reached within the agreed extended time was a nullity. This important limitation on an adjudicator's jurisdiction is discussed in greater detail in paragraphs 2.91–2.107 above.

The Relevance of Earlier Adjudication Decisions

7.71 Once an adjudicator has reached his decision then, until that decision is challenged, either in arbitration or in court, it is binding on the parties. This can create practical difficulties in long-running contracts, where there may be a series of disputes which, over time, need to be referred to the same or different adjudicators. It is clear beyond doubt that a second adjudicator cannot open up any matters decided by the first adjudicator. If he purports to do so, the decision of the second adjudicator will be a nullity.

7.72 Of course, the first practical problem that arises for the court is the nature of its investigation in circumstances where one party is alleging that the second adjudicator trespassed on the decision of the first. In *Sherwood & Casson Ltd v McKenzie*,[114] HHJ Thornton QC gave detailed consideration to the approach the court should adopt when enquiring whether the two disputes were substantially similar or not. He said that, in conducting that enquiry, the court would give considerable weight to the decision of the adjudicator and would only embark on a jurisdictional enquiry in the first place where there were real grounds for concluding that the

---

[112] [2005] EWCA Civ 1358.
[113] [2005] SLDT 341.
[114] [2000] TCLR 418.

adjudicator had erred in concluding that there was no substantial overlap. He commented that it would be a rare adjudication where the conditions were present which would necessitate such an enquiry. On the facts of that case, he decided that there was no substantial overlap between the first adjudication (which was concerned with interim applications and contra charges), and the subsequent adjudication, which was concerned with Sherwood's claim for a final account. The Judge concluded that, although the variation claims were similar in factual content in both disputes, they comprised separate disputes, because the first claim was being treated in the context of an interim valuation without loss and expense, whilst the latter claim was being treated as part of a final account re-measurement exercise, together with a claim for loss and expense.

7.73 Similarly, in another early case, *VHE Construction Plc v RBSTB Trust Co*,[115] the first adjudicator decided that, because no VAT invoice had been issued, the employer was currently under no obligation to pay the sum claimed of £1 million odd but that, because the employer had served no withholding notices, the contractor was entitled to be paid the full amount applied for within 28 days of the issue of such a VAT invoice. A VAT invoice was then issued and again there was no withholding notice. However, the second adjudicator concluded that he had power to order repayment of any sum in excess of that which ought properly to have been applied for by the contractor. He reduced the amount due to the contractor to about £¼ million. HHJ Hicks QC held that, although the second adjudicator had no jurisdiction to set aside, revise or vary the first adjudicator's decision, he had never been asked to do so, and had been conspicuously careful to avoid any form of words which might convey the contrary impression. Thus, whilst the obligation under the first adjudicator's decision remained, the second decision was also valid and enforceable. As a matter of practical reality, since the contractor had limited its demands to the net sum, namely the sum which it would have retained had payment first been made in accordance with the first adjudicator's decision, and then repayment made in accordance with the second adjudicator's decision, it was the second decision which was enforced. Although the effect of the two decisions was that the contractor was paid the net sum found due by the second adjudicator, there was, on the facts, no question of the second adjudicator having modified or altered the decision of the first.

7.74 Generally speaking, the courts have found that subsequent adjudicators' decisions have not trespassed on the province of earlier decisions.[116] Thus, in *Holt Insulation*

---

[115] [2000] BLR 187.
[116] Other relevant cases on this topic, referred to elsewhere in this book, but not in this section, include: *Naylor v Greenacres* [2001] Outer Court of Session P514/01; *AMEC v Whitefriars* [2004] EWCA Civ 1535; *David McLean v The Albany* [2005] TCC 101/05; *HG Construction v Ashwell Homes* [2007] EWHC 144 (TCC) and *Castle Inns (Stirling) v Clark Contracts Ltd* [2007] CSOH 21.

Ltd v Colt International Ltd[117] a sub-contractor's claim was referred to adjudication where it was rejected. The claim was reformulated and, in a second adjudication, it was decided that the sub-contractor was entitled to payment. The contractor argued that where a sub-contractor had claimed a large sum in adjudication and failed, for whatever reason, it could not reshape the claim in the light of the first decision, claim a smaller sum, and then seek a second adjudication on that second, smaller claim. The TCC Judge concluded that, whilst the references to the adjudicator related to the same matters, they did not relate to the same dispute. Although they were both concerned with the sub-contractor's entitlement to claim in respect of work done, the disputes were crucially different because, on the second occasion, the claims were put in a way that ensured their success, whilst the earlier claims had failed.

Similarly, in *Mivan Ltd v Lighting Technology Projects Ltd*[118] the claim had been successful in the first adjudication because there were no withholding notices. The responding party paid the sums found due by the adjudicator, and then subsequently issued its own withholding notice and notice of adjudication and sought to recover the sums that it said it had overpaid. The adjudicator made an order in those terms but LTP refused to repay the money, saying that the adjudicator had no jurisdiction to deal with the second adjudication because it was effectively a re-run of the first. HHJ Seymour QC concluded that the adjudicator had the necessary jurisdiction to deal substantively with the second adjudication. He said that the first adjudication dealt with a narrow dispute as to whether the invoices were payable, whilst the second adjudication was concerned with the matters raised in the withholding notices and was therefore 'a separate and distinct dispute'. Again, in *Skanska Construction UK Ltd v The ERDC Group Ltd*,[119] the first adjudication had failed because the adjudicator found there was insufficient information to support the claims. Thereafter there was a second adjudication relating to the final account, at which time further information relating to the claims was made available. The court rejected the submission that the second adjudication trespassed on the first, and concluded that the second adjudicator had the necessary jurisdiction to decide the dispute that had been referred to him. Again the court referred to the fact that, by the time of the second adjudication, a different stage in the contract had been reached; by then, different contractual provisions applied; considerably more information was available by the date of the issue of the final account than had been available at the time of the first adjudication; and that 'different considerations and perspectives may apply' in the second adjudication. In consequence of the court's conclusion that

7.75

---

[117] TCC, Liverpool District Registry, HHJ MacKay QC, 23.7.01 LVOI 5929.
[118] [2001] ADJCS 04/09; TCC, 9 April 2001.
[119] [2003] SCLR 296.

'the fundamental nature and parameters of the dispute' were different, the challenge to the adjudicator's decision was rejected.[120]

7.76 It is instructive to note that, just as with the cases in which the argument has been advanced that the adjudicator dealt with more than one dispute and therefore did not have the appropriate jurisdiction, the submission that the adjudicator was dealing with a matter previously decided by another adjudicator, although regularly made, has also been largely unsuccessful. *Michael John Construction v Richard Henry Golledge & Ors*[121] is a case in point. There, the claimant contractor carried out work for St Peter's RFC in Cardiff. Although the club was named as the employer in the contract, it was an unincorporated association of individuals, with no separate legal identity or status. The contract was signed by the fourth defendant, who was then the director of development and subsequently became a trustee of the club, although he was not a trustee at the time that the contract was signed. The contractor made a claim for unpaid monies which was referred to adjudication. The adjudicator found that the fourth defendant was liable to the claimant. No sums were paid so the claimant commenced a second adjudication against the three trustees, as well as the fourth defendant. The claims consultant acting for the defendants in the second adjudication refused to deal with the merits of the claims at all, and confined his challenge in the second adjudication entirely to jurisdictional points. The adjudicator found that the trustees were liable to the claimant contractor and that, alternatively, the fourth defendant was liable as agent. In the enforcement proceedings, the defendants took the point that the adjudicator had no jurisdiction to decide the second adjudication because he had decided the same dispute in the first adjudication. The Judge rejected that submission. In respect of the first, second and third defendants, they had never been a party to any adjudication and thus the question of any liability on their part could not have been an issue that had ever been adjudicated before. As to the fourth defendant, he was pursued in the second adjudication because he had refused to accept liability arising out of the first, and had in fact raised points as to his potential liability to pay. The issue that arose in the second adjudication, namely whether the fourth defendant was personally liable because he signed the contract and/or because he was acting as the agent of the first, second and third defendants was not a point which had been expressly decided in the first adjudication and the Judge concluded that it was entirely appropriate for it to be decided in the second adjudication. That jurisdictional challenge therefore failed.

---

[120] See also *Prentice Island Ltd v Castle Contracting Ltd*, 15 December 2003, decision of the Sheriff Principal.
[121] [2006] EWHC 71 (TCC).

General Principles

7.77 There is extensive overlap between the argument that the adjudicator did not have the necessary jurisdiction to decide point A (because it had already been decided in an earlier adjudication), and the contention that the adjudicator's failure to decide point A was a breach of natural justice (because, on a proper analysis, the point had not been decided in that earlier adjudication). This latter point is dealt with at paragraphs 9.38–9.41 below. The leading case of *Quietfield Ltd v Vascroft Construction Ltd*[122] makes clear that the court will examine closely any material which the adjudicator declined to look at, to see if it really did concern an issue which, because of an earlier adjudication, the adjudicator had no jurisdiction to decide.

Ousting the Jurisdiction of the Adjudicator in Other Ways

7.78 It will sometimes be the case that the jurisdiction of the adjudicator will be ousted in other ways, usually by the agreement (whether express or implied) of the parties themselves. An example of this is *Sheppard Construction Ltd v Mecright Ltd*.[123] On 15 March 2000 the parties had reached a compromise agreement which resulted in a payment of about £75,000 by Sheppard to Mecright. Then, on 3 July 2000, Mecright purported to make a further claim for £277,000 odd and made no mention of the compromise agreement. Mecright's claims consultants argued that the settlement agreement had been entered into under duress and should be set aside. Sheppard issued proceedings in the TCC claiming a declaration that the adjudicator had no jurisdiction to resolve the dispute referred to him, on the grounds that the terms of the settlement agreement meant that there was no dispute. In addition they argued that the 'duress' point was not referable to adjudication in any event. HHJ Lloyd QC found that, where parties had reached an agreement which settled their dispute, there was therefore no longer any dispute to be referred to adjudication. He held that that was the situation on 3 July, so that Mecright had no right to seek adjudication, and the adjudicator had no jurisdiction to consider or act upon the notice. He went on to make clear that a dispute about a settlement agreement of this kind could not be said to be a dispute under the sub-contract, since the effect of the settlement agreement was that it replaced the original agreement. The only subsisting obligation was the obligation to pay pursuant to the settlement agreement. He said that such a settlement agreement was not a construction contract within the meaning of s108 and that a dispute about an agreement which purports to settle a dispute or

---

[122] [2007] BLR 67.
[123] [2000] BLR 489. See also paragraph 7.21 above.

disputes under a construction contract is not a dispute *under* that contract.[124] The Judge distinguished between the word 'under' which, he said, was much more limited than the wider reach of expressions such as 'in connection with' or 'arising out of'.[125] A similar decision was reached in *Quality Street Properties (Trading) Ltd v Elmwood (Glasgow) Ltd*[126] where the court concluded that the disputes had been settled by the compromise agreement and that the adjudicator had no jurisdiction. These cases must, however, now be read in the light of the fuller analysis of compromise agreements in *L Brown* and *McConnell Dowell*, discussed in paragraphs 7.22–7.24 above.

7.79 Of course, in cases where the defendant seeks to challenge the jurisdiction of the adjudicator on the grounds that the purported disputes have in fact been compromised, the burden is on the defendant to demonstrate, on the balance of probabilities, that the claims have indeed been compromised. Thus, in any court hearing of the enforcement application, the court will need to undertake an enquiry into that issue. In *JW Hughes Building Contractors Ltd v GB Metal Work Ltd*[127] it was submitted on behalf of JWH that GBM had compromised all of their claims. Forbes J considered the correspondence, found that it was clear from that correspondence that there had been no compromise and that therefore this jurisdictional challenge failed. Although Forbes J went on to find at paragraph 12 of his judgment that, since the adjudicator had decided this point himself, it was not open to the parties to challenge it, it is respectfully submitted that that finding appears to be linked to the later finding that the parties had reached an ad hoc agreement to give the adjudicator the necessary jurisdiction to make a binding determination on his own jurisdiction. It is thought that, in the ordinary case, the adjudicator's investigation of his own jurisdiction in such a situation would not give rise to a ruling which would be binding on the parties, but which would instead require the court, in accordance with the procedure outlined by HHJ Thornton QC in *Fastrack* and *Sherwood and Casson*, to undertake at least some investigation into whether or not the adjudicator had rightly concluded that the matter fell within his jurisdiction.

7.80 It should also be noted that, generally, an adjudicator does not have the jurisdiction to modify the terms of the contract. In *David McLean Housing Contractors Ltd v Swansea Housing Association Ltd*[128] HHJ Lloyd QC said in terms

---

[124] A similar view was expressed by His Honour Judge MacKay QC in *Lathom Construction Ltd v Cross*, 29 October 1999, TCC, Liverpool District Registry, reported at [1999] CILL 1568.
[125] See *Ashville Investments Ltd v Elmer Contracting Ltd* [1988] 3 WLR 867 and paragraph 7.23 above.
[126] [2002] CILL 1922.
[127] [2003] EWHC 2421 (TCC).
[128] [2002] BLR 125.

that the Scheme for Construction Contracts, and, as far as he was aware, other standard forms of contract, did not confer on an adjudicator a right to adapt, vary or otherwise modify the contract. The adjudicator's decision had to be limited to the rights and liabilities of the parties pursuant to the contract in question. The only potential exception to that was concerned with the time for compliance; since the Scheme (and other standard form contractual provisions) provided that the time for compliance with an adjudicator's decision must be set out expressly, this might alter the time within which a payment might otherwise have to be made under the contract. Thus, the Judge concluded, the Scheme permitted the possible alteration of the time within which payments were to be made, but it was only to that extent that the strict terms of the contract might be modified by the adjudicator. In addition, an adjudicator appears to have the power to open up, revise and review any decision or certificate of a contract administrator but was not empowered to issue a certificate himself.[129]

Making a Valid Objection on Jurisdiction

A point which often arises when the courts have to consider a jurisdictional objection at an enforcement hearing is the extent, if at all, to which the objection was raised at the time of the adjudicator's appointment. If the objection was not taken at that time, then, as we have seen,[130] there is a strong chance that the courts will find that the parties agreed to give the adjudicator an ad hoc jurisdiction, so that the objection cannot be taken later, or that the right to take the objection has been waived. What then should a party do who wishes to make such an objection? **7.81**

The best thing, of course, is to make the sort of detailed objection to the adjudicator's jurisdiction that was made, for example, in *The Project Consultancy*,[131] in which the responding party made clear how and why the adjudicator had no jurisdiction, and that their continued participation in the adjudication was subject to this fundamental objection. But it seems that a general reservation of the responding party's position as to the adjudicator's jurisdiction may be sufficient: on the application for permission to appeal in *Bothma*,[132] Waller LJ said that the employer's written reservation as to the adjudicator's jurisdiction was so wide that it covered the particular ground that was successful in front of the Judge, even though that particular ground (multiple disputes) was not specifically **7.82**

---

[129] *Vaultrise Ltd v Paul Cook* [2004] ADJCS 04/06.
[130] See Chapter 5 above.
[131] [1999] BLR 377.
[132] [2007] EWCA Civ 527.

referred to in the letter. However, caution is advisable when making a general reservation in relation to jurisdictional matters: in *Ale Heavy Lift v MSD (Darlington) Ltd*,[133] HHJ Toulmin CMG QC held that, where the jurisdiction of the adjudicator had not been challenged on a particular ground, a jurisdictional challenge on that ground had thus been waived.

Summary of Principles Relating to Jurisdiction

7.83 The alleged absence of jurisdiction has, thus far, proved to be the most common ground on which a defendant relies to seek to avoid the decision of an adjudicator. Such a jurisdictional challenge must be taken expressly and clearly at the time of the appointment of the adjudicator. The adjudicator can investigate his own jurisdiction but, unless the parties have agreed otherwise, his ruling on his jurisdiction will not be binding and can be reviewed by the court. The appointment of the adjudicator must be valid and therefore in accordance, either with the 1996 Act, or the relevant contractual provisions. The terms of the construction contract must be in writing. As to the dispute which the adjudicator decides, he only has jurisdiction to decide the dispute that is referred for decision by the notice of adjudication. Furthermore that dispute must have crystallised prior to the service of the notice of intention to refer, although the court will take a generous view as to whether or not it can be said that, at that date, a dispute had arisen. The dispute must be a single dispute although, again, the vast majority of disputes that arise in connection with construction contracts can be presented as a single dispute, even if they contain a whole series of diverse elements. It is important that the adjudicator does not trespass beyond the dispute that is referred to him. Thus, there must be a clear connection between the dispute that is referred to him and his ultimate decision. Moreover, the adjudicator must not go back over or reconsider any matters decided in earlier adjudications that have arisen under the same contract between the same parties. If the answer to a claim is the suggestion that it has already been compromised, then the adjudicator will investigate the substance of that challenge and rule on it. If he concludes that the claim has been compromised then he may have no jurisdiction, depending on the terms of the original contract and the terms of any second, settlement agreement. If the adjudicator concludes that the dispute has not been compromised and/or that the dispute as to settlement arises under a construction contract, or a contract which otherwise provides him with jurisdiction, he can decide the underlying dispute, although (if his jurisdiction continues to be challenged) his decision may then be subject to the review of the court on the enforcement proceedings.

---

[133] [2006] EWHC 2080 (TCC).

General Principles

In *Carillion Construction Ltd v Devonport Royal Dockyard Ltd*[134] the Court of Appeal cited with approval four general and five more specific propositions as to the jurisdiction of adjudicators which had been identified by Jackson J at first instance, at paragraphs 80 and 81 of his judgment. The four general propositions are set out at paragraph 52 of the judgment of Chadwick LJ and have been set out verbatim in paragraph 7.04 above. The five more specific propositions are set out at paragraph 53 of the judgment of Chadwick LJ and have been set out verbatim at paragraphs 3.63 and 3.83 above. At paragraph 84 of his judgment in the Court of Appeal, Chadwick LJ stated that the court was in broad agreement with both those general and more specific propositions, which were indicative of the approach which the courts should adopt when required to address a jurisdictional challenge to the decision of an adjudicator appointed under the 1996 Act. He went on to emphasise in clear terms that the court's approach to enforcement applications must be that, save in rare cases, the decision was to be respected and enforced and that complaints of 'excess of jurisdiction' were unlikely to succeed and were likely only to lead to a substantial waste of time and expense.

7.84

The relevant parts of the judgment of Chadwick LJ serve as a clear summary of the courts' approach to disputes as to jurisdiction. He said this:

7.85

> 85. The objective which underlies the Act and the statutory scheme requires the courts to respect and enforce the adjudicator's decision unless it is plain that the question which he has decided was not the question referred to him or the manner in which he has gone about his task is obviously unfair. It should be only in rare circumstances that the courts will interfere with the decision of an adjudicator. The courts should give no encouragement to the approach adopted by DML in the present case; which (contrary to DML's outline submissions, to which we have referred in paragraph 66 of this judgment) may, indeed, aptly be described as "simply scrabbling around to find some argument, however tenuous, to resist payment".

> 86. It is only too easy in a complex case for a party who is dissatisfied with the decision of an adjudicator to comb through the adjudicator's reasons and identify points upon which to present a challenge under the labels "excess of jurisdiction" or "breach of natural justice". It must be kept in mind that the majority of adjudicators are not chosen for their expertise as lawyers. Their skills are as likely (if not more likely) to lie in other disciplines. The task of the adjudicator is not to act as arbitrator or judge. The time constraints within which he is expected to operate are proof of that. The task of the adjudicator is to find an interim solution which meets the needs of the case. Parliament may be taken to have recognised that, in the absence of an interim solution, the contractor (or sub-contractor) or his sub-contractors will be driven into insolvency through a wrongful withholding of payments properly due. The statutory scheme provides a means of meeting the legitimate cash-flow requirements of contractors and their subcontractors. The need to have the "right" answer has been subordinated to the need to have an answer quickly. The scheme was not

---

[134] [2005] EWCA Civ 1358.

enacted in order to provide definitive answers to complex questions. Indeed, it may be open to doubt whether Parliament contemplated that disputes involving difficult questions of law would be referred to adjudication under the statutory scheme; or whether such disputes are suitable for adjudication under the scheme. We have every sympathy for an adjudicator faced with the need to reach a decision in a case like the present.

87. In short, in the overwhelming majority of cases, the proper course for the party who is unsuccessful in an adjudication under the scheme must be to pay the amount that he has been ordered to pay by the adjudicator. If he does not accept the adjudicator's decision as correct (whether on the facts or in law), he can take legal or arbitration proceedings in order to establish the true position. To seek to challenge the adjudicator's decision on the ground that he has exceeded his jurisdiction or breached the rules of natural justice (save in the plainest cases) is likely to lead to a substantial waste of time and expense—as, we suspect, the costs incurred in the present case will demonstrate only too clearly.

This chapter has dealt with those challenges that might, in the words of Chadwick LJ, be labelled 'excess of jurisdiction'. The next chapter deals with the courts' approach to errors of law and fact and Chapter 9 considers the question of the adjudicator's obligation to follow the rules of natural justice, the other common area of challenge to the adjudicator's decision addressed by Chadwick LJ in *Carillion*.

8

ERRORS OF LAW AND FACT

Introduction	8.01	Errors of Fact	8.18
Errors of Law/General	8.04	'Slips'	8.24
Errors of Law/Jurisdiction	8.14		

'The purpose of the Scheme is to provide a speedy mechanism for settling disputes in construction contracts on a provisional interim basis and by requiring decisions of Adjudicators to be enforced pending final determination of disputes by arbitration, litigation or agreement, whether those decisions are wrong in point of law or fact, if within the terms of the reference. It is a robust and summary procedure and there may be casualties although the determinations are provisional and not final.'

His Honour Judge David Wilcox in
Absolute Rentals Limited v Glencor Enterprises Ltd (2000) CILL 1637

Introduction

The alert reader will have noticed by now that the adjudicator is generally entitled to make errors of law and fact in reaching his decision, and that such errors will not invalidate that decision or render it a nullity.[1] In those circumstances, it may be thought to be superfluous to have a chapter, however short, concerned with errors of law and fact. Despite that, the purpose of this chapter is twofold: first, to demonstrate the sorts of errors which the courts have said that an adjudicator (with the appropriate jurisdiction) is permitted to make; secondly, to identify those errors which might—at least potentially—affect the adjudicator's jurisdiction, and thus render his decision unenforceable.

8.01

---

[1] The basis for the discussion below as to errors of law and fact is that set out in footnote 1 to Chapter 7.

8.02 The starting point for any discussion of this topic is not a case concerned with adjudication at all. In *Nikko Hotels (UK) Ltd v MEPC plc*[2] a rent review case, the lease contained a formula for increasing the rent which necessitated the determination of the average hotel room rate. The independent expert, whose determination of the issue was provided for by the terms of the lease, construed that expression as meaning the average of the published prices at which rooms were said to be available, rather than the average room rate actually achieved. This interpretation of the lease naturally meant that the rate was higher than it would otherwise have been, and the tenants issued an originating summons, alleging that the decision was a nullity because it was based on a misconstruction of the rent review clause. Knox J dismissed the summons and held that the expert's decision was conclusive and could not be reviewed on the grounds that it was erroneous in law, unless it could be shown that the expert had not performed the task that had been given to him. The Judge said that:

> If he has answered the right question in the wrong way, his decision will be binding. If he has answered the wrong question, his decision will be a nullity.

8.03 This passage was cited by Dyson J (as he then was) in *Bouygues (UK) Ltd v Dahl-Jensen (UK) Ltd*[3] who said that there was a reasonably close analogy between expert valuation cases and adjudication cases. When *Bouygues* went to the Court of Appeal,[4] Buxton LJ approved this approach, recording his understanding that this statement was not disputed by Bouygues. Furthermore, that approach was also expressly endorsed by Sir Murray Stuart-Smith in *C & B Scene Concept Design Ltd v Isobars Ltd*[5] who stated in terms that errors of procedure, fact or law were not sufficient to prevent enforcement of an adjudicator's decision by summary judgment. The Court of Appeal made plain in *C & B Scene* that errors of law could not prevent the enforcement of an adjudicator's decision 'unless the Adjudicator has purported to decide matters that are not referred to him'.

Errors of Law/General

8.04 The issue as to whether an adjudicator's error of law invalidated his decision lay at the heart of the first reported adjudication case, *Macob Civil Engineering Ltd v Morrison Construction Ltd*.[6] The defendant contended that the reference to a 'decision' in the 1996 Act meant a lawful and valid decision, so that, where the validity of a decision was challenged, it was not binding and enforceable until it

---

[2] [1991] 2 EGLR 103.
[3] [2000] BLR 49.
[4] [2000] BLR 522.
[5] [2002] BLR 93.
[6] [1999] BLR 93.

had been determined or agreed that the decision was valid. Dyson J rejected that argument; if it were right, he said, it would substantially undermine the effectiveness of the 1996 Act. He said that, on that basis, an unsuccessful party in the adjudication only had to assert some sort of failure on the part of the adjudicator to be able to argue that there had been no proper 'decision', and the enforcement application would fail. The Judge found that the word 'decision' was not qualified, so that 'if his decision on the issue referred to him is wrong, whether because he erred on the facts or the law, or because in reaching his decision he made a procedural error which invalidates the decision, it is still a decision on the issue'. It was this approach which the same Judge reiterated in *Bouygues*, and which was approved by the Court of Appeal in that case. It is also the approach which the Court of Appeal has reiterated in clear terms in *Carillion Construction Ltd v Devonport Royal Dockyard Ltd*.[7] Chadwick LJ's clear warning that the courts will be obliged to enforce the vast majority of the decisions of adjudicators, regardless of so-called errors of law, is set out in paragraphs 85–87 of his judgment in that case, reproduced at paragraph 7.85 above.

8.05 It can, therefore, be said with some confidence that errors of law which do not affect the adjudicator's jurisdiction and do not give rise to some argument as to impartiality or natural justice, will not prevent the enforcement of an adjudicator's decision. Following the decisions in *Macob* and *Bouygues*, it has been rare for it even to be argued that an error of law makes the decision invalid. When the point is canvassed, it is usually by reference to the House of Lords' decision in *Anisminic v Foreign Compensation Commission*.[8] In that case the Foreign Compensation Commission considered and rejected the appellant's claim to be entitled to participate in an Egyptian Compensation Fund. When that decision was challenged in the courts, the Commission contended that the courts had no jurisdiction to entertain the proceedings. This was rejected by the House of Lords. Lord Wilberforce said that, whilst the court had a duty to attribute autonomy of decision to the Commission within the area designated to it, the counterpart of that autonomy was that the courts had to ensure that the limits of the designated area were observed. Lord Reid said that the courts were not prevented from inquiring into whether the order of the Commission was a nullity. In the subsequent House of Lords decision of *O'Reilly v Mackman*,[9] Lord Diplock referred back to the *Anisminic* case to say that the House of Lords had recognised that if a tribunal, whose jurisdiction was limited by statute or subordinate legislation, mistook the law applicable to the facts as it had found them, then it must have asked itself the wrong question and therefore had no jurisdiction.

---

[7] [2005] EWCA Civ 1358; [2006] BLR 15.
[8] [1969] 2 AC 147.
[9] [1983] 2 AC 287.

8.06 It is thought that, on a close analysis, both of these House of Lords' decisions, and the other non-adjudication cases sometimes relied on to suggest that any error of law made by an adjudicator renders his decision a nullity,[10] simply demonstrate that the courts will only interfere in the decisions of an autonomous tribunal where that tribunal has acted outside its jurisdiction. The point made in these cases is that the tribunal may have had the jurisdiction to enter on its inquiry in the first place but, if it did or failed to do something in the course of the inquiry which was of such a nature that it took the tribunal outside its jurisdiction, then the tribunal's subsequent decision would be a nullity. Therefore, as Lord Reid explained in *Anisminic*, there may have been a want of jurisdiction, not at the outset but subsequently, because, for example, the tribunal made a decision which it had no power to make, or it failed in the course of the inquiry to comply with the requirements of natural justice, or it misconstrued the provisions giving it power to act with the result that it failed to deal with the question remitted to it and decided some question which was not remitted to it. Likewise, he said, the tribunal may have refused to take into account something which it was required to take into account, or it may have based its decision on some matter which, under the statutory provisions setting up the tribunal, it had no right to take into account. All of these were ways, according to Lord Reid, in which the prima facie jurisdiction of the tribunal might have been lost as a result of the way in which the tribunal conducted itself.

8.07 Lord Reid concluded his examination of the jurisdiction question in *Anisminic* by saying:

> but if [the tribunal] decides a question remitted to it for decision without committing any of these errors it is as much entitled to decide that question wrongly as it is to decide it rightly.

It is submitted, therefore, that on a careful analysis of *Anisimic* (and the other public law cases), the approach approved by the House of Lords and adopted by the courts to errors of law by an independent or statutory tribunal is very similar to the approach that should be adopted by the courts to errors of law made by an adjudicator, whether appointed under the terms of the contract, or under the 1996 Act. Accordingly, it is suggested that, of themselves, errors of law cannot invalidate the adjudicator's decision or deprive the adjudicator of jurisdiction. The adjudicator is just as entitled to make errors of law as to avoid such errors, when determining the dispute that has been referred to him. The only way in which his decision can be impeached is if he never had the jurisdiction to consider the dispute or, if he had the necessary jurisdiction at the outset as Lord Reid

---

[10] Other cases which have been cited in support of this proposition include *R v Lord President of the Privy Council ex parte Page* [1993] AC 682; *Racal Communications Ltd* [1981] AC 374; *Boddington v B T Police* [1999] AC 143; *R v Wicks* [1998] AC 92.

explained, he did something or failed to do something at some stage during the adjudication itself which took him beyond the proper determination of the dispute which was referred to him.

8.08 The principal case in which it was argued that, on the basis of *Anisminic*, and the other cases noted above, errors of law invalidated the adjudicator's decision, was *London and Amsterdam Properties v Waterman Partnership*.[11] The argument was that the Judge was not bound by *Bouygues* and *C & B Scene* because they were *per incuriam* and in conflict with *Anisminic* and *O'Reilly*. HHJ Wilcox considered those decisions in detail and rejected the submission, finding instead that the adjudication cases, which stressed that an adjudicator could make errors of law, provided that he was answering the question that had been referred to him, were entirely consistent with the approach of the House of Lords in *Anisminic* and *O'Reilly*.

8.09 It might be thought that one of the most fundamental matters in any adjudication would be the issue as to the correct contract terms. However, a potential error by an Adjudicator in ascertaining the correct contract terms will not ordinarily be a matter which goes to his jurisdiction. In *C & B Scene Concept Design Ltd v Isobars Ltd*[12] the adjudicator acceded to the contractor's claim on the basis that the JCT form of contract was incorporated into the agreement between the parties. However, because the parties had not completed the provisions of clause 30 of that standard form, the contractual mechanism fell away and the provisions of the Scheme for Construction Contracts applied instead. Accordingly, the defendant resisted enforcement on the basis that the adjudicator failed to appreciate that the contractual provisions had been superseded by the Scheme, and had therefore exceeded his jurisdiction by addressing himself to the wrong question. At first instance, the Recorder considered that this was an arguable defence, and therefore gave the defendant permission to defend. The Court of Appeal allowed the appeal, concluding that the dispute that was referred to the adjudicator concerned the contractor's entitlement to receive payment pursuant to their applications for interim payment numbered 4, 5 and 6, and that this valuation dispute had been dealt with by the adjudicator on the face of his decision. In order to determine that dispute, the adjudicator had had to resolve, as a matter of law, whether the JCT clauses applied or not and, if they did, what the effect was of a failure to serve a timeous withholding notice by the employer. The Court of Appeal held that the

---

[11] [2004] BLR 179 at paragraphs 191–207 of the judgment. Other cases where the point arose, directly or indirectly, include *Allied London & Scottish Properties PLC v Riverbrae Construction Ltd* [1999] BLR 246; *Ballast Construction Ltd v Burrell Ltd* [2001] BLR 529; *Dean & Dyball v Kenneth Grubb Associates* [2003] BLR 2465; *Gillies Ramsey Diamond v PJW Enterprises* [2003] BLR 48; and *Tim Butler Contractors Ltd v Merewood Homes* [2000] TCC 10/00, a decision of HHJ Gilliland QC.

[12] [2002] BLR 93.

adjudicator had done that too. Even if the adjudicator was wrong as to the applicable contract conditions, the Court of Appeal concluded that such an error did not affect his jurisdiction.

8.10 The opposite factual situation gave rise to the same result in *Allen Wilson Shopfitters v Anthony Buckingham*[13] There, interim payment applications were dealt with by the contract administrator, who issued interim certificates. When the administrator was sacked, the claimant contractors were unsure as to how to put their claim arising out of interim valuations 12 and 13, and in their reference to adjudication, they put the claim by reference to the Scheme for Construction Contracts. The defendant immediately took the point that, by reference to s106 of the 1996 Act, he was not a residential occupier, so the Scheme could not apply. The TCC Judge rejected that argument. He said that the adjudicator derived his jurisdiction from the terms of the contract and the notice of adjudication. The adjudicator's conclusion that the sums claimed in valuations 12 and 13 were due and payable was a conclusion that was within his jurisdiction; any inquiry into the precise status of valuations 12 and 13 was entirely a matter for the adjudicator and, right or wrong, his decision could not be impeached. The Judge referred to and relied on *C & B Scene*, concluding that, on one analysis, the most that could be said was that here the adjudicator had done the exact opposite of what the adjudicator did in *C & B Scene*, because he applied the Scheme rather than the contract payment mechanism. However, the point of principle was precisely the same because, although his choice of payment mechanism may have been incorrect, it could not affect his jurisdiction and he had answered the question that had been referred to him.

8.11 The decisions in *C & B Scene* and *Allen v Buckingham* are, perhaps, to be contrasted with the decision of HHJ Thornton QC in *Joinery Plus Ltd v Laing Ltd*.[14] In that case, there was no dispute that the relevant sub-contract conditions were the DOM/2 conditions. In error, the adjudicator referred throughout his decision to the JCT Works form of sub-contract. The claimant sub-contractor said that, in consequence, the decision was not a decision on the dispute referred to the adjudicator. The Judge acceded to this submission, holding that the decision had every appearance of having been decided by reference to the wrong conditions of contract and without recourse to the correct contractual documentation. Thus he held that the errors went to the heart of his jurisdiction, which was to decide the referred dispute. The errors were fundamental and were not capable of being corrected under his implied power to correct accidental slips. More controversially, the Judge sought to distinguish *C & B Scene* as a case where the correct contract provisions were misconstrued by the adjudicator. On analysis, it is thought

---

[13] [2005] EWHC 1165 (TCC).
[14] [2003] BLR 184.

that this attempt to distinguish *C & B Scene* is rather difficult, since, as the judgment of Sir Murray Stuart-Smith makes plain in *C & B Scene*, the only point available to the defendant was that the adjudicator was applying the JCT contract conditions rather than the Scheme. Accordingly, it is submitted that *Joinery Plus* is perhaps best treated as a case on its own specific facts, where the adjudicator reached a decision on the contract terms that was contrary to the agreed position of both parties. That point certainly did make it different from the situation in *C & B Scene*. Furthermore, all of these cases as to errors in connection with the contract terms must be read in the light of the important decision of the Court of Appeal in *Pegram Shopfitters Ltd v Tally Weijl (UK) Ltd*[15] which is dealt with in detail in paragraphs 8.14–8.16 below.

8.12 Another case in which an error of law was said to go, ultimately, to the adjudicator's jurisdiction, is *Ballast Plc v The Burrell Co (Construction Management) Ltd*.[16] There it appears that the adjudicator concluded that he could not carry out the valuation requested because the parties had departed from the terms of the contract in a number of respects and the variations and waivers meant that he was unable to reach a decision on any sum due. In the words of Lord Reid, it appears that the adjudicator considered that 'it was impossible, as a matter of construction of his powers, for him to take into consideration, within the framework of adjudication, even the possibility that the parties might depart from the terms of the JCT conditions'. Lord Reid considered that that approach was wrong in law and that, given that there were allegations that variations had been instructed otherwise than in the form stipulated in the contract, as well as allegations of bad faith, the adjudicator's error was material. Lord Reid concluded that as a result of that error, the adjudicator misconstrued his powers, and in consequence failed to exercise his jurisdiction to determine the dispute. He therefore concluded that the decision was a nullity.

8.13 However, it follows from the principles noted above that, in the usual case, a losing party will have no grounds for resisting enforcement of an adjudicator's decision if the adjudicator correctly decided not to consider a particular claim or element of the dispute, even if his particular reasons for arriving at that correct decision were, on analysis, plainly wrong. In *Northern Developments Cumbria Ltd v J & J Nichol*[17] the adjudicator had not considered the repudiation claim because he said that such matters did not arise under the contract. HHJ Bowsher QC noted that counsel had accepted that the adjudicator's reasons for rejecting the repudiatory breach issues were wrong in law. However the Judge concluded that the repudiation issues formed no part of the notice of arbitration and therefore

---

[15] [2003] EWCA Civ 1750.
[16] [2001] BLR 529.
[17] [2000] BLR 158.

were not within the adjudicator's jurisdiction in any event. Accordingly, because the adjudicator was quite right to exclude such matters from his consideration (because he had no jurisdiction to consider those issues), his decision could not be impeached, even if his reasons for so doing were accepted as being wrong.

Errors of Law/Jurisdiction

8.14 Although the general position, as explained above, is that an adjudicator can make errors of law which do not affect the validity of his decision, different considerations may apply if those errors of law touch upon the question of the adjudicator's jurisdiction. Reference has already been made in paragraph 8.12 above to the decision in *Ballast PLC v The Burrell Co (Construction Management) Ltd* in which the court ruled that the particular error made by the adjudicator rendered his decision a nullity. In *Pegram Shopfitters Ltd v Tally Wiejl (UK) Ltd* at first instance[18] the claimant commenced adjudication proceedings and an adjudicator was appointed pursuant to the Scheme for Construction Contracts. The adjudicator provided a decision in the claimant's favour. The defendant refused to pay, contending that, if there was a contract, it was not the one found by the adjudicator but one which incorporated the JCT Prime Cost 1998 Conditions. If they were right about that, it meant that the adjudicator had not been validly appointed, because he had been appointed pursuant to the different procedure required by the Scheme for Construction Contracts. If they were wrong about the contract incorporating the JCT conditions, then the defendant said that there was no contract at all. It was therefore argued (as it had been argued before the adjudicator) that the adjudicator did not have the necessary jurisdiction. HHJ Thornton QC found that it was clear from the correspondence and the decision that both parties were contending that there was a written contract in existence and that the defendant was not now permitted to oppose enforcement of the award on the basis that there was in fact no contract. The Judge decided that, if no clear contract terms were identified and agreed, the parties had not produced a contract in accordance with s108, and therefore the Scheme applied. The defendant appealed.

8.15 May LJ gave the principal judgment in the Court of Appeal.[19] He said that it was an over-simplification to say, as the Judge had done, that although it was not clear-cut which set of conditions had been incorporated into the construction contract, there was no dispute between the parties that there was in any event a construction contract of some kind in existence. Instead, as May LJ observed, it was the defendants' crystal clear contention, both before the adjudicator and

---

[18] [2003] BLR 296.
[19] [2003] EWCA Civ 1750.

before the Judge, that if no contract was concluded on the JCT Prime Cost Conditions, there was no contract at all, with the result that the claimant was simply entitled to be paid a reasonable sum for the work that he had carried out. May LJ said that this contention was not a fanciful alternative argument, but was a submission that had a realistic prospect of success. Moreover, this was a material element of the dispute because, if the alternative argument were right and there was no contract, there could be no construction contract in writing from which the adjudicator's jurisdiction could derive, since any contract for payment on a *quantum meruit* basis would not have been a construction contract in writing within s107 of the 1996 Act. May LJ therefore found that the Judge had been wrong to say that both parties agreed that their relationship was governed by a construction contract, and had been wrong to preclude the defendant from contending in the alternative that there was no contract at all. In those circumstances, the Court of Appeal allowed the appeal and set aside the summary judgment on the adjudicator's decision. Although, at paragraph 33 of his judgment, May LJ accepted that the courts should be vigilant to examine jurisdiction arguments to ensure that they were not insubstantial or advanced just for tactical reasons, he stressed that there would be cases where legal principle had to prevail over broad brush policy, and that this was such a case.

8.16 Accordingly, the position appears to be that, where the adjudicator is offered two conflicting sets of contract conditions, each of which comprised a construction contract in writing with either an express or implied series of adjudication provisions, his choice of one set of conditions over the other will usually be regarded by the courts as part and parcel of his answer to the question that he had the jurisdiction to answer, and will not therefore invalidate his decision. If, on the other hand, the adjudicator is given a choice between a contractual situation which would give him jurisdiction, and a contractual situation which would not, then the adjudicator's investigation and ruling on that point is not determinative, and can be reviewed subsequently by the courts. Moreover if, on that review, the court came to the conclusion that the argument in support of the contractual position which would deprive the adjudicator of jurisdiction was not fanciful but instead had a reasonable prospect of success, then the adjudicator's decision would not be summarily enforced.[20]

8.17 It is, however, important to emphasise that the sort of jurisdictional difficulty that arose in *Pegram* will not often arise and, in most cases, even if the court suspects that an adjudicator may have reached the wrong conclusions in law concerning the operation of the contract provisions, such doubts will not result in a failure to enforce the adjudicator's decision. Thus, in *Carl Construction (Scotland) Ltd v Sweeney Civil*

---

20 See also *Thomas-Frederic's Construction Ltd v Keith Wilson* [2003] EWCA Civ 1494.

Engineering (Scotland) Ltd,[21] Lord Caplan commented that he did not find the reasons for the adjudicator's finding (that the payment provisions in the contract were inadequate) to be clearly set out in the decision and felt 'uncomfortable' with the result, but he concluded that these problems represented potential mistakes the adjudicator had made in her treatment of the referral, rather than a venture beyond her jurisdiction. Similarly, in *William Verry Ltd v North West London Communal Mikvar*,[22] at paragraph 40 onwards of his judgment, HHJ Thornton QC identified a series of errors made by the adjudicator in dealing with the matters referred. Somewhat reluctantly, the Judge concluded that the decision should be enforced because it was both valid and enforceable, but he directed that the resulting judgment was not to be drawn up for six weeks from the date of handing down, so that if there was a subsequent adjudication between the parties, dealing with some of the matters omitted by the first adjudicator, one decision could be set against another with only a balancing figure being paid to the net winner. This was certainly a creative way of seeking to do justice between the parties in the light of the court's concerns about the matters which the adjudicator had apparently ignored but, perhaps because such a court-sponsored stay could be seen to be contrary to the required swiftness of the adjudication process, it is not a procedure which has been adopted in other cases.

Errors of Fact

8.18 Perhaps the most glaring error of fact which an adjudicator can commit is to make a decision against a responding party who is not, in fact, a party to the underlying construction contract. There have been a number of decisions on this factual premise, and the TCC judges have adopted a relatively robust approach. Thus, in *A J Brenton T/A Manton Electrical Components v Jack Palmer*,[23] the adjudicator had required the defendant, Mr Palmer, to make a payment to the claimant. On the enforcement application, the defendant contended that the adjudicator had no jurisdiction to make that award because the correct party to the contract was a company called Lords of Princetown Ltd. HHJ Havery QC held that this was a matter that had been raised in the adjudication and the adjudicator had ruled upon it. By reference to the decisions in *Macob* and *Project Consultancy Group v The Trustees of the Grey Trust*[24] Judge Havery concluded that the adjudicator's decision, including his decision as to who was the appropriate party to the contract, and therefore the appropriate party to the adjudication, was a decision which

---

[21] [2001] SCLR 95.
[22] [2004] 1300 EWHC (TCC).
[23] (TCC, 19 January 2001).
[24] [1999] BLR 377.

he was empowered to make under the 1996 Act. If, therefore, the adjudicator had made an error in coming to that decision, it was an error of fact which it was within his jurisdiction to determine. Accordingly Judge Havery concluded that the adjudicator had the necessary jurisdiction to reach his decision, even if he was wrong about the identity of the defendant, and the decision had to be enforced. A similar result occurred in *Nolan Davis Ltd v Stephen Catton*[25] where again the defendant contended that the contract was with one of his companies, rather than with him personally. HHJ Wilcox said that because the adjudicator had ruled on this question and that it was a matter which he had the jurisdiction to decide, the adjudicator's decision should be enforced.

8.19 There is the suggestion that, in his judgment in *Nolan Davis*, Judge Wilcox assumed that, because the question of which party contracted with the claimant was a matter referred to the adjudicator, the parties had in some way agreed to be bound by his decision on that point. For the reasons explored in paragraphs 7.10–7.11 above, that may not be an entirely accurate statement of the law, and it may have been open to the judge to review the adjudicator's determination of that issue. If there had been any doubt about this, the point was confirmed by Simon Brown LJ in *Thomas-Frederic's Construction Ltd v Keith Wilson*.[26] There, he concluded that it was tolerably plain that the adjudicator had reached the wrong conclusion as to the true identity of the contracting parties. However, he made it clear that the adjudicator's decision would still be binding if it could be shown that the parties had agreed to accept his ruling on that point. Since, however, they had not so agreed in *Thomas-Frederic's*, and a respectable case had been made out for disputing the adjudicator's jurisdiction, the decision in that case was not enforced.

8.20 Accordingly, it is submitted that, if the adjudicator makes an error as to the identity of the contracting parties, then the subsequent enforcement of that decision may turn on the nature of the dispute that had originally been referred to him and the strength of the argument to the effect that he had reached a decision against the wrong party. If the parties had agreed to be bound by the adjudicator's decision, or if the adjudicator's ruling on the jurisdictional issue was plainly right, then the decision will be enforced: see *Brenton*, *Nolan Davis*, and paragraph 32 of the judgment of Simon Brown LJ in *Thomas-Frederic's*. If, however, the parties did not agree to be bound by the adjudicator's ruling on the point, and if the defendant raised a respectable case that the adjudicator was wrong as to the identities of the contracting parties, then the decision will not be enforced (see in particular paragraphs 20 and 33 of the judgment of Simon Brown LJ in *Thomas-Frederic's*).

---

[25] (Unreported, 2000 TCC No 590).
[26] [2003] EWCA Civ 1494.

8.21 In the reported cases, the errors of fact made by adjudicators have divided broadly into two categories. First, there are the errors of computation, including circumstances in which the adjudicator has misunderstood precisely what was being claimed. The best-known example of this is *Bouygues*, discussed above. There is usually nothing that a party can do who is on the receiving end of such an error, particularly if it is not accepted as an error by the adjudicator.

8.22 The second category of error which features in the reported authorities concerns the situation where the adjudicator allegedly erred in failing to take into account some particular argument or point. An example of this can be found in *Shimizu Europe Ltd v Automajor Ltd*.[27] In that case, the adjudicator awarded the claiming party £161,996.89 in respect of alleged variations to smoke ventilation works. It appeared that he did so on the basis that the parties had accepted that there could be no challenge to that element of the claim. Following publication of his decision, the defendant complained that it had at no time accepted that the sum claimed in respect of the variations could not be challenged. In the subsequent enforcement proceedings, HHJ Seymour QC had to rule on whether or not the adjudicator had made an error and, if so, whether that affected his jurisdiction. The Judge seemed unimpressed with the suggestion of an error but, in any event, went on to conclude that, even if the adjudicator had made a mistake, it was in connection with a matter relevant, or possibly relevant, to the evaluation of what sum, if any, should be paid by the defendant to the claimant under the contract. It was not a mistake as to what he was being asked to decide. He therefore asked himself the correct question and he answered that question. If he got the answer wrong, because he misunderstood the submissions being made to him, then the proper mechanism for correcting the error would be in the course of the subsequent final account negotiations or in arbitration proceedings. Such an error (if that is what it was) did not permit a challenge to the award on jurisdictional grounds, because the adjudicator had the jurisdiction to make such a mistake.

8.23 The decision in *Shimizu* is also of interest because of the Judge's views on the alternative argument put forward by the claiming party. They contended that, even if the adjudicator had exceeded his jurisdiction in basing his decision on his misunderstanding of the agreed value of the variations, any right which there would otherwise have been on the part of the defendant to raise an objection on this ground had been waived when the defendant made a part-payment of the sum awarded by the adjudicator and/or when the defendant invited him to correct the award as a result of the alleged mistake. Judge Seymour made the point, which can be found in other reported cases,[28] that a party cannot simultaneously

---

[27] [2002] BLR 113.
[28] See, for example, *Redworth Construction Ltd v Brookdale Healthcare Ltd* [2006] EWHC 1994 (TCC) and *RJ Knapman v Richards and Others* [2006] EWHC 2518 (TCC).

approbate and reprobate a decision of the adjudicator. He decided that, by inviting the adjudicator to correct the decision under the slip rule, the defendant's solicitor was accepting that the decision was valid (ie it was one that the adjudicator had the jurisdiction to make). Since the point that they raised as to his alleged error went to the adjudicator's jurisdiction, it followed that, if they were right, the decision, or at least the relevant part of it, was a nullity and there was nothing that needed to be corrected. The Judge therefore expressly accepted the alternative submission that the invitation to the adjudicator to correct the decision under the slip rule was only consistent with the defendant's recognition of it as a valid decision. He reached the same conclusion in respect of the part payment. Thus, it is important for any disgruntled party, who seeks to get the adjudicator to correct his decision, to make sure that, if he does so, he does not waive his right to complain that the adjudicator did not have the necessary jurisdiction to make the decision in the first place.

'Slips'

8.24 What happens when an adjudicator produces a decision which includes an obvious mistake which he then corrects or expresses the desire to correct? Is an adjudicator permitted to correct his decision at all? The answer will always depend on the facts, although much may turn on whether the adjudicator himself acknowledges and accepts that an error has been made, and the promptness of any purported correction.

8.25 The starting point is of course *Bouygues (UK) Ltd v Dahl-Jensen (UK) Ltd*.[29] In that case the adjudicator had calculated a sum in favour of Dahl-Jensen of about £200,000. However, he made a mistake in his calculations by utilising, on one side of the equation, a contract sum which included retention, and deducted money from it which did not include retention. The net effect of the decision was to release all the retention to Dahl-Jensen, even though there was no dispute that Dahl-Jensen were not, at that stage, entitled to that retention. If the calculation had been correctly carried out, the net result would have been a payment in favour of Bouygues of about £140,000 odd. Bouygues' solicitors invited the adjudicator to amend the decision under the slip rule but this was opposed by Dahl-Jensen's solicitors, who claimed that there was no jurisdiction for him to do so. The adjudicator confirmed in writing that he had not made a clerical slip or error. Both Dyson J and the Court of Appeal said that, although they considered that the adjudicator had made an error, it was an error made when he was acting within his jurisdiction. Thus, the decision in *Bouygues* would appear to suggest that, once the

---

[29] First Instance: [2000] BLR 49; Court of Appeal: [2000] BLR 522.

8.26 However, a different result, on superficially similar facts, was reached in *Bloor Construction (UK) Ltd v Bowmer & Kirkland (London) Ltd.*[30] There, the adjudicator identified the sum payable by Bowmer to Bloor, but his original decision failed to deduct the payments on account that had already been made by Bowmer. Within an hour and a half of the production of his first decision, the adjudicator produced a revised decision which took into account the payments on account and effectively determined that Bloor was entitled to no further payment. Bloor's application to enforce the first (and uncorrected) decision was rejected. HHJ Toulmin CMG QC held that the error that had been made was in the category of a slip. He said that, in the absence of any specific agreement to the contrary, a term can and should be implied into the contract referring the dispute to adjudication, to the effect that the adjudicator may, on his own initiative or on the application of a party, correct an error arising from an accidental error or omission. He concluded that parties acting in good faith would be bound to agree at the start of the adjudication that the adjudicator could correct an obvious mistake of the sort which he made in this case.[31] It is submitted that, in circumstances where a clear error has been made, which the adjudicator has corrected within a very short time, without any prejudice to either side, there is room for the implication of the term suggested. It is therefore difficult to disagree with the practical common sense that underpins Judge Toulmin's conclusion.

8.27 Save for one exception, the decision in *Bloor* has not been further considered in other cases. The exception is the decision of Dyson J in *Edmund Nuttall Ltd v Sevenoaks District Council*[32] which was decided shortly after the judgment in *Bloor* had been handed down. Dyson J said that 'putting the matter at its lowest, it is at least arguable that it [the decision in *Bloor*] is right'. Furthermore, it is apparent from other cases that it is a procedure which the parties in adjudication, and adjudicators themselves, regularly adopt in order to correct obvious errors. It may be that the point has not been further challenged because everyone with experience of the UK adjudication industry accepts that, in certain circumstances, Judge Toulmin's mechanism, first outlined in *Bloor*, is a useful way of avoiding even temporary injustice.

---

[30] [2000] BLR 314.
[31] The judge's reasoning relied on a number of cases as to accidental slips or omissions, including *The Montan* [1985] 1 Lloyd's Rep 189 and *R v Cripps ex parte Muldoon* [1984] QB 686 and *King v Thomas McKenna Ltd* [1991] 1 All ER 653.
[32] Unreported 14 April 2000.

Errors of Law and Fact

8.28 Thus in *Cubitt Building & Interiors Ltd v Fleetglade Ltd*[33] the adjudicator's decision was completed on the final day of the extended period and provided to the parties halfway through the following day. The TCC Judge concluded that such a decision was not a nullity, although it was communicated to the parties at the very last moment. The Judge noted that, following representations from the parties, the adjudicator had corrected that decision by deducting a figure of £5,000 which had been included twice. Neither party took the point that this sensible correction of the original decision was outside the adjudicator's jurisdiction.[34]

8.29 However, it should be emphasised that the rule in *Bloor* will be of limited application, and in particular can probably apply only in those circumstances where the adjudicator has himself admitted that there was an obvious error and sought to correct it. In *CIB Properties Ltd v Birse Construction Ltd*[35] HHJ Toulmin QC held that, in cases involving a slip or alleged slip, there were two questions. Firstly, was the adjudicator prepared to acknowledge that he had made a mistake and correct it? Secondly, was the mistake a genuine slip which failed to give effect to his first thoughts? It was only if the answer to both those questions was yes that, subject to the important considerations as to the time within which the correction was made, and questions of prejudice, the court could give effect to the amendment to rectify the slip if the justice of the case required it. On the facts of *CIB*, the Judge refused to extend the principle to circumstances where the adjudicator declined to make any correction, although he had made a reference to the impending review of his decision by the court. Judge Toulmin concluded that, even if the adjudicator had invited the court to carry out a review of his lengthy decision, the court should decline to do so. In any event, the Judge concluded that there had in fact been no slip at all and that the adjudicator's decision was explicable by the figures set out in his conclusion. Accordingly, in that case, the 'slip' point failed.

8.30 One final word of warning is appropriate regarding the rule in *Bloor*. As noted in paragraph 8.23 above, a party who seeks to persuade the adjudicator to correct an error under the so-called 'slip' rule must be satisfied that, without the error, the adjudicator had the jurisdiction to make the decision which he has just communicated to the parties. If he fails to make this distinction plain, the party seeking the correction runs the risk that by requesting the change he is accepting the validity of the decision and waiving any right to challenge the decision on jurisdictional grounds, as was found to have occurred in *Shimizu*.[36]

---

[33] [2006] EWHC 3413 (TCC); 110 Con LR 36.
[34] Despite the fact that a slip rule has developed in practice, the DTI 2nd Consultation Report suggests that the 1996 Act should be amended to provide expressly for the correction of errors: see paragraphs 19.31–19.32 below.
[35] [2004] EWHC 2365 (TCC); [2005] 1 WLR 2252.
[36] [2002] BLR 113.

9

FAIRNESS

Introduction	9.01	Taking Advice from Others	9.30
Fairness/General	9.02	Indication of Preliminary View	9.33
Size/Nature of Claim	9.04	Ambush	9.36
Bias	9.11	Effect of Earlier Adjudications	9.38
Natural Justice/General	9.16	Miscellaneous	9.42
Natural Justice/Specific Instances	9.23	**Human Rights**	9.44
Separate Communications with the Parties	9.23	**Unfair Terms in Consumer Contracts Regulations**	9.49
Failure to Consult	9.26		

'It is now well established that the purpose of adjudication is not to be thwarted by an overly sensitive concern for procedural niceties...Adjudication under the 1996 Act is necessarily crude in its resolution of disputes . . . It is now clear that the construction industry regards adjudication not simply as a staging post towards the final resolution of the dispute in arbitration or litigation but as having in itself considerable weight and impact that in practice goes beyond the legal requirement that the decision has for the time being to be observed. Lack of impartiality or fairness in adjudication must be considered in that light. . . . It has become all the more necessary that, within the rough nature of the process, decisions are still made in a basically fair manner so that the system itself continues to enjoy the confidence it now has apparently earned. . . . However the time limits, the nature of the process and the ultimately non-binding nature of the decision, all mean that the standard required in practice is not that which is expected of an arbitrator.'

His Honour Judge Humphrey Lloyd QC in *Balfour Beatty Construction Ltd v The Mayor & Burgesses of the London Borough of Lambeth* [2002] EWHC 597 (TCC).

Introduction

9.01 In his judgment in *Carillion Construction Ltd v Devonport Royal Dockyard Ltd*[1] Chadwick LJ said that it was only too easy in a complex case for a party who was dissatisfied with the adjudicator's decision to comb through his reasons and identify points upon which to present a challenge under the labels 'excessive jurisdiction' or 'breach of natural justice'. He went on to say that to seek to challenge the adjudicator's decision on either of these grounds was likely, save in the plainest cases, to lead to a substantial waste of time and expense. The specific warning in relation to allegations of unfairness echoed that of Dyson LJ in *AMEC v Whitefriars*,[2] who said that it will only be in the rarest cases that a court will refuse to enforce an adjudicator's decision because there was a real risk that the adjudicator was either biased or failed to act impartially.

Fairness/General

9.02 The mere fact that the decision itself might be unfair is not a ground for resisting enforcement. This is a fundamental principle of adjudication enforcement. The best example of this is still *Bouygues (UK) Ltd v Dahl-Jensen (UK) Ltd*,[3] where the adjudicator's error was not in respect of a small sum; the retention fund was in the region of £350,000, with the result that the adjudicator erroneously awarded a sum to Dahl-Jensen when, had he made the proper deduction for retention, a similar sum would in fact have been due to Bouygues. Despite all of that, the Court of Appeal ruled that, because the adjudicator had the jurisdiction to reach that decision, the unfair result would not prevent enforcement of the decision.

9.03 It is submitted that the nature of the adjudication process carries with it a risk of unfairness, both in respect of the way in which the adjudication is conducted, and in the result. There are two particular reasons for this. The first, of course, is the speed with which an adjudication has to be completed. In such circumstances, with the need to have the 'right' answer subordinated to the need to have an answer quickly,[4] there will always be a greater risk that both the process and its end product will or might be unfair. Secondly, under the Scheme and many of the standard forms of contract, the adjudicator is entitled to 'take the initiative in

---

[1] [2005] EWCA Civ 1358. The relevant comments are cited at paragraph 7.85 above.
[2] [2004] EWCA Civ 1418.
[3] 1st Instance: [2000] BLR 49; Court of Appeal: [2000] BLR 522.
[4] See paragraph 86 of the judgment of Chadwick LJ in *Carillion Construction v Devonport Royal Dockyard Ltd* [2005] EWCA Civ 1358.

ascertaining the facts and the law necessary to determine the dispute'.[5] Most adjudicators are not lawyers. Thus there is the risk that the adjudicator, in taking the initiative as he is entitled to do, will adopt a procedure that is or might be unfair. Provided that it can be shown that, within the limitations of the adjudication process, the adjudicator acted generally in accordance with the usual rules relating to bias and natural justice, his decision is likely to be enforced. The potential limitations on the adjudicator's role as an inquisitor rather than a referee are identified in paragraphs 17.28–17.29 below.

Size/Nature of Claim

9.04 One constant feature of adjudication disputes, which in a number of the reported cases sits like the proverbial elephant in the room, obvious to all and mentioned by no-one, concerns the use of the adjudication process for complex factual and legal disputes and multi-million pound final account claims. The (usually) unexpressed concerns to which this situation gives rise are obvious: adjudication was intended for simple, straightforward, singular disputes which could be properly dealt with and decided within 28 days; the adjudication process was not designed for the consideration of complicated, multi-million pound claims which rely on scores of lever arch files, which have taken the claiming party months to prepare, and which the responding party is then obliged to deal with in a matter of days, in order to allow the adjudicator sufficient time to consider both the claim and the response, and then provide his (lengthy) decision in writing. It might be said with some force that such a situation was not what the framers of the 1996 Act had in mind when creating the adjudication process, and that the use of the adjudication process to resolve such claims is demonstrably wrong and unfair.[6] The complaint is, therefore, that the mere reference of such a claim to adjudication is unfair, and any decision resulting from such an adjudication must be unfair, and unenforceable.

9.05 In *London & Amsterdam Properties v Waterman Partnership Ltd*[7] HHJ Wilcox said, at paragraph 146 of his judgment, that there may be some disputes, particularly arising at the end of a project, which are too complex to permit a fair adjudication process within the time limits of the scheme. On the facts of that case, he refused to enforce the adjudicator's decision, but that refusal was apparently based not on

---

[5] See Part 1, paragraph 13 of the Scheme for Construction Contracts.
[6] It is noteworthy that, at the end of his lengthy judgment in *Carillion* explaining how and why the adjudicator's decision should be enforced, Chadwick LJ doubted whether 'Parliament contemplated that disputes involving difficult questions of law would be referred to adjudication under the statutory scheme; or whether such disputes are suitable for adjudication under the scheme'.
[7] [2004] BLR 179.

the grounds of complexity, but instead on the specific ground that material had been served late upon the responding party which they had not had an opportunity to address. There was therefore a triable issue as to whether the adjudicator had acted impartially. Similarly, in *AWG Construction Services Ltd v Rockingham Motor Speedway Ltd*[8] HHJ Toulmin CMG QC, at paragraph 123 of his judgment, raised the possibility that there may be disputes which are so complex, and the advantages so weighted against a defendant, that there was a conflict between the adjudicator's duty to provide a decision and his duty to act impartially. Again, however, the Judge refused to enforce the adjudicator's decision, not on this ground, but on the alternative basis that the adjudicator's decision dealt with and relied on matters which were not properly the subject of the notice of adjudication, and that there had been a serious procedural failure, in that AWG did not have a sufficient opportunity to consider the new issues and new material belatedly introduced by the referring party.

9.06 A case in which the size and the nature of the claim was at the forefront of the challenge to the adjudicator's ultimate decision was *CIB Properties Ltd v Birse Construction Ltd*.[9] There, the first adjudicator decided in August 2002 that CIB had been entitled to terminate Birse's contract. Almost a year later, in July 2003, CIB demanded consequential payment in a sum in excess of £16.6 million. The claim was referred to adjudication in November 2003, and consisted of about 50 lever arch files. During the adjudication, both Birse and CIB provided extensive further disclosure of documents so that, in the end, there was something like 150 lever arch files relevant to the adjudication. The adjudicator's time for reaching a decision was extended on a number of occasions and the decision itself was not provided until 24 February 2004, when CIB were awarded £2,164,892 out of a claim for approximately £16 million. One of the grounds for the challenge to the adjudicator's decision was that the size and complexity of the dispute made it impossible for it to be resolved fairly by adjudication.

9.07 Judge Toulmin CMG QC said that the test was not whether the dispute was too complicated to refer to adjudication, but whether the adjudicator was able to reach a fair decision within the time limits allowed by the parties. The Judge concluded that the adjudicator was able to reach such a decision, notwithstanding the size and complexity of the claim and the supporting documentation. He concluded that the adjudicator was, at all stages, careful to consider how he could conduct the adjudication fairly and he succeeded in doing so, discharging fully his duty not only to act fairly but to reach a fair determination on the evidence. At all times the adjudicator gave the parties a fair opportunity to deploy their cases

---

[8] [2004] EWHC 888 (TCC).
[9] [2004] EWHC 2365 (TCC); [2005] 1 WLR 2252.

before him. The size and nature of a claim, the Judge said,[10] was only relevant if it meant that the adjudicator could not discharge his duty to reach a decision impartially and fairly within the time limit. On the facts of *CIB*, the adjudicator had been able to discharge that duty. It should also be noted that this was a case where the responding party had agreed to various extensions of time to the statutory period in which the decision had to be completed. As Judge Toulmin makes plain, a responding party is not bound to agree to extend time beyond the time limits laid down in the 1996 Act, even if such a refusal renders the adjudicator's task impossible, as would apparently have been the position in *CIB*.

9.08 It is not uncommon for contractors and sub-contractors to identify, as the single dispute with which they want the adjudicator to deal, their final account claim. It is sometimes thought that a claiming party has a distinct advantage in adopting the adjudication procedure to pursue such a final account claim or (which is just as common) the claim based upon his last interim application for payment. Whilst the claiming party might have spent weeks and months preparing his final account claim, or last interim application, an adjudication reference following hard on the heels of the submission of the claim itself would allow the responding party little time to deal with the detail. Again, the authorities demonstrate that, provided that the claim can be dealt with fairly by the adjudicator, the adoption of such a procedure will not, of itself, be regarded as unfair.

9.09 However, the adjudication process can involve significant risks to the referring party just as much as to the responding party. For example, in *William Verry (Glazing Systems) Ltd v Furlong Homes Ltd*.[11] Furlong, the main contractor, had its own reasons for thinking that it was to its advantage to refer to adjudication the entirety of its sub-contractor (Verry's) final account claim. This had the effect of requiring the adjudicator, during the statutory 28 days, to reach decisions about disputed variations, extensions of time, loss and expense, and liquidated damages—in other words, all the potential disputes which can arise under a building contract. The TCC Judge described that as a 'kitchen sink' final account adjudication. The result rebounded on Furlong, because the adjudicator's decision was not in its favour and instead found sums and an extension of time due to Verry which Furlong had opposed. As the Judge said, 'a referring party should think very carefully before using the adjudication process to try and obtain some sort of perceived tactical advantage in final account negotiations and, in so doing, squeezing a wide-ranging final account dispute into a procedure for which it is fundamentally unsuited'. Another, related point that arose in *Verry* stemmed from the adjudicator's comment in his decision that there had been so much material provided

---

[10] See paragraph 199 of his judgment.
[11] [2005] EWHC 138 (TCC).

to him that, in the timescale required by adjudication, even with the extensions of time that had been granted to him, it had not been possible for him to make a full analysis of that evidence, of the kind that would have been appropriate in litigation or arbitration. The Judge accepted the proposition that, if an adjudicator runs out of time and cannot produce a fair decision within the statutory time limit, he should say so, and not go on to reach an unfair decision. However the Judge also concluded that, on the facts in *Verry*, the adjudicator had patently not reached an unfair result, and his comment about the absence of a full analysis was merely demonstrative of the difference between the speedy adjudication process and the more considered (and slower) business of arbitration or litigation. It was held that the adjudicator had produced a detailed and painstaking decision which properly reflected all the material with which he had been provided.

9.10 Accordingly, although it is a complaint that has arisen from time to time, there is no reported case in which the court has concluded that the claim advanced in the adjudication was so complicated and/or so large that, for that reason alone, it was inherently unsuitable for the adjudication process from the outset. Although that has not stopped the courts from questioning whether adjudication was appropriate for such disputes, validity and enforcement would appear always to boil down to whether or not the adjudicator had been able to deal fairly with the dispute referred to him.

Bias

9.11 The leading case on the appropriate test for bias was set out by Lord Phillips of Worth Matravers in *In Re Medicaments*.[12] After considering a number of recent decisions on the point, including the House of Lords in *R v Gough*[13] and *Locabail v Bayfield*[14] Lord Phillips said:

> 'The court must first ascertain all the circumstances which have a bearing on the suggestion that the judge was biased. It must then ask whether those circumstances would lead a fair-minded and informed observer to conclude that there was a real possibility, or a real danger, the two being the same, that the tribunal was biased.'[15]

He went on to say that the material circumstances would include any explanation given by the judge/tribunal under review as to his knowledge or appreciation of those circumstances. Where that explanation was accepted by the complainant,

---

[12] [2001] 1 WLR 700 at 726, 727.
[13] [1993] AC 646.
[14] [2000] QB 451.
[15] See also **Director** *General of Fair Trading v Proprietary Association of Great Britain* [2000] All ER (D) **2425**.

it could be treated as accurate. Where it was not accepted, it became one further matter to be considered from the viewpoint of the fair-minded observer. The court did not have to rule whether the explanation should be accepted or rejected. Rather it had to decide whether or not the fair-minded observer would consider that there was a real danger of bias, notwithstanding the explanation that had been advanced.

9.12 The first adjudication case to consider questions of apparent bias was actually decided before *In Re Medicaments*. In that case, *Glencot Development v Ben Barrett*[16] HHJ Lloyd QC applied the test in *R v Gough*, holding that the views of the person against whom the allegation of bias had been made were either irrelevant and/or not determinative of the issue; what mattered was whether the circumstances would lead a fair-minded and informed observer to conclude that there was a real possibility, or a real danger, that the tribunal was biased. In that case, the adjudicator was also asked to mediate between the parties in respect of a specific point as to the applicability of a discount. However, when it became apparent that other elements of the claim were also not agreed, the adjudicator again purported to act as a mediator to try and resolve those elements too, and arranged separate meetings with those acting for each side. He subsequently produced a decision in the adjudication, the validity of which was challenged. The Judge concluded that the adjudicator's participation in these separate discussions would lead a fair-minded observer to conclude that there was a real possibility of bias on his part. The adjudicator went to and fro between the parties, speaking to them privately, and there was nothing to indicate what he had said, heard or learnt. He was under no strict obligation to report such matters to the parties as the meetings continued, and since everything was without prejudice anyway, there could be no inquiry into what had happened. As the Judge pointed out, a private discussion with one party could have conveyed material or impressions which subsequently influenced the adjudicator's decision, and the other party would have had no opportunity to deal with such matters at all; in fact, that other party would not even know what they were. The decision was therefore not enforced.

9.13 There are particular problems when the same adjudicator acts in a number of different adjudications involving the same parties and the same contract. In *R G Carter Ltd v Edmund Nuttall Ltd (No 2)*[17] an adjudicator, in his fourth decision arising out of the same contract, concluded that a substantial sum of money was due to be paid by Carter to Nuttall. There were disputed enforcement proceedings which led to HHJ Seymour QC's conclusion that the adjudicator did

---

[16] [2001] BLR 207.
[17] [2002] BLR 359.

not have jurisdiction, so that the fourth decision was unenforceable.[18] On the same day that Judge Seymour concluded that the decision in Nuttall's favour was not to be enforced, Carter gave notice of a fifth adjudication between the parties and sought the appointment of a different adjudicator from the adjudicator whose decision had just been held to have been made without jurisdiction. However, despite this, the same adjudicator was appointed for the fifth adjudication. Carter made an application to set aside the appointment on the basis that the adjudicator was prejudiced as a result of the previous adjudication. The application was refused. HHJ Bowsher QC rejected the suggestion that the adjudicator's mind had been poisoned by deciding the earlier dispute in excess of his jurisdiction. He said that he did not see that the fair-minded and informed observer could or would think that the adjudicator was biased or acted unfairly in proceeding with the fourth, nor with the fifth, adjudication. He rejected the criticisms of the adjudicator as not being in any way justified.

9.14 A similar result occurred in *Michael John Construction Ltd v Richard Henry Golledge and others*,[19] dealt with in detail at paragraph 7.76 above. Given that the defendants in that case never made any submissions at all about valuation in the second adjudication, but limited themselves entirely to ill-founded criticisms relating to jurisdiction and fairness, it was unsurprising that the adjudicator reached the same decision on the figures as he had reached in the first adjudication. The TCC Judge rejected the allegation of bias and enforced the decision.

9.15 One of the points made by the Judge in *Michael John Construction* was that it was wrong to say that the mere fact that an adjudicator had already decided earlier issues was enough to justify a conclusion of apparent bias in a subsequent adjudication. In that, he was following the important decision of the Court of Appeal in *AMEC Projects Ltd v Whitefriars City Estates Ltd*.[20] In that case, a Mr B was appointed as adjudicator but the court ruled that his decision was a nullity because the contract had identified somebody entirely different to act as the adjudicator. There was then a second notice of adjudication. On the discovery that the named adjudicator in the contract had died, Mr B was again appointed as adjudicator in the second adjudication. At first instance, the Judge decided that, in all the circumstances of the case, there was an apparent risk of bias and failed to enforce his decision. That conclusion was overturned by the Court of Appeal. Dyson LJ said that the mere fact that the tribunal had previously decided the issue was not of itself sufficient to justify a conclusion of apparent bias and that something more was required. Furthermore, if the second adjudication was a re-run of the first,

---

[18] See the first *Carter v Nuttall* decision at [2002] BLR 312, referred to at paragraph 7.50 above.
[19] [2006] EWHC 71 (TCC).
[20] [2004] EWCA Civ 1418; [2005] BLR 1.

it would be unrealistic, indeed absurd, to expect the adjudicator to ignore his earlier decision and not to be inclined to come to the same conclusion as before, particularly if the previous decision was carefully reasoned. The vice which the law had to guard against was that the adjudicator might approach the re-hearing with a closed mind. Provided, however, it can be demonstrated that he did not, there was no apparent bias inherent in an adjudicator reconsidering a question that he had previously considered but which, for some jurisdictional reason, led to an unenforceable decision. In addition, Dyson LJ rejected the contention that there was a risk of bias because Amec's solicitor had indicated to the adjudicator that the reason why the dispute was being referred to Mr B was his familiarity with the facts, which would save time and costs. As Dyson LJ pointed out, even if he had not been given this reason, he would have been likely to infer that that was indeed the reason for the reference back to him.

Natural Justice/General

9.16 Many of the standard form contracts, and the Scheme for Construction Contracts, expressly require the adjudicator to act impartially. The authorities make clear that this is broadly synonymous with acting without bias (see above) and in accordance with the rules of natural justice. Thus the expressions 'impartial' and 'in accordance with natural justice' have been used synonymously in the reported cases.

9.17 There was originally some doubt as to whether the rules of natural justice applied to adjudications. It will be recalled that, in *Macob Civil Engineering Ltd v Morrison Construction Ltd* [21] Dyson J said that a decision could not be impeached, even if the adjudicator 'in reaching his decision . . . made a procedural error which invalidates the decision' provided that he had the jurisdiction to do so. The fact that a procedural error would not invalidate the decision was echoed by Sir Murray Stuart-Smith in *C & B Scene*[22] when he said at paragraph 26 that 'errors of procedure . . . are not sufficient to prevent enforcement of an adjudicator's decision by summary judgment'. In consequence of these comments, it was argued in some quarters that the adjudicator could act in breach of natural justice with impunity, and his decision would still be enforced.

9.18 This argument was expressly rejected by HHJ Bowsher QC in *Discain Project Services Ltd v Opecprime Development Ltd*.[23] Having said, at paragraph 31 of his judgment, that he was not sure what was meant by the word 'procedural' in Dyson J's

---

[21] [1999] BLR 93.
[22] [2002] BLR 93.
[23] [2001] BLR 287.

judgment, he went on to say that he certainly rejected any submission that Dyson J was holding that the rules of natural justice did not apply to adjudication.[24] He also rejected the submission that a breach of natural justice was to be regarded as a 'procedural error':

> 'One can test that proposition by thinking the unthinkable, going to an extreme and asking what would be the approach if it were shown that an adjudicator refused to read the written submissions of one party because they were typed with single rather than double spacing. It would never happen. But if it did, his decision would not be enforced. So there must be some breaches of natural justice that would persuade the court not to enforce the decision of an adjudicator. How is that line to be drawn?'[25]

The Judge referred to the decision of HHJ Lloyd QC in *Glencot Development and Design Co Ltd v Ben Barratt & Sons (Contractors) Ltd*[26] where the Judge had said that it was accepted that the adjudicator 'has to conduct the proceedings in accordance with the rules of natural justice or as fairly as the limitations imposed by Parliament permit'. Judge Bowsher expressly agreed with that statement.

9.19 Judge Bowsher's judgment in *Discain*, referred to above, was actually his second judgment on the issues created in that adjudication, reached after a full trial. The trial arose because of the Judge's earlier decision to refuse summary judgment, in the course of which he also considered the applicability of the rules of natural justice within the limited timescale of the average adjudication. In the judgment in which he gave the defendant permission to defend, he said:[27]

> '... I do understand that adjudicators have great difficulties in operating this statutory scheme, and I am not in any way detracting from the decision in *Macob*. It would be quite wrong for parties to search around for breaches of the rules of natural justice. It is a question of fact and degree in each case... The Scheme [for Construction Contracts] makes regard for the rules of natural justice more rather than less important. Because there is no appeal on fact or law from the adjudicator's decision, it is all the more important that the manner in which he reaches his decision should be beyond reproach. At the same time, one has to recognise that the adjudicator is working under pressure of time and circumstance which make it extremely difficult to comply with the rules of natural justice in the manner of a court or an arbitrator. Repugnant as it may be to one's approach to judicial decision making, I think that the system created by the [1996] Act can only be made to work in practice if some

---

[24] See Chapter 2 above.
[25] Judge Bowsher also quoted with approval an article by Mr Ian Duncan Wallace QC in the Construction Law Journal (2000) 16 Const LJ 102 in which the author said that it was a 'startling proposition' that an adjudicator's decision, if arrived at in serious breach of a principle of natural justice, 'must as a matter of law nevertheless be enforced in circumstances where payment under an invalid decision could easily turn out to be irretrievable and precipitate to the insolvency of the party affected...'
[26] [2001] BLR 207.
[27] [2000] BLR 402.

breaches of the rules of natural justice which have no demonstrable consequence are disregarded.'

Although this formulation has been the subject of minor refinement in subsequent cases, it is submitted that it still remains the most practical guide, for parties and adjudicators alike, as to the requirement to act in accordance with natural justice to the extent that, within the constraints of adjudication, such conduct is possible. It was cited with approval by HHJ LLoyd QC in *Balfour Beatty Construction Ltd v The Mayor and Burgesses of the London Borough of Lambeth*[28] where he stressed that the purpose of adjudication is not to be thwarted 'by an overly sensitive concern for procedural niceties'. He also said that, where the complaint was that some important material was not drawn to the attention of the parties by the adjudicator prior to the eventual decision, that material had to be either decisive or of considerable potential importance to the outcome and not peripheral or irrelevant. He reiterated, however, that, within the rough nature of the process, decisions still had to be made in a basically fair manner so that the whole process of adjudication continued to enjoy the confidence which it had now earned.[29] The facts of this important case are analysed in greater detail in paragraph 9.27 below.

9.20 In *RSL (Southwest) Ltd v Stansell Ltd*.[30] it was argued that the adjudicator's decision was not binding because it had been reached in breach of the rules of natural justice. Stansell's complaint was that the adjudicator had failed to give the parties an opportunity to comment upon the report, which the adjudicator himself had commissioned, and which dealt with the delay and loss and expense claims that lay at the heart of the adjudication. RSL argued that there can have been no breach of the rules of natural justice because the report was not made available to them either. HHJ Seymour QC said this:

> 'The introduction of systems of adjudication has undoubtedly brought many benefits to the construction industry in this country, but at a price. The price, which Parliament, and to a large extent the industry, has considered justified, is that the procedure adopted in the interests of speed is inevitably somewhat rough and ready and carries with it the risk of significant injustice. That risk can be minimised by adjudicators maintaining a firm grasp upon the principles of natural justice and applying them without fear or favour. The risk is increased if attempts are made to explore the boundaries of the proper scope and function of adjudication with a view to commercial advantage . . . The duty to act impartially is, in its essence, a duty to observe the rules of natural justice. It is not simply a duty not to show bias.'

---

[28] [2002] EWHC 597 (TCC).
[29] Other cases where the courts have summarised the general applicability of the rules of natural justice to the adjudication process include *AWG Construction Services Ltd v Rockingham Motor Speedway Ltd* [2004] EWHC 888 (TCC); and *Palmac v Park Lane Estates* [2005] EWHC 919 (TCC).
[30] [2003] EWHC 1390 (TCC).

The Judge concluded that the adjudicator should not have had any regard to the final report that he had commissioned without giving both parties the chance to consider the contents of that report and to comment upon it. If an extension of time was necessary to allow such a process, then the adjudicator should have explained that to the parties and sought their consent to such an extension. This case is analysed further in paragraph 9.28 below.

9.21 The point made by Judge Lloyd in *Balfour Beatty*, to the effect that it must be demonstrated that the alleged breach of the rules of natural justice was significant and/or causative of potential prejudice has been emphasised in four later cases. The first was *Carillion Construction Ltd v Devonport Royal Dockyard Ltd*.[31] At first instance, Jackson J had concluded that an adjudicator's decision to decline to consider evidence which, on his analysis of the facts and/or the law, was irrelevant, was not a breach of the rules of natural justice. That conclusion was expressly approved by the Court of Appeal.[32] Furthermore in *Kier Regional Ltd (t/a Wallis) v City & General (Holborn) Ltd*[33] the same Judge reached the same conclusion despite the fact that he saw 'considerable force' in the contention that the adjudicator ought to have taken into account two experts' reports which he had declined to read, on the basis that they had not been available to the contract administrator when he had produced the relevant evaluation. However, Jackson J went on to say that it was unnecessary for him to decide that point, because the error allegedly made by the adjudicator was not one which could invalidate his decision. He found that, on the basis of the adjudicator's decision as a whole, he had considered each of the arguments advanced by City & General in its written response. At worst, that was an error of law which caused him to disregard two pieces of relevant evidence but, in the light of the decision of the Court of Appeal in *Carillion*[34] that error would not render the adjudicator's decision invalid. The other two recent cases on this point, *Ardmore Construction Limited v Taylor Woodrow Construction Ltd*[35] and *Humes Building Contracts Ltd v Charlotte Homes (Surrey) Ltd*,[36] are both addressed at paragraph 9.34 below.

9.22 Accordingly, it is safe to conclude that, whilst an argument that the adjudicator has failed to comply with the rules of natural justice will be considered with a certain amount of scepticism by the court,[37] where elementary and basic principles of natural justice have not been observed, with a resulting serious effect upon the

---

[31] [2005] EWHC 778 (TCC).
[32] See paragraph 84 of the judgment of Chadwick LJ.
[33] [2006] EWHC 848 (TCC).
[34] [2005] EWCA Civ 1358.
[35] [2006] CSOH 3, Opinion of Lord Clarke.
[36] 4.1.07, a decision of HHJ Gilliland QC, sitting at the TCC in Salford.
[37] A recent example of this approach can be found in the decision of HHJ Wilcox in *South West Contractors Limited v Birakos Enterprises Limited* [2006] EWHC 2794 (TCC) where the Judge

decision in question, the courts will be prepared to refuse to enforce summarily that decision. Due allowance will be given to the adjudicator's obligation to take the initiative to find the relevant facts and the law, and the constraints of the tight timetable in which he is operating. Furthermore, any prima facie failure to comply with the rules of natural justice must be causative and/or significant. It is not enough for there to be a breach of the rules; that breach must have had a significant and detrimental effect on the complaining party and the outcome of the adjudication. In short, the alleged breach must be both obvious and important. It is therefore instructive now to go on to consider some specific instances in which the courts have considered an alleged failure to comply with the rules of natural justice.

Natural Justice/Specific Instances

Separate Communications with the Parties

9.23 An adjudicator must take care not to engage in separate dealings with the parties unless, for some reason, it is unavoidable. Over the course of many years, arbitrators have developed procedural systems so as to ensure that they only speak to the representatives of one party in the presence of the representatives of the other party, and that any correspondence which they receive from one party is immediately copied to the other. An adjudicator must adopt the same procedures. Importantly, an adjudicator must not endeavour to confuse his role as adjudicator with the very different role of a mediator. The two forms of dispute resolution are, bluntly, incompatible. Mediators can, and often will, have closed meetings with one side before going on to have a similar meeting with the other. Such a procedure has no place in adjudication, which is designed to replicate, in miniature and at very high speed, an arbitration or a court case.

9.24 It is, perhaps, a matter of surprise that a number of adjudicators have endeavoured to conduct adjudications in clear breach of these relatively simple guidelines. Thus, in *Glencot Development & Design Co Ltd v Ben Barratt & Son (Contractors) Ltd*[38] the adjudicator endeavoured to act as both an adjudicator and a mediator, and purported to hold discussions with the parties separately. HHJ Lloyd QC concluded that, in going to and fro between the parties, and having separate discussions with them, the adjudicator had failed to act in accordance with the rules of natural justice. Similarly, in *Woods Hardwick Ltd v Chiltern Air-Conditioning Ltd*[39] the adjudicator, on his own initiative, consulted representatives of Woods

---

reiterated that it was 'not permissible for this court to minutely examine the reasons for an award to see if an adjudicator might have made a mistake'.

[38] [2001] BLR 207: see paragraph 9.12 above.
[39] [2001] BLR 23.

Hardwick, and with Chiltern's sub-contractors, without informing Chiltern either that he had obtained information from those sources, or telling them the content of that information. HHJ Thornton QC considered that the failure to make available to both parties the information obtained by him from Woods Hardwick and the sub-contractors meant that he had not acted impartially and he declined to enforce the decision. The adjudicator compounded the difficulties by providing a witness statement which sought to argue Woods Hardwick's case in favour of enforcement, and purported to elaborate on his reasons for making adverse findings against Chiltern.

9.25 However, it will not always be the case that separate discussions will result in a finding that the adjudicator has acted in breach of natural justice. It may depend on the terms of the particular contract in question. In *Dean & Dyball Construction Ltd v Kenneth Grubb Associates Ltd*[40] the adjudication had been conducted in accordance with the CIC Model Adjudication Procedure which expressly permitted separate interviews with the parties and their respective experts. HHJ Seymour QC concluded that natural justice did not necessarily require that the evidence from witnesses of one party had to be taken in the presence of the opposite party or its representatives, provided that the tribunal taking evidence indicated to the opposite party what that evidence was, and gave that other party an opportunity to deal with the evidence, particularly in respect of matters to which the tribunal was minded to attribute importance. Although the Judge said that he had grave difficulty in seeing that adopting such a course could ever be appropriate without the tribunal indicating to the absent party what had been said, and providing an opportunity for a response, he considered that the procedure adopted by the adjudicator in *Dean & Dyball*, in which all the relevant information obtained by this process had been provided to the other side, and they had been given an opportunity to deal with it, was entirely fair. The Judge concluded that no dispassionate observer, aware of the particular circumstances of the case, would consider that there was a risk of actual unfairness on the part of the adjudicator.

Failure to Consult

9.26 A related difficulty is the adjudicator's failure to consult with the parties, either about a communication he has received from one party, or about a view or approach he has formed independently of both. Thus in *Discain Project Services Ltd v Opecprime Development Ltd (No 1)*[41] one of the claimant's personnel contacted the adjudicator and had a conversation in which some of the substantive issues in the adjudication were discussed. That conversation was neither recorded by the

---

[40] [2003] EWHC 2465 (TCC).
[41] [2000] BLR 402.

adjudicator, nor was its substance communicated to the defendant. There was a later conversation, also between the adjudicator and the claimant's employee. HHJ Bowsher QC considered that there was a very serious risk, if not of bias, then at least of a failure on the part of the adjudicator to follow the rules of natural justice, namely a failure to consult with one party on important submissions which had been made by the other party. He said that he found such a situation 'distasteful' and could not bring himself to enforce an adjudication decision which had been arrived at in that way. When the matter was fully tried out[42] the Judge concluded on the evidence that he should decline to enforce the decision because it had been reached after a substantial and relevant breach of natural justice.

9.27 A number of the reported cases concern an adjudicator who has failed to share with the parties his approach to the particular dispute he has to resolve. Thus, in *Balfour Beatty Construction Ltd v The Mayor & Burgesses of the London Borough of Lambeth*[43] the adjudicator was concerned with a dispute as to extensions of time. The dispute was complicated, and involved various debates about the proper approach to the critical path. The adjudicator sought help from a programming expert, who adopted a particular methodology when analysing the delay, which was then included by the adjudicator in his decision. It was a methodology which had not been agreed, or even commented on, by either party; in fact, neither party was aware of the particular approach taken by the adjudicator until they saw his decision. In particular, the adjudicator failed to invite the parties' comments on whether his as-built programme was a suitable basis from which to derive a retrospective critical path analysis. In the circumstances, the HHJ LLoyd QC held that the decision was invalid and that the adjudicator had not acted impartially. He said that an observer would conclude that, by making good the deficiencies in the contractor's case, and by overcoming the absence of a sustainable as-built programme (and the complete lack of any analysis by the contractor as to which of the relevant events were critical and non-critical) with his own analysis on which he had not even asked the parties to comment, the adjudicator moved into the danger zone of being partial, or at least liable to the accusation of 'apparent bias'. The Judge said that the burden of proof remained on the contractor who was claiming the extension of time, so that the defendant employer was entitled to have the dispute decided on the contractor's own terms, namely on the material that it had provided, and not on a basis devised by the adjudicator which had not been made known to the parties. That perceived lack of impartiality or apparent bias could have been cured by disclosure to the parties of what the adjudicator was doing, and what he considered to be the right approach to the critical path. He should have told both parties what he had in mind so as to give them an

---

[42] *Discain Project Services Ltd v Opecprime Development Ltd* [2001] BLR 287.
[43] [2002] EWHC 597 (TCC).

opportunity of either endorsing his approach or deflecting him from his chosen course.[44] His failure to do so was fatal to the validity of his decision.

9.28 Similarly, in *RSL (Southwest) Ltd v Stansell Ltd*[45] the adjudicator had relied on the report of a separate independent expert which he had commissioned. HHJ Seymour QC concluded that the adjudicator should not have had any regard to the final report without giving both parties the chance to consider the contents of that report and to comment upon it. His failure to do so was a breach of natural justice. It was also a relevant breach because, so the Judge concluded, the evidence demonstrated that the adjudicator took into account the report in reaching his decision in relation to extensions of time for completion of the sub-contract works. Also in similar vein, the TCC Judge in *Pring & St Hill Ltd v C J Hafner (T/A Southern Erectors)*[46] found that the adjudicator carried forward from an earlier adjudication (between different parties) not merely what he had seen or been told, but also the judgments which he had formed and the opinions which he had reached, all of which led him to reach a particular conclusion in that other adjudication. The Judge concluded that the adjudicator should have made available to the defendant his thought processes as to why some of his earlier conclusions in the previous adjudication were relevant, and that his failure to do so was a breach of the principles of natural justice.[47] In addition, it should also be noted that the adjudicator's directions in respect of the final submissions were a complete muddle, with each party sending their final submissions to the adjudicator but not providing them to one another. The judge described such a procedure as 'very unwise' although he added that it was 'one of the hazards of adjudication and one which was self-inflicted'. That point alone, therefore, would not have amounted to a breach of the rules of natural justice.

9.29 It will be a matter of fact as to whether the adjudicator adopted his own methodology in determining the dispute between the parties, and the extent, if at all, to which he was obliged to share that approach with the parties. This will often require a very detailed analysis of the issues by the court. Thus, in *Multiplex Constructions (UK) Limited v West India Quay Development Company (Eastern) Limited*,[48] it was said that the adjudicator's decision on the contractor's extension of time claim decided a case not put to him, and adopted an approach which the parties were not given an opportunity to address. Ramsey J considered in detail the issues in the adjudication, and the adjudicator's determination of those issues,

---

[44] This is one of a number of cases where it might be said that the adjudicator was trying too hard to be helpful. A good example of this trend is *McAlpine PPS Pipelines Systems Joint Venture v Transco Plc* (TCC, unreported, 12 May 2004) referred to at paragraphs 3.57–3.58 and 7.68 above.
[45] [2003] EWHC 1390 (TCC).
[46] [2002] EWHC 1775 (TCC).
[47] As the Judge put it, 'it is always going to be difficult for a party in the position of SE to challenge an award made off stage in another adjudication . . .'.
[48] [2006] EWHC 1569 (TCC).

and concluded that, unlike the adjudicator in *Balfour Beatty*, he had not adopted his own methodology, but had instead carefully assessed the contractor's own programming analysis, and made due allowance for his concerns about their claim and the basis for it. There had been no breach of the rules of natural justice.

Taking Advice from Others

9.30 Another related theme, which arose (for example) in *RSL*, concerns the not uncommon practice adopted by some adjudicators of seeking third party assistance in order to arrive at a decision on the dispute. The first reported instance of this was the case noted in paragraph 9.27 above, *Balfour Beatty Construction Ltd v The Mayor and Burgesses of the London Borough of Lambeth*.[49] There the adjudicator employed somebody else to carry out a critical path analysis. His failure to invite the parties' comments on his new methodology led to his decision being unenforceable. In paragraph 41 of his judgment, the Judge also dealt with the use of third party assistance. HHJ Lloyd QC concluded that the adjudicator had sought and obtained assistance from others in a manner which was not authorised by the original agreement or the JCT rules. However, although this was therefore a breach of the rules, the Judge could not draw the conclusion that this breach had any material effect on the decision itself, or that there was any material prejudice to the employer, or substantial injustice as a result. Thus, if the natural justice point had been limited to the unauthorised use of third party assistance (as opposed to the failure to consult the parties) the Judge would have enforced the adjudicator's decision.

9.31 There are a number of other cases on this topic, often concerned with disputed claims for extensions of time. In *Try Construction Ltd v Eton Town House Group Ltd*[50] the adjudicator obtained assistance from a programming expert. The parties agreed to such assistance being provided and also agreed that the programming expert could contact the parties' respective programming experts independently. Eton's defence to the subsequent enforcement application of the adjudicator's decision was based on the particular methodology adopted by the programming expert. HHJ Wilcox said that there had been no breach of natural justice during the adjudication, because the parties had agreed to the appointment of the expert, and took a full part in the process which gave rise to the decision. Importantly, he found that both parties had had the opportunity to respond to all issues arising out of the methodology used in the expert's analysis, and that therefore there had been no breach of the principles of natural justice. Judge Wilcox distinguished the situation in *Balfour Beatty* on the basis that, in that case, no analysis at all had been put forward by the contractor, and the

---

[49] [2002] EWHC 597 (TCC).
[50] [2003] CILL 1982.

adjudicator, without agreement or notice, used an entirely independent analysis and devised his own critical path. Furthermore, unlike the situation in *Try*, the responding party in *Balfour Beatty* had not had the opportunity to deal with the relevant points. Indeed, in *Try*, both parties had had a proper opportunity to deal with the analyst's exercise; it was a wholly transparent process and was therefore entirely legitimate. As noted in paragraph 9.28 above, *RSL* was, on the facts, more akin to the situation in *Balfour Beatty* than the events which occurred in *Try*.

9.32 In *BAL (1996) Ltd v Taylor Woodrow Construction Ltd*[51] the adjudicator obtained his own legal advice without telling the parties when he was going to meet with his legal advisers, what material he would provide to them, or even if the advice he received would be in writing. His decision was in the referring party's favour but did not disclose the advice that he had received. HHJ Wilcox concluded that, on these facts, there had been a breach of natural justice. Furthermore, he rejected the argument that, in some way, the responding party had acquiesced in the proposed procedure, saying that the significance of the procedure might not have been immediately apparent and the rapid time limits in adjudication left little time to consider the full implications of that which the adjudicator had suggested. The Judge said that acquiescence had to be clear, informed and unambiguous and there was no suggestion of that in the case under review. The decision was therefore not enforced.[52]

Indication of Preliminary View

9.33 The authorities make clear that the adjudicator is not generally obliged to indicate to the parties that he has formed a particular preliminary view, in order to seek their express comments upon it, unless (as explored in paragraphs 9.26–9.32 above) his view is based on a new approach which neither party could have anticipated.[53] Whether the failure to share his preliminary views will amount to a serious breach of the rules of natural justice on the part of the adjudicator will always depend on the facts. If, for example, the referring party contends that the delay was due to reason A, and the responding party claims that it was due to reason B, then, if the adjudicator forms a strong preliminary view that the referring party is right and the delay was caused by reason A, he will not need to make that view known to the other side; the responding party is already aware, and has

---

[51] [2004] All ER (D) 218 (Feb).

[52] For an example of a situation where the adjudicator obtained legal advice from counsel, and there was no breach of natural justice, see *Michael John Construction v Golledge and Others* [2006] EWHC 71 (TCC).

[53] In *Carillion*, Chadwick LJ, citing Jackson J at first instance, reiterated that it is often not practicable for an adjudicator to put his provisional views to the parties and it would only be in an exceptional case, like *Balfour Beatty*, that a failure to share provisional conclusions with the parties will amount to a breach of natural justice.

prepared a case to meet, the allegation that the delay was due to reason A. If, on the other hand, the adjudicator has considered all the material and reached the conclusion that, in truth, the cause of the delay was reason C, then it is thought that he would be obliged to make that plain to the parties, in order to get them to deal with it. Thus, in *Shimizu Europe Ltd v LBJ Fabrications Ltd*.[54] the parties had agreed that their contractual relationship was based on a letter of intent. The terms of the contract were not, therefore, in issue. However, the adjudicator decided that LBJ's entitlement to payment was not capped by reference to the letter of intent but could be ascertained in a different way. HHJ Kirkham decided that the adjudicator did not have jurisdiction to reach such a conclusion, because it went outside the parameters agreed by the parties. However, in the alternative, the Judge said that at the very least, prior to his decision, the adjudicator should have made clear to the parties that, although they had agreed that they had contracted on the basis of the letter of intent, he was proposing to decide whether or not that was so, and he should have given them the opportunity to make submissions on the question of contract formation. By not doing so, the adjudicator acted in breach of the rules of natural justice, with the consequence that the court would be slow to give summary judgment to enforce his decision.

9.34 Two further examples can be taken of situations where the court concluded that the adjudicator should have indicated to the parties, in advance of his decision, the basis of his conclusions, and where his failure to do so amounted to a breach of natural justice.

(a) In *Ardmore Construction Ltd v Taylor Woodrow Ltd*.[55] the part of the claim in the adjudication concerned with overtime was based solely on the construction of a particular letter. The eventual decision on the point, however, was based upon the adjudicator's summation of discussions which had taken place at a meeting which the adjudicator had convened, and which the court described as 'more of an open-ended discussion than a controlled, structured meeting'. Notwithstanding that, the adjudicator had used those discussions to make findings of acquiescence and verbal instructions wholly independent of the letter. The defendant had been given no opportunity to investigate such matters or to place relevant evidence before the adjudicator. The Outer House of the Court of Session, although indicating that it was mindful of the dangers of picking over decisions and adjudicators' procedures too critically, held that this was a clear breach of natural justice, with the result that that part of the decision dealing with the overtime claim was reduced. The alternative approach should have been put to the defendant in advance of the decision.

---

[54] [2003] BLR 381.
[55] (2006) CILL 2309.

(b) The same criticism was upheld in *Humes Building Contracts Limited v Charlotte Homes (Surrey) Ltd*,[56] where the adjudicator based his decision on a view of the law which had not been argued by or put to either party. The TCC Judge found that whether the interests of fairness required an adjudicator to put a matter, that had not previously been raised, to the parties for comment would depend on the circumstances, and no hard and fast rule could be laid down. In that case, he concluded that the adjudicator's failure to put to the parties his view that the absence of a withholding notice meant the defendant could not rely on a set-off based upon extensive evidence of defective work carried out by the claimant was a breach of natural justice. It meant that the adjudicator had excluded a substantial part of the defence without consideration of its merits, for reasons which were wrong in law. The decision was not summarily enforced.

9.35 A topic inextricably linked to the adjudicator's duty, in certain circumstances, to share and invite comments upon his preliminary views is the question of his or her own expertise and the role that it might play in the decision-making process. In many technical cases, the adjudicator will have been chosen for his or her particular knowledge and experience in that specialist field. If the adjudicator then brings that knowledge and experience to bear on the evidence that is presented, then it has been held that, unsurprisingly perhaps, such a process cannot on its own be a legitimate ground for complaint. In *Dr Rankilor v Perco Engineering Service Ltd and Another*,[57] the dispute concerned ground conditions. The contractor said that they were unexpected; the employer disagreed, contending that the tender indicated that the ground would be clay, and that was what was encountered on site. The adjudicator, who was an expert, concluded that the particular conditions were unexpected. He reached that view by relying, at least in part, on his own geological expertise and applying it to the evidence. HHJ Gilliland QC held that it was unnecessary for the adjudicator to share all his preliminary views with the parties, particularly in circumstances where they were based entirely upon the technical data which had been provided in the course of the adjudication. His conclusions were not at odds with the evidence, and his decisions were summarily enforced. In addition, as the Judge pointed out, it was inevitable that the adjudicator's decision would be influenced/guided by his personal knowledge, experience and understanding, such that this could never be, of itself, a legitimate ground for complaint.

---

[56] 4.1.07, a decision of HHJ Gilliland QC sitting at the TCC in Salford.
[57] [2006] Adj LR 01/27.

Ambush

Another theme related to those discussed above is the question of ambush, and in particular the provision, late in the 28 day period, of further information (often by the referring party) which the adjudicator takes into account without giving the responding party an opportunity to deal properly with that information. In *London and Amsterdam Properties Ltd v Waterman Partnership Ltd*[58] substantial information and evidence was provided to Waterman for the first time during the latter stages of the adjudication. This material, which related to important aspects of the quantum of the claim, was served late, with the result that Waterman did not have an opportunity to address it. Despite the fact that Waterman had not been given that opportunity, the information was used as the basis for important elements of the adjudicator's decision. The responding party therefore demonstrated a substantial, live and triable issue as to the impartiality of the adjudicator.

9.36

There are a number of other cases on this same point. In *McAlpine PPS Pipeline Systems Joint Venture v Transco plc*,[59] the facts of which are set out at paragraphs 3.57–3.58 above, HHJ Toulmin CMG QC found that Transco had a realistic prospect of arguing at trial that it was not afforded a fair opportunity to respond to the evidence about the compensation events, which had been served at such a late stage of the adjudication process. He therefore concluded that the adjudicator had acted unfairly and that, since that unfairness created a real prospect of prejudice, he would not enforce the adjudicator's decision. Similarly, although HHJ Seymour QC's decision in *Edmund Nuttall Ltd v R G Carter Ltd*[60] was principally concerned with whether or not the dispute that the adjudicator decided was the dispute which had crystallised between the parties at the time of the notice of adjudication, the Judge also dealt with the underlying fairness of the situation in which the responding party found itself facing, for the first time in the adjudication, a claim which the Judge considered was radically different to that which had been debated between the parties prior to the adjudication.

9.37

Effect of Earlier Adjudications

It is often difficult for an adjudicator, appointed in a subsequent adjudication, to work out what, if any, limits or restraints have been placed upon him as a result of earlier decisions. A review of the authorities suggests that adjudicators can be caught between two inflexible rules: they must not reach a decision which qualifies or alters, even implicitly, any earlier adjudication decisions but, at the same time, they cannot assume that the mere fact that a point has arisen in an earlier

9.38

---

[58] [2004] BLR 179.
[59] TCC, unreported, 12 May 2004. This case is discussed in detail at paragraphs 3.57–3.58 and 7.68 above.
[60] [2002] BLR 312.

adjudication means that they cannot consider it afresh. If they do purport to decide something which has already been decided in a previous adjudication, they may well have acted unfairly in so doing.

9.39 The difficulties are well illustrated in the case of *Quietfield Ltd v Vascroft Construction Ltd*,[61] the facts of which are set out in detail in paragraphs 12.30–12.32 below. In short, in a second adjudication, an employer claimed liquidated damages for a period of delay for which an application by the contractor for an extension of time on particular grounds had been refused by the first adjudicator. The contractor defended himself by reference to an entitlement to an extension of time that relied on material ('Appendix C') that had not been referred to in the first adjudication. Jackson J referred to a number of authorities, including the decision in *William Verry (Glazing Systems) Ltd v Furlong Homes Ltd*.[62] in which the TCC Judge had held that where a claim was made in adjudication, the responding party could employ all available defences to that claim. Jackson J decided that Vascroft's alleged entitlement to an extension of time, as set out in Appendix C, was substantially different from the claims for an extension of time which were advanced, considered and rejected in the first adjudication. He concluded that Appendix C ought to have been considered in the third adjudication and that, as a result, the decision in that adjudication could not be enforced because the adjudicator failed to abide by the rules of natural justice.

9.40 Quietfield appealed, but their appeal was dismissed.[63] May LJ said that it was as clear as may be that the dispute referred to the first adjudication was Vascroft's disputed claim for extension of time on the grounds advanced in their two earlier letters. Since Vascroft's Appendix C in the third adjudication identified a number of causes of delay which did not feature in the two letters and were substantially different from the claims for extension of time which were advanced, considered and rejected in the first adjudication, the adjudicator was wrong in the third adjudication not to consider Appendix C. Dyson LJ delivered a concurring judgment.[64]

9.41 The decision in *Quietfield* was considered by Ramsey J in *HG Construction Ltd v Ashwell Homes (East Anglia) Ltd*,[65] the facts of which are set out in paragraphs 12.33–12.34 below. In that case, the second adjudicator acted outside his jurisdiction and/or unfairly, because the dispute about the liquidated damages

---

[61] At first instance, this case is reported at [2006] EWHC 174 (TCC). In the Court of Appeal, this case is reported at [2007] BLR 67.
[62] [2005] EWHC 138 (TCC); see paragraph 9.09 above.
[63] [2007] BLR 67.
[64] The decision in *Quietfield* is also important on the extent to which a subsequent adjudicator is bound by the findings of an earlier adjudicator. This is a point dealt with above at paragraphs 7.71–7.77 above.
[65] [2007] EWHC 144 (TCC).

provisions which he purported to decide was substantially the same as the dispute which had already been decided by the first adjudicator.

Miscellaneous

9.42 There are a number of other decisions which are useful pointers to the limits of a natural justice argument arising out of an adjudicator's decision. At one end of the spectrum is *J W Hughes Building Contractors Ltd v G B Metalwork Ltd*[66] where Forbes J rejected the submission that the failure on the part of JWH's solicitors to provide their own clients with documents served during the course of the adjudication somehow resulted from unfairness on the part of the adjudicator. He found that there was nothing in the adjudicator's decision which gave any indication that the adjudicator was aware of any embarrassment being experienced by JWH in dealing with the matter due to the failure of JWH's own solicitors to provide them with a copy of the original referral documentation. The Judge pointed to the strict timetable that applied in adjudications and observed that the adjudicator had to deal with the case as best he could within the constraints of that timetable. Although the adjudicator was aware that JWH had some problems with regard to missing paperwork, he satisfied himself that GBM had done what they were required to do by way of service of documentation on JWH's solicitors. JWH had been invited to raise the matter further some six days in advance of the adjudication meeting, but they did not do so. In those circumstances, there was simply nothing more that the adjudicator could have done.

9.43 At the other end of the spectrum is the decision of HHJ Seymour QC in *A & S Enterprises Ltd v Kema Holdings Ltd*.[67] In that case the adjudicator suggested a meeting. Because of the short notice, a Mr Overend of Kema was unable to attend that meeting, although the suggestion had been made that he join the meeting by way of conference call. In fact the meeting went ahead with another representative of Kema attending by telephone. The adjudicator's decision, which was in favour of A & S, criticised Mr Overend for 'choosing not to make himself available by telephone' and therefore playing no part in the meeting. The adjudicator described his failure to take part in the meeting as 'very unhelpful' and he said that he had viewed Kema's submissions and arguments which they had put forward 'in this light'. Judge Seymour had no difficulty in concluding that the adjudicator's conduct revealed both a real possibility of bias and a breach of natural justice. He found that the adjudicator did not make clear to the parties at any stage before his decision that Mr Overend's attendance was necessary or that his non-attendance would prejudice the defendant. If the adjudicator felt that it was important that

---

[66] [2003] EWHC 2421 (TCC).
[67] [2004] CILL 2165.

Mr Overend attend the meeting, then he had to make that clear to Kema, in order to give them an opportunity to deal with it. His failure to do so meant that his decision did not comply with the requirements of natural justice and was therefore unenforceable.[68]

Human Rights

9.44 When the 1996 Act came into force, there was a lingering uneasiness as to whether the swift and summary nature of the adjudication process was entirely compatible with the European Convention on Human Rights. Article 6 of the Convention provides that:

> 'In the determination of his civil rights and obligations . . . everyone is entitled to a fair and public hearing within a reasonable time by an independent and impartial tribunal established by law. Judgment shall be announced publicly . . .'

In some ways, a comparison between the adjudication process and this entitlement demonstrates two completely opposite imperatives in operation. If Article 6 does not apply to adjudications, because the adjudicator's decision is only of temporary effect, then it might be argued that Article 6 does not apply to any orders of the court, such as interim custody orders, which are not intended to have a permanent effect. If that were right, Article 6 would be significantly reduced in scope. If, on the other hand, Article 6 applied to adjudication then there would be numerous challenges to the adjudicator's decision on the basis that, very often for reasons inherent in the adjudication process itself, there had not been 'a fair trial'. In *Elanay Contracts Ltd v The Vestry*[69] the defendant claimed that the adjudicator's decision was unenforceable because it had not been provided with a fair hearing. In particular it was said that the principal person involved in the relevant events on behalf of the defendant spent most of the 28 days in hospital, visiting his dying mother, which difficulties were compounded by the late delivery of documents produced by the claimant. HHJ Havery QC noted that the procedure had to be completed within the required period, and whilst that may well be inherently unfair, it was the time limit pursuant to which the adjudicator had to comply. As to Article 6, Judge Havery pointed out that the proceedings

---

[68] In *Vaultrise v Paul Cook* [2004] ADJCS 04/06 the adjudicator ruled that a meeting previously arranged for 12 February would go ahead on that date because otherwise he did not have sufficient time to produce the decision. The defendant was represented at the hearing although his solicitor was not available. The defendant subsequently alleged that this procedure was unfair. The court concluded that, because the defendant was represented and had plenty of opportunity to arrange alternative representation, the adjudicator could not be criticised for going ahead with the meeting and not adjourning it to a later date when the first-choice solicitor was available. Again, the reason for this was the adjudicator's statutory deadline.
[69] [2001] BLR 33.

before an adjudicator were not in public. More significantly, he concluded that Article 6 did not apply to an adjudicator's decision or to proceedings before an adjudicator because, although the adjudicator was concerned with a decision or determination of civil rights, the decision was not in any sense a final determination. Thus, he said, the fact that the procedure before the adjudicator is very much a rough and ready procedure cannot, of itself, be regarded as a reason for not ordering summary judgment. He also made the point that, if Article 6 did apply to adjudications, then 'it is manifest that a coach and horses is driven through the whole of the 1996 Act'.

9.45 A much fuller consideration of the correlation between Article 6 of the Convention on the one hand, and the adjudication process on the other, was provided by HHJ Bowsher QC in *Austin Hall Building Ltd v Buckland Securities Ltd*.[70] Austin Hall, with an adjudicator's decision in their favour, took steps to enforce that decision. Buckland resisted the application, complaining that, as the responding party, they had had no proper and equal opportunity to respond the claims made in the adjudication, that the time allowed for the adjudication had been insufficient, and that there was no public hearing and pronouncement of the decision. Therefore, they contended that the adjudication had been conducted in breach of Article 6 of the Convention. Judge Bowsher rejected all of those points. He concluded that adjudication proceedings were not legal proceedings and did not result in a judgment which, in itself, could be enforced. A decision of an adjudicator was not itself enforceable; the successful party had to issue a separate application in court in order to enforce the decision. Moreover, the judge said, an adjudicator under the 1996 Act was not a public authority and was not bound by the Human Rights Act.

9.46 Perhaps more importantly, the Judge concluded that, even if the adjudicator was a public authority under the Human Rights Act, all the requirements of Article 6 of the Convention were satisfied, if the adjudication process was looked at in the round. At paragraph 45 of his judgment, he said:

> If one considers the whole of that process, including the court proceedings necessary to enforce the decision then there is necessarily a public hearing before the decision is enforced (if enforcement be necessary) and all the other requirements of Article 6 are satisfied. To illustrate the principle behind that decision one need look no further than consider the long standing process of the court granting an interim injunction without notice, or *ex parte* as it used to be said. An injunction granted without notice to the defendant, if viewed on its own, is made in breach of the rules of natural justice and in breach of Article 6 of the Convention. To test whether there is a breach of Article 6 or of the rules of natural justice, one must look at the process as a whole, including the urgency of the situation, the safeguards ordered by the court including

---

[70] [2001] BLR 274.

a cross-undertaking in damages, and, more importantly, an order limiting the length of the injunction in time until an early public hearing on notice to the defendant. One has to balance against those safeguards the consideration that the rights of the citizen, such as the rights of a newspaper's rights of freedom of expression, may be seriously limited and the short period of the limitation of those rights may be very important . . .

The Judge went on to find, on the facts of that case, that the adjudicator's conduct was not unlawful and there was no breach of the Convention. Part of the reasoning behind that conclusion was, of course, the short period in which the adjudication was required by statute to be carried out and completed. The time limits that the adjudicator had set for the proper disposition of the adjudication were tight, but they were necessary in order for him to comply with the 28 day time limit for his decision, and that was imposed upon him by the 1996 Act.

9.47 A further factor in Judge Bowsher's decision was his re-statement of the principle that he had set out in *Discain* (and Judge Lloyd had repeated in *Glencot*), to the effect that the rules of natural justice applied to adjudications. Thus, said Judge Bowsher, in practice adjudications were governed by the rules of natural justice which were not very different from Article 6 of the Convention, except for the requirement of a public hearing and the public pronouncement of the decision. The time limits which were the subject of Buckland's attack were also generally subject to the rules of natural justice, but as the Judge pointed out, there could be no question of an Act of Parliament being attacked in the courts as being itself in breach of the rules of natural justice. Since the adjudicator was constrained by the 1996 Act to impose the time limits that he did, he could not be criticised for breaching the rules of natural justice in so doing.

9.48 It would appear that, certainly for the moment, Judge Bowsher's judgment in *Austin Hall* has dealt comprehensively with the suggestion that adjudication itself is contrary to the Human Rights Act. Indeed, the only subsequent decision in which the point has arisen was *R G Carter Ltd v Edmund Nuttall Ltd (No 2)*[71] in which Judge Bowsher referred to his own decision in *Austin Hall* and reiterated his view that he did not believe that the Human Rights Act 1998 applied to adjudication but that, even if it did, there was no breach of the Act. He concluded that he did not believe that the Human Rights Act made any difference in that case.

---

[71] [2002] BLR 359.

Unfair Terms in Consumer Contracts Regulations

9.49 As their names suggest, the *Unfair Terms in Consumer Contracts Regulations* ('UTCCR') are designed to provide a measure of protection to consumers in their dealings with larger commercial organisations. Regulation 5(i) provides that:

> 'A contractual term which has not been individually negotiated should be regarded as unfair if, contrary to the requirement of good faith, it causes a significant imbalance in the party's rights and obligations arising under the contract to the detriment of the consumer.'

Regulation 5(ii) goes on to say:

> A term shall always be regarded as not having been individually negotiated where it has been drafted in advance and the consumer has, therefore, not been able to influence the substance of the terms.

9.50 There have been a number of cases in which an employer, who has found himself on the receiving end of an adjudicator's decision in favour of the contractor, has sought to rely on the UTCCR in order to resist enforcement and strike down the adjudication provisions. Before turning to the adjudication cases, it should be noted that the test of 'significant imbalance', which is a vital ingredient of any attack based on the Regulations, was the subject of consideration by the House of Lords in *Director General of Fair Trading v First National Bank plc*.[72] Lord Bingham of Cornhill said that:

> The requirement of significant imbalance is met if a term is so weighted in favour of the supplier as to tilt the parties' rights and obligations under the contract significantly in his favour. This may be by the granting to the supplier of a beneficial option or discretional power, or by the imposing on the consumer of a disadvantageous burden or risk or duty . . . This involves looking at the contract as a whole. But the imbalance must be to the detriment of the consumer.

9.51 The first case in which the UTCCR were considered in the context of adjudication was *Picardi v Cuniberti & Cuniberti*.[73] In that case the architect claimed that he had been engaged by the defendants pursuant to the RIBA Conditions of Engagement, which included an adjudication clause. The subsequent fee dispute was referred to adjudication and the adjudicator awarded the sum of about £50,000 in favour of the claimant architect. The TCC Judge refused to enforce the decision on the basis that, on the evidence before him, the contract between the parties did not include the RIBA Conditions, and therefore did not include any express adjudication provisions. Since the work involved the employer's own residence, the 1996 Act did not apply (by operation of s106), so the Scheme for

---

[72] [2002] 1 AC 481.
[73] [2003] BLR 487.

Construction Contracts could not be implied into the contract either. That, of course, was sufficient to deal with the case. However, the Judge went on to consider the operation of the UTCCR. He concluded that, because the work in question involved a private dwelling house which was excluded from the 1996 Act, a contractual provision that, despite this exclusion, adjudication was to be the initial method of dispute resolution, was clearly an unusual provision which had to be brought to the specific attention of the lay party if it was later to be validly invoked. He concluded that a procedure which the consumer was required to follow, and which would cause irrecoverable expenditure in either prosecuting or defending a claim brought pursuant to it, was something which may hinder the consumer's right to take legal action. The fact that, in this particular case, the consumer, as a residential occupier, was excluded from the 1996 Act, reinforced that view. The Judge also referred to the fact that the RIBA Guidance required their members individually to negotiate adjudication clauses with their employer. Although he thought that they were right to recommend the giving of such guidance, the architect in the instant case had not done so. Accordingly the Judge concluded that if, contrary to his view, the adjudication provisions had been incorporated into the contract with the defendants, they would have been excluded by reason of the UTCCR.

9.52 The decision in *Picardi* was considered almost immediately by HHJ Moseley QC in *Lovell Projects Ltd v Legg & Carver*.[74] The facts were superficially similar, in that the defendants were the employers and the claimant, who was successful in the adjudication, was the contractor. The contract incorporated the JCT Minor Works Form, and therefore included a set of express adjudication provisions. The defendants sought to resist the enforcement by reference to the UTCCR. Judge Moseley rejected the argument that the adjudication provisions were unfair. He said that, to be unfair, the terms must cause a significant imbalance in the parties' rights and obligations under the contract, to the detriment of the consumer. Furthermore, that significant imbalance had to be caused by the adjudication provisions contrary to the requirement of good faith. He concluded that neither requirement was satisfied in the instant case. This was because the adjudication terms in the JCT Form applied equally both to contractors and employers, and that there had been no breach of the requirement of openness, because the adjudication terms were fully, clearly and legibly set out in the contract and contained no concealed pitfalls or traps. As for the requirement of fair dealing, the contractor did not, either deliberately or unconsciously, take advantage of the consumer's necessity, indigence, lack of experience, unfamiliarity with the subject matter of the contract, weak bargaining position or any other factor listed in the Schedule to the Regulations. The Judge also pointed to a factor, which will commonly be

---

[74] [2003] BLR 452.

present and which will often be decisive of this point, namely that the contract form containing the adjudication provisions had been required by the architect acting on behalf of the employer himself. It was very difficult to argue that the employer was prejudiced by contract terms proffered by his own agent.

9.53 This important point was one of the reasons which led Judge Moseley to distinguish the factual situation in *Lovell* from that in *Picardi*. He pointed out that the adjudication provisions in *Picardi* had not been the subject of clear advice from the employer's architect; indeed, his dispute was with the architect who should have provided that advice. Judge Moseley said that, whilst he entirely accepted the correctness of that decision, it had no application to a case where the form of contract was insisted on by the employers, who had available both advice from solicitors and from the architect, who was their nominated contract administrator. It is respectfully submitted that Judge Moseley was right, on the facts of *Lovell*, not to follow Judge Toilmin's *obiter* remarks in *Picardi*. Furthermore, the facts of *Lovell* are more likely to recur in the future than those in *Picardi*, which is perhaps best regarded as a case on its own particular facts.

9.54 Judge Moseley's approach has been followed in a number of subsequent cases. In *Westminster Building Co Ltd v Beckingham*[75] the employer engaged the claimant contractor to carry out works to his house. The principal contract document was a specification, which contained a provision that the contract would be the JCT IFC form, a standard form of building contract which included a set of express adjudication provisions. The contractor signed the form that had been sent to him by the defendant's surveyors, and although the defendant never signed it, he did not inform his surveyors that he had any objection to its form or content. HHJ Thornton QC concluded that those contractual provisions applied. As to the attack based on UTCCR, the Judge rejected it. He said that, although the contract terms were not individually negotiated, they were couched in plain and intelligible language. Moreover, those terms had been decided upon by the surveyors who were Mr Beckingham's agents, and thus Mr Beckingham had available to him competent and objective advice as to the existence and effect of the adjudication clause before he proffered and entered into the contract. Westminster did no more than accept the contract terms offered, and had no reasonable need to draw to Mr Beckingham's attention the potential pitfalls to be found in the adjudication clause and its operation during the course of the work. The clause did not therefore contravene the requirement of good faith. Furthermore, the Judge agreed with Judge Moseley that the adjudication provisions did not constitute a significant imbalance as to Mr Beckingham's rights,

---

[75] [2004] BLR 163.

and did not significantly exclude or hinder the consumer's right to take legal action or other legal remedy, or restrict the evidence available to him.

9.55 In *Bryen & Langley Ltd v Martin Rodney Boston*,[76] HHJ Seymour QC reached a similar view. In that case, the Judge pointed out that one of the important features in *Picardi* was that the form of contract which contained the provisions which the Judge considered to be unfair was put forward by the architect claimant, who was then seeking to rely on them if he established the contract for which he contended. That was not the case in either *Lovell* or *Westminster*. Judge Seymour concluded that, on the facts in *Bryen & Langley*, the UTCCR were of no application. He stressed the importance of the professional advice that would have been given to the employer as to the proposed form of contract, saying that, in English law, it was not normally the function of a party negotiating a contract to protect the other party in the negotiations from the consequences of his own folly, or from the negligence of third parties, such as the professional advisers to the other party. Thus, the Judge reasoned, it would be an unusual case in which it would not be a complete answer, to any suggestion that a building contractor had acted in bad faith in letting a consumer choose to use a particular standard form of building contract, to point out that the consumer had made his own decision, with or without the advice of a third party.

9.56 For other reasons, Judge Seymour did not enforce the adjudicator's decision on jurisdiction grounds. When the case went to the Court of Appeal, that other part of his judgment was overturned.[77] However, on the points arising under the UTCCR, the Court of Appeal agreed with Judge Seymour's analysis. Rimer J, who gave the principal judgment in the Court of Appeal, said that it was necessary to consider not merely the commercial effects of the term on the relative rights of the parties but, in particular, whether the term had been imposed on the consumer in circumstances which justified a conclusion that the supplier had fallen short of the requirements of fair dealing. Thus, he said, Mr Boston faced exactly the same difficulties as did the consumers in the *Lovell* and *Beckingham* cases: the relevant provisions were not imposed upon him by the supplier; instead it was Mr Boston, the consumer, acting through his agent, who imposed those conditions on the supplier. Even on the assumption that Mr Boston played no part in the preparation of the invitation to tender and did not receive advice as to the adjudication provisions, he had had the opportunity to influence the terms on which the contractors were being invited to tender. Rimer J concluded that, since it was Mr Boston (by his agent) who had imposed the terms, the suggestion that there was any lack of good faith or fair dealing by the contractor, with regard to the

---

[76] [2004] EWHC 2450 (TCC).
[77] [2005] EWCA Civ 973.

ultimate incorporation of those terms into the contract, was 'repugnant to common sense'.

9.57 The more recent cases on this point have followed this approach.[78] In *Steve Domsalla (t/a Domsalla Building Services) v Kenneth Dyason*,[79] HHJ Thornton QC held that the adjudication provisions themselves did not substantially alter the balance of the parties' rights and obligations and so were not caught by the Regulations. However, because Mr Dyason was the employer in name only, the contract having been negotiated and administered by his insurers or their agent, the Judge concluded that the withholding notice provisions were unfair and not binding. He said that Mr Dyason was unable to avoid the effect of an adverse adjudication decision relating to unpaid certificates, even where there were good cross-claims for defects and delay, because (through no fault of his) no withholding notices had been served. The adjudicator's decision, which had given effect to the withholding notice provisions, and had therefore ignored the detail of Mr Dyason's cross-claim, was not summarily enforced. Permission to appeal against this judgment has been granted.

9.58 It is therefore submitted that, unless it can be demonstrated as a matter of fact that the adjudication provisions were imposed by the contractor on the employer, the UTCCR argument will be difficult to get off the ground. Moreover, from a wider perspective, it might be difficult to argue that, even then, the incorporation of the adjudication provisions was somehow to the detriment of the consumer. It is thought that possibly only in cases where the consumer would otherwise fall outside the sphere of adjudication altogether (because, for example, the works were concerned with a private dwelling house, as in *Picardi*) will such an argument even be available. Thus, for the vast majority of cases, it would appear that a party who has been unsuccessful in adjudication will be unable to avoid the consequences of that failure by reference to the UTCCR.

---

[78] See, for example, *Cartwright v Fey* (unreported, 9 February 2005, Bath County Court) and *Allen Wilson Shopfitters v Mr Anthony Buckingham* [2005] EWHC 1165 (TCC).
[79] [2007] EWHC 1174 (TCC).

10

ABATEMENT AND SET-OFF

The Problem	10.01	Set-Off Against the Adjudicator's Decision	10.20
Abatement/Set-Off Against a Sum Certified/Determined as Due	10.06	The General Rule	10.21
		The Exceptions	10.33
Abatement/Set-Off Against Sums Claimed	10.13	Liquidated Damages	10.35
		Summary	10.38

'"Cashflow" is the lifeblood of the village grocer too, though he may not need so large a transfusion from his customers as the shipbuilder in *Mondel v Steel* or the sub-contractor in the instant appeal. It is also the lifeblood of the contractor whose own cash flow has been reduced by the expense to which he has been put by the sub-contractor's breaches of contract. It is not to be supposed that so elementary and economic proposition as the need for cash flow in business enterprises escaped the attention of judges throughout the 130 years which had elapsed between *Mondel v Steel* and *Dawnays*' case in 1971 . . .'

Lord Diplock in *Gilbert-Ash v Modern Engineering (Bristol) Ltd*
[1973] 3 WLR 421 at page 444D

The Problem

The financial difficulties created for a smaller contractor by the larger or more powerful main contractor or employer with whom he contracts have been the subject of much hand-wringing and not a little legislation since the days of Victorian 'laissez-faire' capitalism. The persistent refusal of the larger company to pay the invoices rendered by the smaller has always been one of many weapons wielded by the larger organisation to ensure that its own cash-flow was given priority over the interests and rights of others. The phenomenon referred to in the media in the early 1990's as 'subbie-bashing' is, sadly, nothing new: larger and more powerful main contractors have always done all that they can to make their

10.01

own contracts as profitable as possible, and it has often been their sub-contractors and suppliers who have suffered. By the same token, as Lord Diplock points out in *Gilbert-Ash*, the main contractor is himself vulnerable to similar machinations on the part of the employer. Of course, one of the principal ways in which a main contractor or employer sought to slide out of his contractual obligations, when faced with a claim for an interim payment, was to seek to rely upon a set-off or cross-claim alleging defective work or delay. Traditionally, provided that such a set-off was at least arguable, the sub-contractor was faced with a very real difficulty. If he sued the main contractor for the money, he might find that he never received work from that main contractor again. Moreover, even if he did decide to take the main contractor to court, the court would usually be obliged, in the face of an arguable set-off and cross-claim, to give the main contractor unconditional leave to defend.

10.02 One of the periodic attempts by the courts to provide assistance to hard-pressed contractors in these situations can be found in the decision of the Court of Appeal in *Dawnays Ltd v F G Minter Ltd*.[1] In that case the Court of Appeal allowed the steelworks sub-contractors to recover the sum due to them pursuant to an interim certificate, holding that, as a matter of construction of the contract, the main contractor was not permitted to deduct unliquidated damages by reference to his disputed claims for delay. In a famous passage, Lord Denning MR said:

> Every businessman knows the reason why interim certificates are issued and why they have to be honoured. It is so that the sub-contractor can have the money in hand to get on with his work and the further work he has to do. Take this very case. The sub-contractor has had to expend his money on steel work and labour. He is out of pocket. He probably has an overdraft at the bank. He cannot go on unless he is paid for what he does as he does it. An interim certificate is to be regarded virtually as cash, like a bill of exchange. It must be honoured. Payment must not be withheld on account of cross-claims whether good or bad—except so far as the contract specifically provides. Otherwise any main contractor could always get out of payment by making all sorts of unfounded cross-claims.

For a while, this decision allowed sub-contractors to recover sums due by way of interim payment, regardless of possible cross-claims.[2]

10.03 These halcyon days (at least for those who wanted to be paid promptly without deduction) were not to last. In *Gilbert-Ash (Northern) Ltd v Modern Engineering (Bristol) Ltd*[3] the House of Lords had to consider the same question that had arisen in *Dawnays*. They concluded that *Dawnays* had been wrongly decided.

---

[1] [1971] 1 WLR 1205; [1971] 2 All ER 1389.
[2] See for example *GKN Foundations Ltd v Wandsworth London Borough Council* [1972] 1 Lloyds Rep 528; and *Fredrick Mark Ltd v Schield* [1972] 1 Lloyds Rep 9.
[3] [1973] 3 WLR 421.

Lord Diplock said he could see no grounds in law to prevent the main contractor from defending the action by setting up the sub-contractor's breach of warranty in doing defective work, even though this involved challenging the architect's certificate that that work had been properly executed. He said that there was no provision in the main contract (which was in a standard form) which excluded the common law remedy of the employer to set up breaches of warranty by the contractor, in diminution or extinction of any instalment of the price, notwithstanding that such instalment had been certified as due from him to the contractor in the certificate issued by the architect. His views as to the 'cashflow' argument, which Lord Denning MR had repeated in the Court of Appeal in *Gilbert-Ash*,[4] are set out verbatim at the start of this chapter. As a result of the decision in *Gilbert-Ash*, for the next 20 years or so, employers and main contractors would habitually raise set-offs and cross-claims in order to avoid payment of sums due to contractors and sub-contractors. By the early 1999's, as discussed in Chapter 1 above,[5] the problem of non-payment was seen in the Latham Report as the principal problem affecting the economic stability of the construction industry. It was implicitly recognised that it was impossible to prevent an employer or a main contractor from setting up a cross-claim of some sort because there would always be cases where the employer or main contractor had a genuine complaint arising out of the contractor's performance. Accordingly, in an attempt to ensure that it was only bona fide set-offs and cross-claims that were raised, the Latham Report concluded that, if an employer or a main contractor was to take advantage of its rights of set-off, it had to do so in a very short period following the issue of the certificate or the request for payment. In other words, if there was a bona fide complaint, that complaint could be, and therefore had to be, registered with the sub-contractor straightaway by way of a written notice. Implicitly, the Report suggested that a bona fide cross-claim would be the subject of a prompt notice, whilst a sham would only occur to the employer or the main contractor much closer to the time when the money had to be paid, and would therefore not be the subject of a timeous notice.

10.04 It was in these circumstances that the withholding notice regime was created. It was the withholding notice mechanism which was designed to ensure that an employer or a main contractor with a genuine set-off could raise it clearly and promptly, so that the sub-contractor knew that the money otherwise due would not be paid because of a particular cross-claim. The adjudicator could then be asked to adjudicate on that claim if that is what either of the parties wanted. The regime endeavoured to ensure that an employer or a main contractor who

---

[4] 71 LGR, at 167, when he said, 'There must be a "cash-flow" in the building trade. It is the very lifeblood of the enterprise.'

[5] See in particular paragraphs 1.11 and 1.12 above.

thought up a cross-claim at the last possible moment in a final attempt to avoid payment would simply not be allowed to do so. Sections 110 and 111 of the 1996 Act[6] set out a clear series of provisions designed to ensure that any set-off was notified fully, clearly and promptly.

10.05 The suspension or prohibition of the parties' usual rights and liabilities as to set-off, and the particular problems thrown up by the withholding notice mechanism, have been one of the most common areas of dispute for adjudicators to decide and have given rise to specific problems as to their jurisdiction. The remainder of this chapter considers the three most common situations which have arisen in this context. They are:

(a) Where a defendant seeks to abate and/or set off against a sum which has been certified or otherwise determined as due and payable under the contract;
(b) Where a defendant seeks to abate and/or set off against a sum claimed as due and payable under the contract;
(c) Where a defendant seeks to abate and/or set off against a sum which has been awarded pursuant to an adjudicator's decision.

Abatement/Set-Off Against a Sum Certified/Determined as Due

10.06 Most standard forms of building and engineering contracts incorporate a complex mechanism by which interim payments are made by the employer to the contractor. These mechanisms usually involve the following:

(a) An interim application for payment by the contractor to the employer's contract administrator;
(b) A detailed consideration of that application by the administrator, usually in conjunction with the employer's quantity surveyor;
(c) The issue of an interim certificate by the administrator, identifying the sum to be paid on an interim basis and the final date for payment.

10.07 If the contract contains the sort of mechanism referred to above then, following the issue of the certificate, the employer has a very short time in which to raise any question of abatement or set-off against the sum certified. This period will usually be provided for in the contract and can be as little as three days after the issue of the interim certificate. Under the Scheme for Construction Contracts the withholding notice must be served five days before the final date for payment.[7]

---

[6] See paragraphs 2.129–2.141 above.
[7] See paragraph 3.112 above.

If no withholding notice is served by the employer by the specified date then the contractor is entitled to be paid the sum certified. This general statement of principle has been questioned following the decision of the House of Lords in *Melville Dundas Ltd v George Wimpey UK Ltd*,[8] a case discussed in detail in paragraphs 2.142–2.147 above. Whilst this decision allows an employer, under a certain standard form of building contract, to withhold sums due to the contractor where, even though there has not been a withholding notice, the contract was determined due to the contractor's insolvency less than 28 days after the sum fell due, it is hard to agree that such an exception is likely to arise on a regular basis. Moreover, in *Pierce International Design Ltd v Mark Johnston and Another*,[9] the TCC Judge interpreted the proviso to the clause in question (which had not been relevant on the facts in *Melville Dundas*) as allowing the contractor to recover, at least where the sums were due more than 28 days before the determination, there had been no withholding notices, and the contractor was not insolvent.

10.08 In *Re: A Company (No 1299 of 2001)*[10] the sub-contractor sought £9,702.47 which had been certified in its favour. There was no notice of intention to withhold payment. The Deputy High Court Judge concluded that the clear intent of s110 and s111 was to preclude the employer, in the absence of a withholding notice with specified content, from contending that all or part of the sum demanded by the contractor was not in fact due. Without a withholding notice, the rule was 'pay now, litigate later'. The Judge went on to find that any other construction of s110 and s111 would rob them of all practical significance.

10.09 The same result occurred in *Clarke Contracts Ltd v The Burrell Co (Construction Management) Ltd*.[11] In that case, Sheriff Taylor concluded that the situation where a sum had been certified as due, which was the position in the case before him, was different to the situation where the interim payment was simply the subject of an application by the contractor. He pointed out that, under the standard form with which he was concerned, the architect would from time to time issue interim certificates, and that the sum which was referred to the adjudicator had originally been certified by the architect. He therefore concluded in *Clarke* that the certified sum became due and payable in accordance with the contract and, in the absence of a withholding notice in respect of that certificate, the responding party could not set up any abatement or set-off. He found that, if the defenders wished to avoid liability to make payment, they were obliged to issue a withholding notice, and the absence of such a notice meant that they were liable to pay the sum found due by the adjudicator.

---

[8] [2007] UKHL 18; [2007] 1 WLR 1136.
[9] [2007] EWHC 1691 (TCC).
[10] [2001] CILL 1745.
[11] Scots Law Times 2002, 103.

10.10 In reaching this conclusion, Sheriff Taylor contrasted the position with another Scottish case, *S L Timber Systems Ltd v Carillion Construction Ltd*.[12] That was a case in which there were no certificates, and the interim payment at issue between the parties was simply the subject of an application by sub-contractor pursuers which had not been scrutinised by any third party. Sheriff Taylor concluded that this was a vital distinction which meant that, in those circumstances, no withholding notice was necessary in order to allow the main contractor to argue how and why elements of the application were not due under the contract. Sheriff Taylor's clear distinction was not perhaps appreciated in some of the subsequent reported cases. However, it lay at the heart of the first Court of Appeal decision on the point in *Rubert Morgan Building Services (LLC) Ltd v Jervis*.[13]

10.11 In *Rubert Morgan*, the builders were in possession of an interim certificate which the employer disputed. There was no withholding notice. The adjudicator found that the certified sum was due, and his decision was enforced by the court. The defendants appealed, arguing that they were entitled to withhold payment because they had an arguable defence, to the effect that the items of work which went to make up the unpaid balance had not been done at all, or were duplications of items already paid, or were charged as extras when they were within the original contract, or represented snagging items which had already been paid for. In rejecting the appeal, Jacob LJ (with whom both Sedley LJ and Schiemann LJ agreed) referred expressly to the judgment of Sheriff Taylor in *Clarke Contracts* which, he said, 'casts a flood of light on the problem'. Jacob LJ pointed out that, pursuant to this contract (like so many of the standard forms) the sum due was determined by the interim certificate. As a result, the contractor was entitled to the money certified right away. The employer's contractual duty was to make immediate payment, and the sum that they had to pay arose because of the certificate. He pointed out that, in any event, the only risk to the employer was an overpayment followed by the insolvency of the builder, and that such risk was one which could be avoided if the certificate was carefully checked and, if any objection arose, the giving of a timeous withholding notice by the employer.

10.12 Jacob LJ drew a clear (and, it is submitted, helpful) distinction between interim payments that had been certified, and were therefore due under the contract, and sums which had not been the subject of any third party scrutiny and which were simply claimed as due by the contractor or sub-contractor in question. He said this was a proper distinction to draw, rather than one which, as had been argued before the Court of Appeal, depended on whether a wide or narrow construction

---

[12] [2002] SLT 997; this case is discussed in greater detail in paragraph 10.17 below.
[13] [2004] 1 WLR 1867.

was placed on section 111 of the 1996 Act. He went on to articulate the advantages of the analysis adopted by Sheriff Taylor, which he expressly endorsed:

14 ...
   (a) It makes irrelevant the problem with the narrow construction—namely that Parliament was setting up a complex and fuzzy line between sums due on the one hand and counterclaims on the other—a line somewhere to be drawn between set-off, claims for breach of contract which do no more than reduce the sum due and claims which go further, abatement and so on.
   (b) It provides a fair solution, preserving the builder's cash flow but not preventing the client who has not issued a withholding notice from raising the disputed items in adjudication or even legal proceedings.
   (c) It requires the client who is going to withhold to be specific in his notice about how much he is withholding and why, thus limiting the amount of withholding to specific points. And these must be raised early.
   (d) It does not preclude the client who has paid from subsequently showing he has overpaid. If he has overpaid on an interim certificate the matter can be put right in subsequent certificates. Otherwise he can raise the matter by way of adjudication or if necessary arbitration or legal proceedings.
   (e) It is directed at the mischief which Section 111(1) was aimed at. This mischief is mentioned in *Keating on Building Contracts*. A report called the Latham Report had identified a problem, namely that "main contractors were abusing their position to wrongfully withhold payment from sub-contractors who were in no position to make any effective protest". Actually the provision has gone further than just dealing with the position between main and sub-contractors since it covers the position between client and main contractor too—but the main contractor will need paying himself so he can pay the sub-contractor. And he may have his own cash flow needs too ...

Thus, where there is a certificate in favour of a main contractor or a sub-contractor, then that main contractor or sub-contractor is entitled to the sums certified, unless there is a withholding notice served within the contractual time limit (and possibly, in cases of determination and contractor insolvency, as per the decision in *Melville Dundas* identified in paragraph 10.07 above). The withholding notice has to raise every point, and in clear detail, as to why the sum certified is not due. Thus, the notice must include points that would be classified in law as matters going to abatement, as well as cross-claims for defects, delay and the like.

Abatement/Set-Off Against Sums Claimed

Is the position different where the sum due has not been certified, but is simply claimed as due by way of an application for interim payment by the contractor or sub-contractor? For the reasons noted above, the answer is Yes. Although a number of the reported cases are not always entirely clear on the point, it would appear that, if the employer or main contractor claims that an interim application is over-stated

10.13

because, for example, it includes items which have already been paid for, or seeks payment by reference to exaggerated rates and prices, no withholding notice is necessary. The position may be less clear in circumstances where what the employer or main contractor disputes is not the application for payment itself, but the subcontractor's entitlement to any payment at all, because of other matters, such as defects or delay, which are not identified in the original application for payment. In those circumstances, the most prudent course is for the employer or the main contractor to issue a withholding notice setting out that cross-claim. The failure to do so might potentially be a breach of s111 or the appropriate contract provisions, and mean that no deduction will be permitted. The authorities dealing with this type of dispute are referred to below.

10.14 From the outset, the position adopted by the TCC Judges in London was that, in circumstances where the sum being claimed had not been certified, and therefore represented simply the claiming party's assessment of what was due, the responding party was not obliged to serve a withholding notice in order to take issue with the detail of the application. Thus, in *Woods Hardwick v Chiltern Conditioning*[14] HHJ Thornton QC noted that, whilst Chiltern had not served a withholding notice in respect of their alleged claims arising out of the loss caused by Woods Hardwick's purported breaches of contract, the sums claimed by Woods Hardwick had not been the subject of any sort of third party assessment or certificate, so that any abatement properly relied on by Chiltern would not require notice under section 111. Thus, notwithstanding the absence of such a notice, Chiltern's abatement defence could, in principle, defeat or reduce Woods Hardwick's claims. A similar view was expressed by HHJ Lloyd QC in *KNS Industrial Services (Birmingham) Ltd v Sindall Ltd*.[15] The Judge concluded that 'one cannot withhold what is not due' and said that, in all the circumstances of that case, including the adjudication notice, the dispute referred to the adjudicator included any ground open to Sindall which would justify not paying KNS. Thus the arguments that the sum claimed was too high did not require a withholding notice.

10.15 As previously noted, the distinction between abatement against a certified sum, and abatement against a sum merely the subject of an interim application, was not always clearly made in the reported cases. Two examples will suffice:

(a) In *Whiteways Contractors (Sussex) Ltd v Impresa Castelli Construction United Kingdom Ltd*[16] HHJ Bowsher QC expressed the view that it made no difference whether deductions were by way of set-off or abatement and that, whichever they might be, notice of such deductions had to be made by way of

---

[14] [2001] BLR 23.
[15] [2001] 17 Const LJ 170.
[16] [2000] 16 Const LJ 453.

withholding notice in accordance with the Act. Accordingly, to the extent that this case suggests that a party seeking to reduce an interim application (because, for example, an element of the application was based on incorrect rates or was not a variation, but part of the contract workscope) has to serve a withholding notice, it is thought that the principle is over-stated in the judgement.

(b) Similarly, it may be that the decision of HHJ Gilliland QC in *Millers Specialist Joinery Co Ltd v Nobels Construction Ltd*[17] should also be treated with caution. In that case, the claimant sought £16,005.96 in respect of invoices for joinery work. There was no certification regime. The defendant opposed the application on the basis that there had been previous over-payment to the claimant, but there had been no withholding notice. The adjudicator produced a decision in favour of the claimant. Judge Gilliland upheld that decision. He said that, whilst ordinarily the claimant would not succeed in obtaining summary judgment because of the issue of over-payment, the absence of a withholding notice deprived the defendant of any right to make a cross-claim in respect of the previous over-payments. The Judge pointed out that, if it were correct that the effect of a failure to serve a withholding notice was that the amount of the invoice was to be regarded as a sum due under the contract then, in all cases without such a notice, neither an adjudicator nor the court could properly refuse to order payment in full, even though it might be clear that the work claimed for had not been carried out. He went on to say that, if the effect of a failure to serve such a notice deprived the payer of the right to refuse payment on the ground that the sum sought was not due and payable, it was difficult to see on what basis the court could refuse to give judgment for the full amount. The Judge concluded that the absence of a withholding notice meant that the recipient had a legal right to be paid on the final date for payment and that the court had to give effect to the failure to serve a notice under s111.

10.16 It is thought that Judge Gilliland perhaps went too far in the terms of his judgment in *Millers*. A claim made on the basis of an invoice, which is disputed by the other side, can be the subject of a dispute as to what, if anything, might actually be due under that invoice, whether or not there is a withholding notice. To the extent that Judge Gilliland suggests otherwise, then it is respectfully suggested that he was wrong to do so, and that he overstated the importance of the withholding notice in such situations. However, it must be said that, on its own particular facts, there is nothing objectionable about the result in *Millers*. That is because the defendant contractor did not actually oppose the sums claimed, or the basis on which those sums were calculated. Instead, the defendant was opposing the application on the basis that it had a separate claim based on previous overpayments.

---

[17] [2001] CILL 1770.

To that extent, it might be said that this separate claim was a true set-off/cross-claim, and therefore did require a withholding notice. It is for that reason that it is thought that an employer or main contractor can only be excused from the obligation to serve a withholding notice where the dispute truly does relate to the particular sum invoiced or claimed by way of an interim application for payment. Any other kind of set-off, such as those discussed in both *Whiteways* and *Millers*, should, out of an abundance of caution, be the subject of a withholding notice.

10.17 The clearest analysis of the position where the claim is not based on a certificate but merely an invoice or an interim application can be found in *S L Timber Systems Ltd v Carillion Construction Ltd*.[18] In that case, the pursuers were specialist timber suppliers. They made interim applications for payment which the defenders refused to pay. The adjudicator upheld the claims for payment in full, relying in part on the absence of any withholding notice in support of his conclusion that he did not have to look at the substance of the applications. Lord MacFadyen concluded that the adjudicator was wrong to adopt this conclusion although he concluded that the adjudicator's errors of law did not take him out of the proper scope of his jurisdiction. Lord MacFadyen's analysis of the particular circumstances in which the responding party was not obliged to serve a withholding notice has the virtue of simplicity and clarity. He pointed out that a withholding notice had to be provided against a sum 'due under the contract' and that those words could not be equated with the words 'sum claimed'. He said that section 111 of the 1996 Act was not concerned with every refusal on the part of one party to pay a sum claimed by the other. It was concerned with the situation where a sum was due under the contract and the party from whom that sum was due sought to withhold payment on some separate ground. He went on to say that a dispute about whether the work, in respect of which the claim was made, had been carried out, or about whether it was properly measured or valued, or about whether some other event (on which a contractual liability to make payment depended) had occurred, all went to the question of whether the sum claimed was due under the contract, and therefore did not involve an attempt to 'withhold . . . a sum due under the contract'. Thus he concluded that such disputes did not require a withholding notice. He contrasted that with the position where there was no dispute that the work had been done and was correctly measured and valued, but where the party wished to advance some separate ground for withholding the payment; in those circumstances, a withholding notice was necessary. Paragraph 22 of his judgment serves as a neat summary of the position where an interim payment has not been certified but is merely the subject of an application:

---

[18] [2001] BLR 516.

In my opinion, the absence of a timeous notice of intention to withhold payment does not relieve the party making the claim of the ordinary burden of showing that he is entitled under the contract to receive the payment he claims. It remains incumbent on the claimant to demonstrate, if the point is disputed, that the sum claimed is contractually due. If he can do that, he is protected, by the absence of a Section 111 notice, from any attempt on the part of the other party to withhold all or part of the sum which is due on the basis that some separate ground justifying that course exists. It is no doubt right, as the adjudicator pointed out, that, if the section did require a notice of intention to withhold payment as the foundation for a dispute as to whether the sum claimed was due under the contract, it would be relatively straight-forward for the party disputing the claim to give such a notice. But that consideration does not, in my view, justify ignoring the fact that the section is expressed as applying to the case where an attempt is made to withhold a sum due under the contract, and not as applying to an attempt to dispute that the sum claimed is due under the contract.

10.18 As previously noted, this approach was contrasted in *Clarke Contracts v Burrell*[19] with the situation where the sum due has been certified. There, Sheriff Taylor rightly pointed out that in *S L Timber* there had been no calculation of the sum sued for by reference to a contractual mechanism, which gave rise to an obligation under the contract to make payment. There had been no more than a claim by the pursuers which claim had not been scrutinised by any third party. Furthermore, as Jacob LJ made plain in *Rupert Morgan*, there was a clear difference between the two situations. In *S L Timber* there was no architect or system of certificates, and the builder simply presented his interim bill for payment. As Jacob LJ concluded, the bill in itself did not make any sums due. Under that contract, what would render the invoiced sums due was just the fact of the work having been done; thus no withholding notice was necessary in respect of works not done, and payment was not due for work not done.

10.19 Accordingly, it can be seen that, in situations where there is no interim certificate, the employer or main contractor does not require to have issued a withholding notice in order to take issue with the detail of the invoice or interim payment application in question. *Woods Hardwick*, *KNS v Sindall*, *S L Timber* and *Rupert Morgan*, all make that plain. To the extent that *Whiteways* and *Millers* suggest to the contrary, then they should be treated with caution. However, the decisions in *Whiteways* and *Millers* are of significance because, in each case, what the main contractor sought to do was to raise the question of pre-existing overpayments. Those were not matters which arose directly out of the particular invoice or interim payment application. Therefore, to the extent that those authorities indicate that a withholding notice is required before an adjudicator has the

---

[19] [2002] SLT 103.

jurisdiction to consider the detail of such cross-claims, they can be regarded as a correct statement of the law.

Set-Off Against the Adjudicator's Decision

10.20 There have been a number of decisions dealing with the losing party's ability to set off, against a sum which they are required to pay pursuant to an adjudicator's decision, a separate claim for damages or delay. Many of these cases date back to the early days of adjudication enforcement, when it was sometimes unclear how the adjudicator's decision fitted in to the existing contractual framework of interim valuations and interim payments. There were also a number of cases which tested the extent to which the party's usual rights of set-off could be said to have been modified and even abrogated by the 1996 Act. Although it is not possible to generalise too far, because each case will turn on the precise contractual provisions agreed by the parties and the precise form of the adjudicator's decision, it is appropriate to conclude that, generally, a party who has been ordered by an adjudicator to pay a specific sum forthwith cannot seek to set-off against that sum a claim for damages or for other losses, even if that claim was not considered in the adjudication itself. Accordingly, the remainder of this chapter deals first with those cases which illustrate the general rule, before going on to address the cases in which a set-off was permitted against an adjudicator's decision, and the particular difficulties created by the employer's cross-claim for liquidated damages.

The General Rule

10.21 One of the earliest significant judgments dealing with questions of set-off as *Allied London & Scottish Properties PLC v Riverbrae Construction Ltd*.[20] In that case, the adjudicator had found that sums were due from the petitioners to the respondents. The petitioners sought unsuccessfully to retain those sums against claims on other contracts between the parties. When that failed, they then sought an order that such sums should be put on deposit, but not paid over to the respondents, so as to allow the petitioners to pursue their other claims against the respondents under those other contracts. The adjudicator rejected the submission, and the petitioners challenged his decision. The Outer House dismissed the petition, finding that, having found sums due to the respondents, and having dismissed the claim for retention, the adjudicator could not logically or lawfully have made an order of the type suggested. Lord Kingarth found that such an order would, in effect, sustain the retention claim which the adjudicator had just rejected, and that, notwithstanding the wide powers given to adjudicators, such an order would

---

[20] [1999] BLR 246.

have been unjustified. Another early case was *VHE Construction Plc v RBSTB Trust Co Ltd*.[21] In that case, following two adjudications, a net sum was due to VHE but, following the second adjudication, RBSTB notified the contractor that they intended to deduct most of that sum by way of liquidated damages for delay. There was no withholding notice. HHJ Hicks QC concluded that, not only did s111 of the 1996 Act exclude the right to set-off in the absence of an effective notice of intention to withhold payment, but that that was one of its principal purposes. He went on to reject the submission that the general right under the contract to deduct liquidated damages overrode the obligation to comply with the adjudicator's decision. Although it was argued that the parties had to comply with the adjudicator's decision 'without prejudice to their other rights under the contract', the Judge said that 'without prejudice to' was the equivalent of 'subject to' and meant 'but leaving unaffected'. He said that RBSTB's construction of the contract, to the effect that they could set-off any other claims against the decision, would destroy the balance between the need, on the one hand, for swift and unconditional compliance with the adjudication decision against, on the other, the preservation of the losing party's right to contend for and, if justified, obtain a different final determination by litigation, arbitration or agreement.

10.22 At paragraph 66 of his judgment in *VHE*, Judge Hicks also rejected the contention advanced by RBSTB that they had a residual right to set-off their liquidated damages claim. He said that such a construction would make a nonsense of the overall purpose of the 1996 Act, particularly if payments required to comply with adjudication decisions were more vulnerable to attack than those simply falling due under the ordinary contractual machinery. He said that the parties had to comply with the adjudicator's decision and that 'comply' in accordance with the contract meant 'comply, without recourse to defences or cross-claims not raised in the adjudication'. Thus, on any view, *VHE* made plain that, in the ordinary course of events, a losing party could not seek to set off a separate claim against the sum awarded by the adjudicator.[22]

10.23 There have been a number of subsequent decisions which have been entirely in line with Judge Hicks' conclusions.[23] They are analysed in greater detail in paragraphs 10.25–10.32 below. However, the next decision on this topic has sometimes been taken as limiting the scope of what Judge Hicks said. That is the Court of Appeal decision in *Parsons Plastics (Research and Development) Ltd v Purac Ltd*.[24] In that case the sub-contractors, Parsons, sought payment of approximately

---

[21] [2000] BLR 187.
[22] See also another early case, *Harwood v Lantrode* (unreported, 24.11.00), a decision of HHJ Seymour QC.
[23] See, for example, *Multiconcept Developments Ltd v Abarus (CI) Ltd* [2002] Adj LR 03/22.
[24] [2002] BLR 334.

323

£250,000, but the defendant main contractors, Purac, refused to pay and complained that the sub-contractors had failed to comply with their contractual obligations. Parsons were subsequently ejected from site. They then took their payment application to adjudication. There was a dispute about whether or not the subcontract work was a construction operation. The adjudicator found that it was, and that sums were due to Parsons. His decision was published on 17 May 2001. Six days later, on 23 May, Purac served an intention to withhold payment of the sum awarded by the adjudicator by reference to their own claim for the reasonable costs of completing the subcontract work. This figure exceeded the sum awarded by the adjudicator. The Judge at first instance refused Parsons' summary judgment application in the amount awarded by the adjudicator and granted Purac summary judgment on their counterclaim. The sub-contractors appealed.

10.24 The Court of Appeal dismissed the appeal. Because it was common ground that the 1996 Act did not apply, this was properly treated as an ad hoc adjudication. Furthermore, the Court of Appeal concluded that the wording of the contract meant that the overriding general right that a party had to set off other sums claimed to be due was not lost or limited, despite the adjudication provisions. Pill LJ, with whom Mummery and Latham LJJ agreed, said that he had not found the question an easy one and that when parties provided a specific procedure by which a claim to withhold payment was to be notified and detailed, it could not readily be concluded that the effect of a general set-off provision (such as clause 31 in that case) was to make the procedure wholly unnecessary. However, he came to the conclusion that the failure to give a withholding notice was not fatal to the main contractor's right to set-off. At paragraph 15 of his judgment, he concluded that, as a matter of the construction of the relevant provisions of the contract, it was open to the respondents to set off against the adjudicator's decision any other claim which they had against the sub-contractors which had not been determined by the adjudicator. At first sight, this is a rather surprising result. It is perhaps best classified, as Jackson J described it in *Balfour Beatty Construction Ltd v Serco Ltd*[25] as a case where 'the contract contained a specific term as to set-off which determined the outcome'.

10.25 A decision more in line with the general principle that to allow the loser to set off against the sum awarded by the adjudicator was contrary to the whole purpose of the 1996 Act was that of HHJ Thornton QC in *Bovis Lend Lease Ltd v Triangle Development Ltd*.[26] There, he said that the decision of an adjudicator that money must be paid gave rise to a second contractual obligation on the part of the paying

---

[25] [2004] EWHC 3336 (TCC).
[26] [2003] BLR 31.

party to comply with that decision within the stipulated period. He went on to say that such an obligation usually precluded the paying party from making withholdings, deductions, set-offs or cross-claims against the sum that had to be paid.

10.26 It should be noted, however, that some of the statements of principle in that judgment were doubted by the Court of Appeal in *Ferson Contractors Ltd v Levolux AT Ltd*,[27] which is now the leading case on this area of the law. In that case, the sub-contractors, Levolux, made a second interim payment application for about £56,000, but Ferson paid only £4,753. They relied upon a withholding notice in respect of the balance. Levolux ceased work and Ferson gave notice to Levolux that it required them to recommence work, failing which Ferson would terminate the contract on the ground that Levolux had wrongly suspended performance. Levolux gave notice of intention to refer the dispute to adjudication. Ferson purported to determine the contract. The matter then went to adjudication. The adjudicator concluded that Levolux were entitled to the balance of their second interim payment, and had been so entitled when Levolux stopped work. The principal issue that he had to decide was whether or not Ferson's withholding notice complied with the 1996 Act. He concluded that if the notice did comply with the 1996 Act, the withholding was lawful and Levolux's claim failed. If it did not comply, then Ferson were not entitled to withhold payment and Levolux's case succeeded. He held that the withholding notice did not comply with the statutory requirements and was therefore invalid. Thus he found for Levolux. That decision was enforced by HHJ Wilcox.

10.27 In the Court of Appeal, it was argued that the adjudicator's decision was limited to whether or not a certain sum was due and owing, and that the adjudicator had not decided whether or not there had been a valid determination of the contract. Thus it was said that this point was available for argument before the Judge on the enforcement application, without in any way resiling from the binding nature of the adjudicator's decision. This argument was rejected by the Court of Appeal. They said that the Judge was plainly right in concluding that it was implicit in the adjudicator's decision that there had been no valid determination, and that such a conclusion followed inexorably from the adjudicator's finding that Ferson had not been entitled to withhold payment. Ferson's alternative argument was that the contract provisions overrode the adjudicator's decision and, in support of this argument, reliance was placed on *Parsons*. Mantell LJ distinguished *Parsons* on the basis that it was not concerned with s108, and instead related to a set-off and counterclaim upon which there had been no adjudication. He went on to say that, in any event, the contract had to be construed so as to give effect to the intention

---

[27] [2003] EWCA Civ 11.

of Parliament rather than to defeat it, and if that could not be achieved by way of construction, then the offending clause must be struck down. The contract clauses dealing with rights and liabilities on determination had to be read as not applying to monies due by reason of an adjudicator's decision. Longmore LJ referred to the parties' agreement to comply with the adjudicator's decision, and that in any event the adjudicator's decision had to take precedence over the contract.

10.28 It is suggested that *Levolux* provides clear guidance as to the position when a party seeks to set-off against an adjudicator's decision. In general terms, the courts will view such an argument as an attempt to frustrate the 1996 Act and, in the ordinary case, will not therefore permit it. This is particularly so where, as in *Levolux*, the subject matter of the purported set-off had implicitly been dealt with in the adjudicator's decision.

10.29 *Levolux* has been followed in a number of subsequent decisions.[28] In *M J Gleeson Group Plc v Devonshire Green Holding Ltd*[29] the TCC Judge decided that a payment ordered by an adjudicator could not be withheld on the basis of a claim which accrued after the commencement of the adjudication. He found that the terms of the contract in question had the same purpose and effect as that set out by the Court of Appeal in *Levolux*. He said that the decision of the adjudicator was binding and had to be complied with by the parties, and the idea that the decision could be defeated by a withholding notice in respect of events which occurred after the commencement of the adjudication seemed to him to be entirely inconsistent with the statutory purpose of providing a quick and effective remedy on an interim basis. He concluded that an adjudicator's decision had to be enforced and complied with, without subtle arguments as to other provisions of the contract.

10.30 In *David MacLean Contractors Ltd v The Albany Building Ltd*[30] the same Judge held that a defendant could not set off its claim for damages for delay against a specific payment ordered by the adjudicator. He held that the defendant could not refuse payment based on a cross-claim in relation to liquidated damages. The Judge referred again to *Levolux* and his own decision in *Gleeson*; although he accepted that the contract did not contain an express prohibition against set-off, he went on to hold that, because the parties had agreed to comply with the adjudicator's decision, that meant that they would not exercise any right of set-off. A set-off would simply delay payment and defeat the purpose of adjudication, which was designed 'to assist cash flow'.

---

[28] See for example *Dumarc Building Services Ltd v Salvador Rico*, Epsom County Court, HHJ Hull QC, unreported, 31.1.03.
[29] HHJ Gilliland QC, sitting at the TCC in Salford, 19 March 2004.
[30] HHJ Gilliland QC, sitting at the TCC in Salford, 10 November 2005.

In *Balfour Beatty Construction Ltd v Serco Ltd*[31] Jackson J reviewed, amongst other authorities, *VHE*, *Bovis Lend Lease*, *Parsons Plastics* and *Fersons v Levolux*. It was a case concerned with an employer's attempt to withhold payment of sums awarded by the adjudicator by reference to a cross-claim for liquidated damages. He derived two principles of law from the authorities which were relevant to the dispute in *Balfour Beatty*. They were summarised at paragraph 53 of his judgment as follows:

10.31

> (a) Where it follows logically from an adjudicator's decision that the employer is entitled to recover a specific sum by way of liquidated and ascertained damages, then the employer may set off that sum against monies payable to the contractor pursuant to the adjudicator's decision, provided that the employer has given proper notice (in so far as required).
>
> (b) Where the entitlement to liquidated and ascertained damages has not been determined either expressly or impliedly by the adjudicator's decision, then the question whether the employer is entitled to set-off liquidated and ascertained damages against sums awarded by the adjudicator will depend upon the terms of the contract and the circumstances of the case.

It is respectfully suggested that there is a third principle to be derived from the authorities, namely that, if the terms of the contract as to set-off are to override the effect of the adjudicator's decision, and deprive the successful party in the adjudication of the sum otherwise due pursuant to the adjudicator's decision, then the terms of contract must clearly provide for such an outcome.

More recent cases have demonstrated that, at least in general terms, a party who asserts a future claim cannot seek to set off the amount of that claim against a sum awarded by an adjudicator. In particular:

10.32

(a) In *Interserve Industrial Services Ltd v Cleveland Bridge UK Ltd*[32] Jackson J was dealing with the situation where the losing party wished to set-off against the sum awarded against him the amount that he reasonably expected to recover in a subsequent adjudication. It was argued that neither the terms of the particular sub-contract in question, nor the words of section 111 of the 1996 Act, could be construed as excluding rights of set-off which did not exist when the subject of the adjudicator's decision crystallised. Jackson J rejected that argument and held that, where the parties to a construction contract engaged in successive adjudications, each focussed upon the party's current rights and remedies, the correct approach was to consider the position at the end of each adjudication. At that point, absent special circumstances, he concluded that the losing party had to comply with the adjudicator's decision

---

[31] [2004] EWHC 3336 (TCC).
[32] [2006] EWHC 741 (TCC).

and could not withhold payment on the ground of his anticipated recovery in a future adjudication, based on different issues.[33]

(b) In *Hillview Industrial Developments (UK) Ltd v Botes Building Ltd*[34] the adjudicator ordered Botes to pay Hillview the sum of £292,650. Botes declined to pay this on the grounds that they were about to issue legal proceedings in respect of their final account which, they said, did not become due and payable until after the adjudication decision had been published. It was argued on behalf of Botes that, although in normal circumstances Hillview would be entitled to summary judgment, on the facts of the case it was open to the court to conclude that the case should be disposed of at trial rather than by way of summary judgment; it was argued that it would be a curious result if Botes was required to pay the sum in the adjudicator's award, only for a substantial part of it to have to be repaid to Botes a short time afterwards. Having considered the decision of Jackson J in *Interserve*, HHJ Toulmin CMG QC agreed with the statements of principle set out above and concluded that, accordingly, Hillview were entitled to judgment immediately, without any set-off. The fact that Botes had a separate claim which was the subject of a future application for summary judgment, which may or may not succeed, could not deprive Hillview of the sums awarded by the adjudicator. Judge Toulmin concluded that there was no possible justification for not granting summary judgment to Hillview. He said it would be an abuse of the process of the court to allow the case to proceed to trial in circumstances where Botes conceded that it had no defence. He observed that the forthcoming application by Botes for summary judgment on their final account was contested, and so it was impossible to say whether or not Botes would succeed. Summary judgment was entered to enforce the adjudicator's decision.

(c) In *RJ Knapman Ltd v Richards & Ors*[35] the adjudicator had awarded a sum of money to the contractor and also found that the contractor was responsible for the defects in the windows and the doors. That latter finding had not given rise to a sum to be paid by the contractor to the employer, and indeed the adjudicator's decision appeared to suggest that, pursuant to the terms of the contract, the contractor had to come back and remedy the defects himself. The TCC Judge enforced the contractor's claim for the money awarded by the adjudicator. He said that, pursuant to the adjudicator's decision, there was no separate financial claim which the employer could set off against the sum found to be due to the contractor. If the employer was right

---

[33] This approach was followed by HHJ Toulmin QC in *Ale Heavy Lift v MSD (Darlington) Ltd* [2006] EWHC 2080 (TCC).
[34] [2006] EWHC 1365 (TCC).
[35] [2006] EWHC 2518 (TCC).

and the contractor was in breach of its contractual obligation to comply with the adjudicator's decision and rectify the defects, then the contract permitted the employer to take legal proceedings to secure compliance. They had not done so. In those circumstances, the Judge concluded that, because the contract provided the employer with a remedy which dealt with the very complaint that the employer now made, it was not appropriate to deprive the contractor of its entitlement as determined by the adjudicator. Merely because there was a possible future claim accruing to the employer, which had not yet been quantified, did not mean that the court should decline to enforce the adjudicator's decision. At paragraph 25 of his judgment, the Judge said:

> It is often the case that, if an adjudicator deals with underlying contractual rights, such as the contractual liability for a particular element of the work, or extensions of time, there will be no immediate financial consequence of that decision, although such consequences may become apparent thereafter, once the decision is complied with or not complied with. This case is no different. The only slight complication here is that there is also a money sum found to be due by the adjudicator to the claimant. In my judgment, arguments about the possible failure to comply with one part of the decision do not affect both parties' obligation to comply with all parts of the decision including, in this instance, the award of the money sum. Compliance and non-compliance are merely easier to identify if the adjudicator decides on a sum of money, rather than a declaration as to contractual rights.

The Exceptions

10.33 An obvious exception to the general rule is the decision of the Court of Appeal in *Parsons Plastic*, where the Court of Appeal concluded that specific contractual terms to set off did allow the overriding of the adjudicator's decision.[36] Three other cases, the first two of which were referred to by Jackson J in *Balfour Beatty Construction Ltd v Serco*, are also relevant.

(a) In *David McLean Housing Ltd v Swansea Housing Association Ltd*[37] the adjudicator issued a corrected decision on 22 March 2001, indicating that a sum should be certified under the contract in favour of the contractors. The following day the employer's agent issued a certificate which reflected that decision. On the same day, the defendant employer wrote to the claimant contractor stating that liquated and ascertained damages would be deducted from the payment due under that certificate. Subsequently, on 16 May 2001 the defendant wrote a further letter to the contractor stating that the contractor was liable to pay liquidated and ascertained damages in the sum of £130,359 and that its primary case was that it was entitled to deduct that sum from such sum as was otherwise due to the contractor under the contract.

---

[36] See paragraphs 10.23–10.24 above.
[37] [2002] BLR 125.

On the enforcement application in respect of the sum indicated in the adjudicator's decision, HHJ Lloyd QC concluded that the employer had realistic prospects of successfully demonstrating that the letter of 23 March complied with Clause 24 of the contract, which was concerned with the payment of liquidated damages for delay. He therefore declined to enforce the decision. Thus, *McLean* was a case where, in all the circumstances, the employer was able to set-off against the sum referred to in the decision. This was partly because of the rather vague notice of adjudication and the Judge's view that the adjudicator's decision could effectively be characterised as guidance as to what should have been certified in response to the specific interim payment application in question, rather than a finding that a specific sum was due and owing. In other words, the adjudicator was telling the parties what the certificate ought to contain and, once his decision was provided, a certificate in that form was then issued. Thus, given the almost advisory nature of the adjudicator's decision, the subsequent certificate that was issued was legitimately the subject of a withholding notice, pursuant to the express terms of the contract, to deduct liquidated damages. It is thought that a different sort of dispute, and a more specific adjudicator's decision, would have given rise to a situation where the decision could not have been the subject of a fresh notice (see, for example, *VHE*).

(b) Indeed, it was in precisely these terms that the decision in *McLean* was described by HHJ Seymour QC in *Solland International Ltd v Daraydan Holdings Ltd*[38] In that case, the Judge decided that, once the adjudicator had reached a conclusion as to whether the contractor was entitled to any, and if so what, extension of time, the employer was entitled to liquidated damages for any part of the period of actual delay for which the contractor had not been found entitled to an extension of time. Subject to the giving of a notice of intention to withhold payment in respect of liquidated and ascertained damages against the sum which the adjudicator had determined was payable to the contractor, there was no reason why a set-off was not appropriate in respect of that period. Accordingly, as Judge Seymour pointed out, the decision in *McLean* was in accordance with the principles outlined by Judge Hicks in *VHE* and the earlier cases.

(c) In *Geris Handelsgesellschaft v Les Constructions Industrielles de la Mediterrannée S.A.*,[39] HHJ Lloyd QC allowed the defendant to avoid summary enforcement of an adjudicator's decision, in which various sums had been found due to Geris, pending the quantification of various sums by way of set-off. Again, rather like the same Judge's decision in *McLean*, the set-off was allowed because of the nature and scope of the decision itself. The adjudicator was

---

[38] [2002] EWHC 220 (TCC).
[39] [2005] EWHC 499 (QB).

unable to resolve all the matters put to him because of jurisdictional difficulties. Therefore his decision included his conclusions as to those matters he could resolve, but was not a definitive statement that one party owed the other a specific sum. Moreover, the Judge concluded that the adjudicator had decided that the defendant was entitled to set off its cross-claims against any sums found due to Geris in other parts of his decision. Thus, the Judge's decision to allow the set-off in that case was in accordance with the express terms of the adjudicator's decision.

Another case which turned on its own particular facts, and the specific contract provisions, was *Connor Engineering Ltd v Les Constructions Industrielles de la Mediterranée*.[40] The principal dispute there was concerned with the proper definition of 'construction operations'. However, a separate point arose in relation to the dates for payment. The adjudicator said that the sums should be paid 14 days after the date of his decision. In accordance with the contract, a withholding notice could have been served not later than seven days before the expiry of that 14 day period; thus, because of the terms of the decision, a withholding notice could be served after the production of the decision, thereby avoiding the need for immediate payment in accordance with that decision. This was again because the adjudicator's decision was declaratory, not only as to amount, but also as to when that amount should be paid. If an adjudicator decides that the sum which he has found to be due should be paid within a period of 14 days or more after the date of the decision, then, depending on the contractual provisions as to the timing of withholding notices, this might allow the losing party to issue a withholding notice, particularly in respect of matters which were not the subject of the adjudication, in order to avoid immediate payment. In an appropriate case, an adjudicator is perhaps better advised to require any payment to be made forthwith, thereby preventing another dispute about the provision of a fresh withholding notice. **10.34**

Liquidated Damages

It will be seen that many of these attempts to set off sums against an adjudicator's decision arise out of the employer's cross-claim for liquidated damages. It has been argued that, following an adjudicator's decision, there is an implied term of the standard form of contract which would permit an employer to deduct liquidated damages from the amount of the award. The argument has been that such a term is necessary because without it, the contract would become unworkable. However, this bold submission was expressly rejected by Dyson J, as he then was, in *Edmund Nuttall Ltd v Sevenoaks District Council*.[41] Dyson J held that the **10.35**

---

[40] [2004] BLR 212.
[41] TCC, unreported, 14 April 2000.

contract worked perfectly satisfactorily without such a term. He was extremely wary about implying a term as to the circumstances in which liquidated and ascertained damages may be deducted from a sum due to the contractor, when the contract contained detailed express provisions which dealt precisely with that issue. The Judge also pointed out the employer's failure to address the claim for liquidated and ascertained damages; the cross-claim should have been advanced in the adjudication, but was not. He concluded that, since liquidated damages were not properly deductible under the contract at the time of the adjudicator's decision, they would not be properly deductible now. The employer's attempt to avoid the summary enforcement of the decision failed.

10.36 As noted above, particular difficulties can arise in circumstances where a contractor has made a claim for an extension of time which has been unsuccessful, either in whole or in part. In those circumstances, the employer naturally wishes to rely on the contractor's failure in order to make a claim for liquidated damages in respect of the period of delay for which no extension of time was awarded. Is the employer entitled to set off his claim for liquidated damages against any sums which the adjudicator may have awarded to the contractor?

10.37 There are three cases in particular which address this issue.

(a) In *The Construction Centre Group Ltd v The Highland Council*,[42] it was held that the employer was not entitled to rely on his cross-claim for liquidated damages, notice of which had been served after the adjudicator had communicated his decision to the parties, to defeat the enforcement claim. The court followed *Levolux*, holding that the adjudicator's decision was intended to have immediate enforceable effect. At paragraph 16 of the Opinion of the Court, Lord Hamilton stressed that it was sufficient to defeat the employer's reliance on the cross-claim for the court to hold that the claim for liquidated damages could have been, but was not, relied on in the adjudication, and that the employer's reliance on the claim for liquidated damages was inconsistent with its contractual obligation to give immediate effect to the adjudicator's decision.

(b) The fullest analysis of this issue can be found at paragraph 53 of the judgment of Jackson J in *Balfour Beatty Construction Ltd v Serco Ltd*.[43] The relevant principles are set out in full at paragraph 10.31 above. In essence, the employer can set off the sum claimed if the entitlement to liquidated damages has been determined, either expressly or impliedly, by the adjudicator's decision. If has not been so determined then it is more difficult, although ultimately it will depend on the precise words of the set-off provisions in the contract.

---

[42] [2003] XA123/02 Extra Division, Inner House, Court of Session.
[43] [2004] EWHC 3336 (TCC).

(c) More recently, in *William Verry Ltd v Mayor and Burgesses of the London Borough of Camden*[44] Ramsey J noted that, following *Levolux*, the right of set-off from an adjudicator's decision was generally excluded. As to the specific question of liquidated damages, at paragraph 29 of his judgment he said:

> The particular issue of whether liquidated damages can be deducted when the adjudicator's decision deals with extensions of time but does not deal with the consequential effect on an undisputed or indisputable claim for liquidated damages raises, I consider, a distinct question of the manner and extent of compliance with the adjudicator's decision. It does not, in my judgment, raise a question as to the ability to set-off sums generally against an adjudicator's decision.

In other words, an employer's ability to set off will probably turn on the contractual provisions relating to compliance with an adjudicator's decision and, in certain cases, the terms of the decision itself.

Summary

10.38 An employer cannot defeat a main contractor's claim, and a main contractor cannot defeat a sub-contractor's claim, by reference to a late and/or unparticularised set-off and counterclaim. A proper set-off and counterclaim must be the subject of a withholding notice and, if there is no such notice, or it is inadequate, the referring party will recover in full in the adjudication. If the sum claimed has been certified, then the absence of a withholding notice will be fatal even to claims for abatement, or allegations that, for whatever reason, the certified sum should not be paid. If, on the other hand, the amount has not been certified, then a withholding notice is not necessary in order to permit the paying party to scrutinise the invoice or interim payment application and to challenge aspects of it pursuant to the contract. A withholding notice will, however, still be necessary to allow the responding party to raise cross-claims for delay, defects and the like.

10.39 Generally it is not possible to set-off cross-claims against the sum that is the subject of an adjudicator's decision. To do so would deprive the 1996 Act of much of its purpose. It will only be possible for a losing party to set off a cross-claim against an adjudicator's decision in circumstances where the contract terms (relating either to set-off or compliance with the adjudicator's decision) clearly permit such a result, or where the adjudicator's decision does not have an immediate effect (where, for example, it is declaratory in nature), thereby allowing the provision of a timeous withholding notice after the completion and communication of the adjudicator's decision.

---

[44] [2006] EWHC 761 (TCC).

11

COSTS AND FEES

Costs	11.01	The Adjudicator's Fees	11.12
The Usual Position	11.01	Lien	11.19
Ad Hoc Jurisdiction to Decide Costs	11.05		
Particular Contract Provisions	11.07		

'A statutorily compliant private agreement in a construction contract for adjudication could sensibly provide that each party should bear their own legal costs and expenses... It is, however, commonplace that some construction contract adjudications are fiercely adversarial and expensive. It is commercially unsurprising if some parties, by adopting a standard form amendment to a standard form, give the adjudicator a jurisdiction to direct the payment of legal costs.'

May LJ in *John Roberts Architects Ltd v Parkcare Homes (No 2) Ltd* [2006] EWCA Civ 64.

Costs

The Usual Position

11.01 Although s108 of the 1996 Act sets out the parties' right to refer disputes to adjudication, and contains a number of specific provisions relating to the adjudicator's role and function, it says nothing about the adjudicator's power to make orders as to the payment of either side's costs at the conclusion of the adjudication. The Scheme for Construction Contracts contains detailed provisions relating to the payment of the adjudicator's fees,[1] but again contains no express power entitling an adjudicator to order one party to pay some or all of the other party's costs.

---

[1] This is discussed in greater detail in paragraphs 11.12–11.17 below.

11.02 In *Northern Developments (Cumbria) Ltd v J&J Nichol*[2] HHJ Bowsher QC pointed to paragraph 25 of the Scheme, which gave the adjudicator power to apportion liability for the payment of his fees as between the parties, and went on to note that nowhere in the 1996 Act or the Scheme was the adjudicator given any similar power to order one party to the adjudication to pay some or all of the costs of the other. He concluded therefore that, generally, an adjudicator had no jurisdiction to decide that one party's costs of the adjudication should be paid by the other party. Unless and until this point is taken to a higher court, the general statement of the law in *Northern Developments* appears to provide a clear answer to this perennial question.

11.03 This result can create considerable hardship to the ultimately successful party. Many adjudications involve a whole raft of complex issues and can require a team of lawyers and experts, working flat out, in order to deal with the numerous points that have arisen within the tight timetable of an adjudication. In litigation or arbitration, the responding party, if it defeats the claims brought against it, would normally be entitled to a costs order in its favour. However, in adjudication, where the costs can often be significant, no such order can be made. Take by way of example the situation where, three years after the event, an employer claims £10 million against the main contractor, for wrongful determination, defects and delay. Assume, after an intense 42 day adjudication, with the main contractor's team working round the clock to prepare a defence on all the detailed points raised, the determination and the defects claim fail, and the delay claim is successful to only a small degree. If that dispute had been fought in litigation or arbitration, the main contractor may well have been entitled to most of its costs on an issue-based approach.[3] However, since the dispute had been referred to adjudication, the main contractor would not be able to recover any of its costs.[4]

11.04 These difficulties explain why there have been a number of ingenious attempts by the successful party in adjudication to recover costs from the other side. Thus, in *Total M&E Services Ltd v ABB Building Technologies Ltd*[5] the successful party argued that their costs were recoverable as damages. The argument was that, if a responding party failed to pay sums due under the contract, it was foreseeable that the referring party would seek to refer the dispute to adjudication and properly incur costs in consequence, and thereafter seek to recover those costs from the responding party. HHJ Wilcox rejected this argument. He said that, since the

---

[2] [2000] BLR 158.
[3] See, for example, *Summit Property Ltd v Pitmans* [2001] EWCA Civ 2020 and *Fulham Leisure Holdings Ltd v Nicholson Graham & Jones* [2006] 2428 (Ch).
[4] Although there is a proposal to amend the 1996 Act in respect of costs, the proposed changes would not assist the main contractor in the example given. Indeed, the proposals would restrict further the ability of one party to recover its costs from another: see paragraphs 19.10–19.13 below.
[5] [2002] CILL 1857.

1996 Act did not provide for the recovery of costs, a claim that sought to categorise those costs as damages was misconceived. He also said that, because the Scheme envisaged that each party might refer a dispute to adjudication, and incur costs which they knew that they could not recover under the Act, it followed that such costs could not be recoverable as damages for breach of contract.

Ad Hoc Jurisdiction to Decide Costs

It is, of course, entirely possible for the parties to agree (either by reference to their contract terms, or in some other way) to give the adjudicator the express power to determine costs and award them against one of the parties. This was precisely what happened in *Northern Developments v J&J Nichol*.[6] In that case, having found that the adjudicator had no general right to order one party to pay the costs of the other, HHJ Bowsher QC went on to find, that on the facts of that particular case, the adjudicator had been granted such jurisdiction by implied agreement of the parties. The Judge observed that one party was represented by experienced solicitors and the other by experienced claims consultants. Each party asked in writing for their respective costs. Neither submitted to the adjudicator that he had no jurisdiction to award such costs. As a consequence, he concluded[7] that the parties had enlarged the jurisdiction of the adjudicator and given him the power to make an order requiring one party to pay the costs of the other party.[8] **11.05**

It is thought that it is in this context that the decision of HHJ Marshall Evans QC in *John Cothliff Ltd v Allen Build (North West) Ltd*[9] should be seen. On one view of the judgment in that case, the Judge appeared to indicate that an adjudicator had a general power to award costs. However, it is suggested that, on a proper analysis, Judge Evans was simply concluding that the adjudicator had such a power at least where, as in that case, costs had been expressly sought in the application before the adjudicator, and where both sides had been properly represented. In other words, his reasoning was very similar to that of Judge Bowsher in *Northern Developments*.[10] Both cases illustrate the dangers of one party expressly seeking their costs in the adjudication; if the they do so, there is at least the risk that this **11.06**

---

6 [2000] BLR 158.
7 The relevant part of his Judgment is set out verbatim at paragraph 3.82 above.
8 It should be noted that, in *John Roberts Architects Ltd v Parkcare Homes (No 2) Ltd* [2006] EWCA Civ 64, May LJ noted that, although both parties were seeking costs from the other, Roberts were not relying on a similar submission to the one that found favour in *Northern Developments*. He said that they were 'correct to refrain from doing so', because that was a decision under the Scheme, which contained no provision as to costs at all, whilst in *Roberts* the contract provided expressly that the adjudicator could make orders as to the costs of the adjudication.
9 [1999] CILL 1530.
10 For another case in which a Judge has expressly followed the reasoning of Judge Bowsher in *Northern Developments*, see the judgment of Judge Wilcox in *Nolan Davis Ltd v Stephen P Catton* (2000) unreported TCC No 590.

will begin a process which will ultimately allow the adjudicator to decide, in an appropriate case (say, where all the claims have failed), to award costs against the referring party or (where all or most of the claims have been successful) to award costs against the responding party.

Particular Contract Provisions

11.07 Some forms of contract (whether in a standard form or bespoke), and some adjudication rules, also provide expressly that the adjudicator can make costs orders against one (or both) of the parties. An early example of such a contract was *Bridgeway Construction Ltd v Tolent Construction Ltd*.[11] The unusual contract in that case required the party serving the notice of adjudication to bear all the costs and expenses incurred by both parties in relation to the adjudication, including but not limited to, all the legal costs and the experts' fees. HHJ MacKay QC upheld the terms of the contract, observing that contracting parties could contract how they liked and, if the result was legally unsatisfactory, the disappointed party could not come to court and seek a declaration that the terms were void. Although the suggestion was that those particular terms would inhibit a party from pursuing adjudication remedies, and that therefore the clauses should be declared void as a matter of policy, the Judge concluded that the provisions were not contrary to the 1996 Act and they could not be unfair because they applied to both parties.

11.08 An example of a case in which the particular adjudication rules which had been adopted gave the adjudicator the power to order costs is the Scottish case of *Deko Scotland Ltd v Edinburgh Royal Joint Venture*.[12] That was a case under the ORSA Adjudication Rules[13] of 1998 which, in Scotland, gave adjudicators the power to make awards of 'expenses', which is the equivalent term for costs. There was no dispute that, pursuant to that contract, the adjudicator had the power to order such costs/expenses to be paid; the argument concerned when such costs fell to be assessed and what they included. Lord Drummond Young held that the sums had to be taxed before they could be recovered in litigation. Moreover, he said that the award of expenses in adjudication should normally be confined to judicial expenses (ie legal costs), and therefore excluded internal costs and the fees paid to claims consultants and surveyors.

11.09 In *John Roberts Architects Ltd v Parkcare Homes (No 2) Ltd*[14] Parkcare employed Roberts to act as architects. Twice, Parkcare exercised its right to refer disputes to adjudication, but each time they abandoned the reference before the decision had

---

[11] [2000] CILL 1662.
[12] [2003] SLT 727.
[13] Now the TeCSA Rules. See paragraphs 4.62–4.70 above.
[14] [2005] EWHC 1637 (TCC); [2005] All ER (D) 341 (Jul).

been provided. Roberts brought proceedings to recover their costs of these abortive adjudications, their position apparently strengthened by the fact that, pursuant to the particular contract under which they were engaged, the adjudicator had a specific power to order legal costs and, at the time of the second abandonment, he had ordered Parkcare to pay Roberts' costs. However, at first instance the claim was rejected. HHJ Havery QC said that Parkcare had done no more than electing to treat the adjudicator as having jurisdiction in accordance with the terms of the contract, and that there was no term, express or implied, by which the adjudicator had power to award costs in the event of discontinuance of the adjudication. He said that any such power was only exercisable as part of a substantive decision. Furthermore, he said, there was no express or implied term of which a party would be in breach if it invoked the adjudication procedure in circumstances where there was no dispute properly referable to adjudication.

11.10 This decision was overturned in the Court of Appeal.[15] May LJ noted that rule 29 of the CIC Model Adjudication Procedure provided that the parties should bear their own costs and expenses incurred in adjudication, but that in this case, the rule had been deleted by Clause 9.2 of the RIBA Standard Conditions and replaced with a provision which allowed the adjudicator to direct the payment of legal costs and expenses of one party by another as part of his decision. This was a clear power which entitled the adjudicator to award costs. The argument on appeal was therefore whether that power was limited to circumstances in which the adjudicator produced a substantive decision on the dispute referred to him following a contested adjudication. May LJ said that it would be very odd indeed if, by their agreement, the parties had given the adjudicator power to direct the payment of legal costs (which could be substantial) only if he went on to make a substantive contested decision. He pointed out that such a conclusion would mean that either party, having generated legal costs by referring an unmeritorious claim to adjudication, or by responding to a claim with an unmeritorious defence, could throw their hand in at the eleventh hour without being at risk of paying the legal costs which their conduct had generated. He therefore concluded that the Judge had been persuaded to adopt the wrong construction of Clause 9.2, and he allowed the appeal.

11.11 It should be noted that, irrespective of the subsequent costs position, it was implicitly accepted by the Court of Appeal in *Roberts* that a party to adjudication could, if they so chose, withdraw/discontinue any claim that they had brought in adjudication proceedings. This was also the result in *Midland Expressway Ltd & Anor v Carillion Construction Ltd & Ors (No 3)*.[16] There, the claimants argued that

---

[15] [2006] EWCA Civ 64.
[16] [2006] EWHC 1505 (TCC).

the defendants, Carillion, were not entitled to withdraw a claim they had made in adjudication. Jackson J reached the unsurprising conclusion that it was impossible to read into either the 1996 Act or the Scheme any restriction prohibiting a party from withdrawing a disputed claim once it had been referred to adjudication. Any other result would have had the bizarre consequence that the referring party would have been forced to press on with a bad claim, which would have led to extensive wasted costs and resources, with no option but to pursue to inevitable defeat. Of course, under a contract which expressly allows the adjudicator to award legal costs against one of the parties, the party who discontinues a claim can expect to be faced with the submission that they should pay all the costs of that discontinued claim. But in the ordinary case, where the adjudicator has no power to make such costs orders, it does mean that a referring party in adjudication is entitled to discontinue a claim at the eleventh hour and avoid any of the usual cost consequences of such conduct.

The Adjudicator's Fees

11.12   In contrast to the position in respect of costs, the Scheme for Construction Contracts contains a number of provisions relating to the adjudicator's fees. If the adjudication is not effective, Paragraph 9(4) of the Scheme makes the parties liable for the adjudicator's fees and expenses in circumstances where the adjudicator resigns because the dispute is the same (or substantially the same) as one which has previously been referred to adjudication, or where the dispute as it emerges during the adjudication varies significantly from the dispute that was originally referred to him in the notice of adjudication, and he is not competent to decide it. More widely, Paragraph 25 of the Scheme expressly entitles the adjudicator to the payment of such reasonable amount as he may determine by way of fees and expenses reasonably incurred by him. It also expressly provides that the parties shall be jointly and severally liable for any sum by way of fees which remained outstanding following the making of any determination on how the payment shall be apportioned.

11.13   In practice, adjudicators will often order that each side pay half his fees. Usually, the parties are jointly and severally liable for those fees. Thus the winner can be held liable to the adjudicator to pay all his fees, and then recover 50 per cent from the loser: see *Donal Pugh v Harris Calman Construction Ltd*.[17] However, in a case where the adjudicator has found wholly or mainly in favour of one party, then it is not uncommon for the adjudicator to order that the successful party can recover his half of the fees from the unsuccessful party. Such an order is perfectly

---

[17] [2003] CLDC 30.6.03.

legitimate, and is one way in which the adjudicator, without the general power to make one side pay the other's costs, can maintain a broadly just and fair balance between the parties, in order to reflect the ultimate outcome of the adjudication. In addition, an adjudicator's decision as to liability to pay fees is final and is not subject to challenge in subsequent arbitration/litigation: see *Castle Inns (Stirling) Ltd v Clark Contracts Ltd*.[18]

11.14 Although the Scheme deals with the position where an adjudicator resigns because the dispute has already been decided in an earlier adjudication, it does not deal with the position where the adjudicator resigns because he has no jurisdiction generally. However, by analogy with paragraph 9(4) it is suggested that an adjudicator is entitled to the fees incurred up to his resignation on the grounds of an absence of jurisdiction. The Scheme provides further support for this approach: in paragraph 11(1) the adjudicator is entitled to his fees if his appointment is revoked by agreement between the parties. The only exception to that, as stated in paragraph 11(2), is where the appointment is revoked due to the default or misconduct of the adjudicator. Thus, in *Paul Jenson Ltd v Staveley Industries Plc*,[19] the adjudicator resigned because he did not have jurisdiction. The District Judge rightly said that whether or not the adjudicator was right or wrong in arriving at this conclusion was irrelevant. On the adjudicator's claim for fees, the District Judge held that, since there was no suggestion of any fault or misconduct on his part, the adjudicator was entitled to the fees incurred up to his resignation.

11.15 What happens when an adjudicator produces a decision in good faith, but it then becomes apparent that he did not, after all, have the necessary jurisdiction to reach that decision? In *Griffin & Anor (t/a K&D Contractors) v Midas Homes Ltd*[20] HHJ Lloyd QC ruled that the adjudicator had the jurisdiction to reach part of his decision, but not jurisdiction as to the remainder. Judge Lloyd then had to deal with the parties' respective liabilities for the fees incurred by the adjudicator in respect of that part of the decision for which he had no jurisdiction. There was apparently no question but that the adjudicator would recover that element of his fees: the only issue was who should pay them. He concluded that the defendant could not be liable for those fees, because the defendant had not caused the reference to the adjudicator of matters in respect of which he had no jurisdiction. The Judge said that only the party who had originally sought adjudication could be liable for the fees, expenses and costs that had been incurred as a consequence of their request for a decision which the adjudicator had no authority to make. Because the referring party was not entitled under the contract to refer one part of the claim, and was therefore in breach of contract in so doing, that party was liable

---

[18] [2005] Scot CS CSOH 178.
[19] 27.9.01, Wigan County Court, Mr District Judge Donnelly.
[20] [2000] 78 Con LR 152.

for that element of the adjudicator's fees. A slightly different result was apparently reached in the Scottish case of *Prentice Island Ltd v Castle Contracting Ltd*.[21] The adjudicator required payment by the defendants to the pursuers of the sum of £1,922.70, being one half of the adjudicator's total fees and VAT in respect of the adjudication. The Judge concluded that, for entirely separate reasons, the adjudicator had, in good faith, fallen into error and continued to act in circumstances in which he ought to have resigned. Nevertheless, it was held that the adjudicator remained in post as a validly appointed adjudicator, and was therefore entitled to be paid his fees, half by each side. The point was not apparently taken that the defenders should not be made liable for their half of the adjudicator's fees, because it was the pursuers who had commenced the adjudication. In addition, it does not seem that the argument was run that, in accordance with *Griffin*, to the extent that fees were incurred in dealing with a claim in respect of which the adjudicator had no jurisdiction, it could only be the pursuers who were liable for those costs. *Griffin*, although a reported case, was not apparently cited to the court in *Prentice Island*. It is submitted that, for these reasons, the latter is a decision which needs to be treated with some caution.

11.16 Pursuant to s108(4) of the 1996 Act, it is stipulated that the contract must provide that the adjudicator is not liable for anything done or omitted in the discharge or purported discharge of his functions as adjudicator, unless the act or omission is in bad faith. This provision finds expression in paragraph 26 of the Scheme for Construction Contracts, which repeats exactly the words of s108(4). Similar provisions are included in the standard forms of contract. An interesting question therefore arises as to whether this provision provides an immunity from a claim by one or both of the parties that the adjudicator's claimed hours and/or remuneration are unreasonable. The better view would appear to be that, if the adjudicator has determined his fees and expenses, it may well not be possible (at least in the ordinary case) for the parties, even if they consider that they have a genuine complaint about the extent of those fees, to seek to open up or review the adjudicator's fee claim. In *Stubbs Rich Architects v WH Tolley & Son Ltd*[22] the adjudicator relied on the immunity to protect himself from the attack made by one of the parties on the scope and scale of his fees. The court concluded that the fees could be challenged if, and only if, the adjudicator had acted in bad faith, and it was not suggested that he had done so. It was also said that there was no statutory regime which could allow the re-examination of the adjudicator's fees and that the immunity therefore applied. In the same case, the Judge also criticised the finding in the court below that the fees were excessive, saying that a court must be

---

[21] [2003] Judgment of Sheriff Principal R A Dunlop QC, unreported.
[22] 8 August 2001, Gloucester County Court, decision of Mr Recorder Lane QC.

very slow indeed to substitute its own view of what constitutes reasonable hours for that reached by the adjudicator.

11.17 Of course, that is not to say that an adjudicator is entitled to his fees, regardless of conduct. In *Dr Peter Rankilor v Perco Engineering Services Ltd and Another*,[23] the TCC Judge concluded that the decision was not in breach of natural justice. However, he went on to observe that it was 'a surprising submission that if an adjudicator's decision had been reached in serious breach of the rules of natural justice and thus would not be enforced by the court, that the adjudicator should nevertheless be entitled to claim payment for producing what was in fact a worthless decision without even any temporary binding legal effect'.

11.18 A related point as to entitlement to fees might arise if the adjudicator fails to produce his decision in the 28 days (or the agreed extended period). In such circumstances, it might be extremely difficult for the adjudicator to argue that he was entitled to be paid fees when his failure to produce the decision in time had led to the production of a decision which was in law a nullity. It may be that in such circumstances, the court would find that there had been a complete failure of consideration, and the adjudicator was not entitled to any fees at all. Furthermore, in such circumstances, an immunity couched in standard terms might be of little assistance to the adjudicator. In *Cubitt Building & Interiors Ltd v Fleetglade Ltd*[24] the TCC Judge concluded that the decision had been completed and communicated in time. However, at paragraph 91 of his judgment, he pointed out that, if he had reached the opposite conclusion, the indemnity in respect of anything done in the discharge of the adjudicator's functions would not have protected him, because the adjudicator's failure to complete the decision within the agreed period would have represented a complete failure on his part to discharge those functions at all.

Lien

11.19 There can be no doubt that the speed of the adjudication process means that, in a usual case, the adjudicator will provide his decision to the parties at a time when he has recovered either none, or a small amount on account, of his fees. Thereafter, it appears that the parties can be slow to pay the outstanding fees and this can cause real hardship for adjudicators. There are a number of reported cases in which adjudicators have been put through all manner of procedural hoops by parties seeking to avoid payment of their fees. A good example of this unfortunate process is *Faithful & Gould Ltd v Arcal Ltd (In Administrative Receivership) & Ors*.[25]

---

[23] 27.1.06, a decision of HHJ Gilliland QC, sitting in the TCC in Salford.
[24] [2006] EWHC 3413 (TCC).
[25] (Unreported) TCC, Newcastle District Registry, No E190023.

There, the first defendant was in administrative receivership and the claim was pursued against the second and third defendants who were the receivers, and employees or partners of Deloitte & Touche. The adjudicator had to issue proceedings for his fees, despite the fact that the defendants had expressly assured him that they would pay his fees before he embarked on the adjudication. The Judge was moved to remark that the defendants had sought to mount 'practically every obstacle to this claim that human ingenuity could devise'. They did so without providing any statement of truth to the court. He rejected all the various points that were taken in opposition to the claim and expressed his surprise and disappointment that Deloitte & Touche should have conducted themselves in such a way.[26]

11.20 In order to try and get round these difficulties in the collection of their fees, adjudicators have in the past sought to exercise a lien on those fees, saying that they will not release their decision until their fees have been paid in full. In arbitration, of course, where there is no statutory deadline, this is a common occurrence. In adjudication, the courts have indicated firmly that, because of the emphasis on speed in adjudication above all things, the purported exercise of a lien will not be permitted.

11.21 The first case in which this point was decided was *St Andrews Bay Development Ltd v HBG Management Ltd*.[27] In that case the adjudicator failed to produce a decision within the time limits but, because the delay was only two days, Lord Wheatley regarded the failure as a technical matter rather than a fundamental error or impropriety eviscerating her entire decision.[28] It appears from the report that at least part of the delay in the communication of the decision arose from the adjudicator's insistence that her fees be paid. At paragraph 19 of his judgment, Lord Wheatley said that she had no entitlement to act in this way. He said there was nothing in the Scheme or the contract which allowed it. Whilst an adjudicator could come to a separate arrangement with the parties concerning the payment of her fees, it was not permissible for such an arrangement to frustrate or impede the progress of the statutory arrangement (adjudication) for resolving the contractual disputes. Any arrangement between the parties and the adjudicator had to be accommodated within the statutory or contractual time limits. The payment of the adjudicator's fees could not be allowed to impede the statutory process or justify a failure to observe its requirements.

---

[26] Another example of this trend is *Cartwright v Fay*, 9 February 2005, Bath County Court. That was another case in which every conceivable point was taken (again unsuccessfully) in opposition to the fees claimed by the adjudicator.

[27] [2003] SLT 740.

[28] This decision has to be read in the light of the later decisions in *Ritchie (PWC) Ltd v Philip* [2005] SLDT 341, a decision in which Lord Wheatley gave the dissenting judgment; *Hart Investments Ltd v Fidler and Another* [2006] EWHC 2857 (TCC); *Cubitt Building & Interiors Ltd v Fleetglade Ltd* [2006] EWHC 3413 (TCC); *Aveat Heating Limited v Jerram Falkus Construction Limited* [2007] EWHC 131 (TCC); and *AC Yule & Son Ltd v Speedwell Roofing & Cladding Limited* [2007] EWHC 1360 (TCC).

In *Cubitt Building & Interiors Ltd v Fleetglade Ltd*[29] the adjudicator's terms of appointment stated expressly that a lien might be exercised over the publication of the decision until receipt of payment by either party. The TCC Judge thought that such an open-ended extension of the statutory period was contrary to the whole principle of adjudication as described in the 1996 Act. He referred to *St Andrews Bay* and concluded that the adjudicator was not entitled to exercise a lien in relation to the decision, either as a matter of contract or as a matter of law. The overriding obligation on the part of the adjudicator was to complete and communicate the decision within the 28 days or the extended period agreed by both parties. A potential lien was contrary to that overriding obligation. **11.22**

Similar reasoning (albeit on a slightly different point) can be found in the decision of His Honour Judge Havery QC in *Epping Electrical Company Limited v Briggs and Forrester (Plumbing Services) Limited*.[30] The Judge found that the 28 day period in the 1996 Act was mandatory and that a contractual provision which suggested otherwise did not comply with the Act. Thus the decision was a nullity. In addition, it appeared that there was a further delay between completion and communication of the decision, brought about by the exercise of a purported lien by the adjudicator, which was subsequently withdrawn. A similar point arose in *Mott MacDonald Ltd v London & Regional Properties Ltd*[31] where, at paragraphs 75–78 of his judgment, HHJ Thornton QC held that the lien that the adjudicator imposed and implemented was contrary to paragraphs 12(a) and 19(3) of the Scheme. On the facts of that case, the Judge also found that the adjudicator appeared to lack impartiality, because he had made it a condition of his appointment that his fees would first have to be paid by the referring party before he delivered his decision to the parties, and then by appearing to enforce that pre-condition. The Judge said, at paragraph 77 of his judgment, that the adjudicator may not be, or appear to be, financially beholden to one party, particularly the referring party, or place himself in the position in which he might appear to be more partial to one side than the other. **11.23**

For the reasons set out above, it seems safe to assume that an adjudicator has no power to exercise a lien over his outstanding fees, if to do so would result in any delay to the completion or communication of the decision. It is recognised that, in consequence, the payment of their fees will remain a problem area for adjudicators but, in the light of the critical emphasis on speed in the 1996 Act, there is little that can obviously be done to alleviate these commercial difficulties. **11.24**

---

[29] [2006] EWHC 3413 (TCC).
[30] [2007] EWHC 4 (TCC).
[31] [2007] EWHC 1055 (TCC).

Part IV

ENFORCEMENT

12. The Status and Effect of an Adjudicator's Decision	349
13. Principles of Enforcement	369
14. Adjudication Business in the TCC	381
15. Stay of Execution	395

12

THE STATUS AND EFFECT OF AN ADJUDICATOR'S DECISION

Introduction	12.01	Temporary Finality/Subsequent	
A Valid Decision	12.04	Adjudications	12.27
Compliance with Time Limits	12.06	Status in Later Court or	
Errors and Slips	12.09	Arbitration Proceedings	12.35
The Decision Itself	12.15	Winding Up/Bankruptcy	12.41
Compliance with the Decision	12.16	Protective Measures in Scotland	12.46
Status of Decision	12.19		
Temporary Finality/Generally	12.24		

'Mr Raynsford: [We are] aiming for a solution that was perfectly expressed in representations to the Minister and Opposition by Professor John Uff QC. In a happy phrase, he expressed concern that the objective should be to ensure 'decisions of temporary finality only'. That is an elegant way of expressing what we all want to achieve.

Mr Robert B Jones: I should like to hear the Professor trying to defend that in the courts.

Mr Raynsford: As a QC, he no doubt has many opportunities to defend such construction. His phrase captures the essence of what we want from adjudication.'

Hansard, 18th June 1996, columns 331–332, Standing Committee F.

Introduction

The sponsors of the original Bill were attracted by the proposition that adjudication in the construction industry would not only be compulsory, but also binding; in other words, they envisaged a situation where the decision of an adjudicator could not be challenged. However, this was met with a chorus of disapproval from almost all directions, the main objection being that, if an

12.01

adjudicator had to decide a dispute within a very short time, mistakes were entirely foreseeable, and it would be grossly unfair if the party who suffered from such a mistake had no opportunity at all to rectify the error. The good sense of this position was quickly acknowledged, but it immediately created another problem: if the decision was not to be binding, what was the purpose of adjudication at all?

12.02 Eventually, it was proposed that, although it was essential that the adjudicator's decision should be binding on the parties, the parties would have the opportunity to re-open the dispute, if they chose to do so, either in arbitration or in litigation. Although it was said in the House of Lords that it was hard to see how a decision could be both binding and temporary,[1] in practice, this concept has given rise to few difficulties. The adjudicator's decision becomes binding on the parties, because that is what the 1996 Act provides or, in a contractual adjudication, what is expressly provided for by the terms of the contract. Thereafter, although the parties can agree to accept the adjudicator's decision as finally determining the dispute, if they do not do so, then the decision remains binding until the dispute is finally determined by legal proceedings or arbitration.[2]

12.03 In most cases, therefore, the position is very straightforward. Assuming that the adjudicator's decision is valid (because he had the necessary jurisdiction to reach that decision and, in so doing, there was no breach of the rules of natural justice) then the parties are bound to comply with that decision. If the losing party does not comply with it, the winning party is entitled to issue enforcement proceedings to ensure compliance. The parties can then agree that the adjudicator's decision has finally determined the particular dispute in question. Even if they have not reached such an agreement, that will be the effect of the adjudicator's decision unless and until the loser reopens the dispute in subsequent arbitration or litigation. At that point, the dispute becomes reopened in its entirety, and the adjudicator's decision has no evidential or legal status. A number of these points are developed in the paragraphs below.

A Valid Decision

12.04 For the reasons set out in Chapter 8 above, the adjudicator's decision will usually be enforced by the courts, even if the reasoning that justified that decision was erroneous in law or fact.[3] However, as HHJ Lloyd QC made plain in

---

[1] In the debate on 23 July 1996, Lord Howie of Troon said: 'I know that I am only a Scot and we look at things somewhat differently, but it is hard to see how it can be both binding and temporary . . .' (Hansard, 23.7.96, page 1342).
[2] Section 108(3).
[3] The basis for the discussion below as to enforcement is that set out in footnote 1 to Chapter 7.

Alstom Signalling Ltd v Jarvis Facilities Ltd[4] the enforcement policy only applies to decisions which are valid, namely decisions which the adjudicator was authorised to reach, in circumstances where that decision was not vitiated by some material failure to comply with basic concepts of fairness. Thus, as the Judge pointed out, it is misleading to speak of a right of enforcement of an adjudicator's decision; such a right is always qualified or contingent on the validity of the decision itself.

In addition to questions of jurisdiction and natural justice, there are two procedural hurdles which need to be cleared by the adjudicator if the decision is not to be regarded as an unenforceable nullity. These are concerned with the adjudicator's obligation to comply with the statutory time limits (as extended by agreement) and his ability, if any, to make corrections to errors in the decision communicated to the parties. **12.05**

Compliance with Time Limits

The time limits for the provision of the referral notice, and the adjudicator's obligation to complete the decision within 28 days (or any extended period) has been dealt with in detail at paragraphs 2.91–2.108 and, in relation to the particular requirements of the Scheme, at paragraphs 3.69–3.71 above. On a careful review of the cases cited there, there is no authority for the proposition that an adjudicator is entitled to take longer than the 28 days (or any extended period agreed by the parties) in order to complete his decision.[5] Indeed the authorities reiterate that both the 1996 Act, and the standard forms of contract, only confer authority on the adjudicator to make a decision within the 28 day period, or such other period as may be agreed: see, for example, paragraph 26 of the judgment of HHJ LLoyd QC in *Barnes & Elliott Ltd v Taylor Woodrow Holdings Ltd*.[6] **12.06**

A number of the most recent cases on the point reiterate that the decision must be completed within the relevant period and that the adjudicator was not entitled unilaterally to award himself some sort of extension of time for completion of the decision. In *Ritchie Bros (PWC) Ltd v David Philp (Commercials) Ltd*[7] the decision was provided over a week late. The Court of Session held, by a majority, **12.07**

---

[4] [2004] EWHC 1285 (TCC), paragraphs 19 and 20.
[5] The only decision which suggests to the contrary, *Simons Construction Ltd v Aardvaark Developments Ltd* [2004] 1 BLR 117, has been expressly doubted and not followed in *Ritchie Bros (PWC) Ltd v David Philp (Commercials) Ltd* [2005] 1 BLR 384 and *Cubitt Building and Interiors Ltd v Fleetglade Ltd* [2006] EWHC 3413 (TCC). The suggestion that what matters is not the language of the 1996 Act, but the consequences of the non-compliance, was rejected for a variety of reasons by the TCC Judge in *AC Yule & Son Ltd v Speedwell Roofing & Cladding Limited* [2007] EWHC 1360 (TCC).
[6] [2004] BLR 111.
[7] [2005] BLR 384.

that the decision was not within the adjudicator's jurisdiction because it was a decision that had been reached out of time. The Court rejected the suggestion that the adjudicator was entitled to reach his decision at any time during an indefinite period after the expiry of the 28 days so long as none of the parties had served a fresh Notice of Adjudication. Lord Nimmo Smith pointed out that if, as was plainly the case, certainty was a principal objective of adjudication, it was not achieved by leaving the parties in doubt as to where they stood after the expiry of the 28 day period.

12.08 This approach and these comments were expressly approved in *Cubitt Building and Interiors Ltd v Fleetglade Ltd*.[8] There the TCC judge referred to his earlier decision of *Hart v Fidler & Another*[9] in which he had expressly said that he considered the decision in *Ritchie* was right. He went on to say that, in his view, adjudicators did not have the jurisdiction to grant themselves extensions of time without the express consent of both parties and that, if their time management was so poor that they failed to provide a decision in the relevant period and had not sought an extension, their decision may well be a nullity, as in *Ritchie*. HHJ Havery QC also came to the same conclusion in both *Aveat Heating Ltd v Jerram Falkus* and *Epping Electrical Co Ltd v Briggs & Forrester (Plumbing Services) Ltd*.[10]

Errors and Slips

12.09 As discussed at length in paragraphs 8.18–8.30 above, the fact that an adjudicator makes an error or slip will not ordinarily invalidate his decision and will not give the losing party any ground for objecting to the enforcement of the subsequent decision. Thus, in the best-known example of this approach, the Court of Appeal held that an adjudicator's decision was enforceable, even though he had muddled together gross and net sums, with the result that he released to the contractor all the retention monies, even though it was not suggested that such retentions were due under the contract.[11] It should be noted that, in that case, the adjudicator wrote to the parties, once the alleged error had been pointed out, and maintained that his calculations correctly reflected his intentions and did not contain a clerical mistake, or an error arising from an accidental slip or omission. He therefore concluded that he would not make any amendment to his decision.

---

[8] [2006] EWHC 3413 (TCC).
[9] [2006] EWHC 2857 (TCC).
[10] There is a full discussion of these, and the other cases on this topic at paragraphs 2.91–2.108 above.
[11] See *Bouygues (UK) Ltd v Dahl-Jensen (UK) Ltd* [2000] BLR 49 (Dyson J); [2000] BLR 522 (Court of Appeal).

12.10 For these reasons, the general position is that an error or a slip by an adjudicator does not invalidate his decision. However, what is the effect of an error or a slip which the adjudicator acknowledges and endeavours promptly to rectify? Is he entitled to rectify such an error, and does either the original error or the purported rectification invalidate the decision?

12.11 Depending on the nature of the error, and the speed with which it is rectified, it is thought that, in some circumstances, an adjudicator does have the power to rectify an error without invalidating the decision. The best-known example of this is *Bloor Construction (UK) Ltd v Bowmer & Kirkland (London) Ltd*[12] where the adjudicator sent out a decision at 3.32 p.m. on 11.2.00 to the effect that Bowmer should pay to Bloor about £122,000. On receipt of that decision, Bowmer pointed out to the adjudicator that he had failed to deduct the payments on account previously made by Bowmer. The adjudicator agreed that he had made an error and, at 5.53 p.m. on the same day, he sent out a corrected decision which, after making due allowance for the previous payments on account, concluded that Bloor were entitled to no further payment. HHJ Toulmin CMG QC concluded that, in the absence of any specific agreement to the contrary, a term should be implied into the contract that an adjudicator might correct a mistake arising from an accidental error or omission and that, although there had to be a time limit within which such corrections could be made, the issue of a corrected decision within three hours of the erroneous decision was within any acceptable time limit. Accordingly, Bloor were not permitted to enforce the adjudicator's first and uncorrected decision and the corrected decision was held to be a valid statement of the position as between the parties.

12.12 Perhaps surprisingly, in view of the sheer volume of cases concerned with adjudication enforcement, there is only one subsequent decision in which the implied term identified by Judge Toulmin in *Bloor* has been further considered. That was *Edmund Nuttall Ltd v Sevenoaks District Council*[13] which was decided shortly after *Bloor*. There, too, the adjudicator had immediately accepted that an error had been made, and took steps to correct it. In considering whether or not there was any residual power to make the correction, Dyson J said that, 'putting the matter at its lowest, it is at least arguable that it [the decision in *Bloor*] is right'. He also stressed that the adjudicator's prompt correction of the error was a feature of the present case which was not present in *Bouygues*.

12.13 It is thought therefore that, in straightforward circumstances, an adjudicator ought to have the power to correct clear and obvious errors. Indeed, many of the

---

[12] [2000] BLR 314.
[13] Unreported, 14 April 2000, a decision of Dyson J.

standard forms of contract expressly provide the adjudicator with such a power.[14] But it is also thought that this power could only be exercised in rare cases, and that often there will be a risk that the purported correction will be invalid or, even worse, might operate to invalidate both the original and the amended decisions. First, it is thought that the original error would have to be accepted as an error by the adjudicator. It should be clear and obvious. Secondly, it should be corrected immediately, as happened in *Bloor*. If the error is pointed out to the adjudicator, and two or three days go by without any rectification, then it will be appropriate for the parties to assume that any power to change the terms of the decision will have lapsed. Sufficient certainty in the adjudication process cannot be provided if an adjudicator is entitled to amend his decision days after it has been sent out and the alleged error pointed out to him.[15]

12.14 Accordingly, it is most unlikely that any sort of slip rule could operate in circumstances where the adjudicator did not expressly accept that an error had occurred. Thus in *CIB Properties Ltd v Birse Construction Ltd*[16] there was no acceptance by the adjudicator that he had made any error, and his written indication that the whole matter would be reviewed by the courts was not to be taken as an admission that there was any error in the first place. And in *Joinery Plus Ltd v Laing Ltd*[17] HHJ Thornton QC held that an adjudicator who had sent out a decision based on an incorrect set of sub-contract terms was not entitled to write to the parties purporting to correct that decision by stating that the error was of no material relevance to the substance of his decision. In that case, the Judge ruled that the original decision, because it was based on the incorrect contract terms, was a nullity.

The Decision Itself

12.15 It should also be noted that, in extreme cases, the court may decline to enforce the decision summarily because of a deficiency in the decision itself. Thus, in *Paul Broadwell (t/a Broadwell Construction) v k3D Property Partnership Ltd*,[18]

---

[14] There is a proposal to amend the 1996 Act to make express provision for a slip rule: see paragraphs 19.31–19.32 below.
[15] There is evidence to suggest that parties to an adjudication operate a commercial and commonsense approach to errors and slips. For example, in *Cubitt Building and Interiors Ltd v Fleetglade Ltd* [2006] EWHC 3413 (TCC) there was a major dispute about whether or not the decision had been completed within the agreed extended period. However this argument was all about the events leading up to the last day of that period and the events in the 12 hours after the expiry of that period. Quite separately, there was an agreed error in the decision, which was pointed out to the adjudicator and caused him to make a subsequent modification to the decision. Neither party took any point on that correction procedure.
[16] [2005] 1 WLR 2252.
[17] [2003] BLR 184.
[18] [2006] Adj CS 04/21.

there had been a number of sub-issues referred to the adjudicator. The decision dealt only with some of these matters, stating simply that 'all other matters had been considered'. HHJ Raynor, sitting at the TCC in Salford, concluded that the adjudicator had failed to deal expressly with all the matters referred to him, including in particular all aspects of the defence, and that the catch-all phrase in the decision was inadequate. The application for summary judgment was refused.

Compliance with the Decision

12.16 Section 108(3) of the 1996 Act provides that the decision of the adjudicator is binding until the dispute is finally determined by legal proceedings or by arbitration. The parties are therefore obliged to comply with the decision. Paragraph 23(2) of the Scheme for Construction Contracts provides that the parties 'shall comply' with the decision of the adjudicator 'until the dispute is finally determined by legal proceedings, by arbitration . . . or by agreement between the parties'. Most of the standard forms of construction and engineering contracts expressly provide that the parties are bound to comply with the adjudicator's decision.

12.17 The general requirement for compliance was spelt out in clear terms by Dyson J in *Macob Civil Engineering Ltd v Morrison Construction Ltd*.[19] He said that the intention of the 1996 Act was to introduce a speedy mechanism for settling disputes in construction contracts on a provisional interim basis and required the decisions of adjudicators to be enforced pending final determination. Absent questions of jurisdiction, natural justice or some sort of procedural question, the parties must comply with the adjudicator's decision. Since most adjudications are about claims for money due, this means that the losing party must pay to the successful party the sum identified by the adjudicator in his decision.

12.18 The presumption that an adjudicator's decision must be complied with forthwith has given rise to procedural issues: what is the best way of enforcing the decision of an adjudicator? One of the earliest cases on this point was *Outwing Construction Ltd v H Randell & Son Ltd*.[20] There the adjudicator's decision was dated 12.2.99 and required the defendant to pay a sum to the claimant. The claimant issued an invoice in that sum on 15.2.99. No money was forthcoming and on 8.3.99, the claimant issued a writ. On 10.3.99 the claimant issued and served a summons returnable on 12.3.99 seeking that the defendant's time for acknowledgment of service be abridged to two days, and that the time for the defendant to serve

---

[19] [1999] BLR 93.
[20] [1999] BLR 156.

evidence in opposition to the claim for summary judgment be abridged to seven days. On the morning of the return day, the defendant paid the claimant the sum claimed plus interest and costs. However the defendant refused to pay the costs of the application, on the ground that payment of the full amount stayed the action and that, since the claimant had indicated that, if payment was made within 14 days the costs would be limited, the claimant was not justified in its conduct and had acted with undue haste. HHJ Lloyd QC rejected this argument, holding that it was justified to abridge time because an action to enforce an adjudicator's decision was not comparable to the process of recovering an apparently undisputed debt. The 1996 Act required that adjudicators' decisions, if not complied with, were to be enforced without delay. He also concluded that there was no reason why a party, who had not voluntarily complied with a decision, should be allowed the best part of a month before the decision was converted into an order of the court. *Outwing* was the start of the special enforcement procedure created by the TCC for the enforcement of adjudicators' decisions, which is explained in greater detail in Chapter 14 below.

Status of Decision

12.19 There has been a good deal of careful consideration as to the nature of a claimant's cause of action when endeavouring to enforce an adjudicator's decision. In *VHE Construction plc v RBSTB Trust Co Ltd*[21] HHJ Hicks QC concluded that enforcement proceedings were proceedings to enforce a contractual obligation, namely the obligation to comply with the adjudicator's decision. The adjudicator's decision did not have the status of a judgment and there was no provision in the 1996 Act which corresponded to section 66 of the Arbitration Act 1996, under which, by leave of the court, judgment may be entered in terms of an arbitral award or the award may be enforced in the same manner as a judgment. Similarly, in *David McLean Housing Contractors Ltd v Swansea Housing Association Ltd*[22] HHJ Lloyd QC said that a decision was not an arbitral award and could not be equated to one. He said that an action to enforce an adjudicator's decision was an action to enforce the right or liability which had been upheld by that decision.

12.20 In *Bovis Lend Lease Ltd v Triangle Development Ltd*[23] HHJ Thornton QC also considered the nature of enforcement proceedings. Although certain aspects of the judgment in that case, concerned with arguments relating to set-off,

---

[21] [2000] BLR 187.
[22] [2002] BLR 125.
[23] [2003] CILL 1939.

were doubted by the Court of Appeal in *Levolux AT Ltd v Ferson Contractors Ltd*[24] it is thought that the Judge's summary of the nature of enforcement proceedings is not only uncontroversial but positively helpful. The Judge said that, ordinarily, a decision of an adjudicator will give rise to a contractual entitlement to immediate payment without deduction, set-off, withholding, reliance on a cross-claim, abatement, or stay of execution. That was because the sum in question was due by virtue of the statutory and contractually-backed provisions requiring compliance and the giving of full effect to the decision of an adjudicator, in addition to it being due by virtue of the underlying contractual provisions. It was for that reason that the courts had repeatedly held that no deduction or withholding would ordinarily be allowed from the sum found due by reference to an adjudicator's decision.

12.21 The point should also be made that an adjudicator's decision is to be treated as a whole, and the parties cannot seek to approbate those parts of it which they like, and reprobate those parts of it which they do not. In *Redworth Construction Ltd v Brookdale Healthcare Ltd*[25] the claimant contractor advanced a particular case in the adjudication as to the make-up of the contract between the parties, in support of its case that the adjudicator had the necessary jurisdiction. The adjudicator acceded to those submissions. The defendant maintained its jurisdictional challenge. In the subsequent enforcement proceedings, the contractor sought to put its case on the contract in a very different way. HHJ Havery QC refused to allow the contractor to go beyond the matters that it had relied on in the adjudication in order to support the adjudicator's conclusion that he had the necessary jurisdiction. He did this on the basis of the principle of election: Redworth had elected to put their case in a particular way, and they could not now resile from it. He reasoned that Redworth had made their election in order to obtain a benefit, namely the decision of an adjudicator in their favour, both as to his jurisdiction and substantively. They had in consequence obtained both those benefits, regardless of whether the same benefits could have been obtained by other arguments, particularly in circumstances where it was not clear that such benefits could have been so obtained. It was therefore unjust to allow Redworth to resile from their election by arguing a different case on contract formation to endeavour to hang on to the money decision in their favour. They could not approbate and reprobate the adjudicator's decision.

12.22 In *Knapman Ltd v Richards & Ors*[26] the argument was advanced that a claimant who was seeking to be paid in accordance with the adjudicator's decision was seeking to approbate and reprobate because the adjudicator had also found that the claimant's supply of the windows and doors had been unsatisfactory

---

[24] [2003] 86 Con LR 98.
[25] [2006] EWHC 1994 (TCC).
[26] [2006] EWHC 2518 (TCC).

and incomplete. However, the TCC Judge concluded that, on the facts, that was not a case where the approbation/reprobation principle was relevant or applicable. Although the adjudicator had decided that the claimant was liable in respect of the doors and windows, this had not crystallised into a financial decision, and the terms on which the contractor would return to site to carry out this work were still under negotiation. It could not be said, therefore, that the contractor had reprobated the adjudicator's decision, and he was entitled to the sum decided by the adjudicator.

12.23 It is, of course, plain beyond argument that a party who accepted and/or relied upon the decision of an adjudicator following its communication to the parties could not, at some later stage, as a result of some change in circumstances, seek to argue that the adjudicator did not have the necessary jurisdiction to reach that decision or that, in some way, it was entitled to reject the validity of the decision which it had earlier accepted: see, by way of example, *Shimuzu Europe Ltd v Automajor Ltd*,[27] discussed at paragraphs 8.22–8.23 above, and *R Durtnell & Sons Ltd v Kaduna Ltd*[28] discussed at paragraph 7.13 above.

Temporary Finality/Generally

12.24 Despite the concerns expressed during the passage of the Bill through Parliament, the construction industry has had little difficulty with the concept of 'temporary finality'. A valid decision will be binding on the parties and will be enforceable in the courts in the usual way. The decision will effectively provide the answer to the dispute between the parties, unless and until one or other of the parties seeks to reopen the dispute in litigation or arbitration, or if the parties reach an agreement as to the binding nature of the decision.

12.25 A number of the authorities have stressed the 'provisional interim basis'[29] of the adjudicator's decision. Thus, in *Bouygues (UK) Ltd v Dahl-Jensen (UK) Ltd*[30] Buxton LJ referred to the purpose of the adjudication procedure as enabling 'a quick and interim, but enforceable, award to be made in advance of the final resolution of what are likely to be complex and expensive disputes'. In the same case, Chadwick LJ stressed that the adjudicator's decision was 'not finally determinative' and was a method 'of providing a summary procedure for the enforcement

---

[27] [2002] BLR 113.
[28] [2003] BLR 225.
[29] The words used by Dyson J in *Macob Civil Engineering Ltd v Morrison Construction Ltd* [1999] BLR 93.
[30] [2000] BLR 522.

of payment provisionally due under a construction contract'.[31] The point has already been made that, even though the adjudicator's decision is not finally determinative, it will regulate the parties' rights and obligations for the short term and, given the volatility of the construction industry, may, at least by default, prove to be determinative after all: the successful contractor may simply not be in existence when the time comes for the final determination of the dispute.

12.26 It is also a little misleading to stress the temporary nature of the adjudicator's decision as if, in some way, its determinative nature will somehow wear off over time. The point has already been made that, once an adjudicator has decided a particular dispute in a particular way, that decision will be binding for all time, unless and until one of the parties seeks to challenge it in subsequent arbitration or litigation. In other words, it is up to one party, almost always the loser in the adjudication, to raise the matter afresh in order for it to be considered again. If there is no challenge, the decision will become binding by default.

Temporary Finality/Subsequent Adjudications

12.27 Particular difficulties can arise on major construction contracts where there may be a series of adjudications between the same parties. Although the decision in adjudication 1 is binding in the subsequent adjudications, what happens if there are changes to the factual position along the way? For example, it is clear that a decision in adjudication 1 to the effect that, as a matter of construction of the contract, the contractor was responsible for the integration of the mechanical and electrical design with the rest of the building, will make it impossible for the contractor, in a subsequent adjudication, to claim additional monies or an extension of time on the basis that he was not contractually responsible for such integration, and carried out this task pursuant to a variation instruction. On the other hand, if the contractor loses an adjudication claim for an extension of time based on delaying factors 1–10, he would not be able to make a subsequent claim for an extension of time based on those same factors, but he could properly make a claim (and, if the claim was not admitted, start a second adjudication) for the same period of delay based on factors 11–20. Furthermore, even if the contractor did not raise factors 11–20 by way of a separate claim, he could defend himself against a claim for liquidated damages for that same period by reference to factors 11–20, or indeed any other factors which had not featured in his original extension of

---

31 In *Carillion Construction v Devonport Royal Dockyard Ltd* [2005] EWCA Civ 1358, the same Judge said 'The task of the adjudicator is to find an interim solution which meets the needs of the case...The statutory scheme provides a means of meeting the legitimate cash-flow requirements of contractors and their subcontractors. The need to have the "right" answer has been subordinated to the need to have an answer quickly. The scheme was not enacted in order to provide definitive answers to complex questions.'

time claim. However, the cases on which this overview has been taken demonstrate that it is not always easy to identify what can and cannot be raised in subsequent adjudications.

12.28 In *Emcor Drake & Skull Ltd v Costaine Construction Ltd*[32] there had been two adjudications. In the first, Emcor claimed an extension of time based on 'the November claim' which was unsuccessful. In the second adjudication Emcor pursued a claim for an extension of time covering the same period as the claim in the first adjudication, but based on different facts and matters, set out in what was called 'the February claim'. The February claim was successful. The adjudicator's decision was enforced, HHJ Havery QC noting that the effect of the first adjudication was not that Emcor were not entitled to any extension of time, but simply that they had not discharged the burden of showing that they were entitled to an extension of time based on the material set out in the November claim. The February claim was based on wider matters and, because the second adjudicator was not invited to trespass on the first adjudicator's decision, and did not do so, the second decision was enforced.

12.29 In *David MacLean Contractors Ltd v The Albany Building Ltd*[33] there were two adjudications before the same adjudicator. In the first, the adjudicator decided that certain withholding notices were valid which entitled the defendant employer to deduct liquidated damages from payments otherwise due to the contractor. In the second adjudication he held that the employer's non-completion certificates were invalid and that, in consequence, £1.3 million liquidated damages had been wrongly withheld and had to be paid back to the contractor. The TCC Judge concluded that the disputes in the two adjudications were different, because in the first the subject matter was the validity of the withholding notices, and in the second it was the validity of the non-completion certificates. Although the adjudicator came to a decision in the first which was against the contractor, and a decision in the second which was against the employer, that was simply the result of the facts of the individual disputes, and the adjudicator did not, in his second decision, trespass upon or modify the temporary finality of the first decision.

12.30 Both these cases were considered by Jackson J in *Quietfield Ltd v Vascroft Contractors Ltd*.[34] In the first adjudication between the parties, Vascroft made a claim for an extension of time based on the facts and matters set out in two specific letters dated September 04 and April 05. The claim failed on the facts. In the third adjudication, the employer, Quietfield, sought liquidated damages for the delay and objected when, as part of Vascroft's defence, they sought to rely on an extensive

---

[32] [2004] EWHC 2439 (TCC); 97 Con LR 142.
[33] HHJ Gilliland QC, sitting as a TCC Judge at Salford District Registry, 10 November 2005..
[34] [2006] EWHC 174 (TCC).

substantiation of the original claim for an extension of time. This extensive substantiation was called Appendix C. Although it contained material that had not been raised in adjudication 1, the adjudicator in adjudication 3 ruled that Appendix C was inadmissible and held that Quietfield were entitled to liquidated damages. Jackson J concluded that the adjudicator had been wrong to exclude Appendix C, finding that, in accordance with *William Verry (Glazing Systems) Ltd v Furlong Homes Ltd*[35] Vascroft were entitled to advance any available defence to the claim against them for liquidated damages, irrespective of whether that defence had been notified when the relevant dispute arose. As the Judge said, Appendix C was 'a far cry' from the two letters that were relied on in the first adjudication and it was 'perhaps regrettable' that Vascroft had not relied on Appendix C before. The Judge said that he was quite satisfied that Vascroft's alleged entitlement to an extension of time as set out in Appendix C was substantially different from the claims for an extension of time which they had advanced in adjudication 1, and which had been considered and rejected in that adjudication. Therefore, he ruled that it did not threaten the temporary finality of the decision in adjudication 1 for the adjudicator to consider Appendix C on its merits in adjudication 3.

12.31 At paragraph 42 of his judgment in *Quietfield*, Jackson J identified four principles that were applicable where there were successive adjudications. He defined them as follows:

(i) Where the contract permits the contractor to make successive applications for extension of time on different grounds, either party, if dissatisfied with the decisions made, can refer those matters to successive adjudications. In each case the difference between the contentions of the aggrieved party and the decision of the architect or contract administrator will constitute the 'dispute' within the meaning of section 108 of the 1996 Act.

(ii) If the contractor makes successive applications for extension of time on the same grounds, the architect or contract administrator will, no doubt, reiterate his original decision. The aggrieved party cannot refer this matter to successive adjudications. He is debarred from doing so by paragraphs 9 and 23 of the Scheme and section 108(3) of the 1996 Act.

(iii) Subject to paragraph (iv) below, where the contractor is resisting a claim for liquidated and ascertained damages in respect of delay, pursued in adjudication proceedings, the contractor may rely by way of defence upon his entitlement to an extension of time.

(iv) However the contractor cannot rely by way of defence in adjudication proceedings upon an alleged entitlement to extension of time which has been considered and rejected in a previous adjudication.

12.32 Quietfield appealed to the Court of Appeal, but their appeal was dismissed.[36] May LJ agreed with Jackson J that adjudication 1 was solely concerned with the

---

[35] [2005] EWHC 138 (TCC).
[36] [2007] BLR 67.

grounds advanced in the two letters, and that the material in Appendix C, which identified a number of causes of delay which did not feature in the two letters and was substantially different from them, should have been considered by the adjudicator in adjudication 3. In his concurring judgment, Dyson LJ expanded upon the first two of the principles outlined by Jackson at first instance. He said that the first principle might appear to suggest that every dispute arising from the rejection of an application for an extension of time may be referred to adjudication. Dyson LJ did not consider that that was necessarily the case: the question of whether a contractor may make successive applications for extensions of time depended on the true construction of clause 25 of the relevant standard form of contract and any term necessary to be implied. The question whether disputes arising from the rejection of successive applications for an extension of time may be referred to adjudication depended on the effect of section 108(3) of the 1996 Act and paragraph 9(2) of the Scheme. Dyson LJ went on to say that, whilst on site, if an architect rejected an application for an extension of time, pointing out a deficiency in the application, which the contractor subsequently made good, it would be absurd if the architect could not grant the application if he now thought that it was justified. By contrast, in adjudication, where referrals can be expensive, the statutory scheme protects respondents from successive referrals to adjudication of what is substantially the same dispute. He went on to say that, whether dispute A is substantially the same as dispute B would always be a question of fact and degree and that, where the only difference between disputes arising from the rejection of two successive applications for an extension of time was that the later application made good the shortcomings of the earlier application, an adjudicator would usually have little difficulty in deciding that the two disputes were substantially the same. On the facts of *Quietfield*, however, Dyson LJ concluded that the disputes were different and that the Judge had reached the right conclusion.

12.33 *HG Construction Ltd v Ashwell Homes (East Anglia) Ltd*[37] was another case about serial adjudications. The first decision concluded that, despite the contractor's arguments that the work scope for each section of the contract was uncertain, the liquidated damages provisions in the contract were valid and enforceable. The contractor then sought a further adjudication, on the basis that liquidated damages had been wrongfully deducted because the employer had taken partial possession. The employer refused to take part in that adjudication, and the second adjudicator found in favour of the contractor. Ramsey J decided, after a careful analysis of the nature, scope and extent of the disputes in both adjudications, that the dispute referred in the second adjudication was the same or substantially the same as the dispute previously referred to (and decided by) the first adjudicator.

---

[37] [2007] EWHC 144 (TCC).

He said that it followed that the second adjudicator's conclusion, in paragraph 96 of his decision, that there was no basis on which the liquidated and ascertained damages could operate, was based on the determination of the same or substantially the same dispute that had been raised and decided in the first adjudication. It was therefore not binding on the parties; it was the first decision, and not the subsequent decision, which had the temporary finality of a valid adjudication decision. The application for summary judgment based on the enforcement of the subsequent decision was dismissed.

Although Ramsey J's conclusions were based on his detailed analysis of the issues in the two adjudications, he referred in some detail to the Court of Appeal's judgments in *Quietfield*. He distinguished *HG* on the facts, saying that it was not a case where there was a changing factual position, where later claims for extensions of time were based on a different set of facts. He also observed that the standard contractual provisions as to adjudication, in that case encapsulated in clause 39A.7.1, were aimed 'at providing a limit to serial adjudications'.   12.34

Status in Later Court or Arbitration Proceedings

If the aggrieved party is unhappy with the adjudicator's decision, he can commence his own proceedings in court, or in arbitration, in order to reverse the decision and, if relevant, to recover the sums paid pursuant to the decision that is now challenged. Neither the 1996 Act, nor the Scheme for Construction Contracts qualifies the right of the aggrieved party to issue that challenge so, on larger projects, it is not uncommon for the proceedings seeking to challenge the decision to be issued shortly after the publication of the decision to the parties. In an appropriate case, where the adjudicator's decision has been concerned with a declaration as to the parties' contractual rights and obligations, the issue of a separate set of proceedings challenging the decision can lead to a binding judgment of the court on the point previously considered by the adjudicator. This process can be seen in a number of the decisions concerned with the design and construction of the new Wembley Stadium.[38]   12.35

By contrast with the 1996 Act, some of the standard forms do place restrictions, usually temporal, upon the aggrieved party's right to challenge the decision. Commonly, these provisions prevent a party from challenging the adjudicator's decision until after practical completion. Whilst this has the advantage of preventing the parties from diverting time and resources to the continuation of a dispute   12.36

---

[38] See, by way of example, *Multiplex Constructions (UK) Ltd v Cleveland Bridge* [2006] EWCA Civ 1834; *Multiplex Constructions (UK) Ltd v Mott Macdonald Ltd* [2007] EWHC 20 (TCC); and *Multiplex Constructions (UK) Ltd v Honeywell Control Systems* [2007] EWHC 236 (TCC).

already decided by the adjudicator, it can allow bad feeling to rankle and fester during an ongoing project, with the aggrieved party looking for any way of getting back at the successful party as the project unfolds on site. It can also have the disadvantage of ensuring that an adjudicator's decision as to the parties' contractual rights and entitlements will continue to bind them until the end of the contract works, no matter how wrong the adjudicator might have gone when arriving at his decision.

12.37 A potentially difficult question concerns the status of the adjudicator's decision in any subsequent litigation or arbitration. Let us take, by way of an example, a claim advanced by a contractor in adjudication that he was entitled to a 20 week extension of time, and assume that this claim was advanced to the satisfaction of the adjudicator, who decided that 20 weeks was a reasonable entitlement, even though there was an absence of detail which, in arbitration or litigation, might have proved fatal to the whole claim. The employer then says that he wishes to challenge the adjudicator's decision, and there is subsequent litigation between the parties. Is the contractor entitled to rely in his pleaded defence upon the adjudicator's decision in support of his claim for an extension of time of 20 weeks, contending that it was for the employer to demonstrate that the adjudicator was wrong in reaching this decision?

12.38 It seems that the unequivocal answer to this question is No. Once the decision has been formally challenged by the issue of subsequent litigation or arbitration, the contractor in the example noted above is not entitled to rely on the existing decision as having any status whatsoever, let alone one that changes or displaces the ordinary burden of proof. In *City Inn Ltd v Shepherd Construction Ltd*,[39] Lord MacFadyen stated that it was no part of the function of an adjudicator's decision to reverse the onus of proof in any arbitration or litigation to which the parties might resort to obtain a final determination of the dispute between them. He said that the burden of proof lay where the law placed it and it was unaffected by the terms of the adjudicator's decision. Thus, in the example previously noted, it would be for the contractor properly to plead and prove his entitlement to the 20 week extension of time.

12.39 The decision in *City Inn* was followed in another Scottish case, *Citex Professional Services Ltd v Kenmore Developments Ltd*.[40] There, the Judge agreed with the reasoning of Lord MacFadyen in *City Inn*. However, in that case, the dispute was principally concerned with the correct interpretation of the contract, and the Judge observed that, as a matter of practicality, he could not conceive that questions as to the burden of proof would play any significant part in the court's

---

[39] [2002] Scots Law Times 781.
[40] [2004] Scot CS 20 (28.1.04).

determination of the issue in any event. That is rather different to the situation in *City Inn*, and in the example postulated above, where the potential difficulties which can arise out of the onus of proof in delay cases are such that a contractor might welcome the opportunity of reversing the normal burden of proof.

A rather unusual case on this topic, again from Scotland, is *Stiell Ltd v Riema Control Systems Ltd*.[41] There an adjudicator awarded the claiming party less than half the sum sought and that sum was duly paid by the defenders. The pursuers were unhappy with the adjudicator's decision. Sums in the hands of a third party were arrested under a warrant for arrestment and the defenders, having paid the sum ordered by the adjudicator, moved that the arrestment should be recalled. However, this was refused by the court on the ground that the action by the pursuer for the remaining part of the sum allegedly due (namely that part not ordered by the adjudicator) was one which involved no conditional contingency, because the sums claimed were outstanding, and thus the debt existed. The court held that the fact that the issue in the action may, in certain circumstances, have to be determined first by an adjudicator did not mean that there was any change in the issue to be determined in the proceedings, and the determination by the adjudicator did not make claims, which were pure, become contingent. It is respectfully suggested that this case turns on the particular operation of Scots law, and that in England and Wales, a different result would have eventuated: because the adjudicator had found that the claimant was not entitled to part of the sum claimed, the claimant would not have been able to conduct itself on the basis that that part of the sum was indeed due. If the claimant purported to do so, the defendant would have been entitled to a declaration to that effect, or to obtain summary judgment on its defence.[42]

12.40

Winding Up/Bankruptcy

As set out in more detail in Chapter 14 below, the TCC has evolved its own procedure applicable to the enforcement of the decisions of adjudicators. In those circumstances, it will rarely be necessary for the successful party to seek to enforce the adjudicator's decision by any other means. Specifically, it will be very rare for the successful party to choose to issue winding-up or bankruptcy proceedings[43] as a means of enforcement. However, there will occasionally be situations in which

12.41

---

[41] [2001] 3 TCLR 9. See also paragraph 4.71 above.
[42] There is no question that *Stiell* is an unusual case. It is difficult not to agree with the commentary in the TCLR which suggests that the case might be seen as authority for the curious proposition that an adjudicator's decision is binding when it is in favour of the claimant, but not otherwise.
[43] In *Harlow & Milner v Linda Teasdale (No 1)* [2006] EWHC 54, the TCC Judge refused to allow the successful party to recover the costs of the (ultimately futile) bankruptcy proceedings.

winding up or bankruptcy proceedings are appropriate and there have been a number of authorities which have considered the status of the adjudicator's decision in such circumstances.

12.42 In *George Parke v The Fenton Gretton Partnership*,[44] FGP obtained an adjudicator's decision in their favour in respect of their outstanding fees, but Mr Parke failed to pay and FGP issued a statutory demand seeking payment of the sum awarded. HHJ Boggis QC, sitting as a Judge of the Chancery Division, held that the adjudicator's decision created a debt which could form the basis of a statutory demand and fell to be treated in the same way as a judgment or order in accordance with paragraph 12.3 of the Insolvency Proceedings Practice Directions. However, he said that, as a matter of principle, a debtor's counterclaim or set-off might be sufficient for the court to set aside the statutory demand and that, on the facts of that case, the statutory demand would indeed be set aside. The Judge concluded that, because Mr Parke had brought TCC proceedings in which he argued that, not only did he not owe the adjudicated figure, but once the final account was properly drawn, it was he who was owed money, there was a valid cross-claim which went to the sum demanded and that there was therefore a genuine triable issue. He therefore found that the statutory demand should be set aside. This decision perhaps illustrates the perils of proceeding by way of a statutory demand rather than by way of straightforward enforcement proceedings. On the general principles set out in Chapter 10 above, the alleged set-off would not normally have prevented the court, in enforcement proceedings, from requiring Mr Parke to pay FGP the sum identified by the adjudicator. However, in the bankruptcy proceedings, where different principles applied, a different result eventuated.

12.43 In *Re a Company (No 1299 of 2001)*[45] the sub-contractor claimed the sum of £9,702.47 that had been certified by the main contractor's surveyor. The sum was not paid because the main contractor alleged that it was entitled to a set-off, even though there had been no withholding notice in accordance with section 111 of the 1996 Act. The Deputy High Court Judge concluded that there was an undisputed debt due to the sub-contractor, because the main contractor's surveyor had certified that sums were due and there was no withholding notice. He also concluded that the existence of a significant cross-claim on the part of the main contractor, alleging defects in the work carried out by the sub-contractor, did not entitle the main contractor to an injunction to restrain the sub-contractor from presenting a winding-up petition. He said that the main contractor could have established its claims by commencing a cross-adjudication as soon as it became

---

[44] [2001] CILL 1713.
[45] [2001] CILL 1745.

aware of the alleged problems with the work. It might be said that the decision in this case is more in line with the authorities cited above, in relation to the enforcement of an adjudicator's decision, than the decision in *Parke*. The Judge based his reasoning on the principle that the absence of a withholding notice meant that there was no ground on which it could be disputed that the £9,702.47 was due and payable. In those circumstances the sub-contractor was to be regarded as a creditor of the main contractor with *locus standi* to present a winding-up petition. As to a consideration of the cross-claim in its own right, the Judge concluded that the main contractor had failed to take any step to litigate a cross-claim for defective work. The Judge concluded that there was at least a significant possibility that a future court, hearing the winding-up petition, might form the view that the main contractor had had a reasonable opportunity to litigate the cross-claim and could therefore, in the exercise of its discretion, properly decide to make a winding-up order. As a result of that conclusion, the Judge could not say that the proposed petition would have no reasonable prospect of success, and therefore considered that he should allow the sub-contractor to present such a petition if it wanted to. He refused the injunction sought by the main contractor.

12.44 In *Guardi Shoes Ltd v Datum Contracts*[46] the contractor, Datum, referred its claim for payment to adjudication. Although the employer, Guardi, alleged that there were defects in Datum's work, there was again no withholding notice under section 111, and the adjudicator therefore decided that Guardi had to pay Datum £108,000. Guardi refused to pay. Datum issued enforcement proceedings and obtained summary judgment. A part of the outstanding sum was paid but, with £78,000 odd still owing, Datum served a statutory demand on Guardi. A winding-up petition was presented. Guardi then obtained an injunction without notice restraining advertisement of the petition, and the matter came before Ferris J on Guardi's application for a continuation of that injunction. He concluded that the injunction should not be continued. He said that Guardi had had an opportunity to serve a section 111 notice but had failed to do so, and that in those circumstances it could not be said that the presentation of the petition was an abuse of process. Nor could it be said that the petition was bound to be dismissed if it were to proceed. He said that the circumstances surrounding the supposed inability on the part of Guardi to litigate in relation to the defects were of crucial importance. Because Datum were entitled to be paid under the contract, unless a witholding notice was served, the failure to provide such a notice was fatal to Guardi's application. Guardi were not permitted to come to court to say that, although they had not operated the contractual machinery under which their obligation on their part to pay Datum would have been suspended, Datum should be put into the same position as if Guardi had operated that

---

[46] [2002] CILL 1934.

contractual machinery. Since Guardi had only itself to blame for this position, the injunction would not be continued.

12.45 Clearly the approach of Ferris J in *Guardi*, like the decision in *In Re A Company*, was much more in line with the approach of the TCC judges and the Court of Appeal in the vast majority of adjudication enforcement proceedings. They are obviously to be contrasted with the decision in *George Parke v The Fenton Gretton Partnership* which might be seen now as a case very much on its own facts.

Protective Measures in Scotland

12.46 Under Scots law, a pursuer can take protective measures by seeking to freeze, in the hands of third parties, monies otherwise owing to the defender: this is known as an arrestment.[47] In *Rentokil Allsa Environmental Ltd v Eastend Civil Engineering Ltd*,[48] the defenders obtained an adjudication decision in their favour. The pursuers belatedly paid up, but simultaneously lodged an arrestment in the defenders' solicitors' hands in a larger sum, said to be due by way of damages. This claim had already been considered in the adjudication. The Sheriff Principal recalled the arrestments, concluding that they were not being used to protect the legitimate interests and rights of the pursuers 'but mainly to embarrass the defenders, defeat the adjudicator's awards and strain the financial credit of the defenders. The use of the arrestments demonstrates an abuse of process which ought to be addressed.' In this way, the purpose of the 1996 Act was preserved and enforced. The decision is perhaps to be contrasted with the result in *Stiell*, discussed at paragraph 12.40 above.

---

[47] See also paragraph 12.40 above and the case of *Stiell* there cited.
[48] (1999) CILL 1506.

13

PRINCIPLES OF ENFORCEMENT

Introduction	13.01	In What Circumstances Might the Adjudicator be Found Guilty of Bias?	13.14
General Approach	13.02		
Was There a Construction Contract?	13.06		
Was the Construction Contract in Writing?	13.08	In What Circumstances Will the Court Consider Breaches of the Rules of Natural Justice?	13.16
Was More Than One Dispute Referred to the Adjudicator?	13.09	Summary Judgment	13.18
In What Circumstances is a Withholding Notice Necessary?	13.10	Summary	13.20
Can the Paying Party Set Off a Separate Claim Against the Sum Awarded by the Adjudicator?	13.12		

'It is only too easy in a complex case for a party who is dissatisfied with the decision of an adjudicator to comb through the adjudicator's reasons and identify points upon which to present a challenge under the labels 'excess of jurisdiction' or 'breach of natural justice' ... To seek to challenge the adjudicator's decision on the ground that he has exceeded his jurisdiction or breached the rules of natural justice (save in the plainest cases) is likely to lead to a substantial waste of time and expense ...'

Chadwick LJ in *Carillion Construction Ltd v Devonport Royal Dockyard Ltd* [2005] EWCA Civ 1358

Introduction

As will already have been noted, a large proportion of the authorities analysed in the preceding chapters arose out of applications to the TCC by the successful party to enforce the decision of the adjudicator. The general principles applied by the courts in such enforcement applications can therefore be discerned from those authorities. In order to avoid undue repetition, the purpose of this chapter is to concentrate on the most commonly argued points that arise in enforcement

13.01

applications and to summarise, almost exclusively by reference to the decisions of the Court of Appeal, the courts' approach to such questions. There are now very few issues arising on enforcement applications which have not been the subject of at least one clear exposition by the Court of Appeal.

General Approach

13.02 The general approach of the courts to enforcement applications can be seen in the two early judgments of Dyson J (as he then was) in *Macob Civil Engineering Ltd v Morrison Construction Ltd*[1] and *Bouygues (UK) Ltd v Dahl-Jensen (UK) Ltd*.[2] In the latter case, despite the clear error made by the adjudicator, the Judge concluded that, in accordance with the adjudication provisions in the contract, the decision had to be enforced. This decision was upheld by the Court of Appeal, with both Buxton and Chadwick LJJ reiterating the point that, because the adjudicator answered the right question, the fact that he answered it in the wrong way did not affect his jurisdiction and did not prevent the summary enforcement of the decision.[3]

13.03 In *Bouygues*, Chadwick LJ said that the purpose of the 1996 Act, and the contractual adjudication provisions which followed, was to provide a speedy method by which disputes under construction contracts could be resolved on a provisional basis. He said that the adjudicator's decision, although not finally determinative, might give rise to an immediate payment obligation which could be enforced by the courts. He said it could be looked upon 'as a method of providing a summary procedure for the enforcement of payment provisionally due under a construction contract'. He said at paragraph 29 of his judgment that adjudicators' decisions ought to be enforced by way of summary judgment.

13.04 Precisely the same approach was adopted by the Court of Appeal in the subsequent case of *C & B Scene Concept Design Ltd v Isobars Ltd*.[4] Sir Murray Stuart-Smith said that, unless the adjudicator had acted outside his jurisdiction, summary judgment should be entered to enforce his decision. This was because the whole purpose of the 1996 Act was to provide a swift and effective means of dispute resolution which was binding during the currency of the contract, until final determination by litigation or arbitration. He said that any dispute could be quickly resolved by the adjudicator and enforced through the courts; if the adjudicator was wrong, the matter could be corrected in subsequent litigation or arbitration.

---

[1] [1999] BLR 93.
[2] [2000] BLR 49.
[3] [2000] BLR 522.
[4] [2002] BLR 93.

Principles of Enforcement

Thus, even if the adjudicator had made errors of law as to the relevant contractual provisions, his decision was binding and enforceable until the matter was corrected at the final determination by the judge or the arbitrator.

Accordingly, the most important question of all in any adjudication, and in any enforcement application, is whether the adjudicator acted within his jurisdiction. There are a number of issues that perennially arise when considering the adjudicator's jurisdiction which can conveniently be framed as questions. Was there a construction contract between the parties? Was that construction contract in writing? Was more than one dispute referred to the adjudicator in the notice of adjudication? The proper approach to these questions is outlined below. **13.05**

Was There a Construction Contract?

There are two decisions of the Court of Appeal which demonstrate that, if there is a real dispute between the parties about whether or not they had agreed a construction contract, such a dispute will mean that, at least arguably, the adjudicator did not have the necessary jurisdiction, and thereby prevent the enforcement of his decision. They are: **13.06**

(a) *Thomas-Frederic's (Construction) Ltd v Keith Wilson*.[5] In that case, there was a clear dispute as to whether the defendant/appellant, Mr Wilson, was ever a party to the relevant contract at all. Although Simon Brown LJ readily recognised the concern that what he called the 'salutary' new statutory power introduced by the 1996 Act to promote early payment in construction contracts might be emasculated by jurisdictional challenges, he concluded that, in that case, the adjudicator's ruling was, on any view, not plainly right and indeed was, if anything, plainly wrong. In those circumstances, he concluded that the application for summary judgment against Mr Wilson, based on the adjudicator's decision to that effect, should have been dismissed.

(b) *Pegram Shopfitters Ltd v Tally Weijl (UK) Ltd*.[6] In that case, although the facts were rather different, the Court of Appeal took the same approach. There was a dispute as to the contract terms, with the defendant contending that, if the contract was not made in the JCT Standard Form of Prime Cost Contract (1998 Edition), there was no agreement between the parties at all. The claimant alleged that there was a contract, but not in the JCT Form, and that it constituted a construction contract and therefore incorporated the implied adjudication provisions set out in the Scheme. The adjudicator had been appointed, and produced his decision, in accordance with the Scheme. In consequence of the defendant's alternative case that there was no contract at

---

[5] [2003] EWCA Civ 1494.
[6] [2003] EWCA Civ 1750.

all, which was at least arguable, May LJ said that both the adjudicator, and the TCC Judge at first instance, had been wrong to proceed on the assumption that both parties were agreed that their relationship was governed by a construction contract. The defendant, he said, had made it crystal clear that, if no contract was concluded on the JCT terms, there was no construction contract at all, and therefore it was arguable that the adjudicator (who had not been appointed under the JCT provisions) did not have the necessary jurisdiction to decide the dispute which had arisen. Like Simon Brown LJ in *Thomas-Frederic's*, May LJ accepted that the court had to be vigilant to examine jurisdictional arguments of this kind 'critically'. However, he concluded that, on the evidence, *Pegram* was a case where legal principle had to prevail over broad brush policy. One or other of the defendants' contentions as to the nature and existence of the contract might well prove to be correct and, in those circumstances, they had a legitimate jurisdictional challenge to an adjudicator appointed under the provisions of the Scheme for Construction Contracts. Again, therefore, the appeal was allowed, and the summary judgment application was refused.

13.07 There are no decisions of the Court of Appeal which deal with the meaning of 'construction operations' and the sorts of disputes which have arisen under s105 of the 1996 Act. Accordingly, the relevant authorities are those referred to in paragraphs 2.23–2.36 above. As to the debate about whether a construction contract with the necessary adjudication and payment provisions is enforceable under the Unfair Terms in Consumer Contracts Regulations, the relevant authorities are those set out at paragraphs 9.49–9.58 above. The Court of Appeal in *Bryen & Langley Ltd v Rodney Martin Boston*[7] upheld the general approach adopted by the TCC, to the effect that, in most cases, where the contract has been proffered by or on behalf of the employer, it will be extremely difficult for him to argue at a later date that the provisions relating to adjudication or payment/withholding were in some way unfair.

Was the Construction Contract in Writing?

13.08 In order for the provisions of the 1996 Act and the Scheme for Construction Contracts to be implied, there has to be a construction contract in writing between the parties. In *RJT Consulting Engineers Ltd v DM Engineering (Northern Ireland) Ltd*[8] the Court of Appeal stressed the importance of the contract being in writing. In the words of Ward LJ, 'writing is important because it provides certainty. Certainty is all the more important when adjudication is envisaged to have to

---

[7] [2005] EWCA Civ 973.
[8] [2002] BLR 217.

take place under a demanding timetable.' On the facts of that case, he concluded that the adjudicator did not derive sufficient jurisdiction merely because there was evidence in writing of the existence of the agreement, its substance, the parties to it, the nature of the work and the price. Ward and Robert Walker LJJ concluded that what has to be evidenced in writing 'is, literally, the agreement, which means all of it, not part of it. A record of the agreement also suggests a complete agreement, not a partial one.' For the reasons explained in detail at paragraphs 2.44–2.73 above, it is thought that the reference by Auld LJ to the need for a written record of 'the *material* terms of the agreement' evidenced a different approach to that of the majority, and that, at least for the present, the only safe basis on which to proceed with an adjudication is to ensure all the terms of the contract are in writing.[9]

Was More Than One Dispute Referred to the Adjudicator?

Some contracts permit the reference of more than one dispute to the adjudicator, but most standard forms do not, and the Scheme for Construction Contracts does not permit the reference to adjudication of more than one dispute at a time. Although it is often argued under such contracts that the adjudicator did not have the necessary jurisdiction because more than one dispute was referred to him under the notice of adjudication, this argument has very rarely succeeded.[10] The reason for this is because the courts have adopted a wide definition of the word 'dispute' with the result that, properly framed, a notice of adjudication will usually be capable of referring one single dispute to the adjudicator, even if that dispute is made up of claims for contract work, variations, extension of time and loss and expense.[11] Although concern has been expressed about this approach,[12] there has been no reported case in which a more restricted definition has been adopted. It should be noted that this point is one of the few arguments which has regularly arisen on adjudication enforcements and which has not yet been taken to the Court of Appeal. Until that happens, it is thought that the point will not remain entirely free from doubt. However, for present purposes, it is suggested that, provided sufficient care is taken in the drafting of the notice of adjudication, it should generally be possible to avoid the complaint that more than one dispute has been referred to the adjudicator at the same time.

13.09

---

[9] As noted in detail in paragraphs 19.03–19.06 below, the DTI presently propose the scrapping of this requirement, so that all construction contracts, written or oral, would be caught by the 1996 Act.
[10] For a fuller discussion of the importance of this requirement, see paragraphs 7.57–7.63 above, and the decision of HHJ Bowsher QC in *Grovedeck Ltd v Capital Demolition Ltd* [2000] BLR 181.
[11] See *Fastrack Contractors Ltd v Morrison Construction Ltd* [2000] BLR 168.
[12] See, by way of example, the comments of Lord MacFadyen in *Barr Ltd v Law Mining* (2001) 80 Con LR 134.

In What Circumstances is a Withholding Notice Necessary?

13.10 Because the concept of the withholding notice was new, there was a certain amount of muddle as to the extent to which the responding party needed to serve a withholding notice in order to defend the detail of the claim being made, with the result that there was a good deal of unhelpful debate about the respective merits of a strict or a liberal approach to the need for such notices where no cross-claim was being asserted. Any lingering confusion was resolved by the Court of Appeal in *Rupert Morgan Building Services (LLC) Ltd v Jervis and Another*.[13] In general terms, the position now is that, if the construction contract provided for a series of interim certificates to be issued by the contract administrator or some other representative of the employer, then the sum due to the contractor on an interim basis was the amount certified by the certifying officer, subject to any valid withholding notice. Thus, where a contractor or sub-contractor was in possession of such a certificate, he was entitled to be paid the sum certified, unless the employer had, within the time limit prescribed by the contract, served a withholding notice seeking to set off, against the sum certified, other sums said to be due to the employer. In the absence of such a withholding notice, the contractor or sub-contractor was entitled to the sum certified right away; pursuant to the contract, the paying party was obliged to pay such sum as had been certified.

13.11 As the Court of Appeal pointed out in *Rupert Morgan*, the position was different where the claim for an interim payment was based simply upon an invoiced amount which had not been certified, but merely asserted as due. In those circumstances, the paying party's contractual obligation was to pay what was due under the contract. Thus, if the paying party considered that the claim was over-stated, because, say, it included inflated rates or a number of duplications, then the paying party could set out its position in writing both before and during the adjudication, and no prior withholding notice was necessary. As Jacob LJ pointed out in *Rupert Morgan*, under that type of contractual regime, no withholding notice was required in respect of works that, on the employer's case, had not been done: payment was not due in respect of work not done, so a withholding notice was unnecessary.

Can the Paying Party Set Off a Separate Claim Against the Sum Awarded by the Adjudicator?

13.12 The relevant authorities are dealt with in detail in Chapter 10 above. Rights of set-off will ultimately depend on the true construction of the contract and the

---

[13] [2003] EWCA Civ 1563; [2004] 1 WLR 1867.

nature of the adjudicator's decision. In general terms, however, it can be said that the paying party will find it extremely difficult to set off against the sum awarded by the adjudicator its own separate claim, particularly in circumstances where that claim could have been raised in the adjudication, but for the absence of a timeous withholding notice. However, in this regard, it should be noted that, in *Parsons Plastics (Research and Development) Ltd v Purac Ltd*,[14] the Court of Appeal decided that the respondents had a set-off against the sum awarded by the adjudicator, even though the respondents had failed to serve a valid withholding notice. The learned editors of the Building Law Reports described this as a 'curious result' and it is respectfully suggested that *Parsons Plastics* is perhaps best regarded as a case confined to the particular terms of the sub-contract in question.

13.13 The decision of the Court of Appeal in *Ferson Contractors Ltd v Levolux A.T. Ltd*[15] is perhaps of more general application. There, Mantell LJ concluded that the purpose of section 108 of the 1996 Act would be defeated if the losing party was permitted to avoid the consequences of defeat by raising a new set-off against the sum awarded by the adjudicator. He said that the contract had to be construed so as to give effect to the intention of Parliament, rather than to defeat it, and that, accordingly, the set-off provisions in the contract had to be read in such a way that meant that they did not apply to monies due by reason of an adjudicator's decision. He distinguished *Parsons Plastics* on the basis that, in that case, the Court of Appeal did not have to consider what impact section 108 of the 1996 Act might have on the construction of the relevant contract provisions concerned with set-off.

In What Circumstances Might the Adjudicator be Found Guilty of Bias?

13.14 There is a discussion of the cases on alleged bias at paragraphs 9.11–9.15 above. The relevant test for bias in adjudication was set out by the Court of Appeal in *AMEC Capital Projects Ltd v Whitefriars City Estates Ltd*.[16] That was a case concerned with the re-appointment of the same adjudicator. Dyson LJ concluded that the mere fact that the tribunal had previously decided the issue was not of itself sufficient to justify a conclusion of apparent bias, and that something more was required. The vice which the law had to guard against was that the tribunal might approach the re-hearing with a closed mind but that, provided that it was

---

[14] [2002] BLR 334.
[15] [2003] EWCA Civ 11.
[16] [2004] EWCA Civ 1418.

clear that the adjudicator had properly reconsidered the matter, it could not be said that the mere fact that he re-heard the same dispute was indicative of bias.

13.15 Actual bias will always be very rare and extremely difficult to prove. Whilst the appearance of bias might be easier to demonstrate, it is still far from straightforward, and the decision in *AMEC* will only make it harder, from a practical perspective, to get a bias argument off the ground. Since almost all the points that might be relied on to support a case of apparent bias would be capable of supporting an alternative claim for breach of natural justice, it is thought that, in the round, most future challenges in this area are likely to be categorised as breaches of the rules of natural justice, rather than as allegations of bias.

In What Circumstances Will the Court Consider Breaches of the Rules of Natural Justice?

13.16 At paragraphs 9.16–9.43 above, there is a detailed analysis of the cases concerned with the alleged failure of the adjudicator to follow the rules of natural justice. Typically, such successful challenges have arisen in circumstances where the adjudicator has had dealings with one party in the absence of another, or where the adjudicator has allowed one party to rely on material with which the other party has had no, or no realistic, opportunity to deal.

13.17 Aside from the decision in *AMEC*, which is principally concerned with bias, there has been no specific Court of Appeal decision giving guidance as to the extent to which an adjudicator must follow the rules of natural justice, and the possible circumstances where a failure to do so might prevent the enforcement of his decision. However, it would be right to note that the Court of Appeal have indicated generally that such challenges are not to be encouraged.[17] In *AMEC*, Dyson LJ said at paragraph 22 of his judgment:

> It is easy enough to make challenges of breach of natural justice against an adjudicator. The purpose of the scheme of the 1996 Act is now well known. It is to provide a speedy mechanism for settling disputes in construction contracts on a provisional interim basis, and requiring the decisions of adjudicators to be enforced pending final determination of disputes by arbitration, litigation or agreement. The intention of Parliament to achieve this purpose will be undermined if allegations of breach of natural justice are not examined critically when they are raised by parties who are seeking to avoid complying with adjudicators' decisions.

---

[17] See, for example, Chadwick LJ in *Carillion v Devonport Royal Dockyard Ltd* [2005] EWCA 1358 at paragraphs 85–87.

However, as noted in paragraph 9.22 above, the first instance authorities establish that:

(a) Where there has been a basic and fundamental failure to follow the rules of natural justice; and
(b) That failure has had a serious effect on the decision-making process;

the courts may well be prepared to reject the application for summary judgment to enforce the decision.

Summary Judgment

13.18 From the outset, the courts have made plain that the right way for a party to enforce the decision of an adjudicator is to seek summary judgment based on the decision. In *Macob*, Dyson J said that, whilst he had no doubt that the court had jurisdiction to grant a mandatory injunction to enforce an adjudicator's decision, the best method of enforcement was by way of summary judgment. He said that the mere fact that the decision may later be revised was not a good reason for saying that summary judgment was inappropriate. The grant of summary judgment did not pre-empt any later decision that an arbitrator or a court might make. It merely reflected the fact that there was no defence to the claim to enforce the decision of the adjudicator *at the time of judgment*.

13.19 The same point was emphasised by the Court of Appeal in *Bouygues*.[18] At paragraph 29 of his judgment in that case, Chadwick LJ said that summary judgment was the proper method of enforcement.

> In the ordinary case I have little doubt that an adjudicator's determination under section 108 of the 1996 Act, or under contractual provisions incorporated by that section, ought to be enforced by summary judgment. The purpose of the Act is to provide a basis upon which payment of an amount found by the adjudicator to be due from one party to the other (albeit that the determination is capable of being re-opened) can be enforced summarily.

Summary

13.20 One of the first cases in which the relevant principles of enforcement were drawn together was in the judgment of HHJ Thornton QC in *Sherwood & Casson Ltd v MacKenzie Ltd*.[19] There, at paragraph 24, he summarised the approach of

---

[18] [2000] BLR 522.
[19] (2000) TCLR 418.

the courts to disputed enforcement applications by reference to the five propositions set out verbatim in paragraph 2.10 above. These include the general rules that:

- A decision of an adjudicator whose validity is challenged as to its factual or legal conclusions or as to procedural error will usually be enforced.
- A decision that is erroneous, even if the error is disclosed by the reasons, will still not ordinarily be capable of being challenged and will usually be enforced.
- A decision may be challenged on the ground that the adjudicator was not empowered by the 1996 Act to make the decision, either because there was no underlying construction contract between the parties or because he had gone outside the terms of reference.
- The court will guard against characterising a mistaken answer to an issue, which is within an adjudicator's jurisdiction, as being an excess of jurisdiction. Furthermore, the court should give a fair, natural and sensible interpretation to the decision in the light of the disputes that are the subject of the reference.
- An issue as to whether a construction contract ever came into existence is a challenge to the jurisdiction of the adjudicator, and so long as it is reasonably and clearly raised, must be determined by the court on the balance of probabilities with, if necessary, oral and documentary evidence.

13.21 Although this summary was provided in the early days of adjudication and adjudication enforcement, it has stood up very well as a guide to the principles which the courts will adopt when considering any application to enforce the decision of an adjudicator. Coming up to date, the most comprehensive recent guidance can be found at paragraphs 80 and 81 of the judgment of Jackson J in *Carillion Construction Ltd v Devonport Royal Dockyard Ltd*.[20] Paragraph 80 contained the four general propositions which are set out verbatim at paragraph 7.04 above. Paragraph 81 included the five more specific propositions which are again set out verbatim at paragraphs 3.63 and 3.83 above. Both these paragraphs were expressly approved by the Court of Appeal.[21] In his own conclusions, at paragraphs 85–87 of his judgment (parts of which are cited verbatim at the outset of this Chapter), Chadwick LJ stated that 'It should be only in rare circumstances that the courts will interfere with the decision of an adjudicator'. Whilst it was only too easy to identify points upon which to present a challenge under the labels 'excess of jurisdiction' or 'breach of natural justice', he emphasised that the courts would give no encouragement to an approach that could be aptly described as 'scrabbling around to find some argument, however tenuous, to resist payment'. He said that the 1996 Act provided a means of meeting the legitimate cash-flow requirements of

---

[20] [2005] All ER (D) 366 (Apr).
[21] [2005] EWCA Civ 1358.

contractors and their sub-contractors; it was not enacted in order to provide definitive answers to complex questions.

13.22 In what is perhaps the plainest indication yet of the courts' approach to enforcement applications, Chadwick LJ said, at paragraph 87 of his judgment, that in the overwhelming majority of cases, the proper course for the unsuccessful party in an adjudication was to pay the amount that the adjudicator had ordered that he should pay. If he did not accept that decision, he could take subsequent legal or arbitral proceedings in order to establish what he considered was the true position. Chadwick LJ made plain that to seek to challenge the adjudicator's decision on the ground that he had exceeded his jurisdiction or breached the rules of natural justice was likely, save in the plainest cases, to lead to a substantial waste of time and expense. Many of the authorities cited in this and earlier chapters only serve to make good that conclusion.

14

ADJUDICATION BUSINESS IN THE TCC

Introduction	14.01	The Consequences of	
Enforcement Generally	14.02	Losing an Adjudication	14.15
Summary Judgment in the TCC	14.05	Injunctions	14.20
Interest and Costs	14.12	Declaratory Relief	14.26
		Staying Court Proceedings For Adjudication	14.30

'The TCC is ordinarily the court in which the enforcement of an adjudicator's decision and any other business connected with adjudication is undertaken. Adjudicators' decisions predominantly arise out of adjudications which are governed by the mandatory provisions of the Housing Grants Construction and Regeneration Act 1996 (HGCRA). These provisions apply automatically to any construction contract as defined in the legislation. Some adjudicators' decisions arise out of standard forms of contract which contain adjudication provisions and others arise from ad-hoc agreements to adjudicate. The TCC enforcement procedure is the same for all three kinds of adjudication.'

The Technology and Construction Court Guide, Second Edition, October 2005, paragraph 9.1.1

Introduction

14.01 The Technology and Construction Court (TCC) is the only nationwide specialist civil court, dealing with all aspects of construction-related litigation. It therefore habitually handles all types of disputes relating to adjudication, and has developed its own specific procedures to dispose efficiently of the various types of adjudication business. Obviously, the most important aspect of this work, in which the TCC in both London and the regions has played a major part in recent years, is in respect of applications for the enforcement of adjudicators' decisions. But the TCC also deals with applications to injunct ongoing adjudication proceedings; applications for declarations arising out of adjudications or the specific decision of the adjudicator; and applications to stay court or arbitration proceedings temporarily in order to allow an adjudication to take place. The relevant practice and procedure in respect of each of these adjudication-related areas of dispute are noted in the remainder of this chapter.

Enforcement Generally

14.02 The principal purpose of adjudication is to resolve the dispute which has arisen between the parties by way of a speedy decision. That decision then becomes temporarily binding, until the underlying dispute is litigated, arbitrated, or settled. In those circumstances, after the 1996 Act came into effect in May 1998, it quickly became apparent that there was a clear need for the courts to provide a similarly swift enforcement procedure, in order to ensure that the victor in the adjudication was not then kept out of his money for months. It has been made clear on many occasions since the 1996 Act came into force that the right approach on enforcement is the issuing of court proceedings in the TCC, coupled with an application for summary judgment pursuant to CPR Part 24.[1] Despite this, in the early days, a number of difficulties arose when the successful party in the adjudication sought to enforce the adjudicator's decision in courts which were unfamiliar with the summary nature of the adjudication process, the general prohibition against set-off, and the concept of 'temporary finality'.

14.03 As noted above, the TCC was and remains therefore the obvious place in which the successful party should seek to enforce the decision of the adjudicator. The TCC has developed its own special procedure, discussed in greater detail below, to enable enforcement proceedings to be disposed of promptly. Since the special procedure operated by the TCC is in force in all of the TCC courts across the country (notably in London, Birmingham, Salford/Manchester, Cardiff, Leeds, Bristol and Newcastle) it is thought that the TCC is the appropriate forum for all adjudication-related proceedings, particularly the enforcement of the adjudicator's decision.

14.04 Because the TCC has a particular procedure for the enforcement of adjudicators' decisions, and because other courts do not, considerable amounts of time and costs can be wasted if the enforcement proceedings are not commenced in

---

[1] See Dyson J in *Macob Civil Engineering Ltd v Morrison Construction Ltd* [1999] BLR 93, 100, second column.

the TCC. By way of example, in *Harlow & Milner Ltd v Linda Teasdale (No 1)*[2] the claimant had originally sought to enforce the adjudicator's decision by issuing a statutory demand and pursuing bankruptcy proceedings in the county court. Six months were wasted, and considerable costs incurred, before the statutory demand was set aside by consent and the parties agreed that the matter would be referred to the TCC. The TCC Judge promptly enforced the decision of the adjudicator. However, he declined to award the claimant the costs of the earlier bankruptcy proceedings, expressing the view that the appropriate method of enforcement was to issue proceedings in the TCC and that, if this course had been followed at the outset, a good deal of time and cost would therefore have been saved. The Judge accepted that the issue of a bankruptcy petition could not, of itself, be described as the wrong way of enforcing the adjudicator's decision but, given that there was a procedure expressly tailored by the TCC to allow the prompt and efficient enforcement of adjudicator's decisions, the court had to consider very carefully an application for the costs of other proceedings, commenced in addition to the enforcement action, particularly where, in the end, it was the enforcement proceedings that had proved to be the right course for the claimant to take.

Summary Judgment in the TCC

14.05 The specific procedure designed to ensure the speedy and just resolution of all disputed enforcement proceedings is set out in the draft directions at Appendix F of the Second Edition of the TCC Guide, published in October 2005. Those draft directions are reproduced here as Appendix D. They presuppose that the claimant will make an application for summary judgment pursuant to CPR Part 24. The important elements of this procedure are analysed briefly below.

14.06 There is no Practice Direction and no claim form specifically designed with adjudication business in mind. Thus, in most cases, because enforcement proceedings are in respect of a sum of money awarded by the adjudicator, CPR Part 7 proceedings are usually appropriate. Only in the rare situation where the enforcement proceedings are known to raise a question which is unlikely to involve a substantial dispute of fact, and no monetary judgment is sought, will it be appropriate for the parties to use CPR Part 8.

14.07 In a typical enforcement case, there will be a short claim form. The claim form should identify the construction contract and, in particular, the terms of that contract which conferred jurisdiction upon the adjudicator. If the adjudication was conducted in accordance with any particular set of procedural rules, those should

---

[2] [2006] EWHC 54 (TCC).

also be identified in the claim form. The claim form will then go on to identify shortly the adjudicator's decision, the fact that the sum identified in that decision has not been paid, and the claim for that sum, together with any relevant interest and other monies due, such as some or all of the adjudicator's fees. The claim form should be accompanied by an application notice setting out in clear terms the procedural directions that are being sought. Those directions should be based upon the standard directions set out in Appendix D.

14.08 It will almost invariably be the case that, alongside the claim form and the application notice setting out the directions that are sought, the claimant will issue an application for summary judgment under CPR Part 24. That application will be accompanied by a short witness statement in support. That statement will identify/exhibit the relevant parts of the contract and the adjudicator's decision. It is usually unnecessary for the statement to contain any further information, although if, for example, the responding party took a point at the start of the reference as to the adjudicator's jurisdiction, and it is obvious to the applicant that this point will be maintained in any subsequent enforcement proceedings, it will usually be helpful for the applicant to identify that point in the statement and to explain how and why, in the applicant's view, the jurisdiction point is a bad one.

14.09 The Judge will consider the application for directions and almost invariably make an order in the general terms set out in Appendix D. In making those directions the Judge will consider a variety of matters including:

(a) The date by which the claim form and summary judgment documentation should be served on the defendant, if that has not already happened;
(b) The abridged period of time in which the defendant must file his acknowledgment of service, usually three days;
(c) The date for service by the defendant of any witness statement in opposition to the enforcement;
(d) The date for service of any further material (if appropriate) from the claimant;
(e) The fixing of the hearing of the summary judgment application, together with dates for the lodging of bundles, skeleton arguments and the like.

It is less wasteful of time if the Judge makes these directions on the basis of the documentation provided to him by the claimant. However, the Judge will always give the defendant liberty to apply, so it is always open to the defendant to inform the court that, because of information unknown to the court at the time that the directions were made, certain variations to the original directions order may be necessary.

14.10 The whole purpose of the particular procedure developed by the TCC for the enforcement of adjudicators' decisions is to ensure that the speed and efficiency of the adjudication process is mirrored in any subsequent enforcement proceedings.

Thus, the TCC endeavours to list an enforcement hearing within 28 days of the issue of the claim form. In a relatively straightforward case, where the claimant has issued its summary judgment application at the same time as the claim form, the Judge will give the defendant about 14 days to put in its own evidence in response, along with the defence. The claimant may then be given a shorter period, say 4 days, in which to put in any further material in reply. Thereafter, bundles can be prepared and skeleton arguments exchanged, so that a hearing can take place within another 7 to 14 days. However, because adjudication enforcement applications are usually listed on a Friday, and the TCC Judges can have notoriously full lists on Fridays (partly, of course, as a result of adjudication enforcement applications), it can sometimes be necessary to list the enforcement application either on a week day or on a Friday five or six weeks after the issue of the claim form. Despite these potential difficulties, the statistics show that the great majority of enforcement applications are heard within 28 days of the issue of the claim form.

14.11 By the time of the enforcement hearing itself, the parties will have exchanged skeleton arguments and the Judge will probably have had an opportunity to go through those arguments with some care in advance of the oral argument. Following the oral argument, the Judge will endeavour to give judgment then and there although, since the points that can be raised at enforcement hearings are many and varied, it is sometimes necessary for the Judge to reserve judgment for a few days and hand down a written judgment, particularly in a case which raised a novel point of wider significance to the adjudication community.

Interest and Costs

14.12 Many construction contracts identify the appropriate rate of interest to be applied to late payment. If the court enforces an adjudicator's decision under such a contract, then the rate of interest applicable from the date on which the sum should have been paid, to the date of the judgment, will usually be the rate of interest stated in the construction contract. If no rate is stated in the contract, it is common for the adjudicator to be asked to decide what rate of interest is appropriate and, if he has identified a rate in his decision, then it will usually be appropriate for the Judge to utilise that rate for the period between the decision and the judgment on enforcement. Another approach is simply to take the judgment rate of interest for the period between the date of the decision and the date of the judgment.

14.13 The costs of any enforcement proceedings are in the discretion of the court. If the claimant is successful in his enforcement application, he will often seek his costs on an indemnity basis. In the ordinary case, if the Judge is not persuaded that

Enforcement

there was any defence to the claim for enforcement, the Judge will award costs on an indemnity basis.[3]

14.14 It is not uncommon for a responding party/defendant to fail to pay on the adjudicator's decision, thereby obliging the claimant to issue enforcement proceedings. The defendant may then remain unco-operative throughout those enforcement proceedings before deciding, a day or two prior to the hearing of the summary judgment application, to offer the clamant the sum identified by the adjudicator. In those circumstances, the court will be readily disposed to order the claimant's costs to be paid on an indemnity basis. In *Gray & Sons Builders (Bedford) Ltd v Essential Box Company Ltd*[4] the defendant indicated the day before the hearing that it did not oppose the application for summary judgment. By reference to a number of cases, including *Wates Construction Ltd v HGP Greentree Allchurch Evans Ltd*[5] the TCC Judge concluded that an order for indemnity costs was appropriate. He said that the defendant knew or ought to have known that it had no defence to the claim to enforce the adjudicator's decision, and that it was unreasonable for the defendant to continue to give the impression that the application was resisted, thereby letting the claimant incur costs and obliging the court to make arrangements for a contested hearing, only for the defendant to concede, the day before the hearing, that they had no valid grounds for contesting the application.

The Consequences of Losing an Adjudication

14.15 The potentially harsh consequences of defeat in adjudication can be illustrated by the case of *Harlow & Milner Ltd v Linda Teasdale*.[6] In that case Mrs Teasdale bought three terraced properties in Leeds as part of a proposed pension plan with her husband. The properties were affected by asbestos contamination. With the help of grants from Leeds City Council, she intended to refurbish the properties, keep two, and sell the third. Mrs Teasdale entered into a contract with Harlow & Milner to carry out the refurbishment works, where the vast bulk of the contract sum was payable by the Council by way of grant monies. Unfortunately, Mrs Teasdale failed to appreciate that, whatever the position as between her and the Council (and their payment of the necessary grants), she was liable under the construction contract to pay Harlow & Milner in respect of their interim payments.

---

[3] See, by way of example, *Harlow & Milner Ltd v Linda Teasdale (No 1)* [2006] EWHC 54 (TCC) and the cases referred to in paragraph 14.14 below.
[4] [2006] EWHC 2520 (TCC).
[5] [2005] EWHC 2174 (TCC); [2006] BLR 45.
[6] *(No 1)* is reported at [2006] EWHC 54 (TCC); *(No 2)* is reported at [2006] EWHC 535 (TCC); and *(No 3)* is reported at [2006] EWHC 1708 (TCC); [2006] BLR 359.

14.16 Almost inevitably, large sums by way of interim payment accrued to Harlow & Milner, whilst the Council failed to pay such sums to Mrs Teasdale. There was a shortfall which Mrs Teasdale could not pay. There was an adjudication, at the conclusion of which the adjudicator decided that Harlow & Milner were entitled to the vast bulk of the monies sought. Mrs Teasdale did not pay and Harlow & Milner (after wasting many months on abortive bankruptcy proceedings) commenced enforcement proceedings in the TCC. Mrs Teasdale did not appear at the summary judgment application and in any event had no defence to the claim. Judgment was therefore given in favour of Harlow & Milner.[7]

14.17 Mrs Teasdale did not pay the judgment sum. Accordingly, Harlow & Milner obtained an interim charging order. At the application to make that order final, Mrs Teasdale's solicitors sent a letter which argued that there was now an ongoing construction arbitration between the parties, and that in those circumstances it would be wrong to make a final charging order. The Judge concluded that such an argument was 'quite hopeless', pointing out that Mrs Teasdale had been ordered by the adjudicator to pay the outstanding sums to Harlow & Milner nine months earlier and she had failed to do so.[8] The Judge said, at paragraph 6 of his judgment:

> The Defendant is not entitled to ignore the judgment of this court and to delay her payment to the Claimant in the hope that 'something may turn up'. Her solicitor's suggestion that the Charging Order should in some way be suspended, until the result of the arbitration is known, would wholly undermine the adjudication process. If it were right, it would mean that any party who was on the receiving end of an adjudicator's decision could, if they wanted to avoid the result, commence arbitration proceedings against the successful party, and then argue that the adjudicator's decision should abide the eventual outcome of that arbitration. It was precisely to avoid such delaying tactics that the statutory adjudication process was created in the first place.

14.18 Inevitably, Harlow & Milner issued an application for an order for sale pursuant to CPR 73.10. That was the first hearing at which Mrs Teasdale was represented, although it was the third and final stage in the enforcement process. Again the principal defence that was raised concerned the ongoing arbitration between Mrs Teasdale and the contractors, and the court was again asked not to make the order because of the possibility that the arbitration would conclude with a decision in Mrs Teasdale's favour. The Judge rejected that approach, pointing out that the authorities were clear: a party who was ordered to make a payment pursuant to an adjudicator's decision could not seek to avoid making such payment by setting off

---

[7] [2006] EWHC 54 (TCC).
[8] [2006] EWHC 535 (TCC).

other claims that it had or might have had.⁹ In addition, the Judge noted that all those decisions went against parties who were in the same position as (or a stronger position than) Mrs Teasdale, because she simply had a claim in the relatively early stages of arbitration. He pointed out that, since the law was that a party with a cross-claim which had accrued after the adjudicator's decision could not set that off against the sum awarded by the adjudicator, then a fortiori a losing party, who simply had the hope that an arbitrator's award somewhere down the line would overturn the adjudicator's original decision, could not be entitled to set off that hope against the sum due pursuant to that decision. The Judge went on to say:

> Standing back from the authorities for a moment, it is worth considering what the effect would be if I acceded to the defendant's request not to make the order for sale because of the on-going arbitration. It would mean that any unsuccessful party in adjudication would know that, if they refused to pay up for long enough, and started their own arbitration, they could effectively render the adjudicator's decision of no effect. It would be condoning, in clear terms, a judgment debtor's persistent default, and its complete refusal to comply with the earlier judgments of the court. For those reasons, it is a position which I am simply unable to adopt.¹⁰

14.19 The Judge therefore made the order for sale against Mrs Teasdale. He said that the case illustrated the sometimes harsh consequences of the system of construction adjudication introduced by the 1996 Act. However, having expressed his considerable sympathy for Mrs Teasdale and the difficulties which she faced, he was obliged to conclude that those difficulties stemmed, not from the adjudication process itself, but from the way in which the contractual arrangements had been set up in the first place. It will often be the case that the decision of an adjudicator will have harsh consequences for the loser but, very often, that will be explicable, not because of some default or unfairness on the part of the adjudicator, but because of the way in which the contractual arrangements had originally been framed.

Injunctions

14.20 A party to an adjudication might seek injunctive relief from the courts in two circumstances. First, as an alternative to the enforcement/summary judgment procedure discussed in the preceding paragraphs, they might seek a mandatory injunction as a means of ensuring that the losing party complies with the adjudicator's decision. Rather less commonly, at an earlier stage in the adjudication

---

⁹ See, for example, *Interserve Industrial Services Ltd v Cleveland Bridge (UK) Ltd* [2006] EWHC 741 and *Hillview Industrial Developments (UK) Ltd v Botes Building Ltd* [2006] EWHC 1365 (TCC).
¹⁰ [2006] EWHC 1708 (TCC); [2006] BLR 359.

proceedings, the responding party might seek to obtain an injunction to restrain the further progress of the adjudication itself.

14.21 As to the former situation, namely the successful party's attempt to enforce an adjudication by way of injunction, this was discussed by Dyson J in his judgment in *Macob Civil Engineering Ltd v Morrison Construction Ltd*.[11] Dyson J held that the mere fact that the adjudicator's decision may later be revised was not a good reason for saying that summary judgment was inappropriate. The grant of summary judgment did not pre-empt any later decision that an arbitrator may make. Although he considered that the court had the jurisdiction to grant a mandatory injunction to enforce an adjudicator's decision, he held that it would rarely be appropriate to grant such injunctive relief to enforce an obligation by one contracting party to pay the other. In particular, he said that a mandatory injunction to enforce a payment obligation carried with it the potential for contempt proceedings in the event of a failure to comply, and it was difficult to see why the sanction for failure to pay in accordance with an adjudicator's decision should be more draconian than for failure to honour a money judgment entered by the court. For these reasons, he concluded that an application for summary judgment was much the better course for the successful party in adjudication to pursue.

14.22 As a result of the decision in *Macob*, and the clear reasoning that underpinned it, it is not suggested that the successful party should ordinarily utilise the injunction mechanism to enforce the adjudicator's decision. The summary judgment process under CPR 24 will usually be a much better option.

14.23 As to the other potential use of injunction proceedings, namely to injunct ongoing adjudication proceedings (because, say, the responding party contends that the adjudicator does not have the necessary jurisdiction), such injunctions have only been granted in the past in fairly limited circumstances. Injunctions have been granted where the court has concluded that the relevant contract was not a construction contract for the purposes of the 1996 Act;[12] and where the adjudicator was found not to have been validly appointed under the relevant contract provisions.[13] However, it is important to note that this jurisdiction will be exercised sparingly. In *Workplace Technologies Plc v E Squared Ltd*[14] HHJ Wilcox was faced with a submission by the claimant that the contract had been concluded before the 1996 Act came into force and was therefore excluded from its operation. The claimant therefore sought an injunction to restrain the adjudicator from

---

[11] [1999] BLR 93.
[12] See for example *ABB Power Construction Ltd v Norwest Holst Engineering Ltd* [2000] TCLR 831.
[13] See, for example, *John Mowlem & Co Plc v Hydra-Tight & Co Plc* [2001] 17 Const LJ 358.
[14] [2000] CILL 1607.

proceeding with the adjudication which the defendant (who alleged that the contract was caught by the 1996 Act) had commenced. Judge Wilcox declined to grant an injunction, saying that the balance of convenience favoured allowing the adjudication process to continue. He pointed out that if the court granted an injunction without determining the issue of the date of the contract, then it inexorably followed that it might be interfering in a valid adjudication, to its clear detriment. The purpose of adjudication would then be frustrated. On the other hand, it was not appropriate for the court to determine the issue as to the date of the contract, since that was the very issue which the adjudicator had to decide.

14.24 If an injunction is sought in respect of an ongoing adjudication, the applicant should generally follow the procedure set out in CPR 25 and, in particular, 25PD. Assuming that the application is urgent, so that no claim form will have been issued by the time of the hearing, the applicant must prepare the application notice, evidence in support (including details of how and why the adjudicator does not have the necessary jurisdiction, or the specific reason why the injunction is being sought) and a draft order, and provide these documents to the court in order that a suitable hearing date can be fixed. It is suggested that these documents should also be served on the respondent, in order that proper notice is given and a mutually convenient hearing date can be fixed. It is important that, in the vast majority of cases at least, notice of the application should be given to the other side: it will only be in the most unusual circumstances that the court will consider an application to injunct an ongoing adjudication in the absence of the respondent. In certain circumstances, it might also be necessary, or at least prudent, to notify the adjudicator of the application for an injunction.

14.25 The court will usually require an undertaking in respect of the service of the claim form, if that has not already happened. In addition, if the injunction sought or granted is interim in nature, cross-undertakings in damages may also be necessary. At the hearing of the application itself, the problem for the court will usually be to decide the issue that lies at the heart of the injunction application (Is this a construction contract? Does the adjudicator have the jurisdiction to decide this dispute?) without trespassing on the issue which has been referred to the adjudicator. This can sometimes be difficult and, if it is, the court is likely to decline the application, for the reasons summarised by Judge Wilcox in *Workplace Technologies*.

Declaratory Relief

14.26 Applications for declaratory relief arising out of adjudication proceedings have commonly arisen in two different ways. First, there may be an application for a declaration by a party who contends that the adjudicator does not have the necessary jurisdiction. In practice, this is simply a variation on the injunction application discussed above. Secondly, there is an application for a declaration by the successful party to an adjudication that the adjudicator's decision is binding on the other party.

14.27 As to the first situation, a party who contests the jurisdiction of the adjudicator has a choice. Either he can raise the jurisdiction issue in the adjudication itself, and make plain that his continued participation in the adjudication is without prejudice to his jurisdictional arguments, or he can instead seek an injunction to restrain the adjudication or a declaration from the TCC that the adjudicator does not have the necessary jurisdiction. In many, perhaps most, cases, there are advantages in maintaining the jurisdictional dispute in the adjudication itself. This is particularly true in circumstances where a party, who contends that the adjudicator does not have the necessary jurisdiction, also considers that he has a good defence on the merits. In that situation, that party may well feel that it is in his interests to run both the jurisdictional point and the merits points together in the adjudication in the hope that, one way or the other, the claim will be defeated. On the other hand, if the adjudication is likely to involve an extensive analysis of a large amount of material, and the responding party is adamant that the adjudicator does not have the jurisdiction to embark on such a process, it may be in the responding party's interests to seek a declaration straight away. That would, of course, be the only way in which the responding party's position on costs could be protected.

14.28 If a party seeks a declaration from the TCC that the adjudicator does not have the necessary jurisdiction to deal with an ongoing adjudication then, in view of the likely urgency of the application, the court will endeavour to ensure that the hearing is fixed as soon as possible. There are a number of instances in which this has been achieved within seven days of the issue of the claim form. Indeed, a claim form is not always required, provided that the necessary undertaking to issue such a document is provided. The process is very similar (and can be seen as an alternative) to an application to injunct an adjudication, as discussed in paragraphs 14.23–14.25 above.

14.29 The second situation in which a declaration might be sought (to confirm the binding nature of the adjudicator's decision), although less common, can sometimes be important, particularly where the dispute concerns accrued contractual rights, not money due. Take the situation where the claiming party seeks a declaration from an adjudicator that he is entitled to a lengthy extension of time. The adjudicator accedes to the claim. The adjudicator's decision is therefore temporarily binding and will have significant knock-on consequences on all kinds of matters, such as the contractor's entitlement to loss and expense and the employer's inability to levy liquidated damages for the period of the extension. It is not uncommon, in such situations, for the employer's team to endeavour to limit the consequences of the adjudicator's decision whilst the contract is being administered on site. In those circumstances, it can often be appropriate for the contractor to seek a declaration from the court that the adjudicator's decision is binding and also, if appropriate, seek particular declarations as to the consequences of that decision. Applications of this kind are treated by the court in a similar way to an application for summary judgment on the basis of an adjudicator's decision, and the court will endeavour to fix such hearings within 28 days of the relevant application.

Staying Court Proceeding for Adjudication

14.30 Assume that A and B have a binding adjudication agreement, but that, in breach of that agreement, A commences proceedings against B in the TCC, without first referring the dispute to adjudication. B may then issue an application in those proceedings for a stay of the court action until the matter has been adjudicated. The application must be supported by a witness statement. The assigned TCC judge will then fix a date for the hearing of the application to stay the proceedings. Again, the TCC recognises the need to arrange such hearings speedily, and they will usually be fixed for a date within 28 days of the original application. Directions are usually necessary as to the preparation of a hearing bundle, and the exchange of skeleton arguments.

14.31 As to whether or not B's application for a stay would be successful in those circumstances, the relevant authorities are set out in the judgment of the TCC Judge in *DGT Steel and Cladding Limited v Cubitt Building and Interiors Ltd*.[15] In short, the position would appear to be that, if a binding adjudication agreement can be demonstrated, the persuasive burden shifts to the party who has commenced the court proceedings in breach of that agreement, to show good reason why the discretion that arises from the inherent jurisdiction of the court should not be exercised in favour of the stay. The reasons for this are set out below.

14.32 The courts' inherent jurisdiction to grant a stay of existing court proceedings, commenced in breach of an agreement to utilise other forms of dispute resolution, was discussed by the House of Lords in *Channel Tunnel Group Limited v Balfour Beatty Construction Limited*.[16] That was a case in which the contract provided for the initial reference of disputes to a panel of experts, with all remaining disputes to be the subject of arbitration in Brussels. In the leading speech, Lord Mustill said that the courts had an inherent, albeit discretionary, power to stay proceedings in

---

[15] [2007] EWHC 1584 (TCC).
[16] [1993] AC 334.

such circumstances. This approach was followed by the Judge in *Cott UK Ltd v F E Barber Ltd*.[17] In that case, the contract contained an agreement that any dispute should be referred to an expert for his determination. The Judge concluded that, in consequence, a stay of the court proceedings could be granted, and that the persuasive burden then shifted to the claimant to demonstrate how or why a stay should not, as a matter of discretion, be granted. On the facts of that case, the claimant discharged that burden and the stay was refused because the expert determination procedure was so unclear as to be unenforceable. In *Cable & Wireless plc v IBM United Kingdom Ltd*,[18] Colman J adopted the same approach in respect of an agreement to refer disputes to alternative dispute resolution. He concluded that the ADR procedure envisaged by the contract was of sufficient certainty to be enforceable and, in the exercise of the court's discretion, the court proceedings were stayed.

14.33 By analogy, it would appear that this approach is appropriate to cases in which the underlying contractual agreement is that, in the first instance, disputes are to be referred to adjudication. There are a number of authorities dealing specifically with adjudication. *Cape Durasteel Ltd v Rosser & Russell Building Services Ltd*[19] was a decision of HHJ Lloyd QC that was concerned with a contractual agreement to adjudicate, and decided before the 1996 Act. The Judge concluded that there was a binding and enforceable agreement to adjudicate and that, having regard to all the circumstances, it was appropriate to order that the action be stayed pending adjudication. Furthermore, the decision of Dyson J in *Herschel Engineering Ltd v Breen Property Ltd*[20] was also concerned with the situation in which there were concurrent court and adjudication proceedings. There, the Judge concluded that the claiming party was entitled to seek a prompt result in adjudication, notwithstanding the existence of the court proceedings, and he therefore refused the application for an injunction restraining the adjudication. He was not asked to grant, and therefore did not consider, a temporary stay of the court proceedings pending the outcome of the adjudication.

14.34 Each of these authorities was considered by the TCC Judge in *DGT Steel Ltd and Cladding v Cubitt Building & Interiors Ltd*.[21] At paragraph 12 of his judgment in that case, the Judge derived from them the following three principles:

(a) The court will not grant an injunction to prevent one party from commencing adjudication proceedings, even if there are already ongoing court or arbitration proceedings in respect of the same dispute (see *Herschel v Breen*).

---

[17] [1997] 3 All ER 540.
[18] [2002] EWHC 2059 (Comm); [2002] 2 All ER (Comm) 1041.
[19] (1995) 46 Con LR 75.
[20] [2000] BLR 272.
[21] [2007] EWHC 1584 (TCC).

(b) The court has an inherent jurisdiction to stay court proceedings issued in breach of an agreement to adjudicate (see *Cape Durasteel*), just as it has the inherent jurisdiction to stay such proceedings where any other enforceable agreement for ADR might exist (see *Channel Tunnel*, *Cott*, and *Cable & Wireless*).

(c) The courts' discretion as to whether or not to grant a stay in such circumstances should be exercised on the basis that, if a binding adjudication agreement has been demonstrated, the persuasive burden is on the party seeking to resist the stay to demonstrate how or why, in all the circumstances, the stay should not be granted (see *Cott* and *Cable & Wireless*).

14.35 In *DGT Steel*, there was considerable debate about whether the adjudication agreement in that case was compulsory, with the parties obliged to submit any dispute to adjudication, or simply optional, with the parties having the right (but not the obligation) to submit disputes to adjudication. The Judge concluded that, ultimately, it made little difference since, even if the agreement was not compulsory, the type of adjudication agreement envisaged by the 1996 Act, which gave each party the right to adjudicate a dispute (no matter which side of the dispute they might be on), constituted a binding agreement which gave each party the right, in appropriate circumstances, to seek to enforce their entitlement by way of an application for a stay.

14.36 In addition to the consideration of the points of principle noted above, the judgment in *DGT Steel* is also of interest because it was dealing with a very common factual situation. The basis of DGT's claim in court was, in essence, their final account claim. However, the dispute encompassed by the earlier adjudication was limited to questions concerned with Cubitt's alleged non-compliance with the interim payment and withholding notice regime provided by the contract. As the adjudicator had correctly pointed out in his decision, the nature of the dispute referred to him meant that he was not required or entitled to consider the underlying merits of DGT's claim. DGT lost on the technical points and subsequently commenced proceedings in the TCC. However, as noted above, their claim in the TCC expressly raised all the underlying issues of valuation, which were disputed by Cubitt on their merits. In seeking to resist the application for a stay, DGT argued that they had already submitted their claim to adjudication, and were therefore entitled to bring that claim to court. However, the Judge ruled that, although the sum of money sought in the court proceedings was the same as that which had been claimed in the adjudication, the principal issue in the court proceedings, namely the merits of DGT's valuation, had never been referred to adjudication and was therefore a new dispute. In all the circumstances, he granted the stay sought by Cubitt.

15

STAY OF EXECUTION

Introduction	15.01
RSC Order 47	15.02
Cross-Claim of Judgment Debtor	15.04
Insolvency of Judgment Creditor	15.06
The Financial Difficulties of the Judgment Creditor	15.09

'In considering what is just and fair in an application for a stay of execution of a summary judgment under Part 24 in circumstances such as these, the court must be careful not to reallocate the commercial risks accepted by the parties who engage in a construction contract mindful of the provisions of the Housing Grants Construction Regeneration Act 1996 and subject to the general safeguards of insolvency law.'

His Honour Judge Wilcox in *Total M&E Services Ltd v ABB Building Technologies Ltd* [2002] EWHC 248 (TCC).

Introduction

15.01 The whole purpose of the 1996 Act, and the Scheme for Construction Contracts, was to provide a quick answer to disputes which would be temporarily binding. In practice, of course, that usually means that the adjudicator decides that one party has to pay a sum of money to the other. On occasion, those sums have been large. In some circumstances, the losing parties have endeavoured to avoid making the required payments. One of the ways in which they have sought to achieve this is by seeking a stay of execution pursuant to RSC Order 47. However, as demonstrated in the authorities set out below, the courts have generally endeavoured to ensure that the stay mechanism is not used in such a way so as to frustrate the purpose of adjudication.

RSC Order 47

15.02 RSC Order 47, preserved in Section A of the Civil Procedure Rules 1998, provides as follows:

> 1–(1) Where a judgment is given or an order made for the payment by any person of money, and the court is satisfied, on an application made at the time of the judgment or order, or at any time thereafter, by the judgment debtor or other party liable to execution—
>
> (a) that there are special circumstances which render it inexpedient to enforce the judgment or order, or
>
> (b) that the applicant is unable from any cause to pay the money,
>
> then, notwithstanding anything in rule 2 or 3, the court may by order stay the execution of the judgment or order by writ of fieri facias either absolutely or for such period and subject to such conditions as the court thinks fit.
>
> (2) An application under this rule, if not made at the time the judgment is given or order made, must be made in accordance with CPR Part 23 and may be so made notwithstanding that the party liable to execution did not acknowledge service of the claim form or serve a defence or take any previous part in the proceedings.
>
> (3) The grounds on which an application under this rule is made must be set out in the application notice and be supported by a witness statement or affidavit made by or on behalf of the applicant substantiating the said grounds and, in particular, where such application is made on the grounds of the applicant's inability to pay, disclosing his income, the nature and value of any property of his and the amount of any other liabilities of his.
>
> (4) The application notice and a copy of the supporting witness statement or affidavit must, not less than four clear days before the hearing, be served on the party entitled to enforce the judgment or order.
>
> (5) An order staying execution under this rule may be varied or revoked by a subsequent order.

15.03 Usually, a stay of execution will be sought in one of two typical cases: if the judgment debtor has a cross-claim which has yet to be determined and which, so it is said, will make it inexpedient to enforce the judgment; or if the financial position of the judgment creditor is such that, in all the circumstances, a stay should be granted. However, the authorities make it clear that slightly different considerations may apply when the judgment that is sought to be stayed is a judgment enforcing the decision of an adjudicator.

Cross-Claim of Judgment Debtor

15.04 Even in an ordinary case, the existence of a cross-claim against the judgment creditor will not usually give rise to a stay of execution: see *Wagner v Laubscher Brothers & Co*[1]

---

[1] [1970] 2 QB 313, CA.

However, there are a number of reported cases where the existence of a separate claim by the losing party, which cuts across the basis of the original judgment, has given rise to a stay: see, for example, *Hillcourt v Teliasonera AB*,[2] where the court stayed execution of a judgment based on an arbitrator's award arising out of a breach of an agreement for lease, in circumstances where later information demonstrated that the judgment debtor had a reasonable case for rescission of the lease.

However, where the judgment is based on the decision of an adjudicator, then it is submitted that, generally, no set-off or cross-claim could justify a stay of execution. In paragraphs 10.20–10.39 above, there is a discussion of those authorities which make plain that a losing party is not generally entitled to raise, against the adjudicator's decision, some sort of set-off and cross-claim. In those circumstances, the principle underlying the decision in *Hillcourt* would simply not be available to the party seeking to stay the execution of a judgment based on an enforceable adjudicator's decision. Generally, and subject of course to the terms of the contract between the parties, to allow the losing party in an adjudication to avoid making prompt payment by raising the existence of a cross-claim would be contrary to the whole purpose and intent of the 1996 Act.

15.05

Insolvency of Judgment Creditor

At the opposite end of the scale, if the judgment creditor is in liquidation, then that is a ground either to refuse summary judgment, or to stay execution. In *Bouygues (UK) Ltd v Dahl-Jensen (UK) Ltd*[3] the Court of Appeal upheld the decision of Dyson J, and said that, although the award contained an error, it was an error that the adjudicator made whilst acting within his jurisdiction, and thus his award would stand and was enforceable. However, in his judgment, Chadwick LJ went on to explain that Dahl-Jensen's liquidation meant that it would be wrong for the sums awarded by the adjudicator to be paid to them. By reference to rule 4.90 of the Insolvency Rules 1986, he concluded that payment of the sums identified in the adjudicator's decision would lead to injustice:

15.06

> 33 . . . If Bouygues is obliged to pay to Dahl-Jensen the amount awarded by the adjudicator, those monies, when received by the liquidator of Dahl-Jensen, will form part of the fund applicable for distribution amongst Dahl-Jenson's creditors. If Bouygues itself has a claim under the construction contract, as it currently asserts, and is required to prove for that claim in the liquidation of Dahl-Jensen, it will receive only a dividend pro rata to the amount of its claim. It will be deprived of the benefit of treating Dahl-Jensen's claim under the adjudicator's determination as security for its own cross-claim . . .

---

[2] [2006] EWHC 508 (Ch).
[3] [2000] BLR 522.

> 35. ... In circumstances such as the present, where there are latent claims and cross-claims between parties, one of which is in liquidation, it seems to me that there is a compelling reason to refuse summary judgment on a claim arising out of an adjudication which is, necessarily, provisional. All claims and cross-claims should be resolved in the liquidation, in which full account can be taken and a balance struck. That is what rule 4.90 of the Insolvency Rules 1986 requires.

15.07 In *Bouygues*, the Court of Appeal did not set aside the summary judgment order because the point about the Insolvency Rules 1986 had not been taken before the Judge and was not embraced by *Bouygues* 'with any enthusiasm' on the appeal. However, the same ultimate effect was achieved by the stay of execution imposed by the Court of Appeal. In *Hart v Fidler and another*[4] the liquidation of the contractor was one of three separate reasons upon which the Court relied in refusing to enforce the decision of the adjudicator. The TCC Judge considered that to enter judgment in such circumstances might amount to an inaccurate assertion of the parties' substantive rights in the liquidation, because such a judgment would be based upon a decision which was only temporarily binding. There was at least a risk of inaccuracy and that therefore, in accordance with the judgment of Chadwick LJ in *Bouygues*, insolvency was a compelling reason to refuse summary judgment.

15.08 In *Harwood Construction Ltd v Lantrode Ltd*[5] the claimant contractor was not in liquidation, but a petition had been presented and was due to be heard some two weeks after the application for summary judgment. The TCC Judge was unable to say whether or not the petition would succeed. Accordingly, the Judge gave judgment for the claimant contractor, but with execution stayed until the hearing of the petition for windingup. If the winding-up order was made at the subsequent hearing, the stay would continue. If the petition was dismissed, then the stay would cease and the contractor would be entitled to immediate payment of the judgment sum.

The Financial Difficulties of the Judgment Creditor

15.09 The greatest difficulties arise in those cases where the party seeking to enforce the decision of the adjudicator is, or is said to be, in financial difficulties. In such circumstances, the judgment debtor will often argue that, since they are seeking a return of the monies awarded by the adjudicator, it would be unfair if they had to pay over that amount now, only to discover, following their success on the ultimate determination of the dispute, that the judgment creditor can no longer afford to pay the money back. As a matter of principle, this argument is open to the judgment debtor in support of a stay of execution of the summary

---

[4] [2006] EWHC 2857 (TCC); [2006] All ER (D) 232 (Nov).
[5] 24.11.00, a decision of HHJ Seymour QC in the TCC in London.

judgment. As a matter of practice, however, this argument can be far from straightforward.

15.10 The first, and most obvious, point to make is that an assertion of financial difficulties is just that, an allegation which may well be disputed, and which cannot therefore result in as clear-cut a situation as where the judgment creditor is in liquidation. The Court then has to embark on a delicate balancing exercise in which the natural instinct to give effect to the adjudicator's efforts must be weighed against any evidence that a real injustice might be perpetrated if the money is paid out to a company which is just about to go into liquidation. It then becomes a matter of discretion as to whether the Court, in considering the evidence as to the judgment creditor's financial difficulties, concludes that they are so severe that any repayment is most unlikely and that, in the round, it is therefore 'inexpedient to enforce the judgment'.

It is suggested that the starting point for any consideration of the way in which the Court should exercise its discretion in these circumstances is the decision of the Court of Appeal in *Sir Lindsay Parkinson & Co v Triplan Ltd*.[6] That was a case concerned with security for costs. However, amongst the matters which Lord Denning MR identified as being relevant to the exercise of the Court's discretion, he referred to the issue of whether the claimant's want of means had been brought about by any conduct on the part of the defendant, such as delays in making payment. That is also directly relevant to the situation where the judgment debtor is seeking to rely on the judgment creditor's financial difficulties in order to obtain a stay, in circumstances where the judgment debtor may be responsible for those self-same financial difficulties. In *Wimbledon Construction Company 2000 Ltd v Derick Vago*[7] the TCC Judge held that the matters listed by Lord Denning in *Sir Lindsay Parkinson*, particularly the possibility that the claimant's want of means had been brought about by the defendant, was of general application to the exercise of the Court's discretion under Order 47 when considering whether or not to grant a stay of execution.

15.11 There can be no doubt that the financial circumstances of the claimant are at least potentially relevant on any application for a stay. In other words, the mere fact that the claimant is entitled to judgment to enforce an adjudicator's decision in his favour does not mean that a stay of execution will automatically be refused. In one of the early enforcement cases, *Herschel Engineering Ltd v Breen Property Ltd*[8] Dyson J refused the application for a stay, because he found that there was no evidence that, if the defendant was successful in the subsequent

---

[6] [1973] QB 609.
[7] [2005] EWHC 1086 (TCC).
[8] [2000] BLR 272.

proceedings, the claimant would be unable to repay the sum awarded by the adjudicator. However, the Judge expressly noted that, had the position been otherwise, and there was a real doubt as to the claimant's ability to repay, he would 'probably have granted a stay of execution' pending the final determination of the separate proceedings.

15.12 In *Rainford House Ltd v Cadogan Ltd*[9] HHJ Seymour QC rejected the submission that a stay of execution should not be granted in principle, because to grant a stay would be to deprive the claimant of the benefit of the 1996 Act. Instead he found that the financial position of the claimant was a matter that could be relied on by the defendant in an application for a stay of execution. In that case, he concluded that the evidence put forward by the defendant raised a strong prima facie case that the claimant was currently insolvent, and that such evidence had not been contradicted or explained. He therefore drew the inference that the present financial position of the claimant meant that they would be unable to repay the amount of the judgment sum if it was later found that the adjudicator's decision was incorrect. A stay of execution was therefore imposed. In *Ashley House Plc v Galliers Southern Ltd*[10] the same Judge found that, although Galliers were entitled to summary judgment in the amount of the adjudicator's decision, their 'parlous financial condition' meant that there would have to be a stay of execution. The stay was ordered on the agreed condition that the amount awarded by the adjudicator would be paid into court. The Judge rejected the contention that Galliers' financial difficulties arose out of Ashley House's conduct.

15.13 How is the Court to exercise its discretion in circumstances where there is evidence and argument from both sides as to the claimant's financial position? The first case in which that problem was considered in any detail was in the second part of the dispute in *Herschel Engineering Ltd v Breen Property Ltd (No 2)*.[11] The TCC Judge held that the test was comparable to that for security for costs and that therefore the points listed by Lord Denning MR in *Sir Lindsay Parkinson* were relevant and applicable. In particular, in *Herschel*, the Judge found that there was no substantial difference between the financial position of the claimant company at the time that it entered into the contract, and the time of the application. At the time of the contract, the Judge said that the claimant company was an unknown entity in financial terms; since that was the company with which the defendant had chosen to contract and had entrusted with the work, it would now be wrong

---

[9] [2001] BLR 416.
[10] [2002] Adj LR 02/15.
[11] A decision of HHJ Lloyd QC, unreported, 28 July 2000, TCC.

for the defendant to take advantage of that position to impose a stay of execution. He concluded:

> 19. In my view, on an application for a stay where a party has entered into a contract with a company whose financial status is or may be uncertain and finds itself liable to pay money to that company under an adjudicator's decision, the question may properly be posed: is this not an inevitable consequence of the commercial activities of the applicant that it finds itself in the position that it is in? It has, as it were, contracted for the result. That is not normally a ground for avoiding the consequences of a debt created by the contractual mechanism (which is how, in the absence of express terms, adjudication operates: see section 114 of the Act). It is very easy (and prudent and relatively inexpensive) to carry out a search or to obtain credit references against a company whose financial status and standing is unknown. Not to do so inevitably places a person at a significant disadvantage. It has only itself to blame if the company selected by it proves not to have been substantial (as opposed to a material deterioration in its finances since the date of contract).

15.14 A similar result was reached in *Michael John Construction v Golledge & Ors*[12] where the TCC Judge concluded from the evidence that the claimant contractor was not in a significantly worse financial position than it had been at the time when the contract was made. Thus the defendant employers 'got the result they contracted for and cannot now use the claimant's financial ill-health to avoid judgment'. A stay of execution was again refused.

15.15 The absence of any significant change in the financial position of the claimant company between the making of the contract and the date of judgment, or the fact that any financial difficulties might be linked back to the defendant's conduct in any event, are the two most common factors which have led the courts to refuse applications for a stay of execution, even where there is evidence of financial difficulties. In *Total M&E Services Ltd v ABB Building Technologies Ltd*[13] HHJ Wilcox set out the competing evidence as to the financial position of the claimant. He concluded that, in the exercise of his discretion, a stay should not be imposed, in part because the capacity of the defendant to pay back the sums in the future was directly linked to its present entitlement to the sums decided by the adjudicator, and in part because there had been no real change in the claimant's financial status since the making of the contract. More widely, he summarised the court's approach to applications for a stay in these terms:

> 52. Where a stay is sought the Court must consider all the circumstances. It must consider whether there are special circumstances which render it inexpedient to enforce the judgment. The risk of an inability to repay on due time is one of a number of factors to be taken account of in the balancing exercise. Where the risk is

---

[12] [2006] EWHC 71 (TCC); [2006] TCLR 3.
[13] [2002] EWHC 248 (TCC).

high, as where there is strong uncontradicted evidence of a present inability to pay or a company is in administration, the stay may be appropriate on terms safeguarding the disputed money. The burden is clearly upon the party seeking a stay to adduce evidence of a very real risk of future non-payment. The balancing exercise is of course subject to the overriding considerations of Part 1 of the CPR ensuring justice and fairness between the parties. In considering what is just and fair in an application for a stay of execution of a summary judgment under Part 24 in circumstances such as these the court must be careful not to re-allocate the commercial risks accepted by the parties who engage in a construction contract mindful of the provisions of the Housing Grants Construction Regeneration Act 1996 and subject to the general safeguards of insolvency law.

That passage was cited with approval by Forbes J in *JW Hughes Building Contractors Ltd v GB Metal Work Ltd*.[14] In that case the Judge found that, on all the evidence, it could not possibly be said that there was a high risk of an inability to repay the money, and the stay was rejected.

15.16 As noted above, a number of the reported cases stress that the burden of demonstrating an entitlement to a stay is firmly on the judgment debtor and that, if the relevant evidence is served late, or if it is unclear on that evidence what the precise financial position of the claimant might be, the stay will usually be refused. Thus in *Absolute Rentals Ltd v Glencor Enterprises Ltd*[15] Judge Wilcox refused an application for a stay because the material questioning the claimant's financial viability was served late and it was impossible to say on the evidence what its precise financial standing was. He made it plain that it was entirely possible that, even if the claimant was impecunious, that derived from the defendant's default.[16] There are a number of other cases in which the same Judge (and other TCC Judges) has refused an application for a stay on the basis of a lack of compelling evidence as to the judgment creditor's alleged financial difficulties.[17]

---

[14] [2003] EWHC 2421 (TCC).
[15] 28.2.2000; CILL July/August 2000.
[16] It has been argued that Judge Wilcox's suggestion, in his judgment in *Absolute Rentals*, that granting a stay would frustrate the Scheme, was contrary to the view expressed by Dyson J and others to the effect that, in appropriate circumstances, a stay could be ordered, notwithstanding the judgment creditor's success in the adjudication. However, it is submitted that Judge Wilcox's comments need to be looked at in the context of his rejection of the application for a stay on the basis of both late and disputed evidence. It is not thought that there is any difference between his approach and that of the other Judges to the principles applicable to applications for a stay.
[17] See two other decisions of HHJ Wilcox in *Nolan Davis v Stephen Catton* (unreported, 2000 TCC No 590); and *Multiconcept Developments v Abacus* (unreported, 2002). In *Multiplex Constructions (UK) Limited v West India Quay Development Company (Eastern) Limited* [2006] EWHC 1569 (TCC), Ramsey J refused a stay, despite the fact that the contractor was 'currently suffering large losses on the Wembley stadium project'. He said that it was being supported by its parent company and there was no evidence that such support was likely to be withdrawn.

Stay of Execution

In *AWG Construction Services Ltd v Rockingham Motor Speedway Ltd*[18] HHJ **15.17**
Toulmin CMG QC observed that, whilst it was not possible to say how far an applicant had to go in putting evidence before a court in support of a stay, it should be noted that the court should not grant a stay unless, consistent with the overriding objective in the CPR, the justice of the case demanded it. He went on to say:

> 186. In general, a court must balance (a) the intention of the legislation that adjudication should be enforced summarily; (b) the right of the successful party not to be prejudiced by being kept out of its money; and (c) in cases where there is a serious risk that a party will not be able to recover the money, that the defendant is not being seriously prejudiced in a way not contemplated by the Act which is silent as to the position where a defendant runs more than a nominal risk of being unable to recover money after trial or arbitration award.

In addition, Judge Toulmin indicated that one matter which the court might consider is the diligence with which the defendant pursued its cross-claim or challenge to the adjudicator's original decision. If the claimant was to be kept out of its money at all, it should be for the shortest reasonable time, so that the right approach might well be to grant a stay for a limited time originally, with extensions depending on the conduct of the parties. By contrast, a failure by the defendant to pursue its cross-claim or challenge with diligence may itself be a bar to a successful application for a stay of execution.

The most recent judgment in which the relevant principles for an application for **15.18**
a stay of execution were considered in detail was *Wimbledon Construction Co 2000 Ltd v Derek Vago*.[19] Having considered a number of the cases set out above, the TCC Judge concluded that the principles applicable to such an application were as follows:

> 26. In a number of the authorities which I have cited above the point has been made that each case must turn on its own facts. Whilst I respectfully agree with that, it does seem to me that there are a number of clear principles which should always govern the exercise of the court's discretion when it is considering a stay of execution in adjudication enforcement proceedings. Those principles can be set out as follows:
>
> > a) Adjudication (whether pursuant to the 1996 Act or the consequential amendments to the standard forms of building and engineering contracts) is designed to be a quick and inexpensive method of arriving at a temporary result in a construction dispute.
> > b) In consequence, adjudicators' decisions are intended to be enforced summarily and the claimant (being the successful party in the adjudication) should not generally be kept out of its money.

---

[18] [2004] EWHC 888 (TCC).
[19] [2005] EWHC 1086 (TCC); [2005] BLR 374.

c) In an application to say the execution of summary judgment arising out of an adjudicator's decision, the Court must exercise its discretion under Order 47 with considerations a) and b) firmly in mind (see *AWG*).

d) The probable inability of the claimant to repay the judgment sum (awarded by the Adjudicator and enforced by way of summary judgment) at the end of the substantive trial, or arbitration hearing, may constitute special circumstances within the meaning of Order 47 rule 1(1)(a) rendering it appropriate to grant a stay (see *Herschel*).

e) If the claimant is in insolvent liquidation, or there is no dispute on the evidence that the claimant is insolvent, then a stay of execution will usually be granted (see *Bouygues* and *Rainford House*).

f) Even if the evidence of the claimant's present financial position suggested that it is probable that it would be unable to repay the judgment sum when it fell due, that would not usually justify the grant of a stay if:

   (i) the claimant's financial position is the same or similar to its financial position at the time that the relevant contract was made (see *Herschel*); or

   (ii) The claimant's financial position is due, either wholly, or in significant part, to the defendant's failure to pay those sums which were awarded by the adjudicator (see *Absolute Rentals*).

15.20 This summary of the applicable principles has been adopted in a number of subsequent decisions. In *Ale Heavy Lift v MSD (Darlington) Ltd*,[20] HHJ Toulmin CMG QC followed this approach. Although, as he put it, 'Ale's accounts are in a state that would give cause for some serious degree of concern', their financial position was the same as, or similar to, the time when the contract had been made. He therefore declined to exercise his discretion in favour of a stay. In reaching this conclusion, he also had regard to the fact that the defendant had not yet commenced any proceedings to recover the sums awarded by the adjudicator.

15.21 In *McConnell Dowell Contractors (Aust) Pty Ltd v National Grid Gas Plc*,[21] a decision of Jackson J, he rejected the application for a stay, but only because McConnell were prepared to offer a bond in respect of monies that might have to be paid back at a later date. In addition, as the learned editors of the Building Law Reports have pointed out,[22] the correct position where the claimant is in insolvent liquidation is that, since the grant of summary judgment is inappropriate, judgment should not be entered at all. There would therefore be nothing for the defendant to seek to stay.[23]

---

[20] [2006] EWHC 2080 (TCC).
[21] [2007] BLR 92.
[22] At pages 375–376 of their report of the *Wimbledon* case.
[23] As discussed in paragraph 15.07 above.

Part V

A PRACTICAL GUIDE TO ADJUDICATION

16. Commencing an Adjudication	407
17. The Adjudication Itself	417
18. The Adjudicator's Decision	427

16

COMMENCING AN ADJUDICATION

Introduction	16.01	Appointment of Adjudicator	16.10
Notice of Adjudication	16.02	A Challenge to the Nominated Adjudicator	16.16
Response to the Notice of Adjudication	16.07	Referral Notice	16.21

Introduction

16.01 There is no shortage of written material purporting to provide guidance as to the best way of approaching and running an adjudication. Inevitably, much of this advice is now out of date, and some of it is of questionable accuracy. However, mention should be made of two helpful Guides prepared by the Construction Umbrella Bodies Adjudication Task Group, in conjunction with the Construction Sector Unit of the Department of Trade & Industry. The first, entitled 'Users' Guide to Adjudication', and published in April 2003, is a useful summary of the various steps in any adjudication. The second is a document entitled 'Guidance for Adjudicators' which, although even older (being produced in July 2002), is nonetheless a helpful summary of the principles which any adjudicator must bear in mind when embarking on an adjudication. These documents are referred to below as, respectively, the Users' Guide and the Guidance for Adjudicators.

Notice of Adjudication

16.02 For the reasons explained in greater detail at paragraphs 3.12–3.15 and 7.35–7.45 above, the notice of intention to refer a dispute to adjudication (which will be referred to throughout as the notice of adjudication) is, in many ways, the most important document in any adjudication, because it defines the dispute which the adjudicator has to decide. In most adjudications, it will be important that the notice of adjudication provides the following information:

(a) a brief description of the contract, together with the names and addresses of the parties to that contract;
(b) a brief description of the dispute that has arisen between the parties;
(c) a clear description of the nature/type of redress being sought in the adjudication, and what the claiming party wants the adjudicator to do.

It is sometimes said that the proper subject of both the notice of adjudication, and the subsequent referral notice, is the dispute itself, and that therefore such notices should set out both sides' opposing positions which have created that dispute. Although it can be sometimes be useful for the referring party to identify, in short order, what it understands the response to its claim to be, it is thought to be unnecessary for the referring party to devote too much time to such an exercise when preparing the notice of adjudication and the referral notice, particularly given that the responding party will have its own opportunity to set out its position in detail when it responds to the referral notice.

16.03 The most important thing for the referring party to ensure is that, unless the form of contract specifically permits the referral of multiple disputes at the same time, the notice of adjudication identifies just one single dispute. Thus the description of the dispute between the parties in the notice must be set out with that requirement in mind. In the vast majority of adjudications, it is wrong in principle, and potentially fatal to the entire adjudication, if the notice of adjudication talks about the existence of disputes (plural) between the parties. Take the common situation where a contractor's application for an interim payment has not been paid (either in whole or in part) by the employer. That interim application for payment might include claims for unpaid contract work, variations, the expenditure of prime cost items, an extension of time, and loss and expense. However, it must be remembered that, despite all those disparate elements, the single dispute between the parties was and remains the employer's failure to pay the sum claimed by way of an interim payment. The notice of adjudication should therefore identify the non-payment of the sum claimed by way of interim payment as comprising the single dispute between the parties. Only then, if it is appropriate, will it be necessary to go on to identify how the unpaid sum has been made up. Any reference in the notice of adjudication to the existence of more than one dispute is likely to lead to a challenge to the adjudicator's jurisdiction by the responding party.

16.04 It is also important to ensure that the notice of adjudication makes quite clear what relief is sought; to identify precisely what the referring party wants the adjudicator to do. It is not enough for a contractor simply to identify the submission of an interim payment application and its non-payment by the employer. The referring party should go on to say that, in consequence of the non-payment, it seeks an order for the payment of the outstanding sum, together with any other consequential matters, such as interest and, more unusually, costs. Similarly, if the contractor claims that he is entitled to a particular period by way of an extension of time, then the notice of adjudication needs to spell out that the contractor is seeking a declaration from the adjudicator to that effect.

16.05 Of course, it is common for an adjudicator to reach a view which gives the referring party some, but by no means all, of his outstanding claim. It can sometimes be said that, if the contractor is claiming £100,000 by way of outstanding payment, and no other relief is sought in the notice of adjudication, the adjudicator does not have the power to award the contractor, say, £35,000. Such technical points can be avoided if, within the notice of adjudication, the referring party makes clear that, in the alternative to his specific claims, he is asking the adjudicator to award such other sum as he sees fit.

16.06 The later, and more detailed, document produced by the referring party is the referral notice, discussed in greater detail at paragraphs 16.21–16.25 below. However, it should be remembered that the referral notice must generally be served within seven days of the notice of adjudication. It is usually sensible, therefore, for the referring party to have prepared his referral notice at the same time as his notice of adjudication, so as to avoid the risk that the referral notice will not be ready in time. A failure to comply with the seven day period might be fatal to the adjudication, and require its re-commencement. If the referring party prepares the documents at the same time, then in practice, it can often make sense for the referral notice to be drafted first, and in detail, so that the notice of adjudication can then be abstracted, almost as a summary, from the referral notice itself. It can be dangerous for a party to issue a notice of adjudication in general terms and only then get down to preparing the detailed referral notice. First, as already noted, there is a risk that the referral notice will not be ready in time. Secondly, there is also the risk that, when the detailed work is done in explaining the individual claims in the referral notice, there may be changes of emphasis or presentation which might reveal that the wording of the notice of adjudication is unclear or even wrong. For these reasons, it is usually appropriate for these two important documents to be drafted simultaneously.

Response to the Notice of Adjudication

16.07 When the responding party receives the notice of adjudication, there are a number of matters which it needs to consider as a matter of urgency. The first is whether there is a contract in existence at all; if so, whether the contract is a construction contract; and/or whether the notice is in accordance with the adjudication provisions in the contract between the parties. If the responding party considers that there is no contract at all, or that the contract is not a construction contract, or that the notice of adjudication is not in accordance with the contract, or there is some other reason that the adjudicator does not have the necessary jurisdiction (for example that the incorrect nominating body has been approached, or someone other than the named adjudicator has been nominated), then the responding party must notify the referring party of this jurisdictional challenge straight away.

16.08 It is often the case that the responding party will feel that the alleged dispute is no such thing, either because the claim being made is not one that has ever been made before, or because the notice of adjudication has followed a matter of days (sometimes just hours) after the submission of the underlying claim, with the result that the responding party considers that he has not had a proper opportunity to consider the claim prior to the service of the notice of adjudication. Again, if the responding party considers that either of those circumstances applies, then he must notify the claiming party immediately, because such complaints also go to jurisdiction. However, whilst the submission of an entirely new claim by way of a notice of adjudication will almost always be illegitimate, the provision of a notice of adjudication hot on the heels of a contractual claim may not give rise to a successful jurisdictional challenge. For the reasons explained in paragraphs 2.77–2.84 and 7.46–7.56 above, the courts have given a wide meaning to the term 'dispute', and the reported cases demonstrate that, provided that the responding party has had at least some time to consider the claim presented under the contract, then a failure to respond to such a claim may well be sufficient to create a dispute between the parties which could then be referred to adjudication.

16.09 It is often said, and with considerable force, that the adjudication process can be slanted in favour of the referring party. Certainly, this is nowhere more apparent than at the commencement of the adjudication. The referring party will have had weeks (if not months) in which to prepare both the detailed referral notice and the notice of adjudication. Once the notice of adjudication has been served, the clock is ticking against the responding party. In such circumstances, it is suggested that the responding party should respond as soon as possible to the notice of adjudication, in clear but concise terms. In the vast majority of cases, the response to the notice of adjudication is not the appropriate place for the responding party to wax lyrical on every detail of the underlying claim: instead, the responding party will almost always get an opportunity to do that in its response to the referral notice. Accordingly, it is important that, at the outset of the adjudication, the responding party concentrates on the bigger picture and, on receipt of the notice of adjudication, confines his response to any headline points concerned with jurisdiction and, if appropriate, the fundamental absence of merit in the claim. However, whilst in the vast majority of cases the key document from the responding party will be the response to the referral notice, it is worth noting that the Scheme for Construction Contracts does not expressly entitle the responding party to submit any such document. That said, it would take considerable courage, or considerable stupidity, for an adjudicator to refuse to allow the responding party to respond to the detail of the referral notice, or to ignore any such response document.

Appointment of Adjudicator

16.10 Some contracts will name the adjudicator. The appointment of that adjudicator to deal with the particular dispute that has subsequently arisen between the parties will then be a straightforward matter. Difficulties only arise if that adjudicator has died or is too ill to deal with the adjudication or, more commonly, if he is too busy to deal with the adjudication in the relevant period. In those circumstances it is very important that the named adjudicator is entirely frank with the parties at the outset. Difficulties have arisen in the reported cases where a named adjudicator has taken on the dispute, possibly because he did not consider that he had an alternative, and then failed to deal with the adjudication in the statutory period. If an adjudicator named in a contract knows that he is unlikely to be able to produce the decision within the relevant period, he should make that plain to the parties at the outset. The parties can then make an informed choice as to whether to utilise the named adjudicator and allow him an extended period to complete his decision or, if not, to activate the default mechanism within the contract for the appointment of an alternative adjudicator.

16.11 Many contracts do not contain provisions as to a named adjudicator. Instead, they will identify an adjudicator nominating body, such as the RICS, RIBA, AICA or TeCSA. In such cases, the referring party will write to the relevant nominating body and ask for an adjudicator to be appointed. That request must be accompanied by a copy of the notice of adjudication.

16.12 As noted above, the 1996 Act, the Scheme for Construction Contracts, and most of the standard forms of construction and engineering contract all identify a seven day period after the service of the notice of adjudication in which the appointment of the adjudicator must be accomplished. That means that the referring party must do all that it possibly can to ensure that any request for nomination, and the notice of adjudication, are provided to the nominating body at the same time as the service of the notice of adjudication on the responding party. All too often, the request to the nominating body is sent off in the post, and sometimes does not arrive for two or three days. This puts the nominating body under unfair pressure, often requiring it to nominate an adjudicator within a day or so of receiving the request. It is therefore recommended that the request to the nominating body and the copy of the notice of adjudication are provided either by hand or by fax to the nominating body at the same time that the notice of adjudication is served on the responding party.

16.13 The nominating body must nominate an adjudicator as soon as possible. It is important to avoid the situation that arose in at least one of the reported cases[1] where the nomination of the adjudicator happened late on day seven and the referral notice was served the following day, thereby allowing the responding party to take a point (which was ultimately unsuccessful) as to the failure to serve the referral notice within the required seven days. However, the seven day period will generally be enforced by the courts,[2] so it is important always to make sure that, if it is possible to do so, the period is observed. Bodies who nominate adjudicators regularly have a procedure and a fixed turn-around time (often five days) for dealing with the nomination process, and it is important that the referring party keeps tabs on the request for nomination so as to ensure that the nominating body acts promptly in identifying the proposed adjudicator.

16.14 A practical difficulty can sometimes arise in the situation where the responding party is anxious to ensure that a particular person is not nominated as the adjudicator. This can happen where there have been a series of adjudications under the same contract and the responding party feels, whether rightly or wrongly, that person X, who has conducted a number of the previous adjudications, has made decisions with which they have been unhappy. If the referring party writes to the nominating body asking them to nominate a particular adjudicator (or, in some cases, not to nominate a particular adjudicator), then it is suggested that such a letter must be copied to the responding party. Failure to do so might give rise to a subsequent debate about the validity of the appointment of a chosen adjudicator in circumstances where the responding party did not know that a particular person was being requested, and would have raised a bona fide objection if they had known.

16.15 If the responding party objects to the person being suggested by the referring party, or wishes to object in any event to the appointment of person X, he should write immediately to the nominating body to say so, and should again ensure that the relevant communication is faxed or emailed. The reasons for the objection should be set out in clear terms. It will then be for the nominating body to reach a conclusion as to the objection, and whether or not, notwithstanding the terms of the objection, person X should be appointed as the adjudicator. There are a number of cases in which, despite the objections of the responding party, person X was appointed as the adjudicator. There are no reported cases in which the responding party has sought to challenge such a decision in the courts, but it is

---

[1] See *Cubitt Building & Interiors Ltd v Fleetglade Ltd* [2006] EWHC 3413 (TCC).
[2] See *Hart Investments v Fidler and Another* [2006] EWHC 2857 (TCC); [2007] BLR 303.

thought that such a challenge might be arguable in appropriate circumstances. It is therefore recommended that the nominating body keeps a short note of the rationale behind its decision to appoint person X as the adjudicator, notwithstanding the responding party's objection to such a nomination.

A Challenge to the Nominated Adjudicator

16.16 Whatever points might have been taken in response to the notice of adjudication, it is very important that, if a responding party has a jurisdictional challenge, he should write to the adjudicator immediately on his appointment setting out the reasons why it is said that the adjudicator does not have the necessary jurisdiction. The jurisdictional challenge should be set out clearly, setting out the specific reasons why, in the events which have occurred, it is said that the adjudicator does not have the necessary jurisdiction. In making its jurisdictional points, the responding party should endeavour to ensure that any references to existing authorities are kept to a minimum. Each case is different and each case turns on its own facts. Furthermore, adjudicators are wary of jurisdictional challenges and can become sceptical as to the merits of any challenge where a half-page point is supported by a lever arch file of legal authorities of questionable relevance.

16.17 Once the responding party has identified his jurisdictional challenge, then it is necessary for the adjudicator to respond promptly. In some cases, the adjudicator will agree with the challenge and resign, although it is common in practice for the adjudicator to allow the referring party to comment on the challenge that has been made before resigning. This is also good practice: it can often be the case that what looks like a cast-iron jurisdictional argument melts away when the referring party has explained it more fully, and provided the adjudicator with copies of those documents not proffered by the responding party. In most of the reported authorities, the adjudicator has concluded that he has the necessary jurisdiction and has continued with the adjudication. In those circumstances, the responding party has three possible choices to make. First, it can refuse to take part in the adjudication altogether. Secondly, it can take part in the adjudication but make it clear that its participation is without prejudice to its objection on jurisdiction. Thirdly, it can agree to be bound by the adjudicator's decision on jurisdiction and/or waive the lack of jurisdiction, and expressly consent to be bound by the result of the adjudication.

16.18 The first option, namely a refusal to take part in the adjudication process altogether, is a high-risk strategy for a responding party to adopt. Indeed, it is not recommended unless it is accompanied by an application to the TCC for a declaration that the adjudicator does not have the necessary jurisdiction. It does not make much commercial sense for a party to refuse to take part in an adjudication process at all, in circumstances where the result might lead to a money award against that party for millions of pounds, no matter how strong the jurisdictional challenge might be thought to be. Much better in most cases will be the second option outlined above, whereby the responding party agrees to take part in the adjudication, but only on the strict understanding that such participation is without prejudice to its jurisdictional challenge. As noted above, this is a particularly effective tactic if, regardless of the jurisdiction position, the responding party believes that it has a good case on the merits of the underlying dispute. Finally, a party with a jurisdictional challenge can choose to waive that challenge or agree to be bound by the adjudicator's view that he has the necessary jurisdiction. This is appropriate in circumstances where the jurisdictional challenge, even though arguably correct, is entirely technical and gives rise to no real benefit to the responding party at all.

16.19 Should the adjudicator consider, of his own volition, and regardless of the points that may or may not have been made by the parties, whether or not he has the necessary jurisdiction? It is thought that he should. If the adjudicator does not have the necessary jurisdiction, then, prima facie, his decision is a nullity, regardless of the lack of an objection at the time. Of course, it is right that the lack of objection may give rise to an ad hoc jurisdiction (see Chapter 5 above), but it is much wiser for the adjudicator to address himself to the question of jurisdiction at the outset of the adjudication, irrespective of the points made by the parties. In *HG Construction Ltd v Ashwell Homes (East Anglia) Ltd*,[3] Ramsey J spoke expressly about the adjudicator considering of his own volition whether he was being asked to decide a matter on which there was already a binding decision by another adjudicator.

16.20 Once the adjudicator has decided that he does have the necessary jurisdiction, it is not recommended that the responding party continues to bombard the adjudicator with further and better ways of putting the jurisdictional challenge. It is surprising how often a responding party will ignore the adjudicator's ruling on jurisdiction and continue, throughout the statutory period, to write endless letters complaining that the adjudicator does not have the necessary jurisdiction. This is counter-productive for two reasons. First, it is most unlikely that an adjudicator, who has concluded that he has the necessary jurisdiction, will change his mind because the point is put in a different way part way through the adjudication process. Secondly, repeated reiterations of the jurisdiction point might lead the adjudicator to conclude that the responding party has no case on the merits at all, and is reduced to arguing purely technical points to try and stave off ultimate defeat. For both these reasons, it is strongly recommended that a responding party who has lost a jurisdiction challenge in front of the adjudicator makes it plain that he does not accept that decision but then goes on, without prejudice to

---

[3] [2007] EWHC 144 (TCC).

Referral Notice

16.21 As explained above, the referral notice is the document in which the referring party should set out in detail the reasons why it should be granted the relief that it seeks in the adjudication. In anything but the simplest of cases, the referral notice should be drafted in a similar way to a Points of Claim, setting out the parties, the contract, and the legal and factual basis of claim. Attached to the referral notice should be all the documents relied on in support of the claim. This will include not only copies of the relevant parts of the contract, but copies of the relevant meeting minutes and letters between the parties, site diaries and the like and, even in an appropriate case, signed witness statements.

16.22 The Users' Guide provides helpful tips as to the correct drafting of a referral notice. It makes plain that the referral notice should be consistent with the notice of adjudication, explain the nature of the dispute and how it arose, detail the facts that are relied on, and provide the documentary evidence to support those facts. It suggests that it is not appropriate to include with the referral notice evidence that the other side has not seen before. In certain circumstances that is wise advice: the inclusion within the referral notice of an expert's report which seeks to explain the 20 week extension of time that has been claimed, in a way that has never before been identified, gives rise to the real risk that the responding party will be able to argue that the referral notice relates to a dispute which has not yet arisen, and the adjudicator therefore has no jurisdiction. On the other hand, it is not always appropriate to exclude evidence that has not been seen before. Take, by way of example, a contractor's claim for work done pursuant to a variation which was instructed orally by the architect, and which the contractor recorded in writing and sent to the architect as a confirmation of a verbal instruction. The referral notice will include that written confirmation of a verbal instruction ('CVI'). However, there could be no possible objection, if it was thought appropriate, for the representative of the contractor to whom the oral instruction was given provided, in addition to the CVI, a short signed statement in which he confirmed the details of the instruction and therefore the correctness of the CVI itself.

---

[4] Section 2 of the Guidance for Adjudicators makes plain that an adjudicator should investigate any jurisdictional challenge and, if the adjudicator concludes that he does have the necessary jurisdiction, proceed with the adjudication, having first obtained confirmation from the referring party that it wishes the adjudication to continue. This is a sensible precaution: sometimes, in the light of a jurisdictional challenge, a referring party might prefer to abandon the first adjudication, get its tackle in order and re-launch a second adjudication at a later date.

16.23 It is important to ensure that the material that is provided with the referral notice has been carefully edited, with only the relevant documentation being attached to the referral notice itself. The problem in construction contracts is that there is often a large amount of minutes, memos and correspondence. It is unwise to include anything other than directly relevant material with the referral notice because of the time constraints and the pressure on the adjudicator to reach his decision promptly; on the other hand, sufficient of the relevant correspondence and minutes ought to be provided so as to ensure that a balanced picture is given to the adjudicator. If a large amount of documentation must be provided with the referral notice, it is a big mistake for the referring party to assume that the material speaks for itself. The adjudicator needs to be taken through that material in the body of the referral notice, so that any documents of particular importance are emphasised. It is never sensible to attach a huge clip of correspondence and expect the adjudicator to struggle through it himself, without a guide, in order to find the particularly relevant documents.

16.24 It is usually sensible for the referral notice, and the material attached to it, to be arranged in chronological order. In this way, the contract will be identified first, and subsequently the particular events and matters of fact which lie at the heart of the dispute which the adjudicator has to decide. Although it can sometimes be tempting to deal, in the referral notice and the supporting documents, with the individual elements of the story one by one, there is a grave risk that, if the overall chronology is departed from, the result will be muddle and confusion.

16.25 The referral notice represents the referring party's best, and often only, opportunity to put its claim in detail. It is commonly assumed that the referring party has a right of reply to the responding party's response. Although the adjudicator will endeavour to ensure that the referring party is given at least a limited right of reply, there may just be insufficient time to allow the preparation of a detailed reply. Moreover, given that the referring party has had a lengthy period in which to prepare a detailed referral notice, responding parties will often complain, with some justification, if they have to respond to the referral notice within a short period of time, only to find that the referring party is then given an additional opportunity to have another go at the material. Accordingly, it is sensible for the referring party to approach the preparation of the referral notice on the basis that it is their one and only opportunity to explain their claim in their own way and by reference to their own documents. Thus the claims in the referral notice should always be kept simple and straightforward, with the cross referencing to the attached documents clear and user-friendly. It can often be a good idea to present a summary of the claim at the outset so that, when working through the detail, the adjudicator can keep in mind the overall shape of the claim. As the Users' Guide rightly points out, the claiming party may have little opportunity to persuade the adjudicator to accept any arguments that have not clearly been set out in the referral notice.

17

THE ADJUDICATION ITSELF

Directions	17.01	Documentation	17.15
Response to Referral Notice	17.04	Timescale and Requested Extensions	17.19
Referring Party's Reply	17.06	Natural Justice	17.23
Meetings, Evidence and Hearings	17.08	Conflict of Interest	17.24
Meetings	17.08	Reciprocity	17.26
Evidence	17.09	Inquisitorial or Adversarial?	17.28
Hearings	17.11	Intimidatory Tactics	17.30
Visits	17.13		

Directions

17.01 Only once the referral notice has been served should the adjudicator make directions for the conduct of the adjudication. He should consider the detail of the referral notice and then consider how the dispute should be managed through to his decision. The most important thing for him to do is to liaise with the parties (either by way of a conference call or, if necessary, a meeting) and set a timetable for the adjudication. This in turn requires consideration of a number of separate matters.

17.02 First, the adjudicator should consider whether or not he can complete the adjudication within the statutory time limit. If he cannot, or he considers that there is a risk that he cannot, he should inform the parties immediately, so as to seek their agreement at an early stage to an extended period. This is dealt with in greater detail in paragraphs 17.19–17.22 below. Thereafter, assuming that he is able to complete the adjudication within the 28 days (or some other extended period) then he should order the responding party to serve a detailed response to the referral notice. This is dealt with in greater detail in paragraphs 17.04–17.05 below. He should then consider whether it would be appropriate to allow the referring party a short period to put in any material in reply; although, as noted in paragraph 16.25 above, the referring party will ordinarily assume that he has the right to put in such a reply, it can often be inappropriate to allow the referring party a second bite of the cherry, and to use up some of the limited time available on such a process. This is dealt with in paragraph 17.06 below.

17.03 Once the adjudicator has made directions for the provision of a detailed response to the referral notice, then he should consider whether or not to hold an oral hearing. Sometimes, particularly in an adjudication which involves complex points of law, it will be important for the adjudicator to give each party the opportunity of making oral submissions as to the relevant principles of law to be applied. Similarly, in a case where it is likely that there will be major disputes of fact which would be difficult to resolve by way of documents alone, he might consider requiring the parties to attend a hearing with the relevant witnesses. These points are also considered in detail below. He may be asked to make orders in respect of further documents although, if the referring party has attached the relevant documents to the referral notice, and the responding party intends to attach any further documents which it considers to be of relevance to his response to the referral notice, then it will not usually be necessary for such further orders relating to documents to be made.

Response to Referral Notice

17.04 Just as the referral notice is the referring party's principal opportunity to set out the detail of its case, so the response to that notice is the key document to be produced by the responding party. The points made above in respect of the referral notice are all equally applicable to the response: the document should be couched in clear and simple language; it should approach the points chronologically; and it should attach those additional documents which the responding party wishes the adjudicator to consider before reaching his decision. It is important that the responding party makes the document as user-friendly as possible. Unless it is impossible or impractical to do so, the responding party should set out its response on a paragraph-by-paragraph or section-by-section basis, so that the adjudicator can see, side by side, the claiming party's assertion and the responding party's response to that assertion.

17.05 Responding parties are often tempted to attach all the relevant documents, regardless of whether or not those documents have already been included with the referral notice. This is usually a mistake; since time is short, the adjudicator cannot be expected to wade through a second mass of documents, most of which he already has. The responding party should consider the documents attached to the referral notice. Where they are complete and clearly numbered, the responding party can refer to those documents in their own response, without needing to copy them again. Where the documents are incomplete, and the omissions are significant,

The Adjudication Itself

then the responding party should copy and attach just the documents that have been omitted. It will only be in the rare case, where so many important documents have been omitted from the referral notice, that a responding party is justified in attaching the whole run of documentation again.

Referring Party's Reply

17.06 As previously noted, referring parties often consider that they have the automatic right to reply to the response to the referral notice. This is incorrect. Indeed, in smaller cases, it is thought that the adjudicator should not automatically grant the referring party any such entitlement. Instead, the adjudicator should give the referring party the opportunity to persuade him that, in all the circumstances, a reply is appropriate. Of course, there will be cases where a reply is vital, because otherwise some entirely new point taken by the responding party will not have been answered. If there has been no previous discussion about a reply, but the adjudicator considers that, in the light of the response, such a document would be assistance, he should endeavour to limit the reply to particular topics or, better still, specific paragraphs in the response. He should also require that document to be served very shortly after the response. In a statutory adjudication with a total period of 28 days, the most important thing is to ensure that the responding party has had sufficient time to respond to the referral notice. In a complex case, that might occupy as much as half of the 28 day period. In those circumstances, the period for a reply should be kept to a few days, otherwise the adjudicator will run out of time. Moreover, this could hardly be said to be unfair, given the time that the referring party has had originally in which to prepare its referral notice.

17.07 Although the procedure identified above has its merits in smaller cases, it is right to note that, in practice, and certainly in larger disputes, it can be more efficient for the adjudicator simply to assume at the outset that a reply will be both useful and necessary. In such circumstances, the adjudicator will normally allow for the service of a reply in the timetable that is agreed/ordered at the commencement of the adjudication. This has the advantage of preventing delays whilst the issue of whether or not a reply should be provided is debated in the correspondence.

Meetings, Evidence and Hearings

Meetings

17.08 Depending on the nature and scope of the adjudication, it will often be the case that the adjudicator does not require any meeting at all with the parties. In some adjudications, he might schedule a meeting at the outset, to discuss and agree the timetable, and possibly a further meeting, after the response has been provided, in which he can ask questions of the parties and their experts, in order to clarify any technical matters or other outstanding issues. The adjudicator will control these meetings, and invite the parties to address him on the specific matters on which he requires assistance. It is usually wise for an adjudicator to provide, in advance of such a meeting, an agenda of the specific matters to be covered. Meetings of this type are primarily to be regarded as part of the adjudicator's investigation into the dispute.

Evidence

17.09 In many adjudications, the only material which the adjudicator will need in order to reach his decision will be the contract and the relevant correspondence, minutes and other contemporaneous documentation attached to the referral notice and/or the response. However, there will be some disputes which cannot be resolved without the production of written evidence. For example, there may be an important dispute about what was said or not said at a particular site meeting which was not minuted. In those circumstances, the referring party may want to provide, with the referral notice, a short signed statement from their representative setting out his recollection of what was said. The responding party may wish to do likewise.

17.10 It will be a rare case which will require extensive expert evidence but, in larger adjudications, it may be necessary for the parties to attach experts' reports to their principal pleadings. For example, a claim for an extension of time, or for financial compensation arising out of unforeseen ground conditions, may not be capable of satisfactory proof unless supported by an expert's report. If the referring party is providing such a report as part of his referral notice then he needs to ensure that at least the substance of that report, if not the report itself, has already been made available to the responding party. A failure to do so might give rise to the argument that the claim being pursued in the adjudication is new and that therefore a dispute has not yet crystallised between the parties.

Hearings

17.11 In a large adjudication, the adjudicator might be asked to decide, or might himself conclude, that such is the scale of the legal and factual differences between the parties, a more formal oral hearing is necessary. Most hearings of this type will be largely taken up with oral submissions by either side in which they elaborate upon the points made in the referral notice and the response. Such submissions will focus on, but not necessarily be confined to, the legal points that have arisen. It is common, however, for the adjudicator to endeavour to control the hearing by identifying those matters on which he wishes to hear the parties, those on which he does not, and limiting the time available to each party for the making of such submissions.

17.12 It is rare for an adjudicator to require oral evidence to be given in an adjudication. However, this is principally because of the time constraints, rather than the existence of any sort of rule that outlaws the reception of such oral evidence in adjudication. Indeed, there will be some disputes in respect of which the adjudicator may have no alternative but to hear oral evidence and make decisions on the basis of which evidence or oral explanation he accepts, if he is going to resolve the dispute properly. Take again the example of the dispute as to what was said at a particular site meeting. If the adjudicator is faced with two entirely conflicting statements as to the contents of the discussions on a particular occasion, he would probably have to arrange for a hearing at which this evidence can be tested orally. It is almost inevitable that he is going to have to conclude that one or other of the parties is mistaken as to what was said at the meeting and it is unlikely, in the absence of any other relevant contemporaneous documentation, that he could reach such a conclusion without hearing oral evidence. Likewise, if extensive experts' reports have been attached by both parties to the referral notice and/or the response, the adjudicator may feel it necessary to arrange a short hearing at which the principal points advocated by each expert can be tested by way of cross examination.

Visits

17.13 Many adjudications arise out of ongoing projects. Furthermore, it will often be the case that the subject matter of the dispute that is being referred to adjudication either arises out of (or can be demonstrated by reference to) the physical situation on site. Disputes as to defects, the physical constraints of a particular site or part of a site, the conditions encountered in the ground, and the proximity of other buildings or amenities, often lie at the heart of adjudication disputes. In all those circumstances, it is plainly desirable for the adjudicator to visit the site and to carry out a detailed inspection.

17.14 If an adjudicator decides on a site visit, then it is sensible for a number of things to happen in connection with the proposed visit. First, he must try and give as much notice of the visit as possible, in order that the necessary arrangements can be made. Secondly, it is always wise for each party to have one representative to attend on the adjudicator at the visit so that they can deal with any questions which the adjudicator might wish to ask. If the adjudicator wants a particular representative to be present, because he considers that he may wish to ask that representative detailed questions as he undertakes his inspection, then he should notify the parties and explain, at least in general terms, what questions he wishes to ask. Thirdly, the adjudicator needs to ensure that the visit goes ahead with a reasonable amount of formality. It is a very dangerous course for the adjudicator to use the opportunity of a site visit to try and speak to the parties on some sort of 'off the record' basis or to endeavour to move the adjudication into some sort of mediation process. The adjudicator should never hold conversations with the representative of one party in the absence of the representative of the other.

Documentation

17.15 The adjudicator must decide what the relevant information is in any given case. He also needs to avoid the situation, which is sadly all too common, in which documents are drip-fed into the process, with new documents being provided by either side shortly before, or even at the expiry of, the 28 day period. Such an uncontrolled 'tit-for-tat' exchange of documentation during the 28 day period might be seen as an indication that the adjudicator is not in control of the adjudication.

17.16 As noted above, the referral notice should contain all the relevant documentation on which the referring party relies in support of its case. If there is some reason to doubt this, the adjudicator is advised to obtain a written assurance from the referring party that that is indeed the case. In order to limit further documentation, the adjudicator should require the responding party to attach all further documentation said to be relevant to the response to the referral notice, with the aim of ensuring that all relevant documents have been exchanged following the submission by the responding party of its response to the referral notice.

17.17 Thereafter, the adjudicator can order that no further documents be exchanged by the parties unless the party who wishes to rely on any such additional documentation has made plain what that documentation is, and how and why it was not previously provided in the adjudication, and the adjudicator has considered such representations and decided to allow in the additional material, giving the other side a proper opportunity to comment upon it.

17.18 The Guidance for Adjudicators suggests that one way of reducing difficulties with documentation is for the adjudicator to limit at the outset the amount of material to be submitted by each party. In simple and more straightforward adjudications this is a good idea. However, in more complicated adjudications, it is not recommended. Any limitation imposed by the adjudicator at the outset will be entirely artificial and arbitrary, and there is a real risk that, in endeavouring to comply with such arbitrary rules, one or both of the parties will not be able to explain their position properly. In extreme cases, it is suggested that this would amount to a breach of natural justice.

Timescale and Requested Extensions

17.19 Once the adjudicator has been nominated, and received the referral notice, he should inform the parties as to whether or not he can complete the adjudication within the statutory period. If he cannot, he should say so immediately and either seek an extension or resign. Assuming that the adjudicator can complete the adjudication within the period then the only other time when he might need to review that conclusion is on receipt of the response to the referral notice. That is the moment when the nature and scale of the dispute in the adjudication should finally have become apparent. It may be that at that point the adjudicator will conclude that he needs further time.

17.20 If, on receipt of the response to the referral notice, the adjudicator considers that he requires an extension of the statutory period, he should immediately say so to the parties, identifying the nature of the extension required and the reasons why it is necessary. It is thought that, if the request for an extension is made at that point, and the extension is not long, the parties ought normally to agree to it. Thereafter, there should be no reason why the adjudicator should not produce his decision within the extended period which he has sought. If an extension has been granted, it is extremely important that the adjudicator meets his side of the bargain. Parties to adjudications are left frustrated and angry when, on day 27, and without any warning, the adjudicator then writes to seek another 14 or 21 days in which to complete his decision.

17.21 It is important that adjudicators are aware that the parties will not automatically consent to the extensions that they seek, particularly if the extensions are sought late and without warning. Neither should an adjudicator endeavour to bully the parties into agreeing the extension, something which has happened in one or two of the reported cases. The best advice for an adjudicator is to ensure that, following receipt of the response to the referral notice, he has blocked out sufficient time to ensure that the decision can be set out within the statutory (or extended) period.

17.22 Of course, there will inevitably be situations when the adjudicator, through no fault of his own, finds himself obliged to ask for more time at a late stage in the process. This will usually occur when one party provides important documentation late on, and the other side reasonably seeks further time to consider, and respond to, that material, leaving the adjudicator with no option but to seek a consequential extension of his own time to complete the decision. In those circumstances, the adjudicator should immediately ask for the shortest extension possible, making it clear that the request is to be treated as part of the application by the recipient of the late documentation for further time. The TCC has made it clear that, in those circumstances, the parties should reply promptly to the adjudicator's request, and in clear terms. A failure by one or both parties to respond at all will, in ordinary circumstances, be treated as an assent to the extension sought.[1]

Natural Justice

17.23 Adjudicators are acutely aware that they must act in accordance with the rules of natural justice. However, because these rules are only ever identified in general terms, some adjudicators are not always familiar with the concepts involved. Set out below is a brief guide to some of the problems that have been known regularly to occur in adjudication.

Conflict of Interest

17.24 The UK construction industry is a relatively small world, and there is always a real possibility that the adjudicator will know those involved in the relevant events on behalf of one of the parties to the adjudication. If the adjudicator has any substantive link or connection with one of the parties, he must draw that connection to the attention of both parties at the outset, making it clear that if either party objected as a result, he would resign. Such offers might rarely be taken up, but the old adage that justice must be seen to be done is of particular importance to the adjudication process, where everything is done so quickly. Providing a clear indication of any connection is the best way of neutering the point at the outset. The risk is always that, if the adjudicator's connection to one of the parties, however trivial, is not identified until after the adjudication has concluded, the loser will endeavour to use it to avoid honouring the decision. For that reason, it is often best for the adjudicator to make plain any connection at all, on the basis that, if it is remote and inconsequential, he can also indicate that he does not consider that it warrants even the offer of resignation.

17.25 Sometimes, the connection will be so obscure as to be unknown to the adjudicator at the time of the appointment, and will emerge at some point part way through the adjudication. If that happens, the advice is again the same: the adjudicator must bring the connection to the attention of the parties and seek their views. If, in either situation, the party with whom there is no connection wishes the adjudicator to resign, even just out of caution, then the adjudicator should consider such a course very carefully.

---

[1] See *AC Yule & Son v Speedwell Roofing & Cladding Limited* [2007] EWHC 1360 (TCC).

Reciprocity

17.26 The adjudicator must continually ask himself whether or not he is acting fairly. One of the ways in which he can test that is by ensuring that each party has had the opportunity of commenting on any documents submitted by the other. Of course, there comes a time, towards the end of the process, when the adjudicator has to stop receiving documents from the parties in order to prepare his decision. It is for that reason that a clear timetable should be set out by the adjudicator at the outset of the adjudication, with a clear 'last date' by which any new material can be provided, with the express warning that any material sent thereafter will not be considered unless that parties also consent to an extension of the 28 day period.

17.27 Reciprocity is also important in relation to all of the adjudicator's communications with the parties. The adjudicator should never communicate with one party in the absence of another, either at meetings or over the telephone. Copies of letters sent to one party should always be sent to the other as well. If, in exceptional circumstances, contact with one party alone is necessary or unavoidable, the adjudicator should keep a detailed record of what was said and then send that record to both parties as soon as practicable. Adjudicators should not field unsolicited telephone calls from one party unless it is of vital importance that he does so. Telephone conferencing is by far the best way for the adjudicator to deal with telephone communications.

Inquisitorial or Adversarial?

17.28 The 1996 Act makes clear that the adjudicator's role is inquisitorial and investigatory. It is therefore up to the adjudicator to investigate the facts that he considers to be relevant and to arrive at his own conclusion as to the answer to the dispute that has arisen. To that extent, the process is different to litigation or arbitration which, at its simplest, is an adversarial process, at the end of which the judge or arbitrator has to choose between the two alternative cases advanced before him.

17.29 However, as a matter of practice, adjudications are not perhaps as different to litigation as might at first be thought. For a start, there are the clear time limits within which the adjudicator must operate. In such a limited timeframe, it is very difficult for the adjudicator to do more than enquire into and consider the information with which he has been provided by both sides. Inevitably, therefore, the adjudication process becomes much more akin to a Judge deciding between two competing cases than a start-from-scratch inquisitorial investigation. Secondly, an adjudicator must be very careful not to stray too far from the information being provided by both parties. There are a number of reported cases in which the adjudicator's decision has been based more on instinct and intuition than on the material with which has been provided in the adjudication. Such decisions may well offend against the rules of natural justice and, if so, they will not be enforced by the courts.

Intimidatory Tactics

17.30 It is interesting to note that section 3 of the Guidance for Adjudicators is entitled 'Intimidatory Tactics'. This warns the adjudicator that some parties in adjudications adopt intimidatory tactics to bully the adjudicator into adopting a particular course of action. The Guide indicates that such tactics may include spurious challenges on jurisdictional grounds; causing delay; deliberate confusion of the adjudicator through the use of technical or esoteric legal arguments; and threatening to take legal action against the adjudicator himself. It is regrettable that such tactics are considered to be so widespread that the Task Group felt it necessary to provide guidance in how to deal with them, but there can be no doubt that, in a small minority of adjudications, the representatives of one (and sometimes both) of the parties bombard the adjudicator with four or five argumentative letters a day, often running to scores of pages. Such tactics are to be depreciated and will be the subject of criticism by the courts.[2]

17.31 Adjudicators who are faced with these tactics must be firm. Whilst they should always receive and consider any submissions received from either party, they should point out in clear terms if they consider that one party is failing to address the underlying issues and is, instead, spending too long on peripheral or jurisdictional matters. If the adjudicator feels that one party is adopting an intimidatory tone, he should ask them to stop, making it clear that such an approach is unhelpful. However, the adjudicator must at all times endeavour to refrain from losing his temper, in part because tactics of this sort are often adopted by one party in the hope that the adjudicator will overreach himself, and do something which will then invalidate his decision. One way in which an adjudicator can test the correctness of any difficult decision that he is about to take is to ask himself: how will this look, and how will my letters read, to a judge who has not had any prior involvement in the dispute when, in two or three months' time, he is studying the papers in advance of the enforcement hearing?

---

[2] In *Michael John Construction v Golledge & others* [2006] TCLR 3, the TCC Judge criticised the lengthy and repetitive letters written to the adjudicator by the claims consultant acting for the responding party, pointing out that the consultant was so keen to make his quasi-legal points to the adjudicator on an almost daily basis, and in great detail, that he omitted to address the real disputes at all.

18

THE ADJUDICATOR'S DECISION

Reasons	18.01	Ancillary Matters	18.09
Completion and Communication	18.03	Fees and Costs	18.09
Errors	18.06	Effect of the Decision	18.12

Reasons

18.01 It is often forgotten that, under the Scheme for Construction Contracts, the adjudicator is not required to give reasons unless at least one of the parties requires them. Thus it is necessary for one or both of the parties to notify the adjudicator as soon as possible that they require him to give reasons for his decision. In a case of any complexity, it is almost always sensible to require the adjudicator to give reasons; otherwise, there will always be at least the risk that the adjudicator has not properly thought through the basis for his decision. Indeed, it is recommended that the adjudicator should make plain to the parties at the outset that, unless they tell him to the contrary, he is proposing to give reasons. This is because, at common law, a reasoned decision is almost always required from any decision-making tribunal; and because the preparation of written reasons will itself improve and focus the process by which the adjudicator comes to his decision.

18.02 Clearly, in a complex dispute, the production by the adjudicator of written reasons will be a lengthy, and therefore time-consuming, task. It is unfair to require the adjudicator to give reasons when notification of such a requirement has only been communicated to him a few days before the expiry of the statutory period. Accordingly, as a matter of practice, it is sensible for adjudicators to ask the parties at the outset of the adjudication whether they require reasons or, alternatively, to fix an early date by which any request to give reasons must be made. As a precaution, it is recommended that adjudicators should always operate on the basis that they will be required to give written reasons, so that they allow sufficient time for the preparation of a fully reasoned decision within the overall 28 day (or extended) period.

Completion and Communication

18.03 The decision must be completed within the 28 days, or any extended period that has been agreed by the parties. It has been suggested in the past that the courts have allowed a certain amount of leeway in connection with the time for completing the decision. This is incorrect; there is no persuasive authority for the proposition that an adjudicator can take any additional time over and above the 28 days (or the extended period) in which to complete his decision. This has been reiterated in a number of recent cases.[1] Accordingly, an adjudicator must ensure that the decision is completed within the relevant period and must provide all necessary directions in order to achieve this result.

18.04 The courts have been a little more relaxed about the time in which the completed decision is then communicated to the parties. If the decision is completed within the 28 days (or the extended period) then, provided that that decision is communicated to the parties as soon as possible thereafter, it will not necessarily be fatal if the decision is not received by the parties until after the expiry of the 28 days, or the agreed extended period. However, it is very important that this is not abused. As the Judge pointed out in *Cubitt Builders & Interiors Ltd v Fleetglade Ltd*,[2] in these days of electronic communication, there really should be very little delay in the communication of the decision itself, once it has been completed. In *Cubitt*, because the decision was completed in the middle of the night, he concluded that communication of the decision at just after noon the following day was acceptable, but observed that any delay in excess of that may well not have amounted to communication of the decision 'forthwith', as required by the terms of the contract in that case.

18.05 For these reasons, adjudicators are well-advised to operate on the basis that, once they have completed their decision, they will send it out electronically and therefore immediately. Accordingly, there ought to be no significant delay in the communication of the decision to the parties. Thus, it is appropriate for adjudicators to plan on sending out their decision to the parties absolutely no later than 4.30 pm on the 28th day following the commencement of the adjudication.

---

[1] See the discussion in Chapter 2 at paragraphs 2.96–2.105 above.
[2] [2006] EWHC 3413 (TCC).

Errors

The point has already been made (see paragraphs 8.18–8.30 above), that, once an adjudicator's decision has been completed and sent out then, prima facie, it becomes enforceable, even if the decision may contain an error or mistake. However, there will be times when the adjudicator will recognise an error almost as soon as the decision has been sent out, either because it has been pointed out to him by the parties or because, on re-reading the decision following its communication, the adjudicator has spotted the mistake for himself. What happens then? Some adjudication agreements give the adjudicator the power to make corrections. If the adjudication agreement contains no such provision, but the adjudicator is satisfied that there is an error, he should correct the error and notify the parties of the correction as soon as possible. **18.06**

It seems to be generally accepted that, depending on the nature of the error and the time in which that error is corrected, an adjudicator may have the power to correct mistakes even after his decision has been sent out to the parties. In *Bloor Construction (UK) Ltd v Bowmer & Kirkland (London) Ltd.*[3] the Judge concluded that the rectification of an error by the adjudicator within hours of the communication of the original decision, in circumstances where both parties and the adjudicator agreed that it was a genuine error, was in accordance with an implied term of the adjudication agreement that such slips could be corrected by the adjudicator in that way.[4] However, it is clear that such a proviso will only work in relatively rare circumstances. One party may consider that an error has been made, but the other may not, whilst the adjudicator may also not be persuaded that he has made any sort of error at all. The so-called slip rule is probably operable only in circumstances where the adjudicator accepts that an error has been made, and neither party could sensibly argue to the contrary. Furthermore, if the mistake is not corrected promptly, it would again be most unlikely that any sort of slip rule could apply. The careful adjudicator is best advised to check and re-check his draft decision before sending it out, so as to ensure that no slips of any kind are contained within it. **18.07**

In the Guidance for Adjudicators, it is suggested that it may sometimes be appropriate for the adjudicator to issue his decision in draft, inviting the parties to scrutinise it for accidental errors. It is thought that this is a potentially dangerous course, given that neither the Act nor the Scheme contains any provision for the **18.08**

---

[3] [2000] BLR 314.
[4] In *Edmond Nuttall Ltd v Sevenoaks District Council* unreported, 14.4.00, Dyson J concluded that the existence of such a slip rule was at least arguable. The point has never been considered by the Court of Appeal.

production of such draft decisions. Furthermore, from a practical perspective, it is difficult to see where, in a 28 day adjudication, a period of days could be found for the provision of a draft decision to the parties; the consideration by the parties of that draft decision; the communication by the parties to the adjudicator of any purported errors (as opposed to the inevitable re-arguing of the points on which, according to the draft decision, one or other party will have lost); the consideration by the adjudicator of the points made by each party on the draft decision; and the issuing of the final decision. For these reasons, therefore, the prudent adjudicator is advised to assume that he will not send out a draft decision to the parties (because he will simply not have the time to do so) and that his decision will have been carefully checked before it is communicated to the parties. If, of course, the adjudicator is concerned about his comprehension of any particular aspect of the dispute before completing his decision, he should seek clarification on that matter some days before the decision is completed.

Ancillary Matters

Fees and Costs

18.09 The adjudicator will require his fees to be paid by the parties, or possibly by the party that he considers has 'lost' the adjudication. Often these fees will appear high (particularly to the party who has to pay them) because, although the adjudicator's hourly rate may have been agreed in advance, there is no effective means by which the parties can limit the amount of time that the adjudicator spends on the dispute. It is thought sensible for an adjudicator to keep the parties informed of the fees that he is incurring as the adjudication progresses and, indeed, many adjudicators issue an invoice part way through the adjudication process with the expectation that at least some of their fees will have been paid by the time that the decision is completed.

18.10 If the adjudicator has notified the parties that he is going to appoint an expert, lawyer or assessor to provide assistance, then the costs of that advice will form part of the adjudicator's fee claim, and will therefore be recoverable in the same way. Again, it is often difficult for the parties to keep any sort of check on these fees until after they have been incurred. However, unless it can be shown that the adjudicator acted outside his jurisdiction in appointing such third parties, it would appear that such fees are also payable.

18.11 The usual position as to the legal costs incurred is that each party to the adjudication will have to pay their own costs. Again, particularly in a complex adjudication, these costs will be quite high. For example, a responding party faced with a final account claim, and given just two or three weeks to respond to the detail, will incur a large amount of costs in dealing with the points raised in such a short amount of time. Unless there is an agreement between the parties to the contrary, those costs will not be recoverable from the other side, no matter how great the success of the responding party in defeating those claims.

Effect of the Decision

18.12 The vast majority of adjudications are about money, and most adjudicators' decisions will identify a sum of money to be paid by one party to the other. In the vast majority of cases, the paying party is entitled to be paid the sum identified in the adjudicator's decision. If the sum is not paid, the payer is entitled to commence enforcement proceedings in the TCC, following the conclusion of which the successful party is likely to recover interest on the sum due at the judgment rate, whilst his costs may well be assessed on an indemnity basis.

18.13 For those reasons, save in exceptional circumstances, the losing party in an adjudication is best advised to pay the sum identified by the adjudicator before further sums by way of interest and costs are incurred by the successful party. The losing party may be extremely aggrieved with the decision and consider it wrong in fact or in law. In those circumstances, having taken advice, the losing party can issue its own proceedings in court in order to recover the sums paid in accordance with the decision. But it is only in those rare cases where an adjudicator has failed to comply with the rules of natural justice, or has reached a decision that was outside his jurisdiction, that a losing party has any prospect at all of being able, lawfully, to hang on to the money ordered to be paid by the adjudicator. In most cases, the losing party should do what the sponsors of the 1996 Act always hoped to achieve: pay now, argue later.

Part VI

THE FUTURE

19. The DTI Review and the Proposed Changes to the 1996 Act — 435

19

THE DTI REVIEW AND THE PROPOSED CHANGES TO THE 1996 ACT

Introduction	19.01	Clarification of the requirement that a Section 110(2) payment notice should be served	19.16
The Second Consultation Report	19.03		
The Adjudication Framework	19.03		
Removing the requirement that the Construction Act should only apply to contracts in writing	19.03	Clarity of the content of payment and withholding notices	19.18
		Clarity of the sum due	19.22
Prohibiting agreements that interim or stage payment decisions will be conclusive	19.07	Prohibiting the use of pay-when-certified clauses	19.25
		Improving the Right to Suspend Performance	19.28
Introduction of a statutory framework for the costs of adjudication	19.10	Other Issues	19.31
The Payment Framework	19.14	**Summary**	19.36
Prevention of unnecessary duplication of payment notices	19.14		

'The proposals are not radical. They are intended to be proportionate amendments to the existing framework. We have only considered further legislative intervention where we believe it is absolutely necessary to achieve the aims of the original legislation—guidance must remain our preferred option to improve the operation of construction contracts.

'Sir Michael Latham (both in the foreword to 'Constructing the Team' and in his 2004 Report to Nigel Griffiths) quoted the Dodo in *Alice's Adventures in Wonderland*—"Everybody has won and all must have prizes". That remains the right background against which to consider the proposals in this document. Taken as a whole, any package of amendments we take forward must benefit all in the industry and its clients.'

The Right Honourable Margaret Hodge MP, MBE
Minister of State for Industry and the Regions,
from the foreword to the DTI Second Consultation Report
on proposals to amend Part II of the HGCRA 1996

Introduction

19.01 In his 2004 Budget Report, the Chancellor of the Exchequer (as he then was) said that

> Following concerns raised by the construction industry about unreasonable delays in payment, the Government will review the adjudication and payment provisions of the Housing Grants Construction and Regeneration Act in order to identify what improvement can be made.

In April 2004 the then Construction Minister appointed Sir Michael Latham to undertake the first stage of the Review. His report was provided in September 2004, and it concluded that the 1996 Act was generally working well. The report identified some areas where further progress was desirable. The subsequent DTI and Welsh Assembly Government's March 2005 Consultation Exercise, entitled 'Improving Payment Practices in the Construction Industry', explored some of these areas in more detail. In January 2006 the DTI issued a consultation analysis which set out the proposed way forward and, thereafter, detailed proposals were developed.

19.02 The intention had been to introduce these proposals under a Legislative Reform Order under the Legislative and Regulatory Reform Act 2006. However, at some point, the DTI concluded that it would be more appropriate to introduce their detailed amendments using primary legislation. As a result, in June 2007, the DTI published their Second Consultation Report on proposals to amend the 1996 Act and the 1998 Scheme. The report identified a number of proposals under four general heading; the adjudication framework; the payment framework; improving the right to suspend performance; and other issues being considered as part of the consultation. The DTI proposals are summarised under each of these headings below.

The Second Consultation Report

The Adjudication Framework

Removing the requirement that the Construction Act should only apply to contracts in writing

19.03 The Second Consultation Report states that, because the 1996 Act and the courts have said that all the contract terms have to be in writing, this requirement has created a particular ground on which the adjudicator's jurisdiction can be challenged.[1] In order to avoid such challenges, the DTI are proposing to remove the restriction of the application of the Construction Act to contracts in writing.

---

[1] See paragraphs 2.44–2.74 and 7.28–7.32 above.

The effect would be that the Act would apply to construction contracts which are agreed wholly in writing, only partly in writing, entirely orally or varied by oral agreement.[2] Although the Report says that certain important contractual provisions required by the Act, such as provisions relating to a contractual adjudication scheme, will continue to need to be in writing, they go on to say that where that is not the case, the relevant provisions of the Scheme will apply.

19.04 The justification for this approach is the suggestion in the Report that 'the practical difficulty of agreeing a full written contract has acted as a barrier to the referral of disputes'. It makes plain that the proposal 'is not intended to encourage more oral or partly oral contracts, nor is it likely to do so'. Curiously, the Second Consultation Report is silent as to why the justification provided by the Court of Appeal in *RJT* for requiring contracts to be in writing in the first place (namely that, in view of the short time period required by statutory adjudication, certainty as to contract terms was a prerequisite if the adjudicator was to complete the task in the allotted time),[3] is or might be wrong. Likewise, the point made by HHJ Bowsher QC in *Grovedeck v Capital Demolitions Ltd*,[4] namely that disputes as to oral agreements are not readily susceptible of resolution by a summary procedure, and that Parliament properly recognised this when stipulating that adjudication was only relevant to contracts in writing, is nowhere addressed, let alone answered, in the Report. The difficulty that many envisage with the DTI proposals is that, if adjudication applies, either expressly or impliedly, to all contracts, whether written or oral, the adjudicator will be faced with the thankless task of trying to sort out what the contract terms were that were agreed, before he even begins to turn his mind to the particular dispute which has arisen between the parties.

19.05 In addition, there is nothing in the Second Consultation Report which explains how an adjudicator can sensibly decide between two opposing cases about contractual terms allegedly agreed orally. If one party says that a term providing for X was agreed at a meeting, and the other party flatly denies it then, in the absence of any relevant documents, the question may well turn on the credibility of those giving the relevant evidence. This would mean that an adjudicator would have to have a hearing, listen to oral evidence (presumably given on oath), and then make up his mind as to which of the two relevant parties was more likely to be telling the truth. Such a degree of formality is not envisaged by the 1996 Act and many (although by no means all) adjudicators would be troubled at having to embark on such an exercise.

---

[2] This would make it similar to the position in New South Wales: see paragraphs 6.06–6.08 above.
[3] See the discussion of *RJT* at paragraph 2.49 and *Grovedeck* at paragraphs 2.70–2.74 above.
[4] [2000] BLR 181.

19.06 In addition, there may be a problem with the restriction on the reference to adjudication of a single issue at any one time, when the claim that is advanced depends upon an oral contract in terms which are very different to those alleged by the responding party. In certain circumstances there might even have to be two adjudications: one to address the contract terms, and one to deal with the disputed claim itself. 'Jurisdictional wrangling' is unlikely to be diminished in such circumstances. Thus, whilst there is no doubt that the change might prevent a handful of jurisdictional challenges every year, it may create other difficulties which are not identified or addressed in the Second Consultation Report. It would also introduce fresh uncertainties into a topic on which, at present, it might be said that the law is tolerably certain.

Prohibiting agreements that interim or stage payment decisions will be conclusive

19.07 The Second Consultation Report points out that some construction contracts provide that a payment decision made under the contract will be conclusive of the amount of the interim or stage payment, and that this thereby prevents the referral of disputes relating to such payments to adjudication. In such circumstances, the decision (of the employer's agent, architect or engineer) has already concluded the matter. The DTI proposal is that an agreement, to the effect that a decision in respect of an instalment, stage or other periodic payment will be conclusive as to the amount of that interim payment, will be excluded from all contracts, in the same way that pay-when-paid clauses have been outlawed.

19.08 The Second Consultation Report suggests that 15 percent of construction contracts provide for conclusive decisions in respect of interim payments and that this should be viewed as a means of avoiding the referral of interim payment disputes to adjudication. The Report says that this practice is contrary to the intention of the 1996 Act and, particularly given the high proportion of adjudications that relate to disputes about interim payments, this method of avoiding the 1996 Act should be addressed. However, there are those who have expressed surprise that such conclusivity arrangements are quite the problem that the DTI have indicated. Others are unhappy at the prospect that such contractual provisions, which are designed to restrict time-consuming and expensive arguments during the currency of construction contracts (so as to ensure that the parties get on with the work in hand), will be rendered ineffective, with the inevitable increase in interim disputes.

19.09 In addition, it is interesting to note that the proposal to make ineffective clauses which make a particular valuation decision conclusive will not extend to final payments. Yet it is very often provisions which make a final certificate conclusive which give rise to all sorts of difficulties and practical problems for contractors and employers alike. In particular, tight time limits on challenging a final certificate can impose undue pressure on a contractor, particularly in circumstances where, if his challenge is made by way of a notice of adjudication, he runs the risk that the eventual decision may, through no fault of his own, be a nullity, which could leave him without any sort of remedy at all.[5]

Introduction of a statutory framework for the costs of adjudication

19.10 The Second Consultation Report recognises that one of the disincentives to a party to a contract in referring disputes to adjudication is the financial cost of doing so. However, instead of going on, as many expected, to allow the adjudicator to decide which party should bear some or all of the costs of the adjudication, the Report proposes to render ineffective those construction contracts whereby, for example, the parties agree that one particular party, or the party whom the adjudicator decides has lost the adjudication, will pay the costs of the adjudication. It is said that such agreements create a disincentive to the party liable for costs to refer disputes to adjudication and, conversely, encourages the other party to escalate costs.

19.11 The DTI Report proposes amendments to the 1996 Act so that parties may not agree before a dispute has arisen and the adjudicator has been appointed that one party will be liable for all or part of the costs of the adjudication. It proposes that agreements that a party should pay the whole or part of the costs of the adjudication, or agreements that the adjudicator should decide that one party should pay the whole or part of the costs of the adjudication, will only be valid if made in writing, and after the appointment of the adjudicator. The proposal is that the adjudicator's power to award costs will be limited to the award of 'only a reasonable amount in respect of costs reasonably incurred by the parties' and 'such reasonable amount as the adjudicator shall determine by way of fees for work reasonably undertaken and expenses reasonably incurred'. In addition, there are proposals to strengthen the adjudicator's ability to recover his reasonable fees and expenses including making the parties jointly and severally liable for those fees. The suggestion is that this would make it unnecessary for an adjudicator to ask the parties to sign an 'adjudication agreement' upon his appointment to secure fees and expenses.

19.12 It seems slightly curious that the Second Consultation Report proposes addressing the question of adjudication costs in the way set out above. There can be no doubt that particular contracts, such as the one in *Bridgeway Construction Ltd v Tolent Construction Ltd*[6] pursuant to which the referring party was obliged to pay the costs of an adjudication whatever the result, are an anomaly, but they are very rare. The present proposals will render ineffective an agreement, reached at the time that the original construction contract was made, that the adjudicator in any future adjudication will have the power to decide the parties' liabilities for costs. Such agreements, although still not very common, are growing increasingly popular,

---

[5] See the discussion at paragraph 2.105 above.
[6] [2000] CILL 1662–1664.

and have been described by the Court of Appeal as commercially unsurprising.[7] More widely, the current inability on the part of the adjudicator, in the absence of such an agreement, to award costs against the unsuccessful party is a major problem in larger adjudications. Many believe that the proposals, that an agreement giving the adjudicator the power to decide who will be liable for the costs of an adjudication will only be valid if made in writing and following the appointment of the adjudicator, will be largely ignored, because the parties will be unlikely to reach such agreements. Since, once the adjudicator has been appointed, the parties might have a pretty good idea of the likely result in the adjudication, the party at the greatest risk of losing is not going to want to enter into an agreement in writing that renders him liable for the costs of the adjudication. The proposals may well mean in practice that agreements covering the costs of adjudication will become very rare. There are many commentators who feel that, unless and until the adjudicator has an unfettered power to award costs against one party either in whole or in part, there will remain, particularly in the larger adjudications, an inherent injustice at the heart of the adjudication process.

19.13 The provisions in respect of the adjudicator's fees are generally to be welcomed because, as pointed out above[8] there is a real problem in adjudicators receiving prompt payment for their fees. That said, it is a little unclear as to how these proposals can really address that problem. Moreover, it is doubted whether adjudicators will waive their standard requirement that their own adjudication agreements are signed by the parties. Even if the Act is amended so that the parties become jointly and severally liable to pay the adjudicator's fees, most adjudicators will still require an express agreement covering hourly rates and the like.

The Payment Framework

Prevention of unnecessary duplication of payment notices

19.14 The Second Consultation Report observed that, although s110(2) requires the payer to issue a payment notice setting out the payments made or proposed to be made not later than five days after the date on which a payment becomes due, under most contracts that provide for interim certificates (or some other formal statement issued by the employer's agent as to the interim sum to be paid) the information in the payment notice only duplicates the information already contained in the certificate. Thus, for those contracts, this requirement represents a needless duplication. The Report goes on to note that the payer is usually happy to pay the sum due as certified, and the information in the notice only duplicates that in the certificate. It claims that there is a significant financial cost associated with the administrative inconvenience of complying with both requirements.

---

[7] May LJ in *John Roberts Architects Ltd v Parkcare Homes (No 2) Ltd* [2007] EWCA Civ 64.
[8] See paragraphs 11.12–11.24 above.

19.15 It is certainly right that there is duplication under this sort of contract.[9] It is unclear what precisely is proposed to remove that duplication or whether this is, in practice, a significant problem. This is important because, under construction contracts which operate on the basis simply of interim claims by the contractor and responses by the employer, the s110(2) notice fulfils a vital function in making plain 'the sum due'. It will be very important to make sure that, in relation to such contracts, this requirement is not affected in any way. In addition, many paying parties (whatever the type of contract) use the s110(2) notice to give an early indication of a sum which they propose to deduct for reasons not set out in the certificate. It is thought that, again, this ability should not be altered.

Clarification of the requirement that a Section 110(2) payment notice should be served

19.16 The Second Consultation Report suggests that the drafting of s110(2) is not ideal and that, specifically, it is not clear that the obligation to issue a payment notice continues even when there is, in fact, no obligation to make payment. The proposal is to make clear that a payment notice is always required if a payment would have become due under the contract. That will be the case even where there is no obligation to make any payment because the work has not been carried out or there has been set-off under the contract, or one or more other contracts, or abatement under the contract.

19.17 The Second Consultation Report suggests that the current drafting of s110(2) may lead the payer to mistakenly conclude that he need not issue a payment notice because of certain deductions that he proposes to make from the sum that would otherwise have been due. However, since payment notices are an important tool in ensuring early communication of payments made or proposed to be made, such notices should be given even when no payment is proposed. Whilst such concern is understandable, because the drafting of s110(2) is not entirely clear, it is again surprising that this point has been suggested as a matter that requires amendment. This is particularly so given the absence of a large number of authorities in which this specific aspect of the drafting of s110(2) has given rise to difficulty. It is often a good test of the efficacy and clarity of a piece of legislation to identify the number of cases that each section or sub-section have given rise to. It is thought that there are very few cases which turned on the issue of a payer mistakenly reaching the wrong conclusion as to the effect of s110(2).

---

[9] It may well be that this point was included in the Report as a result of Lord Hoffmann's comments in *Melville Dundas*: see paragraph 2.134 above.

Clarity of the content of payment and withholding notices

19.18 The Second Consultation Report suggests that there is confusion in the industry about the payment provisions in s110(2) and the withholding notice provisions in s111 relate to each other. It suggests that this lack of clarity can lead to the needless issue of two separate notices when a single payment notice would have sufficed. The Report suggests amendments which would create a clear connection between the information in the s110(2) notice and that required to withhold payment in accordance with s111. The proposal is that the payer must set out in the payment notice the amount (if any) that he has paid or proposes to pay. Under a contract with a certification regime, it is thought that that would be the certificate. Where the sum to be paid is different from the amount that has been certified, the payer must set out the grounds for paying less than the amount certified. It is thought that that is already covered by the s111(1) notice.

19.19 Therefore, it may be that, although the Report does not expressly say so, these proposals are again aimed principally at contracts without a certification regime. In such circumstances, the proposal is that the payment notice should identify the amount that would have been paid if:

- the payee carried out his obligations under the contract;
- no set-off was permitted by reference to any sum claimed under the contract or other contract; and
- no abatement was permitted in respect of the work.

Then, if the payer proposed to pay less than the amount calculated in accordance with this formula, the payer will have to explain how and why the deductions arise.

19.20 In all cases, the proposal is that the withholding notice should be in the same format as a notice under s110(2) so that the withholding notice becomes a revision of the payment notice. The proposal is also to make clear that the withholding requirement is in respect of any amount (ie including abatement) and not just withholding 'of a sum due' as at present which, says the Report, is thought by many only to relate to set-offs.

19.21 Improving the correlation between the payment notice and the withholding notice is a good idea in principle, because there is no doubt that many find the mechanism in the 1996 Act unduly cumbersome. However, it must be doubtful whether, now that the 1996 Act is up and running so successfully, it is altogether wise to make amendments to the detailed provisions of sections 110 and 111 in the manner suggested. After all, the number of enforcement applications in the TCC and elsewhere has fallen considerably, in part because the parties to construction contracts have got used to these detailed provisions and the way in which they are intended to operate. Many doubt whether changing these provisions will

Clarity of the sum due

19.22 The Second Consultation Report identifies the problem in identifying 'the sum due' in contracts where there are no certificates. The proposal is that, where the payer has issued a payment notice as described above, this amount becomes the sum due which can then be subject to withholding. Non-payment of the remainder (if any) would provide the payee with the right to suspend performance.

19.23 In circumstances where there is no payment notice, it is proposed that the sum due is determined by a new fall-back provision. In such circumstances the sum due would be the amount in a claim by the payee issued before the final date for payment. There are also changes proposed to the timetable for final payment of the sums due.

19.24 There is no doubt that the ascertainment of 'the sum due' in contracts where there is no provision for certificates has been a difficulty[10] and that this proposal, following on from the earlier points noted above, may provide more clarity. However, in the round, what is proposed is not very different to the way in which s110(2) has been interpreted by the courts.

Prohibiting the use of pay-when-certified clauses

19.25 In the first round of consultation undertaken for the purposes of the Review, it was apparently suggested that pay-when-certified clauses were a way for the main contractor to shift the burden of non-payment to the sub-contractor. The Second Consultation Report identifies the unfairness of such a provision, particularly in circumstances where a sub-contractor has no way of knowing whether a main contract certificate has been issued, or what its contents might be, or whether the payer had grounds under the pay-when-certified clause to withhold payment.

19.26 The proposal is that a certificate covering work under one contract cannot act as a mechanism to determine the timing of payment for work done under another contract. In effect, the proposal is to prohibit pay-when-certified clauses. The Report indicates that, although this may mean that the main contractor has to pay the sub-contractor before he himself is paid under the main contract, such an arrangement is in keeping with the purpose of the 1996 Act. It would mean that funds would be distributed promptly through the construction supply chain.

19.27 Given that pay-when-paid clauses were outlawed by the 1996 Act, it was always rather surprising that pay-when-certified clauses remained valid: in many ways,

---

[10] See paragraphs 10.13–10.19 above.

The Future

they give rise to the same inherent unfairness. It is thought that it is both logical and consistent to prohibit pay-when-certified clauses as well.

Improving the Right to Suspend Performance

19.28 The point has already been made that, whilst the 1996 Act gives the payee the statutory right to suspend performance in cases of non-payment, there have been few reported cases where this option has been exercised.[11] The Second Consultation Report identifies a number of disincentives to the claimant in exercising this right. These include the costs of spending and remobilising performance under a construction contract; the inconvenience and cost of remobilising immediately upon payment of the outstanding debt; and the inconvenience and cost of having to suspend all obligations under the contract.

19.29 The proposal is that the existing right to suspend performance will be made a more effective remedy by reducing the burden of the party who exercises that right. The detailed proposals involve making clear that a party need not suspend all of his obligations to the party in default when exercising the statutory right. They also provide a clear statutory right for the suspended party to be compensated for reasonable losses caused by the suspension and provide an extension of time for any delay caused by the exercise of the right to suspend.

19.30 There can be no doubt that contractors have not been attracted to the idea of routinely suspending work in cases of non-payment. Equally, it seems clear that, if the proposed amendments to the 1996 Act are made, then suspending work may become more attractive to the party awaiting payment. However, this is something of a double-edged sword, because the suspension of work on a construction site, particularly on a complex and high-value contract, inevitably raises the stakes, and can cause an irredeemable breakdown of relations between the contractor and the employer or the main contractor and his sub-contractors. It is therefore slightly surprising that the Second Consultation Report is prepared to embrace an increase in such suspensions. Although the Report indicates that the proposed amendments 'should ensure that payment is made on time more often in future' there is a clear risk that, if suspending work is made easier, more contractors will adopt that option, with potentially disastrous consequences.

Other Issues

19.31 There are two further issues which have been considered as part of the Second Consultation and which are worthy of comment. First, there is the correction of errors. The Scottish Executive's report of its consultation on 'Improving

---

[11] See paragraphs 2.154–2.157 above.

Adjudication in the Construction Industry' suggested that the Act should contain a slip rule allowing adjudicators power to correct their decisions so as to remove any clerical, arithmetical mistake or other error that had arisen from an accidental slip or omission. The proposal is that corrections be made not later than seven days after the issue of the decision. The Report seeks views on this, noting that, in England and Wales, it has not been necessary to introduce a slip rule because of the implication of such a rule by the courts.[12] The Report recognises that, if amendments were made, it would remove the courts' current discretion as to the time limits and applicability of a slip rule.

19.32 It is thought that some sort of slip rule ought to be included in the amendments to the 1996 Act. For the reasons noted above, whilst the slip rule has operated in practice, it has yet to be endorsed by the Court of Appeal and its omission from the Act can still create practical difficulty. In addition, it might be better for the parties to have specific time limits than rely on the court's discretion, which is not a very certain mechanism. As to the detail, seven days seems a little long: that is, after all, one-quarter of the statutory period for the whole adjudication. In addition, it will be important to ensure that the slip rule is not used to extend the adjudication process without consent.

19.33 The other matter raised concerns the decision in *Melville Dundas v George Wimpey*.[13] That case is dealt with in detail at paragraphs 2.142–2.147 above. The Outer House of the Court of Session in Scotland refused to enforce the payment because, although the final date for payment to Melville Dundas was 16 May, and the termination of the contract did not happen until 30 May, the contractual provisions as to termination meant that Wimpey were not obliged to pay any payment due which accrued less than 28 days before the earliest date that Wimpey could have first given notice to terminate (22 May). Although the Inner House of the Court of Session overruled that decision, the House of Lords restored Lord Clarke's original judgment by a majority of three to two. They concluded that the determination clause allowed the payment to be withheld in cases of administration and that a final payment would be determined taking into consideration all of the parties' respective entitlements. The effect was that the interim payment that had been due was no longer due and instead a final payment would become due following the determination of those respective entitlements.

19.34 The Second Consultation Report indicated that the House of Lords decision raised two areas of uncertainty: whether s111 applied in all cases where the contract was determined, or only where it was determined in cases of insolvency; and whether s111 applied to other grounds for withholding in respect of final payments.

---

[12] See *Bloor v Bowmer & Kirkland* and paragraphs 8.24–8.30 above.
[13] [2007] UKHL 18.

The Future

As to the first point, the Report considered that the courts will not enforce the decision of the adjudicator in cases where the payee is insolvent and that the application of s111 was comparable. As to the second circumstance, the Report said that s111 should apply to all other grounds for withholding in respect of all payments (including final payments) while a construction contract was in operation. The Consultation Response Form required responses as to whether the Act should provide an exception to s111 in cases where the payee was insolvent and whether the Act should be amended to make clear that s111 applied to all other grounds for withholding in respect of all payments.

19.35 The decision in *Melville Dundas* has given rise to a concern that an unscrupulous employer might seek to justify his non-payment of sums due by determining the contract at a later stage. It is therefore unsurprising that the matter has been raised in the Second Consultation Report by the DTI. Clarification may well be appropriate. However, it should be remembered that the decision was limited to one clause in one standard form of contract, and its effect is in any event ameliorated by a proviso in that clause (which was not relevant on the facts in *Melville Dundas*) which allows the contractor in certain circumstances to recover the sums due, notwithstanding the subsequent determination: see *Pierce International Design v Johnston*.[14]

Summary

19.36 In many ways, the limited matters identified in the Second Consultation Report as constituting proposed amendments to the 1996 Act reveal eloquently just how successful the legislation has been. After a tidal wave of disputed enforcement applications, the 1996 Act has settled down in the last year or so, and the number of enforcement applications is falling. Parties know the extent of their rights and liabilities under the new legislation and it has proved an extremely workable and efficient solution to many of the problems that affected the UK construction industry a decade or so ago. In those circumstances, it might be thought that there is a good case for keeping any changes to the Act to a minimum, so as to avoid another round of new points for the courts to resolve on disputed enforcement applications. If it isn't broken . . .

---

[14] [2007] EWHC 1691 (TCC) and paragraph 2.147 above.

APPENDICES

Appendix A: Part II of the Housing Grants, Construction and Regeneration Act 1996 — 449

Appendix B: Statutory Instrument 1998 No 648 — 457

Appendix C: Statutory Instrument 1998 No 649 — 461

Appendix D: Draft Directions in Adjudication Enforcement Proceedings — 469

APPENDIX A

Part II of The Housing Grants, Construction and Regeneration Act 1996

[CONSTRUCTION CONTRACTS]

[Introductory provisions]

104 Construction contracts.

(1) In this Part a "construction contract" means an agreement with a person for any of the following-
   (a) the carrying out of construction operations;
   (b) arranging for the carrying out of construction operations by others, whether under sub-contract to him or otherwise;
   (c) providing his own labour, or the labour of others, for the carrying out of construction operations.

(2) References in this Part to a construction contract include an agreement—
   (a) to do architectural, design, or surveying work, or
   (b) to provide advice on building, engineering, interior or exterior decoration or on the laying-out of landscape,
   in relation to construction operations.

(3) References in this Part to a construction contract do not include a contract of employment (within the meaning of the Employment Rights Act 1996).

(4) The Secretary of State may by order add to, amend or repeal any of the provisions of subsection (1), (2) or (3) as to the agreements which are construction contracts for the purposes of this Part or are to be taken or not to be taken as included in references to such contracts.

No such order shall be made unless a draft of it has been laid before and approved by a resolution of each of House of Parliament.

(5) Where an agreement relates to construction operations and other matters, this Part applies to it only so far as it relates to construction operations.

An agreement relates to construction operations so far as it makes provision of any kind within subsection (1) or (2).

(6) This Part applies only to construction contracts which—
   (a) are entered into after the commencement of this Part, and
   (b) relate to the carrying out of construction operations in England, Wales or Scotland.

(7) This Part applies whether or not the law of England and Wales or Scotland is otherwise the applicable law in relation to the contract.

105 Meaning of "construction operations".

(1) In this Part "construction operations" means, subject as follows, operations of any of the following descriptions—
   (a) construction, alteration, repair, maintenance, extension, demolition or dismantling of buildings, or structures forming, or to form, part of the land (whether permanent or not);
   (b) construction, alteration, repair, maintenance, extension, demolition or dismantling of any works forming, or to form, part of the land, including (without prejudice to the foregoing) walls, roadworks, power-lines, telecommunication apparatus, aircraft runways, docks and

harbours, railways, inland waterways, pipe-lines, reservoirs, water-mains, wells, sewers, industrial plant and installations for purposes of land drainage, coast protection or defence;
- (c) installation in any building or structure of fittings forming part of the land, including (without prejudice to the foregoing) systems of heating, lighting, air-conditioning, ventilation, power supply, drainage, sanitation, water supply or fire protection, or security or communications systems;
- (d) external or internal cleaning of buildings and structures, so far as carried out in the course of their construction, alteration, repair, extension or restoration;
- (e) operations which form an integral part of, or are preparatory to, or are for rendering complete, such operations as are previously described in this subsection, including site clearance, earth-moving, excavation, tunnelling and boring, laying of foundations, erection, maintenance or dismantling of scaffolding, site restoration, landscaping and the provision of roadways and other access works;
- (f) painting or decorating the internal or external surfaces of any building or structure.

(2) The following operations are not construction operations within the meaning of this Part—
- (a) drilling for, or extraction of, oil or natural gas;
- (b) extraction (whether by underground or surface working) of minerals; tunnelling or boring, or construction of underground works, for this purpose;
- (c) assembly, installation or demolition of plant or machinery, or erection or demolition of steelwork for the purposes of supporting or providing access to plant or machinery, on a site where the primary activity is—
  - (i) nuclear processing, power generation, or water or effluent treatment, or
  - (ii) the production, transmission, processing or bulk storage (other than warehousing) of chemicals, pharmaceuticals, oil, gas, steel or food and drink;
- (d) manufacture or delivery to site of—
  - (i) building or engineering components or equipment,
  - (ii) materials, plant or machinery, or
  - (iii) components for systems of heating, lighting, air-conditioning, ventilation, power supply, drainage, sanitation, water supply or fire protection, or for security or communications systems,

  except under a contract which also provides for their installation;
- (e) the making, installation and repair of artistic works, being sculptures, murals and other works which are wholly artistic in nature.

(3) The Secretary of State may by order add to, amend or repeal any of the provisions of subsection (1) or (2) as to the operations and work to be treated as construction operations for the purposes of this Part.

(4) No such order shall be made unless a draft of it has been laid before and approved by a resolution of each House of Parliament.

106 Provisions not applicable to contract with residential occupier.

(1) This Part does not apply—
- (a) to a construction contract with a residential occupier (see below), or
- (b) to any other description of construction contract excluded from the operation of this Part by order of the Secretary of State.

(2) A construction contract with a residential occupier means a construction contract which principally relates to operations on a dwelling which one of the parties to the contract occupies, or intends to occupy, as his residence.

In this subsection "dwelling" means a dwelling-house or a flat; and for this purpose—

"dwelling-house" does not include a building containing a flat; and

"flat" means separate and self-contained premises constructed or adapted for use for residential purposes and forming part of a building from some other part of which the premises are divided horizontally.

(3) The Secretary of State may by order amend subsection (2).

(4) No order under this section shall be made unless a draft of it has been laid before and approved by a resolution of each House of Parliament.

107 Provisions applicable only to agreements in writing.

(1) The provisions of this Part apply only where the construction contract is in writing, and any other agreement between the parties as to any matter is effective for the purposes of this Part only if in writing.

The expressions "agreement", "agree" and "agreed" shall be construed accordingly.

(2) There is an agreement in writing—
- (a) if the agreement is made in writing (whether or not it is signed by the parties),
- (b) if the agreement is made by exchange of communications in writing, or
- (c) if the agreement is evidenced in writing.

(3) Where parties agree otherwise than in writing by reference to terms which are in writing, they make an agreement in writing.

(4) An agreement is evidenced in writing if an agreement made otherwise than in writing is recorded by one of the parties, or by a third party, with the authority of the parties to the agreement.

(5) An exchange of written submissions in adjudication proceedings, or in arbitral or legal proceedings in which the existence of an agreement otherwise than in writing is alleged by one party against another party and not denied by the other party in his response constitutes as between those parties an agreement in writing to the effect alleged.

(6) References in this Part to anything being written or in writing include its being recorded by any means.

Adjudication

108 Right to refer disputes to adjudication.

(1) A party to a construction contract has the right to refer a dispute arising under the contract for adjudication under a procedure complying with this section.

For this purpose "dispute" includes any difference.

(2) The contract shall—
- (a) enable a party to give notice at any time of his intention to refer a dispute to adjudication;
- (b) provide a timetable with the object of securing the appointment of the adjudicator and referral of the dispute to him within 7 days of such notice;
- (c) require the adjudicator to reach a decision within 28 days of referral or such longer period as is agreed by the parties after the dispute has been referred;
- (d) allow the adjudicator to extend the period of 28 days by up to 14 days, with the consent of the party by whom the dispute was referred;
- (e) impose a duty on the adjudicator to act impartially; and
- (f) enable the adjudicator to take the initiative in ascertaining the facts and the law.

(3) The contract shall provide that the decision of the adjudicator is binding until the dispute is finally determined by legal proceedings, by arbitration (if the contract provides for arbitration or the parties otherwise agree to arbitration) or by agreement.

The parties may agree to accept the decision of the adjudicator as finally determining the dispute.

(4) The contract shall also provide that the adjudicator is not liable for anything done or omitted in the discharge or purported discharge of his functions as adjudicator unless the act or omission is in bad faith, and that any employee or agent of the adjudicator is similarly protected from liability.

(5) If the contract does not comply with the requirements of subsections (1) to (4), the adjudication provisions of the Scheme for Construction Contracts apply.

(6) For England and Wales, the Scheme may apply the provisions of the Arbitration Act 1996 with such adaptations and modifications as appear to the Minister making the scheme to be appropriate.

For Scotland, the Scheme may include provision conferring powers on courts in relation to adjudication and provision relating to the enforcement of the adjudicator's decision.

Payment

109 Entitlement to stage payments.

(1) A party to a construction contract is entitled to payment by instalments, stage payments or other periodic payments for any work under the contract unless—
 (a) it is specified in the contract that the duration of the work is to be less than 45 days, or
 (b) it is agreed between the parties that the duration of the work is estimated to be less than 45 days.
(2) The parties are free to agree the amounts of the payments and the intervals at which, or circumstances in which, they become due.
(3) In the absence of such agreement, the relevant provisions of the Scheme for Construction Contracts apply.
(4) References in the following sections to a payment under the contract include a payment by virtue of this section.

110 Dates for payment.

(1) Every construction contract shall—
 (a) provide an adequate mechanism for determining what payments become due under the contract, and when, and
 (b) provide for a final date for payment in relation to any sum which becomes due.
 The parties are free to agree how long the period is to be between the date on which a sum becomes due and the final date for payment.
(2) Every construction contract shall provide for the giving of notice by a party not later than five days after the date on which a payment becomes due from him under the contract, or would have become due if—
 (a) the other party had carried out his obligations under the contract, and
 (b) no set-off or abatement was permitted by reference to any sum claimed to be due under one or more other contracts,
 specifying the amount (if any) of the payment made or proposed to be made, and the basis on which that amount was calculated.
(3) If or to the extent that a contract does not contain such provision as is mentioned in subsection (1) or (2), the relevant provisions of the Scheme for Construction Contracts apply.

111 Notice of intention to withhold payment.

(1) A party to a construction contract may not withhold payment after the final date for payment of a sum due under the contract unless he has given an effective notice of intention to withhold payment.
 The notice mentioned in section 110(2) may suffice as a notice of intention to withhold payment if it complies with the requirements of this section.
(2) To be effective such a notice must specify—
 (a) the amount proposed to be withheld and the ground for withholding payment, or
 (b) if there is more than one ground, each ground and the amount attributable to it,
 and must be given not later than the prescribed period before the final date for payment.
(3) The parties are free to agree what that prescribed period is to be.
 In the absence of such agreement, the period shall be that provided by the Scheme for Construction Contracts.

(4) Where an effective notice of intention to withhold payment is given, but on the matter being referred to adjudication it is decided that the whole or part of the amount should be paid, the decision shall be construed as requiring payment not later than—
   (a) seven days from the date of the decision, or
   (b) the date which apart from the notice would have been the final date for payment,
   whichever is the later.

112 Right to suspend performance for non-payment.

(1) Where a sum due under a construction contract is not paid in full by the final date for payment and no effective notice to withhold payment has been given, the person to whom the sum is due has the right (without prejudice to any other right or remedy) to suspend performance of his obligations under the contract to the party by whom payment ought to have been made ("the party in default").
(2) The right may not be exercised without first giving to the party in default at least seven days' notice of intention to suspend performance, stating the ground or grounds on which it is intended to suspend performance.
(3) The right to suspend performance ceases when the party in default makes payment in full of the amount due.
(4) Any period during which performance is suspended in pursuance of the right conferred by this section shall be disregarded in computing for the purposes of any contractual time limit the time taken, by the party exercising the right or by a third party, to complete any work directly or indirectly affected by the exercise of the right.
    Where the contractual time limit is set by reference to a date rather than a period, the date shall be adjusted accordingly.

113 Prohibition of conditional payment provisions.

(1) A provision making payment under a construction contract conditional on the payer receiving payment from a third person is ineffective, unless that third person, or any other person payment by whom is under the contract (directly or indirectly) a condition of payment by that third person, is insolvent.
(2) For the purposes of this section a company becomes insolvent—
   (a) on the making of an administration order against it under Part II of the Insolvency Act 1986,
   (b) on the appointment of an administrative receiver or a receiver or manager of its property under Chapter I of Part III of that Act, or the appointment of a receiver under Chapter II of that Part,
   (c) on the passing of a resolution for voluntary winding-up without a declaration of solvency under section 89 of that Act, or
   (d) on the making of a winding-up order under Part IV or V of that Act.
(3) For the purposes of this section a partnership becomes insolvent—
   (a) on the making of a winding-up order against it under any provision of the Insolvency Act 1986 as applied by an order under section 420 of that Act, or
   (b) when sequestration is awarded on the estate of the partnership under section 12 of the Bankruptcy (Scotland) Act 1985 or the partnership grants a trust deed for its creditors.
(4) For the purposes of this section an individual becomes insolvent—
   (a) on the making of a bankruptcy order against him under Part IX of the Insolvency Act 1986, or
   (b) on the sequestration of his estate under the Bankruptcy (Scotland) Act 1985 or when he grants a trust deed for his creditors.
(5) A company, partnership or individual shall also be treated as insolvent on the occurrence of any event corresponding to those specified in subsection (2), (3) or (4) under the law of Northern Ireland or of a country outside the United Kingdom.

(6) Where a provision is rendered ineffective by subsection (1), the parties are free to agree other terms for payment.

In the absence of such agreement, the relevant provisions of the Scheme for Construction Contracts apply.

Supplementary provisions

114 The Scheme for Construction Contracts.

(1) The Minister shall by regulations make a scheme ("the Scheme for Construction Contracts") containing provision about the matters referred to in the preceding provisions of this Part.
(2) Before making any regulations under this section the Minister shall consult such persons as he thinks fit.
(3) In this section "the Minister" means—
   (a) for England and Wales, the Secretary of State, and
   (b) for Scotland, the Lord Advocate.
(4) Where any provisions of the Scheme for Construction Contracts apply by virtue of this Part in default of contractual provision agreed by the parties, they have effect as implied terms of the contract concerned.
(5) Regulations under this section shall not be made unless a draft of them has been approved by resolution of each House of Parliament.

115 Service of notices, &c.

(1) The parties are free to agree on the manner of service of any notice or other document required or authorised to be served in pursuance of the construction contract or for any of the purposes of this Part.
(2) If or to the extent that there is no such agreement the following provisions apply.
(3) A notice or other document may be served on a person by any effective means.
(4) If a notice or other document is addressed, pre-paid and delivered by post—
   (a) to the addressee's last known principal residence or, if he is or has been carrying on a trade, profession or business, his last known principal business address, or
   (b) where the addressee is a body corporate, to the body's registered or principal office,
   it shall be treated as effectively served.
(5) This section does not apply to the service of documents for the purposes of legal proceedings, for which provision is made by rules of court.
(6) References in this Part to a notice or other document include any form of communication in writing and references to service shall be construed accordingly.

116 Reckoning periods of time.

(1) For the purposes of this Part periods of time shall be reckoned as follows.
(2) Where an act is required to be done within a specified period after or from a specified date, the period begins immediately after that date.
(3) Where the period would include Christmas Day, Good Friday or a day which under the Banking and Financial Dealings Act 1971 is a bank holiday in England and Wales or, as the case may be, in Scotland, that day shall be excluded.

117 Crown application.

(1) This Part applies to a construction contract entered into by or on behalf of the Crown otherwise than by or on behalf of Her Majesty in her private capacity.
(2) This Part applies to a construction contract entered into on behalf of the Duchy of Cornwall notwithstanding any Crown interest.
(3) Where a construction contract is entered into by or on behalf of Her Majesty in right of the Duchy of Lancaster, Her Majesty shall be represented, for the purposes of any adjudication or

other proceedings arising out of the contract by virtue of this Part, by the Chancellor of the Duchy or such person as he may appoint.

(4) Where a construction contract is entered into on behalf of the Duchy of Cornwall, the Duke of Cornwall or the possessor for the time being of the Duchy shall be represented, for the purposes of any adjudication or other proceedings arising out of the contract by virtue of this Part, by such person as he may appoint.

APPENDIX B

Statutory Instrument 1998 No 648
Construction, England and Wales

THE CONSTRUCTION CONTRACTS (ENGLAND AND WALES)
EXCLUSION ORDER 1998

Made   *6th March 1998*

Coming into force in accordance with article 1(1)

The Secretary of State, in exercise of the powers conferred on him by sections 106(1)(b) and 146(1) of the Housing Grants, Construction and Regeneration Act 1996[1] and of all other powers enabling him in that behalf, hereby makes the following Order, a draft of which has been laid before and approved by resolution of, each House of Parliament:

Citation, commencement and extent

1. (1) This Order may be cited as the Construction Contracts (England and Wales) Exclusion Order 1998 and shall come into force at the end of the period of 8 weeks beginning with the day on which it is made ("the commencement date").
(2) This Order shall extend to England and Wales only.

Interpretation

2. In this Order, "Part II" means Part II of the Housing Grants, Construction and Regeneration Act 1996.

Agreements under statute

3. A construction contract is excluded from the operation of Part II if it is—
    (a) an agreement under section 38 (power of highway authorities to adopt by agreement) or section 278 (agreements as to execution of works) of the Highways Act 1980;[2]
    (b) an agreement under section 106 (planning obligations), 106A (modification or discharge of planning obligations) or 299A (Crown planning obligations) of the Town and Country Planning Act 1990;[3]
    (c) an agreement under section 104 of the Water Industry Act 1991[4] (agreements to adopt sewer, drain or sewage disposal works); or

---

[1] 1996 c.53.
[2] 1980 c.66: section 38 was amended by and section 278 substituted by the New Roads and Street Works Act 1991 (c.22) sections 22 and 23.
[3] 1990 c.8: section 106 was substituted and the other sections inserted by section 12 of the Planning and Compensation Act 1991 (c.34).
[4] 1991 c.56.

(d) an externally financed development agreement within the meaning of section 1 of the National Health Service (Private Finance) Act 1997[5] (powers of NHS Trusts to enter into agreements).

Private finance initiative

4. (1) A construction contract is excluded from the operation of Part II if it is a contract entered into under the private finance initiative, within the meaning given below.

(2) A contract is entered into under the private finance initiative if all the following conditions are fulfilled—
   (a) it contains a statement that it is entered into under that initiative or, as the case may be, under a project applying similar principles;
   (b) the consideration due under the contract is determined at least in part by reference to one or more of the following—
      (i) the standards attained in the performance of a service, the provision of which is the principal purpose or one of the principal purposes for which the building or structure is constructed;
      (ii) the extent, rate or intensity of use of all or any part of the building or structure in question; or
      (iii) the right to operate any facility in connection with the building or structure in question; and
   (c) one of the parties to the contract is—
      (i) a Minister of the Crown;
      (ii) a department in respect of which appropriation accounts are required to be prepared under the Exchequer and Audit Departments Act 1866[6];
      (iii) any other authority or body whose accounts are required to be examined and certified by or are open to the inspection of the Comptroller and Auditor General by virtue of an agreement entered into before the commencement date or by virtue of any enactment;
      (iv) any authority or body listed in Schedule 4 to the National Audit Act 1983[7] (nationalised industries and other public authorities);
      (v) a body whose accounts are subject to audit by auditors appointed by the Audit Commission;
      (vi) the governing body or trustees of a voluntary school within the meaning of section 31 of the Education Act 1996[8] (county schools and voluntary schools), or
      (vii) a company wholly owned by any of the bodies described in paragraphs (i) to (v).

Finance agreements

5. (1) A construction contract is excluded from the operation of Part II if it is a finance agreement, within the meaning given below.

(2) A contract is a finance agreement if it is any one of the following—
   (a) any contract of insurance;
   (b) any contract under which the principal obligations include the formation or dissolution of a company, unincorporated association or partnership;

---

[5] 1997 c.56.
[6] 1866 c.39.
[7] 1983 c.44: amended by the Telecommunications Act 1984, (c.12) Schedule 7, Part III; the Oil and Pipelines Act (c.42) Schedule 20, paragraph 36, S.I. 1991/510, article 5(4) and the Coal Industry Act 1994, (c.21) Schedule 9, paragraph 29.
[8] 1996 c.56.

(c) any contract under which the principal obligations include the creation or transfer of securities or any right or interest in securities;
(d) any contract under which the principal obligations include the lending of money;
(e) any contract under which the principal obligations include an undertaking by a person to be responsible as surety for the debt or default of another person, including a fidelity bond, advance payment bond, retention bond or performance bond.

Development agreements

6. (1) A construction contract is excluded from the operation of Part II if it is a development agreement, within the meaning given below.

(2) A contract is a development agreement if it includes provision for the grant or disposal of a relevant interest in the land on which take place the principal construction operations to which the contract relates.

(3) In paragraph (2) above, a relevant interest in land means—
(a) a freehold; or
(b) a leasehold for a period which is to expire no earlier than 12 months after the completion of the construction operations under the contract.

Signed by authority of the Secretary of State

Nick Raynsford
Parliamentary Under-Secretary of State, Department of the Environment, Transport and the Regions

6th March 1998

APPENDIX C

Statutory Instrument 1998 No 649
Construction, England and Wales

The Scheme for Construction Contracts (England and Wales) Regulations 1998

Made—6th March 1998

Coming into force—1st May 1998

The Secretary of State, in exercise of the powers conferred on him by sections 108(6), 114 and 146(1) and (2) of the Housing Grants, Construction and Regeneration Act 1996,[1] and of all other powers enabling him in that behalf, having consulted such persons as he thinks fit, and draft Regulations having been approved by both Houses of Parliament, hereby makes the following Regulations:

Citation, commencement, extent and interpretation

1. (1) These Regulations may be cited as the Scheme for Construction Contracts (England and Wales) Regulations 1998 and shall come into force at the end of the period of 8 weeks beginning with the day on which they are made (the "commencement date").
   (2) These Regulations shall extend only to England and Wales.
   (3) In these Regulations, "the Act" means the Housing Grants, Construction and Regeneration Act 1996.

The Scheme for Construction Contracts

2. Where a construction contract does not comply with the requirements of section 108(1) to (4) of the Act, the adjudication provisions in Part I of the Schedule to these Regulations shall apply.
3. Where—
   (a) the parties to a construction contract are unable to reach agreement for the purposes mentioned respectively in sections 109, 111 and 113 of the Act, or
   (b) a construction contract does not make provision as required by section 110 of the Act,
   the relevant provisions in Part II of the Schedule to these Regulations shall apply.
4. The provisions in the Schedule to these Regulations shall be the Scheme for Construction Contracts for the purposes of section 114 of the Act.

Signed by authority of the Secretary of State

Nick Raynsford

Parliamentary Under-Secretary of State, Department of the Environment, Transport and the Regions

6th March 1998

---

[1] 1996 c.53.

Appendix C

Schedule

Regulations 2, 3 and 4

The Scheme for Construction Contracts
Part I -

Adjudication

Notice of Intention to seek Adjudication

1. (1) Any party to a construction contract (the "referring party") may give written notice (the "notice of adjudication") of his intention to refer any dispute arising under the contract, to adjudication.
(2) The notice of adjudication shall be given to every other party to the contract.
(3) The notice of adjudication shall set out briefly—
   (a) the nature and a brief description of the dispute and of the parties involved,
   (b) details of where and when the dispute has arisen,
   (c) the nature of the redress which is sought, and
   (d) the names and addresses of the parties to the contract (including, where appropriate, the addresses which the parties have specified for the giving of notices).
2. (1) Following the giving of a notice of adjudication and subject to any agreement between the parties to the dispute as to who shall act as adjudicator—
   (a) the referring party shall request the person (if any) specified in the contract to act as adjudicator, or
   (b) if no person is named in the contract or the person named has already indicated that he is unwilling or unable to act, and the contract provides for a specified nominating body to select a person, the referring party shall request the nominating body named in the contract to select a person to act as adjudicator, or
   (c) where neither paragraph (a) nor (b) above applies, or where the person referred to in (a) has already indicated that he is unwilling or unable to act and (b) does not apply, the referring party shall request an adjudicator nominating body to select a person to act as adjudicator.
(2) A person requested to act as adjudicator in accordance with the provisions of paragraph (1) shall indicate whether or not he is willing to act within two days of receiving the request.
(3) In this paragraph, and in paragraphs 5 and 6 below, an "adjudicator nominating body" shall mean a body (not being a natural person and not being a party to the dispute) which holds itself out publicly as a body which will select an adjudicator when requested to do so by a referring party.
3. The request referred to in paragraphs 2, 5 and 6 shall be accompanied by a copy of the notice of adjudication.
4. Any person requested or selected to act as adjudicator in accordance with paragraphs 2, 5 or 6 shall be a natural person acting in his personal capacity. A person requested or selected to act as an adjudicator shall not be an employee of any of the parties to the dispute and shall declare any interest, financial or otherwise, in any matter relating to the dispute.
5. (1) The nominating body referred to in paragraphs 2(1)(b) and 6(1)(b) or the adjudicator nominating body referred to in paragraphs 2(1)(c), 5(2)(b) and 6(1)(c) must communicate the selection of an adjudicator to the referring party within five days of receiving a request to do so.
(2) Where the nominating body or the adjudicator nominating body fails to comply with paragraph (1), the referring party may—
   (a) agree with the other party to the dispute to request a specified person to act as adjudicator, or
   (b) request any other adjudicator nominating body to select a person to act as adjudicator.

(3) The person requested to act as adjudicator in accordance with the provisions of paragraphs (1) or (2) shall indicate whether or not he is willing to act within two days of receiving the request.

6. (1) Where an adjudicator who is named in the contract indicates to the parties that he is unable or unwilling to act, or where he fails to respond in accordance with paragraph 2(2), the referring party may—
   (a) request another person (if any) specified in the contract to act as adjudicator, or
   (b) request the nominating body (if any) referred to in the contract to select a person to act as adjudicator, or
   (c) request any other adjudicator nominating body to select a person to act as adjudicator.

(2) The person requested to act in accordance with the provisions of paragraph (1) shall indicate whether or not he is willing to act within two days of receiving the request.

7. (1) Where an adjudicator has been selected in accordance with paragraphs 2, 5 or 6, the referring party shall, not later than seven days from the date of the notice of adjudication, refer the dispute in writing (the "referral notice") to the adjudicator.

(2) A referral notice shall be accompanied by copies of, or relevant extracts from, the construction contract and such other documents as the referring party intends to rely upon.

(3) The referring party shall, at the same time as he sends to the adjudicator the documents referred to in paragraphs (1) and (2), send copies of those documents to every other party to the dispute.

8. (1) The adjudicator may, with the consent of all the parties to those disputes, adjudicate at the same time on more than one dispute under the same contract.

   (2) The adjudicator may, with the consent of all the parties to those disputes, adjudicate at the same time on related disputes under different contracts, whether or not one or more of those parties is a party to those disputes.

   (3) All the parties in paragraphs (1) and (2) respectively may agree to extend the period within which the adjudicator may reach a decision in relation to all or any of these disputes.

   (4) Where an adjudicator ceases to act because a dispute is to be adjudicated on by another person in terms of this paragraph, that adjudicator's fees and expenses shall be determined in accordance with paragraph 25.

9. (1) An adjudicator may resign at any time on giving notice in writing to the parties to the dispute.

(2) An adjudicator must resign where the dispute is the same or substantially the same as one which has previously been referred to adjudication, and a decision has been taken in that adjudication.

(3) Where an adjudicator ceases to act under paragraph 9(1)—
   (a) the referring party may serve a fresh notice under paragraph 1 and shall request an adjudicator to act in accordance with paragraphs 2 to 7; and
   (b) if requested by the new adjudicator and insofar as it is reasonably practicable, the parties shall supply him with copies of all documents which they had made available to the previous adjudicator.

(4) Where an adjudicator resigns in the circumstances referred to in paragraph (2), or where a dispute varies significantly from the dispute referred to him in the referral notice and for that reason he is not competent to decide it, the adjudicator shall be entitled to the payment of such reasonable amount as he may determine by way of fees and expenses reasonably incurred by him. The parties shall be jointly and severally liable for any sum which remains outstanding following the making of any determination on how the payment shall be apportioned.

10. Where any party to the dispute objects to the appointment of a particular person as adjudicator, that objection shall not invalidate the adjudicator's appointment nor any decision he may reach in accordance with paragraph 20.

11. (1) The parties to a dispute may at any time agree to revoke the appointment of the adjudicator. The adjudicator shall be entitled to the payment of such reasonable amount as he may determine by way of fees and expenses incurred by him. The parties shall be jointly and severally liable for any sum which remains outstanding following the making of any determination on how the payment shall be apportioned.
(2) Where the revocation of the appointment of the adjudicator is due to the default or misconduct of the adjudicator, the parties shall not be liable to pay the adjudicator's fees and expenses.

Powers of the adjudicator

12. The adjudicator shall—
    (a) act impartially in carrying out his duties and shall do so in accordance with any relevant terms of the contract and shall reach his decision in accordance with the applicable law in relation to the contract; and
    (b) avoid incurring unnecessary expense.
13. The adjudicator may take the initiative in ascertaining the facts and the law necessary to determine the dispute, and shall decide on the procedure to be followed in the adjudication. In particular he may—
    (a) request any party to the contract to supply him with such documents as he may reasonably require including, if he so directs, any written statement from any party to the contract supporting or supplementing the referral notice and any other documents given under paragraph 7(2),
    (b) decide the language or languages to be used in the adjudication and whether a translation of any document is to be provided and if so by whom,
    (c) meet and question any of the parties to the contract and their representatives,
    (d) subject to obtaining any necessary consent from a third party or parties, make such site visits and inspections as he considers appropriate, whether accompanied by the parties or not,
    (e) subject to obtaining any necessary consent from a third party or parties, carry out any tests or experiments,
    (f) obtain and consider such representations and submissions as he requires, and, provided he has notified the parties of his intention, appoint experts, assessors or legal advisers,
    (g) give directions as to the timetable for the adjudication, any deadlines, or limits as to the length of written documents or oral representations to be complied with, and
    (h) issue other directions relating to the conduct of the adjudication.
14. The parties shall comply with any request or direction of the adjudicator in relation to the adjudication.
15. If, without showing sufficient cause, a party fails to comply with any request, direction or timetable of the adjudicator made in accordance with his powers, fails to produce any document or written statement requested by the adjudicator, or in any other way fails to comply with a requirement under these provisions relating to the adjudication, the adjudicator may—
    (a) continue the adjudication in the absence of that party or of the document or written statement requested,
    (b) draw such inferences from that failure to comply as circumstances may, in the adjudicator's opinion, be justified, and
    (c) make a decision on the basis of the information before him attaching such weight as he thinks fit to any evidence submitted to him outside any period he may have requested or directed.
16. (1) Subject to any agreement between the parties to the contrary, and to the terms of paragraph (2) below, any party to the dispute may be assisted by, or represented by, such advisers or representatives (whether legally qualified or not) as he considers appropriate.

(2) Where the adjudicator is considering oral evidence or representations, a party to the dispute may not be represented by more than one person, unless the adjudicator gives directions to the contrary.

17. The adjudicator shall consider any relevant information submitted to him by any of the parties to the dispute and shall make available to them any information to be taken into account in reaching his decision.

18. The adjudicator and any party to the dispute shall not disclose to any other person any information or document provided to him in connection with the adjudication which the party supplying it has indicated is to be treated as confidential, except to the extent that it is necessary for the purposes of, or in connection with, the adjudication.

19. (1) The adjudicator shall reach his decision not later than—
    (a) twenty eight days after the date of the referral notice mentioned in paragraph 7(1), or
    (b) forty two days after the date of the referral notice if the referring party so consents, or
    (c) such period exceeding twenty eight days after the referral notice as the parties to the dispute may, after the giving of that notice, agree.

(2) Where the adjudicator fails, for any reason, to reach his decision in accordance with paragraph (1)
    (a) any of the parties to the dispute may serve a fresh notice under paragraph 1 and shall request an adjudicator to act in accordance with paragraphs 2 to 7; and
    (b) if requested by the new adjudicator and insofar as it is reasonably practicable, the parties shall supply him with copies of all documents which they had made available to the previous adjudicator.

(3) As soon as possible after he has reached a decision, the adjudicator shall deliver a copy of that decision to each of the parties to the contract.

Adjudicator's decision

20. The adjudicator shall decide the matters in dispute. He may take into account any other matters which the parties to the dispute agree should be within the scope of the adjudication or which are matters under the contract which he considers are necessarily connected with the dispute. In particular, he may—
    (a) open up, revise and review any decision taken or any certificate given by any person referred to in the contract unless the contract states that the decision or certificate is final and conclusive,
    (b) decide that any of the parties to the dispute is liable to make a payment under the contract (whether in sterling or some other currency) and, subject to section 111(4) of the Act, when that payment is due and the final date for payment,
    (c) having regard to any term of the contract relating to the payment of interest decide the circumstances in which, and the rates at which, and the periods for which simple or compound rates of interest shall be paid.

21. In the absence of any directions by the adjudicator relating to the time for performance of his decision, the parties shall be required to comply with any decision of the adjudicator immediately on delivery of the decision to the parties in accordance with this paragraph.

22. If requested by one of the parties to the dispute, the adjudicator shall provide reasons for his decision.

Effects of the decision

23. (1) In his decision, the adjudicator may, if he thinks fit, order any of the parties to comply peremptorily with his decision or any part of it.

(2) The decision of the adjudicator shall be binding on the parties, and they shall comply with it until the dispute is finally determined by legal proceedings, by arbitration (if the contract provides for arbitration or the parties otherwise agree to arbitration) or by agreement between the parties.

24. Section 42 of the Arbitration Act 1996 shall apply to this Scheme subject to the following modifications—
    (a) in subsection (2) for the word "tribunal" wherever it appears there shall be substituted the word "adjudicator",
    (b) in subparagraph (b) of subsection (2) for the words "arbitral proceedings" there shall be substituted the word "adjudication",
    (c) subparagraph (c) of subsection (2) shall be deleted, and
    (d) subsection (3) shall be deleted.
25. The adjudicator shall be entitled to the payment of such reasonable amount as he may determine by way of fees and expenses reasonably incurred by him. The parties shall be jointly and severally liable for any sum which remains outstanding following the making of any determination on how the payment shall be apportioned.
26. The adjudicator shall not be liable for anything done or omitted in the discharge or purported discharge of his functions as adjudicator unless the act or omission is in bad faith, and any employee or agent of the adjudicator shall be similarly protected from liability.

Part II -

Payment

Entitlement to and amount of stage payments

1. Where the parties to a relevant construction contract fail to agree—
    (a) the amount of any instalment or stage or periodic payment for any work under the contract, or
    (b) the intervals at which, or circumstances in which, such payments become due under that contract, or
    (c) both of the matters mentioned in sub-paragraphs (a) and (b) above,
    the relevant provisions of paragraphs 2 to 4 below shall apply.
2. (1) The amount of any payment by way of instalments or stage or periodic payments in respect of a relevant period shall be the difference between the amount determined in accordance with sub-paragraph (2) and the amount determined in accordance with sub-paragraph (3).
   (2) The aggregate of the following amounts—
    (a) an amount equal to the value of any work performed in accordance with the relevant construction contract during the period from the commencement of the contract to the end of the relevant period (excluding any amount calculated in accordance with sub-paragraph (b)),
    (b) where the contract provides for payment for materials, an amount equal to the value of any materials manufactured on site or brought onto site for the purposes of the works during the period from the commencement of the contract to the end of the relevant period, and
    (c) any other amount or sum which the contract specifies shall be payable during or in respect of the period from the commencement of the contract to the end of the relevant period.
   (3) The aggregate of any sums which have been paid or are due for payment by way of instalments, stage or periodic payments during the period from the commencement of the contract to the end of the relevant period.
   (4) An amount calculated in accordance with this paragraph shall not exceed the difference between—
    (a) the contract price, and
    (b) the aggregate of the instalments or stage or periodic payments which have become due.

Dates for payment

3. Where the parties to a construction contract fail to provide an adequate mechanism for determining either what payments become due under the contract, or when they become due for payment, or both, the relevant provisions of paragraphs 4 to 7 shall apply.

4. Any payment of a kind mentioned in paragraph 2 above shall become due on whichever of the following dates occurs later—
   (a) the expiry of 7 days following the relevant period mentioned in paragraph 2(1) above, or
   (b) the making of a claim by the payee.
5. The final payment payable under a relevant construction contract, namely the payment of an amount equal to the difference (if any) between—
   (a) the contract price, and
   (b) the aggregate of any instalment or stage or periodic payments which have become due under the contract,
   shall become due on the expiry of—
   (a) 30 days following completion of the work, or
   (b) the making of a claim by the payee,
   whichever is the later.
6. Payment of the contract price under a construction contract (not being a relevant construction contract) shall become due on
   (a) the expiry of 30 days following the completion of the work, or
   (b) the making of a claim by the payee,
   whichever is the later.
7. Any other payment under a construction contract shall become due
   (a) on the expiry of 7 days following the completion of the work to which the payment relates, or
   (b) the making of a claim by the payee,
   whichever is the later.

Final date for payment

8. (1) Where the parties to a construction contract fail to provide a final date for payment in relation to any sum which becomes due under a construction contract, the provisions of this paragraph shall apply.
   (2) The final date for the making of any payment of a kind mentioned in paragraphs 2, 5, 6 or 7, shall be 17 days from the date that payment becomes due.

Notice specifying amount of payment

9. A party to a construction contract shall, not later than 5 days after the date on which any payment—
   (a) becomes due from him, or
   (b) would have become due, if—
       (i) the other party had carried out his obligations under the contract, and
       (ii) no set-off or abatement was permitted by reference to any sum claimed to be due under one or more other contracts,
   give notice to the other party to the contract specifying the amount (if any) of the payment he has made or proposes to make, specifying to what the payment relates and the basis on which that amount is calculated.

Notice of intention to withhold payment

10. Any notice of intention to withhold payment mentioned in section 111 of the Act shall be given not later than the prescribed period, which is to say not later than 7 days before the final date for payment determined either in accordance with the construction contract, or where no such provision is made in the contract, in accordance with paragraph 8 above.

Prohibition of conditional payment provisions

11. Where a provision making payment under a construction contract conditional on the payer receiving payment from a third person is ineffective as mentioned in section 113 of the Act, and the parties have not agreed other terms for payment, the relevant provisions of—
    (a) paragraphs 2, 4, 5, 7, 8, 9 and 10 shall apply in the case of a relevant construction contract, and
    (b) paragraphs 6, 7, 8, 9 and 10 shall apply in the case of any other construction contract.

Interpretation

12. In this Part of the Scheme for Construction Contracts—

    "claim by the payee" means a written notice given by the party carrying out work under a construction contract to the other party specifying the amount of any payment or payments which he considers to be due and the basis on which it is, or they are calculated;

    "contract price" means the entire sum payable under the construction contract in respect of the work;

    "relevant construction contract" means any construction contract other than one—
    (a) which specifies that the duration of the work is to be less than 45 days, or
    (b) in respect of which the parties agree that the duration of the work is estimated to be less than 45 days;

    "relevant period" means a period which is specified in, or is calculated by reference to the construction contract or where no such period is so specified or is so calculable, a period of 28 days;

    "value of work" means an amount determined in accordance with the construction contract under which the work is performed or where the contract contains no such provision, the cost of any work performed in accordance with that contract together with an amount equal to any overhead or profit included in the contract price;

    "work" means any of the work or services mentioned in section 104 of the Act.

    Note:

    [1] 1996 c.53.

APPENDIX D

Draft Directions in Adjudication Enforcement Proceedings

Upon reading the Claim Form, Particulars of Claim, the Claimant's without notice application dated the day of 200 and the evidence in support thereof

IT IS ORDERED THAT:

1. The Claimant's solicitor shall [as soon as practicable after receipt of this Order/ by 4pm on day of] serve upon the Defendant
   a. The Claim Form and Response Pack
   b. This Order
   c. The Claimant's Application Pursuant to Part 24 and the Claimant's evidence in support.
2. The time for the Defendant to file its acknowledgement of service is abridged to [] days.
3. The Claimant hereby has permission to issue an application pursuant to CPR Part 24 without an acknowledgement of service or Defence having been filed.
4. The Part 24 application will be heard on the day of at am/pm at. Estimated Length of Hearing hours]
5. Any further evidence in relation to the Part 24 Application shall be served and filed
   a. By the Defendant, [14 days after the service of the documents in Paragraph 1 above/ at least 5 working days before the date fixed for the hearing of the Application] [on day the day of]
   b. By the Claimant, in response to that of the Defendant, [at least 3 working days before the date fixed for the hearing of the Application] [on day the day of 200] and in either case no later than 4.00pm upon that day.
6. The Claimant's solicitor shall file a paginated bundle comprising
   a. The witness statements provided in support of the application, together with any exhibits;
   b. The witness statements provided in opposition to the application together with exhibits;
   c. Any witness statements in reply, together with exhibits;
   d. Photocopies of relevant authorities.

This bundle is to be provided no later than [2 working days before the hearing of the Application] [on day of].

7. The parties shall file and serve skeleton arguments by no later than [4.00pm one clear working day before the hearing/ 1pm the last working day before the hearing]* [on day the day of]
8. The costs of and incidental to these directions are reserved to the Part 24 hearing. Permission to apply in respect of such costs in the absence of such hearing.
9. The parties have permission to apply to the court on 48 hours written notice to the other to seek to set aside or vary these directions.

   * Depending whether the hearing is estimated to last in excess of ½ day or not

INDEX

abatement
   set-off against a sum certified/determined as due 10.06–10.12
   set-off against sums claimed 10.13–10.19
ad hoc adjudication 5.01–5.11, 7.02
adjudication 1.13 *see also* ad hoc adjudication, adjudication decisions, adjudication rules, adjudicators, compulsory adjudication, contractual adjudication, JCT Adjudication Agreement, notices
   Australia 6.25–6.27
   awards
      interest 3.77–3.80
   cooling off period 1.14
   consequences of losing adjudication 14.15–14.19
   determination 4.26, 4.43, 4.52
      New South Wales 6.18–6.19
   documentation 17.15–17.18
   directions 17.01–17.03
   evidence 17.09–17.10
   fair and public hearing 9.44–9.48
   hearings 17.11–17.12
   implementation 1.16
   insufficient connection between dispute and decision 7.64–7.70
   intimidatory tactics 17.30–17.31
   meetings 17.08
   more than one dispute 4.16, 13.09
   New South Wales 6.13–6.17
   New Zealand 6.35–6.36
   notice of adjudication 3.12–3.15, 7.35–7.45, 7.63n, 16.02–16.06
      at any time 2.76, 2.85, 2.87, 2.90
      response to 16.07–16.09
   purpose of 2.04, 2.15
   parties 7.33–7.34
   pay now argue later philosophy 2.13
   procedural relief 4.18
   referral within 7 days 4.11–4.15
   restriction on issues referred to adjudication 1.14, 1.17
   service of documents 2.164–2.167
   scope under TeCSA rules 4.63
   Singapore 6.29–6.34
   visits to site 17.13–17.14
adjudication decisions 3.73, 12.15 *see also* adjudication, adjudication rules, adjudicators
   28 day time limit 2.76, 2.91–2.97, 2.99–2.102, 2.104–2.105, 3.66–3.72, 4.19–4.22, 4.33, 4.53, 4.73, 12.06, 17.19–17.22, 18.03
   communication of decision 2.106–2.108, 3.72, 18.04–18.05
   compliance 3.90, 12.16–12.18
   delay 4.48
   effect of the decision 3.85, 18.12–18.13
      final and binding 1.15, 1.24–1.25, 2.116–2.117, 2.119, 3.89, 3.91, 4.64, 4.66–4.68, 4.71, 6.28, 7.71, 12.02
      temporary finality 2.108–2.111, 3.86, 4.23–4.24, 12.24–12.26, 14.02
      temporary finality/subsequent adjudications 12.27–12.34
   enforcement 4.68
      arrestment 12.46
      New South Wales 6.20–6.22
      principles of 13.01–13.22
      status of decision 12.19–12.23
      summary judgment 13.18–13.19, 14.05–14.11
      TCC procedure 14.02–14.04
      winding up and bankruptcy 12.41–12.45
   errors 2.06–2.08, 18.06–18.08
      correction of errors 2.117–2.119
      errors as to jurisdiction 2.10, 2.12, 3.92, 4.46–4.47, 7.01, 8.14–8.17
      errors as to matters of fact 8.01–8.03, 8.18–8.22, 12.04
      errors as to matters of law 2.10, 2.12, 3.92, 7.01, 8.01–8.13, 12.04
      errors as to procedure 7.01, 9.18
      slips 8.24–8.30, 12.09–12.14, 19.31–19.32
   fairness 9.02–9.03
      bias 9.11–9.15
      natural justice 9.16–9.43
      size/nature of claim 9.04–9.10
   limits to later challenge 1.31
   opening up, revising and reviewing 3.74–3.76

Index

adjudication decisions (*cont.*)
  reasons 3.83–3.84
    obligation to give 4.70, 18.01–18.02
  set-off 10.20
    general rule 10.21–10.32
    exceptions to general rule 10.33–10.34
  severability 4.45
    in later court or arbitration proceedings 12.35–12.40
    status of decision 12.19–12.23
  stay for arbitration 2.148, 2.151, 3.87–3.88
  validity 12.04–12.05
    compliance with time limits 12.06–12.08
adjudication rules
  CEDR Rules
    paras 12–13 4.71
  CIC Model Adjudication Procedure 4.74, 9.25
    para 1 4.72
    para 4 4.72
    para 5 4.72
    para 8 4.72
    para 14 4.72
    para 20 4.72
    para 25 4.73
    paras 28–29 4.75
  TeCSA Rules
    App 8 para 2.1 4.67
    App 8 para 2.1(f) 4.68
    r 11 4.63, 4.65
    r 12 4.63, 4.64–4.66
    r 14 4.67
    r 21A 4.69
    r 27 4.70
    r 28A 4.67
    r 33 4.65
adjudicators *see also* adjudication, adjudication decisions, natural justice
  ability to adjudicate on more than one dispute 3.34–3.38
  appointment 3.16–3.25, 4.09–4.10, 7.25–7.27, 16.10–16.14
    objection to appointment 3.48–3.49, 16.15
    inability to accept 4.10
    revocation of appointment 3.50–3.51
  bias 9.11–9.22, 13.14–13.15
  conflict of interest 17.24–17.25
  consideration of relevant information 3.60–3.65
  fees 4.33, 11.12–11.18
  impartiality 2.110, 2.113, 3.54–3.56, 4.17, 9.16
  inquisitorial approach 3.59, 17.28–17.29
  jurisdiction 4.46–4.47, 7.01, 7.03, 7.83–7.85, 16.16–16.20

    ad hoc jurisdiction 5.02–5.11, 7.02, 11.05–11.06
    insufficient connection between dispute and decision 7.64–7.70
    investigation by adjudicator of own powers 7.09–7.15
    investigation by court of jurisdictional challenge 7.16–7.17, 7.72
    general principles 7.04–7.05
    objection to 5.14–5.15, 7.81–7.82
    options when jurisdiction challenged 7.05–7.08
    ousting jurisdiction 7.78–7.80
    relevance of earlier decisions 7.71–7.77, 9.38–9.41, 12.27
  lien 11.19–11.24
  nomination 4.07–4.08
  non-compliance with adjudicator's requirements 4.18
  powers 3.52
    to investigate own jurisdiction 7.09–7.15
  reciprocity 17.26–17.27
  resignation 3.39–3.47
  taking the initiative 3.57–3.59
arbitration 1.26
  time limits 2.103
Australia
  New South Wales 6.01–6.22

Building Employers Confederation 1.26

Canary Wharf 1.12
CEDR Rules *see* adjudication rules
certificates
  certificates of practical completion 4.31
  final certificates 4.25, 4.31
CIC Model Adjudication Procedure *see* adjudication rules
claims
  cross-claims 10.03–10.04, 10.13
  of judgment debtor 15.04–15.05
compulsory adjudication 1.03
concurrent proceedings 2.87–2.88
Confederation of Construction Specialists 1.12
construction activities 1.19–1.20
construction contracts 2.16–2.36, 7.20, 13.06–13.07 *see also* construction operations, payment, standard forms of construction and engineering contracts, sub-contracts
  acceptance of existence during adjudication 2.69–2.74
  adjudication provisions 4.01–4.03
  agreements in writing 2.44–2.46, 2.48–2.50

Index

construction contracts (cont.)
  certificates identifying sums to be paid 3.102
  contract price 3.103
  contract in writing 7.28–7.32, 13.08
    proposed removal of requirement 19.03–19.06
  contract terms
    implied terms 2.67–2.68, 2.163–2.163, 3.105, 4.04
    material terms 2.47–2.48, 2.51
  costs provisions 11.07–11.11
  definition 2.17
  New South Wales 6.06–6.07
  oral contracts 2.47
  oral variations 2.62–2.63, 2.66
  parties 7.33–7.34
  pay when certified clauses
    proposed prohibition 19.25–19.27
  pay when paid clauses 2.158–2.161, 3.114–3.115
    Australia 6.24
  for professional services 4.61
  settlement agreements 7.21–7.24
  suspension of work 2.154–2.157
    proposals for change 19.28–19.30
  value of work 3.100, 3.102
construction industry 1.01
  high cost 1.05
  as proportion of GDP 1.06
  recession 1.04
  volatility 1.02
construction operations 1.19, 1.22, 1.28, 2.17–2.19, 2.25, 3.03
  assembly and fixing to the land of industrial plant 2.26
  definition 2.23
  installation of plant 2.33
  offshore installations 2.30
  power generation 2.32–2.33, 2.35–2.36
  provision of professional services 2.19–2.20
  repair and maintenance of heating systems 2.29
  shopfitting 2.21, 2.28
Constructors Liaison Group 1.12, 1.26
consumer contracts
  unfair terms 9.49
contract administration services 2.18
contractors
  insolvency 2.146, 2.147
contractual adjudication 4.01–4.05
  errors as to law and fact 4.05
costs 3.81–3.82, 4.69, 4.75, 11.01–11.04, 14.13–14.14, 18.11
  jurisdiction to decide
    ad hoc jurisdiction 11.05–11.07

    contractual provision 11.05–11.11
  proposals for change 19.10–19.13

damages
  liquidated damages 4.30, 4.58, 7.40, 10.20, 10.35–10.37
declaratory relief 14.26–14.29
Department of Trade and Industry
  proposals for change to HGCRA 19.03–19.35
  development agreements 2.37–2.39
dispute 2.76, 2.78–2.82, 2.93, 4.38–4.39, 4.49
  crystallisation 2.77, 7.46–7.51
  multiple disputes 3.34–3.38, 4.16, 13.09
  pragmatic interpretation 7.54–7.56
  restrictive interpretation 7.52–7.54
  scope and extent 7.35–7.45
  single dispute 7.57–7.63, 9.08
dispute resolution 1.13, 14.02
  ICE Conditions 4.56

enforcement *see* adjudication decisions
errors *see* adjudication decisions
estoppel 2.87, 2.101
  estoppel by convention 5.12–5.13
  statutory estoppel 2.69–2.74

fairness *see* adjudication decisions, human rights
fees *see also* adjudicators
  adjudicator's fees 3.95–3.96, 4.33, 4.75, 18.09–18.10
finance agreements 2.37

GC/Works Contract and Sub-Contracts 4.51–4.53, 4.73
  cl 29 4.52
  cl 38A 4.53
  cl 38A.5 4.53

Hatfield Galleria 1.12
Housing Grants Construction and Regeneration Bill 1996 1.19
  Committee stage 1.28
  debates 1.27, 1.30
  exclusions 1.21
human rights 2.114
  fair and public hearing 9.44–9.48

ICE Form of Engineering Contract 4.54
  ICE Conditions 4.54
  cl 60 4.54
  cl 66 4.54, 4.56, 4.59
injunctions 14.20–14.25

Index

insolvency 2.142–2.147, 4.26
  of judgment creditor 15.06–15.08
  proposals for change 19.33–19.35
instalments *see* payment
Institute of Civil Engineers 1.26
interest
  adjudication awards 3.77–3.79
  late payment 3.80
Intermediate Form 4.31, 9.54

JCT Adjudication Agreement 4.32–4.33
JCT IFC Form *see* Intermediate Form
JCT Minor Works Form 4.28–4.29
  cl 2.3 4.30
  Supplemental Condition D7.2 4.30
JCT Standard Form of building contract
  cl 27.6.5.1 2.142, 2.143, 2.144, 2.146, 2.147
  cl 41A 3.33n, 4.06, 4.16, 4.22
  cl 41A.4.1 4.14, 4.15
  cl 41A.2 4.07
  cl 41A.2.2 4.11, 4.14, 4.15
  cl 41A.5.3 4.19
  cl 41A.5.5 4.17
  cl 41A.5.6 4.18
  cl 41A.8 4.33
  cl 42A.4.1 4.13
  final certificates 4.25
JCT Standard Form of building contract with contractor's design 4.03, 4.20
  cl 30 3.05
Joint Review of Procurement and Contractual Arrangements in the United Kingdom Construction Industry 1.07
judicial expenses 4.69
jurisdiction *see* adjudicators

Latham Report 1.07–1.08, 10.03
  Ch 9 1.13
  interim report (Trust and Money) 1.07
  para 5.17(2) 1.10n
  para 5.17(4) 1.10n
  para 5.18 1.10n
  para 8.9 1.11
  para 8.10 1.12
  para 9.3 1.13
  para 9.4 1.13
  para 9.5 1.14
  para 9.7 1.15
  para 9.7(2) 1.16
  para 9.14 1.17
letters of intent 2.60, 2.72

natural justice 2.109, 2.111–2.112, 2.115, 3.59, 9.16–9.22, 9.42–9.43, 9.47, 13.16–13.17, 17.23
  DOM/2 4.50
  adjudicator's failure to consult 9.26–9.29
  adjudicator's indication or preliminary view 9.33–9.35
  adjudicator's separate communication with the parties 9.23–9.25, 17.27
  adjudicator's taking advice from others 9.30–9.32
  ambush 9.36–9.37
  effect of earlier adjudications 9.38–9.41
NEC/2
  Option Y (UK) 2
  cll 90.1–90.4 4.60
New South Wales *see* Australia
New Zealand
  adjudication 6.35–6.36
notices
  notice of adjudication 3.12–3.15, 7.35–7.45, 16.02–16.06
  at any time 2.76, 2.85, 2.87, 2.90
  drafting 7.63n
  response to notice 16.07–16.09
  payment notices 3.111–3.113
  referral notice 3.26–3.28, 4.44, 16.21–16.25
  referral within 7 days 3.29–3.33
  response to notice 17.04–17.05
  right to reply to response 17.06–17.07
withholding notices 3.111–3.113, 4.26, 4.42, 4.51, 4.57, 10.04, 10.07, 10.13, 13.10–13.11
  proposals for change 19.18–19.21

Official Referee's Solicitors Association 1.26
  see also TeCSA
orders
  peremptory orders
    enforcement 3.94

payment 2.121, 2.129–2.135, 4.41 *see also* abatement, set-off
  cash flow 10.01–10.03, 10.30
  dates for payment 3.104–3.107
    final date for payment 2.122, 2.126–2.127, 3.106, 3.108–3.110
  determination 4.26, 4.43, 4.52
    New South Wales 6.18–6.19
  interest on late payment 14.12
  interim payments 1.02–1.03, 2.121, 4.04, 4.26, 10.06
    proposals for change 19.07–19.09

Index

payment (cont.)
  New South Wales 6.10–6.12
  overpayments 10.19
  payment notices
    proposals for change 19.14–19.17
  relationship of contract terms with ss109–111
    HGCRA 1996 2.142–2.147
  stage payments 2.123–2.125, 3.105
    cap 3.103
    entitlement to and amount 3.98–3.103
    value of work 3.100, 3.102
  sums claimed 2.130, 2.133
    proposals for change 19.22–19.24
  sums certified 2.132–2.133
  withholding notices 2.122–2.123, 2.131, 4.41, 4.42, 4.51
plant 2.31, 2.33, 2.36
private finance initiatives 2.37
professional services
  connection with construction operations 2.19–2.20

residential occupiers 2.40–2.43, 4.28–4.29

Scheme for Construction Contracts 2.162–2.163, 3.01–3.02, 4.01–4.02, 4.16, 4.35, 9.16, 10.07, 12.35, 15.01, 16.12
  application 3.03–3.10, 7.20, 7.80
  as implied term 4.04, 9.51, 13.08
  interrelationship with any given contract 3.04
  Pt I
    para 1 3.12, 3.14
    para 2 3.16
    para 2(1)(a) 3.17
    para 2(1)(b) 3.24
    para 2(1)(c) 3.20, 3.21
    para 2(2) 3.18
    para 3 3.16
    para 4 3.16, 3.18
    paras 5–6 3.16, 3.19
    para 7 3.13, 3.26
    para 7(1) 3.19
    para 8 3.34
    para 8(1) 7.62
    para 8(2) 3.37, 3.49, 7.26
    para 9 3.39
    para 9(1) 3.40, 3.51
    para 9(2) 3.42, 3.44, 3.47, 3.96, 12.32
    para 9(4) 3.96, 11.12
    para 10 3.48–3.49
    para 11 3.50–3.51
    paras 12–19 3.52
    para 13 3.57, 3.58
    para 17 3.60, 3.61
    para 19 3.66, 3.69
    para 19(1) 3.71
    para 19(3) 3.72
    para 20 3.14, 3.73, 3.81
    para 20(a) 3.74
    para 20(c) 3.77
    para 21 3.73
    para 22 3.73, 3.83
    para 23(2) 3.89, 3.90, 12.16
    para 24 3.94
    para 25 3.81, 3.95–3.96, 11.02, 11.12
    para 26 11.16
  Pt II 3.97
    paras 1–2 3.98–3.99
    para 2(1) 3.109
    para 2(2) 3.100
    para 2(2)(a) 3.101
    para 2(3) 3.100
    para 2(4) 3.103
    para 3 3.99, 3.104
    para 4 3.99, 3.104, 3.105, 3.115
    para 4(a) 3.107
    para 5 3.104, 3.106, 3.115
    para 5(b) 3.110
    para 6 3.104, 3.106, 3.115
    para 7 3.104, 3.107
    para 8 3.108, 3.109
    para 8(2) 3.07
    para 9 3.111
    para 10 3.111, 3.112
    para 11 3.114–3.115
    para 12 3.100, 3.101, 3.103, 3.105
  payment of adjudicator's fees 11.01
service of documents 2.164–2.167
set-off 2.136–2.137, 4.30, 4.42, 4.51, 10.01–10.05 *see also* abatement, claims
  against adjudicator's decision 10.20, 13.12–13.13
  general rule 10.21–10.32
  exceptions to general rule 10.33–10.34
Singapore
  adjudication 6.29–6.34
standard forms of construction and engineering contracts 1.17, 3.02, 4.01, 4.03A, 10.06 *see also* GC/Works contract and Sub-Contracts, ICE Form of Engineering Contract, JCT Standard Form of building contract, NEC/2, sub-contracts
  adjudication provisions 2.41
  applicability 1.10

standard forms of construction and engineering
    contracts (cont.)
  impartiality 9.16
  pay when paid clauses 1.12
  sub-contracts
    DOM/1 4.34–4.43
    DOM/2 4.44–4.50, 7.40
  unfair conditions 1.11
stay of execution 15.01–15.03
  cross-claim against judgment
    debtor 15.04–15.05
  financial difficulties of judgment
    creditor 15.09–15.21
  insolvency of judgment creditor 15.06–15.08
stay of proceedings
  stay for adjudication 2.152
  stay for arbitration 2.148, 2.151
sub-contracts
  DOM/1 4.34–4.35
    cl 21 4.42
    cl 29 4.43
    cl 29.6.3 4.43
    cl 38A 4.37
    cl 38A.5.6 4.36
  DOM/2 4.44–4.50
    cl 11 4.48
    cl 11.7 4.48
    cl 38A 4.44
    cl 38A.5.5 4.50
sub-contractors
  right to adjudication 2.27

Technology and Construction Court
  declaratory relief 14.26–14.29
  enforcement procedure 14.01–14.04
    summary judgment 14.05–14.11
  injunctive relief 14.20–14.25
  stay of proceedings for adjudication 14.30–14.36
TeCSA Rules *see* adjudication rules
time limits
  28 day time limit 2.76, 2.91–2.97, 2.99–2.102,
    2.104–2.105, 3.66–3.72, 4.19–4.22, 17.19
  compliance with time limits 12.06–12.08
  extension of time 4.48, 17.20–17.22

Uff CBE QC, Professor John 1.29